W9-AFF-274

1) Mr. Budd Wi
2) The Lady Ga
3) T men   4) K.C. contin
4) Where The Sidewalk Ends
5) California Split
6) Gilda
7) The Big Heat
8) Macao
9) His Kind of Woman
9) Dead Reckoning
10) Any Number
    Can play
11) The Big Town

Frisco
Jenny

The Longest
Day

The Lusty
Men

+

Pale Flower
Bob le Flambeur
The Fire Within
Les Tricheurs
The Shanghai Gesture
The Gambler
Cincinnati Kid
The Hustler
Dark City
Seven Thieves
The ..... Thief
Odds Against Tomorrow
All ... Drive
The Asphalt Jungle
Johnny Eager
The Phenix City Story
The Gangster
Cockfighter
Force of Evil
Scene of the Crime
The Killing! The Criminal
Brighton Rock
Killing of a Chinese Bookie
Croupier
Railroaded woman
His Kind of woman
Robert Rossen
Budd Boetticher

Film Noir
FAQ

Series Editor: Robert Rodriguez

Billy Wilder
Orson Welles
G.W. Pabst
John Brahm
Jean Negulesco
Scorcese
Sam Fuller

Anthony Mann
Stanley Kubrick
Max Ophuls

Jean Pierre Melville
Joseph Losey
Nicholas Ray
Douglas Sirk
Robert Siodmak
Edgar G. Ulmer
Fritz Lang
Fassbinder
Jules Dassin
Kurosawa

Joseph H. Lewis
Mario Bava
F.W. Murnau
Joseph Von Sternberg
John Huston
Basil Dearden

Film Noir
FAQ

All That's Left to Know About Hollywood's Golden Age of Dames, Detectives, and Danger

David J. Hogan

APPLAUSE
THEATRE & CINEMA BOOKS
An Imprint of Hal Leonard Corporation

Published in 2013 by Applause Theatre & Cinema Books
An Imprint of Hal Leonard Corporation
7777 West Bluemound Road
Milwaukee, WI 53213

Trade Book Division Editorial Offices
33 Plymouth St., Montclair, NJ 07042

All images are from the personal collection of the author.

The FAQ series was conceived by Robert Rodriguez and developed with Stuart Shea.

Printed in the United States of America

Book design by Snow Creative Services

Library of Congress Cataloging-in-Publication Data

Hogan, David J.
    Film noir FAQ : all that's left to know about Hollywood's golden age of dames, detectives, and danger / David J. Hogan.
        pages cm
    Includes bibliographical references and index.
    ISBN 978-1-55783-855-1 (paperback)
1. Film noir—United States—History and criticism. I. Title.
    PN1995.9.F54H58 2013
    791.43'6556—dc23
                                                                        2012048283

www.applausebooks.com

For Kim, always the femme fatale

LIZABETH SCOTT

As an Actress, I found it fascinating and exhilarating to be part of Film Noir.

It represented REALITY. Audiences agreed by finding Film Noir in all its facets intriguing, enlightening, and entertaining.

Lizabeth Scott

A special note from Lizabeth Scott for readers of *Film Noir FAQ*

Contents

Acknowledgments

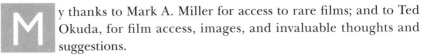y thanks to Mark A. Miller for access to rare films; and to Ted Okuda, for film access, images, and invaluable thoughts and suggestions.

Thanks also to the Film Noir Foundation (www.filmnoirfoundation.org) for returning so many of these movies to the big screen, where they belong.

Special thanks to Lizabeth Scott, for her active interest in this project.

Introduction

Negotiating the Night

The weather in LA is cool, but Mike Hammer cuts through the darkness in his Jaguar convertible, top down. When a young blonde wearing nothing but a trench coat suddenly dashes into the lonely road, Hammer wrenches the wheel in order not to splash her. The Jag slides onto the shoulder in a shower of dust and gravel. Hammer is still muttering when the dame approaches. She's breathing hard and she's desperate for a ride. Hammer is disgusted. "Get in," he says.

They drive, Hammer nearly silent but the blonde going on about poetry, the rocky terrain of man-woman relations, and a special entreaty: "Remember me."

Minutes later, the Jag is cut off by a black Caddy, big as a house. Hammer is sapped and the woman is taken from his car. The Caddy positions its I-beam of a bumper behind the Jag and nudges forward. In a moment, Hammer and his little car jounce down a steep, overgrown grade, and near the bottom, something is ripped open and an evil blossom of flame explodes beneath the car's chassis. Hammer may have bought it this time. He's a prosperous louse—a conniving bedroom dick who specializes in divorce cases—but that's not a capital offense. And anyway, Hammer had never laid eyes on the dame before she forced him to stop. He'd just been driving from here to there, minding his own business, and got sucked into something mean, and isn't that a hell of a way to wrap up an evening?

Kiss Me Deadly, and scores more movies from the 1940s and '50s that we now call film noir, force us to acknowledge that the presumably solid foundation upon which we base our assumptions and our very lives is temporal and dangerously unstable. It's likely to not merely shift beneath our feet, but give way completely, turning the routine of our lives upside-down and annihilating our expectations. We're plunged into a disorienting place where everything we thought we knew is wrong.

This is the fact and the fearsome allure of film noir—black, or bleak, film—a genre that established itself in Hollywood in the early 1940s and that found its fullest expression during World War II and the immediate postwar era. *Film Noir FAQ* is your guide to some two hundred noir thrillers—what they mean, who made them and who starred in them, and how each came to be. It's mostly a story of low- to mid-budget moviemaking, and genre pictures that resonate strongly today, when many mainstream "prestige" releases of the noir period are long forgotten.

Before Italian-born French essayist and critic Nino Frank coined the term *film noir* in about 1945 (when noir was still developing), these movies were just thrillers, heavily steeped in crime, duplicity, and other bad behavior. Like any artistic movement or other cultural artifact, the films came from *somewhere*. Things larger than just the movies shaped these stories. Once upon a time, there was an origin.

Chaos and Disappointment

As we'll see, noir's genesis can be traced to specific events, but it's important to begin by emphasizing that the key motivators of noir stories—fear, greed, hatred, and revenge, plus the complicating factor of sex—aren't events at all but ingredients of the soup called "human beings," and have existed since time immemorial. Film noir is a landscape of mainly urban places that is returned to again and again, but, mainly, noir exists in the landscape of the mind. Noir, regrettably, is what is inside all of us.

The specific events that helped shape film noir are clear: the carnage of two world wars; the scarifying economic depression that separated those wars; bloody, hate-filled regional conflicts that flared across Europe and Asia even before World War II was officially over; the unnerving power of atomic weaponry; an escalating Cold War; and a feeling that our destinies were no longer in our hands. Even our institutions and leaders seemed inadequately prepared (or just disinclined) to prevent further mayhem.

As if to distract Americans from that sort of pessimistic thought, manufacturing and an increasingly sophisticated advertising industry enlarged upon the small taste of material comfort that had emerged during the illusory prosperity of the 1920s. While laborious rebuilding occupied Europe and Asia, America reveled in consumerism. People developed fresh aspirations. They had cars and mobility. The nation's realignment from a rural to an urban society accelerated. Cities became increasingly significant to commerce and culture. The American imagination lived and fed in cities. "City" became synonymous with "America."

Of course, the bible relates that history's first city was established by Cain, history's first murderer. In fact and symbol, Cain linked himself to that first city by calling it Enoch, after his son. Enoch was the city of Cain.

In American cities of the 1940s and '50s, a lot more than just shopping was going on. The public knew it, and so did Hollywood.

The Movies React

What was later called film noir developed and evolved during 1940–60, and for four general reasons: 1) as a reflection of anxiety produced by the events noted above; 2) because the films that best reflected that anxiety could be produced on low budgets (this is one reason why perpetually underfunded RKO had smashing success with noir); 3) the rise of "hard-boiled" crime and detective fiction in pulps, mainstream magazines, and books; and 4) the influx and influence of expatriate German filmmakers steeped in expressionism, fatalism, and psychological melodrama.

As noir evolved, themes became increasingly familiar. *You do not control the circumstances of your life. Choices you agonize over are likely to be bad ones. Choices you make without thinking are likely to be worse. Whatever you love and value can be taken from you at any moment. Forces greater than you, and greater even than your leaders, can conspire to destroy you. Those forces are no smarter than you, but they have the power and you don't. You are not a true participant in events, only an observer. If you are particularly foolish, or just unlucky, you will be a victim.*

"Fate," the hapless protagonist of Martin Goldsmith and Edgar G. Ulmer's *Detour* (1945) dourly observes, "can put its finger on you, or on me, for no reason at all."

This new bleakness was expressed on film via the lingua franca of the new American city, where (the movies repeatedly insisted) menace waits around every dark corner. Every alley is an invitation to have a sap levered against your head, and every automobile is a potential missile that can take your life. Your business partner will cheat you, and your spouse or lover will cheat *on* you. The police are incompetent, in the dark, or corrupt. Here's a buck for cab fare and good luck.

Don't Turn Away

A significant ancillary effect of the rise of noir is that Hollywood felt encouraged to continually push against the limits of the Production Code, becoming increasingly bold in suggestions of sex and (especially) violence. Many famed noir moments are remembered because of their unprecedented brutality: the wheelchair-bound woman who is pushed down a flight of stairs in *Kiss of Death*; the faces splashed with scalding coffee in *The Big Heat*; the ghastly beating administered to Alan Ladd in *The Glass Key*. Noir pulses with uncountable comparable moments. War had inured audiences to violence, and the Code, while mounting a defense, had no choice but to allow the boundaries of what was permissible to be dramatically expanded.

In this regard, film noir is an affirmation of modernity, and a predictor of the content and tone of movies made today.

It All Happens After Dark

Noir's preferred landscape is the night, that playground of our conscious fears and subconscious desires, the period of time when we're simultaneously at our most apprehensive and reckless. At three a.m., dog-tired in rumpled clothes and with the acidic remains of a long-ago cup of coffee burning our stomachs, many things may appear reasonable: a recklessly big score or a poorly considered betrayal . . . or murder. At three a.m., the careless brain contemplates war, scaled down from nations and continents to a city block or a bedroom or a jeweler's safe.

Jean Genet wrote, "A man must dream a long time in order to act with grandeur, and dreaming is nursed in darkness."

At night, while you sit on the edge of your bed, cross-hatched in shadow, perhaps bathed by the neon from somewhere outside your window, monumentally dumb ideas can seem to acquire a twisted grandeur—the grandeur of the foolish, the megalomaniacal, the wicked, the desperate. Night is when schemes are hatched in the back rooms of warehouses, in greasy diners, in after-hours joints, in the maddening solitude of your own tiny apartment when you feel as if you're the only person still awake on earth.

You may have sufficient powers of self-reflection to realize that you might be setting yourself up for a serious existential dilemma—a problem or challenge that, depending on the decisions you make, may cause you to abandon long-held beliefs or principles, and even bring harm to other people. By pursuing a particular course of action, you might simultaneously win and lose, build and destroy.

You may have bad history with people who figure in your present. Past mistakes or fundamental weaknesses of character may come back to haunt somebody. You may be consumed with a desire for revenge, or another person might live only to take vengeance on you.

The violence that you make or that is levied against you is apt to be horrifying. Whatever you set in motion probably won't culminate with a simple fist in the eye. Instead, somebody could end up crushed, tortured, or set ablaze (all of which happen in a single noir thriller, the inimitable *Kiss Me Deadly*).

If you're lucky (or not), you have a companion: a person of the opposite sex whom you love or desire or tolerate or hate. One of you somehow goads the other forward. Whether with explicit or implicit encouragement, your companion often is the key that starts up your own little engine of war.

And sometimes, when you believe you don't need the key anymore, you snap it off.

Night, the city. Small people, big ideas. Gender combat. Guilt, fear. Noir is psychological sickness. Noir is bad luck, bad decisions, and explosive, unanticipated outcomes.

Welcome to nighttime in America.

How This Book Works

Because of my definition of noir, and because of constraints of length (I wasn't allowed to write anything as thick as a phone book), I've elected to focus on American movies made from about 1940 to 1960. The sole exception is Fritz Lang's 1936 revenge melodrama *Fury*, which is probably the first film noir.

Material is divided into seven chapters: *The War Between Men and Women, Act I*; *The War Between Men and Women, Act II*; *The Private Dick*; *A Cop's Life*; *The Best-Laid Plans*; *Victims of Circumstance*; and *The Unsprung Mind*.

A brief Afterword looks at the neo-noir phenomenon of 1960 to the present.

The main text is supplemented with more than seventy sidebars discussing directors, performers, writers, and cinematographers.

Some of the sidebars are devoted to issues, but generally, noir themes and stylistics are examined in the main text, in discussions of individual films. Within each chapter, films are treated chronologically, so that the reader can see how noir unfolded and evolved.

Among the approximately seventy-five illustrations are film stills, candids, and posters and other promotional material.

Making the Selections

I didn't agonize over which films to include in this book, but I did pause to think about some that didn't make the cut. Existing noir reference books and Web sources, as well as analytical studies of the genre, typically agree on the titles that everybody agrees on. *The Maltese Falcon*? It's in. *Gun Crazy*? Check. The trouble begins when the definition of noir is aggressively expanded by people who are carelessly excited about the genre. (Also, some home-video companies that hope to sell a few more DVDs may market any old movie as film noir, willy-nilly.)

Lovers of noir discern the genre's themes and patterns and then sometimes imagine they see those things in crime exposés (*New York Confidential*), police procedurals (*C-Man*), adventure thrillers (*Split Second*), social-problem dramas (*The Blackboard Jungle*), Red-scare films (*Shack Out on 101*), prison dramas (*Caged*), suspense thrillers (*The Steel Trap*), caper films (*5 Against the House*), simple mysteries (*Pier 23*), suspense stories (*The Mask of Dijon*), teenpics (*Teenage Doll*), and even westerns (*Little Big Horn*). Each of the preceding appears on various lists of noir films.

Because of growing interest in film noir, and the understandable eagerness to be the first to "discover" something, many hundreds of movies have been added to the core group of about 250 noir titles. This book looks at about 200. On the other hand, a noir title list posted on a very popular movie Web site has *more than 700* titles. That's just silly.

Naturally, a lot of what determines one's definition of noir is subjective. Some readers of this book may wonder what I was thinking when I decided to include a social-problem melodrama (*Storm Warning*), a Deanna Durbin movie (*Lady on a Train*), and even a cartoon (*The Great Piggy Bank Robbery*). Well, I had my reasons, and I explain them.

Some smartly crafted films that I like very much, such as *Cry Danger, The Scarf*, and *Without Warning*, only flirt with noir, and were thus excluded. In those cases, and in similar ones, I felt bad.

I'll get over it, and I hope the reader will, too.

Victims of their obsessions, cut off from a society that never allowed them a proper place, the doomed lovers (John Dall, Peggy Cummins) of *Gun Crazy* (1950) desperately search for a place to hide from their pursuers.

Noir and Truth

My interest in movies is archaeological as well as visual and aural—which is a roundabout way of saying that I think movies are priceless signposts that direct viewers to what was happening in the culture that produced them. Filmmakers are no less exempt from broader cultural influences than the rest of us, so movies inevitably invoke contemporaneous issues and concerns. It works out that way—whether the filmmakers are aware of it or not. Whatever filmmakers' intentions, movies are reflections of all of us.

Film noir has proved to be one of the most durable movie genres. Its lasting popularity and undiminished artistic integrity are due partly to the films' lively invocations of a modern world that is now past—fashions, cars, architecture, the way people walked and talked, the alternately jaunty and treacherous nature of city life. But the films also endure because they spin compelling entertainment from threads of truth. The pain and shock of real life inform the lives and fates of the fictional hopefuls, schemers, and innocents that populate noir. This genre with style and attitude to spare reveals who and what we were. When we watch the films today, we're challenged, and forced to reflect about things that are untidy and uncomfortable. That's what film noir does, and if that sounds like the definition of art, I'll be the last person to disagree.

David J. Hogan
Arlington Heights, IL

The War Between Men and Women, Act I

"I've wanted to laugh in your face ever since I first met you. You're old and ugly and I'm sick of you. Sick, sick, sick!"

—Joan Bennett to Edward G. Robinson, *Scarlet Street* (1945)

Laura

T he central issue of Otto Preminger's *Laura* (1944) isn't Laura's murder (though murder motivates the plot), but the distorting quality of the male romantic imagination. The title character, played by the breathtaking Gene Tierney, is a fully formed human being, her own person. Yet because she's been molded and guided by famed columnist, radio personality, and fussy epicure Waldo Lydecker (Clifton Webb), he has awarded himself a proprietary interest in Laura's life. He imagines Laura is his own creation and that without him there would be no Laura at all.

To trench-coated police detective Mark McPherson (Dana Andrews), the late Laura is his feminine ideal, whom he studies in a full-length portrait that hangs above her fireplace. McPherson pokes around Laura's *objets d'art* and even her underthings (the last a clever idea of 20th Century-Fox chief Darryl F. Zanuck), developing an obsessive love for, as Lydecker tartly puts it, "a corpse."

In one of the best, and best-known, movie "reveals," Laura unexpectedly—and matter-of-factly—returns to her apartment, very much alive, causing McPherson to rub his eyes in disbelief. The dream girl of two very different men has returned.

Laura was based on the Vera Caspary novel, in which a major preoccupation is McPherson's confusion and resentment at being thrust into a glib Park Avenue milieu when he's accustomed to more direct, rough-and-tumble parts of town. The script by Jay Dratler, Samuel Hoffenstein, and Betty Reinhardt retains McPherson's resentment, giving the film a dark hum of class warfare. Very much against his natural inclinations, then, McPherson falls for a woman who moves among the rich and powerful.

Dialogue establishes that the scrawny, aging Lydecker has a hatred of muscular young men like McPherson (despite Lydecker's apparent homosexuality). For all of his intellect and way with words, he feels threatened and inadequate. He's shocked when McPherson refers to women as "dames," and finally can't abide the thought of Laura in McPherson's arms, just as he had been unable to reconcile Laura with her smarmy beau, Shelby Carpenter (Vincent Price). He muffed his earlier opportunity to have the last word with Laura, and now he wants to rectify that mistake.

Preminger and cinematographer Joseph LaShelle shot the picture with a sort of restrained aggression, packing frames densely from front to rear, making judicious use of camera movement, and shooting many tense sequences in rooms flooded with sunlight—a neat turnabout on noir convention. Scenes on rainy streets and in shadowed rooms are edgily effective.

Preminger calls attention to the camera just once—and very smartly—with a sudden swish-pan to Laura's kitchen door as Lydecker silently pushes it open, intending to commit mayhem on the woman who obsesses him. Joseph LaShelle's lighting is especially dramatic later, as Lydecker enters Laura's bedroom, his own voice coming from the radio in a prerecorded broadcast. "Love is eternal," Lydecker's voice reads. "It has been the strongest motivation for human actions throughout centuries."

David Raksin's score emphasizes that sort of elevated romanticism. The title theme went on to become a standard.

Fox wanted Jennifer Jones for the title role, but because she wasn't available, the part was given to Tierney. She shot for eighteen days with producer Otto Preminger and director Rouben Mamoulian. Preminger was a notoriously prickly character, and he clashed with Mamoulian, who found himself dismissed. Preminger assumed directorial duties and began filming from scratch.

Laura propelled twenty-four-year-old Tierney into the top rank of Hollywood's leading ladies. The actress's beauty is obvious, as is the intelligence she brings to the role. (LaShelle lit her eyes so that they look opalescent, deep, and knowing.) As McPherson is pleased to discover, Laura is considerably more than the beauty in the portrait.

Case File: Otto Preminger (1905–86)

One of the very few directors of his day whose name had box-office value, Vienna-born Otto Preminger aggressively pursued a varied film career that stretched from 1931 to 1980. Although trained as an attorney, Preminger worked in Viennese theater as a producer, director, and actor before coming to Hollywood in 1936. As a director, he had a false start at 20th Century-Fox but had a triumph at that studio with the 1944 noir classic *Laura*, which he produced as well as directed. Preminger went on to produce most of the remainder of his projects and became known for bringing his pictures in on time and on budget. He could be tough on actors but pulled out strong performances. Other noir projects include *Fallen Angel*, *Where the Sidewalk Ends*, and *Angel Face*.

Preminger made films in many genres; among his other notable titles are *Forever Amber*, *River of No Return*, *Carmen Jones*, *Exodus*, *Advise and Consent*, and *Bunny Lake Is Missing*. Three of Preminger's projects pushed the limits of what was then acceptable on the screen, *The Moon Is Blue* (language), *The Man with the Golden Arm* (depictions of drug use), and *Anatomy of a Murder* (sexual frankness).

Otto Preminger's Laura (1944): Police detective Dana Andrews finally gets his hands on the mysterious beauty (Gene Tierney) who has seized his romantic imagination. But every good cop should know that nearly everything is more complicated than it seems.

Dana Andrews is direct and gruffly appealing, while stage actor Clifton Webb, in his first screen role in nineteen years, is paradoxically wonderful as Waldo Lydecker. Even in 1944, the characterization was arch and affected, and it only seems more so to today's viewers. The beauty of the performance is Webb's consistency. Lydecker is almost entirely self-created; you get the sense that, growing up, he never was who or what he wished to be, and that's he's spent his adult life cultivating something—somebody—better. In the end, he becomes a tragic figure, driven to murder by his sense of his own inadequacies. Webb's performance is one of the most vivid and perversely amusing of the 1940s. And Laura, although neither as visibly dark nor as eventful as some other noir thrillers, is nevertheless timeless.

You're Almost Never as Smart as You Think You Are *Double Indemnity*

Billy Wilder's acerbic *Double Indemnity* was released in 1944, when millions of American women went to work every day in factories and other unglamorous places. Unpretentious and self-sufficient, they looked after themselves while their men were away at war.

And then there were women like Phyllis Dietrichson (Barbara Stanwyck), who were married to older men who had not gone away to war and did not work themselves. Idle and often bored, some, like the fictional Mrs. Dietrichson, began to think of things beyond the boundaries of marriage. Things like murder.

If there is an emblematic film noir, it is *Double Indemnity*. In its plot (from a superior hard-boiled novel by James M. Cain), its tone and stylistics, its high-voltage dialogue, and its perverse unwholesomeness, the film is the one you want a novice to see first in order to experience noir.

When Phyllis effortlessly seduces an ambitious and self-assured insurance salesman named Walter Neff (Fred MacMurray), she senses a kindred soul: somebody who will kill for lust and for profit. She's sick to death of her querulous husband (Tom Powers), who is steadily losing money in California's oil fields. What if she could insure his life without his knowing, and what if he subsequently died?

Neff has a better idea. Policies have a double indemnity clause by which the insurance company pays double for deaths that are statistically improbable . . . like a fall from a train. Neff explains to Phyllis that the clause is just a come-on to lure customers, but it's legal and binding and it can be made to pay—*if* the perpetrators are smart about it.

Neff is clever, and although he fancies himself a canny reader of people, he can't read Phyllis at all. Breathless and wide-eyed, vaguely cheap with her peroxide blonde hair and monogrammed anklet, she plays Neff like a trout.

Case File: James M. Cain (1892–1977)

Noir novelist James M. Cain dabbled in Hollywood screenwriting in the late 1930s, but generally thereafter was content to take the money when studios came calling to adapt his prose for the big screen. Audiences were blistered by Billy Wilder's adaptation of *Double Indemnity*, and enjoyed further interpretations of Cain with *Mildred Pierce* and *The Postman Always Rings Twice*. Briefly back in the Hollywood trenches again in 1947, Cain worked without screen credit to tweak Daniel Mainwaring's script for *Out of the Past*.

Cain's early novels don't suggest that the author had any fondness for women, but the books certainly display a great and unwholesome interest in them. Actresses Barbara Stanwyck and Lana Turner prettified the female protagonists of *Double Indemnity* and *Postman*, respectively, but the books' first-person male narrators can barely make sense of what draws them to these hard dames. The women aren't pleasant, they're not even good looking—but the hapless men pursue them anyway, and take a fall.

Mildred Pierce was Cain's first novel written in the third person. The title character is sympathetic; this time, it's the hardworking Mildred's teenage daughter who's the monster that toys with men. The novel (written in 1941) is set in 1931, when economic circumstance and a failed, unloving husband prompt Mildred to teach herself how to earn her own way. The independent, gutsy dames who figure strongly in so many noir films, then, may have been invented by James M. Cain.

He's in lust, and may even fancy that he's in love, but mainly he's in it for the payoff and—in an intriguing touch—for an opportunity to flummox his office's chief claims analyst, Keyes (Edward G. Robinson), who asserts that he can spot a phony setup every time.

The greater part of *Double Indemnity* is a virtual textbook on how quickly perpetrators' exhilaration turns to unease, and then to fear, and finally to paranoia, betrayal, and more death. In the movie's most suspenseful sequence, Neff invites Phyllis to his apartment after the murder. When she's on her way up, Keyes arrives. If he sees Neff and Mrs. Dietrichson together, he'll know everything in an instant. As Neff stands in his doorway to speak to Keyes, Phyllis is in the hallway, hiding silently behind the open door. Keyes keeps approaching the door and then backing away. In shadow, Phyllis's eyes gleam like white marbles. She's already thinking of how to rid herself of her coconspirator.

Inevitably, the final confrontation of the two ends in an exchange of bullets that suggests the uncomfortably close relationship of love and hate.

The ultimate irony of *Double Indemnity* is that it really is a love story—not one between Neff and Phyllis but between Neff and Keyes. Keyes likes Neff and wants to mentor him—wants to make him his assistant, in fact. When Keyes looks down at his slumped protégé and says, "Walter, you're all washed up," his voice has genuine regret.

Case File: Barbara Stanwyck (1907–90)

Barbara Stanwyck is noir's hardscrabble gal, a hands-on-hips survivor who takes what she wants from men and mows down other women or simply ignores them altogether.

Born Ruby Stevens, she rose from a tenuous, orphaned existence in Brooklyn to stints as a Ziegfeld Follies chorus dancer and then to Broadway leads before she was twenty. Stanwyck dabbled in film in New York in 1927, and later went west to work for Columbia and Warner Bros. She became a star because of her unconventional beauty, aura of tough-minded independence, and an understated acting style that remains startlingly modern. A thorough professional whose byword was "preparedeness," Stanwyck excelled early on as shop girls, secretaries, and ambitious "other women" (pre-Code melodramas *Illicit*, *Night Nurse*, and *Baby Face* are sterling examples of the young Stanwyck's gifts). As she passed through her thirties and approached forty, her sex appeal became more intelligent and took on an aura of danger, making her an ideal noir protagonist. She's justly famed for her somewhat atypical histrionics in *Sorry, Wrong Number*. She's even better in *Double Indemnity*, *The Strange Love of Martha Ivers*, *No Man of Her Own*, and *Witness to Murder*.

Stanwyck also was a superb comic actress (*The Lady Eve*, *Ball of Fire*) and a commanding presence in such straight dramas as *East Side, West Side* and *Executive Suite*. Unhappy in love (a marriage to vaudevillian Frank Fay helped inspire *A Star Is Born*, and a later union with matinee idol Robert Taylor was deeply unsatisfying for her), Stanwyck defined "perseverance" and remained a star for more than fifty years.

In Billy Wilder's *Double Indemnity* (1944), greedy L.A. housewife Phyllis Dietrichson (Barbara Stanwyck) selects thickheaded insurance agent Walter Neff (Fred MacMurray) to help with the murder of her husband. Neff enthusiastically goes along, laboring under the delusion that he's in the driver's seat.

John Seitz's cinematography captures the oppressive atmosphere of the Dietrichson home, and the warm nights outside magically capture the oppressive humidity. In one beautifully lit moment that grips Neff's face in close-up, a fine sheen of perspiration masks his features, and you know he doesn't really have the constitution for what he's getting into.

But he *is* into it, and it's going to be his undoing.

A Castle and Some Kings

Phyllis Dietrichson can't wait to rid herself of her husband. That's an ambition typical of noir antiheroines, of course, but every once in a while a woman is frantic to hang on to her spouse—even when she barely knows him. That's the case with Millie Baxter (Kim Hunter), a guileless youngster who has impulsively married Paul, a much older man. She tells a kindly former boyfriend, Fred (Robert Mitchum), that Paul was called away on a sales trip almost immediately after the ceremony. So now she and Frank wait hopefully for Paul to join her in New York. Meanwhile, in Philadelphia, a drunken conventioneer flush with cash is robbed and brutally strangled with a silk stocking. The police are (as we like to say) baffled. Back in New York, just when it seems that Paul (Dean Jagger) will never arrive, he shows up. But why does another person's name identify his apartment, and why is Paul evasive about his sales territory and his recent whereabouts? Who is he really? Deeply curious rather than frightened, Millie is determined to uncover the truth about the man she loves.

When Strangers Marry (1944) was directed by William Castle, a competent technician who made his name in the late 1950s as the hard-sell producer-director of gimmicky horror thrillers. In 1944, he was thirty years old and under contract to Columbia. He had directed only three pictures, including *The Whistler* (1944), a smart, stylish programmer based on the popular radio program (Castle would direct four of the eight Whistler thrillers). When told by Columbia chief Harry Cohn that he had been loaned out to Frank and Maurice King, no-budget producers at Monogram, Castle felt he'd been demoted. But the King brothers, who'd made their money in the vending machine business in Chicago, understood story and promotion. They liked the plot idea Castle hashed out with screenwriter Philip Yordan and assigned the picture a budget of $50,000. Castle was told to complete the shoot in seven days.

The tiny budget of *When Strangers Marry* is apparent but not a detriment, due partly to low-key acting (particularly from Hunter and Jagger); intriguingly wide, simply dressed sets by F. Paul Sylos; and other solid technical credits: cinematography (Ira Morgan), editing (Martin Cohn), and score (Dimitri Tiomkin). And William Castle strove for some *Whistler*-like visual effects, such as a cool gray palette in quiet scenes and dramatic shadowplay and striking compositions during tense moments. For instance, although we're with the killer in Philadelphia, we see him only from behind. His creepily anonymous hat and shoulders dominate the frame as the doomed conventioneer (Dick Elliott) chortles in the middle ground. There is a marvelous frisson later, when Millie glances back at a restaurant and observes the back of a seated patron who wears the hat and coat we saw earlier.

One obvious influence on *When Strangers Marry* is RKO producer Val Lewton, who had begun his string of psycho-horror thrillers two years earlier. A sequence in which Millie is illuminated by an enormous neon sign that flashes DANCE just feet from her hotel window recalls the claustrophobic unease of Lewton's *The Seventh Victim* (1943), and another sequence, in which Millie hurries alone through an oddly lit pedestrian tunnel, captures much of the everyday weirdness of Lewton's *Cat People* (1942).

The narrative road has a couple of potholes. A sequence involving a phony mind reader is supposed to evoke tension but doesn't, and Millie and Paul's visit to a Negro juke joint adds a little flavor but has no point, other than to place the couple in a place that, to white audiences in 1944, might seem fraught with danger.

The climax feels a little rote but is redeemed because Castle shifts quickly from surprise to suspense, forcing our attention to an important letter that has become stuck in an office-building mail chute. We see it and the killer sees it, but the investigating policeman (Neil Hamilton) does not. If the letter becomes unstuck and falls to the bottom, the killer will be nabbed on the spot.

Because the title *When Strangers Marry* has the ring of roadshow exploitation (*She Shoulda Said No, The Road to Ruin, Damaged Lives*, et al.), the film was rereleased as *Betrayed*, a title that's more evocative of the story's drama, but that does nothing to suggest Yordan and Castle's take on young love and naïveté.

Let's Feel Good About Murder   *The Suspect*

Via the Breen Office, Hollywood's self-policing body, the Production Code, mandated that wrongdoers be punished for their crimes. Intriguingly, Robert Siodmak's *The Suspect* (1944) merely suggests that that will be the case. Indeed, by film's end the decision has been left entirely to the wrongdoer himself.

In London in 1902, a gentle, mildly prosperous shopkeeper named Philip Marshall (Charles Laughton) begins a platonic relationship with a sweet, much younger woman, Mary Gray (Ella Raines). Marshall feels encouraged to do this because the endurance race he's been running with his carping, malicious wife, Cora (Rosalind Ivan), is effectively over.

Not long after Cora discovers her husband's increasingly romantic friendship and threatens to reveal it in order to ruin Marshall and Mary, she dies

Philip Marshall (Charles Laughton) has allowed himself to be browbeaten by wife Cora (Rosalind Ivan) for years. Lately, though, he's acted strangely, and Cora isn't sure why. She'll find out soon enough in *The Suspect* (1944).

in a household fall down the stairs. Despite the subsequent upset caused by occasional visits from an aggressively curious Scotland Yard inspector named Huxley (Stanley Ridges), Mary and Marshall wed a few months later. Just as the couple prepares to emigrate to Canada, a drunken, layabout neighbor, Simmons (Henry Daniell), announces to Marshall that unless he's regularly paid off, he will falsely claim that he heard Marshall kill his wife.

To this point, *The Suspect* concerns a man who is literally just a suspect and nothing more. Although we *surmise* that Marshall killed his wife (much like Dr. Crippen, a real figure whose 1910 arrest for the murder of his wife inspired a few superficial aspects of *The Suspect*), we neither see him commit a crime nor speak of it. His wife fell and broke her head; there's the ragged stairstep that tripped her, and that's that. Even Huxley admits he has no evidence. But the blackmail proposed by Simmons prompts Marshall to kill his neighbor with poisoned whiskey. We *do* observe this death, and now, very late in the story, Marshall is no longer just a suspect but, definitively, a perpetrator. Then again, he's rid the world of a terrible man.

There is a marvelous perversion at work here which, although encouraged by the film, isn't *in* the film—it's in *us*. We love Marshall. In fact, we adore him. We take pleasure in his numberless kindnesses and heartily support the devotion he gives to Mary—a gem of a girl, as it might have been put in 1902. We yearn for them to be together and happy. Naturally, our yearning makes us complicit in murder. *The Suspect* frees us to feel good about criminal homicide.

The film's morality becomes considerably more complex when Marshall is led to believe that the gentle Mrs. Simmons has been accused of her husband's murder. So: Marshall can sail with Mary and hope that Mrs. Simmons won't be convicted for something she didn't do—or he can get off the boat and make *sure* that she isn't.

Robert Siodmak's direction and Bernard Millhauser's screenplay (from the 1939 novel *This Way Out*, by James Ronald) manage a deft balance of domestic drama, love story, and thriller. Sequences in which Marshall walks at night while being trailed by various people are moody and tense, and the slow, painless murder of Simmons—as Marshall's face grows increasingly more expectant—is devastating, and not because anyone is going to grieve the victim. Paul Ivano's cinematography is mostly unmannered, as Siodmak was apparently more interested in the story's emotional and moral issues than in too many shots of dark, foggy streets and shadowed doorways (all of it created with flair on the Universal back lot).

Laughton's innate kindness (he was reading aloud to hospitalized children and servicemen during the time he shot the picture) is evident in Marshall, one of the actor's most subtle and endearing creations.

Ella Raines shows her quick-witted intelligence and wry humor, and Henry Daniell is a superlative no-good. Rosalind Ivan is a perfect horror as Cora, and lovely Molly Lamont brings dignity to the underwritten role of Mrs. Simmons.

The film's most problematic figure is Inspector Huxley. The fine character player Stanley Ridges captures Huxley's skill, imagination, and doggedness— and that's precisely why we don't care for him. He's a threat to our vicarious happiness.

A Watery Kind of Romance   *Johnny Angel*

Johnny Angel (1945) is a minor but not uninteresting noir mystery in which sea captain Angel (George Raft) investigates the death of his father and runs into an old flame who wants to betray her husband. The film opens strongly, in a fog at sea, as Angel's ship encounters a derelict that has been torn apart and plundered, leaving not a trace of the crew. The derelict is the SS *Emmaline Quincy*, and the senior Angel had been its captain, so Johnny has very personal reasons to explore the mystery.

Johnny's ship and his father's are owned by Gustafson Lines, headed by pudgy, weak-willed "Gusty" Gustafson (Marvin Miller) and his bored, disinterested wife Lylah (Claire Trevor), who is happy to try to rekindle old passions with Johnny. Johnny isn't buying but Lylah persists.

Onboard the *Quincy*, Johnny finds a woman's shoe—an effective moment because the tiny pump is absurdly incongruous in this place of rusted metal, immense machinery, and scattered debris. Later investigation throughout New Orleans's French Quarter brings Johnny to Paulette (Signe Hasso), who denies knowing anything about the *Quincy* until Johnny grabs her ankle and slips the shoe on her foot. With information from Paulette and facts gleaned from his own snooping, Johnny learns that the *Quincy* was carrying $5 million in French gold bullion, and that when the crew mutinied and killed his father, a mysterious stowaway made off with the gold after murdering all of his accomplices.

In the setup to the film's best moment, Lylah slips a letter opener up her sleeve as she prepares to tell Gusty good night. Not long after, after telling Johnny that the two of them can take the gold and sail to Rio, Gusty turns up, badly wounded and sick with the sting of betrayal. He has a gun, too. To this point, actor Marvin Miller has played Gusty as a hopeless weakling, so the worm-turns nature of the situation is startling and very well played by Miller, who looks absolutely, blubberingly miserable—and mad as hell—about his wife's betrayal.

Lylah is spared rough justice because of the intercession of Miss Drum (Margaret Wycherly), a middle-aged spinster who is the real brains of Gustafson Lines and the person who loves Gusty best.

Journeyman director Edwin L. Marin (*A Christmas Carol*, 1938 version; *Tall in the Saddle*) matched well with Raft, a stiff but compelling presence who specialized in direct-to-the-gut melodrama and seldom worked in noir. Johnny strides through the film with resolute purpose but is always a half-step behind, always in a gray fog of uncertainty. If this bothered Raft, it doesn't show. His performance is lively and sure-footed.

Dependable Claire Trevor, at thirty-six, is a lubricious sex kitten for grown-ups, and Marvin Miller—best known for voice-over work and the vocalizings of Robby the Robot in *Forbidden Planet*—is a revelation as Gusty. He's pathetic, beaten, and disgusted by his own weakness. The ultimate horror is that he loves a woman who wants him dead.

Motherhood and Murder   *Mildred Pierce*

Michael Curtiz's *Mildred Pierce* (1945) is notable for being told exclusively from a woman's point of view. Key conflicts in Ranald MacDougall's carefully wrought screenplay are uniquely female: the struggle to support oneself in "pink ghetto" jobs, various tragedies and disappointments of motherhood, uncommunicative or duplicitous men in one's romantic and business lives, the social dangers of being as career-minded as a man, and the search for respect that's grounded in more than good looks or a fat bank book. It's easy to see why Joan Crawford, always a fighter, was attracted to the project.

Typical of Warner Bros. productions of the period, *Mildred Pierce* opens powerfully, at a shadowy beach house where a violent, kinetically staged murder shoves us headlong into the narrative. We learn later that the beach house belongs to Mildred (Joan Crawford) and the victim, her husband, a dissolute playboy named Monte Beragon (Zachary Scott). In short order, the police have a wealth of suspects: Mildred; Mildred's sullen ex-husband, Bert Pierce (Bruce Bennett); and Mildred's old friend Wally (Jack Carson), a sharpie who has a business relationship with Mildred. Bert encourages the cops to think he killed Monte, and Mildred makes an out-and-out confession. Neither is being truthful.

Mildred's bitchy, ungrateful older daughter, Veda (Ann Blyth), is an especially colorful character and is central to what really interested scripter MacDougall and director Michael Curtiz: the sharp evolution of the key characters. Mildred pulls herself up from single motherhood to ownership of a fabulously successful chain of restaurants. Monte evolves from charmer to heel, and Wally metamorphoses from a flirty old friend who becomes complicit in Monte's takeover of Mildred's business. Ex-husband Bert, who begins as a lout, finally becomes Mildred's closest friend. And Veda . . .

. . . well, what to say about Veda? She's one of the great creations of noir, a character who begins as a spoiled kid; becomes a manipulative, rather lubricious pseudo-sophisticate who openly despises her selfless mother; and finally assures her own destruction.

Actress Ann Blyth came to movies as a singer and light actress, and in fact much of her career followed that pattern. Veda was a different sort of role—the role of a lifetime, in fact, and Blyth is horrifyingly good in it. Perpetually conniving, she hates her mother even as she takes everything her mother sacrifices to give her. Just seventeen when *Mildred Pierce* was released, Blyth is tiny (smaller even than the relatively diminutive Crawford) but shapes Veda into pure, ferocious id. Sexy with her baby face, pillowy lips, and taut little figure, Veda is a gaily decorated box of poisonous candy.

Crawford is impressively intense as Mildred, the role that put the actress back on top after being dismissed by MGM. (Warner had penciled in contract player Ann Sheridan to star, but Crawford won the role after agreeing to a screen test.) Crawford's portrayal isn't the false intensity of histrionics but the genuine on-screen commitment to character that comes from a performer who really lives the role—as Crawford, the ambitious ex-chorus girl, undoubtedly did.

Cinematographer Ernest Haller shot the picture with a full chromatic range, from bright sunlight to artfully choreographed interior shadows. Firelight effects inside the beach house are disquietingly effective, and Haller carefully lit Crawford to bring out her flashing eyes and the planes of her marvelous face.

For Michael Curtiz, a Hungarian émigré with a long, pre-Hollywood career in European silents, *Mildred Pierce* was another superior film in an expansive career that bulges with them. A peerless craftsman rather than an auteur, Curtiz was a key player (arguably *the* key creative player) in Warner Bros.' artistic and box-office dominance in the 1930s and '40s. And yet, despite its smooth gloss, *Mildred Pierce* has an almost unbearable edge of ragged emotion. The picture is as emotionally honest as it is slick, and that's not easy to pull off.

"Paint me, Chris."

Fritz Lang's *Scarlet Street* (1945) exists at the intersection of art, longing, deceit, debasement, and murder. Deceptively familiar, even light, for some of its running time, the film eventually rises on its hind legs and pitches the protagonist—and audiences—over a cliff. With superficial narrative similarities to Lang's *The Woman in the Window* (1944; see Chapter 6), *Scarlet Street* sets up a well-worn premise: A henpecked middle-aged man falls for a younger woman and gets into serious trouble. The similarities between the two films are made more pointed because in both the same three actors take the leads, Edward G. Robinson, Joan Bennett, and Dan Duryea.

Christopher Cross (Robinson) is a meek, unhappily married cashier at a prosperous company. He's held the same job for twenty-five years and has fallen into a rut of presumed contentment. He's a talented amateur painter who takes pleasure in that avocation, but he's consumed by quiet longing, wondering how it would feel if a young woman looked at him with love. His wife, Adele (Rosalind Ivan), is a complete shrew, so cashiering and painting are Chris's only escapes.

Alone in the city, Chris summons the courage to knock down a man who has been beating a woman in the street. The incident occurs at night in a bad part of town, the man is flashily dressed, and the woman seems less concerned with the beating than with making sure her assailant gets away. In 1945 it was difficult for studio movies to say, "This is a prostitute and this is her pimp," but that's precisely the situation here. In his innocence, Chris is oblivious to all of that. Subsequent conversation with the girl, Kitty Marsh (Bennett), leads to a fundamental misunderstanding: Because he's a little bit tongue-tied, Chris inadvertently allows Kitty to assume that he's a successful gallery artist whose paintings sell for $50,000 a pop. Well, that sounds better than "I'm a cashier," so Chris allows the charade to develop. He wants to see Kitty again.

She wants to see Chris, too, not for romance but because she's tagged him as a mark. For romance, she depends on her pimp, Johnny Prince (Duryea), who enjoys slapping her because he knows that she'll not only take it but enjoys it. With Johnny's blessing, Kitty strings Chris along, wheedling money from him, tempting him to steal from his good-hearted employer and saying "Paint me, Chris," as she hands across nail polish and sticks out her naked foot (a moment that was cut by censorship boards in some states).

Kitty finally signs her name to Chris's paintings and finds unexpected gallery success. Because love can be a dulling narcotic, Chris is ecstatic rather than furious. People are seeing his work, and Kitty appears happy. At the very least, she can continue to be a lazy slob without suffering abuse about it from Johnny.

Everything begins to collapse when Chris witnesses Kitty and Johnny embracing and kissing. "Jeepers, I love you, Johnny," Kitty says idiotically.

Alone with Kitty soon after, Chris forgives her and asks her to marry him. Kitty flings herself onto her bed and sobs. Chris comforts her until he sees that Kitty isn't sobbing at all but laughing. She's tickled by what she sees as Chris's ridiculousness. She angrily tells him he's an ugly old man and that she and Johnny have always been together and always will be. Chris is a joke, a sucker. With that, Chris loses his senses. (In an absurd aside, newspaper headlines from the next day refer to Kitty as "Famous Painter.")

The fact that Chris is never pinched by the police—that is, he suffers no traditional punishment—was a concession by Hollywood's Production Code, which invariably demanded clear-cut comeuppance for wrongdoers. Chris is free but he's tormented by guilt—a comeuppance that Code administrators found acceptable.

Scarlet Street was scripted by Oscar-winner Dudley Nichols (*The Informer*), adapting a play and novel by Georges de la Fouchardiere called *La Chienne* (*The Bitch*). (The book was translated and published in America by Knopf in 1930 and was titled, appropriately enough, *The Poor Sap.*) The picture was shot by Lang and cinematographer Milton Krasner almost exclusively on stages, which has the unexpected effect of heightening the realism of the characters and their motivations. The film looks dark and enclosed, and captures agitated lives in miniature, perfectly appropriate for a tale set in a hothouse of emotion. Lang moves his camera with easy, considered confidence along false-front streets and cramped interiors; much of the story is set in Greenwich Village, which seems a desperate rather than joyous place.

The voices that plague Chris during the picture's final sequences unmistakably reference the voices that drive Peter Lorre to kill in Lang's *M* (1931). Of course, the Lorre character is a killer of children, so although we regard him with sick fascination, we give him no sympathy. Chris Cross, on the other hand, wants to connect with another human heart and imagines that he does, only to be slapped down in the cruelest way imaginable.

In *Scarlet Street*'s final moments, Chris is captured in a crane shot on a sidewalk crowded with shoppers. A slow dissolve causes all the people but Chris to disappear. He's alone yet again, a small figure with his back turned to us, shuffling into a miserable future, his head and the soundtrack echoing with the foolish refrain, "Jeepers, I love you, Johnny!"

Six Days to Doom

European cineastes discovered Edgar G. Ulmer's *Detour* (1945) in the 1960s, and much of the praise from that period suggested that many of the commentators had never seen the film. Some asserted that Ulmer put the picture together on one or two sets and in front of process screens, and with a cast of three. The film's undeniable ferocity was accurately noted, but the suggestion was that Ulmer had concocted the whole thing out of nothing at all.

The picture was produced and released by PRC (Producers Releasing Corporation), which existed near the bottom of Hollywood's Poverty Row—a step above laughable shoestring outfits like Tiffany and Chesterfield but not nearly as prestigious as tiny but prolific Monogram. *Detour* was indeed low-budget ($85,000 is a reasonable guess), and Ulmer shot it in just six days, but the film looks no more poverty-stricken than any other B-minus production of the time. Key roles are provided for nine actors, and the film has numerous secondary players and extras. There is some process work (typical even for A-pictures, of course), but much of the script was shot outdoors in LA and in the surrounding desert. And although *Detour* is clearly inexpensive, it never looks threadbare.

Al Roberts (Tom Neal) is a New York nightclub pianist who wants to follow his girlfriend, Sue (Claudia Drake), to Los Angeles. Broke, he has no choice but to thumb it and quickly becomes wearied by the road. Then, in a lucky stroke, a new convertible piloted by an amiable fellow named Haskell (Edmund MacDonald) pulls over and gives Roberts a lift. After Haskell is suddenly stricken by a heart attack, Roberts foolishly assumes the dead man's identity and his bankroll.

Confident after a night in a motel, Roberts drives on and picks up a ratty, tubercular female hitchhiker, Vera (Ann Savage). She sits in silence for a long while and then abruptly demands to know what Roberts did with Haskell's body. *She knows!* Haskell had picked her up earlier (and been badly clawed for his trouble), so Vera is familiar with the car and with Haskell. Roberts is shocked and cowed.

From this point, *Detour* becomes a perverse satire of domesticity, as Vera joins herself to Roberts at the hip, badgering him in motel rooms and threatening to turn him in unless he does as she says. Vera claims to be convinced that Roberts is a murderer. He isn't, of course, and it's his fundamental decency that prevents

Case File: Edgar G. Ulmer (1904–72)

An Austrian intellectual who was shoehorned into Hollywood's fringes, Ulmer had early experience as a stage actor and set designer in Vienna and Berlin before the rise of Hitler. He was associated with Max Reinhardt and F. W. Murnau, and made periodic professional visits to Hollywood before settling there in 1930. He began directing in 1933. From the start, Ulmer's American career was filled with below-the-radar projects: Yiddish- and Ukrainian-language dramas and musicals, sexploitation the likes of *Damaged Goods*, black-cast pictures, and public-service short subjects. *The Black Cat*, an Expressionist thriller Ulmer made for Universal, is a classic of the golden age of Hollywood horror, but Ulmer never gained traction as a studio director. He worked frequently for B- and C-level independent companies, turning out an occasional gem, such as *Bluebeard* (1944) and *Strange Illusion* (1945). The Ulmer cult that began to take hold in Europe in the 1960s is based mainly on *Detour* (1945), a masterpiece of poverty-row noir that's also one of the most disturbingly fatalistic films ever made. Other noir thrillers by Ulmer: *The Strange Woman* and *Ruthless*. He directed some intriguing science-fiction adventures, too, including the inexpensive but atmospheric *The Man from Planet X* (1951). Ulmer continued to work until the mid-1960s.

Detour (1945), directed by Edgar G. Ulmer: Materializing on a desert road as if by fate, the hateful Vera (Ann Savage) manipulates Al Roberts (Tom Neal) like a marionette. She accuses him of a crime he didn't commit and then cooks up a big-money scheme fit for idiots. Al just wants out.

Case File: Tom Neal & Ann Savage

The importance of Tom Neal (1914–72) to film history rests entirely on his performance in Edgar G. Ulmer's *Detour* (1945), as a hapless, well-meaning guy bedeviled by his own poor choices and by a female hitchhiker who makes his life a living hell. Compact, sturdy, and handsome, Neal had an Ivy League education, small experience as a college boxer, and a brief stage background before coming to Hollywood in the late 1930s. Signed by MGM, he had bits in features and larger parts in short subjects. After being dropped by Metro, Neal freelanced at Universal, Columbia, and RKO. Even steadier work was offered by Republic, Monogram, PRC, and Lippert. Neal starred or had featured roles in low-budget crime thrillers, westerns, serials, jungle adventures, and a pair of wartime oddities, Edward Dmytryk's *Behind the Rising Sun* (as a Japanese soldier) and Gordon Douglas's *First Yank into Tokyo* (as an American disguised by plastic surgery to appear Japanese).

Neal's modest career began to peter out around 1950 and was effectively ended in 1951, after he nearly beat actor Franchot Tone to death in a fistfight over claims to party girl/starlet Barbara Payton. In 1965, while working as a landscape architect in Palm Springs, Neal was convicted of involuntary manslaughter in the shooting death of his third wife. He spent seven years in prison and died just months after his release.

Slender, apple-cheeked Ann Savage (1914–2008) was a confident, versatile actress—so versatile, in fact, that she had an almost chameleonic quality that apparently baffled studio executives and casting directors. She played blonde, she played brunette; she could be lighthearted, she could be intimidating; she was a romantic lead, she shaded into character parts. Because she never established (or was allowed to establish) an Ann Savage "brand," she became an industry floater who could handle starring roles in B movies and small parts and bits in bigger pictures. Her belated and lasting fame as the tubercular, ill-tempered Vera of *Detour* is well deserved but hardly suggestive of the range of her talent. To her credit, Savage accepted her cultish fame and occasionally appeared at *Detour* retrospectives, reminiscing, answering questions, and enjoying fans' admiration.

Savage appeared in three other films with Tom Neal in the mid-1940s, *Two-Man Submarine*, *Klondike Kate*, and *The Unwritten Code*. She moved into television in 1950 and did guest spots until 1956, when she left the business. However, she came out of retirement in 2007 to take the lead role in Guy Maddin's quasi-experimental feature *My Winnipeg*.

him from slugging Vera and taking his chances. He wants her to know that he's innocent.

After Vera comes up with a harebrained scheme to collect an inheritance that involves Roberts passing himself off as Haskell, she becomes drunk and threatens to go to the police if Roberts doesn't play along. To emphasize her point, she locks herself in the bedroom with the telephone. Roberts bangs on the locked door and then tugs at the phone cord, attempting to break it, unaware that it's tangled itself around Vera's neck. Was Vera serious about her threat? Well, it hardly matters now because she's dead.

Detour has a framing device, a diner in which Roberts sits as the film opens, his memory jogged by a jukebox tune. Now, at the end, we return to the diner, where police pick him up. He muses in voice-over that "fate or some mysterious force can put a finger on you or me for no good reason at all."

Martin Goldsmith and the uncredited Martin Mooney adapted Goldsmith's blunt 1939 novel. As filmed, *Detour* is just sixty-seven minutes long and frankly unforgettable. Rugged B-actor Neal never appeared in a better film, or gave a better performance. Roberts is utterly, convincingly defeated, and Neal has earned his place in movie history.

Ann Savage is terrifying. A beautiful woman transformed by makeup artist Bud Westmore and wardrobe mistress Mona Barry into a dissolute creature of the road, Savage gives a star-making performance in a minor film that the Hollywood establishment never saw and never cared to see. Vaguely comical at first (she pointlessly brushes her lusterless hair after Roberts gives her the lift), Vera quickly becomes fate's own blunt instrument, a perfect bully who wears Roberts out with unending carping and bossiness. She's unsympathetic but pathetic, as well, and it's sad that she's already been ground down by life.

Ulmer and cinematographer Benjamin Kline (a longtime employee of Columbia Pictures who frequently worked with the Three Stooges) shot exteriors in pitiless bright light and brought chiaroscuro mood to interiors. During the framing device, Roberts's face is captured in gloomy, shadowed close-up, a horizontal band of light illuminating his eyes. (There could be no such light source in the diner, so the audacious device is purely existential.) After Roberts strangles Vera, the subjective camera captures his gaze as it moves around the motel room, going in and out of focus as Roberts's brain struggles to process what has happened.

Ulmer shot with care and thoughtfulness during his meager six days. *Detour* was ignored by all but trade publications upon release. Its reputation has steadily grown, and while the film has yet to be fully restored, progressively better prints have surfaced since the year 2000.

Itchy

The most celebrated moment in *The Postman Always Rings Twice* (1946) is our first look at Cora Smith (Lana Turner). Her lipstick has rolled across the floor and is picked up by drifter Frank Chambers (John Garfield). The camera eye mimics his gaze, traveling upward along Cora's naked legs before a cut to her full figure, resplendent in white short-shorts, midriff-baring white top, and a white turban. Frank has always prided himself for having "itchy feet"—the urge to stay on the move—but this time he's hooked, and he knows it and so do we.

Postman was the first time Lana Turner played a "bad girl." Although she seldom took such roles during her career, she became so closely identified with

Cora Smith that she was forever after known as a femme fatale. The film also was Turner's only experience with John Garfield. With Turner in one ironically white outfit after another, the pair strikes sparks on-screen, and although changing mores have stripped *Postman* of much of its sexual charge, the film remains a powerful cautionary tale about the hazards of lust.

As written by Harry Riskin and Niven Busch from James L. Cain's celebrated 1934 novel, Frank accepts a job at a roadside restaurant called Twin Oaks. The owner, Nick Smith (Cecil Kellaway), is an amiable fellow in late middle age who provides Cora with the security she wants but bores her stiff. Pheromones and bad judgment being what they are, Frank and Cora fall in love and scheme to kill Nick. They succeed, but through a series of clever legal maneuvers that drives them apart and seems to kill their love, Cora is sentenced to probation and Frank walks. But in a grim twist that causes Frank to be wrongly convicted for another murder, it appears that Nick will be avenged.

At 113 minutes, and directed with only occasional flair by Tay Garnett, *Postman* overstays its welcome. The run-up to the murder of Nick, and the act itself, is thrilling, but the jurisprudence nature of most that follows seems anticlimactic. Audrey Totter has a good bit late in the film as a trampy piece of work picked up by Frank in a weak moment, and burly character actor Alan Reed (later the voice of TV's Fred Flintstone) is disagreeably amusing as a private investigator turned blackmailer. So much footage, though, is devoted to the warring attorneys (Leon Ames and Hume Cronyn) that the film's sexual charge is diminished. After the murder, *Postman* becomes a different movie.

An aborted early attempt on Nick's life involves a sock full of ball bearings and an electrocuted cat. The lovers are successful later, as Cora pilots the car while Frank nervously waits in the backseat for an opportune moment to clobber his drunk boss with a bottle. The large soundstage dressed to look like the winding, mountainous road to Malibu is beautifully lit for night by cinematographer Sidney Wagner, and a miniature road and cars are used effectively in long shots. Subsequent action, when Frank takes an unwilling tumble down the mountain in the car with Nick, is a good shock and will give the schemers plenty to worry about later.

Lana Turner was never celebrated for her dramatic skill, and she had her hands full acting opposite a trained actor the caliber of Garfield. To Turner's credit, she holds her own and is credible except in one or two very brief moments. She has no trouble looking beautiful and handles her dialogue— which ranges from amorous to venomous—generally well. She seems very engaged with the character.

In 1945 (when *Postman* was shot), James M. Cain's scandalous novel could not be filmed as written. (It was adapted again, to frank but unmoving effect, in 1981, with Jack Nicholson and Jessica Lange.) Much of the film's steaminess resides in Frank's face, as he speculatively eyes Cora and gives Nick curious, appraising glances. Garfield also used his body well, suggesting that Frank's "itchiness" has spread to more than just his feet. Without being at all graphic (even the pair's kisses are chaste, unlike the sadomasochistic encounters of the novel), the film successfully suggests the animal sexuality of these two young people.

This lively German poster for *The Postman Always Rings Twice* (1946) celebrates John Garfield, Lana Turner, lust, and murder.

The script changes the book's Nick Papadakis to the inexplicably Anglicized Nick Smith. Cecil Kellaway plays Nick with a twinkle in his eye and isn't at all like the vulgar oaf created by Cain. Readers of the novel weren't sad to see Nick go. The movie Nick is sweet and harmless, so Frank becomes particularly unsympathetic. He (and we) can't even pretend he's doing Cora the service of a rescue.

The fact that Frank is stung for a murder he didn't commit is a nice bit of irony, of course, and also reflects the "doubling" effect of the film's title. The metaphorical postman didn't bring Frank anything the first time around, but now the postman is back, and he's ringing the bell twice to be sure Frank gets the message.

The Aphrodisiac of Hate

Stripped to its bare essentials, *Gilda* (1946) is familiar B-movie stuff, in which a young guy in Buenos Aires bumps into an old flame who happens to be married to the young guy's boss—a love triangle. But as developed by scripters Jo Eisinger and Marion Parsonnet, and two uncredited writers, Ben Hecht and the film's producer, Virginia Van Upp (all working from a story by E. A. Ellington), *Gilda* is deliciously, startlingly perverse. The former lovers are Gilda (Rita Hayworth) and Johnny Farrell (Glenn Ford), and they don't share the expected sort of passion—they share hatred. Something went disastrously wrong in their past relationship, and now they despise each other with such fervor that their sexual longing is rekindled.

"I hate you," Johnny whispers to Gilda when they finally allow themselves to clinch. "I hate you, too, Johnny," Gilda answers. "I hate you so much I think I'm going to die from it." Heavy kiss. Gilda (softer): "I think I'm going to die from it."

By this time, Gilda's husband, casino owner Ballin Mundson (George Macready, in a sterling performance) grasps the intense, reciprocal nature of Johnny and Gilda's relationship. To him, it's a double betrayal, because Gilda is his wife and because he took Johnny from back-alley crap games, dressed him in a tuxedo, and turned him into his number-one boy—and if you think there's a gay subtext there, you're probably right. (Think, for instance, about Mundson's sword cane, which Mundson and Johnny repeatedly refer to as a person.) Mundson rightfully feels betrayed, so there's going to be trouble.

In a sunnier time, Mundson wants Johnny to meet his new bride. This will be our first glimpse of her, too. In a line pregnant with meaning, Mundson calls, "Gilda, are you decent?" Gilda (unseen): "Me?" At that, her face and fabulous mane of hair arc from the bottom of the frame and into our view. She's breathtaking and exchanges a brief, surprised glance with Johnny. Then she smiles hugely. "Sure I'm decent!"

Hayworth does two musical numbers, a lively rumba called "Amada Mio" and the film's signature set piece, Gilda's sizzling, quasi-striptease to "Put the Blame on Mame." Gilda does the latter (with uncredited vocal by Anita Ellis) at her husband's casino late in the film, after she's been abandoned and reviled by both of the men in her life. She's despondent and wants to debase herself. Hayworth plays the sequence brilliantly in black opera gloves and a shiny black gown that has almost no top at all. Gilda is emphatically, aggressively sexy, but there's an edge of hysteria to her behavior, and she's too eager to invite men from the audience to come up and help her undo her zippers. Johnny must finally rescue her from herself. It's a timeless sequence that's at once exhilarating and tragic. (Neither "Amada Mio" nor "Put the Blame on Mame" were in the original script. Songwriters Doris Fisher and Allan Roberts banged out the superior tunes very quickly, and both sequences were shot after principal photography had wrapped.)

The power of *Gilda* is paradoxically the film's undoing. Everything rides on the assumption—often asserted by Gilda herself—that she's a heedless roundheels who has slept with numberless men. For instance, not long after being thrust back into Johnny's world, Gilda infuriates him by flirting with an Argentine local.

JOHNNY

You can't talk to men down here like you would at home,
they don't understand it.

GILDA

Understand what?

JOHNNY

They think you mean it.

GILDA

Mean what?

JOHNNY

Doesn't it bother you at all that you're married?

GILDA

What I want to know is, does it bother you?

Gilda's purported cheap sexual behavior explains Johnny's disdain, as well as the depth of his desire for her. Her heedlessness is the engine that creates the miasma of hatred that swirls around this troubled couple. But at the end, in a nod to the Production Code, Gilda reveals that she's been a good girl all along. That makes Johnny happy but takes a lot of sting from the movie's tail.

Director Charles Vidor was a taskmaster on his sets, and although he was reasonably deferential to stars, he nevertheless worked them hard. As Gilda, Rita Hayworth is everything—and more—that Vidor or anyone else could have wanted. The circumspection imposed by censors undercuts the movie's premise, but it also allows us to *imagine* things that no actor could duplicate. *Gilda* soars because of what we do not see.

In *Gilda* (1946), Rita Hayworth isn't as amoral as she likes to pretend. But because former lover Johnny Farrell (Glenn Ford) thinks otherwise, their love is expressed most passionately as mutual hatred.

Icy Ambitiousness at Monogram

Like *Gilda*, Monogram Pictures' *Suspense* (1946) has a show-business backdrop involving a married woman who pursues an affair with one of her husband's employees. Because the film stars the British ice-skating phenomenon Belita (an appealing, soft-spoken woman whose real name was Gladys Belita Jepson-Turner), many of the dramatic set pieces revolve around a magnificent ice arena that showman Frank Leonard (Albert Dekker) has built to celebrate and promote his ice-skating wife, Roberta Elva. The fact that Roberta's professional surname is different from her husband's may mean nothing. Then again, it may suggest that the marriage is less than solid.

The latter possibility is what motivates Joe Morgan (Barry Sullivan), a hustler who ingratiates himself with Leonard and works his way up from peanut vendor to minor executive. Leonard isn't blind to Joe's interest in Roberta, however, and finally gets fed up. His scheme to commit murder backfires—fatally, it seems—which allows Joe and Roberta to pursue their romance over the subsequent months. But is Leonard really dead? And if he isn't, what's he going to do about his wife and his employee?

Monogram made its (small) fortune with very low-budget comedies, westerns, thrillers, and musicals. The pictures were rigidly formulaic and could be churned out quickly, almost as if from standardized templates. The studio gave work to young performers on the way up (Barry Sullivan is a good example); the occasional big name on the way down (Kay Francis was one); established character players like Albert Dekker, who moved easily between big and small studios; and a vast army of freelance actors and bit players whose faces might ring a bell with inveterate moviegoers. There was nothing unprofessional about the Monogram product, but no one who labored there imagined that the place was anything but the anteroom of real moviemaking.

Every once in a while, though, if a star or vehicle showed particular promise, Monogram would marshal its resources to create what was, for Monogram, an "A" picture. The studio's handsome 1934 adaptation of *Jane Eyre* is the most celebrated of these "A" releases. Although *Suspense* is neither as "legitimate" nor as prestigious as *Jane Eyre*, it does suggest that, when inspired, the little studio could create pictures equal to, say, B-unit productions from Columbia or Universal.

Suspense is lovely to look at, thanks to the imagination of director Frank Tuttle (best known for *This Gun for Hire* [1942; see Chapter 5]), and the artistry of cinematographer Karl Struss, an industry giant who won an Academy Award for *Sunrise* (1927).

For *Suspense*, Tuttle and Struss simulated a big-budget picture with clever (and frankly brazen) use of matte paintings, forced perspective, rear projection, and painted cycloramas. To suggest the ice palace's exterior, brief establishing shots of Hollywood's fabulous, streamline *moderne* Pan-Pacific Auditorium were used.

Leonard's murder scheme, supposedly set in the High Sierras, combines back projection, miniatures, and a beautifully detailed pine forest and lake set.

Ice-dancing sequences choreographed by Nick Castle were shot on ice that shimmers richly with the skaters' reflections. The camera soars and dips, pans and tracks. In especially kinetic moments, skaters deliver their bodies right to the camera lens.

Something called the Jaws of Death—a blazing, knife-edged hoop through which Roberta hurls her body at the climax of her act—is another arresting element of the picture's production design. When Joe ponders murder, the shadow of the Jaws of Death is suddenly everywhere: on the ice, outside Joe's upstairs office, on a wall behind a metal staircase. In a literal sense, the ubiquity of the shadow is absurd, but as a metaphor for Joe's growing madness, the device is magnificent.

Joe can't bring himself to kill Roberta, but that doesn't make him a nice guy. Although *Suspense* seems to tell the story of a good fellow who goes bad, the reality is that a crumb has temporarily become "good" before reverting to his true self. (In this, and in the faintly disreputable show-business setting, *Suspense* anticipates the following year's *Nightmare Alley*; see Chapter 5.)

There is a reckoning for Joe, and it comes in the form of an ill-tempered former lover (Bonita Granville) who has dogged her target throughout much of his relationship with Roberta. After justice is served, Joe's assistant (frog-voiced Eugene Pallette) pronounces, "He should have stuck to his peanuts."

Dark Secrets in Iverstown

A love triangle based on terrible, secret knowledge is at the core of *The Strange Love of Martha Ivers* (1946), an impeccably well-crafted noir set not in a big city but in a small one. In 1928, Iverstown is growing rapidly because of a millworks owned by a single family, but in the Ivers mansion things are rocky. Adolescent Martha Ivers (Janis Wilson) is a chronic runaway who refuses to live with her dark, domineering aunt (Judith Anderson). Martha's allies are a restless boy named Sam Masterson (Darryl Hickman) and a timid, ambitious youth named Walter O'Neil (Mickey Kuhn). When Martha half-intentionally kills her aunt by whacking her on the head with her own cane and sending her tumbling down a staircase, Walter backs up Martha's assertion that the fall was an accident and nothing more. Worse, false testimony by Walter and Martha sends an innocent man to the gallows.

Flash forward to the present. Martha (Barbara Stanwyck) runs the now-mammoth millworks and is the most powerful person in the city. She has married Walter (Kirk Douglas), a spineless secret alcoholic who has become the town's busybody district attorney. Their marriage is stiff, formal, and joyless.

Into this peculiar situation comes Sam (Van Heflin), an itinerant professional gambler who stops at Iverstown because he happens to be in the area. He's curious about what has changed since he abandoned the city as a boy. Inevitably, old feelings are rekindled when he sees Martha, much to the unhappiness of Walter, who uses his considerable power to have Sam beaten and rousted out of town. But Sam returns and romances a sweet-natured ex-convict named Toni (Lizabeth Scott). By the time all the high emotion plays itself out, two people are dead.

Martha Ivers was written by Robert Rossen and directed by Lewis Milestone. The two had teamed the previous year on an acclaimed war picture, *A Walk in the Sun*, which was set in Italy. *Martha Ivers* is very different and peculiarly American in its examination of money, the dynamics of local power, and what time does to youthful ambition.

The Strange Love of Martha Ivers (1946): Martha (Barbara Stanwyck) runs Iverstown so that her dark secrets remain hidden. She'd like to run Sam (Van Heflin), too.

Walter is living his adolescent dream, but the reality is sour. Sam Masterson, free and easy as a kid, has continued on that course, gambling for big money across the country and as unconcerned with his sterling war record as he is about his brushes with the law. Sam slips and slides through life—much like the coin that he unconsciously manipulates back and forth along the tops of his fingers.

The film's 1928 sequences aren't noir but Gothic. The dark, mahogany-trimmed Ivers mansion is an oppressive place, rather in the manner of Manderly in Hitchcock's *Rebecca* (1940; continuity between that film and *Martha Ivers* is provided by actress Judith Anderson, who is an unpleasant figure in both).

The present-day portion that comprises the greater part of *Martha Ivers* is pure noir, with many scenes taking place at night (the evocative cinematography is by Victor Milner), as moody conflict shifts between grimy garages, bus stations, seedy dives, and Martha's citadel of wealth. Iverstown seems to have no middle class. Martha has created a sealed world designed to favor only her. Barbara Stanwyck is thrilling in the role, by turns defiant, wistful, and unbalanced. Her performance is subtle and measured, and is among the best and most complex she ever gave. The climax, which brings Martha and Walter together in shared guilt and a sick parody of love and physical intimacy, is shattering.

Portions of *The Strange Love of Martha Ivers* were shot during an acrimonious and violent Hollywood craft-union strike. When Lewis Milestone left the studio to chat with the strikers, he elected not break the picket lines in order to return. As a result, capable journeyman Byron Haskin directed sections of the film. On the set, Stanwyck was helpful to Douglas but warned Heflin that if he did his coin trick during her dialogue scenes, she'd upstage him by raising her skirt.

That's another kind of local power.

Hitchcock and Love's Distorted Lens

If *Gilda* is informed by hate, then Alfred Hitchcock's *Notorious* (1946) is dominated by guilt by association, and by deep antipathy that pulls a man and a woman closer, even as it threatens to drive them apart forever. Alicia Huberman (Ingrid Bergman) is recruited in Los Angeles by a government agency interested in Nazi activity in postwar Rio. Alicia seems a good choice because her father has been convicted as a Nazi. Alicia herself claims to be apolitical and frankly disinterested in American-style patriotism. But in secret agency recordings, she lambastes her father for his unregenerate Nazism and proclaims her love for the United States. She assures her contact, agent Devlin (Cary Grant), that she'll do as his agency requests.

Regardless, Devlin doesn't trust Alicia, particularly after she announces that Sebastian (Claude Rains), the wealthy man she's spying on, wants to marry her. She also says she'll go through with the marriage. In other words, she'll prostitute herself to gain a life of ease and (she says) assist Devlin and Uncle Sam.

In the most celebrated single moment of *Notorious*, Alicia awaits Devlin during a dinner party at the home she shares with Sebastian. The camera is on a very high crane, looking down on Alicia as she stands in an enormous vestibule. The crane begins to move downward, adjusting to emphasize Alicia, and finally positioning itself so that the screen is filled with the image of her hand, the edge of a riskily purloined key barely visible in her clenched palm. This is bravura filmmaking with enormous dramatic impact.

Still, the espionage angle is all part of Hitchcock's MacGuffin—expository material that grounds the plot and moves the narrative forward, but that isn't at all what the film is really about. What interested Hitchcock was the ambivalent passion shared by a man who suspects his love object is morally corrupt and a woman whose understandable defensiveness and resentment may destroy the affair before it can properly begin. One of the picture's great set pieces—the pair's discovery of ore-filled bottles in Sebastian's wine cellar—is unbearably suspenseful (Alicia has stolen the key from her husband, and one of the bottles threatens to fall onto the floor as Devlin's poking fingers nudge it closer to the edge of a shelf). The power of the sequence, though, comes from its denouement, when Devlin realizes Sebastian is watching. How to throw him off? "Kiss me," Devlin whispers to Alicia, and when she obeys, Hitch and cinematographer Ted Tetzlaff come in on Dev and Alicia's faces so closely that you can feel the steam of their released, long-suppressed passion. It's as forcefully intimate a moment as any in a Hollywood studio film of the period—or ever, proving that on-screen explicitness is not a prerequisite for the suggestion of sexual heat.

Like *The Strange Love of Martha Ivers*, *Notorious* is related from a woman's point of view. (The script is by Ben Hecht, from a story by John Taintor Foote, and with an uncredited assist by Clifford Odets.) Alicia is the central character. Devlin and Sebastian are powerful in that masterful kind of way (even their names are superficially similar, and commanding), but Alicia is the figure that evolves the most, and most dramatically. In the end, her real nemesis isn't her essentially weak husband but her bloodless mother-in-law (Leopoldine Konstantin), who suggests that Sebastian might be rid of his problem if he were to slowly poison Alicia. Because we feel we know Alicia since we are so close to her physically, we become hugely invested in her predicament. Late in the film, as Alicia is slowly dying from poison, Tetzlaff lights her from above, giving her face a peculiar, sickly pallor that, in close-up, is shocking.

When Devlin finally arrives to spirit Alicia from the house, Sebastian is struck mute with terror. His bloodless associates watch with undisguised suspicion as Devlin helps Alicia down the stairs and into a waiting taxi. Another member of the plot has been murdered simply because he made a fuss when he spied a champagne bottle on a mantle during a party. When Devlin locks the taxi door to keep Sebastian out, the schemer's fate is sealed.

Sebastian and his mother (like the sons and mothers in Hitchcock's *Psycho* [see Chapter 7] and *The Birds*) are unwholesomely linked. The point is beautifully made with a subjective shot as Alicia struggles to focus on the two of them as she's feeling the effects of the poison. The figures of Sebastian and Mother blacken and shift, and in a moment it's impossible to tell which is which.

That the tale concludes on a note of triumphant, damaged love may say as much about Hitchcock and postwar ambivalence as about the familiar aspects of noir. Emotionally mature and daring, *Notorious* is one of the best American movies of the '40s.

Booze, Memory, and Murder

Black Angel (1946) is a minor but nicely crafted thriller with a clever twist and a solid lead performance by Dan Duryea. Another asset is the film's narrative simplicity: A blackmailer named Mavis (Constance Dowling) has been found strangled in her apartment, and a male visitor who discovers her body is later identified by a maid as he leaves the building. In a trial that's concisely told via montage, the hapless innocent Kirk Bennett (John Phillips) is found guilty, and in short order he's on death row. His loyal wife, Kathy (June Vincent), allies herself with Marty Blair (Dan Duryea), a successful but seriously alcoholic songwriter who tried to visit the victim on the evening of her murder but was turned away by the doorman. But another visitor, Marko (Peter Lorre), was ushered right inside.

Kathy sets her sights on the sinister Marko as the obvious suspect and teams with Blair to take a piano-and-singer gig at Marko's club. (Okay, that's unlikely, but it moves the narrative forward.) Some suspenseful snooping by Kathy in Marko's office suggests additional links to the victim, but in the end Marty Blair, coming off a terrible drunk in a psych ward, has visions of killing the woman himself.

And now the crux of the drama: Can Marty convince the authorities of his guilt, and can he prevent the imminent execution of Kirk Bennett?

Black Angel is the work of Universal contract producer-director Roy William Neill, who helmed the fabulous Sherlock Holmes film series with Basil Rathbone and Nigel Bruce throughout much of the 1940s. Horror fans know him for his solid work on *Frankenstein Meets the Wolf Man* (1943), one of the crazier entries in Universal's monster cycle. Neill was not exceptionally imaginative, but he could tell a story clearly and with visuals that kept audiences interested. His *Black Angel* collaborators are screenwriter Roy Chansler (adapting Cornell Woolrich's considerably darker novel) and cinematographer Paul Ivano, who brings a glossy, frequently menacing look to the film.

Duryea and the indefatigable Lorre are perfectly cast: Duryea with his reed-thin dissipation, Lorre with his unique style of silky menace. Veteran character player Wallace Ford has a solid bit as the friend whose job it is to lock the drunken Marty in his room so he can't hurt himself. (In a bleak little irony, the climax reveals that the custodian had charged Marty a quarter to let him out of his room on the night of the murder. Twenty-five cents, and a woman is dead.)

Constance Dowling is fiery as the doomed Mavis, and you wish she could have had the Kathy Bennett part because star June Vincent is subdued and a little colorless. Stone-faced Freddie Steele makes an impression as Marko's

Case File: Dan Duryea (1907–68)

Dan Duryea's slicked blond hair, slender build, and thin, high voice don't mark him as immediately intimidating. Look closer, though, and you see the sly intelligence, the bulge beneath his jacket, and a completely unashamed nature. When Dan Duryea played the bad guy, the bad guy had gall.

The actor is probably best recalled for his roles as skunks in a pair of Fritz Lang gems, *Scarlet Street* and *The Woman in the Window*. He also had key roles in *Lady on a Train* (providing a disconcerting contrast to leading lady Deanna Durbin) and *Criss Cross*. He did conventional crime dramas, too, including *The Underworld Story*, *Johnny Stool Pigeon*, and *Slaughter on Tenth Avenue*. As Duryea shaded toward fifty, his face and manner became even more intriguing, as witness his fine, carefully modulated performance as an aging box man in Paul Wendkos's *The Burglar*. Duryea also made an indelible mark in westerns, notably as the feral gunfighter in Anthony Mann's groundbreaking *Winchester '73*, and in *Night Passage*, as the antagonist of James Stewart and Audie Murphy.

bouncer/bodyguard, and Broderick Crawford, as a tough but sympathetic cop, finds more in his role than is apparent in the script.

Black Angel becomes particularly tart when Marty, behaving a bit like a wet-brain, hits on Kathy when her husband is hours away from execution and then can't understand why she rejects him. Noir has plenty of protagonists that aren't completely sympathetic, and Marty is one of them. His approach to romance isn't as awful as murder, of course, but it's pretty egregious, nonetheless—and pleasingly believable.

She Loved Herself Best of All

Within a year of directing *Detour*, a very low-budget quickie, Edgar G. Ulmer was working for coproducers Hunt Stromberg and Hedy Lamarr on a United Artists release, *The Strange Woman* (1946), a nicely budgeted costume melodrama that brings noir to Maine in the mid-nineteenth century. Lamarr had grown tired of unchallenging roles, and was eager to prove herself as an actress.

She did.

Jenny Hager is an unusually complex character with multiple, often conflicting motivations. The fever-pitch story, about a young beauty who rises from nothing to great wealth by manipulating men, was a congenial one for Ulmer and allowed Lamarr to throw herself into a role. A flashback establishes Jenny as the daughter of Bangor's ill-tempered town drunk. She's a deceitful, cruel child who shoves a timid companion, Ephraim, into a river, watches as he nearly drowns, and then saves him. Jenny gets no approval from her father, so she'll manufacture it.

Grown to a young woman, Jenny attracts the attention of the richest man in town, middle-aged timber magnate Isaiah Poster (Gene Lockhart). Poster has no designs on the girl; it's Jenny who beguiles him by playing on his sympathy and his understandable attraction to her flesh. Jenny becomes an agreeable wife who is active with charity work (more approval) but who nevertheless seduces Poster's son, the grown-up Ephraim (Louis Hayward). Timorous as a boy and weakly indecisive as a man, Ephraim carries on the affair in his father's house and remains oblivious when Jenny sets her sights on Isaiah's foreman, John Everett (George Sanders).

Jenny exploits Ephraim's fear of water to maneuver him into killing Isaiah during a canoe trip. Ephraim can't bring himself to commit murder, but a real accident occurs during the trip and Isaiah dies anyway. Despondent when he returns home, Ephraim greets Jenny at the door. She is not pleased to see him. "You can't come into this house, you wretched coward. You killed your father."

With Ephraim forced out of the picture (as the widow, Jenny owns the house and can banish whomever she wishes), our maladjusted heroine steals John from his sweetly loyal fiancée, Meg (Hillary Brooke). Jenny agrees when John asks to tell Meg about the new romance—and then hurries to tell Meg herself. Ulmer's suggestion is that Jenny breaks the news partly to control the situation and partly to torment the woman who has been a devoted friend.

A late religious conversion triggered by a raving evangelist causes Jenny to become crushed by paranoid guilt. In a violent accident that is put into motion by her madness, Jenny loses control of a wagon and is smashed to pieces. As she dies, she tells John she loves him.

The fascinating quality of Jenny is her moral ambiguity. Does she mean her last words, or is she simply hiding the depth of her venality? Did she ever love John at all, or did she take him from her friend only because she could?

As delineated in Herb Meadow's script (adapting Ben Ames Williams's seven-hundred-page 1941 novel), Jenny is a chameleon who never truly reveals herself. What we can see with our own eyes is enticing (Lamarr was known at the time, and not without some justification, as "The Most Beautiful Woman in the World"), but the real Jenny is a confusion of honesty and deceit, kindness and cruelty, dominance and shame. At the very least, she's in love with herself, nicely established in the film's opening moments as adolescent Jenny (Jo Ann Marlowe) admires her reflection in the river.

Most profoundly, Jenny is an agent of passion, which is made clear with marvelous overstatement as Jenny and John embrace in a forest lit with fire caused by an explosive lightning strike. Few emotions are small in *The Strange Woman*; rather, this is a tale of selfish love and weak men told in broad, heavy strokes.

Much of the Jenny characterization comes straight from Scarlett O'Hara, the endlessly clever and not entirely likeable heroine of *Gone With the Wind*. "I'm strong," Jenny pronounces in a moment of crisis. "Stronger than you think." The words echo Scarlett's vow of strength as the Civil War turns against the South. And the overrunning of the whole of Bangor by raping, shooting lumbermen is similar to (if on a much smaller scale) the rape of Atlanta.

Contemporary critics were impressed by Lamarr's performance and gave her what *she* had craved: acceptance as an actress. Lamarr and Ulmer saw to it that George Sanders's powerful personality never dominates a scene, and cinematographer Lucien Andriot elaborated on Lamarr's startling beauty with subtle emphasis of her eyes and the planes of her face. *The Strange Woman* grossed $2.8 million, making it one of the most successful pictures of 1946—and a rare foray into "A" moviemaking for the usually underemployed Ulmer.

A Cocktail of Methylene Blue

For unadulterated lunacy, there is nothing in the noir canon to approach *Decoy* (1946). In rough outline the film's story seems familiar enough: scheming beauty Margo (Jean Gillie) appeals to her boyfriend Frankie (Robert Armstrong) to reveal where he's stashed the dough from an armored car robbery. It's important that he do this because he's on death row, and when he's executed, the money will be lost forever. As befits a noir femme fatale, Margo keeps a lover on the side, Jim Vincent (Edward Norris), who badgers her to get the lowdown on the loot. Unmoved, Frankie goes to the gas chamber without revealing his secret.

But wait. We're only about twenty minutes into this tidy seventy-six-minute thriller. What next?

Margo meets an idealistic Skid Row physician, Dr. Craig (Herbert Rudley), who has discovered that a chemical compound called methylene blue reverses the effect of cyanide gas. Margo wasn't born yesterday, so she begins to romance the doctor.

Do you see where this is going?

After a quick hijack of Frankie's body, an IV, some electrodes, and a good dose of methylene blue, Frankie is stunned to find himself alive again. The money won't be lost after all.

The twist is that as soon as Frankie makes the mistake of drawing a map, Vincent shoots him in the back, with Margo's hearty approval. Dr. Craig is forced to become Margo and Vincent's driver. The woman contrives a flat tire and bumpily runs over Vincent as soon as he's finished changing it. At the site located on the map, Craig digs until he uncovers a box. Margo gleefully disposes of him.

And you thought the metal ducks in a shooting gallery get knocked over in a hurry.

As scripted by Ned Young, *Decoy* uses a framing device in which, minutes after the film begins, the wounded Dr. Craig bursts into Margo's apartment and shoots her. At film's end, we're back in the apartment. Sgt. Joseph "Jo Jo" Portugal (Sheldon Leonard) attends to the dying Margo. The box is with her, and inside are scraps of blank paper, a note, and some cash. "For you who double-crossed me," the note reads, "I leave this dollar for your trouble. The rest of the dough, I leave to the worms."

The twice-dead Frankie has the last laugh.

Decoy was produced by Jack Bernhard and Bernard Brandt, and directed by Bernhard, for the most prosperous of Hollywood's Poverty Row outfits, Monogram. Of course, "prosperous" is a relative word, and there's no denying that, in moments, the picture looks a little threadbare. But it's obvious that the studio put extra money and effort into the production. In general, *Decoy* is only marginally more modest than a throwaway picture from one of the major studios' B-picture units.

Blonde British actress Jean Gillie, a shapely, intelligent presence appearing in her first Hollywood film after a prolific career in Britain, is terrific. As a protégé of British light actor Jack Buchanan, Gillie made her mark in comedies. She met American director Jack Bernhard and came with him to Hollywood. *Decoy* was Gillie's first American film, and she threw herself into it. Margo is marvelously malign and unrepentant, with a glare that's withering and an expressive voice that can be turned to seduction in a heartbeat. She squashes Vincent without a moment's hesitation—and even has the moxie to run back to check the body and collect the tire jack. After Dr. Craig has uncovered the money box (on a handsome, misty set by designer Dave Milton, atmospherically shot by prolific cinematographer L. W. O'Connell), Margo plugs him twice, laughing demonically. "It's mine!" she shouts. "It's mine!"

At the conclusion, as she lies dying on a sofa, Margo summons Sgt. Portugal closer. "Jo Jo, just this once, come down to my level." Portugal is tough but not heartless, so he bends closer—only to have Margo laugh in his face! As we said: unrepentant.

Besides *Decoy*, Jack Bernhard is best remembered for a pair of 1948 releases, a wonky dinosaur adventure called *Unknown Island* and a provocative noir, *Blonde Ice* (see Chapter 2). Bernhard wasn't a great stylist, but he could tell a story. The opening portion of the framing device is particularly intriguing, as the camera focuses on a pair of bloody hands that struggle to wash themselves at a filthy sink. The hands belong to the wounded Dr. Craig, whose robotic walk, one arm held to his side, is echoed later by Frankie's stumbling resurrection, as he tentatively moves around Craig's office to get blood pumping again in dormant muscles. Robert Armstrong, the promoter Carl Denham in *King Kong* (1933) and a solid general-purpose actor, expresses with unexpected conviction the jaw-dropping surprise of coming back from the dead. He's simultaneously horrified, astonished, and exultant.

After *Decoy*, Jean Gillie won a supporting role in an A-picture, *The Macomber Affair* (1947). It was her last film work. The actress died of pneumonia in 1949, just thirty-three years old. Had she lived, she almost certainly would have enjoyed a significant career.

The War Between Men and Women, Act II

"Oh, Jeff, you ought to have killed me for what I did a minute ago."

"There's still time."

— Jane Greer and Robert Mitchum, *Out of the Past* (1947)

S o perfect an explosion of intergender warfare is *Out of the Past* (1947) that the film is a natural start point for additional discussion of the noir war between men and women. Although not the most overtly vicious such display (*Detour* must remain the champ in that regard), *Out of the Past* is unusually rich with scheming and duplicity. Jane Greer's thoroughly self-absorbed Kathie Moffat is the perfect survivor, transferring affection and allegiance from man to man as it suits her purposes, warm to the touch but with a core of ice. Small-boned, almost fragile, she's tough enough to use a .45 and clever enough to keep smart guys guessing. Kathie is a brilliant invention.

In broad outline, gas-station owner Jeff Bailey (Robert Mitchum) is an ex-private detective who is hired by an old associate, Whit (Kirk Douglas), to locate Kathie, who has gone missing after putting a couple bullets into Whit and leaving him for dead. She also ran off with $40,000 of Whit's money. Jeff tracks the girl to Mexico, falls in love with her, and subsequently tries to shield her from Whit. But Kathie is bad news, involving Whit in murder and dumping him at the first opportunity. She returns to Whit, but Jeff can't stay away. Finally, Kathie shoots Whit again—this time fatally—and runs off with Jeff. But Jeff has called the cops, who throw up a roadblock. Enraged, Kathie turns her fury against Jeff and mounts a last stand against the police.

The outrageous melodrama is told in flashback, as a counterpoint to the quiet life Jeff has found in a small California town. Running the gas station agrees with him, and he's in love with a fine local girl named Ann (Virginia Huston). These present-day sequences bracket the film and let the hyperdramatic main story unfold within a believable framework.

Besides Kathie, Whit has trouble with a missing tax document that could put him in prison. Jeff becomes involved in the search for the document, and for Whit's slippery accountant, a fellow aptly named Eels (Ken Niles). A further complication is Jeff's old partner, Fisher (Steve Brodie), who wants a piece of whatever it is Jeff is involved in. Kathie calmly shoots Fisher to death and later signs an affidavit for Whit that claims that Fisher was killed by Jeff.

Isn't Kathie great? Isn't she good? She's always two steps ahead.

In *Out of the Past* (1947), Jeff (Robert Mitchum) ponders old entanglements that won't completely go away. Kathie (Jane Greer) knows she has the bait needed to keep Jeff on the hook.

Out of the Past was directed by Jacques Tourneur and scripted by Daniel Mainwaring. Mainwaring is credited as Geoffrey Homes and adapted his own 1946 novel *Build My Gallows High*. (James M. Cain and journeyman screenwriter Frank Fenton had hands in the script, too, both uncredited.) Despite the density of plot, events move easily from rural California to Mexico to San Francisco, and then back to the hinterlands.

Jacques Tourneur had excelled as part of Val Lewton's B-picture unit at RKO, and he knew how to tell a story with grace and visual interest. Equally comfortable with day or night shooting, and as skilled on location as on a stage, Tourneur worked crisply and intelligently. He also understood pacing. *Out of the Past* is remarkable for its richness of plot and incident, and although you have to pay close attention, you never feel rushed or overwhelmed. The script is very organic, and develops within itself like a living thing, never overstepping its self-imposed limits. One incident follows logically (if perversely) from another.

There's a lot of death in *Out of the Past*, but the bodies don't pile up like cordwood. They pile up like the bodies of people who used to be alive. Each death has emotional and psychological weight. Reflecting on a recent kill, a gunsel muses, "He just stood there shaking so hard he couldn't even pray. I never saw anyone so afraid to die."

Jeff knows that Kathie has tried to frame him for the murder of Eels, but Jeff's friend Ann (Virginia Huston) can hardly believe that Kathie is beyond redemption.

> ANN
> She can't be all bad. No one is.

> JEFF
> Well, she comes the closest.

There's something primal about Kathie's allure. She's very difficult to resist. After she's knocked off Whit, she flaunts her charms to Jeff, imploring him to come with her to Mexico and start over again. "You're no good and neither am I," she says. "That's why we deserve each other."

In a small but significant way, *Out of the Past* is about redemption. At the conclusion, after Jeff and Kathie have dealt with each other and the cops, Ann asks Jeff's deaf-mute garage assistant (Dickie Moore) if Jeff and Kathie were really going away. The kid hesitates, and then nods. We don't know whether he gives that answer on his own or if Jeff had instructed him, but it's a mercy directed at Ann. She can break with Jeff's memory and build a fresh life.

Finally, of course, the film is about the impossibility of walking away from one's past. Wherever you go, there it is, walking with you and inside you. You *are* your past, and when the past comes calling, you may feel compelled to answer.

Stop Us If You've Seen This Before

There's no reason to assume that every film discussed in a genre survey is great, good, or even interesting. And that, I suppose, is sufficient prelude to an examination of *Dead Reckoning* (1947), a brazenly derivative and oddly languid noir thriller from Columbia, made when the picture's star, Humphrey Bogart, was on loan-out from Warner. If you've seen *The Maltese Falcon, Casablanca, The Big Sleep,* and *To Have and Have Not,* you've already seen *Dead Reckoning.*

Mustered out of the army at last, pals Rip Murdock (Bogart) and Johnny Drake (William Prince) are on their way to Washington, where Sgt. Drake will receive the Medal of Honor and Capt. Murdock the Distinguished Service Cross. But after Johnny mysteriously hops from the train, Rip learns that his friend had joined the army under a false name, to escape punishment for a puzzling murder to which he'd already confessed.

Essentially functioning as a private eye, Rip follows leads to Gulf City, Florida, where he meets a suspicious cop (Charles Cane), a predatory nightclub owner (Morris Carnovsky), a psychotic goon (Marvin Miller), an amiable box man (Wallace Ford), and a wealthy, throaty-voiced blonde (Lizabeth Scott) whose husband was the murder victim.

Very nearly the entire story unfolds in flashback, after Rip ducks into a church and is approached by a priest (still in chaplain's uniform) who is willing to listen. The religious angle may have been intended by scripters Oliver H. P. Garrett and Steve Fisher to carry some symbolic or philosophical freight, but it ultimately amounts to nothing, particularly because it's not a confession (Rip hasn't done anything wrong).

Typical of many noir films, and of many earlier Bogart pictures, too, scenes unfold in a nightclub, in an illegal gambling den, at a mysterious beach house,

Case File: Val Lewton and Horror Noir

French-born Hollywood director Jacques Tourneur is justly famed for his deft direction of a noir classic, *Out of the Past*, but he has assumed equal importance for a series of moody horror thrillers he directed for the Val Lewton unit at RKO earlier in the '40s: *Cat People*, *I Walked with a Zombie*, and *The Leopard Man*. It is these movies, probably more than any other, that clarify the link between noir and horror. In each, troubled, often morally compromised characters exist in intimidating landscapes of light and shadow. They suffer the terrors of physical and emotional isolation (as during the swimming pool sequence of *Cat People*), and are forced to deal with creeping danger that's amplified by people who are disinclined to help (see the locked door in *The Leopard Man*).

Much of the resolute intelligence of these films came from producer Lewton (1904–51), a prolific novelist and onetime screenwriter who guided Tourneur and fellow directors Robert Wise, Mark Robson, and Gunther von Fritsch as they made highly psychological, mostly present-day horror-noir thrillers that remain revered for their mood, restraint, and peerless entertainment value. Other Lewton-RKO films in this cycle are *The Ghost Ship*, *The Curse of the Cat People*, *The Body Snatcher* (the best film interpretation of the Burke and Hare story), *Isle of the Dead*, *Bedlam*, and Robson's *The Seventh Victim*, a masterpiece of noirish urban paranoia and isolation that revolves around a modern-day cult of witches.

Naturally, Lewton wasn't operating from a vacuum. His aesthetic had been influenced by Expressionist crime and horror thrillers from silent- and early-sound-era Germany (Fritz Lang's *M* and *Spies*, Joe May's *Asphalt*, and G. W. Pabst's *Pandora's Box*, et al.). When important German directors began to come to Hollywood in the late 1920s, they created highly visual thrillers that combined horror themes with the moral ambivalence that would inform what would later be called film noir. Hollywood pictures in this group include Paul Leni's *Waxworks* and *The Man Who Laughs*, Erle C. Kenton's splendidly unwholesome *Island of Lost Souls*, William Wellman's *Safe in Hell*, Roy William Neill's *Black Moon*, and unwholesome horror and suspense thrillers directed by Tod Browning: *The Unholy Three* (silent and sound versions), *Freaks*, and *The Unknown*. Edgar G. Ulmer's *The Black Cat*, and two by Robert Florey, *Murders in the Rue Morgue* and *The Face Behind the Mask*, also link horror to the later noir movement.

The horror-noir link carried on into the science-horror boom of the 1950s (Edgar G. Ulmer's *The Man from Planet X* and Howard Hawks's *The Thing from Another World* [direction credited to Christian Nyby] are strong examples), and into the Gothic revival of the late '50s, most vividly in John Moxey's *City of the Dead* and Tourneur's *Night of the Demon*.

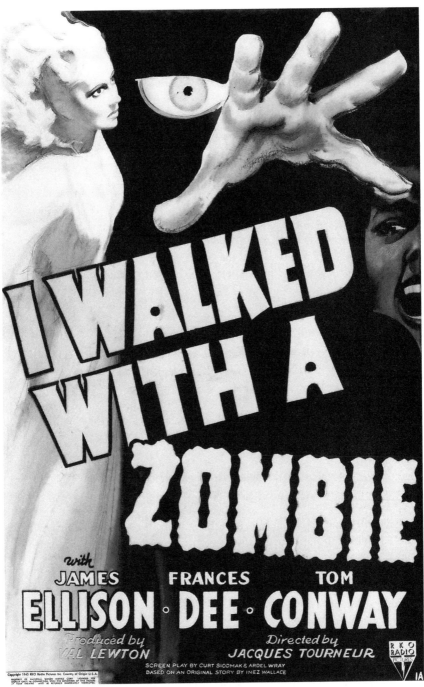

Moody menace, Lewton-style.

in a private office with a wall safe, at a mansion, in hotel rooms, on a train, and on very dark and rainy city streets and suburban roads.

Much is made of the fact, to tiresome effect, that Rip is an ex-soldier, via tossed-off but contrived dialogue the likes of, "That was a great bivouac," "while you were breaking camp," "once I get clear of the beachhead," and the risibly overused "Geronimo."

Dead Reckoning really hits the rocks when dialogue written by Garrett and Fisher becomes 1) archly high-flown, and 2) derivatively Bogartian. After Rip's relationship with Coral (Scott) hits a bad patch, a key exchange goes like this:

> CORAL
> Oh, Rip, what does a girl have to do with you?

> *RIP (with a cynical smile)*
> You know, you do awful good. I came here to—go ahead, put
> Christmas in your eyes and keep your voice low and tell me
> all about Paradise and all the things I'm missing, I haven't had
> a good laugh since before Johnny was murdered.

> CORAL
> Oh, Rip.

> RIP
> I'm not the type that tears do anything to. I'm the brass
> knucks in the teeth, the dime-dance type.

Later, after Rip has taken to calling Coral "Mike," in the vein of Bogart's wry on-screen relationships with Lauren Bacall (whom Scott is clearly intended to evoke), he kisses Coral, at last.

> RIP
> A few minutes ago I didn't dare do this. Now I can, Mike. I'm
> doing it so that you *know* that I can.

Later still, the script makes a daylight raid on *The Maltese Falcon*, as Rip lets Coral know he's unhappy with her:

> RIP
> Then there's Johnny. When a guy's pal is killed, he ought to
> do something about it.

But Rip loves Coral. Won't he miss her?

> *RIP (to Coral)*
> That's the tough part of it. But it'll pass. These things do in
> time. And there's one more thing. I loved him more.

Three of the principal characters are not at all who or what they seem to be, and by the time it's all sorted out, Rip has endured a doped drink (another larcenous assault on *The Maltese Falcon*), a beating, a car crash, a bullet, and pursuit by police.

Leo Tover's cinematography is suitably moody, but John Cromwell's direction is draggy, and individual sequences have little fire. Lizabeth Scott, in just her third picture, is physically intriguing and shows some of the charisma that would blossom later. She holds her own with Bogart but suffers unfairly because so much of her dialogue seems familiar.

Bogart is Bogart—that is to say, he's fine as Rip (silly name, by the way). At this juncture, Bogart was the highest-paid movie actor in the world. He was newly and happily married, and had had enough of keenly cynical roles that smelled of Sam Spade, Rick Blaine, and Philip Marlowe. Notable characterizations by the great actor during the remaining decade of his life would be markedly different from Rip, and all the better for it.

"Oh, Rip." Oh, imitation. Humphrey Bogart and the intriguingly sultry Lizabeth Scott try hard to make something of *Dead Reckoning* (1947), a serviceable thriller that borrows rather brazenly from earlier Bogart vehicles.

Stanwyck Pulls Out the Stops

The emotional misery caused by great, unearned privilege is at the center of *Sorry, Wrong Number* (1948). An ambitious poor man who marries a wealthy woman becomes trapped in a meaningless existence as an unnecessary executive in the enormous company owned by his father-in-law. The husband resents his wife's offhanded way of tossing cash at him, as if he were a child, and becomes furious after learning that the heart disease that has turned his wife into a disagreeable invalid is psychosomatic. When the husband's scheme to steal his father-in-law's industrial pharmaceuticals runs off the rails, he must come up with $200,000 in order to satisfy a dangerous partner. But the husband has no money of his own . . . except for the fat payout he'll get if his wife dies. In a crossed-wires phone conversation that opens the film, the wife overhears some details of a murder plot. Before the night is over—and after flashbacks, and flashbacks within flashbacks—she realizes that the woman to be murdered is she.

In a final irony, she dies while on the phone with her frantic husband, who no longer needs the money and warns her to save herself.

Sorry, Wrong Number runs eighty-nine minutes, not long for an A-picture but far longer than the film's twenty-two-minute source material, a radio play of the same name by Lucille Fletcher. That play, first broadcast on *Suspense* in 1943 with Agnes Moorehead in the lead, was a sensation that Moorehead reprised on radio seven times during the next five years.

The radio play does without much of the backstory indicated above. Instead, neither microphone nor listener leaves the woman's bedroom. Although the central character, Leona Stevenson, isn't entirely likable (she's awfully imperious at the beginning of her radio misadventure), the enforced proximity to her makes her unavoidably sympathetic. We listeners are trapped in that bed with her, reacting, when she does, to voices that have no faces. When she's terrified, we're terrified.

Fletcher adapted her play to the screen, facing the obvious challenge of how to open up the action so the story runs long enough to be a movie and so that it *looks* like a movie. Besides the enormous elaboration of the history and nature of the film husband, Henry Stevenson (Burt Lancaster), and the details of his scheme, the narrative encompasses a wide variety of locations that includes Leona's Manhattan apartment, a subway station, a campus dance, a mysterious clapboard house on a beach, an industrial chemistry lab, a rainy city street, old man Stevenson's Chicago mansion, a seedy hotel room—even (in montage) the major cities of Europe! None of this is awful; the beach sequences, in fact, are satisfyingly eerie. If the radio play never existed, everybody would go home satisfied. But by 1948, the radio version of *Sorry, Wrong Number* was practically folklore, so the camera's excursions hither and yon have the effect of telling us more but giving us less.

Bedridden Leona (Barbara Stanwyck) is off the screen for long stretches, and while we don't forget about her during those interludes (the healthier, ambulatory Leona is central to many flashbacks), we're constantly dragged away from the bed. With each transition back to the present, we have to climb back into the bed and redevelop our fear for her—and that's not as easy as with the play, not simply because of the lack of continual proximity but because the broadened narrative establishes and elaborates on Leona's many bad points. We certainly never *want* her to be murdered, but because she's an arrogant, whiny, manipulative, and self-centered daddy's girl, she definitely rubs us the wrong way.

Common wisdom about the husband is that he's weak, but little in the script or in Lancaster's performance suggests that. To the contrary, he's very strong-willed. His main failings are procrastination (he takes abuse for far longer than is good for him) and foolishness.

Leona is interpreted by Stanwyck in a performance that's best described as fulsome. Between flashbacks and the development of the bedroom predicament, the actress moves from smiling confidence to all-out, frenzied terror, complete with perspiring face, lank hair, and plenty of hoarse screaming. Stanwyck was at her best when playing characters who are hip to their situations and a step ahead of everybody else. (*The Lady Eve* springs to mind.) Here, the structure of the basic story forces Stanwyck to become someone who's continually playing catch-up, and who grows more frantic as she fits the puzzle pieces together.

Director Anatole Litvak encouraged cinematographer Sol Polito to light some sequences for mood. Cleverly, the hired killer in Leona's apartment is reduced to a dark, out-of-focus blur in the kitchen, an ascending shadow on the stairway wall, and a pair of hands clad in white gloves. The killer's face doesn't matter because he's Death, and Death is inevitable, no matter what he looks like.

Leona's murder is mostly offscreen, though we see the killer's shadow as it crosses Leona's face and her flailing hand as she's being dispatched. Henry, with the police literally right behind him, remains on the phone, frantic.

HENRY (through Leona's phone receiver)
Hello! Hello! Leona!

KILLER
Sorry, wrong number.

But of course, it's not the wrong number at all.

Murder at Sea, and a New Hair Color for Rita

Orson Welles, already shading toward the fleshy, is the two-fisted hero of *The Lady from Shanghai* (1948). He was tall but baby-faced at thirty-three, and while his vaguely tough Irish brogue may put us in mind of James Mason in the previous year's *Odd Man Out*, his heft and peculiarly plodding gait suggest a much older man. But never mind: In the film's opening minutes, after a "meet cute" in Central Park, itinerant seaman Michael O'Hara (Welles) beats the hell out of three men who attack Elsa Bannister (Rita Hayworth), the unhappy wife of a famous trial lawyer. In short order, O'Hara is brought to meet Bannister (Everett Sloane) and is hired to crew on the Bannister yacht. On the sea and at various ports of call, relationships grow increasingly tense and peculiar, until finally assorted murder schemes collide.

Along for the sea voyage are various moles and misfits, including Bannister's partner, Grisby (Glenn Anders), a leering, giggling alcoholic who continually thrusts his sweating face into O'Hara's to make elliptical small talk about killing. Anders's performance is potent, but it seems to have dropped in from another movie. Welles the director allowed Anders to mug and chortle, striving for a purposely off-putting effect that is ultimately just odd.

Grisby claims to want to fake his death and disappear, and offers O'Hara $5,000 to go along. In the movie's one unforgivable lapse of logic, O'Hara agrees to sign a fake confession that says he's Grisby's killer.

This is movie logic. In real life, Michael—*anybody*—would be out the door in a heartbeat. But Michael signs the paper, which allows the audience plenty of time to see what Michael cannot: that he's going to be the fall guy in something larger than just a faked disappearance. The signature on the confession undercuts all of Michael's strength and smarts as a character, and the remainder of the film plays out (with an admittedly bravura final sequence in a hall of mirrors) as a kind of disappointing dribble.

The Lady from Shanghai isn't completely successful, but it's fascinating to watch. At the very least, it's engaging as travelogue. Welles, who also wrote, produced, and directed, filmed the lengthy seagoing sequences off the coast of Mexico onboard the *Zaca*, the handsome yacht belonging to actor Errol Flynn. As you might expect, Welles mixed his shots beautifully, revealing the boat from many angles that emphasize the changing sea and sky, the craft's speed, and the beauty of its prow and enormous sails. Many land sequences were shot in Acapulco (when that place was still fairly undeveloped), and other location shooting was done in Sausalito, San Francisco, and New York City. The film is at its best, and most modern, during the location scenes, particularly when crowds of people are about and Welles and other characters move among them. In this, it approaches the naturalistic power of Jules Dassin's great police procedural *The Naked City* (1948).

Welles and cinematographer Charles Lawton Jr. were apparently simpatico, for *The Lady from Shanghai* bristles with aggressive tracking setups, dolly shots, and, most dramatically, extreme close-ups. Faces fill the frame, top to bottom and side to side. The effect is intentionally claustrophobic and inserts us uncomfortably close to this cadre of schemers.

Columbia boss Harry Cohn claimed to be unhappy with the raw footage he saw, and insisted that inserts be shot in Hollywood, on soundstages and in front of process screens. The free hopping from natural light and breeze to the deadened gloss of a stage suggests two different movies altogether, so it's not difficult to imagine Welles's displeasure with the finished product. Hayworth will be seen in a windblown medium shot, for instance, in full sunlight, and when there's a cut to a close-up, her face is artfully, artificially lit, mask-like, with a blank background behind. Then we cut back to the location. Welles intended the picture to have a dreamlike quality, and although these jumps from location to soundstage weren't part of his plan, they contribute to that effect.

Cohn's decision to aggressively meddle arose partly from pique. Hayworth was Columbia's most valued asset, and the studio boss was furious when Welles cut the actress's hair and dyed it blonde. Cohn also resented that Welles and Hayworth were married (though estranged) during the shoot, and he couldn't abide the level of creative control Welles had negotiated for himself. Cohn was determined to undermine his wunderkind.

Welles was obviously searching as an artist when he made *The Lady from Shanghai*, struggling to make art out of pulp and looking for a commercial hit, too. Although he had offers to direct in Europe, his American opportunities were drying up. In Hollywood, no one is resented and hated more than the precocious, gifted, and obstinate—and Welles was all three..

She Played Her Man Like a Piano

A minor fuss was made in 2003 when Jack Bernhard's *Blonde Ice* (1948), a presumed lost classic of film noir, was located, digitally cleaned up, and released to DVD. It's a "black widow" thriller, shot on the cheap on cramped sets and originally released by Film Classics, an organization involved mainly in the distribution of major-studio rereleases. There's no cleverness to the script, but the film does have the virtue of bluntness and a lively central performance.

Seductive Claire Cummings (Leslie Brooks) is a newspaper society columnist who marries a wealthy man for his money, even though she's long been attracted to a fellow columnist, Les Burns (Robert Paige). In a murder contrived to look like suicide, Claire rids herself of her new husband (but not his estate) and resumes her romance with Les, a likable, faintly hapless pawn. Les is ready to tie the knot, but Claire becomes interested in yet another man, Mason (Michael Whalen), an ambitious fellow favored to win a House seat. Power and position are important to Claire, so our heroine dumps Les a second time and becomes engaged to the would-be congressman. But Claire can't keep herself out of Les's arms, and when Mason sees the two in an embrace, the engagement is off. Claire immediately stabs her ex-fiancé to death and fingers Les as the killer. Things don't look good for Les, but Kippinger (David Leonard), a suspicious psychiatrist, hatches a scheme to expose Claire. Not surprisingly, the murderess takes umbrage at that and makes plans to settle some accounts.

Blonde Ice is fun because of some critical illogic. The first murder is ruled a suicide even though the victim shows no powder burns and the gun reveals no fingerprints. Reasonable viewers will conclude that those anomalies are not consistent with suicide—but who wants to argue with the medical examiner? Nevertheless, doubts about the suicide ruling receive plenty of press coverage—so why does a would-be congressman want to come within ten miles of Claire? She's the definition of "political baggage."

Director Jack Bernhard shot *Blonde Ice* mainly in static two- and three-shots. Work by cinematographer George Robinson, a mainstay of Universal horror thrillers in the late 1930s and '40s, is unremarkable here, so the burden of carrying the film fell to the cast. As the angel-faced fiend, Leslie Brooks is alternately sweet and venomous. Although she wasn't an exceptional actress (she spent her career in Bs and in supporting roles in bigger films), she had screen presence, energy, and focus. Her eyes have a hard, slightly crazed quality, even as her mouth is oh-so kissable. Claire isn't completely memorable, but Brooks brought qualities that aren't in the script.

Russ Vincent, a roadshow Bogart type, is amusing as a blackmailer, and Michael Whalen is suitably unctuous as the pea-brained politician. The best performance is by general-purpose actor Robert Paige, who gives Les an approachable Everyman quality. He's smart enough to occasionally get fed up with Claire but human enough to be unable to completely disentangle himself from her. (Horror fans will recall Paige as the unhappy lover in *Son of Dracula* [1943].)

In a 1970 interview with Peter Bogdanovich, director Edgar G. Ulmer said he worked on an early treatment of *Blonde Ice*. No evidence supports the claim, and it's likely that Ulmer was thinking of another project.

Big Love, Small People

Blonde Ice, though it goes through the motions of noir, is mannered and superficial. For emotional and thematic complexity, look to Robert Siodmak's brazenly bleak *Criss Cross* (1949). It is ostensibly a heist thriller, in which armored-car driver Steve Thompson (Burt Lancaster) comes up with a scheme to act as inside man and allow a gang of thieves to plunder the cargo. In a typical crime thriller of the period, the robbery would be the indisputable highlight, but in the world of noir and *Criss Cross*, it's only a way station to another, more awful set of circumstances.

An important fillip is that Steve's partner, professional criminal Slim Dundee (Dan Duryea), is married to Steve's ex-wife, Anna (Yvonne De Carlo). Steve remains so stupidly obsessed with Anna that he can't see that Slim plans to betray him during the robbery.

The robbery goes down badly, with an innocent guard slaughtered by Slim and half the loot inadvertently rescued by Steve. In a tidy irony, the newspapers declare him a hero. But an old friend, police detective Ramirez (Stephen McNally), thinks the whole thing stinks.

The surface aspects of the narrative don't even hint at the style brought to *Criss Cross* by director Siodmak and cinematographer Franz Planer. The film opens with an omniscient, high-angle view of LA that invites us to consider the whole place as small, trivial, and pointless. But emotional close-ups of De Carlo and Lancaster create a startling and uncomfortable intimacy. Anna and Steve's fever becomes our fever, as well.

In scene after scene, the faces of key participants glow with a sheen of light that demands our attention. The technique is classic noir: a stylized, hyperreal visual approach mated to a realistically downbeat exploration of emotion. Siodmak wanted to burn these characters into our brains, and he succeeded.

The daylight robbery sequence begins in documentary fashion, with flatly objective cuts to the gang members, variously disguised as utility workers and an ice-cream man. The approach of the armored car along a narrow, crowded street is shot from above—a clear reference to the bleakly omniscient view that opens the film. The bird's-eye camera tracks the armored car, then tilts oddly, forcing us to twist our heads to follow the truck, which looks for a moment as if it's going to slide right off the screen. The effect is disconcerting and disorienting, and suggests that the whole scheme is headed for some sort of disaster.

The robbery itself is a minimalist, almost surreal landscape of impenetrable white smoke laid down by the robbers' gas bombs, moving figures only barely glimpsed, and Slim, in overalls and a gas mask, prowling around like a murderous man from Mars, intent on removing Steve from Anna's life. The entire tableau looks like a particularly unpleasant day in purgatory.

Much later, Steve goes to Anna, who's been given what remains of the loot for safekeeping. He's still starry-eyed, but she's not. She just wants out.

ANNA
Love, *love*. You have to watch out for yourself. I'm sorry. You
just don't know what kind of a world it is.

When confronted inside the hideout by Slim (a long look at the empty doorway has encouraged us to hope that the visitor is Ramirez), Anna screams twice in mortal terror and flings herself into Steve's lap. The moment is shocking and difficult to watch.

Slim fires three times, ending Anna's cynical sense of survival and Steve's naïveté.

Lancaster is intriguingly cast against type as a fellow with physical strength but intellectual and emotional weakness. He's under the thumb of his mother and seems woefully ill equipped to deal with Anna's sensuality. During a kinetic and well-edited rumba number that recalls the jive-music sequence Siodmak devised for *Phantom Lady* (1944; see Chapter 6), Anna abandons herself to the rhythm. All Steve can do is watch, bemusedly.

Anna is a signature role for Yvonne De Carlo. As for Dan Duryea—well, nobody did Dan Duryea better than Duryea. In the world of *Criss Cross*, he has what it takes to be a survivor.

The Parole Officer Is a Sucker

Much of Douglas Sirk's *Shockproof* (1949) is defined by environment, specifically, the neat, ordered office of parole officer Griff Marat (Cornel Wilde) and the tidy older home he shares with his blind mother. There must be no physical surprises in a space occupied by a blind person, of course, and Griff sees that his home and workspace are similarly predictable. When he's handed paroled murderess Jenny Marsh (Patricia Knight), he brusquely recites the rules, not just to give his new charge the checklist but to make clear that her life is no longer completely her own. She will take a job that has been arranged for her. Without Griff's permission, she can't quit her job, travel, or marry. She must not carry a firearm, and she cannot associate with criminals or people of questionable reputation.

And yet before *Shockproof* is half over, Griff has fallen in love with Jenny. Worse, he's abandoned his home, office, and job in order to go on the run with her after she shoots Harry (John Baragrey), a former lover. In a gala of parole and professional violations (including marriage), the couple rides freight cars and hides out in a tumble of shacks slapped up by an oil company that employs Griff as a laborer.

Discovered at last, Jenny is exonerated because the recovering Harry says she shot in self-defense. Griff gets a pass because Jenny was in his custody during her adventure, that is, with her parole officer. Griff's life and career will go on, but now with love.

And on the Big Rock Candy Mountain, the jails are made of tin and you can walk right out again.

To say that the conclusion of *Shockproof* is ridiculous is like saying that things get drafty during a hurricane. The first-draft script was written by Sam Fuller, who called the story *The Lovers*. Fuller's background as a crime reporter and novelist inevitably pulled him toward the sharply dramatic, and at the climax of his script, Griff is killed when he shoots it out with police. Columbia liked some of what Fuller had done—the script had a bit of Bonnie and Clyde, and the lovers-on-the-run narrative evoked the doomed youngsters of Nick Ray's *They Live by Night* (1949; see Chapter 6). But the studio was looking for an upbeat ending. The script was handed to writer Helen Deutsch, who came up with the cheerful—and wildly improbable—conclusion.

For German-born director Douglas Sirk, the film was another assignment in a Hollywood career that had yet to blossom. Still, the progressively more fevered pitch of Cornel Wilde's performance hints at the great romantic melodramas Sirk would direct just a few years later. *All I Desire* (1953) was the first, and was followed a year later by *Magnificent Obsession* (1954), another tale of romance and guilt. A multitude of others followed.

Little of what might be called "Sirkian" is on view in *Shockproof*; for starters, the film is in black and white rather than lush Technicolor. Still, some recognizable visual motifs, such as frames within frames and action reflected in mirrors, pop up. And Sirk himself commented about his use of close-ups and intimate angles to ensure the audience is emotionally linked to his beautiful protagonists.

Cornel Wilde, tidy of face and physique as well as of home and office, is well cast as Griff. He thinks he's a hardnose, but his heart is made of caramel. Angular beauty Patricia Knight, though not an exceptional actress, brings an effective edge to Jenny, particularly in early scenes when she cynically strings along the smitten Griff while breaking parole to consort on the sly with Harry.

Lean, good-looking John Baragrey dominates every scene he's in. Harry is intrinsically more interesting than Griff—a true smoothie where Griff is playing a role, a wealthy player where Griff is just a working stiff. It's nice to see decency win out, but *Shockproof* needs more consequences and punishment.

Special Delivery from Hell

Like Claire in *Shockproof*, Jane Palmer has an inflated view of herself that includes her presumed right to expensive clothes and other nifty things. And like Claire, she's a little cavalier with other people's lives. Jane (Lizabeth Scott) is the dominant figure of *Too Late for Tears* (1949), a minor but entertaining noir directed by the accomplished journeyman Byron Haskin.

The setup is established in the film's opening moments, and it's a good one: As Jane and Alan Palmer (Arthur Kennedy) pilot their convertible along a dark, winding mountain road above Los Angeles, someone in a car going the opposite way hurls a valise into the Palmers' backseat. It's a neat, obviously prearranged handover, but the Palmers have no idea why it happened. The valise is stuffed with old, nonsequential greenbacks—$60,000 worth, as we learn later.

Case File: Lizabeth Scott (b. 1922)

Common wisdom is that husky-voiced Lizabeth Scott was Paramount's "answer" to Lauren Bacall, as if Scott were somehow not the real thing. Like Bacall, she had modeling and Broadway experience, but Scott's background as an actress was considerably deeper than Bacall's, and she successfully projected a variety of film personas, from "good girl" to man-eating villainess. Scott certainly had the physical equipment: wide-set, piercing blue eyes; blonde hair; an intriguingly long upper lip (and a sexy lisp); and the requisite slim figure. When she's on-screen, your eyes inevitably gravitate in her direction. Scott is in good-guy mode as the beleaguered Toni Marachek in her first noir, *The Strange Love of Martha Ivers*. Shortly after, she registered well opposite Bogart in *Dead Reckoning*. Scott quickly became a staple of noir, appearing in *The Racket*, *Too Late for Tears* (as a masochistic schemer with a dreadful past), and *Dark City*. Outside of the genre, Lizabeth was a game foil for Martin and Lewis in a haunted house comedy, *Scared Stiff*, and gave Elvis Presley something formidable to play against in *Loving You*. She retired in the mid-1960s but came back in 1972 for a featured role in Mike Hodges's *Pulp*.

Alan wants to take the valise straight to the police, but Jane would rather hang on to it. Just for a while. In the meantime, the Palmer car barely escapes a third one that pursues it at high speed. Alan is a war vet who apparently learned nothing about reasonable risk. Although he reasons that the chase car got a look at his license plate, he acquiesces to his wife's scheme and checks the valise at the train station. Before long the consequences of that begin to fall like concrete blocks. Danny Fuller (Dan Duryea), a blackmailer who was the intended recipient of the money, tracks Jane down and visits her at home. He slaps Jane around, whipping her head from side to side.

In a queasy portent of things to come, Jane enjoys the abuse.

Subsequent events unfold quickly, and with dark hilarity: There's a big .45 automatic that goes off when it's pointed at the wrong person; grim, watery mischief at Westlake Park; a poisoning; a scowling police detective (Barry Kelley); a trip to Mexico; and a gigolo. One of Alan's old Air Corps buddies, Don (Don DeFore), shows up and then won't go away. Why not? Because a long time ago Jane was a very bad girl. Finally, there's a hotel balcony with a very low railing.

Roy Huggins, who later became successful as a developer of TV's *Maverick*, *77 Sunset Strip*, *The Fugitive*, and others, scripted *Too Late for Tears*, adapting his own 1947 novel. The story is dense and forces the viewer to pay close attention. Jane's parallel relationships with her husband, sister-in-law, Danny, and Don are intriguingly sketched, but Jane's motivation for her pattern of murder (she was deprived of things as child) is glib and weak.

Much of the picture's success is due to Lizabeth Scott, who's a charmer one moment and a murder machine the next. Jane kills you even as she gives you a warm smile. She's a creature without conscience, and we like that because we can tell ourselves we're very different from her.

Scott was under contract to producer Hal Wallis. She was the first choice of *Too Late for Tears* producer Hunt Stromberg, but she was expensive. Stromberg listened when Haskin made a proposal: *Let cinematographer William Mellor and me save money by eliminating portions of sets the audience will never see.* In the end, some $40,000 was cut from the budget, and Scott was hired.

Two Women and the Man with the Double Life

Imagine looking in the mirror and seeing someone you recognize—and hate. You hate the person reflected back at you because the person is small, timid, and vacillating. You hate the heavy spectacles and the foolish smock. And you hate how the person in the mirror is in love with a woman who manipulates and despises him. This is the setup of the underappreciated *Tension* (1949) and the predicament of pharmacist Warren Quimby (Richard Basehart), who is so in love with his no-good wife Claire (Audrey Totter) that he's petrified to demand her fidelity.

To look in the mirror is hardly easier for Claire. She sees a good-looking dame with a taste for fine things who lives in a small apartment above a drug-store. She sees someone suffocating between four walls.

Two additional players step into this bad situation: Claire's lover, a Malibu playboy named Barney Deager (Lloyd Gough), and a charming career girl, Mary Chanler (Cyd Charisse), who becomes attracted to Warren—even though she knows him as "Paul Southern." Warren has invented Southern, establishing an identity and even a separate residence. Where Warren is mousy and reserved, Southern is fashionably dressed and confident. Warren wears glasses; Southern wears contact lenses. Warren lives above the drugstore; Southern occupies a valley apartment on the weekends.

Southern becomes real because Warren knows he can't kill Deager himself. The motive is too obvious. But if Warren can summon the nerve, *Southern* can do the murder and get away with it. The linchpin of the scheme is a phone call

Tension (1949) pits pharmacist Warren Quimby (Richard Basehart) against his no-good wife, Claire (Audrey Totter). Claire turns on the charm when it suits her but really can't change her spots. Warren, though, changes so completely that he literally becomes somebody else.

to Deager's home, taken by his houseboy, in which Warren identifies himself as Paul Southern and threatens to "get" Deager. With the call, and via interaction with Mary and the apartment manager, Paul Southern is real, but after Deager is dead, Southern can disappear. The crime will go unsolved, and Warren will go back to being himself. Claire will have to come back to him.

Warren fails to reckon with the possibility that Paul Southern may become *too* real. Sure enough, Mary Chanler falls in love with him, and Paul Southern falls for her.

Deager turns up dead one day. Warren's problem is solved, except that he's still married to Claire. And because of Mary, Paul Southern can't just go away. Now what?

And who killed Deager? A clever homicide detective (Barry Sullivan) thinks he might know.

Tension was an MGM "Silver Anniversary" release, and part of a new studio philosophy. Production executive Dore Schary realized that the expectations of sophisticated, faintly jaded postwar audiences were far different from those of earlier moviegoers. Glossy romances and picket-fence family films had their places but now had to be balanced with more urgent, adult films.

When *Tension* was shot during the late spring of 1949, MGM's Hollywood operations were still run by Louis B. Mayer, who had guided the studio to industry preeminence with just the sorts of movies Schary wanted to supersede. Mayer hated the new realism, but MGM's New York office agreed with Schary. Mayer was relieved of his duties in 1950, and Schary became the studio's top Hollywood executive. In light of all this, *Tension* is an intriguing signpost on MGM's journey to a changed market.

It's also a very competent, entertaining movie. Richard Basehart had made a big impact as the calculating murderer in Eagle-Lion's *He Walked By Night* (1948; see Chapter 5). Subsequently signed to MGM, he starred in *Fourteen Hours* and *The House on Telegraph Hill* (both 1951) and others. He was a cerebral actor of great versatility, and that may be why audiences were unable to get a handle on him. In time, Basehart became a popular and respected character player. His performance as Warren/Paul is satisfying because it's not a standard Jekyll-Hyde approach. Instead, it's considerably more subtle—a sort of Jekyll I/Jekyll II approach. Each persona is appealing. Although Paul Southern has been created to do mayhem, Paul himself is sweet, cheerful, and accessible (on weekends, anyway). That's why Mary falls in love with him. Warren is one of those poor saps who believe that reason and decency will win the day. His murder scheme certainly makes him more interesting than before, but we're relieved when he's unable to kill Deager when an opportunity presents itself (in a moody beach house tableau illuminated by a flickering fireplace).

Sensual Audrey Totter, as Claire, is a marvel of bad intentions. Alternately cooing and viper-tongued, she's the original material girl. Clever without being intelligent, her laziness alone marks her as a bad match for the industrious Warren, whose hard work she barely acknowledges and certainly doesn't

---

Case File: Audrey Totter (b. 1918)

Audrey Totter's seductive way with a page of dialogue helped bring her early success as a radio actress, but the full Totter effect is enjoyed only when you see as well as hear her. On-screen, she's blonde, decisive, and blessed with a cynical, appraising intelligence. She looks at lovers and marks alike with knowing bedroom eyes set above a round nose and an expressively shapely mouth that simultaneously suggests *Come and get it, big boy* and *One more step and there's going to be trouble*. She has a wonderful cameo in *The Postman Always Rings Twice* (1946) as a flirty gal who temporarily distracts John Garfield from his liaison with Lana Turner, and really came into her own the following year as Robert Montgomery's chief antagonist in *Lady in the Lake*. Totter is at her best in that one; likewise in *Tension*, in which she burns up the screen as Richard Basehart's selfish, round-heeled wife. Totter's other noir films include *The Unsuspected* and *The Set-Up* (in a movingly sympathetic role).

Although Totter is well known to film fans today, and revered for her contributions to noir, she was a prominent figure for only a short time, from her debut in 1945 to about 1950. For nearly the next thirty years, she devoted the greater part of her energy to episodic television and worked only sporadically on the big screen.

---

appreciate. In a heartbreaking scene, Warren drives Claire to a new housing development. He's so full of excitement he nearly bursts. He stops and shows Claire the house he wants to buy for the two of them. Breathlessly, he begins to describe its features and how wonderful it will be to be away from the city. He steps onto the sidewalk and keeps talking.

Claire pointedly stays in the car. She's not interested. When Warren continues to talk, Claire slides into the driver's seat and lets her body fall against the horn ring. Warren is crushed.

Tension was directed by John Berry, a journeyman filmmaker who directed John Garfield's final film, *He Ran All the Way* (1951), worked in Europe, and hung around long enough to direct *The Bad News Bears Go to Japan* (1978). He was a good storyteller, though the *Tension* script by Allen Rivkin allows the picture to go a little slack at about the eighty-minute mark.

Andre Previn contributed a lively, occasionally dissonant score, and cinematographer Harry Stradling did beautiful work, making the flesh of Totter and Charisse look like satin during romantic moments, and purposely overlighting Totter when Claire is put on the spot for Deager's death.

Decency is sorely tested in *Tension*, but in the end, it wins out.

Just an Old-Fashioned Girl

Flaxy Martin (1949) is a Warner Bros. release that came to theaters the same year as the studio's *White Heat* (see Chapter 7). The latter, with its elevation of a mother-obsessed psychotic to antihero status, stunned audiences with its modernity. But *Flaxy Martin* looks back instead of forward and seems a product of an earlier era. Besides Warner Bros., the only thing that connects *Flaxy* and *White Heat* is leading lady Virginia Mayo.

Cynical attorney Walter Colby (Zachary Scott) is sick and tired of working his courtroom legerdemain to free thugs belonging to mob boss Hap Richie (Douglas Kennedy). Only one thing keeps Colby hanging around: his lover, Flaxy (Mayo). When one of Hap's goons murders a blackmailing perjurer moments after Flaxy has been seen arguing with the victim, Colby knows that Flaxy could be convicted on circumstantial evidence. In one of those preposterous brainstorms that often occur to people in the movies, Colby decides to head off Flaxy's trouble by making a false confession and later get himself off the hook by wowing the jury at his trial.

Two problems: Flaxy is a conniver who allows herself be romanced by Hap, and Colby can't manipulate the jury as he'd assumed because Hap and Flaxy conspire to put *another* perjurer on the stand. Colby is convicted.

Colby's daring escape from custody, his chance meeting with a sweet librarian named Nora Carson (Dorothy Malone), and an almost fatal tussle with Hap's number-one assassin, Roper (Elisha Cook Jr.), lead the exhausted attorney back to Hap and Flaxy. Finally outsmarted by her own cleverness, Flaxy commits a murder that will be her downfall.

When *Flaxy Martin* was released early in 1949, millions of American women had already learned the value of independence by going to work during World War II. Flaxy must have been sitting out the conflict, however, because she's a gold digger very much in the mold of "kept women" of the 1920s and '30s. Tall, stylish, and thoroughly gorgeous, she figures she has all the natural equipment needed to free her from the worry of work. To that end, she plays Colby and Hap against each other, getting what she can from each and looking forward to yet another month in her fabulous, rent-free apartment.

Certainly such women as Flaxy still existed in 1949. There were plenty of men who were willing to support such women. But the best movies look forward, offering progressive, mature views of their principal characters. Flaxy—who is, after all, the title character of *Flaxy Martin*—has no backstory. Other than that she's a club singer who likes money, we know nothing about her. It's clear enough that she plays men, but what is it *inside her* that leads her down that road? David Lang's glib script doesn't offer a hint.

The unfortunate irony is that Mayo was one of the best and most versatile screen actresses of her era. *Flaxy Martin* exploits Mayo's gifts only superficially—and in fact, she's a decidedly secondary character in a tale that focuses most sharply on the attorney, Colby.

Dorothy Malone is sweetly appealing as the librarian Nora, who functions as a pointed contrast to Flaxy, and helps Colby before knowing he's a fugitive, and then falls for him. Warner had put Malone under contract in 1945 but never utilized her to her best advantage. (She was finally allowed to show her talent in the 1950s, at Universal-International.)

The picture was well shot by Carl Guthrie and directed in the slick, truculent Warner house style by the technically capable Richard L. Bare, whose greatest artistic success was as writer-director of more than sixty perfectly wonderful "Joe McDoakes" one-reel Warner comedy shorts made between 1942 and 1956. Comedy was Bare's forte; he also directed every episode of TV's farcically surreal *Green Acres*. He's certainly not at sea with *Flaxy Martin*, but the wildly strident performance of the usually understated Elisha Cook Jr. suggests that Bare's affinity for broad playing came naturally and was difficult for him to suppress. Some sequences, such as a chiller when Colby and Nora are forced to watch as their graves are being dug in a remote forest, are vivid, and Zachary Scott and Douglas Kennedy (who should have had a better career) are solid, convincing antagonists. Additional bite is provided by the young character actress Helen Westcott, who is splendid as a greedy slattern who comes to a bad end.

The preclimax, Colby's furious rooftop struggle with Roper, is lively, but obvious use of stunt doubles is a big flaw, and because the ledge that surrounds the roof is pretty low, it's easy to anticipate how the fight will play out.

True to its old-fashioned underpinnings, *Flaxy Martin* gives us the blunt pleasure of cheering for a too-smart guy who receives a jolt of reality before being redeemed.

She's Not Ethel Anymore

The ambitious Flaxy Martin pursues her fortune while whirling through a landscape of urban comfort. The heroine of Vincent Sherman's *The Damned Don't Cry* (1950) begins a long journey in the Texas oil fields, where the derricks pump day and night outside the simple cottages that house the workers and their families, and where husbands come home filthy and dispirited. For Ethel Whitehead (Joan Crawford) the situation is tolerable—barely, and only because of her little boy. Her husband, Roy (Richard Egan), is an unloving lout obsessively disappointed with his puny pay and resentful of Ethel's modest spending of it. When the boy is killed in a freak bicycle accident, nothing remains to hold Ethel. Careworn yet strangely innocent, she leaves for the big city.

An awareness of social class (and Ethel's lack in that department) motivates three men who become central to Ethel's life in the city: Marty Blackford (Kent Smith), a mild and underpaid CPA who sacrifices his ideals to become chief accountant for the Syndicate; sophisticated Syndicate boss George Castleman (David Brian), once a lowly Mob soldier; and West Coast overseer Nick Prenta (Steve Cochran), who endured a childhood swimming in the filth of the East River.

Castleman is knowledgeable about Etruscan urns, fine art, and gourmet food. He's remade himself, and because he takes a sexual interest in Ethel's beauty and spirit, he wants to remake her, too. The first thing to go is "Ethel Whitehead." Ethel's new name is Lorna Hanson Forbes. Lorna quickly learns about fine things, too, and how to comport herself like a lady.

The Damned Don't Cry (1950): Ethel Whitehead (Joan Crawford) remakes herself, abandoning her past and falling in with high-level hoodlums, including West Coast syndicate boss Nick Prenta (Steve Cochran). Selena Royle is at right.

Besides class, the driving force of *The Damned Don't Cry* is sex. Ethel/Lorna's first real job in the city is to model clothes for buyers and then accompany them on nighttime "dates." Later, she becomes the married Castleman's secret lover. Castleman finally instructs Lorna to go the coast, ingratiate herself with Prenta, and report back on what his underling is up to. A chunk of the Syndicate's money comes from prostitution, and that's what Castleman is proposing to Lorna. It's a cleaned-up proposal, with furs and money and an opportunity to remain Castleman's lover, but the essence of the scheme is that Lorna will give her body to Prenta and then betray him.

Confused and heartbroken, Lorna makes the trip. She never betrays Prenta, but he's soon dead by Castleman's hand anyway. Lorna flees for her life.

Harold Medford and Jerome Weldman's script is a flashback bracketed by present-day sequences at Lorna's humble childhood home in oil country. At the climax, Marty unexpectedly shows up there, with a gun.

And then Castleman arrives. He has a gun, too.

Unarmed, Lorna marches onto the porch to confront Castleman, who can't wait to shoot her. But Marty (who has apparently recovered some of his self-respect) has another idea.

Vincent Sherman was a prolific director of no discernible philosophy but of great professionalism and an understanding of the Warner Bros. house style. *The*

Damned Don't Cry is as good-looking a film as the studio ever produced, thanks to Sherman's smoothly gliding camera, mid-century-modern sets by art director Robert Haas, and gorgeously evocative lighting by cinematographer Ted McCord (romantic scenes involving Lorna and Castleman are vividly intimate).

Location shooting encompasses oil fields, the nighttime desert (notably for a body dump that's the picture's first sequence), and sunny party scenes. Early sequences at Ethel's house are harshly lit; later, when Lorna is ensconced in Prenta's Desert Springs palazzo, tonal values range up and down the scale, from shimmering, silvery light to queerly shifting shadows. Many scenes are shot from a low angle, to emphasize the place's expansiveness (and ironic loneliness). The house is symbolic of how far Prenta and the rest have come. It's also a monument to the new, dangerous criminal mind embodied by Prenta and a sharp contrast to the leather and dark mahogany of Castleman's traditional New York home. We see for ourselves that the future is in the west.

At forty-four, Joan Crawford is too mature for her role, and is certainly too tiny to work as a model. But the actress was still riding the comeback generated five years earlier by *Mildred Pierce*, and dominates the screen with her face and personality. Her performance is rich and nicely varied; she's convincing as the mousy oil-field wife and blistering as Lorna. A softer side comes out in love scenes with David Brian (suitably aggressive and physically intimidating) and Steve Cochran (provocatively sensual and unpredictable).

At the end, Lorna is shaken by the conclusion of her adventure. Can she ever bring herself to become Ethel again? Two reporters who show up at the Whitehead house provide the answer:

> REPORTER #1
> Well, it must be pretty tough, livin' in a place like this.
>
> REPORTER #2
> You'd gotta get out. Think she'll try it again?
>
> REPORTER #1
> Wouldn't you?

Only the Chimp Got Off Easy

Sunset Boulevard (1950) isn't exactly a hate letter to Hollywood—its exuberance makes an impossibility of that—but it is undeniably a backhanded slap in the face at the business that had brought director/cowriter Billy Wilder fame and wealth. In its examination of dreams and misplaced desire, *Sunset Boulevard* (the title, by the way, appears on the screen as a curb stencil: *Sunset Blvd.*) is nightmarish and wickedly funny.

Young, third-rate screenwriter Joe Gillis (William Holden) has written a couple of B pictures but has now hit the wall, unable to sell even an "original story." He occupies a tiny flat above Hollywood and is woefully behind in his car payments. When he hides his convertible in the garage of an old mansion on Sunset Boulevard, he meets and inadvertently charms the middle-aged owner, onetime silent-screen idol Norma Desmond (silent star Gloria Swanson). Norma hasn't worked in years, and although she's wealthy, the mansion and its grounds have gone to seed. Imprisoned by her memories, Norma has retreated inside her home, ruminating about the past, distressed by the present, and full of completely unrealistic notions about her future. Her longtime companion is her dour, aging butler, Max (silent-screen filmmaker Erich Von Stroheim), who quietly endures Norma's moods and verbal abuse.

Gillis's downfall begins when money, lavish gifts, and a roof over his head (things a gigolo might expect) persuade him to collaborate with Norma on a rewrite of her dreadful script for a remake of the Salome story, which she envisions as her comeback. (John the Baptist's noggin ends up on a silver platter in that little fable. If Gillis's instincts had been more acute, he would have put distance between himself and Norma immediately.)

Gillis knows Norma's project is hopeless but becomes trapped by his financial dependency and essential laziness. Finally sick of himself after months have gone by, he attempts to break with Norma by shouting the sandpapery truth: that the script is awful, and that her friend and former director Cecil B. De Mille (playing himself) has been humoring her. Gillis unwisely adds that he can't stand the sight of Norma, or the morbidly suffocating mansion, for another instant. He stalks from the house with his suitcase. Norma, by now panicked and completely unhinged, follows with a pistol and shoots him three times. Gillis collapses into the swimming pool, dead.

The writer's violent end (perpetrated by Norma out of fear rather than malevolence) is staged with shocking effectiveness but isn't a complete surprise because *Sunset Boulevard* opens with Joe Gillis already dead, afloat in the pool, sharing his story in voice-over emanating from somewhere in the afterlife. (In an early idea that Wilder abandoned, the dead Gillis stirs in the morgue and relates his tale to the other corpses.)

Exceptionally effective location shooting in Hollywood, on the Paramount lot, and the wealthy end of Sunset (the mansion was real and is now gone) gives weight to some memorable set pieces and revelations: Gillis's furious race up Sunset, a pair of auto repo men close behind; the ghoulish midnight burial, in a child's white coffin, of Norma's departed chimpanzee; and a New Year's Eve party at which Gillis and a giddy Norma are the only guests. During movie night in the mansion's museum-like living room, Norma unconsciously takes Gillis's hand as she gazes upon her earlier self (a clip from the 1928 Von Stroheim silent *Queen Kelly*). Pointed insert shots of interior doors with neither knobs nor locks, so that Norma can be rescued if she falls back into the habit of attempting suicide, are unsettling; and Norma's visit to Paramount, where she's feted by De Mille and old-timers among the crew, is awful because she's unaware that the studio doesn't want her but her antique car. Max dispassionately reveals to Gillis that he was Norma's first husband, that he directed her pictures during her glory days, and that whatever fan letters Norma receives are written and posted by him.

Most famously, there is the arrival of newsreel cameramen after the murder and Norma's demented glide down her staircase. Max "directs" as Norma's face floats into the camera eye and finally overwhelms it in a nimbus of hazy, overpowering light that's at once beautiful and horrific. Franz Waxman's score is one of Hollywood's greatest, a testament to sweeping melodrama that cleverly incorporates exotic motifs suggestive of Norma's alter ego, Salome. The beautiful final theme, as Norma descends the stairs, is frightening in its implications.

Wilder's first inclination was to hire Mae West to play Norma, but West, fifty-eight in 1950, balked at the notion of playing a character whose age disturbs a younger man. Wilder subsequently approached silent-screen goddess Mary Pickford, who had been adored for her on-screen wholesomeness and thought Wilder was out of his mind. Then Swanson's name came up. The legendary actress hadn't done a picture since 1941, and the gap before that stretched back to 1934. Norma was a triumph for Swanson, who was rewarded with an Oscar nomination and a bit of a comeback.

William Holden had been in pictures since 1939. He was likable on-screen and popular around town but had yet to have a breakout role. Joe Gillis was it. Three years later, again working with Wilder, he won an Academy Award for his performance in *Stalag 17*.

Tech and other contributions are peerless. John F. Seitz's photography brings dimension to musty interiors and sunlit exteriors. Wilder's numberless close-ups on Norma's face are pathetic and stirring in their silken intimacy, and the astonishing final sequence with the newsreel men has rightly entered film legend.

Art direction and set design (Hans Dreier & John Meehan and Sam Comer & Ray Moyer, respectively) are exceptional.

Case File: John F. Seitz (1893–1979)

A leading Hollywood cinematographer and inventor, Seitz entered the business in 1916 and photographed major films until his retirement in 1960. He altered his style to suit changing tastes, but more than that, he helped to *define* what postwar cinematography should be. Of his noir pictures, *The Big Clock* is shot with particular boldness. Other noir thrillers shot by Seitz: *This Gun for Hire*, *Double Indemnity* (a visually perfect California noir), *Night Has a Thousand Eyes*, *Sunset Boulevard*, and *Rogue Cop*.

Like many of his peers, Seitz was a good all-rounder, with experience on Shirley Temple films and Preston Sturges comedies; costume pictures and westerns. Fans of science fiction admire Seitz's evocative color work on *Invaders from Mars* and *When Worlds Collide*.

In an odd twist, young actress Yvette Vickers, who appears in a *Sunset Boulevard* party sequence as a giggly blonde on the telephone, enjoyed a bit of a career in the 1950s and '60s and became a cult actress, only to die alone in her overgrown and dilapidated Benedict Canyon home in 2010 or 2011, at eighty-two. Her body lay in the house for so long that it became mummified.

Hooray for Hollywood.

"Goin' Someplace, Sweetie?"

Noir isn't just a genre—it's occasionally a flavorful seasoning, a philosophical and visual style that can be trotted out for atmospheric effect in pictures that are not, in the main, noir. That's the case with Andrew Stone's *Highway 301* (1950), an enormously competent docudrama based on the real-life depredations of George Legenza's Tri-State Gang, which plundered banks and armored cars throughout the upper South in the 1930s.

Highway 301 is a late-period example of the Warner Bros. house style, headed by a contract player, Steve Cochran (just coming off his success as Big Ed in *White Heat*), and shot on a mix of LA-area locations and the studio's "urban-streets" back lot. In this, the picture is very like the Warner crime melodramas of the 1930s: brutally "real" with moody, carefully controlled visual effects of light and dark. Confidently lit by cinematographer Carl Guthrie and scored with lusty, masculine abandon by the underrated William Lava, *Highway 301* (which is set in contemporary 1950) gives us a good, hard look at the personal and professional styles of career criminals.

A pair of set pieces—a daring daylight bank robbery and a daytime hit on a cash-rich railway express truck—are vividly staged and suggest that even pros can be suckered. The bank heist is a success, but the attack on the currency truck turns into a disaster of murder. The robbers subsequently discover that their $2 million haul is old "cut money" that has been sliced lengthwise for delivery to Washington, for burning. Legenza (Cochran) is so cross he pretends to congratulate his inside man and then shoots him dead.

Legenza has a couple of other problems, too: a pair of women who threaten the gang's future. It's with this man vs. woman preoccupation that *Highway 301* slips effectively into noir. Legenza's first bother is his own squeeze, Madeline (popular serial actress Aline Towne), who is disgusted with crime's heavy risk, Legenza's disagreeable temperament, and the boredom of trundling from one hideout to another. When she makes the mistake of shooting off her mouth to a new girlfriend of one of the gang members, she and Legenza simultaneously realize that Madeline has overstayed her welcome. In a tense, protracted sequence of attempted escape, Madeline hurries to her apartment, where she throws things in a suitcase and waits for the elevator. When it arrives, Legenza is inside. We see him full-figure for just an instant before his face—eyebrows to chin—fills the screen with cool, unperturbed menace. "Goin' someplace,

Case File: Steve Cochran (1917–65)

Darkly brooding Steve Cochran enjoyed a busy career as a prominent supporting player and leading man. Rakish black hair, sensual features, and a heavy air of violence and sexual menace restricted him mainly to villainous roles, which he played with relish and style. He's amusing in one of his early pictures, *Wonder Man* (1945), in scenes with Danny Kaye, and began to come into his own a year later as a wife-stealer in *The Best Years of Our Lives*, and as a quietly crazy criminal in *The Chase*, Cochran's first noir. He's a powerful presence in *White Heat, The Damned Don't Cry, Highway 301, Storm Warning* (his best performance, as a dimwitted Klan member), and *Private Hell 36*.

Cochran established his own production company in 1953 and starred in Michelangelo Antonioni's *Il Grido (The Cry)* four years later. Cochran wrote, produced, directed, and starred in his final film, an elegiac romance called *Tell Me in the Sunlight* (1965). Before the picture could be released, Cochran died of respiratory failure aboard his forty-foot schooner, *Rogue*, while off the coast of Guatemala. None of the three women onboard with him had a clue about operating the boat, which drifted for ten days. Cochran left a twenty-three-year-old wife, his third. Merle Oberon—one of many name actresses with whom Cochran had had a love affair—tried unsuccessfully to encourage an investigation into possible criminal wrongdoing in his death.

sweetie?" Madeline's face, also in *über*-close-up, freezes in terror, eyes as wide as saucers.

"George!"

When she turns to run, Legenza comes out with a revolver and shoots her in the back, sending her into a sliding, face-first tumble to the bottom of the stairs.

Legenza turns to the diminutive, very nervous elevator operator. "Get goin'," he says.

With Madeline decisively disposed of, Legenza turns his attention to Lee (Gaby Rogers), a French-Canadian beauty who has become the fiancée of the gang's Romeo, a young smoothie named Phillips (Robert Webber, in a very early role). Lee is in love (her sweetie has led her to believe he sells cosmetics), but she's not an idiot, so before much more of *Highway 301* unreels, she's on the run from Legenza in the dark, rain-slicked streets of Richmond—which apparently rolls up its sidewalks at 9:00 pm. In the crime-film genre, few pursued women have seemed as utterly, desperately alone as Lee.

Cat-and-mouse stuff that incorporates the click-clack of Lee's heels; a deserted, weirdly shadowed park; the steps to a basement apartment; and an unexpected crowd of late-night merrymakers culminates in Lee's escape in a cab—which is piloted by Legenza. He stops the car and coolly aims his gun over his shoulder, putting a bullet into Lee at point-blank range.

This concludes the noir portions of *Highway 301*, but if you're wondering, things begin to break bad for Legenza and the others when they go to the local hospital intending to clean up some unfinished business. After just a minute or two, there's more lead in the air than dust motes, and Legenza barely manages to escape. But on a rise topped with railroad tracks, Legenza is stitched by police machine-gun fire and falls alive onto the tracks, where he's squashed by a speeding train.

The Mobster, the Mortician, and the Missing Buddy

The success of *White Heat* (see Chapter 7) boosted Steve Cochran's status at Warner and also did good things for the careers of costars Edmond O'Brien and Virginia Mayo, and cowriters (and longtime partners) Ben Roberts and Ivan Goff—all of whom came together for a 1950 Warner release, *Backfire*. If the film isn't familiar to noir fans, the reason is that it's not particularly distinguished. Despite the talent noted above, plus moody cinematography by Carl Guthrie and effective direction by the great (if stylistically anonymous) craftsman Vincent Sherman, *Backfire* doesn't come together.

The setup is simple: An ex-GI whose dream (like that of so many returned vets) is to go into business with his buddy, searches the length and breadth of Los Angeles when his pal vanishes after inexplicably taking a job with a racketeer and becoming a suspect in the Bugsy Siegel–style rubout of a notorious gambler. The racketeer who employs the pal is married, and woe unto any man who looks at his wife. As you might guess, the missing buddy took a good, *long* look, fell in love, and got himself into trouble that's even worse than the murder rap.

The scenario is noir-familiar, and with a direct treatment it could have had some blunt power. But because Roberts, Goff, and cowriter Larry Marcus (who spent most of his career in television) were encouraged to replicate the complexity of an earlier Warner noir, *The Big Sleep* (1946; see Chapter 3), *Backfire* pulls us into a narrative that, while as confusingly elliptical as the one that drives *The Big Sleep*, isn't nearly as satisfying. Endless flashbacks involving every principal character and a lot of secondary ones pop up with the regularity of summer dandelions and finally make you long for a scorecard. After a while, your attention flags, and you absorb the flashbacks as discrete set pieces and not as parts of a larger puzzle—precisely the reaction the filmmakers *didn't* want.

Most of the casting is good. Edmond O'Brien is Steve, the engaging old pal who goes missing, and young Gordon MacRae (in a rare nonmusical role) is Bob, who searches for his friend with guileless, open-faced earnestness. His honest nature contrasts effectively with the grim types who fill out much of the plot. Virginia Mayo is game and appealing in the underwritten role of Julie, a spunky VA nurse who helps Bob ferret out what's become of Steve. (The actress is at her best in a peculiar and unnerving nighttime sequence in which she connives her way into the locked office of an unscrupulous doctor [Mack Williams], only to be caught red-handed.)

Dane Clark plays another army pal, Ben; and Viveca Lindfors is Lysa, the wife of the seldom-glimpsed racketeer Lou Walsh.

Dane Clark came to films from the stage. Like many Warner leading men, he was essentially a character actor, and from the start of his prolific career at the studio, he was intended to evoke another, more popular Warner star, John Garfield. And the Swedish Lindfors was the studio's transparent attempt to replicate the beauty and intelligence of Ingrid Bergman. Neither of those casting schemes quite works, so in addition to its familiar plot, *Backfire* suggests the second-hand or second-best—which is really no knock on Clark or Lindfors; both are effective and well-suited for their roles. They're just not Garfield and Bergman.

Better to have cast the versatile and powerful Virginia Mayo as Mrs. Walsh and given the nurse's role to the quirkily appealing starlet Sheila Stephens (later Sheila MacRae—yes, *that* MacRae), who is brashly funny as a what-the-hell dame who reveals to Bob (via the inevitable flashback) a great deal about Walsh.

Much is made of the mysterious nature of Mr. Walsh. Director Sherman takes pains to show only the character's legs, or to reveal him merely as a small figure in very shadowed long shots as he skulks outside windows. *Who is Lou Walsh?!* Well, Dane Clark's Ben, an amiable, successful mortician, has little reason to be in the movie except to function as a minor ally of Bob. That might suggest something about the baffling Mr. Walsh.

Two set pieces stand out: When Steve is crushed against a garage by Walsh's car and, much later, when Walsh's plan to rub out Bob is sidetracked when Steve—locked into an above-the-waist body cast and a hideous metal chin-and-neck support—comes trundling down the stairs like the Golem and hurls himself onto Walsh's back.

The racketeer is finally cut down when he foolishly engages Lt. Garcia (Ed Begley) and a platoon of uniformed cops in a gun battle on his front lawn. Steve is spirited away in an ambulance, attended by Julie and Bob. "We're out of the jungle now," Steve says wearily—and that should have been the fade-out. However (and unfortunately), *Backfire* has an absurd coda, perhaps generated by audience preview cards, in which a rejuvenated Steve skips down the hospital steps and into a Jeep with Julie and Bob. They're off to that business of their own, a ranch. Oh, boy, it's great to be together again.

The Man Who Heard Too Much

Numerous starlets of the 1950s eyed Marilyn Monroe, particularly MM's come-hither look and vividly blonde hair, and decided (or were advised) to remake themselves in Monroe's image. Chief among these were Jayne Mansfield and Mamie Van Doren, each of whom demonstrated an agreeable personality to go along with the requisite, if overstated, sex appeal. And then there were such lesser lights as Cleo Moore, Joi Lansing, and Barbara Nichols. One of the earliest imitators was lanky Beverly Michaels, whose screen persona isn't just sexy but very funny. She played the Bad Girl many times but never with more cheapness and venom than in *Pickup* (1951). She's hilariously wonderful.

At railroad Tank Stop 47, somewhere in the California desert, Czech widower Jan Horak (Hugo Haas) works as a track inspector. Middle-aged and a little stout, he sees almost no one. His dog has died, and his only friend is an erudite bum called the Professor (Howland Chamberlin), who stops by to make conversation and cadge a cup of coffee. The Professor offers to find Jan a puppy, but Jan declines.

In town, he watches a long-legged girl ride side-saddle on a carousel, her skirt hiked above her knees. This is Betty (Michaels), a no-good, emotionally volatile gold digger who peeks at Jan's bankbook and comes to covet his $7,300. Turning on her modest charm and exploiting Jan's loneliness, Betty maneuvers the older man into marriage. Problem: Betty won't get her hands on the money until Jan retires—in six years.

Fate deals a hand in Betty's favor when Jan is suddenly struck deaf. As Betty sees it, Jan will *have* to retire, and the two of them can move to town.

While Jan's deafness is diagnosed, the railroad brings in a much younger man, a handsome fellow named Steve (Allan Nixon). Steve isn't a bad sort, but he can't resist when Betty paws him like an oversexed she-wolf. Soon, he has to listen to Betty's scheme to get rid of Jan. A railroad bridge with no railing is on the route of Jan's daily inspection. Would it be so awful, or so hard, to give Jan a little push? No one would ever know it wasn't an accident, and Steve could go away with Betty and help her spend Jan's money.

The pleasing hook of *Pickup* is that, after a minor accident, Jan's hearing returns. Excited to tell Betty, he rushes home, where he's shocked when he hears her rail against him to Steve, right in front of him, expressing her anger and contempt. Jan is as curious as he is hurt, and continues to play deaf.

In a clever sequence, Betty's cruel insults are separated—and emphasized— by repeated shock cuts to footage of a locomotive racing at the camera, with horizontal wipes that return us to the house and the next bit of invective. Finally, Betty and Steve sit across from Jan at the kitchen table.

> **BETTY**
> Look at him, that old spider, staring at me. What does he
> want? [Betty gives Jan a toothy smile, then laughs] You
> sucker, I married your bank account, but the trouble is, I
> can't get at it, ain't that a joke?

Betty's face splits with laughter, and she doesn't know that the sound is as bitter to Jan as it is to her. In a moment that recalls the silent-screen pathos of Emil Jannings or Lon Chaney, Jan forces himself to echo his wife's laughter. Haas (who directed and cowrote *Pickup*) filmed himself in close-up, his mouth and eyes revealing his horror and shame. It's a fine moment in a small film.

Betty eventually wears Steve down about doing murder, but at the last moment he can't bring himself to go through with it. Disgusted, Betty cats around all night, and when she returns Steve begins to throttle her. Jan listens impassively for long moments. After all, he's deaf. No one could blame him because he didn't hear the sounds of his beloved wife being murdered.

But Jan is no killer, not even by proxy. He pulls Steve away. When the phone rings, Jan answers it. Now Betty knows he can hear. The call is about an emergency that causes Steve to rush from the house. Betty, on her own once again, isn't far behind.

When the Professor brings a puppy later, Jan says, "That's what I should have brought home in the first place."

Hugo Haas was a Czech actor who came to Hollywood in the late 1930s and established a successful career as a featured character actor. He changed the focus of his livelihood after 1950, becoming writer-producer-director of fevered, arguably misogynistic tales of sexual misery and deceit, nearly always starring himself as an unfairly betrayed husband. He prospered at this masochism for a decade, with such low-budgets pictures as *The Girl on the Bridge*, *Strange Fascination*, *Bait*, *Thy Neighbor's Wife*, *The Other Woman*, and *One Girl's Confession*. The overtly sexy Beverly Michaels was Haas's first muse; she was followed by the equally over-the-top Cleo Moore.

In the pictures Haas made with Michaels, he cannily allowed her performances to come right to the brink of parody—and no further. The characters she plays are larger than life but not improbable. You realize, with considerable discomfiture, that people like Betty are running around all over, thinking too much and not too clearly, aware of the briefness of youth and determined to score.

The Actor's Guide to Murder

Wealthy playwright Myra Hudson (Joan Crawford) marries an impoverished actor (Jack Palance), only to discover that he and his lover (Gloria Grahame) are conspiring to kill her. Myra wants to foil and punish the two schemers—but how? RKO's *Sudden Fear* (1952) is predicated on very familiar noir material but has some freshness because the film is as much about the nature of art as it is about the art of murder.

During a New York reading for her latest play, Myra decides that actor Lester Blaine (Palance), though talented, hasn't the romantic appeal needed to "sell" the character. Myra orders that Blaine be dismissed. When she runs into the actor weeks later on a train taking her home to San Francisco, Myra discovers for herself that Lester has plenty of romantic appeal—so much, in fact, that the two are married after a brief courtship.

The focus of Myra's life is fiction. She lives to create and guide the characters in her plays. Her disinterest in power over real people marks her as a sympathetic figure. Further, because she's accustomed to inventing stories that work out as she wishes, she's not predisposed to think that her husband—like every actor, a professional impersonator—might be dishonest and manipulative.

Lester says he wants to find meaningful work. He doesn't want to live off Myra's fortune. Myra loves him for that. What a happy couple.

A guest at a swanky dinner party is a blonde stunner named Irene Neves (Grahame). In short order, we discover that Irene and Lester have 1) a torrid sexual past, 2) every intention of pursuing a torrid sexual present and future, and 3) a fierce desire to help themselves to big chunks of Myra's fortune. Because Lester misinterprets a draft of Myra's will, he thinks he has just three days to kill her.

Myra discovers the pair's plot while listening to playback from the Dictaphone she uses to write her plays. She recoils in disbelief and sorrow as the tinny voices of Lester and Irene come from the machine (which Myra forgot to turn off when last using it).

> LESTER
> Sometimes when I'm with her it's all I can do to keep from saying, "Be yourself, wise up. Love you? I've never loved you. Not for one moment." Hnh. I'd like to see her face....
>
> IRENE
> Kiss me. Kiss me! Hard!
>
> LESTER
> I'm crazy about you. I could just break your bones.

This dialogue is awful (the stuff that Myra writes is awful, too), but it's in keeping with Joan Crawford's larger-than-life persona. She was a movie star who also was *emblematic* of a movie star, so the details of her predicament have to be emblematic, too. If you want to rephrase that and say "over the top," that's fine, and not inaccurate.

Although the Dictaphone business is contrived (and clumsily telegraphed in a much earlier scene), it does emphasize the peculiar power of dialogue—an oblique reference to Myra's profession. Indeed, *Sudden Fear* is preoccupied with dialogue and the art of acting: Lester's continued impersonation of an adoring husband, and a performance by Myra that must not only conceal her fear and disgust but appear to reciprocate the false feelings put forth by Lester.

Myra is shaken but not defeated. She isn't going to go quietly. In fact, if she has anything to say about it, she isn't going to go at all. Because she's a professional dramatist, she comes up with a baroque scheme of her own, involving a pair of forged notes that she'll deposit with Lester and Irene, a midnight rendezvous, and Irene's nickel-plated .38. In her imagination, it all works out perfectly, but in a final twist that displays additional differences between life and art, almost nothing of Myra's plan works out. No one shoots anybody, people answer telephones that they have no business answering, and Myra has a change of heart that causes her to become trapped in Irene's closet while Lester sits just ten feet away. (He absently fiddles with a windup toy dog, and in one of the oddest and most unnerving sequences in all of noir, he sets the toy loose on the shadowed floor, forcing Myra to watch helplessly as the doggie waddles directly toward the closet. When the toy finally stops, director David Miller and cinematographer Charles B. Lang Jr. contrive things so that only a portion of the dog's head, and one tiny, gleaming eye, are visible from inside the closet.)

Events come to a climax during a lively, starkly lit nighttime chase. Myra runs the deserted streets on foot while Lester pursues her in his Packard. He stops the car and dashes up some stairs, falls from a low balcony, and hurries back to the car. Meanwhile, Myra steps on a cat's tail (*Mrrowwwr!*) and noisily rattles a garbage can. If you'd never seen a movie before, you'd be riveted.

In a final contrivance, Myra and Irene happen to wear identical coats and scarves. Lester spots one of the women and—well, let's just say that Irene's days as a hot blonde are over, and Lester wouldn't have been around to enjoy her anyway.

Sudden Fear was made when Joan Crawford needed a hit. She'd been hanging on through sheer grit and willpower but now was challenged not only by younger actresses but by new *styles* of acting. The *Sudden Fear* script (by Lenore Coffee and Robert Smith, from Edna Sherry's 1948 novel) appealed to her. She wanted Clark Gable or Robert Taylor as Lester, but director David Miller held out for Palance, the rare actor, Miller felt, who could believably menace Joan Crawford. Crawford thought the casting idea was awful (because Palance was "ugly," or because he was a newcomer, depending on which account you examine), but when she saw test footage, she changed her mind. During the film's early sequences, Palance wears a nose appliance and a false hairline that soften his appearance. As his villainy is revealed, the makeup is removed. By the late stages of the story, Palance's peculiarly stark features (the result of a wartime injury) look like a death's head. Crawford has the antagonist she needs.

The public made *Sudden Fear* an enormous box-office success. Audiences had seen much of it before but seldom with as much old-style vigor.

Murder on the Rebound

Of the eleven films directed by Fritz Lang in the 1950s, *The Blue Gardenia* (1953) is the least successful. Its premise—that a woman has committed a murder she can't remember—has possibilities, but plot contrivance and an air of budget-cutting chop it off at the knees and leave viewers disappointed.

Norah Larkin (Anne Baxter) is a switchboard operator who shares an apartment with Crystal (Ann Sothern) and Sally (Jeff Donnell). The switchboard is enormous and staffed by a multitude of women. To overbearing commercial artist Harry Prebble (Raymond Burr), it's like a candy store, and he spends hours chatting up Norah and others, doing beautiful impromptu portraits while pretending not to flirt. When Norah receives a devastating "Dear Joan" letter from her boyfriend in Korea, she goes out with Prebble, who smilingly gets her very drunk at the Blue Gardenia restaurant. At his apartment later, Prebble turns into an aggressive octopus, and Norah reacts in a well-designed shock-cut montage (shot by Ted McCord and edited by Edward Mann) of fireplace poker, shattered fragments of mirror, and Prebble's death scream. Norah flees, leaving behind her shoes and a crushed blue gardenia.

Norah wakes up in her own bed the next morning, hung over and with only a fragmentary memory of the night before. Finally, Norah forces herself to approach columnist Casey Mayo (Richard Conte), who has written a "Letter to an Unknown Murderess" that promises to deliver the "Blue Gardenia" killer to the authorities with complete legal representation and to tell her story exactly as it happened.

To this point, *The Blue Gardenia* is engaging, and sailing along pretty smoothly. The fatal misstep in Charles Hoffman's screenplay (from the short story "Gardenia," by Vera Caspary) is that the streetwise and cynical Mayo believes Norah when she tells him her "friend" is the killer, and wants to turn herself in. Norah's retelling of her "friend's" tale is so emphatic and emotional that only Norah could be the suspect, but Mayo—who apparently just fell off the turnip truck—has no suspicion at all that he's listening to the woman he's been looking for. And when he finds out, he's devastated. Mayo is the most naïve hard-bitten columnist in the history of journalism.

Oversexed commercial artist Harry Prebble (Raymond Burr) takes Norah Larkin (Anne Baxter) to *The Blue Gardenia* (1953) in order to get her drunk. When Prebble is found dead later, Norah can't be certain she's not responsible.

The yellow press occupied Fritz Lang in a later picture, *While the City Sleeps* (see Chapter 7), and it is a subtext in the director's *Beyond a Reasonable Doubt* (see Chapter 5). *While the City Sleeps* is particularly cynical in its look at rough politicking for the top job at a sheet that's making hay with a series about a thrill killer. *The Blue Gardenia* expresses a bit of similar cynicism, as Mayo's paper plays the killing as a circus spectacle. Every scruple goes out the window when Mayo confesses to Norah that his paper isn't going to help the murderess at all.

Looked at in a certain way, the movie is an indictment of the bad behavior of men: the boyfriend who jilts Norah long-distance, the pushy and crudely oversexed Prebble (who specializes in leg art), and the columnist who, in the end, stands for nothing that's good. But at the same time, the script suggests that women trapped in the pink ghetto of meaningless work must be more careful about their choices of male companions, and that an urge to get married isn't enough to guarantee a suitable mate. (Ann Sothern's Crystal, amusing with her ironic wit and cigarette perpetually dangled from her lip, has already been married and divorced.)

Lang got a solid performance from Anne Baxter, who holds her own against the scene-stealing Raymond Burr—no small feat. Norah's progression from gaiety to emotional collapse and finally to desperation is convincing; Baxter is at once modulated and suitably melodramatic. Raymond Burr is darkly menacing in what was for him a typical sort of role, and Richard Conte brings some energy to the part of the columnist.

Pretty character actress Jeff Donnell, though, overacts terribly as Norah's perky, man-crazy roommate Sally (Sally also loves gory murder fiction), and bland George Reeves is simply an actor impersonating a frustrated police captain.

As a record-store clerk who figures in the story's denouement, angular Ruth Storey is agitated in the extreme, but because she drops in from nowhere at the eleventh hour, and because the nature of her character and her history with Prebble aren't revealed to us, we can't judge the appropriateness of Storey's performance.

Regrettably, this Alex Gottlieb/Blue Gardenia Productions project picked up for distribution by Warner Bros. was shot on the cheap. When Mayo looks from his office window and comments on a rainstorm, only a flat field of gray paint is visible from our oblique view. In another moment, a door opens to reveal a clumsily painted flat that is supposed to represent the city. A few sets seem underdressed. Shortcomings like these hurt because they're unnecessarily distracting. Fritz Lang would have better luck with other projects from his latter-day Hollywood career.

Nature in the Raw

Marilyn Monroe played a delusional but sympathetic babysitter in *Don't Bother to Knock* (1952), but in her next picture, *Niagara* (1953), she took the role of an out-and-out villainess. The actress was never more lushly beautiful on-screen, and she seems comfortable with the script of this Technicolor noir.

Monroe's very presence, though, is problematic. Although paired with a strong, charismatic leading man, Joseph Cotten, Marilyn effortlessly dominates every scene she's in. Few screen stars have had her sheer photographic presence. She's obviously not functioning at Cotten's level of talent, but you can't take your eyes off her. Her performance is better than adequate, her presence thrilling. Fox publicity promoted the picture as the pairing of two great natural wonders—Niagara Falls and MM—and for once the hype wasn't exaggerated. *Niagara* is dominated by two titans of nature.

Rose and George Loomis (Monroe and Cotten) are finishing up an unhappy stay at Niagara Falls. The maddeningly jealous George (who appears to be at least twenty years older than his wife) is in faltering recovery from shell shock, and Rose has a boyfriend. Worse, Rose and her lover have cooked up a smart scheme to kill George. The well-adjusted vacationers next door, Polly and Ray Cutler (Jean Peters and Casey Adams), become peripherally involved with Rose and George, at first with simple bemusement and later with considerable annoyance, as George's rages and Rose's hysteria turn the small resort upside down.

After the murder scheme fails, George kills his wife and (in an act that unwisely changes the film's complexion) attempts a run by speedboat to the American side, with Polly Cutler an unwilling passenger. When the boat runs out of gas, George and Polly are adrift in the rapids with nowhere to go but over the falls.

Niagara was directed by one of Hollywood's most capable craftsmen, Henry Hathaway. He came up in the 1920s (initially as an actor) concurrent with such figures as Victor Fleming, Howard Hawks, and William Wellman. In 1935, Hathaway had his first significant directorial success, *Lives of a Bengal Lancer*, and for the next thirty-seven years he adroitly moved among westerns, domestic drama, war films, and historical adventures. Hathaway was not an agenda- or theme-driven auteur but a peerless storyteller who personified Hollywood's professional ethic.

Niagara is a carefully contrived showcase for the relatively inexperienced Monroe, but because Hathaway had been an actor, he was able to guide his unsure star with firm, helpful paternalism. The success of Hathaway's approach is evident in Marilyn's performance, which is confident and forceful. Rose Loomis (as created by writers Charles Brackett [who also produced], Walter Reisch, and Richard Breen) is amoral and unsympathetic, with startling beauty that invites us to believe she can't be as bad as she seems.

Oh, yes, she can.

Most significantly, she's not the familiar noir fortune seeker. To the contrary, she's motivated purely by lust, as we see for ourselves when she phones her handsome lover (Richard Allan), who takes the call from his tiny room in a boardinghouse. The only payoff Rose is going to get from her scheme is sex, and that's the way she wants it. Indeed, she seems defined by sex. We first see her as

In Henry Hathaway's *Niagara* (1953), Rose Loomis (Marilyn Monroe) is on holiday at the Falls with her older husband (Joseph Cotten) and her secret lover. She wants to see her husband dead, but first, a spin on the phonograph of Rose's favorite song, a humid number called "Kiss."

she sleepily writhes beneath her sheets, apparently naked, trying hard to ignore George. (An implicit suggestion is that George is impotent.) In the picture's most celebrated sequence, Rose steps from her cabin attired in a form-fitting scarlet dress, which is apparently worn without undergarments. The dress is stunning, and so is Monroe. Her sexuality was never more brazenly exploited, nor turned to such impressive purpose. She really *is* the match of the Falls.

For other sequences, costumer Dorothy Jeakins put Monroe in a variety of somewhat more subdued but no less eye-catching outfits, with strappy heels, cinched jackets, and skirts designed to hobble her walk and emphasize her gorgeous behind. Monroe soon wearied of being a sex symbol, but the fact is that, in her era, she was unmatched. It's because of her that *Niagara* is a well-remembered noir.

Cinematographer Joe MacDonald deftly manipulated the rich Technicolor film stock, infusing the film with subdued violets, lavenders, cool blues, and reds. Many scenes are in evocative shadow, and even views of the falling water have depth and tonal values not seen in other movies set at the Falls. Soundstage setups are lit with great skill. Although an astute viewer will see that these are stages, the moments cut in well.

Dialogue is propulsive and often amusing. When Polly inadvertently sees Rose and the lover kissing at the base of the Falls, she's both shocked and tickled.

POLLY
Didn't that Mrs. Loomis say she was going shopping?

RAY
Yeah. Why?

POLLY
Well, she sure got herself an armload of groceries.

The lovers' method of signaling each other by requesting that their favorite song, a steamy ballad called "Kiss," be played by the Falls bell tower is clever. It is in the locked bell tower that *Niagara* reaches its first, and only truly important, climax. Rose dashes up floor after floor, panicked and hoping for a way out. George, his fierce love overcome by hurt and rage, is close behind. What follows is pure cinema and pure noir:

George steps through the final door to accost Rose, his body crisscrossed in shadow. "Too bad they can't play it for you now, Rose," he says, as he moves to strangle his wife, who's trapped against a red wall that seems to glow.

George steps beyond our view, and the camera pans upward along the wall until the top of the frame is filled with giant bells. For the next minute or so, Hathaway cuts between silent, static shots of the bells from different points of view and, finally, Rose's body as it slumps to the floor far below, crisscrossed in shadow and situated so that Rose seems to have been somehow affixed to a wall, like a prized butterfly.

Common wisdom is that no director utilized Monroe as effectively as Billy Wilder (*The Seven Year Itch, Some Like It Hot*). Wilder and MM did marvelous work together, but the Monroe-Hathaway team gives up nothing to Wilder. Its flaw of construction aside, *Niagara* is formidable.

Looking Out for Number One

Writer-director Sam Fuller's early professional experience as a crime-beat newspaper reporter introduced him to a multitude of "characters": cops, petty criminals, dopers, working girls, strong-arm men, grifters, murderers. Because he had an astute ear for dialogue, his crime films have a reality and depth of motivation that other screenwriters simply couldn't match. (The same goes for Fuller's war films.) The principal characters of Fuller's *Pickup on South Street* (1953) exist on the margins as criminals, or as police who try to contain criminal activity. Professional criminals are specialists with carefully honed skills. Cops are specialists, too. This highly topical film with a potently adversarial man-woman relationship at its center is set entirely within the rarefied world of crime and investigation. There are no civilians here.

While riding the New York City subway, Candy (Jean Peters) loses her wallet to an expert pickpocket, Skip McCoy (Richard Widmark). But here's the kicker: Candy has been working as a courier for what she thinks is a group involved in everyday industrial espionage. Inside her wallet is a strip of microfilm. Because of Skip, she can't make a scheduled delivery—and that's bad because the only business her handlers are in is communism. To use the argot of the day, Candy is a Red dupe.

Part of the genius of *Pickup on South Street* is that the Communist angle doesn't affect the arc of the narrative. It doesn't matter. Although communism puts the film right in the middle of a then-raging fear and controversy (Joe McCarthy was still riding high when the picture was released), Fuller uses politics merely as a device. And anyway, Skip is no patriot. Hauled in by police after hiding the wallet and film, Skip stares at an FBI agent (Willis Bouchey) who makes an appeal to Skip's Americanism. The pickpocket is smirking, arrogant, taunting. He can't believe what he's hearing. "Are you wavin' the flag at *me*?"

From Skip's perspective, incredulity is the sensible reaction. After all, the only thing the system ever did for him is kick him around and send him up three times for practicing his craft. That makes him a three-time loser, and under the rules of the system Skip goes away for life if he's pinched and convicted again. That strikes him—not unreasonably—as absurd and unfair. So to hell with cooperating.

Candy is no less a criminal than Skip (Fuller invites us to consider that Candy may have dabbled in prostitution), but she has an aversion to communism that's not shared by her handler and ex-boyfriend Joey (Richard Kiley, in a rare villainous role). Attracted equally by money and doctrine, Joey makes life even more difficult for Candy than the cops make it for Skip. By degrees, Joey's treatment of Candy grows more aggressive, and finally cruelly physical. In the end, Skip confronts Joey and beats the hell out of him, recovering the microfilm. But Skip is never motivated by patriotism. He puts his neck on the line because of his reluctant fondness for the woman, who risked her life to shield him. Indeed, when the FBI orders that Skip's convictions be erased, Skip feels more triumphant than grateful or humbled. He's played the system and won.

The conclusion puts Skip and Candy in each other's arms. That's romantic, but you wonder how long it can last. In an earlier sequence, Skip sweet-talks Candy and kisses her—before inevitably bringing the pillow talk back around to the microfilm and how much it's going to pay off for him. (Joey is willing to pay $500. Skip wants $25,000.) Fuller shot in extreme close-up and in delicate shadow as mouth explores mouth and Skip's hand cups Candy's chin. Visually, this is frank and hugely romantic, and Fuller's joke on all of us—including the hapless Candy—is that the dialogue and physical action function in complete counterpoint to what's going on in Skip's brain. The words aren't love talk but money talk. It's what's-in-it-for-me talk.

A fourth major character gives *Pickup on South Street* its heart and a mature preoccupation with human dignity: Moe (Thelma Ritter), the aging informer who sells tips to the cops and hawks neckties on the side, a buck apiece. Moe is alone in the world, and you wonder whether she wants it that way or if it just happened. The only thing she wants now is to save enough money so that she won't be buried in Potter's Field. She yearns for a proper funeral. In key dialogue when Candy has learned that Moe fingered Skip to the cops, Fuller gets at the gulf between the criminal world and ours.

> CANDY
> You sold him out for fifty bucks?
>
> MOE (a little wearily)
> Oh, look, some people peddle apples, lamb chops, lumber—I
> peddle information. He ain't sore, he understands. We live in
> a different kind of a world.

For his part, Skip only remarks, "Ah, Moe's all right, she's gotta eat."

Dialogue is clipped and street-smart. When Candy is in Skip's arms, she dreamily asks, "How'd you get to be a pickpocket?" Skip angrily pushes her away and spits, "How'd I get to be a pickpocket?! How'd you get to be what you are? Things happen, that's all."

Cinematographer Joe MacDonald, who shot *Niagara* in Technicolor, gave *Pickup on South Street* black-and-white street cred, even though most of the picture was filmed in Hollywood on beautifully designed stages. Aesthetically, MacDonald's work exists about halfway between police procedural and noir.

Skip is one of the most intriguingly developed characters in the career of the invariably engaging Richard Widmark, and Candy is the best role the underrated Jean Peters ever had. Appearing the same year as a wholesome wife in another

Fox production, *Niagara*, she's emphatically carnal here. If you thought Peters couldn't play sexy, you'll change your mind in a hurry.

It may be tempting to call *Pickup on South Street* a tale of redemption, but Sam Fuller was smarter and better than that. Gut emotion fascinated him throughout his career, and although his pictures express sentiment, they are rarely sentimental. Skip and Candy may be able to rise above old habits of self-interest and deception, and if they don't, well, that's just men and women.

Billie Plays the Angles

Lanky Beverly Michaels returned to low-budget noir in *Wicked Woman* (1954), another of the numberless melodramas inspired by *Double Indemnity*. A long-distance bus pauses in a small town to disgorge Billie Nash (Michaels), who is down to her last ten-spot. Days after landing a job as a cocktail waitress in a bar owned by Matt and Dora Bannister (Richard Egan and Evelyn Scott), Billie and Matt entwine themselves around each other like lovestruck boa constrictors and discuss how to put Dora out of the picture.

Dora is an alcoholic who feels right at home in the bar. But she's a querulous drunk who gets on Matt's nerves. Luckily for her, neither Matt nor Billie is quite capable of murder, but they do come up with another, even dumber scheme: sell the bar out from under Dora, take the twenty-five Gs, and split for Mexico. When Matt's attorney requests that Mrs. Bannister be present at the signing, Matt hurriedly tutors Billie in all things Dora, so that Billie can pull off an impersonation. The ruse works, but the pair must wait three or four days for the cash to come out of escrow. In the meantime, Dora is still at the bar, which makes for added tension when the bar's new owner drops in.

Adding to the complications is a hunchbacked, aging little man named Charlie (Percy Helton), who lives across the hall from Billie in a grungy boardinghouse. Stuck on Billie from the start, he gamely tries to strike up a romance, which Billie encourages in order to cadge meals, twenty-dollar loans, and free alterations of a dress (Charlie is a tailor). After a blowup with Matt, Billie finally tells Charlie that he's a little creep and she wouldn't be seen dead with him. Not long after, Charlie overhears the lovers discussing their scheme.

The illicit relationship goes blooey when Matt discovers Charlie busily kissing Billie's neck—tribute demanded by the old guy so that he'll keep his mouth shut. Matt just thinks Billie's a tramp, and walks out on her. At the end, Billie boards another bus. She's blown into town like the measles, and now she's on her way to find somebody else to infect.

Wicked Woman was written and directed by Russell Rouse, who made a splash in 1949 as the screenwriter of *D.O.A.* and again in 1951 as writer of a social-problem melodrama called *The Well*. Rouse spent the remainder of the '50s as a writer-director responsible for *The Thief* (an espionage drama in which not one word of dialogue is spoken), *New York Confidential*, and *The Fastest Gun Alive*. All of those suggest a certain seriousness of intent as well as good commercial

Case File: Percy Helton (1894–1971)

The son of vaudevillians, ubiquitous character player Percy Helton had some experience in silent films but worked mainly on Broadway until the late 1940s, when he began to focus on the movie career that kept him busy until his death. Small and stooped, Helton had particularly movie-friendly assets: a raspy, high-pitched voice (he also had trouble with the "r" sound) and tiny, squinting eyes well suited to suggestions of desperation or general shiftiness. Helton had featured roles and bits in more than two hundred movies, in all genres and budget levels. In his noir work, he's memorable as the brave little man who lives in a warehouse in *The Crooked Way*; as the obnoxious, never-say-die suitor of Beverly Michaels in *Wicked Woman*; and as the unscrupulous coroner of *Kiss Me Deadly*, who holds his hand out for a bribe and has it crushed in a desk drawer by Ralph Meeker. Helton is also seen in *The Set-up*, *Criss Cross*, and *Thieves' Highway*, as well as in many westerns and twenty years of episodic television.

In *Wicked Woman* (1954), long, lean Billie (Beverly Michaels) blows into town and sets her sights on a married man. But her diminutive neighbor (Percy Helton) is consumed by thoughts of romance and won't leave her alone. Billie is less than thrilled.

instincts, so you're compelled to wonder where *Wicked Woman* came from. It's commercial and nothing more, and seems just as forlorn as Billie's room at the boardinghouse. Very nearly all the action is set indoors; sets are small, simple, and obviously inexpensive. Edward Fitzgerald's cinematography is perfunctory, and Buddy Baker's score is often inappropriately perky. The inane title tune is belted out by Herb Jeffries with pretentious gusto.

Then there's Beverly Michaels, on hand to save the day. Although some sources list her as standing 5'9", a better guess is 5'10" or 5'11." In shoes with a very modest heel she's just as tall as Richard Egan, and she makes little Percy Helton look like a garden gnome.

Michaels wasn't just tall but busty and (otherwise) skinny. She had a pretty face with hooded eyes and a tangy way with unpleasant dialogue. At least as directed by Rouse (whom she later married), Michaels doesn't walk—she slumps and glides, and at a snail's pace, too. She looks exhausted, bored, and hot to trot, all at once.

Costar Richard Egan later became a reasonably popular leading man. Russell Rouse went on to cowrite (with Harlan Ellison) and direct *The Oscar* (1966), an unintentionally funny melodrama about a Hollywood heel.

Train Wreck

Railroads have a powerful quality of inevitability about them. Linear, geometric, and predetermined, they lead to destinations that cannot be altered. You can ride a train part way or to the end of the line, your choice. In Fritz Lang's *Human Desire* (1954), that sense of order appeals to army vet Jeff Warren (Glenn Ford), who resumes his job as an engineer after three years in Korea and Japan. But when he runs into alcoholic, assistant yardmaster Carl Buckley (Broderick Crawford) and Buckley's young wife, Vicki (Gloria Grahame), his existence goes off the rails. He falls for Vicki, and the two of them conspire to kill Carl.

Screenwriter Alfred Hayes based *Human Desire* on *La Bête Humaine* (*The Human Beast*), French naturalist Emil Zola's 1890 novel about sexual obsession, adultery, madness, and mass murder. Jean Renoir filmed the novel in France in 1938 as *La Bête Humaine*, with Jean Gabin and Simone Simon. Renoir followed the book closely, including the engineer's sexual love for his engine. Such fictions were permissible on European screens, but much of the story could not have been duplicated under the Production Code that still ruled Hollywood in 1954. Alfred Hayes's script streamlines the book and earlier film version, turning the story into a clear-cut (if brutish) love triangle.

Director Fritz Lang was generous in his use of subjective shots of train tracks unreeling beneath Jeff's engine, intercut with shots of Jeff in the engineer's compartment, looking pleased, even complacent. His engine isn't his lover, but it's obviously a place of peace and meditation. The literal geometry of the tracks is reassuring. Jeff is confident that he knows exactly where he's going.

The script hints, however, that Jeff's time in Korea warped his sensibilities and coarsened him. Ellen (Kathleen Case), the young, very beautiful daughter of Jeff's friend Alec (Edgar Buchanan), clearly adores him, but Jeff has no romantic interest in the ingenuous, clear-eyed girl. However, Vicki Buckley—worldly and overtly sexy—catches his eye.

Vicki is repulsed by her husband, and like some other antiheroines of noir, she doesn't contemplate murder with the promise of a monetary payoff. She just wants out.

Carl is pathetically dependent on Vicki, not least for getting his job back for him after he clashes with the yardmaster. Carl insists that Vicki see John Owens (Grandon Rhodes), a wealthy man with influence at the railroad, and who employed Vicki's mother as a housekeeper many years ago.

Vicki sets things right, but Carl becomes suspicious about just *how* she did it. With Vicki's coerced assistance, Carl traps Owens in a train compartment and stabs him to death. A love note to Owens that Carl forces Vicki to write is his instrument of blackmail. Now Vicki will stay with him, and will belong to no one else. At least, that's Carl's view of things.

Jeff and Vicki see the situation through a different lens. Their plan is for Jeff to ambush Carl at night in the train yard and beat him to death. Lang sets up Jeff's cat-and-mouse pursuit of Carl in overhead shots of tracks and train cars. Jeff quickly steals closer, a heavy tool in his hand, and catches up to Carl just as a passing freight rumbles in front of the men, cutting off our view of them.

Soon after, Jeff tells Vicki he didn't do it. He didn't kill Carl.

JEFF
I'd have done anything for you. Except that! Yes. Yes, except that.

VICKI
You killed before!

JEFF
Before? Oh, the war, huh? I almost forgot. You thought I could do it because of that. Well, there's a difference. In a war you fire in the darkness, something moving on a ridge. Position, uniform, enemy. But a man coming home helpless, drunk. That takes a different kind of killing.

The beautifully subtle thing about Jeff's response is the way it makes clear that life and death in combat—like railroad tracks and trains—are carefully ordered. There are rules of engagement and moments during which it's all right to kill. The relationship of soldier to enemy is almost geometric. Push, pull. Kill, survive. Negotiate the grid and live.

In the film's coda, Vicki boards a train that will take her out of town, only to be surprised in her compartment by Carl, who ends their relationship in a final spasm of rage.

Jeff, perhaps ready to accept the love of the girl, Ellen, pushes his engine ahead, unaware of what has happened in the car far behind him.

Human Desire was shot at the Santa Fe rail junction in Reno, Oklahoma. The place is as gritty and unglamorous as you expect a rail yard to be; the modest house shared by Vicki and Carl is just feet away from a maze of switching tracks and gives the proscribed lives of these characters a physical perspective.

Lang wanted to display his players in close-up, particularly Grahame, so cinematographer Burnett Guffey lit the actress's face carefully, bringing out her catlike eyes and that marvelously expressive mouth that was a combination of nature and the surgeon's art. Glenn Ford, one of the finest and most understated film actors of his generation, *is* Jeff. Ford is "acting," but you never catch him doing it.

Just five years after his Oscar-winning turn as Willie Stark in *All the King's Men*, Broderick Crawford is third-billed in a showy role that the actor makes simultaneously sympathetic and repellent. Struck stupid with love for a woman who hates him, he staggers through this story of lines and grids at a perilous angle.

Violent Colors of Forbidden Love

If anybody but writer-director Sam Fuller knew that his 1955 noir for Darryl Zanuck and 20th Century-Fox, *House of Bamboo*, is a gay love story, they didn't let it leak. Although a woman is a peripheral character, the sexual dynamics that identify the picture with film noir are played out by men. Issues of love, passion, and betrayal loom very large.

Sandy Dawson (Robert Ryan) is an American expat in Tokyo who heads up an aggressive robbery gang financed by a string of pachinko parlors. A scruffy, brazen newcomer, Eddie Spannier (Robert Stack), tries to sell protection to parlor operators and gets kicked around by Sandy and Sandy's "number-one boy," Griff (Cameron Mitchell). Because Sandy has an informant at Tokyo police headquarters, he gets his hands on Eddie's record: ex-soldier and wartime "stockade hound" repeatedly punished for assault and the theft of a military payroll. Sandy is always looking for recruits and invites Eddie to join his operation.

We use the word "recruits" advisedly. *House of Bamboo* (the first Hollywood picture filmed in Japan after the war) was based on Harry Kleiner's script for *The Street with No Name* (1948; see Chapter 4). Although the *House of Bamboo* credits cite Kleiner as the screenwriter, with Fuller as contributor of "additional dialogue," the earlier script was in fact completely rewritten by Fuller. He liked the paramilitary aspect of Kleiner's story but had his own ideas about the story's themes and undercurrents.

Sandy's insistence that his men have military backgrounds is almost fetish-istic. As he briefs his troops on the next "objective," he conducts himself like an officer, pointing with authority to a pull-down wall map and describing "photographs of terrain," "immediate withdrawals," and "pull back." At the kickoff of one ambitious robbery, the gang arrives at dock by speedboat—it's an amphibious landing!

Sandy insists that his men keep "kimono girls" to provide R&R, but he seems disinterested in taking a woman himself. This could be interpreted as the willful self-denial of a leader who knows he must remain sharp and undistracted. It can also be viewed as the decision of a man who has no personal interest in women.

Sandy is a smart, disciplined operator, but he's not omnipotent: Although he quickly takes a liking to Eddie, he's unaware that Eddie is an undercover man, a sergeant with the U.S. Army Military Police assigned to infiltrate the gang. (We don't know this ourselves until about a third of the film has passed.)

When Griff realizes that Eddie is elbowing him aside, he erupts in temper fits suggestive of a frustrated lover who has good reason to feel threatened. His outbursts are purple with rage, and they're shrill, too, like the bad behavior of a lovestruck adolescent girl. Sandy finally sends Griff home to rest, as a business-man might exile a peckish mistress to her apartment.

When a complex robbery goes wrong, Sandy assumes the cops were tipped by Griff. (The police had been alerted by Eddie.) In the sort of sequence enacted in many films noir, but with an actor and an actress rather than two actors, Sandy surprises the bathing Griff and pumps him full of 9mm slugs.

What immediately follows gets to the crux of Sandy's relationship with Griff. The corpse is slumped in the water, one arm hung over the side of the wooden tub. Sandy speaks to his former number one with tenderness and understanding. More than once, as Griff's head drops toward the water, Sandy carefully lifts his face, regarding it as a melancholy man regards his dead mistress.

SANDY (gently)
And I knew, Griff. I *knew*. I wish I hadn't been right. But I was
Griff, like always.

When the police informer tells Sandy not long after that Eddie Spannier is a fake and a plant, Sandy is forced to deal not just with a betrayal of love but with his own quickness to assume betrayal from another man he loved, and killed.

The remainder of *House of Bamboo* is a protracted, very well-staged chase atop Tokyo rooftops that culminates on the tipsy, wheel-like carousel atop a department store. Eddie and Tokyo cops fire tentatively with their revolvers; Sandy responds with furious bursts from clip after clip thrust into his much-loved Walther P-38. *Bang!* goes a cop's gun, and then comes Sandy's response: *Bangbangbangbangbangbang!* To the end, he's potent and dangerous.

Fuller and cinematographer Joe MacDonald shot *House of Bamboo* in full daylight, in DeLuxe color and CinemaScope. Encompassing lively shops, tradi-tional Japanese dance, a geisha party, and overhead shots of Sandy's red bus as it moves through monochromatic traffic, the film is a riot of color and thus of bare emotion. Fuller uses the dramatically horizontal 'Scope frame to emphasize the Japanese love of the horizontal in architecture and interior design. *House of Bamboo* has a visual excitement that is unique to noir. And although its theme of betrayal is familiar, the purposely provocative particulars of its love story remain fresh and intriguing.

A side note: Fuller claims in his autobiography that *House of Bamboo* is the first mainstream film to deal with interracial romance; and one of Robert Ryan's biographers states that the picture was Shirley Yamaguchi's first. In fact, Yamaguchi (who plays Eddie's love interest) had starred opposite Don Taylor in a reasonably bold 1952 programmer (directed by King Vidor!) called *Japanese War Bride*.

Climbing the Walls in Suburbia

Barbara Stanwyck believed in story. She described it as the "foundation" of any film, and so she must have been pleased to learn that Jo Eisinger, who had helped write *Gilda* (see Chapter 1), had done the script for what would become Stanwyck's next project, *Crime of Passion* (1956).

Kathy Ferguson (Stanwyck) is a hotshot, very popular advice columnist with a San Francisco daily. When she assists a pair of visiting Los Angeles police detectives in the apprehension of a murderess, she becomes attracted to one of them, Lt. Bill Doyle (Sterling Hayden). Kathy quits her job, and she and Bill quickly marry. Home is now an innocuous but barren housing development in the San Fernando Valley—America's postwar purgatory. At first, Kathy bubbles about the joy she'll find in mending Bill's socks and making his breakfast—but because she's an active, ambitious woman, her romantic haze quickly melts away and she finds herself trapped with the relatively unambitious Bill—and the vapid, blabbering wives of Bill's coworkers—in the mediocrity that Kathy once addressed in her advice column.

Finally sublimating her career desires to Bill's (much like the wives who drive her crazy), Kathy inserts herself into the life of Inspector Pope (Raymond Burr), who commands Bill's division. Pope tells Kathy he may retire soon. In an overheated moment of false passion, Pope and Kathy kiss, and the inspector says he'll consider Bill as his replacement.

All of that wisps away with the light of day, and Pope distances himself from Kathy. After a shouted nighttime confrontation at Pope's home, during which he declares that Bill's name is off the table, Kathy shoots the inspector in the head.

Pope had thought that Bill wasn't skilled enough to even be considered for the promotion. Now Bill wants to find his boss's killer, and we'll see how sharp he really is.

The film's conflict is rooted in the divergent natures of Kathy and Bill. The situation is one of role reversal, of course, with Kathy the aggressively "male" figure and Bill the passive "female" one. (Implicit in the story is a negative view of so-called career women.) Because Kathy has given up her profession, she tries to find vicarious success through her husband. He becomes the vessel by which Kathy hopes to recapture the excitement of her previous life.

Because the script is in a hurry to get to the melodrama, Bill and Kathy's courtship is presented as a mere sketch, and the subsequent marriage happens far too quickly to be believable. One minute Kathy wants to own the world, and the next she can't wait to become Bill's handmaiden. We never know *why* Kathy falls for the man for whom she will eventually commit murder. Because that is never properly explicated, *Crime of Passion* is a story only half told.

Although directing just his third feature, Gerd Oswald showed a solid visual sense, particularly in intriguing deep-focus setups he created with cinematographer Joseph LaShelle and in moody nighttime interiors and exteriors. His command of his actors is less sure. Stanwyck really emotes. Kathy's frustration with her suburban-wife life, and with Bill's dull contentment, is driving her crazy, and she uncorks a lot of big emotion. The pitch of Stanwyck's performance is entertaining, but Hayden and even Burr are quite low-key, so Kathy's fervor seems a little hysterical.

Crime of Passion was produced by Herman Cohen, who had already done a clever, low-budget science-fiction thriller called *Target Earth* (1954), and who would go on to produce a pair of pictures that encouraged dramatic changes in the film industry, *I Was a Teenage Werewolf* and *I Was a Teenage Frankenstein* (both 1957). Cohen was a cynical visionary who could put together a presentable product with little money. *Crime of Passion* obviously isn't an "A" picture, but its production values are as good as they need to be.

The Private Dick

"Look, Mike, I like you. I like the way you handle yourself. You seem like a reasonable man. Why don't we make a deal? What's it worth to you to drag your considerable talents back to the gutter you crawled out of?"

—Paul Stewart to Ralph Meeker, *Kiss Me Deadly* (1955)

During our first look at private detective Sam Spade in *The Maltese Falcon* (1941), Spade (Humphrey Bogart) is rolling a cigarette. This small, seemingly inconsequential visual detail tells us a few things about Spade: he's a smoker and he's self-reliant. Self-reliance has become a habit with him (surely it's easier just to go to the cigar stand and buy cigarettes), and he's unselfconsciously at ease with it. We're invited to consider that Spade's personality has been molded in the ethics and personal independence of an earlier, earthier era. Spade is direct, and he's not always interested in the easy way.

A moment later Spade meets his first client of the day, a beautiful, faintly jittery woman who calls herself Miss Wonderly—and from there it's off to the races, as Spade and his client—real name Brigid O'Shaughnessy (Mary Astor)—become enmeshed in a mad swirl of a search for a fabulous, jewel-encrusted falcon statuette that dates from sixteenth-century Europe, when it was already a priceless remnant of the Crusades and Malta's Knights Templar.

Brigid wants to get her hands on the falcon, and so do an odd-couple pair of partners, prissy Joel Cairo (Peter Lorre) and an endlessly shrewd fat man called Kaspar Gutman (Sydney Greenstreet).

Before the adventure is over, Spade is braced by the cops (numerous times), his business partner is murdered, and an enormous ship at dock is set ablaze. Spade falls in love with Brigid, people continually pull guns on each other, Spade is drugged and kicked, and people tell more lies than can be counted.

The bird finally comes into Spade's hands, and the bitterly funny revelation is that the thing is a worthless fake, and that the true falcon is still out there, somewhere.

Cairo and Gutman agree to continue their search, but Brigid won't be going with them. Although Spade is very much in love with Brigid, he nevertheless is going to hand her over to the cops for knocking off his partner.

> SPADE
> Yes, Angel, I'm gonna send you over. The chances are you'll
> get off with life. That means if you're a good girl you'll be out
> in twenty years. I'll be waiting for you. If they hang you, I'll
> always remember you.

BRIGID *(with a girlish wrinkle of her nose)*
Don't, Sam! Don't say that, even in fun! Oh, I was frightened
for a minute. I really thought—you do such wild and
unpredictable things.

SPADE *(dead serious)*
Now, don't be silly. You're taking the fall.

The earlier era that has apparently informed Spade's morality gives him no choice. "When a man's partner is killed," Spade tells Brigid, "he's supposed to do something about it. It doesn't make any difference what you thought of him. He was your partner, and you're supposed to do something about it."

Writer-director John Huston's adaptation of the famed Dashiell Hammett novel is deliciously convoluted and roundabout. By focusing sharply on Spade's personal morality, and because Huston elicited a star-making performance from the remarkable Humphrey Bogart, the film scores its dramatic and philosophical points while avoiding some of the unfilmable aspects of the book: Cairo's sexual attraction to Gutman's gunsel, Wilmer (played with dimwitted venom in the film by Elisha Cook Jr.); Spade's steamy relationship with his secretary (played on-screen by the grinning Lee Patrick); and the killing of Gutman by Wilmer. (In Huston's adaptation, Gutman agrees to make Wilmer the fall guy for some of the mayhem surrounding the search.) One character, Gutman's daughter, is eliminated altogether, and the novel's most bluntly sensational scene, in which Spade strips Brigid bare while searching for a missing $1,000 bill, was of course never filmed.

Case File: Humphrey Bogart (1899–1957)

To generations of film fans, Humphrey Bogart is the greatest and most iconic male star ever produced by Hollywood. Dedicated to his craft and inevitably impatient to claim better and more varied sorts of roles, he possessed the intelligence, ability for keen self-appraisal, and independence that characterize so many of the characters he played. Bogie was of average height and rather slight, with thinning hair and an intriguing lisp. None of this marked him as star material, but following stage experience and small film roles at a variety of studios, Bogart landed at Warner Bros. in 1936, to reprise his Broadway role as gangster Duke Mantee in *The Petrified Forest*. Warner routinely elevated character actors to star status. Bogart thus joined a stable that included Paul Muni, Edward G. Robinson, James Cagney, and George Raft. (John Garfield arrived a short time later. Warner's only all-glamour male star was the inimitable Errol Flynn.)

Bogart's noir roles helped to define the genre, particularly movies' idea of private detectives. In this respect, Bogart is nearly as important a cultural figure as Dashiell Hammett and Raymond Chandler. Enjoy Bogie's noir exploits in *The Maltese Falcon*, *The Big Sleep*, *Dead Reckoning*, *Dark Passage*, and *In a Lonely Place*. Some other vehicles, like *Key Largo* and *Deadline U.S.A.*, are intriguing quasi-noir.

When *The Maltese Falcon* went before the cameras in 1940, John Huston had been a successful screenwriter for nine years. He scripted *High Sierra* (1940), the crime thriller that gave Bogart an early nudge toward true stardom. But Huston had never directed until *Falcon*, so he came to the set with a full set of detailed storyboards. He was scared to death of making a fool of himself in front of the magnificently professional Warner Bros. cast and crew.

Hammett's novel had been filmed two times previously, very well in 1931 with Ricardo Cortez, Bebe Daniels, and Thelma Todd; and, loosely and with disappointing results, in 1936 as *Satan is a Lady*, with Warren William and Bette Davis. Huston's version towers over the others and is still brilliant today. Huston may have been nervous, but he had an instinctive grasp of the director's art, in particular a flair for camera placement and the relationship of visuals to dialogue. He also understood silence (as when Gutman and the others decide to make Wilmer the fall guy, and the camera cuts between close-ups on the faces of Wilmer and his persecutors). And there's something *right* about how Spade dominates every scene he's in, even when he's not the most prominent visual element.

The film has a propulsive quality that denies the viewer the time needed to process all the plot points—but then, plot hardly matters because *The Maltese Falcon* is a morality play and character study.

Case File: Dashiell Hammett (1894–1961)

The PI Sam Spade was introduced in Dashiell Hammett's 1930 novel *The Maltese Falcon*—after the writer had already created another indelible investigator, the Continental Op, whose first short story adventure was published in 1922. Another important Hammett novel, *The Glass Key*, was published in 1931, and *The Thin Man* (which introduced married sleuths Nick and Nora Charles) arrived in 1934.

Hammett had been an investigator with Pinkerton before and after World War I, moving among lowlifes and musing about the criminal mind. When he began to write, it was with an egalitarian approach to criminality that was later a great influence on film noir. He removed crime fiction from drawing rooms and put it into the everyday contexts of eateries and the gutter. An admirer, Raymond Chandler, noted that Hammett wrote for and about people who "were not afraid of the seamy side of things; they lived there. Violence did not dismay them; it was right down their street. Hammett gave murder back to the kind of people that commit it for reasons. . . ."

Boozing virtually ended Hammett's output after 1934. He worked for a year with artist Alex Raymond on a popular comic strip, *Secret Agent X-9*, and adapted *Watch on the Rhine*, a play written by his lover, Lillian Hellman, into a good screenplay in 1943.

Left-leaning personal politics got Hammett into trouble with HUAC in 1951, and he went to prison, for contempt of court, for five months. The ordeal fractured his health (he had picked up TB in the army during World War I), and he spent the next decade in irreversible decline.

Case File: Arthur Edeson (1891–1970)

Edeson, a founding member of the American Society of Cinematographers, began his career on the East Coast as a still photographer around the time of World War I and made the transition to cinematographer in 1914. His Hollywood career began in 1917, and by the early 1920s he was working with Douglas Fairbanks on such famously lively projects as *The Three Musketeers, Robin Hood*, and *The Thief of Bagdad*. Edeson came on staff at Warner Bros. around 1935 and photographed musicals, light mysteries, and comedies, as well as such Warner triumphs as *Each Dawn I Die, Castle on the Hudson, They Drive by Night, Casablanca*, and *Across the Pacific*. He also was the cinematographer on a trio of moody noir dramas: *The Maltese Falcon, The Mask of Dimitrios*, and *Three Strangers*. Typical of Warner contract shooters, Edeson was extraordinarily versatile and is thus difficult to pigeonhole stylistically. His greatest asset may have been his ability to assist writers and directors with the visual aspects of characterizations. Warner players photographed by Edeson invariably looked their best and were able to "sell" their roles with style.

Huston and Bogart's interpretation of Spade became a template that's still used today: the private dick as tough, concise, strangely principled, and unafraid to take a beating.

Astor's Brigid O'Shaughnessy immediately defined the duplicitous beauty that every subsequent PI, in books and on the screen, has had to deal with ever since. In this, Huston's film has become archetypal and folkloric. We've come to *know* these characters.

The degree to which Huston depended on cinematographer Arthur Edeson is unknown, but it's clear that Edeson contributed mightily to the picture's success. Dramatic and evocative shadowplay had been seen in Hollywood crime thrillers since *Scarface* (1931), and before that in German silents and early talkies from the Weimar era. Edeson absorbed all of that and dialed the style down a few notches, creating atmosphere but seeing that it worked in the service of the story and characters. Although *The Maltese Falcon* is strikingly moody, the visuals never call attention to themselves.

So successful was *The Maltese Falcon* that some talk of a sequel went around the Warner lot. That might have been a great film, too, but it really wasn't needed. All by itself, Huston's picture definitively established what a private-eye movie should be.

Marlowe and Powell, Reinvented

As in many films noir, the action of *Murder, My Sweet* (1944) is motivated by a search for a woman. The assignment strikes private investigator Philip Marlowe (Dick Powell) as being reasonably straightforward—other than that his well-dressed client, Moose Malloy (former wrestler Mike Mazurki), is a soft-spoken

The almost-mythic artifact called *The Maltese Falcon* (1941) is desired by many, including congenital liar Brigid O'Shaughnessy (Mary Astor). When the partner of private eye Sam Spade (Humphrey Bogart) is killed, Spade is sucked into a whirligig chase that bubbles with cross and double-cross, and that defines *film noir*. Adapted by writer-director John Huston from the novel by Dashiell Hammett. This poster art borrows a Bogart image from *High Sierra*.

giant given to impatient outbursts of violence. Well, no one is ever the ideal client, and anyway, Moose is pretty generous with the greenbacks. Plus, Moose says that the woman, Velma, is "cute as lace pants." Things seem more promising by the minute.

Soon, though, Marlowe's search leads him into a tangled scheme involving a stolen jade necklace, an old man with a much younger—and unfaithful—wife, a resentful grown stepdaughter, testy cops, a fraudulent psychic healer, and goons who are alarmingly skilled with saps and hypodermics.

A lot of people assume Marlowe knows where the necklace has been stashed (he doesn't) and give him a hard time because he won't spill. In one of the most weirdly wonderful movie sequences of the 1940s, Marlowe is abducted and injected with bug juice that gives him (literally) hellacious nightmares and hallucinations. Even when he comes back to consciousness, his vision, and ours, is obscured by a stubborn veil of webby mist. For three days and nights he endures the tortures of the damned, and when he cracks a guy's head and gets the drop on somebody else on his way out, we're simultaneously excited and enormously relieved. Much more punishment and Marlowe's mind would have been a soft-boiled egg, permanently.

You have to pay close attention to understand how everything plays out, but even if you don't, the ride is satisfying and great fun because of Edward Dmytryk's directorial flourishes, an enthusiastic cast, Harry J. Wild's imaginative cinematography, a splendid score by the perennially underrated composer Roy

Case File: Edward Dmytryk (1908–99)

The life and career of this important director are defined by art and politics. Dmytryk found gofer work in Hollywood while still a teenager and became a director in 1935. He did capable work on *The Devil Commands* and other horror programmers, and on low-budget thrillers in the Falcon, Lone Wolf, and Boston Blackie series, before breaking out in 1943 with *Hitler's Children*, a powerful anti-Fascist statement. With *Murder, My Sweet*, Dmytryk helped to define and shape film noir. He revisited the genre with *Crossfire* and *The Sniper*, films of unusual and uncompromising power.

Dmytryk's best films combine a declarative, aggressive visual sense with a flair for pointed characterizations, but none of that helped when he became tangled in HUAC's investigations of Hollywood in the late 1940s and early '50s. As one of the so-called Hollywood Ten, a group of writers and directors that refused to assist the committee's Red-baiting agenda, Dmytryk was sent to prison in 1951. But months behind bars encouraged a change of heart, and he went back before the committee and named names of other left-leaning Hollywood figures. That decision had a deleterious effect on Dmytryk's career, which became increasingly less important after the mid-1960s. Still, he directed some notable movies after HUAC: *Eight Iron Men*, *The Caine Mutiny*, *Broken Lance*, *Raintree County*, *The Young Lions*, *Warlock*, and one of Hollywood's most entertaining guilty pleasures, *The Carpetbaggers*. Dmytryk retired from filmmaking in the mid-1970s and made a new career in academia.

Case File: Harry J. Wild (1901–61)

A fifteen-year association with RKO (following early work for economy-minded Republic) encouraged this busy, versatile cinematographer to light quickly and atmospherically. From 1938 to 1942, he photographed more than two dozen lively B westerns starring (alternately) George O'Brien and Tim Holt. After genre-defining work on *Murder, My Sweet*, Wild segued into higher-quality westerns, and noir thrillers that include *Johnny Angel*, *Nocturne*, *Pitfall*, and the frankly gorgeous *His Kind of Woman*. Wild also did good work on pictures as varied as *Cornered*, *Till the End of Time*, *The Conqueror*, *Son of Paleface*, *Macao*, and *Gentleman Prefer Blondes* (he was a longtime favorite of actress Jane Russell). Like many contract cinematographers, Wild moved into television in the mid-1950s, working steadily there until his death.

Webb, and—most especially—a tough and sardonically funny performance by Powell as Marlowe. In noir's PI subgenre, in fact, Powell stands second only to Bogart.

Twenty-nine-year-old Dick Powell had been in movies for only a year when he had his first great success, the Warner Bros. backstage musical *42nd Street* (1933). Baby-faced, of average height, and with boyishly sparkling eyes, Powell was a pleasant crooner who became typecast in what used to be called "juvenile" roles. By the 1940s he had refashioned himself into a nonsinging light leading man in such pictures as *Christmas in July* and *It Happened Tomorrow*. *Murder, My Sweet* was a startling departure; indeed, the movie's trailer proclaims, "Starring Dick Powell, in an amazing new type of role!"

Much of Marlowe's appeal in *Murder, My Sweet* is rooted in his size. He's not at all a large man, and when costar Claire Trevor spies him in his undershirt and says he has a nice build for a private detective, you wonder what she's looking at because Marlowe looks vaguely out of shape and a little dumpy. But the power of the character, and the genius of Dick Powell and Edward Dmytryk, is that Marlowe doesn't have to be a bruiser because he's a natural scrapper who keeps charging ahead, even when he's scared. Like Bogart's Sam Spade, Marlowe is principled, with toughness that comes from deep inside.

In a clever stroke by screenwriter John Paxton, adapting the overtly sexual Chandler novel *Farewell, My Lovely*, the story begins in the present and is related in flashback, via Marlowe's voice-over. Marlowe is in police custody as the film opens, installed in an interrogation room, his eyes covered by a tightly wrapped bandage or towel. Why, we don't know. Marlowe is apparently on the hook for at least one murder, and maybe for theft, too, so the ninety-minute flashback isn't just a provocative tale but Marlowe's opportunity to clear himself.

Moose Malloy is predictable enough in his unpredictability; it's other people who give Marlowe fits, partly because no one can tell a straight story. A gigolo/bagman named Marriott (Douglas Walton) hires Marlowe to protect him during a nighttime exchange of money in a deserted canyon, but Marlowe ends up conked on the head, and when he comes to, he finds Marriott in the backseat

Raymond Chandler's sardonic PI, Philip Marlowe, got pitch-perfect treatment from Dick Powell in Edward Dmytryk's *Murder My Sweet* (1944). With this superior thriller, Powell changed the direction of his career, and Claire Trevor cemented her status as a key figure of noir.

of the car, savagely bludgeoned. The owner of the jade necklace, Mrs. Grayle (Claire Trevor), is a sexy blonde married to an old man and happy about it only for the *things* that her lovestruck husband can give her. Old Mr. Grayle (Miles Mander) is alternately morose and self-pitying, and you want to tell him to get a backbone.

Grayle's daughter, Ann (a sparkling Anne Shirley), can't stomach her step-mother, and it's a long time until we learn if Ann is working on her father's behalf or against him.

The mastermind of the jewel-theft ring is a phony healer named Jules Anthor (Otto Kruger), another physically slight man who radiates a lot of power; when he abruptly cracks Marlowe full in the face with the edge of a revolver, we're a little undone.

Icing on the cake is a Germanic fellow in a lab coat, Dr. Sonderborg (Ralf Haralde), who works for Anthor and injects Marlowe with the hallucinogen that nearly destroys him.

Case File: Dick Powell (1904–63)

In 1944, this onetime Warner musical star with the round face and modest tenor voice surprised audiences with his iconic, tough-guy portrayal of investigator Philip Marlowe in *Murder, My Sweet*. For the next ten years, Powell excelled as a blunt, wisecracking antagonist of criminals and double-crossing dames, as well as a roadblock to politicians, military men, and other authority figures. Although neither large nor muscled, Powell was a convincing hard guy; the characters he played fight with their wits as well as with their fists. Powell is a compelling presence in *Johnny O'Clock*, *Cornered*, *To the Ends of the Earth*, *Pitfall*, *Cry Danger*, and *The Bad and the Beautiful* (as a pleasantly cynical film director). In a change of pace, Powell is charming in *You Never Can Tell* as a murdered German shepherd who is reincarnated as private detective Rex Shepherd—and investigates his own murder! Powell made a successful transition to director in 1953 with the agonizingly suspenseful A-bomb thriller *Split Second*. Others that he directed include *The Enemy Below* and *The Conqueror*.

Powell left features in the mid-1950s for television production, cofounding and eventually becoming president of Four Star Television, which was responsible for *The Dick Powell Theatre*, *The Rifleman*, *Four Star Playhouse*, *Wanted: Dead or Alive*, *Burke's Law*, and *Richard Diamond, Private Detective*. (Powell's Four Star Partners were Ida Lupino, David Niven, Charles Boyer, and David Charnay.)

Because Powell had shot *The Conqueror* in Utah, downwind of U.S. atomic-test sites, he and nearly one hundred others in that film's cast and crew later contracted cancer. Many of those who did, including Powell and stars John Wayne and Susan Hayward, died of the ailment.

Claire Trevor makes the venal and greedy Mrs. Grayle almost cuddly, and Marlowe isn't completely immune to her charms. The most remarkable person in Marlowe's adventure, though, is Moose, whose determination that Marlowe find Velma only *seems* to be simpleminded. In reality, he's just obsessively focused, and whether he has to peel off more bills for Marlowe or bounce the PI around like a tennis ball, it's all the same to him. He just wants results.

In the end, and as we've suspected, Mrs. Grayle is the long-lost Velma, and by the time Moose is reunited with her, she's dead. In a startling moment at the climax, Marlowe is blinded by the muzzle flash of a gun that goes off too close to his face—hence the bandages later.

Esther Howard has a nice featured bit as the drunken widow of the owner of a club where Velma may have worked, and Don Douglas is suitably cynical as police Lt. Randall, who is still interrogating Marlowe as the flashback concludes.

Murder, My Sweet (the title replaced the original *Farewell, My Lovely* because RKO worried that the latter might be mistaken for a musical) retains the famously Chandleresque dialogue. We could quote it endlessly, but we'll leave it at a brief, and wonderfully funny, exchange between Marriott and Marlowe, who have got off on the wrong foot in Marlowe's office.

MARRIOTT
How would you like a swift punch on the nose?

MARLOWE (dryly)
I tremble at the thought of such violence.

Marlowe Meets Men from Mars

Marlowe returned in *The Big Sleep* (1946), shot by director Howard Hawks in 1944–45 but not released until more than a year later. Bogart took the role this time, and it's to his credit that his conception isn't just different from Dick Powell's but that it's far removed from Bogart's conception of Sam Spade. The Raymond Chandler source material is more stylized and "writerly" than Hammett, but credit also must go to Hawks and his writers, William Faulkner, Jules Furthman, and Leigh Brackett. Bogart's Marlowe is a bit of a cynic, but he's a better, more patient listener than Spade. He has an antic edge, too, as when he impersonates a fluttery bookworm—something we can't imagine Spade doing.

The Big Sleep is beloved partly because of its supposed incomprehensibility. In essence, the adventure is one of blackmail perpetrated against one of LA's wealthiest and influential families, the Sternwoods. The nymphomaniac younger daughter, Carmen (the amusing, perpetually open-mouthed Martha Vickers), has committed some sort of sexual indiscretion, and the family has been told that incriminating photographs can be purchased for a fat ransom. Aged and ill General Sternwood (Charles Waldron), who warms his blood by parking his wheelchair in a hothouse filled with orchids, hires Marlowe to get his daughter out of trouble.

The older daughter, Vivian (Lauren Bacall), is wrapping up an unsuccessful marriage and has a dim view of men, including Marlowe. The story develops to encompass a missing chauffeur, the murdered owner of a peculiar bookstore (in Chandler's novel, the place sells pornography in the back), General Sternwood's vanished aide, a prosperous—and cuckolded—gambler named Eddie Mars (John Ridgely), and the vanished Mrs. Mars. There's also a cold-blooded professional killer called Canino (Bob Steele), a little guy (Elisha Cook Jr.) who trails Marlowe and later dies when Canino forces him to drink poison, a beautiful but bitchy bookstore clerk named Agnes (Sonia Darrin), and the presumed blackmailer, a lightweight named Joe Brody (Louis Jean Heydt). The lubricious Carmen Sternwood shows up again near the climax to make yet another unsuccessful play for Marlowe, and Eddie Mars is forced by Marlowe to take the hardest of all falls for whatever it is Mars has been doing.

Oh, and Marlowe and Vivian fall in love and are going to be a couple.

Are you pooped just reading all that? Responsible viewers who make the mistake of keeping careful mental notes, or even written ones, will grow even more exhausted, but the beauty of *The Big Sleep* is that the plot confusion and issues of why-is-he/she-doing-this don't matter. To the contrary, the picture succeeds for a reason that would sink other films that had less talent behind them: *The Big Sleep* isn't really a linear narrative at all but a series of colorful vignettes. They don't quite tie together because 1) Jules Furthman and Leigh Brackett so furiously rewrote William Faulkner's basic structure (after the great and weary author had returned home) that they confused themselves and everybody else on the set, and 2) director Howard Hawks literally tore pages from the finished script when he was under the gun to complete the shoot. The climax, for instance, as finally filmed, couldn't have taken up more than four or five script pages but went on far longer—and with more clarity—in the original draft, before Hawks started throwing away pages.

Sid Hickox's pitch-perfect photography is another of the film's many strong points; in numerous key scenes, the lighting is such that the features of Marlowe and other important characters are suffused with a glow that fades into shadow below their faces, forcing our attention to the emotion in their eyes and mouths. Sometimes the faces look like pieces of Renaissance art.

Lively incidental and minor characters are other reasons the vignettes succeed. Beloved cowboy star Bob Steele, cast wildly against type, is completely chilling as Canino, wrapped tight in a form-fitting overcoat and waving a .45 that's as big as a toaster. (When Canino strikes Marlowe flush in the face while gripping a fistful of nickels, you wince.)

Elisha Cook, as the fellow who shadows Marlowe to protect him from Mars's goons (he fails at that, by the way), dissolves into fright when he knows Canino is about to kill him, but he doesn't give up his girlfriend, the no-good Agnes. When Marlowe fails to learn anything at Agnes's bookstore, he saunters to one across the street and makes time with a very pretty and delightfully self-possessed young clerk (Dorothy Malone), who removes her glasses and literally lets her hair down as Marlowe keeps an eye on Agnes's place.

A young brunette actress named Joy Barlowe is a treat as an affably sexy cab driver who hands Marlowe her card and tells him to call her night or day if he needs a cab. "Which is better?" Marlowe inquires. "Nights," the girl says, "I work during the day." (Not all of America's GIs had returned from the war when *The Big Sleep* was shot, which provides a logical rationale for the female cabbie.)

The vignettes, like the film's frequently overlapping dialogue, hurry us from one locale to the next without giving us time to breathe or properly assimilate information. Characters are constantly coming and going, and from among the great wealth of sets, only one or two are visited more than once. *The Big Sleep* runs us ragged, and we're pleased to have the exercise.

Bogart and Bacall were a couple when the picture was shot but not yet married. (Bogart was trying mightily to extricate himself from his marriage to volatile actress Mayo Methot. It was a difficult and noisy process, and Bogart missed many days of work because of his drinking.) Bogie and Baby (Bacall had become a star with the recent release of her debut, *To Have and Have Not*) sparkle on-screen. You like Vivian's open-minded nature, and you get the impression that Vivian and Marlowe are equals, despite the age difference. Each is capable of keeping pace with the other.

At the climax, in which Eddie Mars has set up Marlowe to be killed by goons waiting outside, Marlowe's eyes and voice spark with real venom. He shoots off a couple rounds to pique the interest of the would-be assassins and then forces Mars to go through the front door. It seems to be a satisfying conclusion to a wildly eventful film that's not really about story at all but about character, attitude, and style.

Camera as Character

Technique, not style, is the hallmark of *Lady in the Lake* (1946), the last Phillip Marlowe adventure of the noir era. (Yes, the end credits spell "Phillip" with two els.) Star-director Robert Montgomery and writer Steve Fisher shaped the Raymond Chandler story so that very near all of it is told via subjective camera, from Marlowe's point of view. We see Marlowe only when he briefly steps in front of mirrors, and in framing sequences and a bridging interlude at the film's midpoint (in which Marlowe sets up or otherwise explains what's going on). Otherwise, *Lady in the Lake* unfolds precisely as Marlowe experiences it. Paul C. Vogel handled the cinematography.

The convoluted plot brings Marlowe to pulp-magazine editor Adrienne Fromsett (Audrey Totter), who claims to want to buy a story Marlowe has submitted to her but really wants to hire him to look for the missing wife of her boss, Mr. Kingsby (Leon Ames), so that Kingsby can serve divorce papers. Before long, Marlowe is told that a woman has been murdered and dumped in a lake near Kingsby's getaway place in the mountains. Local cops say the victim is named Muriel Chess, but the name may be phony. In fact, the woman's name may be Mildred Hallorhan. Or the victim may be Crystal Kingsby. Then again, maybe not.

Marlowe taps Avery (Dick Simmons), a smarmy gigolo with a fake Southern accent, as the killer, but when Avery is shot dead in his shower, it appears that somebody else is responsible for the lake murder and is now doing cover-up chores. Marlowe discovers one of Adrienne's monogrammed handkerchiefs at Avery's, so his employer is now a suspect, and Mr. Kingsby isn't entirely off the hook, either. And an LA police detective named DeGarmot (Lloyd Nolan) is so hostile to Marlowe that the PI wonders whether DeGarmot is mixed up in the killing.

Marlowe takes a lot of physical abuse as the mystery unfolds. It's unusual to see a fist or other implement aimed right at the camera, and when the camera eye falters, clouds over, and then collapses toward the floor, you feel the blow almost as stingingly as Marlowe does.

The subjective camera is an intriguing novelty, and you really want to love it—and you do, mostly. Characters who address Marlowe seldom face a stationary

Case File: Raymond Chandler (1888–1959)

"From thirty feet away she looked like a lot of class. From ten feet away she looked like something made up to be seen from thirty feet away." That's a textual quote from writer Raymond Chandler, whose jaundiced wit, impressive feel for telling detail, and impeccable expressions of character and place elevated detective fiction from throwaway pulp to art. A sensual writer attuned to sights, sounds, and scents, Chandler invented much of what we now accept as California noir. Casting his characters' misadventures on the dark playground of wartime and postwar Los Angeles, Chandler explored corruption as well as heroism, which he regarded as a quiet, unostentatious quality displayed by everyday men forced to confront extraordinary circumstances. The hero may be confused by his adversaries, he may be verbally or physically abused, but when the day is done, the hero still has a firm hold on his sense of self. He also knows that his ultimate destination isn't as important as the decisions he makes during the journey. This point of view was naturally attractive to Hollywood, which not only adapted *Farewell, My Lovely*, *The Long Goodbye*, *The High Window*, *The Big Sleep*, *Lady in the Lake*, and *The Little Sister* but hired Chandler, for big money, as a screenwriter and script doctor. Like Nathanael West and other prominent authors who took a whirl on the Hollywood merry-go-round, Chandler was quickly disillusioned and bored by the picture business. His alcoholism, which began to take hold around 1930, didn't help his disposition or his prospects. But his screenplay for *Double Indemnity* (adapting James M. Cain) is a gem, and his script for *The Blue Dahlia* (a film original) has moments of brilliance.

Chandler scripted *Strangers on a Train* (1951; from Patricia Highsmith) for Alfred Hitchcock, but by that time his tenure with features had run out. Until his death, Chandler toiled in television, some of it good (*Robert Montgomery Presents*) and some of it indifferent, at best (*77 Sunset Strip*).

camera; Montgomery was clever enough to frequently move the camera during otherwise static setups, as though Marlowe's attention has been caught by something other than the person speaking to him. (Frequently, the distraction is Kingsby's receptionist, played by svelte Lila Leeds, who was famously busted with Robert Mitchum for weed in 1948.)

But many moments that would have been explicated quickly with a traditional approach take forever with the subjective technique and undercut the film's pace. When Marlowe walks up a flight of stairs, for instance, the suspense of the climb isn't nearly as important as what might be up there, so the slow, step-by-step "through Marlowe's eyes" approach just seems laborious and unrewarding. Similarly, when Marlowe pulls himself across a dirt road on hands and knees, the (admittedly unusual) sequence of one hand, and then the other, coming from the bottom of the frame to grip the dirt becomes so protracted that you nearly forget where Marlowe is trying to go. It's as if Montgomery felt obligated to play out the string in every subjective sequence.

Much of the film's frequent slowness happens for purely physical reasons. Cameras of the day were large, heavy, and cumbersome. The Steadicam and other portable conveniences were many years away. Just to maneuver a camera up a flight of steps and around the bend of a landing, or through the door of a car and into the driver's seat, were impressive achievements. But technical success doesn't guarantee effective pacing or that viewer interest will be maintained.

The film's central performance is another rub. One challenge of subjective-camera acting is that, if the camera is you, you'll have to give your performance a little extra oomph to push it across. After all, the audience can't see you. Montgomery's decision to make his voice unusually sharp and speak very succinctly allows him to dominate the story but also makes him a little artificial. His performance would have been fine on radio, where a declarative style was the norm (at least until Jack Webb and *Dragnet* came along in 1949). Marlowe is a bit too loud, a little too exclamatory. In moments, Lord help him, his voice has the same timbre of radio comic Fred Allen's.

Still, the script's fondness for the snappy comeback gives Montgomery a lot of opportunities to be funny

Robert Montgomery starred in and directed *The Lady in the Lake* (1946), an enjoyably cynical but visually cumbersome Philip Marlowe thriller explicated via subjective camera; we see only what Marlowe sees. The PI is occasionally glimpsed in mirrors, as in this scene with Audrey Totter.

> ADRIENNE
> What would you say your story is full of, Mr. Marlowe?
>
> MARLOWE
> Short sentences.

A bit later:

> ADRIENNE
> I need help.
>
> MARLOWE
> Like I need four thumbs.

And later still:

> ADRIENNE
> Why didn't you phone first?
>
> MARLOWE
> I didn't have a nickel.

Because we're not supposed to get a handle on Adrienne until very late in the film, the blonde is the picture's most intriguing character. Audrey Totter's on-screen persona, softness with a hard edge, is effectively exploited. Adrienne is alternately sweet and calculating, tender and cynical. Because Montgomery's Marlowe is an incurable wiseass who delights in keeping Adrienne at arm's length, he's the main cause of her mood swings. (In the midst of some lovey-dovey chitchat with Adrienne, Marlowe abruptly comes out with, "Did you bump that guy off?") Adrienne is more than just an impatient foil; she has real dimension.

Marlowe's jibes reveal the natures of other characters, as well. Jayne Meadows has fun as a landlady who feels unfairly provoked, and Lloyd Nolan, as DeGarmot, nearly walks off with the movie. Although not a large man, he suggests intimidation and danger. It's a star-caliber performance, and it's easy to see why Nolan starred in his own series of PI pictures in the '40s, the Michael Shayne mysteries.

In its best moments, *Lady in the Lake* is a grim explication of PI travail and the eternal battle of the sexes—what Marlowe sagely describes as "petticoat fever."

Waldo Lydecker, Redux

For a brief period in the 1940s, 20th Century-Fox saw star potential in Mark Stevens, a trim, compact actor with regular features and a steely gaze. Real stardom never developed for Stevens, but he was a leading man for more than twenty years and even made forays into producing and directing. His two best vehicles, *The Dark Corner* (1946) and *The Street with No Name* (1948; see Chapter

4), are noir thrillers produced by Fox. *The Street with No Name* is the more novel of the two, but *The Dark Corner* has its own (calculatedly derivative) charms.

New York private detective Brad Galt (Stevens) and his gal Friday, Kathy (Lucille Ball), have put together a pretty successful practice. Galt wears decent suits, works out of a reasonably spacious office, and appears to be in control of events. But it's partly illusion, because not long ago in San Francisco Galt got behind the wheel of a car while drunk and killed a truck driver. Convicted of manslaughter, he served two years in prison.

Only trouble is, Galt never was drunk. He was the victim of his then-partner, an attorney named Jardine. Slugged, doused with booze, and set off in his car, Galt was a victim, a patsy created by Jardine because Galt had discovered that Jardine was blackmailing clients. Based now on the East Coast, Galt aches to start fresh but is frequently reminded of his past by a New York cop named Reeves (Reed Hadley), who warns Galt that he'll be keeping an eye on him. "You're an impulsive youth, you know," Reeves says dryly.

Galt gets the upper hand on a strong-arm boy named Foss (William Bendix) who's been hired by Jardine to shadow him. Jardine (Swiss actor Kurt Kreuger) is now based in New York, hooked up with a wealthy fine-art dealer named Cathcart (Clifton Webb), and blackmailing Cathcart's wealthy clients.

Jardine being Jardine, he's having an affair with Mari Cathcart (Cathy Downs), the very young wife of the middle-aged art dealer. Mari has been giving Jardine money; now she offers him her jewels—anything so that the two of them can run away together.

Cathcart's discovery of the affair causes him to arrange Jardine's murder, for which the already tainted Galt will be blamed. After that, Cathcart will have just one loose end to tidy up: Foss.

Clifton Webb had been a sensation as arch, lovestruck Waldo Lydecker in *Laura* (1944; see Chapter 1) and essentially reprises that role in *The Dark Corner*. (Like *Laura*, *The Dark Corner* has a mild preoccupation with classism.) Once again attired mainly in formal evening wear, and given to cynical *bon mots*, Cathcart is Lydecker all over again—including his unhealthy love for a woman.

The picture's other familiar element is William Bendix, who had impressed audiences in *The Glass Key* (1942; see Chapter 5) as a bloodthirsty thug. He's similarly intimidating as Foss (which turns out not to be his real name), dispatching Jardine and setting up Galt with professional ease.

Directed by top Hollywood craftsman Henry Hathaway (see discussion of *Niagara*, Chapter 2), *The Dark Corner* is smooth, assured, and consistently absorbing. A mobile camera and imaginative blocking of static scenes bring consistent visual interest. Individual scenes are perfectly paced.

In moments, Mark Stevens is a little lifeless as Galt. When he complains, "I feel all dead inside. I'm backed up in a dark corner and I don't know who's hitting me," Galt's predicament is nicely encapsulated, but the reading hasn't the conviction needed to really push the sentiment across. Lucille Ball, Bendix, and most other supporting players are bright-eyed and engaged; young actress

Cathy Downs, though, is flat as Mari Cathcart, and skates by on the strength of her considerable, camera-friendly beauty.

Joe MacDonald's chiaroscuro cinematography brings rich mood and visual depth, and the art direction of James Basevi and Leland Fuller takes us into places as diverse as squalid tenements and Cathcart's enormous Park Avenue gallery. The picture was shot in LA, but good second-unit work in New York by William Eckhardt, particularly during a rousing police chase after Galt has stolen a cab, effectively invokes Manhattan.

Four explosions of violence distinguish the film. The most memorable happens when Foss, his chores apparently completed, meets Cathcart for his payoff. Cathcart fumbles some bills that flutter to the floor, and when Foss bends down to retrieve them, Cathcart suddenly shoves up and back—and pitches his enforcer right through a window. Mind you, they're on the thirtieth floor, so Foss's shriek, and a brief, slick optical of his body plummeting toward the pavement, are wildly shocking.

Scripters Jay Dratler and Bernard Schoenfeld, working from a story by Leo Rosten, don't exactly depend on the familiar, but their work isn't entirely fresh, either. They produced a solid, workmanlike script for a stimulating thriller that could have been even better.

Marlowe Lite

Leslie Halliwell's *Filmgoer's Companion* describes rugged leading man George Montgomery as "genial." That's a fair assessment—and it's also a big reason why *The Brasher Doubloon* (1947) is by far the weakest of the Philip Marlowe adaptations of the 1940s. The other reason, as we'll see, is a flawed script.

Marlowe takes himself out to upper-crust Pasadena to meet with a disagreeable old matron named Mrs. Murdock (Florence Bates). The Brasher doubloon, a rare coin that had been part of her late husband's collection, has been stolen. She believes somebody in the house, possibly her dissolute son, Leslie (Conrad Janis), has taken it. However the coin went missing, Mrs. Murdock wants it retrieved without the knowledge or involvement of anybody outside of the family. Marlowe knows that's a ridiculous request, but he takes the case anyway.

Marlowe learns later that previous owners of the doubloon have come to bad ends. A droopy-eyed little guy named Eddie Prune (Alfred Linder) comes by Marlowe's office to warn him off the case, waves a gun, and has it taken away from him. Marlowe has a dryly unpleasant meeting with an elderly numismatist named Morningstar (Houseley Stevenson) and later discovers a Morningstar associate, murdered.

Other suspects include Mrs. Murdock's timid secretary, Merle Davis (Nancy Guild), a blackmailer named Vennier (Fritz Kortner), a reasonably prosperous hood called Blaire (Marvin Miller), and, of course, old Mrs. Murdock herself.

The source material, Raymond Chandler's *The High Window*, has grim fun with Merle Davis's pathological aversion to men and to being touched, and it's to the credit of screenwriter Dorothy Hannah that some of Merle's odd pathology remains in the film. But the Production Code prevented the film from explicating the unwholesome reason for the young woman's troubled mind, as explicated by Chandler. Instead, it's suggested that a great deal of Merle's difficulty arises from having seen Mr. Murdock take a fatal tumble from a window five years before. She's haunted by it.

We eventually realize that the doubloon is just a plot device; it really doesn't matter much. The real issue is that Mr. Murdock's fall (as he observed the Rose Parade) was no accident but the result of a good shove from Mrs. Murdock. In the film's best moment, director John Brahm reveals the crime via enlarged frames from long-hidden newsreel footage of the killing. The victim's drop from the window is horrifying, and sure enough, there's a ferociously grimacing Mrs. Murdock in the room right behind him.

George Montgomery had been a boxer, and had a light-heavyweight's height and broad-shouldered physique. He's a good-looking hero but an inappropriate-seeming Marlowe, whom Chandler never described as an unusually large or fit man.

The greater problem is that Montgomery isn't much of an actor. He's professional but little more, rushing through his lines so rapidly that words are occasionally lost, and not really connecting with the other characters. He exists mainly to wait for moments to utter unmemorable quips ("This thing [the coin] really sends you, doesn't it?" "Oh, for the lova Mike!" "How I hate to find a stiff!").

Montgomery can't suggest much of Marlowe's canny turn of mind and commits the even worse sin of being uninteresting. He's just a good-looking lug.

Nancy Guild suggests Merle Davis's psychological problems in a performance that begins as mousy and gradually becomes more assertive. Guild was an adequate actress, with unconventional good looks, but had the liability of a thin speaking voice. The character is intriguing but hasn't much presence.

Merle finally holds Marlowe at gunpoint and demands that he hand over the doubloon, which he's hidden inside his tobacco pouch. Merle fails to find it and then insists that Marlowe undress. When Marlowe laughs at the absurdity of it all, Montgomery's barks of amusement are embarrassingly false—the sound of delight as expressed by a novice actor in summer stock. And then, just to compound this shortfall, Marlowe and Merle are in each other's arms a moment later, lip-locked, everything apparently forgiven, and Merle on her way to a cure.

Does that seem likely?

Beefy Florence Bates is a rudely assertive Mrs. Murdock and captures the unpleasantness of appearance and demeanor that's beautifully described by Chandler in the novel. (The old lady's explanation of why she swills port, and why she isn't offering any to Marlowe, is hilarious.)

The film's best dialogue exchange isn't from Chandler but is purely the invention of Dorothy Hannah:

MRS. MURDOCK
To tell you the truth, I expected an older man, someone
more intelligent looking.

MARLOWE

I'm wearing a disguise.

German-born director John (Hans) Brahm was a legitimate talent whose flair for atmosphere is obvious in his best films, *The Lodger* (1944), *Hangover Square* (1945), and the somewhat less successful *The Locket* (1946; see Chapter 1). Brahm had taste and a good eye but seems to have been defeated by this independent production. The film isn't noticeably low-budget, but it has a needy, slightly careworn look. Cinematographer Lloyd Ahern does journeyman's work, with occasional moody setups, but nothing startling or memorable.

Besides the fatal limitations of George Montgomery, *The Brasher Doubloon* is hurt by inevitable and unflattering comparisons to John Huston's *The Maltese Falcon*—another PI adventure in which a motley group of people engages in a mad search. What may be most regrettable, though, is that Pasadena never flashes to life as a character, as in the novel. In the 1940s, Pasadena was a well-established, old-money town populated by rich people who disdained Los Angeles. Great power was wielded from behind Pasadena's locked doors. In the novel, the dusty affluence of the Murdock mansion establishes an unhealthy tone that's barely hinted at in the film. Because it's from this place of money and desperate propriety that all of the mayhem originates, the town—or at least its guiding attitudes—needs to be sharply delineated on-screen. It isn't, so *The Brasher Doubloon* lacks what every good film needs: a point of view.

McGraw, Plus Fun for Car Buffs

Your first take on Joe Peters (Charles McGraw) in *Roadblock* (1951) is that he's a thug. After all, he's just gunned down a running man in front of a bystander. But it's all an elaborate bit of playacting designed to force the witness, a bank robber, to uncover his hidden stash in exchange for his life.

The ploy works, and Peters shows a badge. He's a Los Angeles insurance investigator sent to retrieve the money. The shooting victim, who happily returns, is Peters's partner. The bank robber has been set up, but good. Case closed. (America had a favorite insurance investigator before *Roadblock* was made, the eponymous hero of CBS radio's *Yours Truly, Johnny Dollar,* "the man with the action-packed expense account.")

Joe Peters isn't precisely what we think of when the term "private dick" is invoked, but that is indeed what he is: an armed, private cop—with arrest powers, no less—whose job is to save a big insurance company the expense of payouts for losses suffered by institutional policyholders. Whenever Peters

Case File: Cartoon Noir

The heavy stylization of film noir naturally lent itself to spoofery but never with the aggressive energy that propels a 1946 Warner Bros. cartoon called *The Great Piggy Bank Robbery*. TGPBR is sharper than a sharp stick because its satire is two-pronged: It sends up Chester Gould's obsessive, intentionally grotesque *Dick Tracy* newspaper strip (which itself borrowed heavily from the movies) by wrapping the seven-minute narrative in the textures and atmosphere of noir. Daffy Duck, playing PI Duck Twacy, is swaddled in a trench coat and fedora. Camera angles are weirdly tilted. The city streets are slick with rain, and the skyscrapers are shrouded in chilly mist. There's a taxicab—which is hailed by Twacy and then roars off without him.

A ride on a weird streetcar that's going to GANGSTER HIDEOUT culminates with Twacy crashing through a basement window. Inside, he follows footprints (picking one up for a closer look) to a teeny mouse hole, where he loudly orders the occupant to show himself. The angry mouse that emerges faster than a Bouncing Betty is freakin' huge and very angry—the Mike Mazurki of rodents!

Finally, Duck Twacy is braced by a rogue's gallery inspired by the work of Chester Gould but made even more extreme by director Bob Clampett and writer Warren Foster. As each villain looms into frame, weirdly hued and slashed with shadow, Twacy's eyes bulge like balloons and dart crazily from side to side. His scrawny chest heaves like a bellows as he recoils from deformities that are better seen than described. It's all Twacy can do to stammer the villains' names: Snake Eyes! Hammerhead! Pussycat Puss! Double Header! Pumpkinhead! Jukebox Jaw! And the most frightening of all, Neon Noodle, a Frankenstein's Monster formed from malignantly glowing swirls of light.

When the whole mob of grotesques chases Duck Twacy through the room, the elongated shadows of these vaguely human creatures leap and cavort on the wall like mad things. Only Duck Twacy's climactic spasm of violence, with machine gun and hand grenade, demolishes the fiends and reveals the cache of stolen piggy banks.

Foster's script is unwholesomely imaginative, and Clampett's direction gives every indication of insanity. The cartoon forgets only one thing: a femme fatale!

Happily, that lack was addressed by others, much later, in the 1988 animated feature *Who Framed Roger Rabbit?*

---

comes through, which is apparently frequently, his employer is off the hook for thousands.

Although Joe grosses a paltry $350 a month (about $4,000 in today's currency), he's content to play on the straight and narrow, tracking and nabbing no-goods and feeling good about himself.

But when he falls for the mistress of a local crime lord, he gives up inside information about a fat currency shipment. Naturally, he finds himself in more trouble than he ever imagined. (Story man Daniel Mainwaring, working under his "Geoffrey Homes" pseudonym, found inspiration in a real-life 1924 case involving a crooked Georgia postal inspector.)

Roadblock is a lesser noir, and certainly the least of the three that Charles McGraw toplined for RKO. Failings and miscalculations are myriad. Chief among them is that Peters abandons his principles with absurd quickness. The essence of this kind of noir situation is that the conflicted antihero must suffer the torments of the damned as he weighs whether or not to go all the way, in the wrong direction, for a dame. As scripted by Steve Fisher (*I Wake Up Screaming, Lady in the Lake, Dead Reckoning*) and George Bricker (*Cry Vengeance*), Peters appears conflicted for two or three heartbeats. There's really no question in his mind that he's going to go bad for his new girl, Diane (Joan Dixon).

That fundamental mistake is compounded because Diane—quite contrary to noir convention and good drama, not to mention early delineation of her character—turns out to be a nice girl after all, who's happy with Peters's anemic bank account. This revelation comes after earlier emphasis on her material ambitions with tired dialogue the likes of, "I'm aiming for the World Series" and "I'm on a ticket to the moon" and "Happiness can't buy money." (All of this is made worse because Dixon, her almost overwhelming beauty aside, was a barely competent actress with an inexpressive, rather thin voice.)

If these turnabouts of fundamental character were intended to be startling ironies, they certainly don't play that way. They're just inexplicable.

On the production side, a meager budget means that sets are small and cramped; the airport interiors look particularly undernourished. Cinematographer Nicholas Musuraca filled a lot of blank walls with subtle patterns of light and shadow, but you still get the impression that if the camera panned a teeny bit left or right, you'd see two-by-fours and the key grip.

Catatonic blocking is another problem. Far too much of the picture is comprised of static two-shots in which the actors speak but barely move. In one embarrassing moment, poor Joan Dixon obviously hasn't a clue as to what to do with her arms and hands. If she looked to director Harold Daniels for help, he didn't offer any.

Budget also led to a couple of unintentional laughs. When a car speeds along a mountain road, the footage is stock stuff showing a heavy sedan from the mid- to late 1930s. The car that pulls up onto the soundstage "exterior" is a different, more recent model. And when Peters conks the driver and gives the car a good shove, the vehicle that overturns (at far too great a rate of speed given the modest push engineered by Peters) is still another one, in stock footage from *High Sierra*!

Because of sterling work by a second unit, *Roadblock* finally comes to life in its last eight minutes, when Peters and Diane take it on the lam in a '50 Plymouth and burn up the concrete of the barely damp LA River as a '50 Nash Airflyte black-and-white jounces in furious pursuit. The sequence is kinetic and expertly shot from stationary cameras and camera cars, and a back-seat camera positioned inches from McGraw and Dixon.

At last, editor Robert Golden has something he can work with. What a disappointment, then, that the climactic spurt of violence is bollixed because of inadequate coverage and becomes momentarily confusing.

Joan Dixon was another RKO contract starlet handpicked for success by studio boss Howard Hughes. That didn't pan out at all, and Dixon would have faded into complete obscurity if not for Charles McGraw, whose authoritative presence guarantees that *Roadblock* will enjoy periodic revivals.

A Bullet to the Gut, in Three Dimensions

Victor Saville was a British director of the late 1920s and '30s whose light, imaginative touch helped make sprightly singer-actress Jessie Matthews a major star in the UK. With Matthews's vehicles (notably *Evergreen*) and numerous other successes under his belt, Saville came to Hollywood in the late 1930s to produce films. Although his output was variable—the Spencer Tracy *Dr. Jekyll and Mr. Hyde* on the one hand, and *The Silver Chalice* on the other—he remained active as a producer (and occasionally as a director) until the early 1960s. Drawn to prestige projects early in his American career, he later developed a shrewd eye for commercial trends.

In 1947, E. P. Dutton published a private-eye novel called *I, the Jury*, featuring a new PI character named Mike Hammer. The author was a former comic-book writer named Mickey Spillane. Spillane's debut novel was unprecedented—at least for an above-the-counter item—in its descriptions of physical mayhem and sexuality and its obvious approval of Hammer's happily bloodthirsty dispensation of vigilante justice.

The novel is blunt and full of narrative brio: Hammer is furious about the Christmastime murder of an old war buddy, Jack, and sets out to find the killer, bracing people who had been with his pal near the end, and finally gut-shooting the perpetrator. Eyebrows were raised, and readers titillated, because the perp is a beautiful woman who stands naked before Hammer, seducing him, as he pulls the trigger. The book's final lines are justifiably famous:

> The roar of the .45 shook the room. Charlotte staggered back a step. Her eyes were a symphony of incredulity, an unbelieving witness to truth. Slowly, she looked down at the ugly swelling in her naked belly where the bullet went in.
> "How could you?" she gasped.
> I had only a moment before talking to a corpse, but I got it in.
> "It was easy," I said.

After Signet's 1948 paperback edition sold millions of copies, Victor Saville saw the commercial possibilities in a film adaptation and produced *I, the Jury* (1953) for his Parklane Productions, for release by United Artists. Screenwriter-director Harry Essex had been most active as a scripter. As a director, he's merely adequate. Some of the blocking is static, and a few too many scenes look as if

Case File: Mickey Spillane (1918–2006)

Few postwar writers of pop fiction can match the commercial success of Mickey Spillane, a onetime comic-book writer who changed the PI genre with his door-crashing creation Mike Hammer and sold more than 220 million books along the way. Spillane's first novel *I, the Jury*, was published in hardcover in 1947. It subsequently sold more than two million copies in paperback, and Spillane was suddenly one of the most popular writers in America. Hammer is a tough and vengeful guy who relates his first-person exploits in a humorless, thoroughly unreflective voice. Hammer is neither cause nor symptom. He just is. Not strictly a noir writer, Spillane is more closely identified with the PI and crime thriller genres. Still, three of his novels were filmed in the noir style: *I, the Jury* (filmed 1953); *The Long Wait* (published 1951, filmed 1954); and *Kiss Me, Deadly* (published 1952, filmed 1955). Significantly, the film versions of *I, the Jury* and *The Long Wait*, which hew closely to the source material, are merely adequate, while *Kiss Me Deadly*, which uses Spillane's novel only as a springboard, is far better than anything created by Mickey.

the camera has been locked down. On the other hand, violent interludes are well staged and convincingly rough. The picture opens with a literal bang, as Hammer's pal is shot in his apartment and then agonizingly pulls himself across the floor toward the camera, one arm outstretched to us (the film was shot in 3-D) as the title and opening credits blast from the screen. The participation of famed cinematographer John Alton is an important asset, and, in a good omen, the 3-D effects are not overdone.

As you might imagine, any adaptation of a Hammer adventure is going to rise or fall on the strength of the actor playing Hammer, and this is where *I, the Jury* comes undone. Victor Saville had seen a thirtyish actor named Biff Elliot in a few television roles dating to 1951 and hired him to be the screen's first Mike Hammer. Elliot, who had been an amateur boxing champ in New England, had a forty-year career ahead of him because he was an "aggressive" type who worked at his craft and became a good actor. But when *I, the Jury* was shot in the spring of 1953, Elliot couldn't overcome his inexperience or Essex's inability to properly guide him.

Dressed mostly in a trench coat with absurdly padded shoulders, Elliot embodies Hammer's physicality and moxie, but his shouted, grimacing performance is strictly one-note and unconvincing. Key to the story is Hammer's developing romance with Dr. Charlotte Manning (Peggie Castle), a blonde, cool-kitty psychiatrist who says she wants to help Hammer solve the murder. Elliot and Castle share many intimate scenes, during which Castle interprets her lines while Elliot recites his. There's no connection between them, as actors or as characters, and it becomes uncomfortable to witness Castle do all the heavy lifting.

Over the course of the picture's seventy-two minutes, Hammer learns that his friend Jack had been privy to the workings of a crime syndicate and was gunned for knowing too much. As Hammer investigates, a conga line of colorful characters crosses his path: Jack's pathetically drunk fiancée (Frances Osborne); oversexed identical twins (Broadway dancers Dran and Tani Seitz); an improbably helpful cop (Preston Foster); a harmless, pop-eyed drunk named Bobo (Elisha Cook Jr.); a gay, comfortably retired fight manager (Alan Reed) and his lover (Bob Cunningham); Hammer's happy-go-lucky elevator operator (Joe Besser); a veterinarian (John Qualen) who despairs over his wayward daughter (Mary Anderson); a crime lord named Marty (Paul Dubov); and a pair of "Spanish" dance instructors (Ron Rondell and Carol Thurston) who are strictly American by way of Brooklyn. Hammer blusters and gesticulates at most of them, and allows the prettiest women to seductively coo in his direction. (When Charlotte greets Hammer for the first time, she steps from her office in a peignoir, like a burlesque queen; and one of the irresistible blonde twins welcomes Hammer with an elongated back-scratcher that she waggles in a promisingly symbolic way.)

Intelligent, dark-eyed Margaret Sheridan (impressive in Howard Hawks's *The Thing from Another World* in 1951) plays Velda, Hammer's secretary and aide, and is wasted, as the script develops no personal relationship between the two characters.

Essex's staging of a titanic, multiperson fistfight inside LA's famously peculiar Bradbury Building is superior, and Charlotte's final moments, as she begins to undress for Hammer, are sensational. When Charlotte says, "The world, Mike! It could be ours!" Hammer's anguished reply—"I never wanted the world! Just—just room enough for the two of us!"—is Biff Elliot's best moment. And the novel's final lines of dialogue are intact and undeniably powerful.

I, the Jury is episodic, with each vignette cleverly introduced with a full-screen Christmas card (and appropriate music) that previews the next location. Things happen at a pretty rapid clip, and the screenplay has the requisite convolutions of plot that don't seem to matter once the punching and shooting start. And Biff Elliot, bless him, tries hard.

Noir Apocalypse

After an interlude of two years, executive producer Victor Saville and United Artists returned to Spillane and Hammer. For much of *Kiss Me Deadly* (1955), prosperous Los Angeles "bedroom dick" Mike Hammer has a predatory gleam in his eye, a signal that he knows he's on to something big, and that he's sharp enough and tough enough to milk it for whatever it's worth. The great, bitter joke of Robert Aldrich and A. I. Bezzerides's adaptation of the popular Mickey Spillane novel is that—unlike the Hammer of the book—our protagonist (Ralph Meeker) is in so far over his head he has no idea he's drowning. He has shrewdness without real smarts, physical bravery without foresight, and greed without a sense of restraint. He has no principles, not even misguided ones, and by the time his adventure climaxes, he's almost certainly doomed himself, and perhaps all of LA, too.

Spillane's 1952 novel is written in the author's by-then-familiar unreflective narrative voice, with Hammer provoking the FBI and the Mafia as he chases down a package of drugs and searches for his gal Friday, Velda, who has been kidnapped. At the climax, Hammer is shot but emerges triumphant, Velda in his arms.

Robert Aldrich and A. I. Bezzerides's *Kiss Me Deadly* (1955) is a brutal and brilliant reboot of Mickey Spillane's flat-footed novel. PI Mike Hammer's greedy search for "the great whatsit" climaxes on a dark beach illuminated by an atomic explosion that destroys a beach house—and may doom all of Los Angeles. The amoral Hammer (Ralph Meeker) has been in over his head from the jump, and now all he and gal Friday Velda (Maxine Cooper) can do is watch the world go up around them.

Its brilliant title aside, *Kiss Me, Deadly* (note the comma) is not a good book. It is as turgid as it is eventful, and one of the only reasons for its enduring fame is that it is part of the brutal, high-octane Spillane canon that changed the face of detective fiction.

The other reason is that the novel loosely inspired the film, for which screenwriter Bezzerides (a novelist himself) threw out nearly everything save the title, Velda's abduction, and the story's chase element. As fashioned by Bezzerides and director-producer Aldrich, nothing as mundane as dope motivates the movie's ceaseless action. This time, Hammer and many others covet a mysterious square, metal box, its lid held fast with leather straps, and with a smaller box inside. And the smaller box is warm to the touch. It contains an unknown item that Velda (Maxine Cooper) cynically calls "the Great Whatsit," a thing with no intrinsic value for which people, nevertheless, are willing to kill. In time, we are allowed to deduce that the Whatsit is a radioactive element that (in a wonderfully bizarre touch) literally growls. This is all the anxiety of the Atomic Age, inadequately confined in a box.

Unlike the scruffy Hammer of the book, the film's Hammer is a sleek creature with a twenty-dollar razor cut, custom-fitted clothes, and a succession of sports cars. He lives in a *moderne*, well-appointed high-rise apartment that has a sunken living room, a piece of modern sculpture that he probably doesn't like or understand, smart furniture, and an answering machine built into the wall. He pays the full-lipped Velda a salary, and is also her lover and her pimp. (Hammer works divorce cases, and Velda gets the blackmail goods on errant husbands.)

In the context of the movie, "culture" is a peculiar concept. We know that consumerism is crass, and although *Kiss Me Deadly* explicates that, it also has pointed interludes of art, literature, and music: modern art, sold to suckers; a poem, poorly understood; ballet, badly practiced; opera, miserably sung. American society seems built only on what may be ignorantly purchased or taken—even women are "goodies." (When Hammer and a blonde beauty [Marian Carr] share a passionate kiss about thirty seconds after laying eyes on each other, the moment isn't an example of Spillane's convictions about rugged virility but a satire of the absurd.)

The main architect of the story's mayhem is a medical doctor named Soberin (Albert Dekker). Initially represented only by his black Cadillac, glimpses of his dark, pinstriped suit, and an archly modulated voice on Hammer's answering machine, he's finally revealed as the ultimate fool: a man of education and high culture who traffics in ugliness that he only *thinks* he understands.

At his beach house near the end of the film, as his sexy but obtuse mistress, Gabrielle (Gaby Rodgers), looks on, Soberin prepares to depart with his prize. Gabrielle repeatedly asks, "What's in the box?" Soberin tells her she's like Pandora, and then invokes Medusa, Cerberus, the "gates of Hell," and "brimstone and ashes." Impatient because impatience is a hallmark of the New American, Gabrielle finally shoots him dead.

Case File: Ernest Laszlo (1898–1984)

Laszlo's career got off to an impressive start with uncredited work on two of the greatest of all aviation films—as a camera operator on *Wings* (1927) and as a second-unit cinematographer on *Hell's Angels* (1930). Although he began to receive screen credit for cinematography as early as 1928, Laszlo continued to do second-unit work throughout the 1930s and didn't hit his stride until 1944, when he shot *The Hitler Gang*, a melodramatic but fact-based look at the criminal government of Germany. Laszlo's first noir assignment was *Impact*, and he followed that with two of the best-liked noir thrillers, *D.O.A.* and Robert Aldrich's *Kiss Me Deadly*. The former is a grim visualization of a man's final hours; the latter is one of the most unrelenting looks at moral and cultural decay ever put on film. Visually stark in its patterns of light and dark, the movie frequently edges toward the experimental. Laszlo and Aldrich had worked together previously, on *Apache* and *Vera Cruz*, and would collaborate later on *The Big Knife* and *Four for Texas*. Laszlo also photographed Fritz Lang's 1956 noir *While the City Sleeps*.

Equally comfortable with color as with black and white, Laszlo worked in all genres, even drive-in exploitation (*Attack of the Puppet People*). In the main, he turned his talent to major projects, including *Road to Rio*, *The Moon Is Blue*, *Fantastic Voyage*, *Airport*, and three for producer-director Stanley Kramer: *Judgment at Nuremburg*, *It's a Mad Mad Mad Mad World*, and Laszlo's last, *The Domino Principle* (1977).

When Hammer arrives for Velda, Gabrielle smiles and turns the gun toward him. Her face is enormous on the screen, her mouth opened in a false smile, her eyes glittering. She's been a commodity, but she's done with all that now.

GABRIELLE *(seductively)*
Kiss me, Mike. Kiss me, Mike. I want you to kiss me. Kiss me.
The liar's kiss that says *I love you*. You're good at giving such
kisses. Kiss. Me.

And then she fires.

Free of the misplaced faith in erudition (Soberin) and the arrogant belief in the powers of personal will (Hammer), Gabrielle opens the box and is turned into a pillar of flame. (In a bit of perfect phrasing, critic-historian Carlos Clarens referred to Gabrielle as a "birdbrained Pandora.") Hammer is able to rouse himself and free Velda. Together, they stagger into the surf as the enormous beach house flashes and growls behind them, and then finally explodes. Hammer has already ensured that he'll get radiation sickness because he opened the box a crack after discovering it in a locker, but now, with radioactive *stuff* freely flying into the atmosphere, he's surely doomed—and he's taken Velda and numberless other people with him. (In an unauthorized edit of the conclusion, which circulated for years without Robert Aldrich's knowledge, Hammer and Velda are never seen leaving the house, and are presumably inside when it explodes.)

Besides its myriad intrigues as a philosophical piece, *Kiss Me Deadly* is a marvel of the visual art of film. Following title credits that scroll in reverse from the top of the screen, the picture creates one indelible image after another: a frightened young woman (Cloris Leachman, in her film debut) who runs along a dark highway in bare feet and clad only in a trench coat; Hammer unconscious on a naked bed, the bedsprings throwing weird shadows onto the floor; Hammer in a hospital bed, the camera tilted so that he's more vertical than horizontal; the sheen of perspiration on Velda's face when Hammer awakens her in the night; a body that tumbles down an impossibly long flight of concrete steps, right into our laps; a battered face that peers from the crack of a barely opened door; a hand crushed in a drawer and Hammer's sadistic sneer of satisfaction; a hand that twists the control of a hydraulic jack, causing the car it supports to drop onto the man beneath; the leer of covetousness on the face of Hammer's car-loving Greek friend (Nick Dennis; "Va va voom! Pretty pow!"); an exploding Jaguar; Hammer's hopeless struggle in the surf with a pair of thugs; Gabrielle's face as the flames begin to consume her, the light dancing and bouncing off the walls; the brilliant flashes of radioactive illumination that envelop Hammer and Velda at the climax.

So visceral is all of this (brilliantly shot by Ernest Laszlo), so avant-garde, that it remains breathtaking some sixty years later. *Kiss Me Deadly* deeply influenced the young filmmakers of France's *nouvelle vague*, and bewildered audiences in America, where the picture was neither a commercial nor a critical success. Its art and implications darted over people's heads like a rush of starlings, and the film didn't begin to be properly understood and appreciated at home until the 1970s.

Robert Aldrich's other films include *Vera Cruz, Attack!, The Big Knife, The Dirty Dozen,* and *Whatever Happened to Baby Jane?* He was drawn to big emotions and the grotesque, and was so successful that he briefly had his own film studio. Aldrich created an impressive body of work, and many of his pictures are classics of their genres. With *Kiss Me Deadly,* though, he created not just a great film noir, not just a great American movie of the 1950s but one of the most vigorous and electrifying films ever.

4

A Cop's Life

"Oh, wake up, Brown. This train is headed straight for the cemetery. But there's another coming along—a gravy train. Let's get on it!"

—Marie Windsor to Charles McGraw, *The Narrow Margin* (1952)

Although Detective Tony Cochrane (William Gargan), the stolid, married cop who dominates Henry Levin's minor but highly charged *Night Editor* (1946), is entangled with a wealthy sexpot, Jill Merrill (Janis Carter), the film uses noir's familiar man vs. woman conflict only as a device. The story's primary interest is betrayal of responsibility and trust, to family and to the force. To be sure, Cochrane and Jill have an emotionally unhealthy relationship that ultimately explodes, with miserable consequences for both players. But the sharp edge to everything is how justice can be stonewalled and even subverted because of a cop's personal corruption and fear.

Night Editor was based on a popular radio series of the same name (starring Hal Burdick). Columbia (which hoped *Night Editor* might be the first of a series) gave Levin little money for the picture, which looks threadbare even for that efficient and cost-conscious studio. But Levin had some advantages going in: the fine character lead William Gargan, firebrand blonde Janis Carter, a lively screenplay by Hal Smith, and a pair of superior and evocative cinematographers, Burnett Guffey and Philip Tannura.

Perhaps the most useful advantage Levin had as he undertook the project was widespread public awareness of serious corruption within the LAPD, particularly among detectives. Throughout the 1940s, many LAPD plainclothesmen spent lavishly, had considerable holdings in real estate, retired early, and dressed so nattily that, as California historian Kevin Starr observed, they were famous for their "dandyism." Detective Cochrane isn't on the take—he's just weak and unmindful of his responsibilities. Still, when *Night Editor* was released in March 1946, audiences, especially on the West Coast, easily believed that a police detective could go bad.

While necking in a car parked amidst wild grass at a beach, Cochrane and Jill witness a man in another car use a tire iron to viciously crush the skull and face of his female companion. Cochrane never gets a clear look at the man. When the killer flees on foot, Cochrane chases after him but can't bring himself to shoot because Jill loudly warns him not to. She doesn't want to be involved, and Cochrane, because of his family, doesn't want to get mixed up in an investigation either.

The balance of *Night Editor* chronicles Cochrane's increasing despondence over his failure to speak up, and the fact that he's compromised his career and endangered his family life for a sick woman who gets an unmistakable sexual charge from bloody violence. Moments after the murder, Jill writhes against Cochrane's arms.

JILL
Tony, I want to see her. I want to see her, Tony! I want to look at her, Tony!

Later, Jill declares that the victim was a "little brat" who deserved to die, and that the innocent tradesman who has been arrested for the murder is a "nobody" that won't be missed. Cochrane has had enough.

COCHRANE (to Jill)
You're rotten. Pure, no good, first-rate high-grade A-number-one rotten!

JILL (visibly aroused)
Tony—I love you!

The ripe dialogue works because of Janis Carter's panting lubriciousness and William Gargan's sudden eruption from his perpetual state of hangdog catatonia. And by way of contrast to Jill, there is Cochrane's sweet, infinitely patient wife (Jeff Donnell), who is steady where Jill is off the rails.

The high melodrama also brings special significance to a not unexpected twist: Cochrane is among the detectives assigned to investigate the murder he witnessed. When Jill greets him as he pays an "official" visit to her at her home, she introduces him to her pompous, much older husband (Roy Gordon) and then deposits herself on a couch, arms spread across the bolster behind her, one foot propped on a coffee table. Her posture is casual yet unmistakably seductive, a challenge to Cochrane and a cruel taunt aimed at her oblivious husband.

It's not too long before Jill dumps Cochrane for Loring (Frank Wilcox), a middle-aged society type who has struck Cochrane as a likely suspect in the murder. (In Cochrane's presence, and in the height of gall, Jill allows Loring to use her as his alibi—when she was with Cochrane that night!)

Cochrane finally confesses his transgressions to another detective, who makes plans to arrest Loring in a raid on Jill's home. In the kitchen, after Jill has demanded one last embrace from Cochrane, she slides an ice pick into his back. Cochrane grips his erstwhile lover's arm and stiffly walks her outside, handing over his badge before collapsing.

Night Editor is a protracted flashback with a framing device. As in the radio program, the tale is a reminiscence of a veteran newspaperman (Charles D. Brown), related to a young, exhausted newshawk (Coulter Irwin) so that the youngster's interest in journalism will be rekindled. In a coda that brings the film's theme full circle, the now-energized young reporter hurries home to his family, passing the graying proprietor of the lobby cigar stand. The older man is Cochrane, seemingly at peace and happy to step outside to wave at his son, now a homicide cop himself.

Henry Levin was a general-purpose filmmaker who worked competently in all genres. Much later in his long career he helmed *Journey to the Center of the Earth* (1959) and two of Dean Martin's cheerfully misogynistic Matt Helm spy spoofs of the 1960s. *Night Editor* is very serious about the importance of vows that encourage us to be faithful to mates and, just as important, to the proper upholding of the law. Cochrane (played by Gargan with a fine, weary dignity) has been lucky. He rediscovered and rescued his soul.

All the Women Are Named Dolores

In Edwin L. Marin's underrated *Nocturne* (1946), LAPD detective Joe Warne (George Raft) is a dedicated, occasionally overzealous cop who happens to live with his mother. Because he has no other woman in his life, he defines himself completely by his job. He's ripe, then, to become obsessed with a woman—or rather, with a whole gallery of women, whose framed glamour portraits line the walls of a home belonging to a wealthy murder victim. Each of the women has brunette hair and similarly smoldering eyes. The victim, a haughty, self-styled Casanova called Keith Vincent, has loved and discarded each of them in turn, keeping the photos as trophies. Warne finds the mementos intriguing, but what really niggles at him is his certainty that one of the women is Vincent's killer.

In a clever touch by scripter Jonathan Latimer, the deceased had the habit of calling each of his lovers "Dolores," so although each portrait is of a different person, each is the same, too. None of the images carry a real name. Simultaneously perplexed and seduced, Warne will return many times during his investigation to gaze at the beautiful, inscrutable faces. He's looking for a murderer, but his unconscious is looking for love.

Image obsession is straight out of *Laura*, of course (in that noir, a police detective is seduced by a painting of the deceased title character). The multiple images of *Nocturne* amplify that sort of obsession in a way that's witty rather than just imitative. The detective in *Laura* wants one woman; the cop of *Nocturne* wants *any* woman. (For more on *Laura*, see Chapter 1.)

With assistance reluctantly provided by Vincent's shapely blonde housekeeper (Myrna Dell) and others, Warne tracks down a few of the former Doloreses, without learning much. Then he finds a Dolores named Frances Ransom (Lynn Bari), whose cynical wit and elliptical remarks mark her as a prime suspect. Others who figure in this portion of Warne's investigation are a nightclub pianist (Joseph Pevney) and Frances's blonde sister (Virginia Huston).

Warne also has some tentative tangles with the giant-sized club bouncer (Bernard Hoffman). The early encounters, mostly feints and insults hurled by Warne, culminate in a savage, sharply edited fight in the confined space of a dressing room. Warne is the person who walks away, but only after resorting to a savage defense. It's as rough a fight as any in noir.

Director Edwin Marin began his screen career as a cameraman not long after World War I. He was a deft, if unremarkable, director of B and B-plus pictures, and is recalled for his solid 1938 adaptation of *A Christmas Carol*. Marin and Raft had worked together successfully on *Johnny Angel* (1945; see Chapter 1) and collaborated later to good effect on *Race Street* (1948). For *Nocturne*, one of Marin's best films, he composed his setups to take full advantage of the then-standard 1.37:1 aspect ratio, often placing heads or other objects in the extreme foreground; because these are slightly out of focus, our eyes are forced right where Marin wanted them to go: the frame's middle ground or background. Camera movement is supple and concise, and Harry J. Wild's lighting is lusciously shadowed. A scene in which Warne discovers a body in the dim studio of a photographer is an unnervingly good mix of shadowed corners, peculiar noises, and outright horror.

Marin, Wild, and special-effects cameraman Russell A. Cully collaborated on a brilliant opening shot that begins beneath the main credits. From a great distance, we have a godlike, nighttime view of a mid-century-modern home set into the side of one of the Hollywood Hills. (This was likely a combination of miniatures, matte paintings, process photography, and live action.) As the camera slowly dollies in from on high, the dark landscape grows more detailed, and a tiny figure moves behind the house's lighted, rectangular picture window. The camera moves lower and closer still, so that we can discern details of the home's exterior and the man inside, who sits at a piano. The camera continues to move forward and down, *passing through the window frame and moving into the room*. The camera eye gracefully swings over the man's left shoulder and around the side of his head—revealing the shadowed figure of a woman in black who sits quietly at the back of the frame. The man is Vincent (Edward Ashley), who directs a few casual words in the woman's direction. Only then does editor Elmo Williams cut to another setup.

Are we impressed?

We are impressed.

Another setup in the same sequence puts Vincent and his piano at the right-side rear of the frame, while the left foreground is dominated by the seated woman's shapely legs and heels. Sex, mystery, unspoken menace: It's pure noir.

George Raft and Lynn Bari play well off each other—Raft with his flattened affect and potent charisma; Bari with her intriguingly wide-set eyes and air of mischievous intelligence. An inside joke of this RKO production is that Bari's Frances toils as a bit player in lamebrained historical epics made by RKO! But the studio lacked the resources to mount many splashy historical films—just one reason why the relative low costs of noir made the genre a congenial one at RKO.

Bad Ways to Die

Although Anthony Mann's *T-Men* (1947) is rightfully celebrated as a crucially important noir, it is actually a hybrid of noir (a genre that *T-Men* helped define) and the police procedural. The latter had come to popularity two years earlier with 20th Century-Fox's *The House on 92nd Street*, a taut, semidocumentary thriller, directed by Henry Hathaway, about FBI agents assigned to bring down Nazi fifth-columnists chasing after A-bomb secrets. The film creates drama not simply from what the FBI men are doing but from *how* they do it. Surveillance, logistics, the management of evidence, informers, investigative science, an undercover agent—all of this creates an "insider" illusion that gives the viewer the impression of being given privileged information.

The House on 92nd Street is smart and involving, and inspired the police-procedural subgenre. Noteworthy follow-ons made by others include Jules Dassin's *Naked City* (1948), Jack Webb's radio and TV incarnations of *Dragnet*, and Mann's *T-Men*.

The "T-Men" of the title are Treasury agents. As ubiquitous voice-over narrator Reed Hadley informs us, counterfeit currency falls under Treasury purview. The story we are about to see is a true "composite case" based on multiple cases handled by Treasury agents.

The Hollywood source material was an unpublished story by Virginia Kellogg, who later contributed to *White Heat* (1949; see Chapter 7) and a fine prison picture, *Caged* (1950). In synopsis, nothing about John C. Higgins's

The dreadful hazards of police undercover work are toughly chronicled in Anthony Mann's *T-Men* (1947). Alfred Ryder (left) and Dennis O'Keefe (far right) are the cops. Wallace Ford is the small-time criminal who comes to a memorably bad end.

screenplay suggests that *T-Men* will be anything but a blunt procedural: Two Treasury agents are assigned to infiltrate a Los Angeles counterfeiting ring. The counterfeiters have fair plates and superb paper; the agents approach the gang with plates that are almost perfect. The counterfeiters jump at the chance to create phony bills that will be virtually undetectable. When carefully orchestrated handovers of plates and cash go down, waiting agents will move in. But plans have to be adjusted on the fly when one of the undercover T-men is unmasked by the counterfeiters and is executed as his partner helplessly watches. Following Treasury pursuit to a ship at dock, where the surviving agent still hopes to complete the transfer, the ring is broken up and its mastermind exposed.

As in *The House on 92nd Street*, *T-Men* emphasizes the training and difficult psychological preparation needed for undercover work. Agents Dennis O'Brien (Dennis O'Keefe) and Tony Genaro (Alfred Ryder) must temporarily abandon friends, lovers, and coworkers. They must live under aliases and phony backgrounds, never knowing if a casual remark or chance meeting will be their undoing.

If *T-Men* had been shot in the straightforward style that characterizes many procedurals, it would have been a lively and engaging picture. But because two young collaborators, director Anthony Mann and cinematographer John Alton, trusted each other, the film has intense, almost unbearable mood and texture that underscore the clever plot points. Although a few process shots are apparent, Mann and Alton filmed mainly on location and frequently at night. Alton shot some nighttime exteriors without added light, and the production company, Eagle-Lion, feared that those sequences wouldn't match with more traditionally

Case File: Anthony Mann (1906–67)

In the pantheon of noir, there are few challengers to director Anthony Mann. His best films, such as *T-Men* and *Raw Deal*, function as pointedly with visuals as with dialogue to suggest the untenable situations of his protagonists. Mann's early show-business experience was as a stage actor, so he was well tuned to character motivation and the ability of faces and bodies to express ranges of emotion. The noir world that Mann developed with cinematographer John Alton and writers John C. Higgins and Sydney Boehm is a masculine one, occasionally informed by courage and selflessness but most usually by a catalog of the worst traits of the male sex: predation, violence, and brutality; greed, revenge, and the love of power. Mann's noir thrillers are sharply concerned with feints, strategy, strike and counterstrike. There are a few leaders, many followers, and a needle's eye of dissenters. Power is held for its own sake. Mann's protagonists are pummeled, and only their rage will save them.

Other films noir by Anthony Mann: *Desperate*, *Railroaded!*, *He Walked by Night* (uncredited), and *Side Street*. Beginning with *Winchester '73* in 1950, Mann shifted his focus to westerns and neurotic quasiheroes who struggle to escape their pasts and tame the thirst for revenge that may consume them.

filmed exteriors. Alton and Mann took risks here, but Alton was convinced that everything would cut together seamlessly. He was right. From the opening scene, in which little but the gleaming eyes of LA enforcer Moxie (Charles McGraw) are visible as he eases his face out of deep shadow, to the climactic sequence aboard the darkened ship, *T-Men* is a stylistic triumph.

Interiors, too, have the ring of gritty authenticity. *T-Men* unfolds mainly in shabby, unglamorous settings: locker rooms, flyspecked Chinese restaurants, warehouses, transient hotels, Turkish baths, the beat-up ship at dock. Although individual tableaus are dynamically blocked and framed, this isn't the arch world of the Thin Man; this is a naturalistic, hyperreal milieu of crummy, murderous people with big ideas.

Some sequences have become justifiably famous. When Moxie seals the aging Schemer (Wallace Ford, giving a superb performance) inside a Turkish bath and cooks him like a lobster, we look at a particularly ugly kind of murder. Moxie braces himself against the door outside as the portly Schemer ineffectually bangs

Case File: John Alton (1901–96)

Cinematographer John Alton was born in Hungary. He worked as a young filmmaker in the United States and then in France and Argentina, before returning to the States in the late 1930s to begin the greater part of his career. Although he photographed films of many types for more than thirty years, Alton is best known for his films noir; indeed, his contribution to the genre is enormous, but he would have been the first to admit that he shaped his style after studying cinematographers, from Hollywood and in Germany, who predated him: Arthur Edeson, Karl Struss, Lee Garmes, Tony Gaudio, Fritz Arno Wagner, John Mescall, Charles Stumar, Günther Rittau, and others. These men shot horror movies, gangster melodramas, and expressionist psychological thrillers. It was Alton who stirred that stew of influences into high-contrast, deep-focus monochrome photography that perfectly suggests fear, tension, and isolation. His famed 1949 book *Painting with Light* is a practical guide to cinematography that reiterates the intriguing paradox of Alton's work: He lit for dramatic tension but also knew what *not* to light. Although his most famous effects are plain to see, the totality of his artistry incorporates what we only think we see, or don't see at all. Alton was particularly adept at working with directors who favored complex blocking, which forced camera and actors to be mindful of areas of light and dark. Alton's effects could be as big and bold as a shadowed boulevard or as sharply focused as the pinpoint of light in an actress's eye. The artistry is breathtaking, and yet because Alton understood story, his effects invariably work in service to the narrative. He was a storyteller.

John Alton's noir projects include *T-Men, Raw Deal, He Walked by Night, The Crooked Way, The Big Combo,* and *I, the Jury.* He also made splendid contributions to such quasi-noir films as *Bury Me Dead, Canon City, Border Incident,* and *Scarlet Street.* Ironically, when Alton was given an Academy Award, it was to acknowledge his luscious color cinematography for the ballet sequence in *An American in Paris.*

at the small window with a stool. Schemer is a crook, but he's not evil. He doesn't deserve to die this way. But he does.

Early on, before O'Brien is accepted by the gang. Moxie slugs him around and then violently boxes his ears—an unbearably painful kind of assault that we'll see again in *Armored Car Robbery* (1950; see Chapter 5).

Suspense and paranoia are built with pitiless close-ups on the agents' faces. Within a single setup, light values may vary from near-black to a glowing, milky white. Static sets, such as staircases and walls, are alive with weirdly angled shadows. Straight procedurals concentrate on *what* and *how,* *T-Men* does that, too, but adds the intimidating landscape of suspicious minds and empty souls.

Indeed, the pothole in the Treasury Department scheme is that to carry off an undercover impersonation is brutalizing. In order to effectively play their roles—in order to survive—the agents must tap their latent capacities for violence. They must become thugs, and remain thugs until their jobs are done. Contrary to the patriotic boilerplate of the Reed Hadley narration, the agents' work is wearying and psychologically murky. Genaro and O'Brien die by degrees.

The murder of agent Genaro, though not as stylistically startling as the Turkish bath sequence, is shocking and an indisputable signature moment of noir. Although the agent is warned that his cover has been blown, he takes a chance and upends Schemer's furnished room, hoping to find a coded account of the workings of the gang. Genaro plays out the string too far, and when he's confronted by Moxie, with O'Brien in tow, all he can do is laugh at O'Brien, call him a sucker, and give him a thin cover. Moxie dispatches Genaro with two slugs to the belly. Because actor Alfred Ryder has had as much screen time as Dennis O'Keefe, his death—and his partner's impotence—sets us back on our heels.

Dennis O'Keefe never became a major star, but he was a dependable, rugged leading man who has been rightfully canonized for his work here and in an

Case File: Dennis O'Keefe (1908–68)

The red-headed Bud Flanagan who did many uncredited movie bits throughout the 1930s finally changed his name to Dennis O'Keefe and became a virile, second-rank star of the '40s and '50s. He never headlined a "big" movie but was a dependable presence in B thrillers, musicals, dramas, and comedies for nearly thirty years. Noir fans recall him as the agitated protagonists of *T-Men* and *Raw Deal*, where he showed not just skill but an edgy, riveting presence that goes a long way toward making these movies classics. O'Keefe had a raw-boned physicality that contrasted well with his wide, easy smile—you never quite know what he's thinking. He and tough-cookie Ann Sheridan are well matched in a San Francisco noir, *Woman on the Run*. O'Keefe gave good accounts of himself, too, in *The Fighting Seabees*, *Walk a Crooked Mile*, *Inside Detroit*, and *Chicago Syndicate*. Like other actors of his generation, O'Keefe worked extensively in television in the 1950s and even top-lined a painfully cute sitcom, *The Dennis O'Keefe Show*, during 1959–60.

almost-concurrent Mann noir, *Raw Deal* (1948; see Chapter 6). And Charles McGraw, though still scrambling to gain a secure foothold as a working actor when *T-Men* was shot, impressed critics and casting directors with his performance as Moxie. He inhabits the role, as he did during his brief bit with William Conrad in *The Killers* (1946; see Chapter 5].

Production company Eagle-Lion rose from the ashes of Poverty Row PRC via a partnership of railroad man Robert R. Young and British producer-distributor J. Arthur Rank. In an amusing twist that's straight out of noir itself, *T-Men* producer Bryan Foy gave West Coast mobster Johnny Rosselli uncredited associate-producer status on the picture. Incredibly, Rosselli had already been on the Eagle-Lion payroll, as a consultant. Precisely what the famed gangster added to *T-Men* is unknown, but it probably didn't involve suggestions about Chinese food.

T-Men was produced for about $425,000 and earned $3 million—a tremendous sum in 1947, particularly for a B picture. The financial return is one kind of legacy. The film's tough-minded artistry is the other.

Undercover in Purgatory

The semidocumentary influence of *The House on 92nd Street* is vigorously apparent in William Keighley's *The Street with No Name* (1948; the picture opens with a printed crawl explaining that the "Street" is any American street where crime flourishes). Considerable time is devoted to FBI resources and methods; location shooting at FBI headquarters in Washington, D.C., and at the Bureau's training facility at Quantico, Virginia, adds to the instructional-film feel of the picture's first fifteen minutes. The link to *92nd Street* is made stronger with the reappearance of a key character from that film, FBI agent George Briggs, played in both pictures by Lloyd Nolan.

Harry Kleiner's script for *The Street with No Name* opens in familiar fashion, with an authoritative voice-over narrator who sets up the central situation in fictional Center City, which is suffering a series of well-orchestrated, big-money heists planned by Alec Stiles (Richard Widmark). Because one of the targets was a bank, the Bureau has been called in. The selection process of an undercover agent, Gene Cordell (Mark Stevens) is carefully delineated. Director William Keighley and cinematographer Joe MacDonald purposely handled these sequences with all the flat competence of an instructional film. It's only when Cordell travels to Center City and slips into his undercover role that *The Street with No Name* executes a stylistic shift into noir.

The undercover portion of the story was shot on location in Los Angeles, mostly at night and to brilliant effect. Cordell and Stiles's violent playground is a dark tapestry of shadowed staircases, dirty sinks, garbage-filled vacant lots, cluttered basements, and insistent neon. Streets reverberate with the noise of shooting galleries and honky-tonk music. Cars crowd the rain-slick streets. Horns blare and moving headlights bring odd illumination to people and buildings. The section of town where Cordell hopes to hook up with the gang tempts locals and visitors with pool rooms, diners, bars, a boxers' gym (admission twenty-five cents), and fleabag hotels. Some of MacDonald's setups appear to have only a single source of ambient light, such as a streetlamp or neon sign. In other moments, oddly illuminated mist or fog suggests an environment that's chilly in more ways than one.

Central to the story is that Stiles, the detail-obsessed leader of the gang, fancies himself a big thinker in the manner of Patton or Eisenhower—and he is, but his character flaws, particularly a violent temper and an unwise fondness for revenge, conspire to bring him down. He diminishes his leadership when he berates and beats his wife (Barbara Lawrence) in front of his boys, and his insistence that the briefly unconscious Cordell be (accidentally) shot by cops causes him to linger too long at a burglarized manufacturing plant—a dizzying maze of corridors, pipes, metal stairways, and catwalks.

Things really go south for Stiles when his unsmiling number-two (Donald Buka) is punched halfway through a window by Cordell and then machine-gunned by cops outside. Stiles might still get away, but because he violates a military precept—*think first before you fling open a door*—he's in big trouble, too. Finally, it's just Stiles and Cordell.

William Keighley was a versatile, polished director who made his reputation at Warner Bros. with such films as *G Men* (a pseudo-documentary precursor to *The Street with No Name*), *Bullets or Ballots*, *The Prince and the Pauper*, *The Fighting 69th*, and *The Man Who Came to Dinner*. By the late 1940s Keighley was at Fox, shifting easily between Shirley Temple vehicles and noir. *The Street with No Name* brings professional competence close to the level of art; camera setups are engaging but not showy, and much of the narrative is moved along on strictly visual terms. For long stretches, there is no dialogue. Quiet "character" moments are handled with as much conviction as the big set pieces.

Case File: Joe MacDonald (1906–68)

Joe MacDonald rose from B pictures (*Charlie Chan in Rio*, *The Big Noise*) to twenty years of work as one of the best cinematographers in Hollywood. He shot beautifully in black and white (*The Dark Corner*, *Pickup on South Street*), and brought vivid style to color noir projects that included *Niagara* and *House of Bamboo*. He was skilled at westerns (*My Darling Clementine*; *Yellow Sky*), farce (*Will Success Spoil Rock Hunter?*), docudrama (*Call Northside 777*), "problem" pictures (*Bigger Than Life*), epics (*The Sand Pebbles*), and over-the-top melodrama (*The Carpetbaggers*). Except for sixty minutes of television shot in 1959, MacDonald worked exclusively in features. He was in demand his entire life because he was one of the best.

Widmark, still typecast because of his 1947 turn as psychotic killer Tommy Udo in *Kiss of Death* (see Chapter 7), had not yet become a leading man. For now, he was the grinning fiend, and he and Keighley made sure the character doesn't slip into burlesque. Top-billed Mark Stevens, enjoying a more clearly delineated role than the perplexed PI he played in *The Dark Corner* (see Chapter 3), is appealing and effective. Stevens never came close to Hollywood's top rank—his compact, tidy frame may have militated against him—but *The Street with No Name* suggests that he probably deserved better than he got.

Star character actor John McIntire (as Cordell's undercover contact) and Donald Buka make strong impressions, and future director Joseph Pevney is amusing as the most upbeat of Stiles's men.

For discussion of the film's refocused 1955 remake, *House of Bamboo*, see Chapter 2.

Conscience and Impersonation

The cops of *T-Men* and *The Street with No Name* do their jobs as squarely as they can, but what happens when a cop makes a bad mistake, tries to cover it up, and inadvertently puts the life of an innocent man at risk? More significantly, what happens if the cop's cover-up is eventually so successful that the innocent man is beyond harm's way? If you're the bad cop, what do you do—confess or walk away clean? These are some of the questions faced by New York police detective Mark Dixon (Dana Andrews) in *Where the Sidewalk Ends* (1950), produced and directed for 20th Century-Fox by Otto Preminger, and written by Ben Hecht, from William L. Stuart's 1948 novel *Night Cry*.

Dixon has a bad personal history: His father was a petty thug, and Dixon has spent his adult life trying to get out from beneath his old man's shadow. He pursues criminals with such fervor that he'll physically abuse anyone who gets in his way, including ordinary citizens. You know that this is a troubled cop going down a dark road. Sure enough, as Dixon works to get the goods on an arrogant mobster named Scalisi (Gary Merrill), and maybe solve a murder along the way, he accidentally kills a Scalisi underling, Paine (Craig Stevens). What now? Get the body out of Paine's apartment and dump it. Maybe Scalisi can take the fall.

Things grow more complicated when Dixon meets Morgan Taylor (Gene Tierney), a design-house mannequin who happens to be the estranged wife of the deceased Mr. Paine. When strong circumstantial evidence suggests that Morgan's father, Jiggs (Tom Tully), schemed to murder Paine, an innocent man is looking at the electric chair.

Dixon has to save Morgan's father. He writes a letter to the inspector, confessing to accidentally killing Paine and orchestrating a cover-up. Now he's going to go after Scalisi. The letter is not to be opened unless Dixon is dead.

During the final confrontation, Scalisi maliciously tells Dixon that his father set him up in the rackets. Dixon's old man created the crook that Dixon hates more than any other. In a perverse way, Dixon and Scalisi are brothers. Dixon's father created them both.

When Scalisi is captured by Dixon, the cop knows that Morgan's father will be cleared. The inspector returns the sealed letter to Dixon, unread, and praises him for fine work. A promotion is in the offing. Morgan is in love with him.

Dixon has pulled it off, all of it.

Can he live with that? He makes a decision.

Where the Sidewalk Ends is intriguing and complex because of its interest in impersonation. Dixon is a dogged cop who secretly feels as if he's just his father all over again, only now pretending to be a policeman. More issues of identity pop up. After getting rid of Paine's body, Dixon dresses in Paine's clothes, calls a cab, and makes sure the lady (Grace Mills) in the basement apartment gets a half-look at him. He sees to it that the cabbie notices the old service bag that clearly says "Paine," and he does likewise with a ticket agent at Grand Central Station. Dixon has become Paine.

In a weird twist when the investigation is still underway, Dixon's boss tells him to get into a trench coat and hat like Paine's and walk up to the sidewalk outside the neighbor lady's window. *Is that what you saw when the man left?*

Dixon's crisis of identity begins to be resolved after he meets Morgan. She married a wrong guy but is working to extricate herself from him. She isn't going to let herself be defined by her no-good husband. Dixon sees that it's possible to become your own person. Character isn't predestined. We can define who we are.

Ben Hecht's script is smart but not showy. Few individual lines of dialogue demand to be quoted. The words are just solid and come together to build a sophisticated, challenging script.

Where the Sidewalk Ends is a reteaming of Andrews and Tierney, who had struck sparks six years before in another Fox noir, *Laura*. Dana Andrews has even more to work with here than in the earlier film and brings believable psychological unease to his usual grim stolidity. Tierney is appealing and suitably world-weary. The role of Morgan doesn't seem to have the complexity of Andrews's, but Tierney's nuanced facial expressions and tone of voice suggest that the character has an extensive backstory and a life that extends beyond the limits of the screen.

Gary Merrill effectively conveys the arrogant nature of Scalisi. (The mobster's quirky use of a menthol inhaler was borrowed from the Richard Widmark character in *The Street with No Name*; the criminal character played by Nick Adams in a small 1956 melodrama from Republic, *A Strange Adventure*, employs the same device.)

Preminger and cinematographer Joseph LaShelle shot on location in Manhattan and Washington Heights and on the well-dressed "New York street" on the Fox back lot. Blocking of many scenes is complex, requiring that actors

Where the Sidewalks Ends (1950) is an edgy and satisfying reunion of director Otto Preminger and two of his *Laura* stars, Dana Andrews (center) and Gene Tierney. Andrews plays a violent cop who covers up his inadvertent killing of a hood. By doing so, he carelessly implicates Tierney's innocent dad. The other cops are Bert Freed (background) and Karl Malden.

walk *into* the camera for a close-up (rather than let the camera come in to them) and then move away obliquely so that the camera can sweep around and follow.

Where the Sidewalk Ends wasn't the financial bonanza Fox had anticipated. In October 1950, about three months after the picture's release, Fox chief Darryl F. Zanuck struck a cautionary note in a memo to another Fox director, Henry King: "In spite of the high quality of such pictures as *Panic in the Streets*, [*The*] *Asphalt Jungle*, *Where the Sidewalk Ends*, etc., etc., these films and all films in this category have proved to be a shocking [box-office] disappointment. . . . There have been twenty-three pictures released in eighteen months in which one or more characters are motivated by psychopathic or psychiatric disorders. . . . Pictures in this category are certainly a very high risk."

Noir would continue at Fox but with less fervor than before.

Oh, Brother

Because Fox's *The Man Who Cheated Himself* (1951) wrapped production just weeks after the studio's July 7, 1950, release of *Where the Sidewalk Ends*, Darryl

Case File: Dana Andrews (1909–92)

"Stolid" and "dependable" describe leading man Dana Andrews, but those words don't take into account his quietly powerful screen presence or his natural, unassuming performance style. After LA stage work in the 1930s, he made his film debut in 1940 and rose quickly through second leads until becoming a full-fledged star in 1944. Andrews flourished at 20th Century-Fox and starred in many of the studio's hits, including the noir classic *Laura*. Other noir appearances include *Fallen Angel*, *Boomerang!*, and *Where the Sidewalk Ends*. Intensely masculine though not traditionally handsome, Andrews was particularly effective as conflicted heroes who struggle with their own shortcomings. His career slipped in the mid-1950s, but he took starring roles in a pair of late noir pictures by Fritz Lang, *While the City Sleeps* and *Beyond a Reasonable Doubt*. From 1960 to his retirement in 1985, Andrews split his time between features and television. Among his other notable pictures are *The Ox-Bow Incident*, *A Walk in the Sun*, *The Best Years of Our Lives*, *Night of the Demon*, and *The Satan Bug*. Beset by alcoholism throughout much of his career, Andrews became a vocal advocate for treatment and understanding of the disease.

Zanuck's memo was a nonissue. Sure enough, *The Man Who Cheated Himself* is another downbeat cop noir.

San Francisco Detective Lieutenant Ed Cullen (Lee J. Cobb) has been carrying on a sexual relationship with a married socialite, Lois Frazer (Jane Wyatt). When Lois bumps off her husband in Cullen's presence, the cop fashions an elaborate alibi for his lover, disposes of the body, and thinks he's gotten away with something—until witnesses begin to come forward.

All of that is familiar noir stuff. The film's modest hook is that Ed Cullen's smart younger brother, Detective Andy Cullen (John Dall), is on the force, too. The final fillip is that Ed, an old hand at homicide, is assigned to mentor Andy during the investigation of Mr. Frazer's death.

Ed had disposed of the murder weapon, but it turns up in the hands of a dumb kind who found it and plugged a liquor-store clerk. Elements of the case fail to add up in Andy's mind, and Ed becomes increasingly desperate. Will Ed allow the liquor-store killer to take the fall for what Lois has done? And can Ed protect himself and Lois without disposing of his brother?

Capable journeyman director Felix Feist (best-recalled today for *Donovan's Brain*) does a workmanlike job with Seton I. Miller and Philip MacDonald's screenplay, and accomplished cinematographer Russell Harlan brings a straightforward, faintly documentary-like visual tone. *The Man Who Cheated Himself* could have been memorable, but quirks of casting trip it up. First, no one is apt to believe that blocky, muscular Ed and reed-like Andy are brothers. Ed has the physiognomy of a bulldog; Andy looks like a greyhound.

Second, perennial sweetheart Jane Wyatt hasn't the fire necessary to convince us that she's worth big throws of the dice by Ed. Wyatt was a skilled, confident actress who was typically cast in good-girl roles for a reason. Lois Frazer is beautiful but looks like a PTA mom dressed up for a big night. She goes through the motions of romancing Ed Cullen, but she's not the sort that brings fever to a man's brow.

An equally bothersome issue is Ed, who, though masculine in the extreme, is underpaid and rough around the edges. What does the sleek socialite see in him? The attraction could be the cop's sexual prowess, but because neither Ed nor Lois strike sparks (and because this a Hollywood picture from 1951), the stallion angle must remain speculative. Like Jane Wyatt, Lee J. Cobb skillfully goes through the motions but seems miles away from passion.

John Dall's Andy is the film's most engaging figure. Although inexperienced, he's a sharp observer and a quick learner. Andy is fun to watch as he unknowingly sniffs around his brother, ferreting out clues and making Ed increasingly nervous. A good moment comes when Andy finally puts two and two together and confronts his brother, who tries to brazen it out. But Andy isn't buying, so Ed slugs him and trusses him like a Christmas goose. Andy gets loose and plays a hunch, locating Ed and Lois at Fort Point, a multilevel brick structure at the base of the Golden Gate Bridge that enjoyed its glory days during the Civil War. By 1951, the fort was empty and in mild disrepair. With its arched casements and novel location, Fort Point is an unusual, highly pictorial setting for the picture's climax. Felix Feist seems to have been more excited by the location than by his actors; he and Harlan prowled the place via a variety of points of view and aggressive compositions that incorporate doorways, support pillars, and those arches. In a particularly striking setup, Andy is shot from ground level as he pauses in the fort's courtyard, an observation tower (which hides Ed and Lois) rearing into the sky behind him.

Ironic, then, that the film finds its greatest power in a location rather than in its principal characters. *The Man Who Cheated Himself* is low-fat noir.

Incorruptible Cop from an Earlier Era

The Racket (1951) is based on a stage play of the same name that came to Broadway in 1927. The writer was Bartlett Cormack, a twenty-nine-year-old Chicagoan with newspaper experience. The play caused an uproar because it suggested that crime is practiced not just by career criminals but by guardians of public safety, specifically, Prohibition agents. Cormack spared no one, and Chicago legend holds that crime boss Al Capone ordered that *The Racket* never be staged in his city.

Cormack wrote the screenplay for a 1928 Paramount adaptation, produced by Howard Hughes and directed by Lewis Milestone. Thomas Meighan and Louis Wolheim starred. Twenty years later, Howard Hughes took ownership of RKO. He remained intrigued with the property and brought it to the screen again in 1951.

Crime boss Nick Scanlon (Robert Ryan) holds onto power the old-fashioned way, with muscle, but the times (as one of his goons muses) are changing. Organized crime now functions in partnership with corrupt politicians and judges, and prefers methods more subtle than Scanlon's. Locally, Scanlon has his hands full with Tom McQuigg (Robert Mitchum), a ramrod-straight police captain who was one of Scanlon's childhood pals. McQuigg gives mob-linked pols the sweats. He's too high-profile to be fired but is continually transferred from one precinct to another, so that his effectiveness is diminished. McQuigg is undeterred and becomes relentless when Johnson (William Talman), one of his best and most principled young patrolmen, is murdered *in the precinct house*. At first, McQuigg does not know that the killer is Scanlon himself.

When Scanlon is cornered and loudly threatens to blow the lid off the whole organization, he's shot and killed by a state's attorney gumshoe (William Conrad) while attempting to escape. McQuigg compounds his victory when he hands subpoenas to the gumshoe and a mob-affiliated candidate for judge (Ray Collins). Officer Johnson's sacrifice may be the beginning of the cleanup the city badly needs.

People who haven't seen *The Racket* in a long time recall it with fondness. The star power of Mitchum and Ryan counts for a lot, but these potent actors are mired in a dated story that, despite the best efforts of director John Cromwell, can't escape its age or its stage origins. Many sequences are shot on location, and two of them—a limousine's doomed attempt to outrun a train and a frantic foot chase and fight atop a building's roof—are pips. In these and similar moments, *The Racket* is kinetic and modern.

Artistic trouble brews in two areas, structure and characterization. The adversarial relationship of Scanlon and McQuigg is shallow, and the fact that they were pals who grew up to pursue wildly opposed occupations (à la *Manhattan Melodrama, Angels with Dirty Faces*, and many other Hollywood crime melodramas) is pat and, by 1951, trite.

When the narrative takes us to McQuigg's station house, the picture slows to a crawl. Characters enter and exit, stage right and stage left, as if they're on Broadway. The blocking is stiff and artificial, and Cromwell moves his camera so little that the vantage point becomes dully constant, as if we're sitting in the eighth row center and can't move.

The script, credited to William Wister Haines and the estimable W. R. Burnett, fails to get at *why* McQuigg is aggressively honest. Stolid and predictable, he never changes. Because the script gives him nothing that he might learn about himself or the system, he's the same at the conclusion of the story as at the beginning, He displeases a lot of politicians but faces no serious internal conflicts. Things unfold just as McQuigg might have expected.

Scanlon, played with venomous vigor by Ryan, is an intimidating but one-note figure. It's a bit of a surprise when he's foolish enough to drill a cop in the precinct house, but he remains convinced he's done what was necessary (and what Officer Johnson asked for). Like McQuigg, Scanlon never evolves. He just gets angrier.

William Talman, cast against type as good-guy Johnson, is the film's most intriguing and charismatic figure. His motivations are obscure, but Talman brings a lot to Johnson that isn't in the script. The actor's piercing pale eyes suggest a sharp intelligence instead of the mere attitude expressed by Mitchum. And when Johnson agrees to a special assignment, he demonstrates a willingness to be surprised. Contrary to first impressions, he's the central figure of the story, and it's to Talman's credit that he gives breath and life to a symbolic role.

Key secondary characters—a mildly scandalous nightclub singer (Lizabeth Scott) and a naive young reporter (Brian Hutton) who loves her—are strictly rote. The sin is compounded because the reporter is an old friend of the doomed Johnson. The puzzle pieces fit too neatly.

Freethinking Sam Fuller wrote the first-draft script for this version of *The Racket*. Predictably enough, he had the good instinct to ignore the play and earlier film adaptation and go his own way. As we'll see throughout this book, Fuller was a potent screenwriter, so Hughes would have been better off using that script. But because Hughes wanted to recreate the 1928 film, Fuller's work was scrapped and screenwriter William Haines was hired to start fresh. Later, Hughes ordered Haines's script rewritten by Burnett.

Even after all of that, Hughes wasn't satisfied and spent hundreds of thousands of dollars on retakes. In the end, he got a 1920s melodrama that should have been left in the 1920s.

Class Distinctions, and Disaster

The criminal activity that engages the attention of Captain McQuigg in *The Racket* involves judges and politicians as well as career criminals. It's *macro* stuff, tentacled and spread out, and with an insidious capacity for further growth. It involves a community. In Joseph Losey and Dalton Trumbo's *The Prowler* (1951), crime exists on the micro level, essentially involving only an unmarried man, a married woman, and the woman's dull husband, who will be murdered. The story's passions, acts, and outcomes are personal and closely proscribed. Other than the principal participants, no one is affected by the crime in a fundamental, visceral way, and even the ripple effect is modest. If *The Racket* and similar noir thrillers are about the business of professional crime on the public stage, *The Prowler* examines amateur criminal activity that is small, furtive, and private.

Uniformed LAPD officer Webb Garwood (Van Heflin) dislikes being a cop. He regrets never having finished college, feels underpaid, and hates that his pad is a rented room. He wants material comfort and longs to be his own boss. When he responds to a nighttime prowler call in an affluent neighborhood, he finds nothing—except good-looking Susan Gilvray (Evelyn Keyes), who phoned because her husband, an all-night radio personality, is at work. She's alone and she's frightened. She also lives well. Webb isn't jealous of the class difference that separates him from Susan—just keenly aware of it.

A calculated follow-up visit (*Any more prowlers? Everything okay?*) sparks an affair. Susan responds to Webb's charm and unconventional good looks. Webb wants Susan, and he wants her husband's money, too. Can Webb kill her husband, get away with it, and be with Susan afterwards?

You bet he can.

In a clever setup, Webb arranges things so that Susan makes yet another call about a prowler. He arrives on the scene, makes a racket in the yard, and fires on middle-aged Mr. Gilvray, who has innocently stepped onto his lawn with gun in hand.

The inquest concludes "accidental death."

Susan allows hope to overpower her better judgment, making herself believe that the shooting was a tragic quirk. After a decent interval, she and Webb are married. Webb quits the force, and Susan's money sets him up with his own business, a motor court. Now he's his own boss. Now he's happy.

A fresh problem crops up, though, and it's a beaut: Susan happily tells Webb she's pregnant. She's long wanted children, but her late husband wasn't able to oblige (whether because of sterility or impotence, we never discover). Webb is happy about the baby, too, until he begins to count backwards. Susan is four months along, which makes it clear that she became pregnant when Gilvray was still alive, because of an illicit affair with Webb—and that's motive for murder.

What to do?

In a move that was no less audacious for Losey and scripter Dalton Trumbo than for Webb and Susan, the couple relocates to an abandoned desert town, where Susan will secretly have their baby. It's a complete change of scene, for them and for us. But sandstorms, an unexpected problem with the delivery, and a suspicious doctor upend the scheme. Worse, Webb makes a verbal slip that reawakens Susan's doubts about her husband's death. Webb's carefully

Case File: Van Heflin (1910–71)

Best remembered for his role as the stalwart homesteader in *Shane*, Van Heflin was an extraordinarily skilled actor who, though a character player at his core, achieved leading-man status. He was a wry, sometimes soulful screen presence, suggestive of physical and moral strength. Heflin established himself in noir as Robert Taylor's loyal, alcoholic friend in *Johnny Eager* (1941) and subsequently took starring roles in *The Strange Love of Martha Ivers*, *Act of Violence*, and, most memorably, *The Prowler*. Although Heflin was a sophisticated presence, his rough-hewn good looks made him well suited to westerns as well as contemporary dramas. Some key films: *Presenting Lily Mars*; *Till the Clouds Roll By*; *Madame Bovary*; *East Side, West Side*; *My Son John*; *They Came to Cordura*; *Patterns*; *3:10 to Yuma*; and *Airport*.

Joseph Losey's *The Prowler* (1951): Webb Garwood (Van Heflin) hates and resents being a police officer. When he falls for bored housewife Susan Gilvray (Evelyn Keyes), he takes it upon himself to kill the woman's husband and pass it off as an accident. Next stop: marriage, a new job—and more trouble than Garwood ever dreamed.

constructed dream unravels, and when local cops close in on the ghost town, Webb tries to escape across the desert on foot.

Joseph Losey had recently completed another film about class conflict, *The Lawless* (1950). The core of that picture is racial hatred. In *The Prowler*, the protagonists are driven by self-regard and aspiration. Webb wants to step up in class. Susan wants the respectability of motherhood and the social acceptance that comes with a husband her own age. Within this framework, *The Prowler* is fluid and visually dynamic. Characters move easily into and away from the camera eye, filling the frame (and the relatively confined sets) with movement. Varied sites used in location shooting provide additional visual interest, as well as a series of effective visual and thematic contrasts. In particular, cinematographer Arthur Miller's night-for-night shooting near Susan's home evokes danger and the seductive quality of those warm Southern California nights (much as in key scenes of *Double Indemnity*; see Chapter 1).

Dalton Trumbo had already been blacklisted because of the HUAC-inspired Hollywood Red scare, so *The Prowler* script is credited to a "beard," Hugo Butler.

Joseph Losey would soon be caught up in the witch hunt himself, and *The Prowler* would be his last American film in a career that would continue for another thirty-four years.

The Prowler fell out of copyright and eventually existed only as scraps of much-abused 16mm film. The comments here are based on the splendid 2010 restoration undertaken by the UCLA Film and Television Archive and the Film Noir Foundation.

Seeing Through Blindness

Shooting of Nicholas Ray's elegant and reflective *On Dangerous Ground* (1952) wrapped at RKO in May 1950, but because few executives at the studio ever liked the troubled-cop melodrama in the first place, the completed picture sat on the shelf for the better part of two years before finally seeing release in February 1952. Despite potent star turns by Robert Ryan, Ida Lupino, and Ward Bond; thoughtful direction by Ray; unusual locations; and striking, high-contrast photography by George Diskant, *On Dangerous Ground* went onto the books showing a loss of $425,000. A few sophisticated magazine critics understood the film, but reviewers who serviced the nabe audiences expressed confusion or ignored the picture altogether.

Some reviewers, and possibly audiences, as well, were put off by the film's sharply bifurcated nature. Approximately the first third of the narrative follows NYPD detective Jim Wilson (Ryan), a capable but angry and unnecessarily violent cop whose spirit has been poisoned by eleven years of daily contact with human "garbage." (The film's first image, a holstered gun lying on a bed, sets the dangerous tone of the New York sequences.) Unlike his partners, Wilson has no wife, no family—just old athletic trophies that sit lonesomely on his bureau.

After knocking the hell out of a hood who might provide a lead on a pair of cop killers, Wilson endures yet another lecture from his captain (Ed Begley). In order to save Wilson's career by getting his boy out of the city, the captain sends Wilson upstate, as a special officer, to assist in the investigation of the murder of a teenage girl. In a very small town held fast in the grip of winter, Wilson sees his own anger reflected in the brute fury of the grieving father (Bond). Later, he discerns some of his own pain and confusion in the face of the killer.

Significantly, the murderer isn't an overgrown fiend but a developmentally disabled teenager (Sumner Williams) who looks like any other blond kid with big ears. The boy is pathetically vulnerable, and Wilson isn't so far gone as to be unable to see that.

The killer's sister, Mary (Ida Lupino), lives with her brother in an isolated house on a spread that she leases to a local farmer. Her brother's emotional and mental deficiencies have made her protective and also encouraged her to develop uncommon empathy. In a clunkily symbolic but tastefully handled fillip, Mary is blind. She's a child of nature, too, a sort of proto-hippie who fills her house with "the outside," especially flowers and twisted, lacquered tree trunks brought by her brother. She accepts her blindness with equanimity, and although she's carefully arranged her home so that she can freely walk within it, she's not in hiding. To the contrary, she understands that sometimes a person has to accept the world as it is, and adapt to it.

A. I. Bezzerides's screenplay, based loosely on Gerald Butler's 1945 British novel *Mad with Much Heart*, is intriguingly light on dialogue, particularly during the rural portion. (Because the film was shot in the springtime, Nick Ray and a forty-person crew traveled to Granby, Colorado, where late snow was still on the ground.) During the city sequences, Wilson spits his words with venom and impatience. He worries and puzzles his partner (Anthony Ross) and has no patience for an underage B-girl (Nita Talbot). Once upstate in a physically expansive environment, he becomes quieter, and less likely to take quick offense. When he finally confronts the boy, he finds he can control his anger. Wilson wants justice, and if that means the boy will be taken to an institution and given help, then so be it. But the moment is destroyed by the sudden, bull-like arrival of the father, which sets off a protracted foot chase across snow, through fir trees, and atop rocks. As Wilson runs, he's determined to get the boy back in one piece, and he can't do that unless he prevents the father from killing him.

The film's first portion has a familiarly visual noir feel, with back alleys, chintzy hotel rooms, crummy taverns, and clogged sidewalks. In the second portion, the screen is dominated by endless vistas of distant mountains, snow-covered fields and forests, a few narrow roads, and isolated houses. Vital to an appreciation of *On Dangerous Ground* is that the rural locale perfectly captures the essence of noir: loneliness, isolation, and latent violence.

Ryan and Lupino act mainly with their faces, which are held in frequent, lengthy close-ups. Ray choreographed violent physical movement like modern dance, presenting it with simultaneous aggression and grace. This almost subliminal stylization gives the film a heightened sort of reality, in which the characters, as well as the actors, are playing roles. For Wilson, redemption comes when he's able to rewrite the role into which he's cast himself.

Gender Wars and Some Big Ideas from Howard Hughes

One of the most highly regarded films noir, RKO's *The Narrow Margin* (1952), came perilously close to oblivion after being completed. During thirteen days in May–June 1950, studio contract director Richard Fleischer shot the suspenseful story of a Chicago police detective who risks his life to transport a hoodlum's wife to Los Angeles, via train, so that she can be a witness in a mob trial.

Most of *The Narrow Margin* is restricted to the train's passenger cars, a marvelous construction of claustrophobic sets (by Albert S. D'Agostino and Jack Okey) with breakaway sections that allowed full camera access. The narrative is tense, and although many interludes are violent, the tale isn't contrived.

After the shoot was complete, RKO owner Howard Hughes suggested, with great enthusiasm, that the male protagonist, Detective Sergeant Walt Brown

Case File: Richard Fleischer (1916–2006)

A list of Hollywood's greatest directors isn't likely to include Richard Fleischer, despite his long and prolific career, impeccable craftsmanship, and professional ethic. The son of animation pioneer Max Fleischer, Richard grew up in the picture business, becoming a straightforward storyteller who respected the subtle qualities of actors and invoked mood and emotion without calling attention to the camera. He had particular artistic success in the noir genre while under contract to RKO: *The Clay Pigeon*, *Follow Me Quietly*, *Armored Car Robbery*, *His Kind of Woman* (uncredited), and *The Narrow Margin*, one of the greatest of all B pictures. A gun for hire after his time at RKO, Fleischer stepped up into the big leagues with *20,000 Leagues Under the Sea* in 1954 and remained there for decades, directing critical and box-office champs that include *The Vikings*, *Compulsion*, *Barabbas*, *Fantastic Voyage*, *The Boston Strangler*, *Tora! Tora! Tora!*, and *The New Centurions*.

In Richard Fleisher's *The Narrow Margin* (1952), a cynical Chicago cop (Charles McGraw) suffers the company of a spiteful mob witness (Marie Windsor), whom he must transport via train to the West Coast. Complication: The train is crawling with hoods sent to assassinate the dame.

(Charles McGraw) leave his charge (Marie Windsor) in order to conduct a (literally) running gun battle with murderous mobsters *on top of the train*, as in innumerable westerns. Though cinematic, the added sequence would have removed the story from the realm of the plausible and turned it into a comic-book adventure. Richard Fleischer thought it was one of the worst ideas he'd ever heard.

Well, Hughes abandoned that notion. Then he came up with a bigger one. Because *The Narrow Margin* had turned out so well, Hughes wanted to scrap all footage with McGraw and Windsor. The editors would salvage as many other sequences as possible, and the leads would be recast with RKO's two biggest assets, Robert Mitchum and Jane Russell. In a commercial sense, the idea wasn't without merit, but it would obviously have meant the destruction of an exceptionally well-done B thriller. Fleischer, still typecast around the studio as a B-picture director, would probably have been cut out of the revamped project. He knew he could do Bs and ached to step up to the A-picture level. Hughes's idea would be a setback to Fleischer's career, particularly because rumors would spread that the McGraw-Windsor footage was deficient.

Fortunately, the ceaseless activity of Howard Hughes's mind brought with it some positive ramifications. Project ideas, endless memos with editorial revisions, a never-ending search for new starlets—all of that and more bubbled in his head like a stew. He eventually decided against—or simply forgot—the Mitchum-Russell idea, but time had passed. *The Narrow Margin* had been sitting on the shelf for nearly eighteen months.

One Hughes idea—and a good one—was implemented: In the original cut, Detective Brown's partner, Gus Forbes (Don Beddoe), is revealed to have been on the take and a facilitator of mob attempts on the woman's life. Hughes didn't like that, so William Cameron Menzies was hired to direct four days of shooting in December 1951 that turned Forbes into a right guy. Also, Menzies directed scenes with character actor Peter Brocco, cast as a corporate-style mobster who unsuccessfully tries to buy Brown's cooperation after Forbes has taken a bullet before setting foot on the train. The alteration streamlined the narrative and kept the focus where it belonged, on Brown, the mob threat, and the woman. (Menzies's work is not credited on-screen.)

Intriguingly, *The Narrow Margin* is secure as a key noir despite its lack of many traditional trappings of the genre. Fleischer and director of photography George Diskant shot nearly all of it in normal light. "Startle" effects, like the rhythmically slashing rectangles of illumination that fill the car from the windows of a train traveling the opposite way, are used sparingly. Although Fleischer's approach isn't in the semidocumentary style, it is well grounded in everyday reality. Sequences in the train's corridors, dining car, and private berths appear as we would see them in life. It's claustrophobia—that is, nowhere to run—rather than shadowplay, that adds voltage and a unique physical dimension to the suspense. (Brown's brutal fistfight with a mobster in a tiny sleeper-compartment bathroom must surely have inspired the similar dustup in *From Russia with Love*.)

The agitated tenseness of Earl Felton's script (based on "Target," a story by Martin [*Detour*] Goldsmith and Jack Leonard) revolves around the mob threat to Mrs. Neil (Windsor) and the imperative that Brown keep thinking ahead. And that's not easy because the mob has sent two hit men, and possibly more, to ride along; and on the highway running parallel to the tracks, a speeding black limousine keeps pace.

Equal tension is produced by the adversarial, snappish relationship of Brown and Mrs. Neil. A dialogue exchange with his partner early in the film makes clear that Brown is predisposed to dislike his witness even before he meets her.

FORBES
What about this dame, Mr. Crystal Ball?

BROWN
A dish.

FORBES
What kind of a dish?

BROWN
Sixty-cent special. Cheap, flashy, strictly poison under the gravy.

FORBES
Amazing. And how do you know all this?

BROWN
Well, she was married to a hood, wasn't she? What kind of a dame would marry a hood?

FORBES (*mildly*)
All kinds.

BROWN
Ah, Gus, at heart you're still a Boy Scout.

When Brown and Forbes take charge of their witness at a cheap hotel, everything Brown has said seems to have been confirmed. The thirtyish Mrs. Neil wears a severely tailored dress, strappy heels, and dangle earrings. She's shapely and aggressively sexy, with a tendency to snap and demand rather than speak. She's a pip.

The greater part of *The Narrow Margin* is a well-plotted and smartly choreographed cat-and-mouse game, as Brown ducks into the odd door and slips around corners in order to keep the gunmen away from the part of the train that holds Mrs. Neil. (The would-be killers have never seen her face.) An accidental meeting with a young mother (Jacqueline White) gives Brown some cover until he realizes that the killers are apt to think she's their target. (Mrs. Neil declares that that would be swell!)

Case File: Charles McGraw (1914–80)

When character lead Charles McGraw thrusts his hawk-like profile into somebody's personal space and issues a threat in that gravel-mixer voice, everybody knows he means business. One of the most emphatic of all noir stars and the focus of cultish admiration, McGraw began his film career in 1942. Uncredited bits gave way to featured supporting roles and finally, while at RKO, to B-picture stardom. Early on, he made a smashing impression as one of the two title characters in *The Killers* and sizzled in *T-Men*, as the sadistic gangster who slow-cooks Wallace Ford. He's a tough cop dedicated to bringing down a clever thief in *Armored Car Robbery* and plays another, even tougher, cop in *The Narrow Margin*. During his thirty-five-year career in features and on television, McGraw played many police officers, sheriffs, and thugs, as well as the occasional judge, doctor, and other authority figures. Watch for him in *Brute Force*, *The Threat*, *Side Street*, *His Kind of Woman*, *Roadblock*, *The Bridges at Toko-Ri*, and *Hang 'em High*, one of his numerous westerns. Although most familiar as a tough guy, McGraw expresses a touching vulnerability in *In Cold Blood* as the aging, dissolute father of murderer Perry Smith.

Finally braced in her drawing room by two thugs, Mrs. Neil reaches for a gun but is shot down. But the story isn't over yet.

Charles McGraw brings life to the familiar tough, decent cop. He's a "company man" who refuses to be bribed and makes use of law enforcement's communication network to give himself an edge. But the mob is sophisticated and organized, too, so even as Brown sends messages to his allies, the thugs send theirs. This central conflict—one man against many, one organization against another—gives *The Narrow Margin* an unexpected depth. And because *The Narrow Margin* has no musical score, a familiarly artificial element of movies, Detective Brown's predicament picks up an added element: not reality, precisely, but the *realness* that a fine filmmaker can create.

Tall, broad-shouldered Marie Windsor—a dame who looks as if she could eat half the men on the planet before breakfast—makes an enormously strong impression. Charles McGraw is imposingly charismatic, but Windsor matches him, gesture for gesture, retort for retort. She's a tough cookie, and when she goes for her gun and is dropped, you reason that she's died the way she lived.

Peculiar Magic

Herbert W. Yates's Republic Pictures made brilliant serials and flavorful westerns, as well as one of the most confounding of all noir thrillers, *City That Never Sleeps* (1953). On the surface, the script by Steve Fisher (*Lady in the Lake*, *Dead Reckoning*) is familiar: Chicago uniformed cop Johnny Kelly (Gig Young) is disenchanted with his job and his marriage. He's taken up with a cooch dancer called Angel Face (Mala Powers) and plans to run away with her. Obstacles: Johnny's wife (Paula Raymond); his father (Otto Hulett), a veteran police detective; and

Penrod Biddel (Edward Arnold), a wealthy political fixer who employs Johnny for quasi-legal "special work." Johnny has no hope of walking away from Biddel unless he does one last job: eliminate another of the fixer's operatives, a clever professional criminal named Hayes Stewart (William Talman).

Many elements come together beautifully in *City That Never Sleeps*—and others just lie there, looking silly. A tuxedoed "mechanical man" (played with touching melancholy by Wally Cassell), who entices passersby from the cramped prison of a nightclub's display window, is a small stroke of genius. Then there is "Sgt. Joe" (Chill Wills), who materializes out of nowhere one night to ride along in Johnny's prowl car. We've already heard Sgt. Joe's deep tones as the film's omniscient, unidentified opening narrator, and now that we see as well as hear him, it's plain that he's a phantasmagorical creation: the spirit of Chicago itself. This pretentious conceit might have been acceptable but for Sgt. Joe's habit of offering a lot of stilted or self-evident observations about life and law enforcement, such as, "In a way, we're like soldiers, an army of policemen." You're amazed that Johnny doesn't lock Sgt. Joe in the trunk.

Johnny's unhappiness with his job and marriage is due mainly to ennui and his sense that everything that defines the respectable part of his life is a bad fit. Although he doesn't enjoy doing errands for Biddel, he has no horrible event in his past that torments him. He just wants out, and that, in its simplicity, is refreshing.

On the other hand, the burley-q dancer Angel Face moans that she once dreamt of becoming a ballerina. "And now look at me." Oh dear.

Case File: Steve Fisher (1912–80)

Pulp writer and sometime Hollywood story man Steve Fisher hit it big in 1941 with his novel *I Wake Up Screaming*, a sordid tale of a corrupt Hollywood cop who schemes to frame an innocent man for murder. The eponymous film (adapted by Dwight Taylor and shifted to a NYC setting), with Victor Mature, Betty Grable, and Carole Landis, was a popular success that propelled 20th Century-Fox into its long and fruitful exploration of film noir. *I Wake Up Screaming* elevated Fisher's stock around town, and after writing the original story for *Destination Tokyo*, he sold his first screenplay, *Johnny Angel* (1945). More noir scripts—some original, others adaptations—followed: *Dead Reckoning*, *Lady in the Lake*, *Roadblock*, *City That Never Sleeps*, *Vicki* (a remake of *I Wake Up Screaming*), and *Hell's Half Acre*.

When *I Wake Up Screaming* was reprinted in paperback in 1960 (following a 1947 paperback release), Fisher updated the text, bringing the tale into the late 1950s and invoking such latter-day phenomena as space travel and Tuesday Weld.

During 1964–68, Fisher hooked up with producer A. C. Lyles to write a series of low-budget westerns with a gimmick: the leading players are aging stars from the 1940s and '50s. Besides westerns and noir, Fisher scripted war films, light mysteries, crime exposé thrillers, and about twenty-five years' worth of episodic television.

Hayes Stewart is an ex-magician. He keeps a white rabbit in a cage on his windowsill and amuses himself with magic tricks. That's clever.

Johnny has no idea that his younger brother, Stubby (Ron Hagerthy), has become Stewart's apprentice in crime. That's as old as melodrama itself.

Biddel takes immature pride in his gorgeous, much younger wife (Marie Windsor), a rehabilitated waitress who hooks up with the magician and betrays her husband. (She breathily informs Stewart that she digs his "magic touch.") *City That Never Sleeps* goes on like this, veering wildly between the tired and the ingenious, the inane and the inspired, as it studies people who feel miscast by life.

Director-producer John H. Auer was a B-movie fixture who parked himself at Republic during the 1950s before getting into episodic TV. He seems to have been a little lost during the film's dialogue sequences. Gig Young is somnambulistic, and some other players have a tendency to pose awkwardly as they deliver their lines. (Talman and Windsor are lively exceptions.)

The picture is considerably more successful during action sequences, when Auer works confidently with cinematographer John L. Russell (who would later shoot *Psycho*). Hayes Stewart's game of cat-and-mouse with Johnny and other cops inside a towering office building is neatly staged, and nighttime exteriors shot in Chicago are pleasingly shadowed and textured (although Chicago

Case File: Marie Windsor (1919–2000)

A not-so-tall leading man, George Raft, claimed not to have been bothered that Marie Windsor towered over him—but directors nevertheless soothed Raft's ego by instructing Marie to bend her knees when the two of them walked side by side. The unconventionally beautiful Windsor stood 5'9"—too tall to pursue a standard Hollywood career, but then, there was nothing standard about Windsor in the first place. Raven-haired, with enormous, wide-set eyes and a seductive mouth, plus a figure to die for, she seems to have been born to play schemers, round-heeled wives, honky-tonk gals, kept women, and other ladies of bad reputation. Her voice was sharply expressive, and on-screen she made many men angry and caused others to wither into impotence.

Windsor began her movie career in 1942, following brief experience on the LA stage. She did mostly uncredited bits until 1948, when she made a strong impression in *Force of Evil*. She subsequently became one of the most familiar faces in noir, crafting potent supporting appearances (and, as in *The Narrow Margin*, the occasional lead) in *The Sniper*, *City That Never Sleeps*, *Hell's Half Acre*, and *The Killing*, in which she shares memorably nasty scenes with Elisha Cook Jr. With more formidable presences the likes of Sterling Hayden, Windsor took full command of her share of the screen. She starred and costarred in numerous westerns and had the female lead in *Cat-Women of the Moon*, a much-loved science-fiction cheapie.

Windsor focused heavily on television after about 1954 but returned to familiar territory in John Flynn's gritty 1973 neo-noir, *The Outfit*.

appears awfully deserted for a city that never sleeps). A climactic chase atop a water tower and onto the el tracks is a rouser that builds and maintains energy with a smart variety of shots and effective cutting by Fred Allen.

Near the climax, as events come to a head outside the mechanical man's display window, loneliness and disassociation are revisited. Night after night, the mechanical man escapes the (literally) dehumanizing monotony of his job by "traveling in my mind" to beautiful places, and he dreams that Angel Face might love him. At last, Angel Face offers some romantically encouraging words. The camera goes to a medium close-up of the mechanical man's face, his silver-painted flesh burnished by the ambient light. The soundtrack is silent. Then we cut to a more intimate close-up. The disconcerting face fills the screen, staring, unreadable—except for a single tear that courses down one silvered cheek. This is a brazenly peculiar, emotionally fraught image worthy of underground cinema. When it was created at the end of 1952, magic happened.

Vengeance Will Kill the Soul

As Columbia contract screenwriter Sydney Boehm worked on his adaptation of William P. McGivern's popular 1953 crime novel *The Big Heat,* he made a smart and significant change. As written by McGivern, the story's central character, police detective sergeant Dave Bannion, is a well-educated fellow whose erudition provides him with a barrier against the effects of the dirt he sees daily. The detective goes about his business with an ironic detachment that helps keep him sane. But as delineated by Boehm, Bannion is sharp but no intellectual. He might have a year or two of college, but you surmise that most of what makes him a dogged and effectively instinctive cop is on-the-job experience. There's certainly no irony about him. To the contrary, he becomes so emotionally and philosophically invested in his latest investigation that he earns himself a suspension from superiors who are cowed by the local mob.

Bannion (Glenn Ford) hates the very idea of wealthy crime boss Mike Lagana (Alexander Scourby). He pursues him with bald aggression, bracing Lagana in his palatial home, roughing up Vince Stone (Lee Marvin) and other Lagana punks, and actively looking for confrontation. Why? Because he's convinced that a B-girl named Lucy Chapman (Dorothy Green) was tortured, killed, and dumped by Lagana's goons before she could tell Bannion more about the mystifying suicide of a top cop.

At home in the suburbs, Bannion is warm and loving with his spirited wife, Katie (Jocelyn Brando), and his little girl, but when he leaves that place of warmth, he strides through the criminal landscape infused with fury. Finally, the mob has had enough of him. In a great shock moment, Katie is killed by a car bomb meant for her husband.

From this point, *The Big Heat* becomes a livid revenge fable in which Bannion—suspension be damned—harasses the Lagana organization with all the vigor of an angry god.

Director Fritz Lang put together a late-career triumph with *The Big Heat* (1953), a harrowing thriller about a police detective (Glenn Ford) who nearly loses his humanity while pursuing the mobsters that murdered his wife. Mob girl Gloria Grahame experiences another kind of suffering and reawakens the cop's better instincts. Although not Grahame's first experience with noir, this is the picture that forever linked this unique actress to the genre.

A well-explicated subplot reveals that the suicidal cop, Duncan, left behind a document that explains his longtime involvement with Lagana *and* the workings of the organization. Widow Bertha Duncan (Jeanette Nolan, in a marvelously unpleasant characterization) keeps the letter from investigators, secreting it in a safety deposit box and using it to extort a fat weekly sum from Lagana. If anything happens to her, the letter will come out and Lagana will be done. (This is the "big heat" of the title.)

Gross villainy is always diverting, but Boehm and director Fritz Lang were most interested in the ambivalent natures of Bannion and Stone's preening girlfriend, Debby (Gloria Grahame). We can see that, since Katie's death, Bannion has closed off his capacities for love and tenderness. Debby is a bit of a contradiction, too. She craves the expensive clothes and travel Stone provides but knows that her boyfriend is a crumb. She knows that he has no real regard for her, so she'd like some validation that she's something more than "Vince Stone's girl."

Case File: Fritz Lang (1890–1976)

This German director who fled the Hitler regime for Hollywood is one of the great psycho-dramatists and pure storytellers of world cinema. Lang was an incurable lover of the pulp sensibility, and was fascinated by emotions and dramatic situations that are larger than life. *M* (1931) is a psychologically intimate examination of an unregenerate murderer of children that remains deeply disturbing (and predictive of noir themes and stylistics). *Metropolis* (1926) is an eye-filling, hugely respected landmark of political science fiction that inspired numberless books and films about dystopian futures where workers are cruelly exploited by lordly masters. Some of Lang's other German films, such as *Spies* and his Dr. Mabuse series, anticipate the gaudy, cliffhanging thrills of the James Bond adventures that arrived more than thirty years later. Lang created a straightforward science-fiction epic with *Woman in the Moon* and waded fearlessly into large-scale, uniquely Germanic epic fantasy with the two-part *Die Nibelungen* (*Siegfried's Death* and *Kriemhild's Revenge*).

Lang's first American movie is *Fury* (1936), which is probably the first film noir, as well. Its primary concerns—criminal psychosis, wronged innocents, and revenge—inform many of the director's subsequent American pictures. During the 1940s, Lang was very important to the definition and development of noir (see in particular *Scarlet Street* and *The Woman in the Window*). Nearly sixty-three when he made *The Big Heat* in 1953, Lang redefined the noir genre by mating it to the postwar preoccupation with personal violence and large-scale corruption. He also took clever advantage of his status as a director of A-minus and B-plus movies by pushing the limits of what was allowable in depictions of physical and emotional violence, as well as sexual tension.

Lang carried an enormous ego, and he could be a martinet on the set. Many of the actors who worked in his films disliked him. Still, his gifts were, and continue to be, appreciated. Even in decline, as in his last American film, *Beyond a Reasonable Doubt*, Lang was eager to provoke audiences.

He returned to Germany in the late 1950s, indulging his unabashed fondness for pulp with a pair of gorgeous and quite underrated "Indian" adventure-fantasy epics (*The Tiger of Eshnapur* and *The Indian Tomb*) and his final film, *The Thousand Eyes of Dr. Mabuse*, a violent and darkly amusing quasiserial that very nearly brought Lang full circle. Other films noir by Fritz Lang: *The Blue Gardenia*, *Human Desire*, and *While the City Sleeps*.

Debby's unwise interest in Bannion eventually leads to one of the supreme—and most brutal—shock moments in all of cinema, when Stone angrily dashes a pot of scalding coffee in Debby's face. After perfunctory medical treatment, Debby flees to Bannion's hotel room, begging for sanctuary and a word of kindness. Bannion's human qualities are revived, and he looks after Debby with the solicitude of a concerned big brother.

Beginning with the film's early sequences, the idea of sanctuary and particularly *home*—and the subversion of that idea—figures prominently. Lagana is keenly proud of his elegant mansion, just as Bannion has been proud of the home he made with his wife and daughter. These opposite poles—mansion

Case File: Gloria Grahame (1923–81)

The word "unique" is an absolute that cannot be modified with superlatives intended to designate degree. There can be no "highly unique." But one is tempted to say that about Gloria Grahame, the acknowledged queen of film noir. Her movie career began in 1944, and in just two years she rose from "pretty girl" bits to important support work in *It's a Wonderful Life*, and finally to a quirky kind of stardom.

Grahame would have been a marvelous actress of the silent screen because so much of her appeal is in her face: sleepy, appraising eyes; an upturned nose; and a small mouth with a provocatively thin upper lip that Gloria herself could not stop fiddling with via surgery. The challenging tilt of Grahame's head and her alternately seductive and exuberant body language also would have served her well in silent movies, but we must consider her voice, which helped make her a great personality of the sound era. It's a honeyed instrument, as sleepy as her eyes, with an amused lilt and a sibilant way with consonants.

Grahame's tragicomic turn as the kept woman Debby in Fritz Lang's *The Big Heat* is practically folklore to movie buffs and as vital to an understanding of the noir/woman connection as Jane Greer's work in *Out of the Past* or Peggy Cummins's in *Gun Crazy*. Debby personifies the easy acquisitiveness of the postwar era and the casual, even heedless, sexuality, too. Debby is excitingly modern because (her financial setup aside) she belongs only to herself. That's why she reaches out to the tormented cop and why she gets herself into a world of trouble.

Grahame played similar characters, often with darker emotional shadings, in other noir films: *Crossfire*, *In a Lonely Place*, *Sudden Fear*, *Human Desire*, *Naked Alibi*, and *Odds Against Tomorrow*.

More versatile than some people realize—she's pure pleasure as Ado Annie in *Oklahoma!* and won a supporting actress Oscar for her performance as Dick Powell's daffy, unfaithful wife in *The Bad and the Beautiful*—Grahame remained busy throughout her short life. She's one of Hollywood's great originals.

versus tidy tract house, ill-gotten gains versus a home earned honestly—inform much of the film's underlying drama.

Debby goes to Bertha Duncan's comfortable home to shoot Bertha dead (after coyly observing that the two of them are "sisters under the mink") and force the release of the incriminating letter. Stone's penthouse apartment is his place of ease and comfort, and it's also where his anger will lead to his undoing.

Fritz Lang made good films in this latter portion of his career, but none have the jolting power and impeccable craft of *The Big Heat*. Lang was attracted to the script's violence (Sydney Boehm had had long experience as a crime reporter) and assured producer Robert Arthur that he could shoot the heaviest scenes and get them past the Production Code. He was right. Because Debby's scalding is achieved with a bit of misdirection (the camera holds mainly on Stone's sadistic grimace of pleasure), Lang gave the moment real horror without being graphic.

Late in the story, Debby surprises Stone with a cascade of boiling coffee to *his* face. What's good for the goose . . . This time, Lang and director of photography Charles Lang held on the *victim's* face because Lang knew that we want to see Stone suffer—and that the Code censors wouldn't mind. He was right about that, too.

The fevered drama of *The Big Heat* is like an assault. (The very first image is of a gun resting on a desk.) In some key sequences, Bannion launches himself into the frame (rather than being followed by the camera), startling us as he reaches to throttle a neck or shove somebody against a wall. The coffee that scalds Stone washes in unexpectedly from frame right. In these very effective moments, Lang saw the frame not just as a place to convey information but as a space that could be emphatically violated for dramatic effect.

Glenn Ford worked amicably with Lang to create a dark, riveting characterization that finally comes round again to Bannion's unkillable humanity.

Gloria Grahame brings real warmth to Debby, emphasizing her quick intelligence and humor, and finally demanding that we regard Debby with an aching sort of tenderness. As on other jobs, Grahame was a free spirit on the set, intensely curious about the nature of the character she played and never willing, or able, to do a take the same way twice. This violated Lang's love of disciplined precision, and because he liked to bully at least one actor on each of his films, Grahame was his victim on this one. But she persisted in her quirkiness and found a protector in Glenn Ford.

Lang may not have known it, but the actress was giving one of the greatest film performances of the 1950s.

Joined at the Hip

Essentially a bad-cop melodrama, Don Siegel's *Private Hell 36* (1954) is regarded by many as noir—due, probably, to the central relationship of the two plain-clothes detectives, Cal Brunner (Steve Cochran) and Jack Farnum (Howard Duff). As is typical of films directed by Siegel, *Private Hell 36* is laudably direct: Some time after a murderous New York City robbery, bills from the heist turn up in and around Los Angeles. As the detectives team up to trace the bills to their source, Cal pursues a romance with nightclub singer Lily Marlowe (Ida Lupino), and Jack (like Bannion in *The Big Heat*) labors to provide a middle-class home and comforts for his wife, Francie (Dorothy Malone), and young daughter. When the partners discover the cache of money (following a highway pursuit and an impressive crash of the suspect's car), Cal pockets about $80,000 off the top. Jack is aghast but seems powerless to effectively resist his partner's scheme, partly because Cal assures Jack that they'll split the take down the middle. Who's to know how much cash the suspect was carrying? The money is hot, but Cal is confident he can sell it on the black market. It's pure profit.

Cal stashes the dough in a small trailer on lot 36 of a run-down trailer park. The money gnaws at the two for different reasons. For the restless Cal, it means an escape with Lily to Mexico; for Jack, it's an existential burden that makes him question his worth as a cop and a man.

By the time the two are found out, Jack has been shot and wounded by Cal, and Cal has been shot and killed by the pair's captain (Dean Jagger), who's been shadowing both of them.

Although *Private Hell 36* has no obvious gay subtext, Cal and Jack neverthe-less pursue many of the niceties and aggravations of marriage. Actor Steve Cochran, with his sturdy frame, brooding good looks, and aura of danger, is the dominant partner. Howard Duff, slightly out of shape and inevitably dressed in light-colored clothing, takes the role of the put-upon, generally ineffectual wife. The pair breakfast together and have dinner together. When one phones, the other immediately joins him. They shave and perform other ablutions together at the station-house locker room, and when they're dog-tired, they find cots at the station and sleep under the same roof. They share private jokes, know the same people, and are familiar with each other's strengths and weaknesses. When the captain or other third parties (including Jack's wife) express doubts about the pair's methods or moods, Jack and Cal present a united front.

Stereotypically, manipulative "husband" Cal has grandiose schemes for the money—travel, gambling, luxury goods—while "wifely" Jack has more modest and sensible ambitions: to get ahead on the house mortgage, to buy nicer clothes for Francie, to lay the groundwork for the baby's future. Cal is a short-term thinker with ideas that exceed his grasp; Jack is the nest-egg type whose eye is on the far horizon.

Cal's betrayal of this faux marriage is hardly different from the act of any other husband who has tired of his wife and feels compelled to dispose of her. The twist, of course, is that these partners are cops, so guns figure prominently in the narrative. When Siegel dollies in on the police revolver in Cal's hand as Jack prepares to step from the trailer, Cal thumbs back the hammer and waits. This isn't just a betrayal but a divorce, and an unpleasant one.

Private Hell 36 was produced by The Filmmakers, an independent production company founded by Ida Lupino and her husband (later ex-husband), writer Collier Young. They collaborated on the screenplay and cast Lupino's then-husband, Howard Duff. The Filmmakers had found moderate box-office success with *Outrage* (1950), *Hard, Fast and Beautiful* (1951), *The Bigamist* (1953), and *The Hitch-Hiker* (1953; see Chapter 7). All of the preceding were directed by Lupino and are models of effective, low-budget storytelling. Lupino and Young had been impressed by Don Siegel's gripping and economical 1954 prison melodrama *Riot in Cell Block 11* and hired him to do *Private Hell 36* because they knew he worked efficiently, and because they sensed he was a kindred spirit. And indeed, Siegel came through with a straightforward narrative approach spiced with effective set pieces that include the car chase, a protracted sequence shot on location at

Hollywood Park, and a wildly kinetic shoot-out and fistfight, involving Cal and a pair of burglars, that opens the film.

Siegel, who had been directing since 1945, had enjoyed the blessings of producer Walter Wanger to do things however he wished on *Riot*. Siegel liked that independence and had his own ideas about methodology and craft, all of which caused him to butt up against Lupino and Young. In one absurd on-set exchange, Lupino demanded that Siegel explain his intellectual reasoning behind a boom shot that was intended to be nothing more than handsome and dramatic.

Except for Dean Jagger, the principal actors drank on the set, which gave Siegel another kind of hangover. Because of the friction, the director claimed to dislike *Private Hell 36*. Although it's not one of Siegel's very best (he later did *Invasion of the Body Snatchers*, *The Lineup* [see Chapter 7], *Dirty Harry*, *Charley Varrick*, and *The Shootist*), the picture has physical energy and a central conflict that explores the limits of friendship, as well as the thin line that, for cops, separates mistakes from full-on catastrophes.

Tough, Irish, and Corrupt

A year after the release of *The Big Heat*, screenwriter Sidney Boehm went to MGM and returned to noir with an adaptation of *Rogue Cop* (1954), another hard-boiled novel by William P. McGivern. Like Dave Bannion in the earlier film, Detective Sergeant Chris Kilvaney (Robert Taylor) spends every day dealing with his own worst instincts. But where Bannion's problem is an inclination to violence, Kilvaney's is a tendency to corruption and easy money ladled out by the mob. And although Bannion battles to control his demons, Kilvaney gives in completely to his—so enthusiastically, in fact, that he's well known around the station house as a crooked cop who has more ready cash than the other officers, lives in a nicer apartment, and dresses like a top-tier business executive rather than a flatfoot. All of that begs the question, *Why is Kelvaney still on the force?* Surely his superiors are as hip as Kilvaney's peers to his shenanigans.

More significantly, the nature of the weakness of character that has encouraged Kilvaney to become a bag man for the mob goes unexplained.

So some important questions are never satisfactorily answered. If they were, Kilvaney would have been off the force ages ago and we wouldn't be watching this movie. So, quite artificially, Kilvaney's career continues.

Rogue Cop has a few other fundamental problems. First, it's trite in its explication of Kilvaney as one of a family of cops, all Irish to the core and many with exemplary records. Kilvaney's late father, Patrick, earned many commendations and lived to see his oldest son go bad. Now Kilvaney's younger brother, Eddie (Steve Forrest), has joined the force. Eddie's mission, at work and in life, is to be honest, which naturally puts him at odds with his older brother. (The kid is so decent, his sweetheart [Janet Leigh] is a reformed mob habitué.) When Eddie

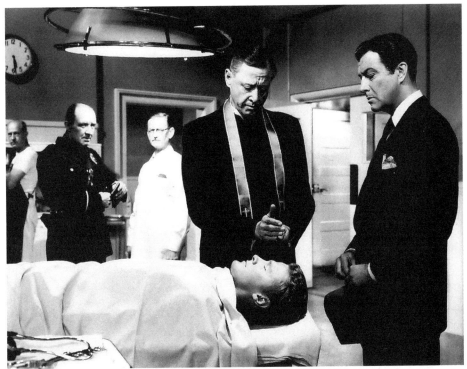

Rogue Cop (1954): A brazenly corrupt police detective (Robert Taylor, far right) inspects the body of his younger brother (Steve Forrest), an honest patrolman murdered by one of his brother's criminal associates. The priest is Anthony Ross.

fingers a murder suspect and prepares to identify him in a lineup, Kilvaney's mob connections, Ackerman (Robert F. Simon) and Dan Beaumonte (George Raft), let him know that if he wants Eddie to stay alive, he'll convince the kid to forget the ID.

As if to let us know that he's really not happy with any of this, Kilvaney fires off endless, peevish *bons mots* instead of real dialogue. ("Don't kid me!" "Oh, grow up!" "Sixty-five bucks'll buy you a pension and a headstone." "I know what kind of dame you are." etc., etc.) The character is motivated almost completely by unexplained cynicism—about the law, women, love, ideals, work, everything. You get the idea that if it ever comes up, Kilvaney will be cynical about pleated pants.

Existing in thematic opposition to Eddie's girl is Nancy (Anne Francis), a gorgeous but pitiable alcoholic who is Beaumonte's mistress. When she drunkenly laughs at him after Kilvaney has knocked him to the floor, Beaumonte finally struggles to his feet. Director Roy Rowland goes to a tight close-up on Nancy's face as she looks up at her furious lover. Her drunken giddiness has vanished, and she begins to grasp what she's done to herself. It's a nice moment for Anne Francis, who suddenly looks like a wounded bird.

Beaumonte orders his boys to "take her to Fonzo's place," which doesn't sound good at all. When Nancy shows up much later at Kilvaney's apartment, bruised, shamed, and disheveled, the implication is that she's been gang-raped. As with Bannion in *The Big Heat*, Kilvaney's better nature—such as it is—is aroused by the abuse levied against the girl.

Kilvaney's redemption continues but at the cost of his younger brother's life.

Director Roy Rowland was a competent yeoman who scored in 1945 with *Our Vines Have Tender Grapes*, an honest, warmhearted look at small-town Americana. Most of Rowland's other films are skillful but unremarkable B-plus product (*Killer McCoy, Scene of the Crime, Affair with a Stranger*), though a 1953 release, *The Five Thousand Fingers of Dr. T*, is a wonkily imaginative visualization of a story by Dr. Seuss.

Other than sequences featuring George Raft and Anne Francis, the best moments of *Rogue Cop* are at the beginning and end. The picture gets off to a fast start with a pretitle, semidocumentary montage of rolling squad cars and cops across the city going about their business. And at the climax, Kilvaney and another detective, Myers (Robert Ellenstein), shoot it out with a suddenly aggressive Beaumonte, who fires from behind the wheel of a parked car. The sequence is visually complex, shot from numerous points of view with a smart variety of close-ups, medium shots, and long shots. Editor James E. Newcom cut it all together with laudable clarity. Two bits of business stand out: a worm's-eye view of the wounded Kilvaney, unconscious on the pavement beneath the car, a tire poised to roll over his head; and Myers's savage gunning of Beaumonte, who lets loose with a shocking shriek of pain as the bullets rip into his body.

Regrettably, most of *Rogue Cop* is told in static two-shots. The camera (supervised by John Seitz) seldom moves, and the actors often seem frozen within the frame. The picture's thoughtful and imaginative moments stand out because they're rare. *Rogue Cop* is competent, but it's almost certainly the least of many crime scripts written by the estimable Sidney Boehm.

The Twisted Art of Murder

The novelist William P. McGivern provided the source material for yet another policeman noir, *Shield for Murder* (1954), adapted for the screen by Richard Alan Simmons and John C. Higgins. Once again, we meet a rogue cop, but with a difference. Unlike Dave Bannion and Chris Kelvaney, Detective Barney Nolan (Edmond O'Brien) actually kills people, and not on principle, either, but for personal aggrandizement and self-protection. He's a murderer with a record of killing suspects who "made a break" or otherwise tempted fate. His captain (Emile Meyer) loathes and distrusts him, and the other detectives in the squad room look at him as if he had two heads. It seems as if he has just one ally, a young cop named Mark Brewster (John Agar). Brewster isn't a Boy Scout, but he is scrupulously principled and honest. A former street kid, he's also Nolan's protégé, so he's willing to strain and give Nolan the benefit of the doubt.

Nolan doesn't deserve Brewster's trust, as we see in the film's nighttime opening sequence, when Nolan grabs a bookmaking suspect, steers him around the corner into an alley, and shoots him dead. Nolan takes a fat roll off the corpse and then shouts, "Police! Halt" He fires two shots in the air and then waits for assistance.

From a second-floor window that overlooks the alley, an old man (David Hughes) witnesses the whole scene unfold. Terrified, he draws back into the darkness, unnoticed.

Unlike the killer cops of some other thrillers, Nolan isn't an asocial loner who's content to live in a boardinghouse. To the contrary, he dreams of happy married life in the suburbs. His girlfriend is Patty (the striking Marla English), and it's clear that Nolan worships her. The killer is in love. And Patty is in love with Nolan. They make an intriguing pair: the curvy, guileless cigarette girl and the burly cop whose cynicism is mitigated by the sweet mush of romance.

Edmond O'Brien in *Shield for Murder* (1954): The killer cop's banal dream of married life ends in the dirt of a postwar housing development. The money he murdered for won't help him now.

Joining the themes of police criminality and romance are uncontrolled anger and self-survival. Of all the bad-cop noirs of the period, *Shield for Murder* verges on pure, unadulterated lunacy, as if Nolan's behavior is literally guided by the moon, or some other cosmic force. He doesn't just "do" murder, he performs it, like an interactive art piece. To kill gives him a twisted pleasure and vindication. In Nolan's mind, his victims aren't dead because he killed them. They're dead because they didn't deserve to live, and because their deaths are to his advantage. Judge, executioner, thief, artiste. Nolan has the bases covered.

By 1954, the reasonably sleek figure presented by Edmond O'Brien in 1949 and 1950 was shading to chubbiness, and he was very near to his transition from two-fisted leading man to portly character actor. *Shield for Murder* suggests that very clearly: Although O'Brien is the picture's ostensible leading man, he takes a character actor's role.

The part of Nolan suits him, and you can see that the actor enjoyed himself—partly, no doubt, because he was the film's codirector, with Howard W. Koch. Some of the film's players, such as John Agar and Marla English (once known around Hollywood as "the poor man's Elizabeth Taylor"), and David Hughes, the actor cast as the doomed old man, bring laudable restraint to their roles. Agar, though never acclaimed for his thesping, is particularly good. You feel the vibration of his devotion to Nolan and his profound disappointment when he learns the truth and tries to bring his friend in.

Edmond O'Brien, on the other hand, runs amuck in a most entertaining way, hurling his thick body through doorways and against other people, grimacing in fevered close-ups and shouting much of his dialogue. He's bigger than life and the villain you love to hate. So unrestrained is his performance that *Shield for Murder* is, to that time, the hysterical apotheosis of the cop gone bad; we wouldn't see his like again for nearly twenty-five years, when character actor/ leading man Harvey Keitel played *The Bad Lieutenant* in 1978. (Some of the Lear-like overplaying also affects Emile Meyer, cast as Nolan's splenetic boss, and composer Paul Dunlap, whose score is often loudly intrusive and thematically inappropriate; Patty's "love theme" turns up so often you begin to hate it.)

Two set pieces grab our attention: Nolan's (possibly) accidental killing of the elderly witness (a miserable and upsetting act) and a fabulous shoot-out at a crowded indoor swimming pool. The money Nolan took from the bookie belongs to a crime boss named Packy Reed (Hugh Sanders), who has sent a private detective, Michaels (Claude Akins), to quietly threaten Nolan and convince him to hand over the dough in exchange for fake passports and a pair of tickets to Argentina. Detective Nolan—by now dressed in his old uniform because half the force is looking for him in his civilian clothes—agrees but hands over cut newspaper in the pool's locker room. In the very well-shot and sharply edited sequence that follows, the private dick chases Nolan around the perimeter of the pool, firing and missing, straining for a clear shot, panicking bathers whose screams echo crazily inside the tiled space. Because O'Brien and Koch varied their setups, we get a nice combination of points of view and subjective images, long shots and close-ups. And all while Nolan and Michaels are constantly moving. Editor John F. Schrever skillfully cut it all together.

Suitably enough for a bad cop with a flamboyant manner, Nolan dies in a big way, illuminated by a phalanx of squad-car headlights at a suburban model home he's bought for Patty and himself (the money is stashed there). He unwisely takes a couple of potshots at the other cops and winds up flat on his face in the dirt that will one day be a lawn. It just won't be his lawn.

One of the officers is Brewster, who plucks the shield from his friend's body and looks at it, as if wondering what it, or anything, means.

Support Your Local Bakery

The first feature directed by journeyman filmmaker Jerry Hopper is *The Atomic City* (1952), a taut, intelligent thriller about the kidnapped son of an American atomic-weapons scientist. Gene Barry plays the scientist, giving a generally understated, nicely modulated performance. Hopper and Barry were reunited for *The Naked Alibi* (1954)—and this time Barry plays the villain. The actor was almost inevitably cast in forthright roles, and it seems apparent that he had particular fun with *The Naked Alibi*. His performance is perfectly mad, a real exercise in carpet chewing. And it's not without philosophical implications.

Al Willis (Barry) owns a successful Los Angeles bakery and appears to be happily married to a sweet, unassuming woman (Marcia Henderson). When Willis is hauled to the precinct house on a routine drunk charge, he becomes belligerent, striking Detective Parks (Casey Adams) and threatening Joe Conroy (Sterling Hayden), the chief of detectives. Willis eventually apologizes and is turned loose, but not long after, Detective Parks is shot dead by an unseen assailant as he stands at a call box. No evidence ties Willis to the killing, but Conroy, who prides himself on his instincts, is convinced that Willis is guilty.

Days after Parks's murder, two more local detectives are blown up in their car, in front of one victim's wife, no less. Not a shred of evidence connects the well-dressed baker to the crimes, but the enraged Conroy leans on Willis so hard that he's booted from the force.

In the tradition of the troubled policemen of *The Big Heat* and *Rogue Cop*, Conroy becomes a vigilante, trailing Willis to a squalid border town, falling for Willis's cooch-joint mistress, Mariana (Gloria Grahame), and alternately taking and delivering beatings as he presses to wring a confession from Willis.

The Naked Alibi is a modestly budgeted Universal-International noir that has the flat, brisk competence of a Columbia thriller; even the main-title card looks like Columbia product. At first glance, this seems a simple revenge tale, but a closer look reveals that the story is propelled by Conroy's certitude (he's not wrong about Willis) and the notion of double lives. Just as Willis masquerades as a happily married baker and good community member, Conroy's impersonation of a team player has made him chief of detectives. But Conroy is a free agent at heart. His relentless mindset certainly rolls over any notion of common sense—after all, he loses his job.

As delineated by Hopper and screenwriter Lawrence Roman, Conroy's propensities for rough stuff and intimidation are presented as good things. He pursues his methods in the face of a growing political investigation of police wrongdoing—unprofessional brazenness that establishes him not as a pariah but as a hero. Conversely, Willis's "good citizen" masquerade is despicable because it deceives the public and installs a monster in the community's midst. (He even has the gall to hide a murder weapon inside one of the town's churches.)

Sequences in the border town, shot night-for-night by cinematographer Russell Metty, are lively and atmospheric, mixing crane shots, tracking shots, rich interplay of light and shadow, deep focus, and long takes. To a modest extent, these sequences anticipate the tawdriness of the cross-border mischief so important to Orson Welles's *Touch of Evil* (1958; discussed later in this chapter). In that film, the local muse is Marlene Dietrich, a quasi-gypsy. In *The Naked Alibi*, the muse is Gloria Grahame's Mariana, a vulgar singer-dancer whose elemental sexuality connects her, as if by alchemy, to Conroy, and to the truth. Grahame has more screen time here than in *The Big Heat*. The Debby character of the earlier film is gorgeous and sprightly; *The Naked Alibi*'s Mariana is more bluntly eroticized (in one interlude, she nibbles Conroy's chin like a strudel) and more haggard, too. Her unwise relationship with Willis has worn her out thoroughly, and as for many bad girls of noir, her ultimate escape is via death.

The climactic nighttime shoot-out across rooftops is exciting and well staged; likewise Conroy's beating at the hands of Willis thugs; Conroy and Willis's ferocious fistfight in the ridiculously cramped rear of a fully packed semitrailer; and (in a clever "left field" moment) Willis's startling and completely gratuitous shove that sends a waiter toppling over a railing.

Willis's brand of criminal dementia is grossly unappealing. *The Naked Alibi* is a minor film, but it does successfully suggest that an avenger with his own touch of the demented is sometimes best suited to put the lock on an irredeemable lawbreaker.

Philosophies of Hate

Philip Yordan and Joseph H. Lewis's *The Big Combo* (1955) is built on a stated foundation of hate. For mob boss Mr. Brown (Richard Conte), hate is life's great motivator. He hates the legitimate world and anybody who blocks his ambition or fails to grasp his philosophy. (He's driven his wife [Helen Walker] to literal insanity.) A dabbler in the fight game, he dismisses a talented boxer because the kid doesn't "know how to hate." Hate is Mr. Brown's sustenance and has elevated him to the dominant position he enjoys.

Police Detective Lt. Leonard Diamond (Cornel Wilde) hates Brown and the criminal organization that profits from ruined lives. Diamond's dislike is exacerbated because the cop has history with the mobster's blonde mistress, Susan Lowell (Jean Wallace).

Diamond especially despises the rules that prevent him from dealing with Brown and other lowlifes as he'd like. Diamond would be very pleased to shoot Brown in the head or beat him to death. But as his captain (Robert Middleton) warns, that isn't a fruitful line of thought.

A maddening *sublimation* of hate consumes Joe McClure (Brian Donlevy), a nattily dressed, hard-of-hearing criminal whose empire has been snatched by Brown, and who now functions as Brown's highly paid but servile associate. McClure absorbs his daily humiliation obsequiously, like an affluent whipped dog. Late in the story, circumstance encourages McClure to become cocky and finally summon the nerve to make a move against Brown. Then, at last, he can express his hate.

Susan Lowell hates, too, though the emotion is considerably muted in her case, as she floats through life in a somnambulistic trance. Pampered with a plush apartment, clothes, and jewels, she's nevertheless another target of Brown's flair for degrading others. She knows that to him, she's an object, a prize. She hates Brown, and, because of what she has allowed herself to become, she hates herself, too. But stuck in emotional limbo, her only rebellion is a half-hearted attempt at suicide, which brings her back into Lt. Diamond's orbit but does nothing to solve her fundamental problem.

As counterpoint to all of this emotional unpleasantness, Lewis and scripter Philip Yordan give us characters who do not hate. Two of them are Brown's devoted torpedoes, Fante and Mingo (Lee Van Cleef and Earl Holliman, respectively, giving insightful, sophisticated performances). They kill easily but respect Mr. Brown and love each other. Much like the bad cops of *Private Hell 36*, Mingo and Fante (whom Mingo calls Fannie) work together, sleep under the same roof in very domestic twin beds, dine together, and, ultimately, die together.

The other principal character not absorbed by hate—although she's plenty cynical—is a startlingly beautiful brunette stripper named Rita (Helene Stanton). She is Diamond's on-again, off-again lover, and although Rita knows she has no reasonable hope of a future with the cop (who treats her, as he shamefacedly admits later, "like a pair of gloves"), she loves him. She accepts his occasional affection and endures his endless, unpleasant barbs. When Diamond calls on her for emotional support, she gives it.

As the denouement of *The Big Combo* approaches, Rita is slaughtered in Diamond's dark apartment by machine-gun fire meant for Diamond. The shooters are Fannie and Mingo, acting on orders from Brown, who has had enough of his longtime nemesis. Because the botched hit leads to bad consequences for the torpedoes, Mingo becomes eager to give Diamond information that will topple Mr. Brown. (True to what has already been established, Mingo snitches not because he hates Brown but because he loves Fannie. It's a lovely consistency of character.)

The Big Combo was shot by John Alton, who apparently understood what Lewis was looking for. Alton's work here is typically artful and audacious, with textured shadowplay, backlighting, and eerie highlights on anguished or conflicted faces. His treatment of actress Jean Wallace—whose features are symmetrically, unnervingly perfect—is particularly effective. In key moments she looks unearthly, like an anemic angel who's lost all hope.

When Diamond is abducted by Brown's boys and strapped to a chair in a warehouse and tortured, the monochrome values are vividly stark black and white, with few grays. But the nighttime climax, shot on a stage dressed to suggest the exterior of a small airfield, is thick with artificial fog that obscures nearly everything in gray. The frame is bracketed by shapes that might be the edges of hangars, and a lonely light beacon pulses in the far distance. Minimalist (and cost-saving) in the extreme, the tableau is visually abstract, as well as a perfect evocation of the psychological and emotional ambivalence of the characters who have gathered there.

In one of noir's most justifiably famous sequences, Brown brings McClure to the airfield for execution. When he gently removes McClure's hearing aid, David Raksin's intense, brilliant score is suspended and the soundtrack goes dead silent. We see an instant of muzzle flash from McClure's point of view but hear nothing.

The killing accomplished, Brown steps forward, his feet audibly scuffing on the asphalt, the sounds of life restored.

Brown himself is later taken at the airport, caught in a spotlight's eye like a terrified rodent. In a satisfying irony that suggests Diamond has put much of his hate aside, he takes Brown alive, even though Brown defiantly insists on being killed. Diamond knows that prison will be worse punishment, and that's just where Brown will go.

In *The Big Combo's* final shot, Diamond and Susan stand in the middle ground with their backs to the camera, their figures silhouetted against the bright fog. Diamond stands stock-still, as if waiting. Susan tentatively moves closer to him.

There may be hope for love after all.

Orson Scares the Suits

The beautiful and innovative creation that is Orson Welles's *Touch of Evil* (1958) exists because of a misapprehension. In 1957, Charlton Heston's agent sent the actor a script (then called *Badge of Evil*), suggesting that his client might do well in the role of a forthright Mexican cop who locks horns with a corrupt American lawman (Welles) in a U.S. border town. Heston, assuming that Welles would also direct the picture, readily accepted the role. When word of the casting coup got back to Universal-International staff producer Albert Zugsmith and studio executives, there was little hesitation: Welles was assigned to direct, with an understanding that *Badge of Evil* could lead to a four- or five-picture director's contract with the studio.

Welles tossed the script (based on Whit Masterson's 1956 novel *Badge of Evil*) and rewrote it. In fact, Welles didn't read the novel until after the film was completed, so what's on-screen is Welles's vision; he used the first script as a framework only.

In its clash of familiar noir archetypes, the setup seems simple. A cross-border murder investigation brings together a bloated, dissolute American lawman named Hank Quinlan (Welles, wearing age makeup, a bulbous false nose, and sixty pounds of body padding) and Mike Vargas (Heston), a high-ranking Mexican police official who's in the area with his American wife, Susie (Janet Leigh), hours after their marriage. Vargas shortly becomes convinced—and rightly so—that Quinlan is a corrupt cop who has framed a Mexican national to take the fall.

Quinlan hates Vargas's interference, and fights back by enlisting a bombastic local crime boss, Grandi (Akim Tamiroff), to abduct Susie and manage events so that she appears to be a drug user. Vargas can't be officially shut down, but he might be derailed by scandal.

Finally, in concert with Quinlan's disillusioned, longtime partner, Menzies (Joseph Calleia), Vargas electronically records Quinlan's words as the big cop walks with Menzies and incriminates himself. But Quinlan discovers the betrayal as it's going down, shooting Menzies and nearly dispatching Vargas before the dying Menzies summons the strength to pull the trigger on his partner and friend.

Touch of Evil (as the studio finally called the picture) is visually and structurally complex, and extraordinarily ambivalent in its morality (much in the manner of Welles's first film, *Citizen Kane* [1941], which set down much of the stylistics and film grammar that were subsequently utilized in noir). Heston's Vargas is the ostensible leading man, but the central figure is Welles's Quinlan. Vargas is honest and straight—so much so that he's more than a little self-righteous, and a bit of a priss, too. He's fearless but gives the impression of being shocked by corruption, as if he's never run into it before. It's also hinted that Vargas has larger aspirations, so although his morality is honest, it squats next to self-promotion and Vargas's acute interest in his image. (You suspect, in fact, that *he* feels as threatened by Susie's predicament as she does.)

Quinlan is a physical and moral horror, bloated by years of drink and candy bars, and so sunk in lawless certitude that he pursues his self-appointed role as judge and jury without question or qualm. He realizes that he may have sent innocent men to prison or even to their deaths, but he feels all of that is more than balanced by his career-long refusal to allow the guilty ones to escape.

Vital to an understanding of Quinlan is that he's been corrupted only by power. After thirty years of work, he owns nothing but a small chicken farm and has almost no money. The job, his conception of self, and his administration of justice by any means—it all defines him. Although he complains bitterly about his financial state, he's never been motivated by money. In that, Quinlan has a

Self-righteous Mexican police official Mike Vargas (Charlton Heston, far right) has a fundamental philosophical dispute with U.S. bordertown cop Hank Quinlan (Orson Welles, far left) in Welles's last great directorial effort, *Touch of Evil* (1958). The other actors are Victor Millan (center, left) and Joseph Calleia.

certain moral purity. In his dishonesty, he's honest, and he may not deserve to be betrayed.

Betrayal is central to a lot of great drama. A violation of trust, no matter the reason, is a profound act, and Menzies commits it with complete, abject misery (which takes *Touch of Evil* into the realm of classical tragedy). Menzies's unhappiness escapes Vargas, who is completely absorbed with nailing Quinlan, clearing his wife, and establishing his own righteousness.

Welles rehearsed *Touch of Evil* for nine days and shot it in about thirty-eight. He had hoped to film in Tijuana but had to settle for Venice, California, which was beautifully re-dressed for night-for-night shooting by art directors Alexander Golitzen and Robert Clatworthy.

The picture is justly revered for Welles's intensely visual storytelling and his collaboration with his brilliant cinematographer, Russell Metty. Most famous, of course, is the four-minute, uninterrupted take that opens the picture, as a convertible that carries a bomb in its trunk slowly wends its way through the streets and across the border into the U.S., where it explodes. Mounted on a boom, the camera tracks not just the car but introduces us to the strolling

Vargas and Susie, coming down from on high to eye level, keeping pace with the couple, pausing when they (or the car) stop for pedestrians or cross traffic, dollying in to pick up their conversation, then craning high above them to again assume a dispassionate view that continues to track their progress as well as the car's. The sequence is astonishing, mind-boggling, and the work of a filmmaker of incomparable confidence and skill. (Another, almost subliminal single-take sequence shows up later, during an interrogation in a small apartment.)

Scenes with Susie at an isolated, whitewashed motel owned by Grandi are perfect horrors of blaring rock 'n' roll and bleating hot rods. (The arriving cars are announced with a bravura exterior crane shot, and precise tracking and shooting from inside the room, through windows and a door frame.) Various leather-jacketed Grandi nephews have taken over the switchboard, and when Susie's room is finally violated, the first person inside is a very butch piece of rough trade (Mercedes McCambridge, in an unforgettable cameo) who says, "I want to watch." A nephew commands, "Hold her legs," and Susie is violently set up for the big frame—on her wedding night! (Significant to the sexual undercurrents of *Touch of Evil* is that Welles continually highlights the contours of Janet Leigh's ample and gorgeous bust, an asset that the actress virtually never exploited during her career. Susie's sexualized, hyperfemale physicality heightens her vulnerability, of course, but also underscores what Quinlan hates: a Mexican who has a gorgeous blonde wife.)

Welles made room for pathos (Marlene Dietrich, as a quasi-Gypsy who loves and admires Quinlan), horror (Grandi's grossly distorted face after Quinlan has strangled him), and for absurd comedy, as well: the mangy toupee that won't stay on Grandi's head; the Grandi nephew who can't stop himself from bobbing up and down to a rock 'n' roll beat; Quinlan's pouty complaint to Menzies: "Didn't you bring any donuts or sweet rolls?"; and the motel night man's flippy, psychosexual nervousness (Dennis Weaver, anticipating, somewhat, a later motel keeper, Hitchcock's Norman Bates; see Chapter 7).

U-I executives who watched the rushes claimed to love what they were seeing, but when they viewed the picture cut together (by Virgil Vogel, whom Welles admired), they were aghast. The visual and thematic darkness bewildered and frightened them, and they couldn't grasp Welles's intriguingly fragmented narrative progression. Suddenly, Welles's hopes for a multipicture director's contract evaporated. He was fired, and the studio hired a B-western and serial director named Harry Keller to shoot a day's worth of bridging scenes to "make sense" of the narrative. The picture was also recut (probably by U-I fixture Edward Curtiss) so that entire sequences—including the darkly comic ones—were excised and others rearranged. Welles's crosscutting was eliminated, which made sequences longer and killed the picture's pace. The film was dumped into American theaters with no buildup or other marketing plan. It was a box-office failure.

Touch of Evil was Welles's first Hollywood picture in ten years. He had high hopes for it, and for the course of his career, but all of that was dashed. Welles never worked in Hollywood as a director again. He continued to make films abroad, but Hollywood now saw him only as an actor for hire.

The critical comments in this book are based on the 1998 restoration undertaken by Universal and produced by Rich Schmidlin and edited by Walter Murch. The restoration allows *Touch of Evil* to be seen as close to how Welles envisioned it as is possible. One example: The opening sequence of the 1958 release was cluttered with title, cast, and credits against a bed of music; in the restoration, all of that information appears as end credits, and the sequence has no score—just the ambient music of the street. Welles's storytelling unreels without distraction.

The restoration is the only way to see *Touch of Evil.*

5

The Best-Laid Plans

"I just wanna be somebody!"

—Richard Widmark, *Night and the City* (1950)

I protect Sheepshead Bay from pirates," announces Harold Goff (John Garfield), the smiling and completely uningratiating extortionist at the center of *Out of the Fog* (1941). Goff bestrides this theater-based mix of early noir and social drama like a puny colossus, deceptively resplendent in well-tailored overcoat and kidskin gloves. His targets du jour are Jonah (Thomas Mitchell) and Olaf (John Qualen), local merchants and devoted friends whose great pleasure is to take their tiny skiff out for fishing in the evenings after work. If they wish to continue that enjoyment, they will pay Mr. Goff five dollars each week. Otherwise, he will burn their boat.

The story is set in December, and an apparently mild one, at that, with the bay represented by a fabulously detailed, fog- and mist-enshrouded sound-stage set by Carl Jules Weyl that is simultaneously expansive and claustrophobic. Director Anatole Litvak, writers Robert Rossen, Jerry Wald, and Richard Macaulay (working from Irwin Shaw's play, *The Gentle People*), and cinematographer James Wong Howe created a watery neighborhood that isn't quite sinister but is far from embracing. Careworn and tired, it's home to what Jonah calls—with no small pride—"ordinary people." Jonah is a pants presser; Olaf runs a diner. Jonah's beautiful daughter, Stella (Ida Lupino), speaks into a headset at the telephone exchange for nine hours a day. Stella's earnest, mild suitor, George (Eddie Albert), is a local auctioneer.

Goff comes boiling into all of this ordinariness as ordinary as a chest cold. He's a strictly local organism, and a disagreeable one. But he has the courage of his warped convictions, and that quality gives him a leg up on the decent people who are his victims. He brims with the confidence that comes from believing that his grift is the best and most logical way for him to make a living. He's even scrupulous about preparing fraudulent paperwork that "explains" his extortion to gullible judges. He knows how to work the system.

In much of this, Goff is a clear stand-in for prewar Germany, which bluffed and bullied its way onto territory to which it had no claim, while its larger, equally powerful neighbors engaged Hitler in inept statecraft and allowed themselves to be cowed and intimidated. Germany knew what it wanted, and it was not going to be deterred.

Not surprisingly, Goff is taken by Stella's beauty and crassly exploits her naïve wishes for nightlife and a dreamed-of trip to Cuba with a visit to a Cuba-themed nightclub. Later, he offers a genuine trip to the island, to be financed with $190 that Goff has extorted from Stella's father.

Decency collides with reality when Jonah and Olaf scheme to lure Goff into their boat, take him into the bay, and drown him after hitting him on the head. If they betray their own better instincts, they can be rid of their tormentor. In the boat (they've offered Goff a shortcut to Stella) they come close to committing murder, but neither man has quite what it takes to kill. But in a propitious turn, Goff tumbles to what's going on, stands and wobbles in the skiff, and topples overboard. He'd liked to thump the place where his heart should be and claim that he "has rocks in here," and he must, for he makes a splash like a boulder and vanishes. Later, investigating cops fail to uncover Goff's ostrich-hide wallet, which Jonah has suspended by line into the water and eventually recovers—with his own money inside and some extra, besides.

Goff, for all of his blustery scheming, is ultimately helpless in the face of family and decent values. He's turned himself into a habitué of the bay, but he's a fish that doesn't belong.

Unlike Sidney Kingsley's famed play *Dead End*, which is concerned mainly with issues of class, *Out of the Fog* is more interested in irony and comeuppance. If Goff is a chest cold, Stella catches the bug: "I get hot and cold all over," she excitedly says of her reaction to her transparent suitor. "I feel like yellin'."

When Jonah briefly defies Goff, he absorbs a terrible beating. "He hit me with a rubber hose," he quietly explains to Olaf later. "It's a little hard to move now."

Stella is in trouble, Jonah is fearful, and evil pushes decent men to the contemplation of evil. If Goff understands that, he's foolishly, dangerously unafraid of it.

Out of the Fog was made when the stars of Garfield and Lupino were on the ascent. They had struck sparks together in *The Sea Wolf*, and Warner executives noticed.

Although Irwin Shaw had written *The Gentle People* as a stage vehicle for Garfield, the actor didn't play the part until the film version. (Franchot Tone—a completely different sort of actor and personality—took the Broadway role.) The film was a box-office disappointment. Garfield may simply have been too unsympathetic for audiences to comfortably absorb.

Johnny Smoothie

The tone and stylistics of noir were still developing in 1941, when MGM released *Johnny Eager*. The title character (Robert Taylor, emphatic, and emphatically handsome) is an ingratiating young fellow who drives a big-city cab. He's on parole and has put together a sterling record since his release from prison. His parole officer (Henry O'Neill) couldn't be more pleased. Johnny, conscientious and deferential, has learned his lesson. Now he wants to go straight.

An errand to an almost-completed new dog track gives us a shock: Johnny owns the place. In an instant, he's out of his cabbie togs and dressed like what he is: a sleek, confident criminal whose $500,000 investment in the track won't pay off until he can finalize deals with the city's crooked politicians and fixers. When that's taken care of, the track will open, and Johnny Eager will make a fortune.

The track isn't Johnny's only enterprise. He controls the town's bookies and slots, and sends his men out to deal with unruly low-ranking associates. In a sequence that combines shock and dark humor, Johnny kills an unfaithful employee by knocking the guy cold, dousing him with liquor, and sending his car careening through a highway bridge to fall upside-down onto railroad tracks far below—where the car is demolished by a passing freight train!

Cabbie-Johnny addresses his parole officer as "Sir," but gangster-Johnny is as chilly and as dangerous as liquid nitrogen.

The film's notion of an obsequious parolee who's really a scheming, fabulously powerful criminal mastermind is frankly risible. It's secret-identity stuff, like Fantômas or the Crimson Ghost. How could responsible authorities fail to connect the two Johnny Eagers? Same name, same face—everything. In this aspect of the story, then, *Johnny Eager* is a naïve, leftover artifact of the 1930s—or earlier. Further, because Johnny moves through most of the film untroubled by conscience or doubt, he's very unlike the more familiar sort of noir protagonist. When an old friend (onetime Warner Bros. contract player Glenda Farrell, in a moving cameo) pleads with him to use his influence to get her patrolman husband moved to a beat closer to home, Johnny coolly refuses. Whatever he felt for this woman is gone, and her husband—with the ironically "lucky" badge number 711—is going to have to suffer right where he is. Johnny isn't plagued by moral conflict or existential doubt, and because he has no emotional core, he's untroubled by former or present relationships.

A naïve sociology student, Lisbeth Bard (Lana Turner), arouses Johnny's interest (she's been introduced to him because he's a model parolee). He knows, however, that he'll put himself at risk if he pursues her, because her stepfather, John Benson Farrell (Edward Arnold), is a crusading prosecutor. The situation is all the more dodgy because Farrell immediately has doubts about parolee-Johnny.

Although Lisbeth is resolutely good, she's no deep thinker. Existential angst is no more a part of her existence than it is of Johnny's. She just wants romance. Although Johnny's feelings for her eventually deepen into a simulacrum of affection, he sees her mainly as a convenient device that might be turned against her stepfather, who's finally tumbled to gangster-Johnny. In a contrived setup involving a revolver loaded with blanks, Lisbeth "kills" one of Eager's boys (Paul Stewart) on the assumption that she's saving Johnny's life. Lisbeth is wracked with guilt, of course, but Johnny feels pretty good about it—as he makes clear to Farrell: *Lay off me or I go to the cops about your daughter.*

Johnny Eager finally traffics in noir with the compromised Farrell character, who is caught between his sense of morality and his love for his daughter. Aggressive yet reluctant to move against Johnny because of Lisbeth, Farrell confronts a dire dilemma of conscience.

The other, even more potent noir figure of *Johnny Eager* is Johnny's only friend, a sweet, pathetically alcoholic attorney named Jeff Hartnett (Van Heflin). Attached to Johnny yet repulsed by the milieu in which he and Johnny move, Jeff is dedicatedly drinking himself to death. He knows he can no longer communicate with Johnny meaningfully—his own fuzzy brain and Johnny's disinclination to listen are insurmountable obstacles—so he limits himself to boozily cynical *bons mots* about the human condition.

The relationship of Johnny and Jeff isn't quite a marriage, but it's indisputably a love affair that detours around its gay subtext to complex issues of devotion and fealty. Johnny finally realizes that he has loved Jeff all along. Much of the film is adolescent, but in this it becomes boldly, unexpectedly mature.

Pricked by conscience at last, Johnny arranges for Lisbeth to come face to face with the man she supposedly killed. He wants to restore his innocence, even if by doing so he'll give Farrell a ready opportunity to crucify him.

Director Mervyn LeRoy had impeccable technical ability. The greater part of *Johnny Eager* is handled with smooth, vaguely detached assurance, but the climactic sequence, in which Johnny purposely walks into a trap set by his business partner, Halligan (Cy Kendall), combines the messy grit of Warner Bros. crime melodramas of a few years earlier with grown-up focus on a protagonist who realizes he's abused the love given him by other people. Johnny wants to be rid of Halligan, and he wants to be rid of himself, too. The sequence was shot at night by LeRoy and cinematographer Harold Rosson on a beautifully dressed section of MGM's "city street" back lot. Johnny is wounded but manages to finish off Halligan's boys and Halligan, too, who dies screaming at the bottom of a concrete stairway that leads down from the street to a locked door.

And then Johnny comes face to face with a cop (Byron Shores) who wears badge 711.

"I killed my luck."

Frank Tuttle's *This Gun for Hire* (1942), a key film in noir's thematic and stylistic development, was a star-making vehicle for a young actor named Alan Ladd. As adapted by Albert Maltz and W. R. Burnett from a 1936 Graham Greene novel called *A Gun for Sale*, it's the story of a professional killer who pursues an assignment, only to be distracted by love. He achieves the final part of his mission, but his concern for a woman who has been his hostage causes him to hesitate during his escape, and he is destroyed. But the killer, a soft-spoken, smooth-faced youth named Raven, gives a good account of himself, revealing an ability to think on his feet and improvise when details go awry.

Raven's employer is an overfed dandy named Willard Gates (Laird Cregar). Gates is mixed up in a baroque scheme to sell secret chemical equations to an enemy power (a strong hint is that it is Japan). Raven has been hired to clean up various messes, but because Gates doesn't want him around too long, he pays for the job in stolen bills. When Raven discovers that he's been tricked, he grows perturbed and sets himself the task of tracking down and killing Gates, as well as the aged chemical magnate, Brewster (Tully Marshall), who's masterminded the whole treasonous scheme.

In an amusing touch, Gates is an inveterate backer of shows and nightclub acts—and this is how we meet Ellen Graham (Veronica Lake), a blonde seductress whose act mixes singing and sleight-of-hand magic. After a variety of agreeable contrivances, including that Ellen is the girlfriend of a police lieutenant (Robert Preston) involved in the chemical case, Raven and the girl encounter each other on a train. When the cops close in, the pair retreat to a shadowy railyard and finally to a sinister, darkened gasworks. Like the hero of a movie serial, Raven gets away and beards Gates and Brewster in the chemical company's executive suite. But before the killer can make his final escape, Raven holds his fire when the girl is in danger of being hit.

This Gun for Hire was the first teaming of Alan Ladd and Veronica Lake, physically perfect diminutives whose soft-spoken personas worked in complement. (For the role of Raven, Ladd's naturally blond hair was dyed black, befitting the character's name.) The script forces us to regard the pair as islands of serene beauty in a sea of stupidity, corruption, and dull stolidity (the cop boyfriend). Although each is very different from the other, they develop a strong and mutual attraction that is considerably more than superficial. Specifically, Raven responds to Ellen's spunk and decency, and she is taken by his pathetic backstory (he was an abused child) and a belief that underneath the trench coat beats the heart of a patriot.

At the very least, Raven is a mass of contradictions. After awakening in the film's first scene, he solicitously feeds milk to a kitten and then slaps around the maid who had given the animal a swat with a towel. In the railyard, Raven happily discovers an orange tomcat. "Cats are good luck," he informs Ellen. But when the cops are momentarily very close, Raven inadvertently presses down too hard on the cat to keep it quiet. "It's dead," he says flatly. "I killed my luck."

His luck and innate cleverness are all he has, at least according to how he sees things. Except for Ellen, other people do little to arouse his better instincts.

GATES
Don't you trust me?

RAVEN
Who trusts anyone?

And later:

GATES
How do you feel when you're doing . . . this?

RAVEN
I feel fine.

VERONICA LAKE · ROBERT PRESTON

THIS GUN FOR HIRE

with LAIRD CREGAR · ALAN LADD

Although fourth-billed on this poster, Alan Ladd was the breakout performer of *This Gun for Hire* (1942). As the somnolent, superstitious hired killer Raven, Ladd intrigued audiences, who also were taken with Veronica Lake. Ladd and Lake would team up again.

B-picture stalwart Frank Tuttle made sure that, in its set pieces, *This Gun for Hire* is very strong. While at Gates's dimly lit home in the Hollywood Hills during a crashing thunderstorm, Raven plants his foot in the chest of Gates's chauffer/stooge (Marc Lawrence) and sends him on a painful tumble down the cellar stairs. At the railyard later, Raven's sleeve is hung up for a long moment on a wire as he struggles to drop out of sight. He disentangles himself the instant before a police searchlight sweeps over the spot where he had been.

A unique pleasure of *This Gun for Hire* is that it isn't pure noir or even a pure crime thriller but a recombining of conventions from various genres. Surrounded in the yard by cops and guns, Raven looks at Ellen and predicts what will happen next: "They'll move in in the morning. Every flatfoot in town." In that moment, we could be experiencing a war film or a western. Musical conventions, as when Ellen warbles her way through her nightclub act, are invoked, as well. The picture is contradictory and fascinating, and keeps the viewer a little off-balance—not least because Raven remains a sympathetic figure even after killing a police officer. And in that, we become nearly as morally compromised as our protagonist.

When he filmed *This Gun for Hire*, Ladd had been kicking around Hollywood as a bit player for nine years. Paramount liked his looks and demeanor, and director Frank Tuttle was a great booster who became a close friend. Tuttle

Case File: Alan Ladd (1913–64)

In *This Gun for Hire*, Alan Ladd's Raven is emotionally and physically scarred by punishments inflicted by an abusive aunt. Ladd's real-life childhood wasn't as dire, but it was nevertheless marked by interludes of near-poverty and emotional uncertainty.

An unusually handsome boy, Ladd stood just 4'9" as he began high school. He was self-conscious about his small stature and yet became a star high school athlete. As an adult, he stood 5'5" or 5'6", and it was no secret in Hollywood that tall actresses played their scenes opposite him while wearing flats or even standing in trenches.

Ladd was a subtle, low-key, instinctive actor who doubted his own talent and whose catastrophic imagination led him to believe that each new film assignment would be his last. *This Gun for Hire* made him a star at 29, and he was teamed three more times with diminutive Veronica Lake: in *The Glass Key*, *The Blue Dahlia*, and *Saigon*.

Ladd remained a top box-office draw throughout most of the 1940s before experiencing the inevitable dip in popularity. He came roaring back as the gunslinger *Shane* in 1953, but his star dimmed again as the 1950s moved into the '60s. Many of his later pictures are high-level melodramatic programmers.

Drinking was a longtime problem, and an "accident" with a handgun nearly took his life in 1962. In 1964, not long after completing a showy but clearly supporting role in *The Carpetbaggers*, Ladd died of an overdose of liquor and barbiturates. He was fifty years old. An investigation found that the death was accidental.

A cool enigma of the 1940s, Ladd was an intriguingly impassive presence during that highly charged decade. He is an enduring icon of noir.

and the studio stuck with Ladd after the actor came down with pneumonia when shooting was only halfway complete. They were rewarded because in the end, *This Gun for Hire* cost less than $500,000 to make and went on to gross an astonishing $12 million. It was remade, with so-so results, in 1957 by director James Cagney as *Short Cut to Hell.*

One Man, Many Faces

Jean Negulesco's *The Mask of Dimitrios* (1944) is noir-exotica that takes viewers to Eastern Europe and the edge of Asia and invites rumination on the differences between fact and fiction, myth and reality. Key to this is that the central figure isn't Dimitrios (Zachary Scott) but a mild, diffident mystery novelist named Cornelius Leyden (Peter Lorre). Leyden has made his modest fortune churning out fiction, but now he's ready to do nonfiction. In Istanbul, he's intrigued when police officials invite him to view a waterlogged corpse identified as Dimitrios Makropoulos, a Greek national and onetime fig packer who transformed himself into a much-feared smuggler, assassin, and spy. Leyden wants to know more and travels across Europe to locate people who had known Dimitrios, and who are willing to talk about him.

Leyden meets Mr. Peters (Sydney Greenstreet), a man of uncertain occupation who thinks Dimitrios may still be alive. And that would suit Mr. Peters just fine, because Dimitrios once cheated him. Piece by piece, through the reminiscences of Mr. Peters and others, we discover that Peters is right. The scoundrel Dimitrios is very much alive.

Naturally, Dimitrios doesn't wish to meet either man.

Deeply separated by basic mindset but united by related goals, Leyden and Mr. Peters surprise each other by becoming convivial partners. Leyden is eventually able to evaluate Dimitrios in the flesh, and Mr. Peters achieves his much-anticipated reckoning with the man he hates.

In the bold design of Frank Gruber's script (based on the 1939 Eric Ambler novel *A Coffin for Dimitrios*), the title character is absent from the screen for long stretches. The story's focus is on Leyden, the fiction writer now absorbed with fact, and Mr. Peters, the cold-blooded pragmatist whose imagination doesn't extend to the make-believe. Leyden wants to learn whether the legend of Dimitrios is real. Mr. Peters knows the legend has been grossly romanticized. Other former associates see Dimitrios as different things: lover, betrayer, fellow schemer. The "mask" of the title refers not simply to artifice and deception but to people's interpretation of the self-created man behind that mask.

Dimitrios is seen mainly in reminiscences shared with Leyden. (This way, Zachary Scott, a screen newcomer, did not have to shoulder the weight of exposition. Dimitrios appears only in the story's "good parts.") Mise-en-scène is heavily faux exotic, as in an earlier Warner film, *Casablanca,* and encourages us to fill in the details of place that helped shape Dimitrios. The work of art director Ted

Peter Lorre, Sydney Greenstreet, and Geraldine Fitzgerald are the *Three Strangers* (1946), an unlikely alliance that, because of each person's innate ability to act freely and make awful decisions, does not hold.

Smith and set designer Walter Tilford is sterling, and Arthur Edeson's cinematography is so smokily moody you can almost smell the incense.

Director Jean Negulesco was a polymath with experience as a painter, stage designer, screenwriter, and director of lightweight shorts. *The Mask of Dimitrios* is his first feature. (Although credited as director of a minor 1941 picture called *Singapore Woman*, he was removed from that project well before its completion.) Although some film historians have criticized Negulesco for encouraging a subdued performance from Lorre, the approach is just right. It was important that Leyden be established as a bit of a dreamer, for whom this new intrigue and danger is unfamiliar and disconcerting. A bombastic Lorre would have destroyed the character's vulnerability and thematic resonance.

Uniquely, the film is dominated by character actors. Neither Lorre nor Greenstreet was a traditional leading man, and Zachary Scott, though handsome, was someone who might be cast today as a crooked lobbyist. Producer Henry Blanke and studio chief Jack Warner were enthusiastic about the elevation of Lorre and Greenstreet, who worked in *Dimitrios* with such fine character

Case File: Sydney Greenstreet (1879–1954)

Famously, this imposingly assembled star character actor didn't make his first film until he was sixty-two. But Greenstreet, a Brit who gave up on a career in business while a very young man, made his London stage debut at twenty-three and was on Broadway at twenty-five. He was occupied exclusively by stage work until 1941, when he appeared in a very important early noir as the endlessly scheming Kasper Gutman, a man obsessed with *The Maltese Falcon*. Warner Bros. signed the actor and made excellent use of him, particularly in *Falcon* and three other teamings with star character actor Peter Lorre: the noir classics *The Mask of Dimitrios* and *Three Strangers*, and an effective non-noir, *The Verdict*.

Frankly obese, Greenstreet may seem to have been an unlikely candidate for stardom, but audiences relished his deep, ruminative voice and the rolling laugh that began somewhere deep within his diaphragm. He was a good-looking man with intent, even hawkish features, and was unmatched in portrayals of formidable connivers who have the saving grace of a (jaundiced) sense of humor.

Greenstreet's unique legacy to noir is obvious enough; he's significant, also, because he showed that seriously overweight actors could become featured players and even stars (as witness Britain's Francis L. Sullivan and Hollywood's Victor Buono).

players as Victor Francen, Steven Geray, Florence Bates, Eduardo Ciannelli, and John Abbott. Special mention must be made of square-jawed beauty Faye Emerson, who is at once tough and pathetic as a woman whose association with Dimitrios has transformed her from an ingenuous charmer into the hardened, world-weary person who speaks with Leyden. Dimitrios is poison.

Your Mess, Your Fault

Lorre and Greenstreet worked together six times, three times as a costarring team. *Three Strangers* (1946), written mainly by the uncredited John Collier and directed by Jean Negulesco, is the summit of that creative partnership. Complex and purposely obtuse, the film also is a perfect schematic of the noir genre, a carefully conceived template for disaster.

In prewar London of 1938, a stylish and intense woman named Crystal Shackleford (Geraldine Fitzgerald) enlists two men she does not know, alcoholic layabout Johnny West (Peter Lorre) and ambitious barrister Jerome K. Arbutny (Sydney Greenstreet), as her partners in a quasimystical scheme to win the Grand National sweepstakes. Crystal is a devotee of the Chinese goddess Kwan Yin, from whom she has divined that "three strangers" can win the sweepstakes if one of them is a believer and all swear to equal shares of the winnings. (Arthur Edeson's moody lighting makes the goddess figurine appear almost alive.)

The deal is made—with good humor by the men and dead seriousness by the woman—and the three strangers part. As the day of the Grand National approaches, each carries on with his or her own life, to disastrous effect. Johnny

Case File: Peter Lorre (1904–64)

This Hungarian character actor is the bracing dash of Tabasco in numerous noir thrillers. Lorre was educated from childhood in Austria and did stage work there and in Germany and Switzerland. In 1931, he was cast by leading German director Fritz Lang as the psychopathic killer of children in *M*, giving an alternately subdued and frenzied central performance that electrified audiences around the world. Like Lang, Lorre departed Germany as the Nazis consolidated power, and settled in Hollywood in 1935. A featured player from the start, he did lively work as a freelancer for Universal, MGM, RKO, Columbia, and Republic. He went to Fox for eight glossy and entertaining "Mr. Moto" mysteries during 1937–39 and shortly after was signed by Warner Bros., where he remained under contract for more than five years. Lorre's first Warner picture was *The Maltese Falcon*, a seminal noir that allowed him to solidify one aspect of his screen persona: the fractious little man with the dangerous little gun.

Lorre was often amusing on-screen, but the chuckles stopped when he played out-and-out villains (such as the sadists of Columbia's *Island of Doomed Men* [1940] and Warner's fifth-column thriller *All Through the Night* [1941]). Perhaps no other actor has so successfully exploited a small stature, a soft speaking voice, puppy-dog eyes, and European exoticism to such entertainingly disconcerting effect. And he could be sympathetic too, as in Robert Florey's unusual crime-suspense thriller *The Face Behind the Mask* (1941).

Weight gain that began to show itself after 1946 altered Lorre's appearance considerably, but he remained popular and very busy. Late in his life, he won a new generation of fans with starring roles in comic-horror thrillers directed by Roger Corman and others for American International.

Lorre's other noir work includes *Stranger on the Third Floor*, *The Mask of Dimitrios* (with screen partner Sydney Greenstreet), *Three Strangers* (with Greenstreet), *Black Angel*, *The Chase*, and *Quicksand*.

is convicted for a murder he didn't commit and is sentenced to die. Arbutny swindles a client out of a great sum and becomes frantic to replace the money before his perfidy is discovered. And Crystal struggles to save her marriage after discovering that her husband has a mistress. On the day of the race, the three strangers are reunited at Crystal's flat. One of them walks away, guiltless. Another is dead, and the third succumbs to hysterical insanity.

The genius of Collier's screenplay (taken from a story by John Huston; late-arriving Howard Koch did some rewrite) is that although *Three Strangers* initially appears to be a monument to determinism, it develops with complete conviction and naturalness into a confirmation of free will. Early on, the deterministic aspects are strong. Repeated insert shots of the Kwan Yin idol Crystal consults on her mantel suggest irresistible occult power. Crystal is a believer, and like a planet, she draws satellites into her orbit. Her life is partially overlapped by Johnny's, and Arbutny's life partially overlaps the other two. No matter whose perspective you take, you have three lives, separate and yet irresistibly linked.

The story progresses via discrete narratives that look more closely at each of the three strangers, and the other lives that intersect theirs. The cast of players expands, giving each of the strangers various antagonists, lovers, and betrayers. We observe the courses of these linked lives and finally see that individual predicaments aren't the product of fate but of poor choices. Crystal has a ferocious belief in Kwan Yin, but her husband's infidelity wasn't predetermined. As he (Alan Napier) explains, it just happened. And although Crystal believes otherwise, it's not been predetermined that she'll win her husband back, either.

Johnny's most serious shortcoming, lassitude, causes him to become mixed up with a murderous thief, Fallon (Robert Shayne). In other words, he's in trouble because of things he unwisely failed to do, and not because of something that was written in the stars. When Johnny is exonerated, it isn't because of fate or an intervention of gods but because of a risk taken by a fine young woman (Joan Lorring) who loves him. (Yes, Peter Lorre is the film's romantic lead.)

Arbutny reasons that if he turns on the charm, he can marry a wealthy client, Lady Rhea (played with a wink by Rosalind Ivan), whom he's swindled, getting himself off the hook for fraud and landing in clover in the bargain. But the wealthy widow turns down Arbutny's proposal because, as she's already made clear, she regularly communicates with her late husband and couldn't possibly abandon him. There's nothing mystical about that, either. It just happens that Lady Rhea has elected to be goofily idiotic.

The charming and soft-spoken Crystal Shackleford we meet at the beginning of the film is soon revealed as a volcano of strident self-interest that even Kwan Yin couldn't control. Crystal discourages her husband's mistress with a simple, rational discussion but reacts with shrill impatience when Arbutny begs for early payment of his share of the winning ticket. A moment later, the heavy idol is in the barrister's hands, and Crystal is dead. Arbutny cradles the idol and swears he had no will of his own, and that his hands acted on their own accord. *Three Strangers* insists that we understand the absurdity of Arbutny's claim.

Because the tale is set in 1938, it's not obligated to invoke the individual powerlessness that comes with war. Nothing was going to interfere with the script's insistence on choice.

Jean Negulesco's direction is measured and elegant. Although the film has a sharp, visceral power, events and characterizations unfold gradually, with a narrative grace that was unusual even for 1946. Negulesco gave editor George Amy the coverage needed to hold on individual cuts for a beat longer than you might anticipate. The consequence is a film that is at once disquieting and languorous. It's really quite elegant.

The Destination Is Death

Ernest Hemingway's short story "The Killers" appeared in *Scribner's* magazine in 1927. Short indeed at just eight magazine pages, the tale is set at a diner that is invaded by a pair of men who announce they've come to town to kill a local, the Swede. A diner customer (Nick Adams, Hemingway's occasional alter ego) escapes to the Swede's rooming house to sound the alert and is shocked when the Swede wearily says he's simply going to wait for the killers to find him.

And there Hemingway's story ends.

The obvious challenge faced by screenwriter Anthony Veiller and his uncredited cowriters, Richard Brooks and John Huston, was how to transform what would have been five minutes of screen time into a feature film. They did it with layers of flashbacks that address the central question of Hemingway's story: Why does Swede (Burt Lancaster) wish to die?

The Killers (1946) was a breakthrough project for director Robert Siodmak, a German émigré who had been working in Hollywood since 1941. His distinctly European fatalism and visual sense bring considerable energy to the pegs of the story: Swede's love for a heist man's girlfriend, Kitty (Ava Gardner); a quarter-million-dollar payroll robbery that is partly bungled; and more than one double-cross. The proxy for the audience is Riordan (Edmond O'Brien), an inveterately curious insurance investigator whose company has a payout policy on the Swede.

Riordan unpeels the Swede's story like an onion, tantalizing us with seemingly unrelated bits of information: the Swede has left a $2,500 bequest to a hotel chambermaid he met only once six years before; Lubinsky, a Philadelphia cop (Sam Levene), grew up with the Swede, liked him, and once put the pinch on him for robbery; the cop's wife (Virginia Christine) had been the Swede's girlfriend until the two of them visited a party where the Swede first laid eyes on Kitty. The Swede once saved Kitty from arrest by claiming that the stolen brooch she wore came from him.

After the robbery, Kitty conspires with the mastermind (and her lover), a crumb named Colfax (Albert Dekker), to cheat Swede and the rest of the gang of their shares. Well, Swede manages to gain the upper hand and walks off with the cash, but *another* double-cross leaves him without a dime. Finally, after the passing of years, Swede is located by the hired killers of the title (Charles McGraw and William Conrad), whose task is to shut Swede up for good.

But Colfax isn't done. He tries yet another double-cross, this time on the investigator Riordan. Colfax's earlier attempt to bump him off, in a crowded restaurant (a kinetic sequence with potent use of dolly and tracking shots), failed, so the mastermind makes his last play. Bullets zing around the inside of Colfax's mansion like angry bees, and Kitty is left out to dry.

Much of *The Killers* unfolds in low illumination, often at night, with carefully placed key lights, but the robbery sequence—which plays out to Riordan's voice-over—is shot documentary-style in overcast daylight, from a high, omniscient point of view. The four gunmen enter the plant's grounds by strolling in with the rest of the employees; they wind their way around and up the stairs to the payroll office, where they grab the money. Loot in hand, they walk with a truck that is leaving the plant and head for separate cars in the parking lot. The armed guard at the gate finally tumbles to what's unfolding and fires, first at one car and then another. Riordan (still doing voice-over) is shot in the groin—a particularly unpleasant detail.

In a typical treatment, the heist would be filmed at ground level, from the points of view of the participants and victims, but Siodmak's elevated camera eye is coolly dispassionate, and for good reason. After all, *The Killers* isn't about the heist but about the Swede's obsession with Kitty and his plan to make her his own. He's a dreamer. So is Kitty, and so is Colfax. They all dream, and a couple of them think too much. Sometimes, crime is easy. It's the aftermath that's usually a bitch.

The title characters (played by Charles McGraw and William Conrad) show up in the film's first sequence, a nighttime tableau that's pregnant with menace, thanks to Siodmak's effectively unhurried pacing, the oddly low-key demeanors of the assassins, and the frightening ease with which they bully the counterman

Robert Siodmak's *The Killers* (1946): Swede (Burt Lancaster) is obsessed with Kitty (Ava Gardner). Kitty, though, isn't interested in the purity of romance. She just wants the money that Swede and others have labored to steal.

Case File: Burt Lancaster (1913–94)

This rugged, imperiously handsome actor had just a dab of stage experience when he was given the central role in *The Killers* (1946). Rather like the baseball phenom who goes from high school to the majors without a day in the minors, Lancaster became a star immediately. He was laudably versatile and managed his career well, establishing his own production company in 1948 and showing a willingness to occasionally spoof his athletic and charismatic persona (see *The Crimson Pirate* and *The Flame and the Arrow*).

But Lancaster's work in noir is dramatic and dark. Much of his effectiveness in the genre comes from the nature of his physical presence, which in most non-noir movies assures a good outcome. How can anyone as handsome and appealing end up back-handed by fate? Because Lancaster wasn't afraid to be unconventional, the characters he plays in *The Killers*, *Sorry, Wrong Number*, *Criss Cross*, and *The Sweet Smell of Success* arrive at places where they'd rather not be and because of mistakes of their own making. But then, that's noir, isn't it? Lancaster understood that perfectly.

He excelled at blunt melodrama the likes of *Brute Force* (a rugged prison film that's classified as noir by some) and in such reasonably complex dramas as *From Here to Eternity*, *Elmer Gantry*, *Judgment at Nuremberg*, and *Birdman of Alcatraz*. As Lancaster passed fifty, he became increasingly adventurous, starring in some superior existential dramas (*The Train*, *The Swimmer*, *The Gypsy Moths*), large-scale westerns (*The Professionals*, *Buffalo Bill and the Indians*), and art-house dramas (*The Leopard*, *Atlantic City*, *1900*). We expect living legends to live forever, so Lancaster's death, though not premature, nevertheless seemed to have arrived far too soon.

(Harry Hayden). High-contrast photography by Woody Bredell throws peculiar shadows and highlights that emphasize the killers' creepy professionalism and the vulnerability of anyone who catches their attention.

The Killers came fairly early in Ava Gardner's career and kept her going on the fast track to stardom. Blessed with what used to be called animal magnetism, she had depth that was too often ignored or underappreciated. Burt Lancaster, a former Broadway player and ex-trapeze artist in his film debut, electrified audiences with his portrayal of the resolute but faintly dim Swede. He was not the first choice for the role (the colorless Wayne Morris and Sonny Tufts were considered first), but few other actors could have matched Lancaster's restless, very physical presence. Producer Mark Hellinger had originally signed Lancaster for a picture called *Desert Fury*, but *The Killers* came to theaters first. A star was born.

Personalities and motives are on collision courses throughout *The Killers*, and in retrospect Swede's scheme seems doomed from the start. When Riordan meets with Swede's old cellmate, he learns that Swede often gazed from his prison window at the heavens. "Him and me," the cellmate recalls, "we had some good talks about the stars."

But the Swede forgot, if he ever knew at all, that the stars are not always in alignment.

Home Is Where the Danger Is

Some sixteen million men and women who served in the U.S. armed forces during World War II were demobbed during 1944–46. Job and housing shortages were epidemic, and returning vets often felt at odds with civilian society. The atmosphere of *The Blue Dahlia* (1946)—a much-anticipated reteaming of Alan Ladd and Veronica Lake—is frantically celebratory, with wartime victory encouraging people to drop their inhibitions and drink too much, dance too amorously, and play the phonograph too loud. It's a society that's at once exhausted and energized, and living on the thin edge of hysteria.

But every vet was hopeful of a better life. As scripted by Raymond Chandler, the picture is, superficially, a "buddy" story about three Navy pals who leave the service and reenter civilian life together. George (Hugh Beaumont) is a rugged, cool-headed attorney. Johnny (Ladd) is a combat hero who hopes to start over with his oddball wife, Helen (Doris Dowling). The wild card is Buzz (William Bendix), a burly, sometimes amiable fella who's come home with a steel plate in his skull.

In Johnny's absence, his dipso wife has been carrying on with Eddie Howard (Howard Da Silva), a slick, connected character who owns a Sunset Strip nightclub called The Blue Dahlia. (In January 1947, nine months after the release of *The Blue Dahlia*, LA would be fascinated by the "Black Dahlia" murder case). Johnny becomes aware of the affair and makes plans to leave Helen, who has a gift for antagonizing just about everybody. When Helen turns up dead at home, shot at point-blank range by Johnny's .45, Johnny is suspect number one.

We see for ourselves that Johnny was nowhere around when the shooting took place (he's been accepting a ride in the rain from Joyce Harwood [Lake], a good-hearted stranger who happens to be Eddie Howard's estranged wife).

Raymond Chandler indulged in a small bit of boldness for the day, developing *The Blue Dahlia* as a four-sided triangle in which the two principals are in love but married to morally flawed spouses who are the paramours of each other. That's even more contrived than the plate in Buzz's head, but it plays out interestingly enough, with Helen full of spite and angry self-loathing, and Eddie sharply amoral with his million-dollar wardrobe and his mob partner, Leo (Don Costello, peculiarly sinister in heavy spectacles).

So who knocked off Helen? Maybe it was Johnny's pal Buzz. When Buzz hears jukebox swing ("monkey music," he calls it), his head throbs and he becomes inclined to violence. Helen plays a lot of monkey music. Loudly. Buzz might have killed her.

Yes, Buzz is a contrived creation but a lively one, too, who continually stokes the fires of aggression. He picks a fight with a music-loving soldier. He resists Johnny and George's repeated suggestions that he calm down. At a police station, he takes perverse delight in needling a detective, and later pronounces—in intense close-up—"I hate cops."

Case File: William Bendix (1906–64)

A character actor who became an important star, William Bendix was an intriguing combination of the physical (he played semi-professional baseball) and the cultured (his father was a conductor of the Metropolitan Opera Orchestra). He worked in regional theater in New York and New Jersey, and went to Broadway in 1939. Three years later, he was a busy film actor, taking roles as goons, comic primitives, and wisecracking friends to the hero. He was especially at home in war films and urban melodramas, and starred in one of the most transparently sanitized of all biopics, *The Babe Ruth Story*. The fact that Bendix achieved his most lasting fame in comedy, as the star of the radio and television incarnations of *The Life of Riley*, is testament to his versatility; in his noir work, he occupies a small, spooky range between unpleasant and monstrous. Playing an amiable sadist, he nearly walks off with *The Glass Key* (in one of numerous roles opposite his close friend Alan Ladd), and makes strong impressions in *The Blue Dahlia* and *The Dark Corner*.

Eddie seems too obvious a suspect. George is a little unreadable and thus hard to figure. Then there's Dad (Will Wright), the aging, bitter house dick at the bungalow court. Dry and wizened, he's sick and tired of his twenty-eight bucks a week, his cheap cigars, and the loathing he gets from every tenant.

Despite the ripe melodrama, *The Blue Dahlia* has a light, almost amiable tone that is cleverly undercut by some key sequences. One is minor but colorful, when Johnny is expected to pay a "helpful citizen" (Frank Faylen) ten bucks for having steered him to a crummy hotel room in the city with no rooms to spare. It's a revealing portrait of the new, postwar predators.

Heavy drama arrives in the form of a major revelation concerning Johnny and Helen's young son, Dickie, who died while Johnny was overseas. Helen has led Johnny to believe that the boy died of illness, but in a fit of pique she spitefully reveals that she caused his death when she loaded him into the car while she was drunk. Dickie's life was ended in a "car smash." If Johnny has a real motive for murder, this is it.

A particularly stylish sequence that's effectively at odds with much of the rest of the movie is Johnny's kidnapping at the hands of Eddie's associate Leo and a stooge (Walter Sande). Johnny doesn't go to the deserted country house easily, and during a rousing fight he injures Leo's foot. Later, the trussed Johnny comes out of unconsciousness. Director George Marshall (who was equally adept at drama and knockabout comedy during his very long career) and cinematographer Lionel Liden shot much of *The Blue Dahlia* in bright or medium light, but for this sequence the room is crisscrossed in shadow. With the camera at floor level, Johnny's upper body is in profile, dominating the foreground of the frame. A table occupies the middle ground, and beyond it is Leo, still nursing his badly damaged foot in a pan of hot water. Johnny gets his hands on the table's legs and upends the thing with a loud crash—sending the sharp edge right onto Leo's foot. Leo howls as if mortally wounded. It's one of noir's better explications of physical pain.

As in *This Gun for Hire*, Lake and Ladd are an appealing, natural-seeming pair. She isn't the actor Ladd is, but she has screen presence that's nearly the equal of his. Small, beautiful, and well formed, the two of them look like the handsome couple on top of a wedding cake. In the midst of amorality and violence, they're endearing.

Pretty Poison

All his life, Eric Stanton (Dana Andrews) has been running away: from fights as a child, from responsibility as an adult. But after he's tossed off a bus in Walton, California, about 150 miles south of San Francisco, he falls hard for a hash house waitress named Stella (Linda Darnell), one of two title characters in Otto Preminger's *Fallen Angel* (1947). Stella is gorgeous and immune to Stanton's small charms. She dates and takes gifts from a variety of men who frequent the diner: Judd (Charles Bickford), a retired New York City cop who's come to Walton for his health, and Adkins (Bruce Cabot), the fellow who comes around to service the diner's jukebox. And then there's Pop (Percy Kilbride), the diner's owner, who gives Stella quiet adoration while putting up with her crummy work ethic.

Stella deserves none of this attention. She's easy on the eyes but is a slack, belligerent dame who goes out of her way to insult customers and the men who desire her.

Stanton, who has never moved in refined circles, is nuts for her. And he's just her type. Late in the film he hides in the shadows near the diner's entrance, backed up against signs that say "BEER Peanuts Ice Cream Popcorn." That's who Stanton seems to be, a beer and popcorn kind of guy, so he's perfect for Stella's peanuts-and-ice-cream kind of woman.

But Stanton also becomes intrigued with one of the town's pillars, June Mills (Alice Faye), an introverted blonde beauty whose looks are matched only by her bankroll. June's older sister, Clara (Anne Revere), has serious (and well-founded) doubts about Stanton, so much of the narrative is a sort of tug-of-war between the grift and respectability.

Harry Kleiner's script (from the 1945 novel by Marty Holland) develops a dangerous parallel course as Stanton simultaneously woos June and tries to make Stella. Finally, in an act of mad impulse, Stanton spirits June to San Francisco and marries her. And June, as kind as she is guileless, promises him that all of her money is now his, too.

Significantly, Stanton does not consummate the marriage—just the sort of quasicontroversial twist that inevitably tickled Preminger, a born instigator.

The parallel course continues but now in unexpected ways. Stanton is surprised to find himself falling for his bride—and deeply concerned when Stella is discovered murdered, her temple crushed by a heavy instrument.

Water seeks its own level, which may explain how Stella (Linda Darnell) and Stanton (Dana Andrews) find each other in Otto Preminger's *Fallen Angel* (1947). Stella is looking for a meal ticket to take her out of the hash house and into respectability. Stanton wants to abandon the peripatetic life of the grift. But Stanton has to deal with Stella's other suitors and his growing attraction to the wealth of another woman.

The balance of *Fallen Angel* is a reptilian contest between the retired cop Judd and local suspects, including Pop, Stanton, and the jukebox man, Adkins. Or perhaps the killer isn't a man at all.

Fallen Angel is about longing and, more specifically, aspiration. Stella wants the home that will let the world believe she's not really cheap. Stanton wants money and, later, love. June wants companionship and love. And half the men in town, it seems, aspire to possess Stella.

One bitterly piquant aspect of the casting of Linda Darnell, arguably the most beautiful Hollywood actress of the 1940s, is that her conception of Stella defies our expectations about beauty. We yearn to believe that exceptionally beautiful women are sweet and kind and that they possess elegance—either hereditary or carefully cultivated—that further distinguishes them. Stella defies all of that. She's selfish, coarse, and inconsiderate. Her face is stunningly beautiful, but it's a sensual mask of defiance that's never in repose. If she has a redeeming quality, it's her blunt honesty, but she's honest mainly about herself and what she wants: a decent husband, a home, children, security. Her honesty is just a manifestation of her appallingly self-centered attitude; the feelings of others are nothing to her.

Dana Andrews, always perfectly cast in noir, is typically stolid yet complex. He's tormented by his past, and he's certainly weary of existing with just a dollar in his pocket. It isn't just that he's unhappy about being broke but that his financial condition is a constant reminder of his failures. In Stella, he sees the possibility of redemption as man. In June, he finds validation as a person.

Director Otto Preminger (doing the first of four pictures he would make with Darnell and the second of four with Andrews), working with cinematographer Joseph LaShelle, directed with urgent aggressiveness, dominating the pre-Scope 1.37:1 frame with an element (most usually a human face) displayed in very tight close-up to one side or the other and balanced by slightly less emphatic close-ups that fill in much of the space leading to the frame's middle ground. The technique puts objects and people right in our laps and increases the tale's emotional urgency.

Preminger's camera also sweeps and pans with sensible grace (everything is done in service to the story), and LaShelle lights many scenes so that they are simultaneously shadowed and edged in a nimbus of light, as when June reclines on her modest honeymoon bed. Other moments are less elegiac, as when Judd carefully pulls on a kidskin glove to beat from Adkins an admission that he gave Stella a watch that was found on her body. The gloved hand is large in the frame, and we stare with dread anticipation.

June is made of better stuff than Judd and most of the others. "Then love alone can make the fallen angel rise," she hopefully quotes to Stanton, "for only two together can enter paradise."

In the end, Stanton's better nature wins out. June takes her husband's arm and asks, "Where to?"

Stanton answers, "Home."

A Prescription for the Doctor

As expressed in Vincent Sherman's *Nora Prentiss* (1947), the wish of the central male figure isn't to create a home but to escape one. Diffident and mild-mannered Dr. Richard Talbot (Kent Smith) has a thriving San Francisco practice and some renown as a surgeon. He dresses conservatively, speaks in low, polite tones, and has a painfully precise mustache. He shares a beautiful (but unostentatious) home with two pleasant, well-scrubbed teens (Wanda Hendrix and Robert Arthur) and his maddeningly proper wife, Lucy (Rosemary de Camp). The couple's relationship is classic passive-aggressive. Lucy has established that she likes Talbot to be home by the same hour each evening. He complies, engaging her in superficial dinner table chitchat while simultaneously ignoring her. This apparently satisfies Lucy, who rewards Talbot with thin smiles and mostly unintentional condescension. Whatever passion the couple may have shared is as dead as petrified wood. Talbot is bored.

Good God, is he bored.

The script by Richard Nash and Philip MacDonald shakes things up when Talbot brings nightclub singer Nora Prentiss (Ann Sheridan) into his downtown office after witnessing an accident that has left Nora with a small injury to her leg. Nora is young, glamorous, and wry. She has a knowing intelligence, and she dresses smashingly (all due credit to Warner Bros. costumer Travilla). When Talbot dabs at Nora's naked thigh, you'd think he'd never seen a thigh before. Nora notices his reticence and is amused by it. We're amused, too, and a little worried.

If *Nora Prentiss* were a typical noir, our worry would be justified. Nora would be a voracious, unprincipled man-eater who would steal Talbot from his wife just because she could. But in an important twist, Nora is kind, principled, and emotionally honest. Her view of life is slightly jaundiced (there's no doubt that she's been around), but she has no interest in taking things that don't belong to her. And she's not looking for a man. To the contrary, she maintains a light relationship with her infatuated employer, a dark-haired smoothie named Phil Dinardo (Robert Alda). Twist number two is that Dinardo is a sweetheart instead of a heel.

After resisting for a while, Nora lets go and falls in love with Dr. Talbot, who already is completely devoted to her. Subsequent plot developments include Talbot's inability to ask his wife for a divorce, a patient who conveniently drops dead in Talbot's office, a car, a can of gasoline, and a cliff.

Talbot takes Nora to a New York hotel, shaves his mustache, and calls himself Thompson. This confuses Nora (twist number three is that Talbot has told her nothing about the identity switch beforehand), but she's patient because Talbot says he doesn't want any publicity. Come again?

The campy tone that began with the useful corpse turns dark when Talbot becomes a paranoid recluse who won't leave the hotel room. His clothes become permanently rumpled, and he stops shaving.

Now *Nora* is bored.

The high melodrama continues: Talbot jealously conks Dinardo on the head and races through traffic. It's night and cops give chase. In Central Park, Talbot collides head-on with a truck.

Fire. Facial burns. Emergency plastic surgery.

The cops ask: *Hey, Thompson, what did you do with Talbot?*

In one of those life-changing moments that happen only in the movies, Talbot is put on trial for murdering himself.

Life is no longer boring.

No one in court, not even Lucy or Talbot's partner (Bruce Bennett), recognizes him. (Perc Westmore's burn makeup is disquieting, but Talbot, to our eyes, is still clearly Talbot. Nevertheless, Sherman and cinematographer James Wong

Howe made a brave stab at convincing us otherwise by shooting Kent Smith in deep shadow and with his head perpetually lowered onto his chest.)

Nora is a presence in the gallery. Although Talbot's face is altered, his voice is unchanged, and so we wonder why Nora doesn't say a word. Talbot and Thompson are the same person, but Nora remains mum.

Nora Prentiss is the great guilty pleasure of film noir. Slick and glossy, it begins as a woman's picture that becomes noir before transmogrifying into a quasi-horror tale. The invariably incisive Ann Sheridan, in one of her most layered roles, adds an earthy sheen. Skilled general-purpose actor and occasional lead Kent Smith captures the complicated inner turmoil of a repressed man. Although Talbot is neither strong nor particularly sympathetic, he rings true as a sexually inexperienced addle-brain.

Nora Prentiss devotes a lot of energy to establishing the irresistible passion that consumes Nora and Talbot (a key sequence is dominated by the symbolic flames of a fireplace), so it's absurd that when the lovers arrive at the New York hotel they take—and stay in—separate hotel rooms. This silliness was mandated, of course, by the film industry's Production Code. In 1947, America just wasn't ready to allow Hollywood to properly film this kind of tale.

Human despite himself

Lucky Gagin (Robert Montgomery), the intensely dominant character of *Ride the Pink Horse* (1947), hardly seems lucky at all—or if he is, he cares not to acknowledge that luck. After arriving in the New Mexico town of San Pablo, Gagin establishes himself as a brusque, unpleasant guy who has shown up to blackmail a gangster who killed Gagin's pal Shorty—who died because he, too, had attempted the same blackmail. Gagin pushes around desk clerks, insults an aging federal cop (Art Smith) who has an eye on the gangster, and dismisses a pretty Mexican girl (Wanda Hendrix) by calling her "Sitting Bull" (amusingly and crassly mixing up his ethnicities). He looks at the girl's plain peasant garb and says, "You look like something out of a sideshow. . . . You look like Zip What-is-it" (a famous sideshow "pinhead").

When he can't immediately meet the gangster, Gagin gut-punches the guy's male secretary and subsequently shows himself immune to the charms of the gangster's woman, Marjorie (Andrea King). Gagin is as focused as a tracer bullet, and when he and the gangster, Frank Hugo (Fred Clark), finally meet, there's virtually no prelude, no dance. As Gagin explains, it's as simple as this: Hugo will hand Gagin $30,000 in cash to purchase a canceled check that proves Hugo had been shortchanging the government during the war. If Hugo refuses, Gagin will turn the check over to the feds.

The war figures importantly in Gagin's recent past. He makes occasional, sour references to his time in New Guinea, where he served with Shorty. He feels shortchanged, having risked his neck for Uncle Sam and gotten very little in return. As he informs the federal cop, Retz, he's unmoved by calls to patriotism.

It slowly becomes clear that Gagin is less a human being than a creature on a mission. He's loyal to the memory of his pal—or maybe he's just pissed off—but beyond that he shows no capacity for human connection. Even the money is almost secondary: Hugo is worth millions, and yet Gagin is content to insist on a paltry $30,000. He calls Pila "Sitting Bull" more than once and isn't impressed by further overtures from Marjorie. But Pila has carefully observed the other woman.

PILA
She's very beautiful.

GAGIN
Yeah. They usually are.

PILA
She has very nice clothes. And diamonds.

GAGIN
Diamonds. And a dead fish where her heart oughta be.
I've known a lot of them babies. . . . You understand what a
human being is?

PILA
Yes.

GAGIN
Well, they're not human beings. They're dead fish with a lotta
perfume on 'em.
You touch 'em and you always get stung. You always lose!

The legendary Ben Hecht and Charles Lederer adapted the 1946 Dorothy B. Hughes novel. Their dialogue snaps and crackles. Gagin seems a lost soul, and yet despite himself he inspires loyalty from Pila and from Pancho (Thomas Gomez), a laughingly philosophical poor man who makes a tenuous living as the owner of a small carousel (a real item that was purchased for the film and reassembled on the set). Gagin is in San Pablo during Fiesta, a noisy bacchanal. The modest carousel seems the only innocent diversion in town.

When Hugo decides not to pay the blackmail, Marjorie leads Gagin into an ambush outside a club, watching with sadistic pleasure as Gagin is badly stabbed in the upper back before breaking the arm of one attacker and killing the other. (Only the beginning of the tussle is shown; the rest is left to our imaginations.)

Suddenly vulnerable, Gagin is sheltered by Pila and Pancho, who hide him beneath a blanket on the turning carousel. When more of Hugo's goons show up, Pancho absorbs a terrible beating but doesn't give Gagin away. It wouldn't be right to betray this refreshingly direct man who has bought him drinks.

Following the wounded Gagin's climactic confrontation with Hugo, the world slowly begins to wobble back to what passes for normal.

Two or three days later, Gagin tells Retz he doesn't know how to say goodbye to Pila. Like Rosebud in *Citizen Kane*, the carousel is symbolic of innocence. The lost soul Gagin has rediscovered his humanity. He frets about Pila's feelings.

But how to say goodbye to her?

The girl takes care of it. "Goodbye," she says simply.

Robert Montgomery began his career as a film actor in 1929 at twenty-five, became a decorated Navy war veteran, and dabbled in behind-the-camera work when he directed himself and John Wayne (without credit) in portions of *They Were Expendable* (1945). He directed himself again in his complete, credited effort *Lady in the Lake* (1946; see Chapter 3). *Ride the Pink Horse* followed a year later.

There is nothing timorous or flatfooted about Montgomery's work as a director. After a brief opening montage of a speeding bus, *Ride the Pink Horse* continues with a bravura three-and-a-half-minute single take—no cuts—as Gagin steps from the bus and enters the train station. He looks around and then sits. He opens a case on his lap, extracts a gun and piece of paper and then walks to a bank of rental lockers. He opens a locker and puts the piece of paper inside, takes the key, and walks to a gum machine. He briefly chews the gum and then uses it to stick the key to the back edge of a waiting-room map. Gagin leaves the station and asks directions outside. During all of this, the camera is tracking, panning, moving in and out on Montgomery, looking at him full-figure and peering over his shoulder. Cinematographer Russell Metty had to compensate on the fly for changes in exterior and interior light. The train station and the area outside swarm with carefully choreographed extras. For most viewers, the effect is subliminal. They don't specifically notice that there are no cuts, but the sequence makes narrative sense because it shows a character who goes about his business smoothly, with a minimum of movement and no hesitation. Almost without realizing it, we accept that Gagin is a determined man and one not to be trifled with.

Other moments are even better. After Gagin is stabbed, Pila searches for him. Montgomery engineers a close-up, from Pila's point of view, of a bloodied hand that sticks from a heavy bush. Inside the foliage, Gagin's face, also in tight close-up, is mashed into the dirt. He's nearly insensible with pain and blood loss.

Gagin shortly scuffs away, and Pila doesn't find him again until he's inside Hugo's hotel room. The gangster can see that Gagin is out on his feet. "Money" is all that Gagin can say. Hugo holds out an empty palm and says, "Right here in my hand."

Star character player Fred Clark, with his large frame and big voice, declarative pencil mustache, bald head, and enormous black hearing aid, turns Hugo into a fine and funny grotesque. Montgomery knew that Gagin needed a potent adversary, and in Clark/Hugo, he got one.

Thomas Gomez is a marvel of fortitude as Pancho, and petite, angel-faced Wanda Hendrix is perfectly endearing as Pila. When she cradles the head of the wounded Gagin against her breast, she's like a Madonna. Hendrix was as adept

Case File: Dorothy B. Hughes (1904–93)

The novel *Ride the Pink Horse* was published in 1946. Because author Dorothy B. Hughes spent much of her life in Santa Fe, New Mexico (where portions of the film version were shot), the book has a confident feel for Hispanic culture and provides a colorful backdrop for the internal and external conflicts of unhappy war veteran Lucky Gagin.

Hughes's first book, published in 1931, was *Dark Certainty*, a prize-winning collection of poetry. Book number two was a nonfiction history of New Mexico, and Hughes did not publish a mystery novel until the faintly mystical *The So Blue Marble* in 1940. She wrote fourteen suspense novels in all, including three that were adapted to film: *Ride the Pink Horse*, *The Fallen Sparrow*, and *In a Lonely Place*. From 1940 to 1950 Hughes produced about a novel a year and then retreated from books for eleven years to become a newspaper critic and, more importantly, a family caretaker.

The effects of emotional transgression and trauma, particularly racism, intrigued Hughes. *In a Lonely Place* is an early and very successful example of the serial-killer genre, and *The Fallen Sparrow*, like *Ride the Pink Horse*, is incidentally preoccupied with the miserable aftereffects of war.

Although a careful, subtle writer, Hughes also was skilled at sudden shifts in tone.

Her last book, a study of Perry Mason creator Erle Stanley Gardner, was published in 1978.

at comedy (*Miss Tatlock's Millions*) as drama and made headlines in the 1950s during her troubled marriage to war hero/movie star Audie Murphy.

Robert Montgomery directed only three more films. He retired from acting in 1951 and moved into television, where he became a powerful producer. *Ride the Pink Horse* is his finest achievement as a director and one of his best as an actor. Utterly without sentimentality, it nevertheless develops a fine sense of sentiment.

Technology That Kills

The Unsuspected was released in 1947, the year Bing Crosby utilized an improvement on wartime German technology to broadcast his radio show via transcription, that is, by recording instead of during a live performance. The technology's capability was important to Crosby, who enjoyed his leisure time and didn't wish to be tied to a studio on fixed days and hours. In *The Unsuspected*, New York–based mystery-radio star Victor Grandison (Claude Rains) utilizes transcription, too, but instead of devoting his free time to golf, he commits murder.

At 103 minutes, this glossy Warner Bros. thriller directed by Michael Curtiz feels long and heavy. The transcription business is designed as a minor mystery that's spelled out for us about thirty minutes into the story. We've been led to believe that Grandison couldn't possibly have murdered his secretary, Roslyn (Barbara Woodell), because he was on the air at the time of the killing. As we're able to figure out for ourselves long before the big reveal at the thirty-minute mark, Grandison's program was prerecorded on the night of the murder. Ironclad alibi or not, he killed Roslyn and then strung up her body to simulate suicide.

Ranald MacDougall's script is busy busy busy, with enough plot and plot twists for three or four movies. You quickly lose track of exactly what has driven Grandison to kill and why he wants to keep on killing, and after awhile, you lose interest. Story elements include supposed amnesia, a secret wedding, clumsy attempts at seduction, severed brake lines, poisoned champagne, servants who are ordered to take the night off, a shipwreck, a steamer trunk, a beady-eyed assassin with a pickup truck, a coveted inheritance, a steam shovel, motorcycle cops, a burning dump in Jersey, gimmicked recordings that fake a murder, and a man who drinks to forget. Whew! Although *The Unsuspected* is gorgeous to look at, most of the plot is explicated through ceaseless, often arch dialogue that is numbing instead of helpful. (When a messenger delivers a telegram, somebody takes it into the living room and says, "Mercury on a bicycle just brought this." Eh?)

The script and pictorial design unwisely incorporate elements that remind us of other, better movies: intense romantic close-ups and the whirling propeller of a plane's engine at startup (*Casablanca*); Claude Rains, a fabulous mansion with a wine cellar, and poison administered to the heroine (*Notorious*); and a gorgeous painted portrait of a dead woman (*Laura*).

Second-unit work in New York and New Jersey (possibly by Robert Vreeland) is capable. A police chase is a corker and very much in the mold of postwar realism, but because most of *The Unsuspected* takes place on mammoth sets and soundstages (including "exteriors" at the mansion), the film gives the impression of having been made much earlier in the decade. The real treats are Rains's plummy performance, Michael Curtiz's inquisitively mobile camera, and Woody Bredell's textured, ravishingly good-looking photography. There's fun to be had, too, with the dense, incredibly detailed art direction and set decoration by Anton Grot and Howard Winterbottom, respectively: arched windows, high ceilings, and fine furniture, plus swirling drapes and a wealth of statuary, pillars, staircases, plants and floral displays, painted lampshades, assorted bric-a-brac—you hardly know where to look.

Audrey Totter, as an unhappy niece, has an edgy bitchiness, and perennial heavy Jack Lambert is spooky as a thug who is (unaccountably) in league with Grandison. Top-billed Joan Caulfield plays the girl whose wealth and beauty set much of the plot in motion. She's lovely but too subdued to be interesting. And male ingénue Michael North, as the putative hero, gives it a good stab but doesn't quite register. (North is livelier in *The Devil Thumbs a Ride*; see Chapter 7. Beginning in 1940, he worked mainly as a bit and small-part actor under the name Ted North before being reintroduced as Michael North in *The Unsuspected*. It was his last film.)

I wonder if he suspected *that*.

The Dark Carnival of the Mind

When an old man sees the nighttime apparition of Dorrie, a young lover who died decades before, he's speechless. Another, much younger man who stands with him speaks: "We're on hallowed ground. Get on your knees with me."

It's a desperately magical moment—and also the ultimate in cynical manipulation, for the young man is a charlatan and the beautiful phantom is his female accomplice. But to the deceiver, it's a moment of personal triumph, the promise of a rich payoff, and the culmination of years of planning. During this interlude, the charlatan is at his zenith.

Edmund Goulding's *Nightmare Alley* (1947) adapts a hard-boiled 1946 novel by William Lindsay Gresham. The book's protagonist, Stan Carlisle, is a carny pitchman and small-time mentalist who hits the big time after developing a "class" mind-reading act based on a very valuable verbal code. He and his girlfriend (who feeds him carefully worded questions from the audience) become headliners in vaudeville. Eventually, Stan passes himself off as a minister and develops a full-blown, high-dollar grift that climaxes with the creation of the ethereal apparition.

But Stan is haunted by his past. In boyhood he developed an unhealthy sexual fixation on his mother (he witnessed her sexual intercourse with her lover) and a hatred of his cruel father. As an adult, he's tormented by nightmares in which he's pursued into dark alleys.

Stan's accomplice, Molly, has serious daddy issues and sees Stan as the embodiment of her kind but crooked father.

Stan's big score is arranged with the help of Lilith Ritter, a beautiful psychologist who provides inside information about the wealthy mark. Lilith fascinates—and dominates—Stan sexually and secretly works to betray him.

In the end, the grift explodes and Stan is a carny again—not a smiling, confident pitchman but a hopeless drunk who agrees to become the carnival's geek, a netherworld creature who exists in an alcoholic haze, raving and biting the heads off chickens for the shocked amusement of customers.

Considerable credit goes to screenwriter Jules Furthman, who preserved the essence of Gresham's fine, unwholesome novel while eliminating elements that could never have passed Hollywood's Production Code. In the film, Stan and Molly are married. Although Lilith Ritter is an aggressive schemer, she's not the dominatrix of the book; Stan is attracted to her mainly by the promise of money. When Stan and Molly hit the big time, it's not in vaudeville but at top hotels.

The movie doesn't explore Oedipus or Electra complexes (though Molly's early carny job is to perform as "Electra" in a startling electricity act), and Stan never impersonates a minister. An improbable sequence, when the mark has sex with "Dorrie," is scuttled. And while the book's conclusion suggests that Stan is doomed, the film allows our antihero to be rediscovered by Molly, who will nurse him back to health.

Nightmare Alley (1947) unfolds in the calculated unreality of carnival life, where Stan (Tyrone Power, standing) schemes to hit the big time with a mind-reading act controlled by Zeena (Joan Blondell, right). Molly (Coleen Gray, standing) is an innocent about to be sucked into Stan's machinations; strongman Bruno (Mike Mazurki) is Molly's protector, so Stan had better grow eyes in the back of his head.

For all the changes, *Nightmare Alley* replicates the novel's peculiarly unique carnival milieu, with most of the action taking place late at night, when the customers have gone and the place is a misty, shadowed maze of tents, false-front attractions, and caravans where the carnies sleep. Acres of the Fox back lot were devoted to the carnival set. Director Goulding and one of Hollywood's most versatile cinematographers, Lee Garmes, created a sort of landscape of the subconscious, where everything seems darkly possible.

The special language of the carnival is retained, and we feel as if we're privileged to observe and listen to these unusual people. A minor complaint is that atmospheric secondary characters from the novel, such as a sadistic midget, a kind boy with withered legs, and a tattooed "sailor," are not part of the script.

Casting helps a lot. Tyrone Power, with his impossible good looks, is potent as the intrinsically rotten Stan, partly because the actor is cast very much against type. Power is in nearly every scene, and if he doesn't quite carry the picture, he comes close. Ingratiating and intelligent, the character is as appealing as he is dangerous.

Case File: Coleen Gray (b. 1922)

Although as important to noir as Audrey Totter, Marie Windsor, and other actresses who projected malice, Coleen Gray is fondly recalled as the redemptive heroine who tries—with varying degrees of success—to save her men from their own mistakes. Petite, sweetly pretty, and blessed with a soft and expressive voice, Gray invariably represents "the light" in the dark world of noir. She's not always strictly on the side of the law (in *Nightmare Alley*, for instance, she is for a long time an active accomplice in a huckster's swindle), but she possesses a self-awareness that's unusual in noir. The characters she plays are subtly dimensional, carrying the burdens of moral ambivalence and aware of the shades of gray that dominate the urban landscape. Despite her small stature and delicate features, Gray holds her own on-screen opposite such physically imposing actors as Victor Mature and Sterling Hayden. *Nightmare Alley* is a flawed classic; Gray's other noir work includes *Kiss of Death*, *Kansas City Confidential*, and *The Killing*.

Joan Blondell is Zeena, the original possessor of the mind-reading code. Although married to a hopeless drunk (Ian Keith), she's Stan's lover and the woman he ultimately abandons. With her grave manner and devotion to her tarot deck, Zeena is a dark eminence. She warns Stan not to exceed his capabilities, little dreaming that he's capable of feeding her husband moonshine so that he dies.

Although thirty-eight when *Nightmare Alley* was released, Blondell gives the impression of a woman in her forties—and a zaftig, sensual one at that, an unusual occurrence in '40s Hollywood, where women weren't allowed to be sexual unless they were younger than thirty.

Noir favorite Coleen Gray shines as Molly, a character who is by turns guileless and very knowing. Her marriage to Stan is sudden and not entirely the idea of either one of them but a notion of the angry strongman, Bruno (Mike Mazurki, in a spooky performance). Bruno has had romantic interest in Molly and insists that Stan do right by her.

Gray is very powerful when she grasps the implications of the dead-girl grift. Molly stares at Stan with luminous intensity. "You're going against God!" she cries. ". . . Do you want Him to strike you dead?" Not unexpectedly, Molly can't bear the old man's reaction to the reappearance of his late lover and impulsively exposes the hoax.

Finally, Helen Walker, with her beautiful cat's eyes, is nothing but hazardous as Lilith. Even when she's confronted by Stan about her cheating him (she's pulled a classic money switch), she's cool enough to recite psychological jargon at him, almost convincing him that *he's* the person who needs some adjustment.

The Production Code that we mentioned earlier insisted that guilty parties in all Hollywood films be punished. Although Stan takes quite a tumble—reduced to holding court in a hobo jungle—Molly's later discovery of him ensures rehabilitation and happiness, despite the fact that Stan is directly responsible for the death of Zeena's husband. It's an interesting lapse in Code enforcement.

Better that the film had ended a few minutes earlier, after Stan has stumbled into a carnival and begged the owner for a job. The owner suggests that Stan might want to fill in for the geek—strictly temporary, of course.

> STAN
> Geek?
>
> OWNER
> You know what a geek is don'tcha?
>
> STAN
> Yeah. Sure, I, I know what a geek is.
>
> OWNER
> Do you think you can handle it?
>
> STAN *(with great resignation)*
> Mister, I was made for it.

Love's Avenging Angel

Nightmare Alley utilizes the "outsider" milieu of the carnival to confirm the perils of ambition without morality. In Edgar G. Ulmer's *Ruthless* (1948), another man sheds his morality to climb to the heights, but in this instance he maneuvers within the socially approved world of business. Horace Vendig (Zachary Scott) claws through the maze of high finance to ownership of a Wall Street brokerage house with enormous holdings in banks, construction, and utilities. But neither his money nor his arrogance can protect him from reminders of his past or from the animus of people he has wronged.

The challenge faced by Ulmer is that American pop culture had been keenly aware of the "robber baron" mentality since the nineteenth century. Ulmer knew that *Ruthless* had nothing fresh to offer in terms of theme. But just as the director rose above despised genres (such as horror) to make fresh, unique films, he also could rise above familiar concepts.

As Vendig deals his way to the top, he uses and discards lovers (he has little interest in physical sex), betrays business partners, and sacrifices lifelong relationships, most dramatically with Martha Burnside (Diana Lynn) and Victor Lambden (Louis Hayward). All three had been devoted childhood friends, and when the adolescent Vendig saves young Martha from drowning, he displays the glory of being human. He suggests a *possible* adult Vendig.

Lambden briefly joins his old friend in business and functions with empathy and principle. But when the inevitably disillusioned Lambden unravels himself from Vendig's enterprise and walks out, the good part of Vendig goes out the door with him.

Ulmer and writers S. K. Lauren and Gordon Kahn (adapting Dayton Stoddart's 1945 novel *Prelude to Night*) suggest yet another possible Vendig—and the most cautionary—in the person of a business rival, Buck Mansfield (Sydney Greenstreet). Mansfield is no less a schemer than Vendig, but he's devoted to his wife, Christa (Lucille Bremer), and has a highly charged libido. (In other words, he hasn't sacrificed everything to business.) But Christa is revolted by Mansfield's girth and age and betrays him to Vendig. The spoils, Christa included, are happily taken by Vendig, who fails to grasp that age comes to everyone and that he invites betrayal no less than Mansfield did.

Lambden and Mansfield's relationships to Vendig allow Ulmer to toy with the conceit of "doubling." The conceit emerges full blown, and hits *Ruthless* like a bombshell, when Lambden reenters Vendig's life with a beautiful woman on his arm. The woman is named Mallory Flagg, and she's played by Diana Lynn, the same, sparkling actress that plays the abandoned Martha.

No explanation for the women's identical appearance is given. Although nothing in the script encourages us to believe that Mallory and Martha are the same person (working, perhaps, to somehow torment Vendig), nothing *discourages* us from believing it, either. One interpretation is that Mallory is a magical figure that exists to remind Vendig that people who are tossed aside seldom return, but if they do, they are different than before. And love, once forsaken, is seldom recaptured.

In any case, Vendig is captivated by Mallory and proclaims his love for her (Christa Mansfield is already yesterday's news!), ignoring that she has a romantic relationship with Lambden. Vendig wants Mallory to go away with him on his boat, and when she follows him to his private pier, you have the sinking feeling that Vendig has won again.

The despondent (and by now ruinously alcoholic) Mansfield has other ideas. Following a ferocious dockside struggle between two titans of business—one of them ruined, the other still on the rise—Vendig is drowned. Lambden embraces Mallory, who had no intention whatever of leaving with Vendig. (This suggests, of course, that Mallory is an avenging angel.)

Lambden and Mallory embrace and kiss. "The End" appears on the screen. The image duplicates the closing shots of numberless other movies, but the perverse joke is that Lambden and Mallory kiss to celebrate a man's death.

Ulmer's direction of *Ruthless* is measured and elegant, with Bert Glennon's camera gliding gracefully through scenes that are paradoxically beautiful when the central character is ugly. One moment—a crane shot of Vendig as he strides away from camera, alone in a shadowed, nearly empty marble ballroom—recalls the spiritual emptiness of similar moments in *Citizen Kane*. Nobody mourns Kane, and some will passionately rejoice in the passing of Horace Vendig.

The Total Criminal

He Walked by Night (1948) is arguably the keenest blending of the police procedural with noir. In its depiction of a citywide hunt for a cop killer, the film reveals much of what is now taken for granted by filmgoers: the precinct switchboards, the dispatchers, the back and forth of police radio, the drudgery of door-to-door canvassing, the stakeout. The young actor Jack Webb appears as a crime-lab tech who demonstrates how the scientific examination of chemicals, metal, guns, and bullets can identify a criminal. In all of this, *He Walked by Night* is similar to another 1948 release, *The Naked City*. But while that film is exclusively about procedure and is not noir, *He Walked by Night* is a rich catalogue of noir stylistics and point of view.

Roy Martin (Richard Basehart) is an accomplished lock-picker who guns down an off-duty police officer after the cop has eyeballed him outside an electronics store. As the subsequent investigation unfolds, the police determine that the suspect is knowledgeable about chemicals (a vial of nitroglycerin is found in his stolen car), weapons, and electronics.

Martin suddenly changes his MO, abandoning electronics theft for liquor-store stickups. In the meantime, he continues to consign modified electronics to a lab that rents or sells the pieces. The lab's unsuspecting owner, Reeves (Whit Bissell), begs Martin to come to work for him as a researcher, but Martin refuses.

A combination of good luck and good police work causes the noose to gradually tighten, and Martin is finally killed after leading police on a protracted foot chase through LA's underground sewer system, a brilliant—and brilliantly shot—location that would not be used as effectively again until Gordon Douglas's *Them!* (1954). Scenes of Martin launching himself on his stomach into curbside storm drains are startling, and it's intriguing to watch as what had been his well-stocked refuge becomes his tomb.

Key to the film's unwholesome allure is the nature of the killer. Intelligent and methodical, he monitors police broadcasts from his car and apartment. His garage holds a cache of stolen license plates and registrations, and the apartment bristles not just with electronics but with guns of all sorts. When engaged in anything related to his criminal pursuits, he wears gloves, even at home.

He's also isolated—by choice, one infers—and has contact with virtually no one but his victims and Reeves. In a nice throwaway moment, a shapely young woman passes Martin on the street. His reaction? Not even a flicker of a glance. Not just violent, he's creepily asexual, too.

When Reeves assists the police in laying an ambush, Martin jumps one cop (Scott Brady) and shoots another, paralyzing him. But that officer puts a bullet into Martin. In a typical cop story about a typical crook, the bullet wound would be the criminal's undoing because he'd be forced to take himself to a hospital. But not Martin. Sweating at his apartment from a combination of pain, concentration, and the steam from a homemade autoclave, he probes his side for the bullet and then pulls it free with forceps. It's a great, mute performance from Richard Basehart, his face a strangely lighted mask of frightful discomfort and determination.

He Walks by Night was shot by John Alton, who literally wrote the book on mood cinematography (*Painting with Light*, 1949). Alton captured the silky nighttime look of dark Los Angeles neighborhoods, and the invasive nature of Martin's presence in them. Repeated deep-focus photography carries our gaze far back into the frame, all the way to the damp, illuminated mists that finally obscure our view. Martin is typically shot in shadow and frequently in tight close-up that masks one side of his face in blackness, the other in ambient light that lets us observe the ceaseless roving of his suspicious eye.

Much of the picture was shot on location, in full dark that was beautifully, and subtly, illuminated by Alton. The tonal values suggest not just the darkness of night but its *feel*, as well. You imagine the scent of the night-blooming jasmine and the whisper of a warm breeze against your skin.

For Jack Webb, the *He Walked by Night* set turned out to be a revelation. Mightily impressed with LAPD technical adviser Detective Marty Wynn, Webb cut himself free from *Pat Novak for Hire*, a private-dick radio show he'd been doing as work for hire, and began development of a procedure-oriented radio drama he called *Dragnet*. In this, *He Walked by Night* is indirectly responsible for letting us learn everything we think we know about police procedure.

The picture also gets at something that Webb's *Dragnet* later explored: the possibly unbridgeable divide between police and civilians. Even well-meaning citizens can be obtuse and impatient, and it's clear that cops and the rest of us exist in separate worlds that frequently overlap but are never the same.

Although *He Walks by Night* is credited to journeyman director Alfred Werker (*House of Rothschild, The Adventures of Sherlock Holmes, A-Haunting We Will Go*), direction was taken over by Anthony Mann, who almost simultaneously did a pair of noir classics, *T-Men* and *Raw Deal*, for Eagle-Lion, the same independent studio that made *He Walked by Night*. With its aggressive framing that puts us inside the minds of Martin and cops alike, the movie is very much in the Mann style.

The film had special piquancy for audiences of 1948 because scripters John C. Higgins and Crane Wilbur based it on the story of Erwin Walker, an electronics expert and cop killer who gave Los Angeles the willies during 1945–46. He freely committed burglaries and robberies and wounded two officers with machine-gun fire before finally killing another. Like Martin, Walker was scrupulous in his habits and escaped police ambushes, sometimes via the sewer system.

Unlike the fictional Martin, Walker was taken alive and was incarcerated in various penitentiaries and mental hospitals until 1974, when he was granted clemency. He changed his name and went off to forge a new life as a chemist. He died in 1982.

To the Bottom of the World

New York mob attorney Joe Morse (John Garfield) dresses and speaks well. When he justifies the nature of his work, he doesn't make empty boasts, like the Goff character played by Garfield in *Out of the Fog*. Instead, Morse lays out a logical and legally irrefutable case for the appropriateness of his activities.

Although not a criminal, he lives in a criminal milieu, protecting men involved in the numbers racket. If to provide legal aid to thugs seems an inconsequential thing, Abraham Polonsky and Ira Wolfert's script for *Force of Evil* (1948; from Wolfert's 1943 novel *Tucker's People*) insists otherwise by making clear that the nickels and dimes taken daily from hopeful bettors help finance the mob's larger operations, which include graft, extortion, prostitution, and murder. When you walk into your neighborhood policy "bank" and put down coins on your three-numeral pick, you're helping to pay off corrupt cops, judges, politicians, and other officials. You're undercutting the social fabric.

Joe knows that his older brother, Leo (Thomas Gomez), a small-time policy banker, is going to be wiped out—along with numberless other minor players— on July 4th, when the mob will ensure that the day's most commonly wagered number, 776, will come up the winner. Some of the wiped-out banks will be refinanced and taken over by the mob, with the original owners allowed to keep a small percentage of the profits. Other banks, like Leo's, will die and stay dead.

Joe can't abandon his client by revealing to Leo (and thus others) what's coming. Instead, he skirts the issue, telling Joe to close the bank for a day.

Leo doesn't get it. Why the hell would he want to do that? Joe won't say more, so Leo is wiped out. Furious by this double betrayal, he disowns Joe and becomes a loose cannon. Finally, in an existentially terrifying moment, Leo's meek and frightened bookkeeper, Bauer (Howland Chamberlin), sets Leo up for abduction and execution.

Naturalistic rather than realistic, *Force of Evil* conjures a stylized, thoughtfully emphatic *interpretation* of reality. In the everyday world of our own lives, people move freely from job to job. In Joe Morse's world, once you're in, you're in. The pathetically cowardly bookkeeper, Bauer (a considerably more central figure in the source novel), discovers this when he attempts to quit Leo's bank and is told by mob fixers that he's not going anywhere. This isn't America but a sick subversion of it.

Much of the *Force of Evil* dialogue is "literary" rather than realistic, and so well is it played by Garfield, Gomez, and others that it rings true. Some passages unreel like tortured stream of consciousness; one should be noted here: After Leo is murdered, Joe decides to turn against the mob, but first he must descend endless stone steps that lead to the river beneath the George Washington Bridge.

> *JOE (voice-over)*
> It was morning by then, dawn, and naturally I was feeling
> very bad there, as I went down there. I just kept going down
> and down there. It was like going down to the bottom of
> the world, to find my brother."

The high-mindedness that encouraged Polonsky and Wolfert to evoke Orpheus's descent into Hell is poetically honest rather than arch. The fact that Joe isn't moved to act until he suffers a personal loss hardly makes him a hero but does suggest the filmmakers' keen insights into human nature. As Joe's dilemma grows uglier, he feels himself dying by inches. John Garfield's face becomes tighter and tighter, until it's a mask of unwilling introspection.

In disquieting contrast, the face of the big boss, Tucker (Roy Roberts), is calm, even placid. If Tucker is troubled by anything, the problems are strictly external. Truly, confidently evil, he seems to have no inner life—which is probably why the gorgeous Mrs. Tucker (Marie Windsor, in a beautifully understated performance) challenges Joe's notions of right and wrong and defiantly offers herself to him. She and Joe might make a good fit, but Joe knows he'll stay with his innocent girl Doris (Beatrice Pearson), whose essential morality may be his lifeline.

Polonsky the director (with cinematographer George Barnes) made *Force of Evil* visually compelling—overcast natural light is used to chilly effect on New York locations, and interior shadowplay is striking and sophisticated. Doorways, walls, and foregrounded elements judiciously divide the 1.37:1 frame. An important, kinetically staged moment, the execution slaying of Bauer at Leo's bank, remains frighteningly potent and difficult to watch. (The razor-sharp editing was done by Arthur Seid.)

Force of Evil was the second production from Enterprise Pictures, an independent, self-financing mini-studio established in 1947 by, among others, producer David Lowe, John Garfield, and Garfield's business manager, Bob Roberts. Enterprise was set up on a profit-sharing basis. Principals ensured that line employees, like assistant director Robert Aldrich, were treated fairly and given modest perks. Grounded in politically liberal ethics, Enterprise wanted to make socially significant films, free of the timid, conservative grip of major studios. *Body and Soul* (see Chapter 6), a fine social drama set against the world of professional boxing and starring Garfield, was the first Enterprise release, but when another project, Lewis Milestone's *Arch of Triumph*, soared over budget,

Case File: John Garfield (1913–52)

Of all the formidable male stars on the Warner lot during the 1940s, John Garfield may have been the most purely gifted. A scrappy product of New York's Lower East Side, he might have been doomed to live and die there if not for an early interest in speech and the theater. He attended drama school on scholarship, did rep, and made the leap to Broadway in 1936. Garfield was signed by Warner in 1938 and made an immediate impression in the domestic drama *Four Daughters*, which earned him an Oscar nomination as best supporting actor. Intense and contemplative, Garfield also had a physicality that made him equally appealing to men and women. The camera loved him, and he quickly taught himself how to subtly play to it. Garfield often portrayed emotionally isolated, even anguished characters and did some of his most significant work in noir: *Out of the Fog*, *The Postman Always Rings Twice*, *Body and Soul* (an Oscar nomination, best actor), and his best, *Force of Evil*.

In the late 1940s, Garfield ran afoul of the opportunistic politicians of HUAC and was informally blacklisted by cowed studio executives. His death from a heart attack at thirty-nine was a shocking loss to the art of film.

Enterprise took a loan from MGM, which cofinanced *Force of Evil* and acted as distributor.

Because of Louis B. Mayer's dislike of realist drama, MGM unenthusiastically tossed *Force of Evil* into the marketplace as a B picture. Although the film received some good critical notice, it died at the box office. Enterprise produced only two more films, *So This Is New York* and *Caught*, before folding in 1949. And by that time, Garfield, Polonsky, and others had fallen under the scrutiny of the House Un-American Activities Committee (HUAC), when that body investigated supposed Communist infiltration of Hollywood.

Polonsky the writer brought an artist's sensibilities to *Force of Evil*, creating accessible art that was beyond the grasp of audiences and movie executives in 1948. The film's reputation grew over the many years, and in 2004, USC and filmmaker Martin Scorsese assembled a brilliantly restored version.

Victory's Pain, Victory's Pride

Heavyweight boxer Stoker Thompson has a plan, and because he's pumped himself up with desperate confidence it strikes him as a good one. He's going to go into the ring and knock the hell out of a twenty-three-year-old up-and-comer named Tiger Nelson. That's the plan—never mind that Stoker is thirty-five, well worn, and barely a step above a faceless club fighter.

Stoker's manager and trainer have a plan, too, by which Stoker will take a dive after the second round. Big money is involved, and so sure are the schemers of Stoker's diminished skills that they don't bother to tell him that he's supposed to lie down. They have every confidence that he just will.

Until *Raging Bull* more than thirty years later, Robert Wise's *The Set-Up* (1949) stood at the pinnacle of boxing movies, and it still may be second only to that Scorsese epic. And in its smaller, more intimate scale, it is probably more personal and intense. At its core are numerous existential questions: Is it possible for personal will to become reality? At what point is human dignity seriously diminished, and when is it gone altogether? Is love sufficient defense against the cold, rapacious forces of the world? And finally: If a man is convinced he is not committing a transgression, has the transgression been committed at all, and does the man deserve to be punished? For you see: Stoker *does* knock the hell out of Tiger Nelson, after finally being told between the second and third rounds that *he's* been tapped to lose.

The Set-Up runs just seventy-two minutes, and in real time, as numerous shots of clock faces remind us. The film's second half is given over almost entirely to the grueling fight, which was impeccably choreographed by fighter John Indrisano, forcefully directed by Wise, and sharply edited by Roland Gross. And of course there are the contributions of scowling young Hal Fieberling as Tiger and Robert Ryan as Stoker. For the rest of his life, Ryan remained particularly proud of the performance. His face, especially his haunted eyes, shows hope and despair, passion and pride, a battered dignity, and a burning core of humanity.

Robert Wise's *The Set-Up* (1949) looks at Stoker Thompson (Robert Ryan), an aging boxer whose skills have nearly deserted him. Regardless, Stoker insists on one more shot at the big time. His devoted lover, Julie (Audrey Totter), is desperately apprehensive. Worse, the fighter has no idea that his manager has sold him out.

Certainly Ryan was well cast. He had been a four-year heavyweight boxing champion at Dartmouth and had honed his body in other ways, too, notably during two years among the "black gang" in the bowels of a steamer and with experience as a Marine Corps drill instructor during World War II. Ryan stood 6'4" and weighed 190 pounds—all of it sinew and muscle. But John Indrisano thought Ryan was a little too lithe to pass as a true heavyweight, so the actor was put on a carb-heavy diet and daily workouts in the gym, adding nearly ten pounds while retaining his leanness.

Stoker looks like quite a package, but his eyes and slightly lined face betray him (Robert Ryan was thirty-nine years old when *The Set-Up* was released; professional boxer and neophyte actor Hal Fieberling, later known as Hal Baylor, was just thirty).

Stoker's woman, Julie (Audrey Totter), begs him not to go through with the match. Stoker is undeterred: "You know somethin'? I can take that guy tonight. I can feel it." He aches to be a contender again. "I'm just one punch away!"

Stoker gives Julie a ticket for the match, and in beautiful defiance of cliché, Julie never shows up. Instead, she wanders the shabby streets of the rinky-dink down, passing tattoo parlors, bars, dance halls, and penny arcades, before finally taking herself to a pedestrian bridge that overlooks a street filled with buses and streetcars. The view from the bridge is a geometric abstraction, and when Wise reverses the angle and shoots up on Julie's face, her head delicately backlit against a black sky by cinematographer Milton Krasner, her humanity is heartbreaking.

She tears the ticket into pieces that flutter onto the street below.

Ultimately, Stoker's victory is at once brilliant and disastrous. He's regained his hope and his dignity, but after dressing he finds the arena dark and empty. The impeccably groomed gambler called Little Boy (Alan Baxter), Tiger, and two other stooges wait for him on the sidewalk outside. Finally trapped in an

Case File: Robert Ryan (1909–73)

As lean and tensile as a strip of leather, former college boxer and Marine drill instructor Robert Ryan brought tortured single-mindedness to film noir. In most of the many movies he made during a thirty-four-year career that followed brief stage experience, he embodied the American quality of aggressive pursuit of goals, more often than not suggesting the dreadful results of overzealousness and tunnel vision. Of all the American movie actors who have had a hyper-masculine presence (Ryan stood 6´4″ and was sleekly muscled), he may be the most complex and challenging. Although well known in his private life as a politically progressive activist, Ryan had an uncanny on-screen ability to get inside the skins of characters that were his opposite numbers: prejudiced, hateful, and small-minded. His portrayal of the murderous, anti-Semitic soldier in Crossfire is a spooky gem of smiling monstrousness. On the other hand, few noir protagonists have the pathetic hope and sheer nobility of character of the aging prizefighter Ryan played in The Set-Up. The actor's other noir work is no less taut and emotionally engaged: Act of Violence; The Racket; On Dangerous Ground; Beware, My Lovely; House of Bamboo; and the literally explosive Odds Against Tomorrow. In The Outfit, a lively neo-noir released the year of Ryan's death, the actor made a strong statement as a bloodless mob boss who is preoccupied with a snarky, much-younger wife and a vengeful hoodlum who wants to kill him.

Outside of the noir genre, Ryan is superb in The Woman on the Beach, Clash by Night, The Naked Spur, Bad Day at Black Rock (one of his best roles, in one of the best American films of the 1950s), The Professionals, The Wild Bunch (another milestone of cinema history), and The Iceman Cometh. Ryan was attracted to downbeat roles, and although he became a major star, he remained a star character player rather than a traditional leading man. If that bothered Ryan, he never let it show on-screen.

alley, Stoker takes the measure of his four attackers but is finally held fast. He slips a grip and gives Little Boy a fair shot in the jaw (Alan Baxter's quiet fury is scary), so the gambler vows that Stoker will never punch with that hand again.

When Julie sees her man stagger from the alley, his hand crushed, she rushes to him. Stoker knows his boxing career is over, but he's maintained his dignity. "I wouldn't do it," he rasps. "I wouldn't do it."

The Set-Up was filmed in just nineteen days at RKO, not long after the studio was purchased by Howard Hughes. Wise had already done sterling work at RKO producer Val Lewton's B-picture unit; this would be Wise's last RKO assignment. The cast is filled out with a brace of emphatic actors in colorful, often piquant roles: George Tobias, Percy Helton, Philip Pine, Paul Dubov, James Edwards, Wallace Ford, and Darryl Hickman.

Inside the ring and out, *The Set-Up* is a testament to craft and extraordinary intelligence.

The Snowball Effect

Garage mechanic Dan Brady (Mickey Rooney) has set himself up with a hot date, but he doesn't get paid until the end of the week and he's broke. Mackey (Art Smith), the skinflint owner of the place, would never give him advance, so after Dan rings up a transaction, he guiltily helps himself to a twenty. The accountant won't come by for a few days, and by that time Dan will have collected on a debt and replaced the Andrew Jackson.

Dan has his date, with a local hard-case cashier named Vera (Jeanne Cagney), and feels great at work the next day—until his pal says he's tapped out and can't repay the loan, and the accountant pulls up outside the garage. A special job has brought him to the place early, so he'll just balance the drawer now.

The clock is ticking. If you were Dan, what would *you* do?

Quicksand (1949) is a neat, tight little noir that Rooney made for Rooney Inc., an entity that was the brainchild of a promoter named Sam Stiefel. Stiefel made a lot of promises he couldn't keep, and neither he nor the corporation were parts of the Mick's life for very long, but *Quicksand* was built to last. Robert Smith's script is a lovely, diagrammatical progression of disaster that builds remorselessly from Dan's attack of sticky fingers.

The accountant is already rooting around in the cash drawer. Dan has an idea. He runs up the street and buys a $100 watch with $10 down, hocks it for $30, and puts the $20 into the drawer as the accountant is finishing. *Look, the twenty was there all along, see?*

Real trouble begins the next day, when a surly finance man (Robert Gallaudet) shows up at the garage and tells Dan that unless he pays off the watch in one day, he'll be pinched for grand larceny. Dan doesn't have anywhere near ninety bucks, so his first bad decisions are shortly compounded by others. Very soon, *Quicksand* blossoms with assault and battery, strong-arm robbery, breaking and entering, burglary, car theft, extortion, a fistfight, blackmail, murder, a carjack, kidnapping, and flight. It all may sound ridiculous, and yet the logical basis for events is all there in the screenplay: deed, intended consequence, *unintended* consequence, deed—the same cycle, over and over, as Dan digs himself in deeper.

The moment when Dan sees Vera wearing a mink coat that she bought with money that Dan *really* needed for another purpose is a pip. Dan is so furious he can barely contain himself. Vera takes umbrage. Isn't she *entitled* to a mink coat? And anyway, she told Dan how to score the cash.

Vera is useless, but Dan has a weightier adversary, a penny-arcade owner and inveterate schemer named Nick Dramoshag (Peter Lorre). Nick is nasty by temperament, but that doesn't prevent him from viewing the world in glass-half-full terms. When he realizes he can coerce Dan into further crime, he forces the issue. (Dan has a habit of leaving physical evidence behind, and Nick is good at picking it up.)

Dan is royally screwed. Where will it all end?

The probably unintentional joke of *Quicksand* is that Vera is no prize. She's the short, blocky type, with a thick neck, an unappealing pageboy, and features that are emphatic rather than pretty. Jeanne Cagney is craftily effective in the role (you suspect that Vera is a cock tease and is just about what Dan deserves), but at no time do you understand why Dan is infatuated with her—particularly since Dan's ex, a pretty sweetheart named Helen (Barbara Bates), wants to rekindle her relationship with our hero.

A chase climax is fun, but an improbably happy ending suggests that Dan won't suffer too horribly for all the mischief he's done. He even gets back with Helen.

Irving Pichel's direction is laudably concise, and Lionel Lindon lit the picture so that back alleys, furnished rooms, and noisy, crowded streets acquire a kind of grungy splendor. Lorre is perfectly repellant, and Rooney—at thirty, already a twenty-four-year veteran of the business—does some of the best work of his career. He's completely natural and engaged. If Rooney had a technique at this time, he never revealed it. You *never* catch him acting.

Rooney has brushed off *Quicksand* and some other very good Bs he made during the same period—*The Strip* and *Drive a Crooked Road* are two of them—probably because of unpleasant memories associated with Stiefel and Rooney, Inc. (Mr. Steifel even got to Peter Lorre and put together Lorre, Inc. As you might guess, it didn't pan out at all.) Rooney should be proud of his work here. Dan is in quicksand up to his nose, and commands our interest through every moment of his struggle.

"A left-handed form of human endeavor"

Kentucky-bred Dix Handley is a big-city "hooligan" who knows how to walk free from a lineup by silently intimidating an eyewitness with a glare. He's an old hand at hooliganism, and few characters in John Huston's *The Asphalt Jungle*

John Huston's *The Asphalt Jungle* (1950) dissects the dreams and failings of the miserable schemers who pull a daring jewelry heist. An accidental shooting during the job foreshadows even worse things to come. Gathered to examine the loot are (from left) Sterling Hayden, Brad Dexter, Louis Calhern, and Sam Jaffe.

(1950) credit him with anything more than a strong back. Dix is one of the more disagreeable habitués of the criminal underworld, a strong-arm boy and hopeless horseplayer who exists on life's—and crime's—margins. To others in the rackets, he's a tool, a device, and to police, he's simple vermin.

The heavy and quite beautiful irony of *The Asphalt Jungle* is that Dix is fully alive: with memories, with longings, and with a dreamer's desire to somehow reclaim the horse farm of his childhood. By gambling on the thoroughbreds, he references the past that he wishes to reclaim.

Crooked attorney Alonzo Emmerich (Louis Calhern) archly refers to crime as "a left-handed form of human endeavor." Well, the people who fall into or near Emmerich's orbit are certainly a bit off the grid: the sweating, obsequious bookie, Coppy (Marc Lawrence); Doll (Jean Hagen), the lovestruck chorus girl who can't keep a job or a roof over her head; Lt. Dietrich (Barry Kelley), the cynical cop who takes money to look the other way; Angela Phinlay (Marilyn Monroe), Emmerich's disarming but impossibly self-involved mistress; Ciavelli (Anthony Caruso), the talented "box man" who blows safes to finance a normal family life with his wife and baby; Brannom (Brad Dexter), the greedy, stupidly confident private detective.

Finally, there is Erwin Riedenschneider (Sam Jaffe), an elderly German-American criminal mastermind who is freshly out of prison and needs a $50,000 stake in order to score half a million.

Two characters in Huston and Ben Maddow's elegant, pitiless script (from the novel by W. R. Burnett) exist in counterpoint to the hustlers. One of them, Gus (James Whitmore), is a hustler himself, a hunchbacked diner owner who participates in the score while also serving as a sort of Greek chorus, astutely reading motives and character, advising Dix and others where they might go wrong, and why.

More familiarly, there is the city's police commissioner (John McIntire), a hardheaded bureaucrat who hates police inaction and public apathy with nearly as much passion as he hates crime. But the lure of crime tells a lot of people what to do.

Riedenschneider gets his stake, but the money comes from Coppy because the lawyer Emmerich is tapped out. Coppy thinks he's merely providing cover for a big man who might be willing to help him later. The other members of the gang have no idea that Emmerich is running on fumes. (Even the sweet and desperately lonely Mrs. Emmerich [Dorothy Tree], an invalid, has no idea of the household's circumstances.)

The robbery is pulled off with military-like precision (and inspired similar set pieces in numberless films that came later, notably *Rififi*). But bad luck and greed eventually step in. Ciavelli is accidentally shot, and Emmerich sees a double-cross as his best way out of his financial mess. His attempt fails, and Dix angrily asks, "What's inside of you? What's keepin' you alive?"

Soon, the police put on the squeeze, and various characters are undone because of their essential flaws of character. For Emmerich, it's the weight of maintaining a luxurious home and the pretense of sophisticated courtliness, as if he's superior to the people whose illegal work he finances. His fondness for Angela also contributes to his fall, for she quickly caves under interrogation. (Marilyn's little-girl-lost performance is a small gem. She was selected for the part by Louis B. Mayer and not, as Huston inevitably claimed, by John Huston.)

The elderly Riedenschneider is captured because of his all-absorbing attraction to good-looking, very young women, whether on calendar pages or in the flesh. He's not a satyr but a voyeur, compelled to look and do nothing more, and when he gazes at a girl for too long at a roadhouse, he gives the cops time to catch up with him.

Most pitiably, Dix remains sunk in his dream of the Kentucky horse farm, owned for years by strangers and beyond his reach. Wounded during the double-cross and now bleeding to death, he forces himself to drive south, Doll begging him to stop. In the inevitable irony of the conclusion, Dix finds freedom not in the city but in the country, in a pasture with horses.

Case File: John Huston (1906–87)

The legendarily larger-than-life polymath who helped invent film noir had determination and talent enough to defy the odds and forge a Hollywood career that lasted a remarkable fifty-eight years. For many of those years, from 1938 until his death in 1987, Huston was a major figure who wowed audiences and his peers as a writer, director, producer, and actor. (He also kept a very lively, often raucous, private life, which didn't diminish his popularity around town.) Huston's script for *The Maltese Falcon*, which was the first film he directed, captured the terse qualities of Dashiell Hammett's plotting and dialogue, and added a compellingly visual dimension. Huston contributed greatly to the career of Humphrey Bogart, with a 1941 script for *High Sierra*, script and direction of *The Maltese Falcon* a year later, and subsequent collaborations on *Across the Pacific*, *The Treasure of the Sierra Madre*, *Key Largo*, *The African Queen*, and *Beat the Devil*.

Huston's interest in deeply ambivalent protagonists found expression in nearly all of his movies, and with particular piquancy in *The Maltese Falcon* and his other noir work: *The Killers* (contributing writer, uncredited), *Three Strangers* (writer), and *The Asphalt Jungle* (producer, cowriter, director). Huston did not return to noir after *The Asphalt Jungle*, except for a stunningly malignant turn as an actor in Roman Polanski's brilliant 1974 neo-noir *Chinatown*.

The Asphalt Jungle is completely absorbing. The principal characters are drawn with such vividness that you empathize with their predicaments even as you damn them for getting into the situations in the first place. John Huston and cinematographer Harold Rosson repeatedly brought the camera very close to the actors' faces, forcing us to accept the humanity of these misfit characters.

A sense of impending doom pervades every frame. The city (unnamed but meant to evoke New York) looks gray and blasted, like a postwar European city that has only recently cleared away the rubble. Situations that various characters believe they control aren't in their control at all. It isn't just the law that's going to crush these people but circumstance and the people themselves. There are very few ways out of this dippy carnival of avarice, desperation, and plain foolishness, and none of them are appealing.

One night, Maria (Teresa Celli), soon to be the box man's widow, listens to a distant police siren. "It sounds like a soul in hell," she says.

Icy, Bold, and Deadly

On August 21, 1934, a gang of unmasked men outside the Rubel Ice Corporation in Brooklyn's Bath Beach section robbed an armored car of $427,000 and escaped cleanly. It was the largest robbery of cash in the United States to that time. In 1950, Robert Angus and Robert Leeds wrote a fictional treatment of the brazen crime. RKO contract writer Earl Felton and Gerald Drayson Adams turned the treatment into an unusually tight, hard-edged screenplay called

Case File: Sterling Hayden (1916–86)

Standing 6'5" and at one time promoted by Paramount as "the blond god," Sterling Hayden despised the industry that made him internationally famous. Why? Because he never aspired to be a performer, and because he spent much of his life not acting at all, but in dangerous pursuits that included professional ship captaincy, wartime intelligence work and guerrilla fighting, and never-ending, financially debilitating battles with ex-wives and the U.S. government that finally mandated a self-imposed exile abroad. An attachment to communism (he was a friend of Yugoslav strongman Josip Broz Tito) came back to bite Hayden in the late 1940s and early '50s, when he was put in a vice by HUAC and pressured to reveal much about his political past. Hayden excoriated himself for that and afterwards worked in movies only when he needed cash.

All of this informs Hayden's on-screen persona, which is paradoxically aloof and dogged; distant and emotionally engaged. He was an ideal noir protagonist in *The Asphalt Jungle*, *Crime Wave*, *Naked Alibi*, and *The Killing*. In each of these, whether outside the law or working on its behalf, Hayden projects fierce personal integrity and a clear-eyed view of the world that is considerably more complex and flavorful than mere cynicism. Rather, the Hayden antihero allows no sentiment for those who are undeserving of it, even as he fights to preserve relationships that are meaningful to him. This duality of character made him an ideal western hero (see Nick Ray's *Johnny Guitar*), and motivates Hayden's most famous role, the deranged general at the center of *Dr. Strangelove*, who busily works to destroy the world even as he longs to save it.

Code 3, which became *Armored Car Robbery* (1950). Not just an early triumph for director Richard Fleischer, the picture helped propel actor Charles McGraw to B-movie stardom. Like Anthony Mann's *T-Men* (1948; see Chapter 4), *Armored Car Robbery* deftly combines elements of the police procedural with the darker tones of noir. Marvelously compact at just sixty-seven minutes, the picture is brisk, tough, and completely engaging.

Assisted by three accomplices, icy criminal mastermind Dave Purvis (William Talman) engineers a daring, half-million-dollar daylight robbery of an armored car in front of Wrigley Field, the minor-league ballpark in South Central Los Angeles. During the melee, a police detective (James Flavin) is killed and one of the robbers, Benny (Douglas Fowley), is gut-shot and badly wounded. All four robbers escape, and it's left to grim, dogged police lieutenant Cordell (McGraw) to chase down the criminals and avenge his partner.

Purvis, though, is a difficult adversary. He moves constantly, changing his addresses and phone numbers like the rest of us change our socks. He's an impeccable dresser who takes a razor blade to every label in every article of his clothing. He's well known in the underworld, but his face is elusive and he has no police record. "Dave Purvis" probably isn't even his real name. And he's as remorseless as a cancer.

Charles McGraw is a potent, righteous force as Lt. Cordell, but *Armored Car Robbery* is dominated by William Talman. Pale-eyed, with close-cropped wavy hair and an improbably high forehead, Talman is frankly intimidating. Purvis never merely looks at anything—he stares at it, evaluates it, decides what to do about it. He leaves nothing to chance, but he's not a paranoiac. He just knows how to protect himself. He's a predator and a survivor.

As Purvis's stripper girlfriend, Adele Jergens is a tall, leggy vision, and good character bits are contributed by hard-boiled actors Douglas Fowley, Gene Evans, and Steve Brodie as Mapes. (When Purvis forces Mapes to his knees and then boxes his ears, the sound is so awful it'll make *your* ears ring.)

Richard Fleischer began his directorial career in 1946. RKO liked his promise well enough to put him under contract. In *Armored Car Robbery*, as throughout his career, Fleischer worked with concise aggressiveness. This was a B film destined to go out as the bottom half of a double bill (with Columbia's antic comedy *The Good Humor Man*). It was a sixteen-day shoot, mainly on location in and around LA: the ballpark, the Valley, and oil fields at Torrance.

No scene or setup is held a moment longer than needed. Desmond Marquette's cutting is exemplary but you get the feeling that Fleischer, working under the gun, didn't expose a lot of film in the first place. The picture is efficient as well as artful.

Self-styled criminal mastermind Dave Purvis (William Talman, left) lays out an *Armored Car Robbery* (1950) for Benny McBride (Douglas Fowley) and McBride's wife, stripper Yvonne LeDoux (Adele Jergens). Benny is receptive because he's greedy and because he has no idea that Purvis and Yvonne have become lovers. Sixty-seven minutes of hardboiled thrills, directed by Richard Fleischer.

Case File: William Talman (1915–68)

Star character player William Talman was an accomplished working actor with Broadway experience, a devoted family man—and the guy who haunts the dreams of many noir heroes. Tall, silken-voiced, and queerly handsome with his large forehead and amphibian eyes, Talman reached the apotheosis of noir notoriety as Emmett Myers, the deranged serial murderer who abducts and terrorizes a pair of hapless Joes in Ida Lupino's *The Hitch-Hiker*. Talman later became famous as district attorney Hamilton Burger in TV's long-running *Perry Mason*, but not before he did a variety of villainous turns that puts him among noir's most intimidating figures. You can creep yourself out by observing him in *Armored Car Robbery* and *City That Never Sleeps*. The other noir on Talman's résumé, *The Racket*, finds him in an atypical sympathetic role, as a straight-arrow policeman. He's very effective, too, in a quasi-noir, *The Woman on Pier 13* aka *I Married a Communist* and in hard-boiled crime thrillers of the '50s: *Big House U.S.A.*, *Crashout*, *The Man Is Armed*, and *Hell on Devil's Island*.

Besides his work in movies and episodic television, Talman is justly famed for a courageous 1968 public-service TV spot, in which he comes out against cigarettes by bluntly announcing that he has lung cancer.

Guy Roe was the director of photography. A bright, flat documentary look informs the daylight activities of the crooks (the robbery, a tense time at a police roadblock in the oil fields, some of Purvis's activities at his motel) and the workings of the cops (surveillance, the crime lab, coordination by radiophone, planting of bugs, interrogations). Nighttime scenes have a bare minimum of illumination, but key lights pick out the details that we need to see. Los Angeles and its environs come to palpable life.

A few sequences have particular force. The robbery is briskly shot in medium close-up with eye-level cameras and quick cuts that put you right in the middle of the action. When Purvis tags Cordell's new partner, Ryan (Don McGuire), as a cop at the docks, he puts a bullet in him. Purvis wants to finish him off, but more cops are coming, and he has to get out of there. Ryan stirs and finally drags himself to the radio in his squad car. The top of his head is in the extreme foreground of the frame, beneath the steering wheel and right in our laps. It's an uncomfortable intimacy.

Other than the robbery, the film's big set piece is the nighttime climax at Metro Airport. Purvis, Yvonne, and the dough are ready to leave, but the pilot is instructed by the tower to hold up. Furious and impatient, Purvis grabs the suitcase and makes a run for it, only to be chopped into pieces by the propeller of another, larger plane.

Purvis has planned so carefully and worked so hard. You want to feel sorry for him.

But you don't.

Seduced by a Punk

Try and Get Me! (1950) strips evil to its banal core, exposing a preening dandy named Jerry Slocum (Lloyd Bridges), who picks up a few bucks here and there as a stickup artist. In his chintzy rented room, he covers himself in cologne ("Only the best! Six-fifty a bottle!") and gazes into the mirror to admire his lean physique. He's found a female dumbbell who celebrates him as "God's gift to women," and he has a new associate, Howard Tyler (Frank Lovejoy). Tyler is a law-abiding Everyman type who's fallen on lean times. In a moment of weakness and desperate to feed his family, he agrees to drive when Slocum does his heists. One haul nets the two of them the gaudy sum of twenty-four dollars.

That's peanuts, but Slocum is a big thinker, a *confident* thinker. He wants real money, and inveigles Tyler to assist in a kidnapping.

The kidnapping goes wrong.

Try and Get Me! is a brutally compelling experience, directed with blunt assurance by Cyril Endfield. Working from a script by Jo Pagano (adapting his own 1947 novel, *The Condemned*), Endfield shot on location in Phoenix to capture the hustle and provincialism of a mid-size American city.

In a couple of amazing sequences, Tyler obeys when Slocum amiably asks for his shoes. Tyler holds Slocum's mirror, hands him his hairbrush, and buttons his shirt cuffs. Slocum parades around naked to the waist, yakking about all the dames he knows when he's actually seducing Tyler—who is indeed seduced. All of this makes for a fascinating sexual aside.

The brute power of *Try and Get Me!* is rooted in the fate of the kidnappers, who are arrested, later dragged from jail by an enormous mob of howling locals, and lynched. This is what happened in 1933 near San Jose, California, to two men arrested for the kidnap murder of a local department-store heir. In the San Jose case, and in Jo Pagano's script, local newspapers exploited the tragedy for monetary gain, effectively trying the suspects on the front pages and inciting the fury of local residents.

Try and Get Me! tosses in a Man of Conscience, an academic (Renzo Cesana) who cautions a newspaper writer (Richard Carlson) about inflammatory language, suggesting that the potential for evil is latent in all of us. (The academic is pointedly European and thus almost certainly speaking from bitter, recent experience.) The reporter ignores the advice.

In a protracted, horrifying sequence shot with documentary-like realism by cinematographer Guy Roe, and that recalls the mob scene in Fritz Lang's *Fury* (see Chapter 6), the press of bodies outside the courthouse ebbs and flows like a dark wave, pushing back the defenders, undulating closer to the building—and finally pouring inside. Tyler is strangely resigned, almost calm as the cell doors are opened, while Slocum erupts in an irrational "Try and get me" rage. He's stripped half-naked by the mob and passed over the top of it by numberless hands. It's *all* hands for a long moment, and no faces. Who among the mob is guilty? The perpetrators are apparently everyone and no one.

In *Try and Get Me!* (1950), a kidnap scheme concocted by a conceited idiot (Lloyd Bridges, right) and abetted by a naïve workingman (Frank Lovejoy, left) goes awry at the outset. That's bad, but unimaginable terrors—and a blot on the soul of a whole town—lie ahead. The muffled victim is Carl Kent.

We don't see Tyler or Slocum again, but not long after their abduction the night air reverberates with the mob's joyous, approving cry. A few moments pass, and then the awful sound comes again. Animal justice has been served.

Lest we forget that the young-adult kidnap victim (Carl Kent) is somebody's son, the film devotes considerable time to Tyler's relationship with his own son, a little boy who doesn't understand why he can't have a bike like the other kids. Mrs. Tyler (Kathleen Ryan) is pregnant, a situation that calls for celebration as well as for fear. How will Tyler take care of this new child? In a peculiar moment, he is about to mail the ransom note when he's beaten to the corner mailbox by a fat little man who wants to post a fistful of birth announcements. He's a father for the first time, and he's thrilled and thankful. Tyler is visibly touched and disturbed by this display.

By audaciously suggesting that a perpetrator of a heinous crime has not just an interior life but a kindly, even reflective one, *Try and Get Me!* provocatively tests the limits of audience tolerance. In *Fury*, the principal character run afoul of the law but is innocent. Here, even though it's Slocum who crushes the kidnapped man's head with repeated blows from a rock, Tyler is no less guilty. He helped plan the kidnapping, and he does nothing to prevent the murder. He continues to go through the motions of daily life until his torment forces him to blurt his guilt to a mousy, love-starved woman (Katherine Locke) who has been paired with Tyler by Jerry, as a sort of nonsensical cover intended to bestow normalcy on a man who departed the normal world some time ago.

Crime Is Best Left to the Professionals

Armored Car Robbery and *Try and Get Me!* explore the schemes and failures of professional criminals. In Anthony Mann's *Side Street* (1950), the amateur enthusiast has his day in the sun—although "hell" is closer to the truth.

Because he steals $30,000 from the office of a New York attorney, part-time mail carrier Joe Norson (Farley Granger) thinks he's lucked into the prosperity that he desperately wants for himself and his bride, Ellen (Cathy O'Donnell). But the theft was a spur of the moment notion; Joe hasn't the mindset or experience needed to avoid the fallout from a police investigation, a blackmail scheme, four murders, and deadly threats to Ellen and himself. (Later in 1950, audiences saw Granger in Mark Robson and Charles Vidor's *Edge of Doom*, a social-problem drama about a young man who kills a Catholic priest because the Church won't give his mother an extravagant funeral. Young Granger apparently had the kind of face that suggests calamitous impulsiveness.)

Sydney Boehm's tight, agonizingly deterministic script suggests that professional criminals sometimes flourish not simply because they know how to go about their business but because they're *willing* to go about it. Georgie Garsell (James Craig), an intimidating ex-con who's in league with the attorney, Backett (Edmon Ryan), is professional through and through. That's why he's able to garrote his ironically named lover, Lucky (Adele Jergens), after she's delivered on her part of the blackmail setup, and why he can throttle a larcenous barkeep who might know where the money has gone. And it's why Georgie can murder another trusting lover, with his bare hands, in the backseat of a taxicab. Georgie is monstrous and remorseless, and by the time he figures out that Joe is the guy he's after, *Side Street* quivers like a bowstring that's been pulled back almost to its breaking point.

Joe has done something damned foolish, but he doesn't deserve Georgie any more than he deserves an asteroid falling on his head. Georgie, naturally enough, thinks differently. Joe reasons that the cash belongs to him because he stole it and because he thought he was stealing only $200. Georgie and Backett feel the money belongs to them because *they* stole it. Crime is all about personal perspective, isn't it?

The moralistic essence of *Side Street* isn't a debate about entitlement, however, but a contention that anybody could be Joe. Even his Everyman name—Joe—is a synecdoche for all of us. Whatever innate weaknesses Joe has are aggravated by his naïve hope to travel with Ellen through Europe and give her a mink coat. Dialogue establishes that Joe has owned and lost a filling station. Now he's trapped in a crummy part-time job, with no prospects and a baby on the way. He keeps a .45 automatic in his dresser, not because he's a criminal but because, like millions of other young men, he's an ex-GI who did his time overseas and returned home with hope that was quickly deflated by joblessness and inflation. He's frustrated and bitter. Society seems to have let him down.

Director Anthony Mann and cinematographer Joseph Ruttenberg shot on location in New York City, mainly eschewing traditional noir shadowplay for natural daylight that brings an objective, documentary-like feel to views of Greenwich Village, the Fulton Fish Market, Battery Park, Central Park, and Wall Street. Vertiginous opening and closing shots filmed from a blimp establish and reiterate New York's spiraling immensity.

Frequent close-ups on faces variously reveal perfidy, fear, and suspicion. When Ellen takes a call from Joe as cops are listening in, the camera rapidly dollies in on her face as she screams, "Run, Joe, run, the police are tracing this call!" It's a fine, unexpected moment.

Frequent use of low angles on Joe doesn't make him seem imposing but helplessly small, because rising behind him are more of the city's enormous buildings. New York is a character, just as emphatically as in Jules Dassin's fine, groundbreaking police procedural *The Naked City* (1948).

For a climactic car chase, Mann put cameras in twenty-story windows to shoot down at the wheeling autos and the vertical stripes of streets that seem to be all that prevent the city's monolithic buildings from falling into each other. Other setups are on street level and allow for cars to swoop past the cameras by inches. The intensity of the action is heightened because Georgie has forced Joe to drive the getaway car and because of Conrad A. Nervig's razor-sharp cutting.

Side Street was one of many hard-hitting, mid-budget MGM dramas that were pushed through in the late 1940s and early '50s by Dore Schary, who became the studio's chief of production in 1948, a year after leaving RKO. (While there, he championed Nicholas Ray's social-conscience noir *They Live by Night*, the first teaming of Farley Granger and Cathy O'Donnell; see Chapter 6.) MGM overlord Louis B. Mayer hated Schary's "message pictures," convinced that they were fundamentally un-American. But to postwar audiences receptive to realism, the films were welcome.

The inherently vulnerable qualities of Granger and O'Donnell make Joe and Ellen's situation particularly compelling and also provide a pointed contrast with the criminals.

Georgie is the best role muscular James Craig had in a thirty-five-year screen career. Edmon Ryan brings an arrogant, disagreeable sneer to the lawyer Backett, and Jean Hagen—promoted in the *Side Street* trailer as "A Coming Hollywood Star"—is at once distasteful and pathetic as an alcoholic, none-too-gifted night-club singer. Joe is unsuited by temperament to consort with such people, but because he does, *Side Street* encourages us to be mindful of our limitations as well as our aspirations.

What's a Girl to Do?

Family is often central to noir. As we've seen in this chapter, *Try and Get Me!*'s Howard Tyler yearns to nurture and provide for his family and chooses a disastrously inappropriate way to go about it. Stella, the morally slack waitress of *Fallen Angel*, wants a husband and a proper home but plays the wrong man and suffers for it. In Mitchell Leisen's *No Man of Her Own* (1950), Helen Ferguson (Barbara Stanwyck) becomes pregnant after a sexual affair and is abandoned by her no-good lover, Steve (Lyle Bettger). While on a train, Helen meets a sweetly charming pregnant woman, Patrice Harkness (Phyllis Thaxter), and the woman's amiable and modestly wealthy husband, Hugh Harkness (Richard Denning). Moments after Patrice asks Helen to hold her wedding ring while she washes her hands, the train is upended in a grinding crash.

In a sobering revelation, the Harknesses (and the unborn Harkness baby) are among the dead, but Helen survives—with Patrice's ring on her finger. Because Helen is groggy after the crash and a subsequent C-section, and unable to properly respond to questions, hospital personnel assume she's Patrice. As Helen's mind clears, she remembers something Patrice had mentioned to her: The Harkness family has never seen Patrice, not even a photograph. With the possibility of a name and a home for her baby boy, Helen gambles that she can pull off an impersonation.

Mother and Father Harkness (Jane Cowl and Henry O'Neill, in appealing performances) accept and love "Patrice" and the baby. The noirish worldview enters when the wolfishly grinning Steve resurfaces to put the touch on Helen for some blackmail money and, worse, to demand that she marry him—right now—so that he'll receive a part of the Harkness fortune when the parents pass on. Backed against that figurative wall and dependent on Hugh's brother Bill (John Lund) for help, Helen puts a bullet into Steve and keeps watch later as Bill dumps the body over a lonely railroad bridge into a freight train passing underneath. The late-breaking twist to the story is that Steve was already dead when Helen shot him. So who killed the blackmailer?

Enjoyably improbable and as sudsy as a soap opera, *No Man of Her Own* examines what was once an untenable predicament for a woman: to be unmarried and pregnant. Because women were neither expected nor given serious opportunities to support themselves, many in Helen's situation were doomed not just to social approbation but to emotional isolation and poverty (that is, if they elected not to risk their lives with a back-alley abortionist). Even the title reflects society's eagerness to place the onus on the woman: *No Man of Her Own*, no man, no man . . .

When the picture was shot in 1949, the illusive virtues that helped motivate America during World War II were very fresh: freedom, home, family, decency, and other faintly self-righteous qualities. Good luck to you if you were a woman in Helen's situation. (The issue of unwed pregnancy is explored from

Case File: Sydney Boehm (1908–90)

This screenwriter with a knack for noir came to movies relatively late in life, at age thirty-eight, after success as a newspaperman. In Hollywood, he wrote a mix of adaptations and originals from 1947 to 1967 and was active in episodic television until 1971. From the beginning of his movie career, Boehm was interested in degrees of guilt, suggesting in screenplay after screenplay that few among us are completely innocent and that we're often complicit in our downfalls. Boehm's noir projects, in particular, focus on flawed protagonists whose impulses threaten to pull down everything they value. His first noir, *Side Street* (a cautionary tale about reckless, spur-of-the-moment decision making), was followed by *The Big Heat* (the unintended fallout of revenge) and *Rogue Cop* (the sorry consequences of personal corruption). Boehm wrote many non-noir crime thrillers, too, including *The High Wall*, *The Undercover Man* (directed by Joseph H. Lewis), *Mystery Street* (directed by John Sturges), *Union Station*, *Black Tuesday*, *Violent Saturday* (directed by Richard Fleischer), and *Six Bridges to Cross*. Boehm also wrote westerns and the adapted screenplay for a science-fiction landmark, *When Worlds Collide*.

a gritty- working-class perspective in Ida Lupino's 1949 directorial debut, *Not Wanted*, with Sally Forrest as the unhappy young mother.)

Director Mitchell Leisen was an accomplished, unpretentious filmmaker who had done one of Stanwyck's best pictures, *Remember the Night* (1940), in which the actress took another outsider role, as an incorrigible shoplifter whose heart is softened by kindness. Leisen also directed a superior Paulette Goddard vehicle, *Kitty* (1945), in which a cultured man takes an eighteenth-century girl of the streets and fashions a lady. Both of those movies are about transformation, and *No Man of Her Own* continues that theme. The culture demands that Helen become someone else. Her deepest flaw isn't the desperation that prompts her to impersonate Patrice but the poor judgment that led her into Steve's arms without weighing consequences.

Bill Harkness intuits almost immediately that "Patrice" is an imposter but says nothing because he's busy falling in love with her. Their side trip into grim criminality will have unhappy consequences that, fortunately, won't be nearly as severe as they might have been. Patrice Harkness will continue to live and prosper.

The 1948 source novel, Cornell Woolrich's *I Married a Dead Man* (published under the author's "William Irish" pseudonym), is practically a screenplay already. When it was adapted by Leisen, and Sally Benson and Catherine Turney, very little was altered. Leisen and cinematographer Daniel L. Fapp brought an edgy darkness to the Helen-Steve scenes in New York and then executed a turnabout by softening the visual style after Helen has met the Harkness couple aboard the train. The visuals switch back again to nightmarish darkness as the train derails and turns over. (For that shocking sequence, Stanwyck and actress Phyllis Thaxter stood in a powder room set that was actually an enormous steel drum that rotated on a gimbal to simulate the ferocious crash. The mechanical effect is as good as any you'll see in any film from the era.)

At home with Mother and Father Harkness, the visual tone again becomes warm and soft-edged, serving to complement the welcoming nature of the large, loving house. When Steve slithers back into Helen's life, harsh shadows return and continue until the story's final moments. Carefully lit stage work that simulates dark, slushy streets is superb and gives the body-disposal sequence a lot of malicious entertainment value. Steve, the rat, gets what he deserves.

A "woman's picture" with noir's bite—that sums up *No Man of Her Own.*

You're Never as Important as You Think

Mal Granger is a smart cookie—smart enough to kiss the LA phone company goodbye and take a job as technical expert for a large bookie operation. He eventually organizes the bookies and takes over the whole setup. Suddenly, he's wealthy and powerful. When the national crime syndicate comes calling, Granger agrees to a partnership. As you might anticipate, the arrangement goes sour, and by the time *711 Ocean Drive* (1950) gallops to its conclusion, Mal is deep within the workings of Boulder Dam, in dutch with the syndicate and running from cops who will shortly kill him.

Although not stylistically aligned with noir, *711 Ocean Drive* deals in a sort of hard-truth irony that reflects an important aspect of the noir sensibility: Not all of your enemies will be punished. You may lose everything, including your life, and the puppet masters will go on. And they won't bother to be smug about it, because the moment you're out of their hair, they will have forgotten about you. To them, you never existed.

To Mal (Edmond O'Brien), nothing is more important or memorable than Mal. His mindset puts him at odds with the big boys and also compromises his love affair with Gail Mason (Joanne Dru), the wife of the syndicate's number-two, Larry Gordon (smarmily well-played by Don Porter). Mal arranges to have Gordon killed, and when Gail presses him about the death later, Mal swears that he had nothing to do with it. The pair's romance continues, based now on Mal's lie. (Mal has cruelly brushed off an earlier girlfriend [Cleo Moore] by telling her to take her "plans" to some other guy. He's a real sweetie, isn't he?)

Another neat irony about the syndicate is that it doesn't have to dispose of Mal itself. It just calls the cops and lets them take care of it. This notion of the establishment being manipulated by forces of lawlessness is bleak, even despairing, and another of the film's links to noir thinking. (But think: The syndicate is just a corporation, and corporations use politicians and police to do their dirty work all the time. Don't they?)

Capable journeyman director Joseph H. Newman (most famous for the 1956 extravaganza *Forbidden Planet*) shot *711 Ocean Drive* on locations in LA, Palm Springs, and, most vividly, at Boulder Dam. Much of the story unfolds in blazing sunlight, but there's no comfort in the brightness. Even the interludes in gorgeous Palm Springs have a sense of menace. Mal thinks highly of himself, but he can't escape his mistakes. Rain or shine, he's going to pay.

The picture was scripted by Robert English and Francis Swann. Two bits of business, nicely framed by Newman and his director of photography, Frank F. Planer (this is Franz Planer, who was frequently credited as Frank), sum up Mal's rise and fall. Relatively early in the story, after Mal has bought himself a Malibu beach house, a throwaway close-up calls brief attention to Mal's wristwatch, a handsome and obviously expensive timepiece with an elegant rectangular case. It's the watch of someone who's arrived. At this stage of the narrative, Mal is happy with Mal. Mal is on the rise.

Near the film's climax, Mal flees Nevada cops in a hopeless attempt to get across to Arizona. He climbs a very narrow, extraordinarily steep, and absurdly long utility staircase located deep within the dam. He climbs and climbs, finally stopping for breath, and then climbs some more. Newman shoots down on Mal as he climbs toward us and then shoots up on Mal as he climbs away. From whichever perspective, Mal doesn't make much progress. His labors aren't exactly Sisyphean (he doesn't tumble back down the steps), but all that effort certainly seems futile. And guess what? It is. Mal is climbing, but he's falling, too.

Newman utilized Boulder Dam and (in an earlier sequence in which Mal addresses all of his bookies) a pipe-choked gas works in much the way Raoul Walsh used the oil-processing plant in *White Heat* (1949; see Chapter 7). These are harsh, mechanized environments that throb with technology (the dam's turbines and access tunnels are remarkable) but that, by design, lack humanity. They are as cold and efficient as Mal has imagined himself to be, but efficiency is of limited value when you've killed your human qualities.

As the ambitious protagonist, Edmond O'Brien is aggressive and innately appealing. He's a crumb, but he has sparkle. Otto Kruger brings oily charm to his role as the syndicate's insouciant Mr. Big, and character actor Robert Osterloh is chilling as the rude, cocksure hit man who does Mal's dirty work—only to be crushed by Mal's car and thrown into the sea after making an unwise demand for hush money.

Dirty money, ambition, living—it's all so real, so urgent and important. But make enough mistakes and it's all over, and everything moves on without you.

A Dream for the Dead

Partly because of location shooting and Max Green's highly textured cinematography, London is explicated just as assuredly in Jules Dassin's *Night and the City* (1950) as New York in *The Asphalt Jungle*, and LA and Palm Springs in *711 Ocean Drive*. This time, though, our doomed antihero isn't a mere hooligan or an overconfident tech expert but an incurable dreamer, a confabulator who is convinced that "a life of ease and plenty" is within his grasp. But his struggle seems unending, and during the long march to his goal, he lies, steals, manipulates, and betrays.

Scripter Jo Eisinger—whom we've already met in discussions of *Gilda* and *Crime of Passion*—adapted Gerald Kersh's wickedly brilliant 1946 novel, eliminating the unfilmable (a subplot about narcotics and the white slave trade) and combining some characters to get at the essence of American expat Harry Fabian (Richard Widmark), an unfulfilled, impoverished schemer who has dabbled in the risky (a dog track) and the absurd (a petrol pill). (The casting of Widmark altered Kersh's conception of Harry, whom the novel describes as an unusually puny man with a sunken chest, narrow shoulders, and an enormous head. Also, Kersh's Harry is a Brit who only pretends to be American.)

Harry lusts for money, but even more than that, he wants to be "a somebody." None of that is news to Harry's long-suffering lover, Mary (Gene Tierney, in a novel working-class role). She's given him money in the past, but now she's fed up. "No! No!" she cries after the latest request.

Phlegmatic, obese Phil Nosseross (Francis L. Sullivan) owns the Silver Fox club, where Harry freelances as a tout and Mary is employed as a B-girl. Phil appreciates Harry's glibness and other minor gifts but mildly accuses him of having a "highly inflamed imagination." Well, one of Harry's fancies *has* come true: a perfunctorily sexual affair with Phil's wife, Helen (Googie Withers). Repulsed by her massive, lovestruck husband, she uses Harry to obtain an operator's license that will allow her to reopen a shuttered club and leave Phil. (As things develop, Harry delivers a license that's spotted by a policeman as a forgery.)

When Phil discovers his wife's affair, his anguish takes the form of revenge—masquerading as a business loan—that helps set up Harry's final arc of triumph, struggle, and downfall (the shape of which recalls one definition of literary tragedy). This is Harry's audacious scheme to stake his claim to a portion of London's pro-wrestling circuit, which is presently controlled by a quietly sinister fellow named Kristo (Herbert Lom). Through guile and audaciousness that you can't help but admire, Harry does an end run around Kristo by forging an alliance with Kristo's aged father, a legendary Greco-Roman grappler named Gregorius (played by former champion wrestler Stanislaus Zbyszko). Harry disingenuously promises Gregorius that Fabian-style wrestling will be clean and classical—not the scripted junk played out by the Strangler (Mike Mazurki) and others in Kristo's stable.

At the climax of a physically intimate sequence that's redolent with sweat, suspense, and dread, Gregorius dies following an impromptu grudge bout that Harry's calculated wheedling has encouraged. Now Harry Fabian is a dead man, and the third act of *Night and the City*, which whirls us up, down, and across ruined London, begins.

Throughout his shoot, Dassin (already under the scrutiny of Red-baiting politicians when the picture was shot in 1949) aggressively worked to pummel us with crane shots, close-ups, furious tracking shots, de Chirico–like shadowplay, queer highlights on faces, and tilted angles. Postwar London, shot at night or beneath bilious, overcast skies, appears blasted and intimidating.

Many shots of Harry and the menacing Phil Nosseross are made from floor level, a decision that is particularly bold because, although it gives Harry height and emphasizes Phil's intimidating bulk, it paradoxically diminishes each man. We literally look up to them, only to see their flaws and failings.

Fabian is one of the best roles Richard Widmark ever had, and from it came one of the actor's most agitated and flavorful performances. Harry really is a terrible person of low morality, and yet he's oddly endearing. Mary sees something in him, and so do we.

Gene Tierney is honest and direct, though her role is small. Other support, particularly from Googie Withers (an important British star with a sly, very unconventional sex appeal), the massive Francis L. Sullivan, and Herbert Lom, is sterling.

Dassin was dead-smart when he decided to find a real wrestler he could teach to act, rather than a burly actor somebody else could teach to wrestle. Stanislaus Zbyszko was seventy years old when *Night and the City* was made. Over the many years, the indomitable wrestler had become a great, ruined monument, with a bald head as large as a frigate's cannonball and a massive chest that faded into an even more massive, solid belly. Fleshy but massive upper arms and forearms suggested incredible strength. Years of pummeling had caused his eyelids to droop (he had retired in 1925), and scar tissue distorted his face and ears. As the story's pillar of integrity, he's beautiful.

The 2005 Criterion DVD release of *Night and the City* includes a documentary about the American and British cuts, which illuminates visual and narrative differences, and particularly differences of musical score: Franz Waxman's for the USA; Benjamin Frankel's for the UK.

Fear, Conscience, and Justice

The 1920s marked a high point for the modern Ku Klux Klan; states as disparate as Texas, Maine, Oklahoma, and Oregon had officeholders with Klan affiliation, and national membership stood at a robust four million. After that, as the nation became preoccupied with the economy and war, Klan membership dropped precipitously. But antiblack, anti-Catholic sentiment never went away, of course, and neither did the Klan. A particularly noxious printed manifestation of Klan sentiment, *Take Your Choice: Separation or Mongrelization*, by Dixiecrat U.S. Senator Theodore Bilbo, was published in 1947. A year later, some seven hundred hooded Klansmen staged a dramatic nighttime rally (complete with de rigueur burning cross) at Stone Mountain, Georgia.

Of all the major studios, Warner Bros. demonstrated the greatest commitment to social issues. A 1936 Warner melodrama, *Black Legion*, condemned a true-life proto-Klan organization. Postwar Klan activity intrigued Warner Bros. staff producer Jerry Wald, who headed production of Stuart Heisler's *Storm Warning* (1951), a thriller that's not simply one of the most viscerally shocking of all noir pictures but that relative rarity: a topical noir.

Shortly after stepping off a nighttime bus to visit her newly married sister in a small Southern town, New York model Marsha Mitchell (Ginger Rogers) witnesses the shotgun murder of an "outsider" reporter, perpetrated outside the local jail by the Ku Klux Klan. As Marsha secretly watches, two of the men remove their hoods to examine their victim. Marsha silently flees. At her sister's house later, Marsha is shocked to discover that one of the men she saw is her grinning, loutish brother-in-law, Hank (Steve Cochran, spookily effective as a dangerous dullard).

For the remainder of Daniel Fuchs and Richard Brooks's nerve-jangling screenplay, Marsha is forced to weigh her conscience and sense of justice against her desire to protect her naïve (and pregnant) sister, Lucy (Doris Day). Pressured by the tough and determined local district attorney, Burt Rainey (Ronald Reagan), and threatened by increasingly suspicious Klansmen, Marsha reneges on a promise to tell the truth, has a later change of heart, and nearly loses her life.

When Marsha lies at the carnival-like inquest, claiming she saw nothing (not even robes), her moral failing becomes one part of the film's philosophical center. Another, equally important part is that the entire town is complicit in the crime, having shut its eyes to the Klan's activities for years. The Klan's scheme of domination has succeeded because the complicity is quiet and easy for townsfolk to pretend to ignore. Rationales are pathetic: When Rainey is visited by a contingent of local leaders, he's urged to soft-pedal the inquest. "It's bad for business, Burt," one man pleads. "Christmas is coming on!"

The Klan counts on the protection provided by the town's fear and self-interest. Not until Marsha is sickened by Hank's drunken preening after the "assailant or assailants unknown" inquest verdict, and after his clumsy attempt to sexually assault her, does she promise to reverse her testimony and tell the truth, identifying Hank and local Klan boss Charlie Barr (Hugh Sanders, in a coolly contemptible characterization). Marsha will speak out because she's been insulted and because she wants to separate her sister from Hank.

Note that Marsha's reversal happens primarily because of personal interest. Like the local businessmen, she's motivated by her own concerns. Even the icy stare of the dead man's widow (Janet Barrett) after the inquest merely shames Marsha; it doesn't move her to honesty. District Attorney Rainey exists in marked contrast, motivated strictly by the morality of the law. He knows local Klansmen personally. He likes a lot of them. But the things they do are wrong, and Rainey will get them.

The film's preoccupation with morality pulses from the screen with calculated power during two set pieces: the opening murder of the helpless, partially trussed reporter; and a climactic nighttime Klan gathering that exists, in symbolic terms, to punish Marsha for her fecklessness. Earlier sequences of the town's darkened, shadowy business district are true to uneasy noir style. The Klan rally melds traditional noir with the high theatrics of horror cinema: guttering light thrown across a vast clearing by a gigantic flaming cross; legions

Case File: Brit Noir

British noir was shaped by conditions and forces that were frankly more pressing than the cultural motivators of American noir. In Britain, enormous urban areas were smashed flat during World War II, and rural economies were upended. Thousands of civilians had perished, and a generation of young boys entered adolescence with absent or deceased fathers. Black markets thrived during years of postwar rationing of food and other commodities. Then there is the fact that Britain's rigidly stratified class system had *not* been swept away by war, as many had hoped. Resentment brewed. Because of all of this, Brit noir has a unique urgency.

More prosaically, postwar production of British B films was encouraged because of a 1948 change to Britain's film-quota system, which now insisted that nearly half of the films exhibited at the top of double bills be British-made; the ruling gave British Bs (the so-called second features) a far better chance at exhibition on double bills with prestige product.

Brit noir deals in subjects familiar to American audiences—adultery, murder of spouses, heists gone wrong, violent jealousy—but with the added fillip of the nation's persistent economic disarray, personified in many movies by black marketeers. In *They Made Me a Fugitive* (1947), one of these opportunistic fellows seeks revenge after having been framed by a woman who tried to goad him into murder. The unaccountably likeable Harry Lime of *The Third Man* (1949) traffics in tainted penicillin, and in *Wide Boy* (1952) a black-market "spiv" makes the mistake of blackmailing a member of Britain's ruling class, so that his acquisitive girlfriend can have the material things she pines for.

For the first two years of World War II, Britain stood alone against Germany, which encouraged a feeling of having been unfairly put upon, and that may help explain why a significant number of Brit noirs concern innocent people wrongly accused of crime and even imprisoned: *Murder in Reverse* (1945; a man is convicted for a killing that never happened), *The October Man* (1947; a false accusation is sparked by paranoid mob mentality), *For Them That Trespass* (1949), *The Long Memory* (1952), *Time Without Pity* (1957), and *Blind Date* (1959; upper-class seductress frames working-class youth).

The British ambivalence about capital punishment is vividly expressed by *Yield to the Night* aka *Blonde Sinner* (1956), a rethinking of the infamous Ruth Ellis murder case. And three pictures—*Brighton Rock* (1947; from the Grahame Greene novel), *Cosh Boy* aka *The Slasher* (1953), and *The Sleeping Tiger* (1954)—are particularly powerful treatments of juvenile delinquency. Unstable minds, another noir trope, are the angry engines of *Wanted for Murder* (1946) and *Mine Own Executioner* (1947).

Some Brit stars became keenly identified with noir: Dirk Bogarde, Stanley Baker, Diana Dors, Richard Attenborough, Googie Withers, Trevor Howard, Margaret Lockwood, John Mills, and James Mason.

As the Hollywood studio system began to break down in the late 1940s, many American actors found work in Britain, often in noir projects. Male imports include Richard Basehart, Lloyd Bridges, Dane Clark, George Raft, Marc Lawrence, Dan Duryea,

Zachary Scott, Tom Neal, and John Ireland. Among the actresses are Gloria Grahame, Lizabeth Scott, Barbara Payton, Hillary Brooke, and Alexis Smith. In addition, low-budget American producer Robert Lippert maintained a British unit that turned out noir and quasi-noir that could be profitably exhibited in the U.S. as well as in Britain.

No single British director became as dominant a noir filmmaker as, say, Anthony Mann or Fritz Lang, but numerous people made significant contributions: Roy Ward Baker, Montgomery Tully, J. Lee Thompson, Peter Graham Scott, Lewis Gilbert, Ken Hughes, Tony Young, and John Gilling. Amusingly, one of the more important directors of Brit noir, Alberto Cavalcanti, was a Brazilian whose formative filmmaking experiences were in France.

Of American directors who made noir films in Britain (after having been pummeled by Hollywood's Red scare), the most notable are Joseph Losey (by far the most important in this regard), Edward Dmytryk, and Cyril Endfield (South African by birth but a product of Hollywood).

The success of playwright John Osborne, novelist John Braine, and other "angry young man" writers at the end of the 1950s caused Brit noir to be superseded by kitchen-sink drama the likes of *Look Back in Anger*, *Saturday Night and Sunday Morning*, *The Loneliness of the Long Distance Runner*, and *Alfie*. Melodrama was out; stylized social realism was in.

The ruined dreams of postwar Britain are embodied by Diana Dors in *Yield to the Night* (1956).

of hooded figures; kneeling initiates who wear peculiar half-masks; Marsha's medieval punishment beneath repeated lashes of a whip. To this point, the film's exteriors were actual "Main Street" locations in Corona, California, but key portions of the rally sequence were shot on an enormous, brilliantly dressed soundstage that allowed for precise audio control (the crack of the whip is sickening) and for a stunning crane setup that shoots down from above the flaming cross as Marsha and others move and struggle below. Is this the eye of an unhappy God? (It's certainly the expertise of a canny director; a skilled cinematographer, Carl Guthrie; and a clever art director, Leo K. Kuter.)

A carefully composed shot of a hooded woman who lifts her similarly garbed child onto her shoulder, so it can see the unfolding action, is pointedly revolting and a backhanded acknowledgment of the Klan's spurious emphasis on Protestant family life. When the police close in, a shovelful of blunt morality is provided via the increasingly panicked Hank, who takes a single shot at Rainey, only to be cut down by a burst from a trooper's machine gun.

But *Storm Warning* isn't done with us yet. Hank's shot was off the mark, and now someone he claimed to love is dead.

The script doesn't explore racism, nor does it get into precisely what this Klan chapter stands for, or even opposes, other than snoopy "outsiders." Although concerns of black life aren't addressed, a few black people are glimpsed in a crowded town square sequence—novel for a studio picture from 1951 and an almost subliminal (and inadequate) way of suggesting the Klan's agenda. Mainstream cinema wasn't yet ready to shout down racism, but in Marsha, who had never troubled herself with reflective thought, we at least have a figure suggestive of part of the problem.

Choose Your Fall Guy with Care

In Phil Karlson's tight and brutal *Kansas City Confidential* (1952), Tim Foster (Preston Foster) is an establishment figure who has turned against the establishment. A former police captain who was forced into early retirement for spurious health reasons, he conceives and carries out an elaborate armored-car heist that he will eventually crack himself, betraying the three thugs he has selected as his accomplices. Trouble is, the scheme involves setting up an innocent man, an ex-con named Joe Rolfe (John Payne). He's the patsy whose floral-delivery van will be duplicated at the crime scene as a diversion. Joe is arrested when the phony van is miles away, tucked in the back of a tractor-trailer. It takes a day and a night and part of the next day—and two or three vicious police beatings—before Joe's innocence is determined.

After all of that, he's on a mission to uncover who set him up.

Joe's predicament is very much in the "victim of circumstance" mode, and although Joe is clearly the film's protagonist, the key character around which everything spins is Foster. It is his carefully wrought but flawed scheme that brings the characters together, propels the action, and encourages violent little dustups between the doomed players.

The film achieves a special weirdness when Foster greets his accomplices, one by one, before the robbery: So that nobody will know who anybody else is until it's time to divide the take, Foster wears a peculiar leather mask, with a formed forehead, eyeholes, and nose but a loose leather flap over the bottom half of his face. In its anatomical strangeness, the mask suggests something from an old dark house thriller or an Edgar Wallace *krimi* about a deformed fiend.

When the three accomplices are together, each wears a mask, too, which further heightens the oddness while preserving the mutual anonymity Foster desires.

Phil Karlson shot the picture's opening sequences on location in LA (doubling for Kansas City) in a documentary-like style, with plenty of natural sunshine, sidewalks crowded with extras, and a dispassionate—if brutally executed—visualization of the robbery. After Joe finds one of the holdup men, beats the hell out of him, and takes his mask and identity, the remainder of the story plays out in Mexico. Karlson and cinematographer George E. Diskant shot these sequences, interiors and exteriors alike, mainly on stages designed to simulate a not-bad resort. Lighting is carefully controlled and is quite different from the look of the early scenes in Kansas City. There's a lot of shadowplay in "Mexico," rich and velvety and suggestive of climatic and emotional humidity.

Foster is there, as "himself"—just a retired cop doing some fishing. He keeps an eye on Joe and the other hard guys: a snake-eyed womanizer named Tony Romano (Lee Van Cleef) and a gum-chewing dandy called Boyd Kane (Neville Brand.) Each of the three warily sizes up the other; after all, none has seen the others' faces and isn't even sure if they're partners.

Romano and Kane eventually go a little stir-crazy and begin pulling guns on Joe, whom they've decided to dislike. Joe gets gut-punched and has to crack a few heads. The conflict is like a dance, choreographed just so, as one guy or another gains a momentary advantage, only to lose it suddenly. Close-ups are used aggressively, and faces are frequently bunched together in the frame and shot from below, suggesting that these agitated characters want to burst from the top of the frame.

Foster schemes to arrange a rendezvous for the split on his boat, the ironically named *Manana*, after he's alerted an old friend from the KCPD about the meet. Because Foster plans not to be aboard, only the stooges (and poor Joe) will be caught with the loot. Foster will get all credit for uncovering the scheme, and will most likely be reinstated. And as a sweet bonus, he'll walk away with the insurance company's reward—a standard 25 percent, which amounts to a cool quarter million.

Kansas City Confidential (the title was inspired by a popular series of "Confidential" tell-all books by journalists Lee Mortimer and Jack Lait) builds to that meeting on the boat and doesn't disappoint. Once onboard, everybody double-crosses everybody else for the cash. Slugs fly, and a lot of jokers end up dead. Foster ends up in a very bad spot, too, but a word from him to an insurance investigator is enough to clear Joe.

The ex-cop has been a smart cookie. He reads the crooks correctly, but his scheme hits the wall because he couldn't grasp the determination of an innocent man.

The Unattainable Blonde

With *Pushover* (1954), Columbia Pictures showcased two rising young contract talents, director Richard Quine and a stunningly good-looking new actress named Kim Novak. Given the B-plus treatment as a sort of coming-out party for Novak, the picture returns top-billed Fred MacMurray to the moral quicksand of an earlier triumph, Billy Wilder's *Double Indemnity* (1944; see Chapter 1). In the Wilder film, MacMurray plays an insurance agent who agrees to help a seductive blonde bump off her husband for the insurance payout. In *Pushover*, MacMurray is a Los Angeles police detective who conspires with the blonde Novak to dispose of her fugitive boyfriend and grab the $210,000 the boyfriend has stolen from a bank. Greed is almost never a good quality, but it's not a difficult one to understand, either. The trouble is that, although MacMurray's Paul Sheridan wants the money, he wants the woman, Leona, more. Because the cop's motivation is ferociously sexual rather than analytical, he works against his own better judgment and engineers his own downfall.

Scripter Roy Huggins created *Pushover* by blending and adapting two existing sources, "The Killer Wore a Badge," a 1951 *Saturday Evening Post* novelette by Thomas Walsh, and *Rafferty*, a 1953 novel by William S. Ballinger. Like Huggins's later creation, TV's *The Fugitive*, *Pushover* is smart and character driven, with a pleasingly convoluted plot and a great deal of almost unbearable suspense. (Example: Sheridan is on stakeout with other detectives, watching Leona in her apartment. When Sheridan steps out for an illicit rendezvous, one of Leona's neighbors happens to see Sheridan where he's not supposed to be. The cop knows that if the neighbor sees him again, he's screwed. Thus begins an anxious game of cat and mouse.)

Leona is being watched because Sheridan's boss, Lt. Eckstrom (E. G. Marshall, essentially reprising the story function handled by Edward G. Robinson in *Double Indemnity*) is convinced that the woman's boyfriend, Wheeler, will come to Leona and try to escape with her and the missing loot. As Sheridan becomes increasingly obsessed with Leona, *Pushover* grows thematically and visually darker, with veteran cinematographer Lester H. White making effective use of night-for-night shooting, rain-slicked streets, and close-ups on shadowed faces caught in expressions of fear and sexual longing. Boom and tracking shots are elegant.

The protracted surveillance sequences that drive the plot are fascinating. Sheridan and other detectives have taken an apartment located directly opposite Leona's. Her phone is tapped, her conversations recorded, but the cops get most of their information from sitting in the dark and gazing at the woman through binoculars. *Pushover* is predicated on sexual desire, and this method of surveillance underscores that. Typical of the day, the detectives are male, and the film suggests that voyeuristic window peeping is a male prerogative. On this assignment, voyeurism is part of the men's jobs, but it's a distinct pleasure for them, too.

Nicely played subplots involve an aging, incompetent detective (Allen Nourse) who figures out what Sheridan is up to and winds up dead; and Sheridan's partner, Detective McAllister (Phil Carey), who can't keep his binoculars off that neighbor we mentioned earlier, a pretty nurse named Ann (Dorothy Malone). The script establishes that neither Sheridan nor McAllister is married and that their gender politics differ enormously. Sheridan has been nothing but cynical about dames; McAllister is perennially hopeful about finding the right woman. The relationships that each cop develops with the respective women function in pleasing, understated counterpoint.

As is usual in noir tales of illicit scheming, events soon overtake Sheridan, who must kill to cover himself. He has a whole laundry list of other chores: brace the bank robber, move the robber's money-stuffed car around the neighborhood, account to Eckstrom for his absences from the stakeout room, and send McAllister on a fool's errand so that Leona will be free to talk on the phone. And Sheridan hopes like hell he doesn't run into the neighbor again.

Well, he does.

MacMurray is no less coiled than in *Double Indemnity*, and Novak (who gets an "And Introducing Kim Novak" title card) begins to create the intriguingly somnambulant persona that served this underrated actress well throughout her career and would shortly turn her into Columbia's number-one asset. (She later had a decade-long romance with director Richard Quine.) Other performances are solid; special mention should be made of Paul Richards, who brings creepy determination to his small but pivotal role as the robber Wheeler; and the aforementioned Allen Nourse, whose portrait of the forlorn but principled Paddy Dolan is heartbreaking.

A Beautiful Plan

Although Stanley Kubrick titled his third feature *Day of Violence*, United Artists, which was distributing, insisted on *The Killing*—and for once the suits got it right. "The Killing" is a grim and lovely title because of its multiplicity of meanings. As scripted by crime novelist Jim Thompson and Kubrick, "the killing" is a successfully executed robbery. It also means the sudden deaths of numerous individuals, the fatal implosion of a marriage, and the annihilation of many dreams. A box-office flop but a critical favorite when released in 1956, *The Killing* still stands tall as one of the best and most haunting American thrillers of that artistically rich decade.

Stanley Kubrick's marvelous *The Killing* (1956) turns on the quiet desperation of small men who make a big score—and then things really get interesting. Key members of the group include (from left) Ted de Corsia, Joe Sawyer, Elisha Cook Jr., Sterling Hayden, and Jay C. Flippen.

Career criminal Johnny Clay (Sterling Hayden) has been practicing his craft for a long time. Now he wants to get out after one last score: an audacious robbery of $2 million from a horse track. Working with men on the inside and the outside, Johnny plots the robbery like a military assault, with diversions, feints, and a keen understanding of the weaknesses of the "enemy." By the time an enormous sack of cash comes sailing from a high window to an accomplice below, it seems that nothing can derail the scheme.

But *The Killing* is very concerned with point of view. Indeed, as in the 1955 source novel, Lionel White's *Clean Break*, the narrative is fragmented, told and retold, so that we witness the run-up to the robbery and the assault itself from five different points of view. Sober, mildly urgent voice-over narration (by Art Gilmore) keeps us apprised of who's who and what's what. (This "Rashomon" quality of exposition told and retold attracted Frank Sinatra, who liked the novel but was slow to option the property.) Each reworking of the narrative reveals a fresh, and frequently ominous, angle, and we see how strongly Thompson and Kubrick's major preoccupation, human nature, is going to figure in the outcome.

Everything begins to come unglued because one of the inside men, George Peatty (Elisha Cook), so desperately wants to impress his no-good wife, Sherry (a luminously creepy Marie Windsor), that he tells her the whole plan. Not unexpectedly, Sherry has a lover, Val (Vince Edwards), who figures that he and an accomplice can burst in on the gang during the split and take the money for themselves.

George and Sherry exist together in domestic hell. Preparation for the score has made George feel queasy, and he complains about it to his wife, who never looks up from her magazine as she lounges on the bed.

GEORGE
I been kinda sick today, I keep gettin' pains in my stomach.

SHERRY (pleasantly)
Maybe you've got a hole in it, George, do you suppose you have?

GEORGE
A hole in it? How would I get a hole in my stomach?

SHERRY
How would you get one in your head? Oh, fix me a drink, George, I think I'm developing some pains myself.

GEORGE
Sherry, can't I ever say anything at all without you joking about it?

SHERRY
Hurry up with that drink, George, the pains are getting worse.

Johnny's longtime relationship with a sweet woman named Fay (Coleen Gray) exists in obvious counterpoint to George and Sherry's. Guileless Fay has adored Johnny since they both were kids. "I've always believed you," she tells Johnny, "everything you ever told me. . . . I'm not pretty and I'm not smart, so please don't leave me alone again." (Piquant dialogue, but the truth is that actress Coleen Gray isn't just pretty but beautiful.)

Another inside man, track bartender O'Reilly (Joe Sawyer), is devoted to his sick wife (Dorothy Adams) and plans to use his cut to take her out of their drafty flat and restore her health. Kubrick's handling of this is honest and touching.

In a daring and unexpected moment, the scheme's aging "bank," Marvin Unger (Jay C. Flippen), tells Johnny he regards him as a son and suggests that the two of them go away together after the split, to relax and "take stock." There had been gay characters in film noir before but never any that engender such compassion and pity in the viewer. Johnny, true to his nature as a decent man and a cool head, pleasantly dismisses the idea.

Two contract men who will take flat fees instead of shares are also involved. One is Maurice (Kola Kwariani), a middle-aged bear of a man who wrestles when he needs money and plays chess when he doesn't. His task is to physically engage track security so that Johnny can slip through a critical door.

The other contract player is Nicky (Timothy Carey), a chicken farmer and lover of MG sports cars and semiautomatic weapons. He's also a deadeye with a sniper rifle and will earn $5,000 for the diversionary shooting of a particular horse as it rounds the far turn.

A lot of people are ventilated when Sherry's lover makes his play. Only Johnny and Fay get out alive, hauling the money in an oversized suitcase as they hurry to the airport.

But the suitcase has a bad latch . . .

The Killing is an excitingly visual movie. Kubrick had been a New York street photographer for *LOOK* magazine during 1945–50 and had an impeccable eye for lighting, composition, and the beauty of black-and-white film stock. Cinematographer on *The Killing* was veteran Lucien Ballard, one of the best in the business and very much a sophisticated creature of Hollywood. (Ballard's wife was movie star Merle Oberon.) Because the rumpled, twenty-eight-year-old Kubrick was very definite about what he wanted, Ballard felt that a stripling was usurping his authority, and although he did as Kubrick instructed, he did so grudgingly and with great resentment. The results, though, are vivid and impressive. Single sources of light (or the illusion of same) illuminate many scenes; when the bartender enters a corridor at the track and pauses beneath a bare bulb, he looks momentarily like a lost soul. Key lights on Marie Windsor's Sherry create an edge of misleadingly warm light on her face and hair, and many scenes—Maurice's epic tussle with track cops; the daily routine of the crooked cop, Randy (Ted de Corsia); Nicky's killing of the horse—have the straightforward, efficient look of documentary.

Kubrick kept the camera in motion, most pointedly in tracking shots that follow characters through rooms and along corridors. Elements placed in the extreme foreground of the frame zip past in a flash, imparting a sense of headlong movement.

Many images, such as Johnny in a grotesque clown's mask as he holds up the money room and George's bloodied face after the shoot-out, are indelible. Kubrick slips only once, when the dead bodies of Johnny's companions are arrayed too artfully on floor and sofa.

Stanley Kubrick spoke more than once about the "meaningless" aspect of life and the ability of film to capture it. Whether he truly believed that life was without purpose is unknown, but *The Killing*, with its pitiless interest in futility, suggests that the director was keenly interested in the idea as a gateway to art.

"That's a weird, crazy idea!"

Beyond a Reasonable Doubt (1956) unreels with the dull competence of a mid-'50s television drama. Flatly directed by Fritz Lang and perfunctorily photographed by William Snyder, the film is a fitfully absorbing disappointment. Lang's star had dimmed in Hollywood by 1956, and this would be his final American effort. (He would go on to make more movies—and good ones—in Europe.) As you look at *Beyond a Reasonable Doubt*, it's difficult to believe that this visually passionless work is from the man who did *The Big Heat* just three years earlier. Lang seems to have been momentarily deflated by age (he was by now approaching sixty-five) or simple frustration.

There are compensations. Although the premise of Douglas Morrow's screenplay is absurd, the script is nevertheless sharp and compelling. Newspaper publisher Austin Spencer (Sidney Blackmer) opposes capital punishment, and his opposition has grown stronger after a guilty verdict in a high-profile murder case that hinged entirely on circumstantial evidence. No witnesses, no smoking gun, just a series of what could have been badly timed coincidences.

Former star reporter turned novelist Bob Garrett (Dana Andrews) is looking for a follow-up to his first book. Spencer suggests a nonfiction blockbuster by which he and Garrett will select a recent murder and manufacture circumstantial evidence that will point to Garrett. So strongly will it point, in fact, that Garrett will be arrested, tried, and convicted. At that point, Spencer will come forward with documentation and photographs showing how the "evidence" was manufactured and planted. Garrett will be freed, and Spencer will have made a powerful point.

By this time, any reasonable man would have been edging toward Spencer's door, but Garrett is just ambitious enough to agree. He wants that blockbuster.

A stripper has been murdered, her body dumped in a rural area. She will be Garrett's "victim." Garrett and Spencer go about their business, planting a lighter and a stocking at the crime scene. (We haven't an inkling as to why the police won't wonder how they overlooked such obvious clues during their early investigation.) Body makeup of the sort used by the victim is industriously rubbed into the upholstery of Garrett's car. He even buys a coat and hat that match what a witness says the barely glimpsed suspect was wearing when he drove off with the victim.

Garrett is painted in court as a very clumsy murderer indeed. Meanwhile, his romantic relationship with Spencer's daughter, Susan (Joan Fontaine), understandably deteriorates (she's been told nothing about the scheme).

When the inevitable happens and Garrett is found guilty, Spencer hurries to the courthouse—only to be killed in a sudden smashup that burns all the photographs and documentation.

Garrett is understandably upset over this turn of events.

Over time, as the date of Garrett's execution looms, Susan searches frantically for anything exculpatory her father might have left. She finally finds it (Spencer's letter to the executor of his estate), and Garrett is readied for a pardon. But when he makes a verbal slip in front of Susan, it's apparent that he had a history with the murdered stripper, and that he's the killer after all! His pardon is never signed, and Garrett is taken back to death row.

Beyond a Reasonable Doubt combines 1930s-style melodrama with a more contemporary torn-from-the-headlines sensibility. The film offers a good explication of the judicial system's flaws as well as the power of the press to insert itself, as it pleases, into prominent cases: After her father's death, Susan takes control of the newspaper and insists that the heretofore objective coverage of the Garrett case become aggressively pro-Garrett and anti–capital punishment. (It's a clever reversal of the "get-the-bastard" tack taken by *Cleveland Press* editor Louis B. Seltzer just two years before, in the circumstantial case against Cleveland osteopath Sam Sheppard, who was on trial for the brutal murder of his wife. The *Press* essentially convicted the young physician with headlines and editorials.)

Despite the static nature of the visuals—for a movie, *Beyond a Reasonable Doubt* doesn't move much—the film does succeed in pulling you along, and rather breathlessly, at that. "That's a weird, crazy idea!" Garrett tells Spencer as the scheme is outlined. "Maybe that's why it intrigues me." The audience is intrigued, too. Because Garrett's risk (the risk made by the "innocent" Garrett, that is) is foolhardy, we want to see how it's going to come out.

The final revelation made, it's clear that Garrett has been banking on the double jeopardy law: If he's pardoned for the stripper's murder, he can never be tried for the crime again. Although that's not to say he couldn't be brought to trial for kidnapping or felonious assault. But that never occurs to our perverse protagonist, and he's willingly swept up in Spencer's risky plan.

Dana Andrews is typically stolid and compelling, but he showed up on the set each day with a terrible hangover and wasn't effective until mid-morning. The film's producer, Burt Friedlob, was very ill during the shoot, and his illness made him querulous. A professional relationship with Lang that had gone reasonably smoothly on another 1956 release, *While the City Sleeps* (see Chapter 7), was suddenly mistrustful and frankly impossible. Friedlob obsessed over every penny and installed spies on the set to keep an eye on Lang and others.

The biggest argument was over Tom Garrett's execution, which Friedlob and RKO wanted to be shot and included in the final cut. (Rather like Billy Wilder's abandoned experiment in shooting the execution of Fred MacMurray in *Double Indemnity*.) Lang refused (such a sequence would have been completely superfluous), and his relationships with Friedlob, the studio, and Hollywood were over—despite not-bad notices and okay box office.

The Art of Larceny

Many of film noir's visual and thematic conventions are at play in *The Burglar* (1957), the first picture directed by Paul Wendkos. Because Wendkos studied film at New York's progressive New School for Social Research—that is, because he was a New Yorker who didn't come up through the Hollywood system—he was inclined to regard film primarily as an art form, and as "product" only secondarily. And indeed, *The Burglar*, which Wendkos directed for Samson Productions (for release by Columbia) when he was thirty-two or thirty-five (accounts of his birth date vary), has the look of an unusually accomplished student effort. Does that mean that the picture is distractingly self-conscious? Yes. But *The Burglar* is never less than stimulating.

Weary professional burglar Nat Harbin (Dan Duryea) heads a small gang that snatches an emerald necklace from the mansion of an oddball philanthropist named Sister Sara. (In a nod to Orson Welles, Sister Sara has a home theater where she watches herself in booming newsreels.) The jumpy member of the group, Baylock (Peter Capell), wants to find a fence and cash in right away, but Nat insists that it's best to wait—the necklace is too hot. The loutish Dohmer (Mickey Shaughnessy) is mellower, except when Nat's companion, Gladden (Jayne Mansfield), enters his field of vision. Then Dohmer becomes a sex maniac. We learn later that Gladden is Nat's stepsister, the daughter of a burglar who took Nat in as a boy. Nat's own innocence was corrupted long ago, so his only link to decency is the soft-spoken young woman.

Growing internal conflict and the unwelcome attentions of a crooked cop (Stewart Bradley) and his curvy accomplice (Martha Vickers) cause the gang to disintegrate.

David Goodis, adapting his own 1953 novel, scripted *The Burglar*. Like Jim Thompson, Goodis had an unremittingly bleak view of fate and human nature. True to form, the events of *The Burglar* are cynical, violent, and dour. Nat is good at what he does, but he's mentally wrung out. Baylock and Dohmer are dangerously unpredictable, and Gladden yearns to spread her wings and explore the world on her own, without Nat's careful oversight. But because she's naïve, she ends up in harm's way. Nat intervenes, but between the doggedness of the legit cops and the murderousness of the crooked one, he hasn't a chance.

In one of those cinematic devices for which Hitchcock expressed disdain, some of the robbery, and all of its immediate aftermath, is shot from inside the safe, through a round aperture that looks onto the room. This may bother you (what's a camera doing inside Sister Sara's safe?), but as a cinematic device it's effective, particularly when the gargling Sister Sara (Phoebe Mackay) walks past the open safe without noticing it; pads across the room going the other way, still oblivious; and finally sees what's happened on her third pass, when she thrusts her face into the camera (the safe).

Wendkos packs *The Burglar* with that sort of self-conscious cleverness. The instant after a TV director drops his arm to signal newscaster John Facenda that he's on the air, we cut to a dark figure dropping over Sister Sara's wall. A pensive Nat is dappled by spotty moonlight that enters through cheap chenille curtains. A dead body tumbles across a speeding car's backseat and right into our laps when the car makes a sudden sharp turn. Heads thrust upward from the bottoms of frames. When the grown-up Gladden is sexually assaulted, Wendkos and editor Herta Horn (probably Wendkos himself) rhythmically, frantically cut between the struggling bodies and the noisy rush of a nearby train.

Sol Kaplan's emphatic score is frequently intrusive, but other sound is utilized to advance the narrative, heighten tension, and add texture. We hear the downstairs television when Nat is upstairs at the safe, the maddening tick of a clock, a shrill tea kettle, and a locomotive's whistle. During the climactic foot chase inside the eerie darkness of an Atlantic City scare-in-the-dark ride (another Welles reference), demonic laughter bounces from one cave-like wall to another, and a recorded voice repeats, "We—the dead—welcome you. We—the dead—welcome you." (In this, it's easy to be reminded of Curtis Harrington, another darkly talented, academically inclined filmmaker with a fondness for overstatement.)

Night-for-night shooting by cinematographer Don Malkames (who was very active during the 1940s and early '50s with all-Negro shorts and features) is raw and intimidating, suggesting the presence of little more than available light. Dan Duryea looks like every one of his fifty years (when Nat says, "I'm thirty-five," you can't help but smile), and Jayne Mansfield, plainly dressed and with no glamour accoutrements, is a peculiar figure that glides in and out of shadow in her bare feet. Mansfield made a career of comic overstatement, but as Gladden, she's soft-spoken, fragile, and convincing.

Paul Wendkos went on to direct the fascinating evangelist drama *Angel Baby* (1960) and *The Mephisto Waltz* (1971), as well as many high-profile TV-movies. He seems to have been dedicated to being unique, and although *The Burglar* is stylistically overwrought, it's an invigorating late noir.

A Box of Poisoned Cookies

Sweet Smell of Success (1957) is ostensibly about the gutter press, but its true interest is in the criminality of the heart. Written by Clifford Odets and Ernest Lehman, and rather remorselessly directed by Alexander Mackendrick, the film dissects the ugliness of ambition and the hubris of ego.

The circulation of the *New York Globe* is dependent on gossip columnist J. J. Hunsecker (Burt Lancaster), who can make or break careers with a mere squib. Like other such columnists, J. J. takes a lot of his material from aggressive press agents, who pester and schmooze endlessly to get their clients' names in print. Self-serving Sidney Falco (Tony Curtis) is one of the less appealing of the press agent pack, endlessly (and desperately) smiling, clapping backs, and spitting venom when people's backs are turned—and often when they're not. He's attached himself to J. J., the most powerful columnist in the city. Although J. J. despises Sidney, he has assigned him a job: break up the romance between J. J.'s much-younger sister and a promising young jazz guitarist. So far, Sidney has failed, and J. J.'s patience is running out. Finally, through baroque machinations by Sidney and some frightful bullying by J. J., the romance seems to have been derailed. But Sidney has been too clever. The sister turns her back on J. J., and now Sidney must do penance.

When *Sweet Smell of Success* was released in 1957, the career of Walter Winchell, the columnist who inspired the fictional Hunsecker, had seen his popularity and power slip almost to nothing. A virtual force of nature during the

1930s and '40s, with print syndication and a national radio show, he overstayed his welcome and allowed time and taste to pass him by. When he was on top, though, Winchell's rat-a-tat style of writing and speaking (complete with cleverly coined new words) enthralled millions. His column was garbage designed for credulous nitwits, but the *New York Daily Mirror* marketed it aggressively, and helped Winchell to gain inordinate, and undeserved, power.

J. J. Hunsecker is Winchell squared. He holds court nightly at 21 and a succession of other top Manhattan clubs, where he's deferred to as if he were a demigod. But his acolytes worship rags and bones—it is established early on that J. J.'s column is a slight, arrogant thing of bad jokes, innuendo, celebrity sightings, and cheap, flag-waving patriotism.

His unwholesome solicitude of his nineteen-year-old sister Susie (baby-faced Susan Harris) borders on the pathological—they live together, and J. J. monitors her life like an obsessive mother, or lover. Typical of such obsessives, J. J. insists to Susie that everything he does is for her when, of course, his meddling is strictly for his own sake. Susie just feels smothered.

Nearly all of *Sweet Smell of Success* takes place at night. The picture was brilliantly shot on location by James Wong Howe in crisp, glittering black and white. New York looks like an alternately hard-edged and smoky amusement park for affluent grown-ups. Chico Hamilton and his Quintet (which includes jazz cello player/composer Fred Katz) is on hand for the sound of authentic jazz, and is where we find the guitarist, Steve (Martin Milner), who loves Susie.

If *Sweet Smell of Success* has a flaw, it's that the characters, though vividly drawn, are utilized as archetypes. Steve is honesty and virtue. Susie is confused innocence. J. J. is power and hatred. Another columnist, Otis (David White), is lechery. The cigarette girl, Rita (Barbara Nichols), is compromised virtue. And Sidney is all of our worst instincts in a good-looking suit.

Much of the film's dialogue is glibly epigrammatic. "I'd hate to take a bite out of you," J. J. says to Sidney. "You're a cookie filled with arsenic." When J. J. wants a light, he offers his cigarette and quietly commands, "Match me, Sidney."

Later, as J. J. dismisses somebody on the other end of a telephone line, Sidney leans across the table to address a dinner guest:

SIDNEY
Senator, do you believe in capital punishment?

SENATOR
Why?

SIDNEY
A man has just been sentenced to death.

That sort of crackling dialogue suggests that the film is almost exclusively about issues larger than the characters. (At the very least, it's about the inflated sense of melodrama that afflicts people living in an insular, incestuous world.)

Sidney, J. J., and the rest are merely devices. Naturally, one could say that about a great deal of fiction, but the artificiality seems particularly apparent here.

None of that diminishes the film's power. J. J. whips across the screen like a rogue power line, and Sidney is despicable. Like J. J., he's completely unsympathetic, but we reluctantly appreciate his small ambition. He sleeps in a shabby office where the secretary-receptionist (pretty character actress Jeff Donnell) is perpetually downcast. She's been infected by Sidney's venality and dully carries on as if she's fighting the flu. Although New York is in the grip of winter, Sidney makes his rounds clad only in his suit because he's can't afford to tip "every hat-check girl in the city."

The role of Sidney was a breakthrough for Tony Curtis, who, though a box-office force, had been an industry lightweight noted mainly for his startling good looks and his marriage to actress Janet Leigh. With *Sweet Smell of Success*, Curtis proved he was an actor. Likewise blonde bombshell Barbara Nichols, whose portrait of Rita is heartbreakingly honest and understated. Excited over a late date with Sidney at his office, Rita is shaken to see that Sidney has the lip-licking columnist Otis in tow. Sidney wants a favor from Otis, and what better way to get it than to pimp the woman who loves him? "What am I?" Rita whispers in mortification, "a bowl of fruit? A tangerine that peels in a minute?"

Although Burt Lancaster is physically miscast—we envision a gossip columnist as a smaller, more dissipated sort—he's cuttingly effective and dominates the narrative like an oppressive curtain. What's fascinating about J. J. is that even when he realizes he's lost the respect and love of his sister, even when he knows that the scheme he insisted Sidney set into motion has backfired, he still strikes out like the viper he is, ordering his "kept cop," the fearsome Lt. Kello (Emile Meyer), to find Sidney and do him serious harm. Struck to the heart, J. J. has developed no insight into himself. He will carry on as before, a little more hollow now but still immersed in self-righteous cynicism.

We're reminded of what Sidney has snarled at his hapless secretary: "This is life, get used to it!"

Keeping Control of the Kill

Because noir is predicated on issues of crime, the genre is inevitably preoccupied with class and social status. Who wants to be (in the argot of *The Asphalt Jungle*) a hooligan? Nobody. Even a hooligan has aspirations. And the hooligan's aspirations, like so many, depend on ready money. The dollar. It's almost always at issue, in noir and in life.

Irving Lerner's simultaneously primitive and complex *Murder by Contract* (1958) was written by Ben Simcoe and the uncredited Ben Maddow. (Maddow was a longtime leftist who coscripted *The Asphalt Jungle* and other major films and often worked as a script doctor, which is apparently the case here. He also had some trouble with the Hollywood blacklist, which caused at least some of his work to be anonymous.) Our protagonist is a handsome young professional assassin named Claude (Vince Edwards), who keeps a tally book that he checks regularly. He's putting together the down payment for a house on the Ohio River, and every hit brings him closer to that dream. He doesn't like the life of a paid killer. He doesn't dislike it, either. The occupation is just a means to an end, and Claude looks at it—and at people and life in general—through analytical, objective eyes. He makes seventy-five dollars a week in his day job as a comptometer operator. Murder is more lucrative, so it's better.

Vince Edwards's unnervingly restrained performance is an incongruent wonder of focus and passivity that revolves around the killer's need to retain control. Claude harangues and humiliates a waiter (Joe Mell) for bringing a coffee cup stained with lipstick—and then tosses the wretch a fat tip. When Claude arrives in Los Angeles to do a job, he directs events by telling his puzzled handlers, "I'd like to see the Pacific Ocean." Days later, after visits to the zoo, the movies, and a driving range, he's still not ready to scope out the federal witness who is his target. Claude says, "Not enough people take time to think."

The perplexed local contacts are George (Herschel Bernardi) and Mark (Phillip Pine). Neither of them can get a handle on Claude, but at least George is willing to go along and see what happens. Mark is aggressively impatient and continually in Claude's face. *What are you doing now? When are you gonna start on this? Shouldn't you check out the house? The trial starts in six days. What's taking you so long?* If all of that bothers Claude, he doesn't show it.

The implicit suggestion is that Claude has been spending his days in the city getting his mind in order, clearing his brain of clutter and cultivating the focus he'll need to do the job. One day, he sits down with Mark and George and explains something.

> CLAUDE
> I wasn't born this way. I trained myself. I eliminate personal feeling.

> MARK
> You're born like everybody else. Flesh and blood. Ya gotta feel!

> CLAUDE
> I feel hot, I feel cold. I get sleepy and I get hungry.

And that's that.

Trouble begins when Claude is informed that his heavily guarded target (with the gender-neutral name of Billie) is a woman. His brow puckers with concern.

CLAUDE

It's not a matter of sex, it's a matter of money. If I'd have known it was a woman I'd have asked double. I don't like women. They don't stand still. When they move it's hard to figure out why or wherefore. They're not dependable. It's tough to kill somebody who's not dependable.

Claude grits his teeth and carries on. Now it's time for people to die.

Murder by Contract was produced on the cheap by Orbit Productions and picked up for distribution by Columbia. Lerner and cinematographer Lucien Ballard shot on location over the span of about a week, almost exclusively in full daylight, in the styleless style of surveillance footage. The film has a marvelous offhanded quality, as if it's not really a proper movie at all but just a filmed record of Claude's comings and goings. Many exteriors were shot silent, and money was saved with occasional process work that's patently false—and thus fascinating. Sets by Jack Poplin (who later did excellent work on TV's *The Outer Limits*) are small, dark, and sparse. The film's general air of impoverishment is wonderful because it suggests the flat objectivity of Claude's mind. The furnished room that is his personal space is a sort of limbo, without adornment or personality. Zoo animals and a bucket of balls are all the stimulation he requires.

The film reveals very little physical violence. A couple of Claude's early murders (including one at a barbershop, where the revolving pole outside says, "You are next") are depicted with considerable circumspection. Later, we hear but don't see Claude's failed first attempt on the witness (a richly absurd scheme involving an exploding television set). A second attempt, involving archery, a brush fire, and a high-powered rifle, pays off, but our vantage point when we see the woman fall is a considerable distance from the body; the psychological detachment continues.

The victim turns out to have been a policewoman. Armed with a plat of survey, Claude makes one more attempt, entering the witness's house via a system of culverts and drainage conduits. The woman (Caprice Toriel, giving a good, high-strung performance) knows he's there, standing behind her at the piano. Claude quietly tells her to keep playing. He undoes his tie and winds it around his hands but cannot put it around her neck. Apparently, his trouble with women is greater than just their undependability. Back inside the culvert, Claude is cut to pieces by police fire from both ends.

The fact that Claude seems to have no existence before his murder career, and certainly no existence afterward, suggests one of those mythic heroes, like Gilgamesh, who isn't fully born until the moment of bloody confrontation. That's a legitimate way of looking at *Murder by Contract*. Another is to ponder the nature of control and failure.

Hate's Incendiary Outcomes

Robert Wise's *Odds Against Tomorrow* (1959), the director's reunion with actor Robert Ryan ten years after *The Set-Up*, is a late noir that stands as one of the best. Unusually hard-edged and challenging, it is a seldom-discussed high point in the career of one of Hollywood's finest studio-system directors. But in this bank-heist thriller, as in so many noir melodramas, the crime is only a device to illuminate theme and character.

On one level a tale of unregenerate racism that brings horrific consequences, a broader view reveals that the film is about the warped self-images of its three perpetrator-protagonists, each of whom is convinced that he's been dealt a bad hand by life—not because of any failure of his own but by people and a system that are out to get him.

Johnny Ingram (Harry Belafonte) owes $7,500 to a bookie. If he doesn't pay up in a day or two, bad things are going to happen. Divorced, paying alimony and child support, and living beyond his means (sports car included), Johnny can't stay away from the track. He explains his mounting losses as bad luck and reasons that if he makes more bets, day after day, he'll snap his streak. Meanwhile, he can barely pay the bookie's $100 daily vig. On the larger stage, Johnny is acutely conscious of America's racial divide, angrily telling his ex, "It's their world and we're just livin' in it!"

Dave Burke (Ed Begley) put in thirty good years as a cop before taking a fall for contempt when he refused to roll over on fellow officers. He hates the system because it turned its back on him when he tried to protect it. Now, stripped of camaraderie and his sense of purpose, he sits and schemes in a small apartment inhabited by a police dog and festooned with awards and photos from his glory years.

Finally, there is Earl Slater (Ryan), the angriest and most dangerous of the group. A child of the Old South (he teasingly calls a young black child a "pickaninny"), Earl is fiftyish and afraid that his moment will soon pass. Once imprisoned for ADW and manslaughter, Earl is panicked at the thought of growing truly old with nothing. Despite the love of a good, if needy, woman, Lorry (Shelley Winters), Earl is completely sunk in resentment and hatred. He has particular animosity toward blacks—which is going to be trouble because a $150,000 after-hours bank job Burke has cased in a small town in the Hudson Valley requires the active participation of Johnny Ingram.

The job isn't badly planned but still goes disastrously wrong, partly because Earl (working contrary to what's best for his survival) refused to trust Johnny with the keys to the getaway car. The old cop Burke is repeatedly shot in the back, finally screaming because to be shot is excruciatingly painful—a reality that was almost never acknowledged by movies of the day. With police all around, Earl and Johnny turn on each other. Finally, atop fuel storage tanks (a big borrow from *White Heat*), they exchange gunfire and blow themselves to atoms. So severe is the conflagration that—in a glib but nevertheless potent irony—almost nothing of their bodies remains.

COP *(lifting blankets to view the corpses)*
Which is which?

COP #2
Take your pick.

Robert Wise produced *Odds Against Tomorrow* in conjunction with Harry Belafonte's production entity, HarBel. Belafonte had risen to great fame earlier in the decade as a calypso singer. He had acted in movies as early as 1953

Odds Against Tomorrow (1959), directed by Robert Wise: During the penultimate moment of a carefully planned robbery, Johnny (Harry Belafonte, left) finally gets fed up with racist accomplice Earl (Robert Ryan) and threatens to cave his head in. Meanwhile, the clock is ticking and time to escape is running out.

Case File: Robert Wise (1914–2005)

A do-anything craftsman whose first significant film job was the edit of *Citizen Kane*, Robert Wise directed forty movies in a fifty-six-year career. He won the best director Oscar twice, for *West Side Story* (shared with dance-sequence supervisor Jerome Kern) and *The Sound of Music*. Although Wise is revered by filmmakers, he troubles historians who cannot reconcile his versatility and commercial success with the auteur theory. All right, then. The fact is that Wise committed himself to each of his projects to a perfectly appropriate degree, deftly telling stories in a variety of genres, including film noir. His involvement with *Kane*, as well as with *The Curse of the Cat People* and *The Body Snatcher*, the moody, scrupulously intelligent horror thrillers he directed in the mid-1940s for RKO producer Val Lewton, gave Wise a technical and psychological grounding that prepared him for the particular nuances of noir. His first in the genre, *Born to Kill*, is a landmark of low-budget thrills. His subsequent noir projects, *The Set-Up* and *Odds Against Tomorrow*, are tough, compassionate pictures that elevated the genre (and that, coincidentally, gave Wise two opportunities to work with noir icon Robert Ryan).

Wise brought noir touches to other films: *Captive City* (1952), *Somebody Up There Likes Me* (1956), and the fact-based capital punishment drama *I Want to Live!* (1958). *The Day the Earth Stood Still* (1951) is a masterpiece of political and religious comment masquerading as a science-fiction thriller. Wise also directed war films, historical epics, mainstream drama, and *The Haunting* (1963), an unsettling gem of psychological horror.

and made a big splash opposite Dorothy Dandridge in *Carmen Jones* (1954). Simultaneously tender and tough on-screen, he holds his own against the vastly more experienced Begley and Ryan. As scripted by Abraham Polonksy and Nelson Giddings (from a 1957 novel by William P. McGivern), Belafonte's Johnny has made a mess of his marriage but still has feelings for his wife (sensitively played by the luminous Kim Hamilton) and adores his little girl. He wants to reconcile but can't because the gambling habit has him by the throat, and his ex-wife knows it. Johnny is present in the lives of the other two people but is no longer *of* those lives.

As for Earl, self-hatred has blinded him to Lorry's love. He hates that she earns a fair living while he brings in nothing, and the loathing he feels for himself is unfairly directed against her. In a brilliant interlude that appears simultaneously seductive and unwholesome, Earl allows himself to be seduced by a neighbor (Gloria Grahame) who has a morbid interest in Earl's manslaughter bust, and what Earl felt when he killed. This, then, is Earl's pathway to physical intimacy: an account of how he felt glad when he took a life. Robert Ryan's interpretation of Earl is simultaneously appalling and pathetic. It's a ferociously good portrait of a vile man—by one of Hollywood's most committed progressives.

Director of photography Joseph Brun gave Wise the deep focus in narrow, confining rooms that suggests traps. Some moments play out in tunnel-like hallways, and two key scenes take place in a tiny elevator. These characters are like big birds in small cages. The score, by John Lewis of the Modern Jazz Quartet, is a solemn, sophisticated creation in minor keys meant to suggest unhappiness rather than excitement.

Much of the picture was shot outdoors, on location in the Bronx and in the Hudson River Valley, during a bright, snowless winter. The air looks cold, with deceptive cheer provided by the sun. Interiors are alternately lit by sunlight or encased in velvet shadow.

With the plan blown to pieces, Earl and Johnny forget about the money. The only job that remains is to annihilate each other.

That's the plan, and they're stuck with it.

6

Victims of Circumstance

"I don't think you fully understand, Bigelow. You've been murdered."

—Frank Gerstle to Edmond O'Brien, *D.O.A.* (1950)

Although never as liberal in his social and political leanings as he enjoyed claiming, director Fritz Lang knew a little about political tyranny. His career in Germany predated the Nazis' rise to power, and by January 1933, when Hitler was appointed chancellor by a naïve political cabal, Lang had had at least one meeting with Minister of Propaganda Joseph Goebbels, during which Lang was asked to become the face of Nazi cinema. Not long after, the director and his mistress, Lily Latté, left Germany for the United States.

By 1934, Lang had been signed to a directorial contract by MGM, but 1934 became 1935, and no assignment had progressed beyond early preproduction. Finally, in the summer of 1935, Lang was assigned to staff producer Joseph L. Mankiewicz, who had worked up an outline from an intriguing story idea by writer Norman Krasna. The subject was lynch law—more specifically, a mob's attack on an innocent man who, despite the mob's best efforts, manages to secretly escape with his life and later manipulate events so that the twenty-two offenders are tried and found guilty of murder. (Krasna had been inspired by a pair of well-publicized, shameful events, a 1933 incident in San Jose where two suspects in a kidnapping were dragged from jail, stripped, and hanged; and, more pointedly, a 1930 Oklahoma lynching that resulted in twenty-three indictments and no convictions.)

The central moral dilemma that was eventually worked out by Lang, Mankiewicz, and skilled dialogue writer Bartlett Cormack is the limits of the victim's rage and revenge: Can he bring himself to allow twenty-two men and women to be imprisoned and possibly executed for that crime that they did not literally commit? (Moral culpability is quite another issue.)

The Krasna-Mankiewicz treatment was called *Mob Rule*; by the time it went before the cameras in the second half of 1935, it had been retitled *Fury*. A 1936 release, it stars Spencer Tracy as amiable working stiff Joe Wilson, who is arrested outside a small town, on circumstantial evidence, as a suspect in a kidnapping. Although the tough sheriff (Edward Ellis) insists on keeping to the letter of the law, cheap, thoughtless gossip that sweeps the town inspires a local bullyboy (Bruce Cabot) and a horde of other grotesques to storm the jail. Although they can't get at Joe's cell, they merrily set the place alight, sabotage the efforts of firemen to put out the blaze, and toss dynamite as a coup de grace. A wall is blown out, and Joe escapes. From here, the story unfolds as devised by Mankiewicz, with the marvelous detail that Joe's sweet-natured fiancée, Katherine (a radiant Sylvia Sidney), eventually learns that Joe is alive. So she, too, faces a thorny moral dilemma.

Fury predates the classic noir era, but in its visual and thematic darkness, its nerve-jangling focus on a terrorized innocent man, and its exploration of the pleasures and costs of revenge, the film is at the very least a template for noir. Of course, much of noir has origins in German cinema of the 1920s and '30s, and during those years, Fritz Lang was German cinema.

The horror film, another strongly Germanic genre that's a clear precursor of noir, also shows its influence in *Fury*. MGM cinematographer Joseph Ruttenberg won the assignment by giving Lang a test reel with bizarre angles and harsh lighting, and it's that kind of nightmarish feel that pervades *Fury*: Joe's gradual realization that his arrest is no joke; the gossiping townies (represented in montage and with bitter inserts of clucking chickens and a grocer's sign that says CALVES BRAINS); the drunken false courage of the mob; and the brazenly violent attack on the jail.

Katherine has tracked Joe down by the time the jail is torched, and Lang intercut close-ups of her horrified reaction with close-ups of the leering, monstrously shadowed faces of the participants and onlookers. Some stare with the dumbfounded fascination of animals; others openly rejoice. It's like something out of *Island of Lost Souls* by way of small-town America—a treatment that's quite atypical of the usual MGM product.

During a protracted and unfailingly engaging trial sequence after the tables have turned, the district attorney (Walter Abel) seals his case against the twenty-two by running footage shot by newsreel cameramen that reveals the frenzied defendants. (With a visual device that's shockingly modern, the newsreel footage is periodically frozen to give clear, damning views of the defendants. In this, Lang and Ruttenberg achieve the awful, irresistible urgency of tabloid crime photography.) Katherine's numb, morally compromised testimony seals the deal, and most of the twenty-two are found guilty.

The defendants shriek and begin to crawl over their seats and each other—until Joe enters the courtroom and strides up the central aisle, causing a sudden silence. His better nature has won out. He cannot become what his murderers allowed themselves to become. In a brief but remarkable sequence, Joe calmly addresses the judge and the wider world:

JOE
The law doesn't know that a lot of things that were very
important to me—silly things, maybe—like a belief in justice
and an idea that men were civilized, and a feeling of pride
that this country of mine was different from all others. The
law doesn't know that those things were burned to death
within me that night.

Fury opens as Joe and Katherine window shop (as people do in Lang's *M*, *The Woman in the Window*, and *Scarlet Street*). They look at furniture, including a bedroom suite. Despite the Depression, the window display promises not just better days but love and peace of mind. By shattering all of that, Lang and his collaborators smash innocence, indict a dark corner of the human spirit, and lay the foundation for twenty years of film noir.

The moral dilemma faced by Joe was replicated in Arthur Lubin's frequently atmospheric *Impact* (1949), in which an industrialist (Brian Donlevy) must decide whether to let his no-good wife (Helen Walker) stand trial for his murder. He makes the right decision but, in a hard-to-swallow turnabout, nearly pays for it with his freedom.

He Worships a Memory

Do you see the photo portrait on the wall? Take a good look at it. Pretty girl, isn't she? Step closer to the photo. Put out your hands. The frame has physical dimension, but the image itself is flat and unresponsive. It has no warmth or physical contour. It's simply a souvenir of a life that now is over. The face belongs to an aspiring actress named Vicki Lynn, the engine that drives the 1941 noir, *I Wake Up Screaming*. Vicki (Carole Landis) has been "discovered" slinging hash by a successful sports and show-business promoter, Frankie Christopher (Victor Mature). He's convinced he can turn the girl into a star, and just as he's close to doing so, Vicki is murdered. For the remainder of this dark adventure, Frankie is mercilessly hounded by a self-righteous police detective, Cornell (Laird Cregar), who wants his head for the murder. Fortunately, Frankie is given moral and practical support by Vicki's sister, Jill (Betty Grable).

Vicki exists in the standard narrative manner early in the film and appears later in numerous flashbacks, as well as in those portraits mentioned above. Look: There she is, framed and beaming, on Jill's wall. There's Vicki in a picture frame again, displayed on Jill's desk. At the police station, when the cops want to unnerve a suspect in Vicki's death, they run motion-picture footage of the girl singing, gesturing, and giving every suggestion of health and vigor. But the cops' snippet of movie film, like the portraits, is a mere simulacrum of life. To us and to Frankie and the others, Vicki is visible but no longer present—and certainly no longer attainable.

None of that deters Detective Cornell, who knows that Frankie had no part in the murder. In fact, Cornell has braced the killer and set him free, all so that he can continue to dog Frankie. Why? Because Cornell resents Frankie's former proximity to Vicki, and resents that Frankie still has access to a world that Cornell—heavy, sullen-faced, and underpaid—will never be privy to.

Vicki is a creature of artifice. We've seen for ourselves that she worked as an anonymous waitress and was built into "something" merely by being squired around town by Frankie and gaining the attention of ham actor Robin Ray (Alan Mowbray), gossip columnist Larry Evans (Allyn Joslyn), and others. Frankie spins big events, such as Vicki's coming-out and well-publicized boxing matches, out of almost nothing at all. Acting. Gossip. Promotion. What in Frankie's world is real?

Jill, fashioned from unpretentious loyalty and kindness, is real (Grable plays her with real warmth), and underneath all the nonsense, Frankie is real, too. He even confesses to Jill that his real name is Botticelli and that he's the son of immigrants. He's refashioned himself with the same energy he brings to the refashioning of others. Contrarily, Cornell is unhealthily absorbed in his work and trapped in his clumsy, big man's body. He's beyond the salvation of artifice. When he stops on a bustling nighttime sidewalk to surreptitiously stare at waitress-Vicki as she works, his mouth slightly agape, he's separated from the girl by the diner's plate-glass window. She'll be no more attainable for him than the later portrait-Vicki, another beautiful thing preserved behind glass.

Director H. Bruce Humberstone (credited here as Bruce Humberstone) rose from Charlie Chan programmers to A pictures that he directed with an economy of style he learned in the Bs. His camera setups, lit by director of photography Edward Cronjager, are forceful but uncluttered, with visual atmosphere parceled out judiciously; when Frankie plasters himself against a wall in Vicki's former apartment house, his body is decorated with a lattice of shadows thrown by some unseen lobby decoration. Spiderlike, he stands stock-still to observe the oddball switchboard man (Elisha Cook Jr.). A sequence in which Jill escapes from her apartment building by taking to the rooftops is splendid in its understated drama, and the final revelation—the perverse and pathetic shrine to Vicki kept by Cornell in his tiny apartment—is a shocker that *whispers* the horror rather than shout it. The lover that Cornell desired but never possessed has left him, but he cannot leave her.

Because of its preoccupation with images and artifice, *I Wake Up Screaming* invites thoughts about the reality of *I Wake Up Screaming*, and about all movies. What is film, after all, but discrete, stationary images that flash before us, twenty-four a second? Movies become real when actors and technicians want to tell a story. They're fundamentally different from Cornell, who imagines that he can *live* one.

I Wake Up Screaming was remade, to flat and listless effect, as *Vicki* (1953), directed by Broadway and film designer Harry Horner. Jean Peters took the title role, with Jeanne Crain as the female lead. Character player and occasional leading man Elliott Reid is a featherweight as Christopher—appropriate enough, since in this version the focus isn't on Christopher's dilemma but on the unscrupulous nature of Vicki (not unlike Anne Baxter's Eve Harrington in *All About Eve* [1950]). A commanding actor, Richard Boone, is Cornell, and although he's a bully, he was asked to suggest none of the surreal menace that's so integral to Laird Cregar's interpretation. With its flat gray tonal palette and two other capable but third-tier male leads, Casey Adams and Alex D'Arcy, *Vicki* seems threadbare.

I'm Not Me

If *Street of Chance* (1942) has fallen off the film noir radar, then the picture's director, Jack Hively, has fallen off the edge of the world. Mystery fans may recall him as the director of three light and lukewarm "Saint" mysteries during 1940–41; and World War II buffs may have seen his 1945 propaganda documentary, *Appointment in Tokyo*. Hively directed nineteen films in all but was much more prolific as an editor of B pictures the likes of *Don't Tell the Wife* (1937). He began his career in 1933, and ended it with second-unit assignments and a couple of forays into early television. *Street of Chance* is the indisputable high point of his career.

Scripter Garrett Fort (who wrote the 1931 *Frankenstein* and other horror thrillers) adapted a 1941 Cornell Woolrich novel, *The Black Curtain*, to tell the story of Frank Thompson (Burgess Meredith), a regular city guy who finds his world upended after being thrown into momentary physical shock when a wall nearly collapses on him. He makes his way home and discovers that his wife has moved out of their apartment. She's living elsewhere, under her maiden name.

Understandably concerned by the profound changes of just one day, Thompson finds his wife (Louise Platt). She's shocked and pleased to see him. After all, it's been a year since he disappeared.

A year?

For the remainder of *Street of Chance*, Thompson tries to reconcile his existence with the life of another man, Danny Nearing. Thompson is Thompson, and Thompson is apparently Nearing, too. Police detective Marucci (Sheldon Leonard) has tabbed Nearing as the murderer of a rich old duff named Diedrich, and if he gets his hands on Nearing, he's going to throw him in jail.

Nearing's fiercely loyal lover, Ruth Dillon (Claire Trevor), wants the two of them to get the hell out of town. During the subsequent cat-and-mouse narrative, Thompson/Nearing learns that Ruth still works in the Diedrich mansion as a maid. The house is occupied by the murder victim's family, a peculiar bunch with various motivations to kill but seemingly unassailable alibis.

The real murderer is finally revealed, of course, and Thompson/Nearing is able to return to being just Thompson. A shock of some sort had led Thompson to believe he was Danny Nearing—a misapprehension that went on long enough for Nearing to meet Ruth and get too close to a murder. The near-miss with the falling wall flipped the amnesia in reverse, banishing Nearing and restoring Thompson. Cornell Woolrich loved this sort of convoluted and unlikely backstory; it's to the great credit of Jack Hively and Garrett Fort that, on-screen, it all makes sense—sort of.

Street of Chance is a Paramount B that nevertheless addresses complex issues of love and self-preservation. Before Thompson begins to explore the Danny Neary mystery, he hustles his wife to her mother's. He loves his wife and doesn't want her to be involved or harmed. Contrarily, Ruth loves Nearing so ferociously that she pulls him closer as the danger he faces threatens to flare out of control. By encouraging him to stay with her and run, she endangers him. Finally, when Ruth stands revealed as the killer (Diedrich caught her stealing his cash), Thompson expresses his weary disbelief:

> THOMPSON
> What kind of a love is it that would send me running away
> from a crime *you* committed? That would have stood by as
> the police take me away to the electric chair?

Ruth has no answer.

Assured, sweeping use is made of enormous, unusually well-dressed sound-stages that are used for all exteriors (except for a single, eyeblink insert of a car pulling up to the Diedrich mansion). Plentiful cars and extras fill the ornate city sets and bring a choked, claustrophobic air that mirrors Thompson's fear and confusion. The central character's unease is compounded by Hively's imaginative camera setups that shoot severely down from roofs and walls (dizzying) or sharply up at them (confining). The city isn't malevolent (as in so many noir thrillers)—just overwhelming. Hively and director of photography Theodor Sparkuhl further juiced the visuals with clever use of pinpoint lighting (particularly a moving flashlight beam) and vigorous tracking shots. Late in the film, a pullback through a second-floor window of the mansion and subsequent crane-down to the front door, where Detective Marucci pauses on the front stoop to light a cigarette, is elegant and dramatically meaningful.

David Buttolph's score is a gem of understatement that's put to smart use. During some highly dramatic moments, such as the shock "reveal" of an old lady's face and Ruth's climactic grip on an automatic in her purse, there is no music at all. The silence is profound.

The everyday, unglamorous appeal of Burgess Meredith is an appealing asset, and it's good to see perennial heavy Sheldon Leonard in a restrained, thoughtful role. More is going on inside Marucci than you may think, and more is going on in this shrewd little film, too.

Thank God for Kansas

Throughout Robert Siodmak's *Phantom Lady* (1944), human figures are photographed in long shot as they stand in large, empty spaces: a deserted subway station; the empty end of a bar; the visitors' room at a prison; a high-ceilinged corridor; the dark, barren intersection of streets. These are images of isolation and vulnerability, and they inform much of the film's central predicament: the murder conviction of an innocent man.

Scott Henderson (Alan Curtis) is an amiable but unhappily married civil engineer who is arrested when his wife turns up strangled. His alibi—that he drank and went to a show with a woman he met that night—falls apart when

Hoping to buck up her wrongfully imprisoned boss (Alan Curtis), Carol (Ella Raines) visits him in jail, promising to locate the *Phantom Lady* (1944) who can clear him of murder. This unusually beautiful noir was director Robert Siodmak's first exploration of the genre.

nobody remembers seeing the woman. Indeed, supposed witnesses are unusually emphatic about it. Henderson never caught his companion's name (she had insisted on that), and without her to corroborate, he's cooked.

The main narrative of *Phantom Lady* focuses on the dogged efforts of Henderson's loyal secretary, Carol (Ella Raines), to comb New York to locate the woman. To do that, she must assume unaccustomed guises and confront the uncooperative witnesses. She's an active, resourceful heroine who moves far from her comfort zone and places herself in physical danger to clear the man she loves. It's established that she's a transplant from Wichita (Henderson calls her "Kansas"), and although she's bright and brave, she's a little out of her element and oblivious to danger. So successfully does she silently haunt an uncooperative bartender (Andrew Tombes) that she's nearly pushed onto subway tracks because the guy objects that she's brazenly followed him underground. (The fact that, for once, a woman is shadowing a panicked man is a neat reversal of tradition.)

Carol dresses like a tart to entice the truth from the stage-show drummer, Cliff (Elisha Cook Jr.). Although her clumsy questioning confirms that Cliff accepted $500 to keep his mouth shut about the mystery woman, he won't say from whom. Drunk, he has enough sense left to realize that he's being pumped, and Carol barely gets out of his apartment in one piece.

Carol is helped in her investigation by a sympathetic police inspector, Burgess (Thomas Gomez), and by Henderson's concerned partner, Jack Marlow (Franchot Tone), who had been on a cruise when the murder occurred. But we discover long before Carol that Marlow *is* the killer and that he's insane, smiling, and waiting for the moment to be rid of her.

Phantom Lady is the first noir directed by German émigré Robert Siodmak. He was obviously simpatico with his director of photography, Woody Bredell, and found fertile material in the script by Bernard C. Schoenfeld, adapting the 1942 novel by William Irish (Cornell Woolrich). Rich with elegant crane shots and dolly-ins, and suffused in soft shadow, it's one of the most purely beautiful of all noir thrillers.

Siodmak effectively broke with tradition by shooting the murder trial while focusing entirely on the gallery, without a single shot of the judge, attorneys, jury, or even Henderson. The trial is bread-and-butter stuff, necessary to the exposition—but no one said it had to be shot traditionally.

The film's celebrated set piece is Carol's visit with the drummer, Cliff, to an after-hours jive joint. The footage, very well cut by editor Arthur Hilton, is a

Case File: Robert Siodmak (1900–73)

The Hollywood career of director Robert Siodmak is bookended by early work in Germany and late-career activity in Germany, France, and Britain. Some three years of experience as a film editor helped him to develop an economy of style and a pictorial approach that's frequently startling in its beauty. Siodmak's considerable reputation rests almost entirely on just a few films from his eleven-year (1941–52) Hollywood output. His earliest American projects are low-budget trifles, but he gained some notice for his intelligent and subtly atmospheric *Son of Dracula* (1943; story by Robert's brother, Curt), a horror fable transposed into a bittersweet love story. The year 1944 brought *Cobra Woman*, wonky Technicolor exotica designed to showcase Universal's gorgeous nonactress Maria Montez. The same year saw the release of *Phantom Lady*, a brilliantly atmospheric and frequently unsettling adaptation of Cornell Woolrich's noir novel about an innocent man whose secretary saves his bacon after he's wrongly accused of murder. This was followed by *The Suspect*, *The Killers*, and *Criss Cross*—amounting to a noir output that's modest only in number.

Siodmak also hit hard with the 1945 psychological thriller *The Spiral Staircase*, *The Dark Mirror*, *Cry of the City*, *The File on Thelma Jordon*, and a delightful costume comedy, *The Crimson Pirate*, which gave Burt Lancaster an opportunity to spoof his heroic image.

A late film, *Nachts, wenn der Teufel kam* (*The Devil Strikes at Night*, 1957), is an intriguing melodrama about the political ramifications of a serial murderer on the loose in Nazi Germany.

magnificent, dizzying mélange of assertive, moving instruments, and hunched musicians, plus close-ups on sweating faces and Carol's attempt to negotiate what is, for her, an alien environment. The sequence's movement and cutting are unusually rapid and insistent, and in the abstract the screen is filled with a succession of shots aggressively cut through with diagonals: arms, instruments,

Case File: Elisha Cook Jr. (1903 or 1906–95)

Noir's resident fall guy worked almost exclusively in vaudeville and legit theater from the time he was a teenager until 1936, when he focused on movies. The skill behind the quirky persona so familiar to film fans, then, was the result of many years of varied professional experience (which included the romantic lead in a 1929 Broadway play called *Her Unborn Child*). Cook's first work in film noir came in 1940's *Stranger on the Third Floor* and was followed by eight more appearances, four of which confirm Cook's status as one of Hollywood's greatest character actors: *The Maltese Falcon* (as the petulant and miserably inept gunman, Wilmer), *Phantom Lady* (the orgiastic swing drummer who appalls Ella Raines), *Born to Kill* (Lawrence Tierney's reasonable—but nevertheless murderous—companion), and *The Killing* (the hapless schlub married to Marie Windsor, the original Wife from Hell). Cook also took prominent supporting roles in *I Wake Up Screaming*, *The Big Sleep*, *Flaxy Martin*, and *I, the Jury*.

He could do comedy and knockabout (*Ball of Fire*, *Up in Arms*), conventional crime (*Dillinger*, *Fall Guy*), and drama (*The Great Gatsby*, *Don't Bother to Knock* [as Marilyn Monroe's nice-guy uncle]), and westerns (*Shane* [one of Cook's best-known performances, as a courageous but overmatched homesteader who takes on gunslinger Jack Palance]). In that role, as in many others, Cook exhibited a wounded kind of dignity.

Cook got into television in 1953 and thereafter divided his time between the small screen and features. In "Semi-Private Eye," a 1954 episode of *The Adventures of Superman*, Cook plays Homer Garrity, a noir-like PI whose skillful methods are disastrously imitated by Jimmy Olsen. Not long before his retirement in the late 1980s, Cook was a semiregular on TV's *Magnum P.I.*

Case File: Woody Bredell (1902–69)

Cinematographer Elwood "Woody" Bredell was a fixture at Universal in the 1930s and '40s, shooting light crime films starring the likes of the Dead End Kids and the adolescent Jackie Cooper. In the early '40s, he was able to explore material that was more atmospheric: *The Invisible Woman*, *Man Made Monster*, Abbott and Costello's *Hold that Ghost*, *The Ghost of Frankenstein* (with Milton Krasner), and *Sherlock Holmes and the Voice of Terror*. Bredell's first noir assignment, the richly shot *Phantom Lady*, was followed by *Lady on a Train*, *The Killers*, and *The Unsuspected*. Bredell's final credit before retirement is *Female Jungle* (1955), a chaotic, no-budget noir that has nothing to offer other than Bredell's stark photography and the novelty of Jayne Mansfield in her feature-film debut.

upper bodies, shadows—and as aural background, a raucously pounding swing tune.

Vital to the sequence is that although Carol has made herself seem cheap and available, she's neither, and every one of her excited smiles, her jive-poppin' finger snapping, her silent sexual entreaties to Cliff, are agonizingly difficult for her. In a particularly impressive moment, Carol goes to a mirror to adjust her lipstick (after Cliff has nearly sickened her by planting his mouth on hers), and must pause and give her head a shake because the music makes the mirror jump on the wall, and the face that stares back at Carol hardly seems to be hers at all.

The sequence climaxes with a drum solo (variously credited to Buddy Rich and Gene Krupa) that sends Cliff to orgiastic ecstasy as he pounds away, his mouth open in a rictus grin, his eyes fastened on Carol. It's as blatant an exhibition of sexual pleasure and release as in any film of the '40s. Elisha Cook is simply superb, all wild eyes and raw libido.

Ella Raines had stunning, catlike eyes and unusual on-screen intelligence. Her complex, many-toned performance gives *Phantom Lady* its legs. Handsome Alan Curtis is a strong presence as the wrongly accused Henderson, and the delicately beautiful Fay Helm is vulnerable and tragic as the title character, whose "disappearance" has been unintentional but inevitable. Only Franchot Tone's Marlow, given to frequent examination of his strangler's hands, seems overplayed.

If there can be a "short list" of indispensable noir, *Phantom Lady* is surely on it.

Old Enough to Know Better

It's surely no accident that in numerous scenes of *The Woman in the Window* (1944), psychology professor Richard Wanley (Edward G. Robinson) is reflected in mirrors and windows. This tale of accidental death, cover-up, and blackmail appears to hinge on Wanley's mild-mannered nature, but it actually turns on his duality. When pushed, he's a resourceful, reasonably cool lawbreaker. His accomplice, Alice Reed (Joan Bennett), is far more worldly than Wanley but hasn't nearly his presence of mind. Her trump card is her beauty, which bewitches the professor.

Middle-aged, prosperous, and profoundly respectable, Wanley has a wife and children who have left New York for the summer. In their absences, Wanley lives a circumspect existence, teaching during the day and enjoying a drink and a cigar at a private, men-only club each evening with his friends, district attorney Frank Lalor (Raymond Massey) and Dr. Barkstone (Edmond Breon).

For some days, Wanley has been transfixed by a portrait of a beautiful woman that's displayed in a show window of the building that houses his club. One night, as Wanley admires the picture, the model's living face appears in the window next to the painted one. Wanley is a mild and engaging conversationalist, and because his family is gone, he feels free to ask Alice out for a drink. Later, he comes to her apartment to see other works by the portraitist. Perhaps Wanley isn't as circumspect as we think.

Another drink and a few pieces of artwork later, the apartment is noisily invaded by a burly man who demands to know who Wanley is and why he's there. In a flash, it's clear: Alice is this man's mistress. The intruder locks his hands around Wanley's throat and throttles him. Alice helpfully places a pair of scissors into Wanley's outstretched hand, and the blades are repeatedly plunged into the attacker's back. Now Wanley and Alice are alone with a dead man on the floor.

German poster art for *The Woman in the Window* (1944), Fritz Lang's tale of art and obsession, violence, and a man's gift for being two people—one kind and law-abiding, the other complicit in murder and eager to cover it up. Edward G. Robinson and Joan Bennett star.

The victim is Claude Mazard (Arthur Loft), a well-known financier. A cover-up isn't going to be easy. The victim wasn't a wino or a second-story man. People are going to be *looking* for this guy.

Director Fritz Lang and writer-producer Nunnally Johnson develop fine tension as Wanley decides to get rid of the body. It's very late. Can he get the blanket-wrapped corpse out of the apartment without anyone seeing? When a policeman pulls Wanley over for driving without his headlights, will the cop glance at the back floor? (In a nicely gruesome touch, the blanket has fallen away from the dead man's face, and he leans against the rear door like a giant doll, an angle of illumination falling across his open, unseeing eyes—effective work by cinematographer Milton Krasner.)

Wanley has more close calls at a toll booth and a red light but finally gets to the country, where he dumps the body in the woods. (All of this is shot on carefully lit, rain-slick stages at "night," with every visual detail as vivid as what might be seen in a dream.)

But wait. Mazard's lieutenants were concerned about their boss's private life and had had him shadowed for months by a private detective. Soon, Heidt (Dan Duryea) drops by Alice's apartment to cheerfully ask for $5,000 in hush money. Heidt says he's patient. He'll wait for a day.

The remainder of *The Woman in the Window* revolves around the mess with Heidt, Wanley's efforts to keep Alice stable, and the growing number of clues: tire marks in the mud near the body, blood and fabric on a section of barbed wire, well-preserved shoe prints, a cop who vaguely remembers a car. Because he's a friend of the DA, Wanley is invited along for much of the investigation, soberly nodding in mute panic as the clues mount against him. In a humorously macabre moment, Wanley feels obligated to explain the cut on *his* hand, and his attack of poison ivy, after a trooper mentions the barbed wire, and points out that poison ivy grows all over the crime scene.

With Wanley's encouragement, Alice tries to kill Heidt with an overdose of barbiturates and fails. Now the furious blackmailer wants another $5,000. It's all too much for Wanley, who sadly dumps what's left of his barbiturate powder into a glass and drinks it. He begins to slip away—only to be awakened at his club. He'd fallen asleep and has been dreaming. He's safe, and if there is a real woman in the window, he's never met her.

In the 1942 source novel, J. H. Wallis's *Once Off Guard*, Wanley is a professor of English, and the book concludes with his suicide. Hollywood's Production Code had a strict prohibition on suicide, so the film version could not end that way. But it *does*, of course, and then again it doesn't—a neat trick that salvages some of the force of the book while managing an upbeat conclusion. Still, almost nobody connected with the film liked the ending, which becomes so precious that the club's hat-check man is Mazard and the doorman is Heidt. It's like *The Wizard of Oz* with a murder twist. Still, the point about the duality of Wanley's nature is made. In his inner mind, at least, he's capable of far more devious thought than anybody would dream.

Case File: Milton Krasner (1904–88)

A prolific and important cinematographer with long employment at Universal, Krasner shot comedies (*Buck Privates*, *The Bank Dick*) and horror thrillers (*The Ghost of Frankenstein* [with Woody Bredell], *The Mad Ghoul*) before a celebrated 1944–45 collaboration with director Fritz Lang on *The Woman in the Window* and *Scarlet Street*, among the most strikingly photographed of all noir thrillers. His other noir credits are *Vicki* and the bleakly beautiful *The Set-Up*. After a move to 20th Century-Fox, Krasner photographed Marilyn Monroe three times (*Monkey Business*, *The Seven Year Itch*, and *Bus Stop*) and shot a variety of powerful dramas, including *The Dark Mirror*, *The Accused*, *A Double Life*, *All About Eve*, *Deadline U.S.A.*, and *Fate Is the Hunter*. Krasner was a six-time Oscar nominee who went home with the statuette in 1954, for *Three Coins in the Fountain*.

The most intriguing aspect of *The Woman in the Window*, which was independently produced by Nunnally Johnson for his International Pictures, is the depth of Alice's villainy. Does she hand Wanley the scissors to that he can avoid being throttled, or does she simply want to ensure that Mazard is going to be dead and out of her life? Is she the lovely spirit conjured by the painting, or is she a malevolent opportunist? The answer is up in the air because Joan Bennett plays Alice as a sort of beautiful blank; you can read whatever motive into her face that you like. An "unfinished" characterization, she's very like someone you would encounter in a dream.

Sailor in a Strange Land

Memory loss following a blackout, an avocational hazard faced by long-term alkies and binge drinkers alike, sparks the plot of Harold Clurman and Clifford Odets's *Deadline at Dawn* (1944), a murder noir that is a Jungian fable, a fairy tale, and a touching exploration of the restorative power of love.

Sailor (Bill Williams) is a guileless innocent adrift in the New York night, with seven hours to kill before the bus that will return him to the navy. (The film's title refers to Sailor's need to be back at base early the next morning; it also evokes the pressing nature of a heroic quest.) Pleasant and polite, Sailor is also vague, particularly in his recollection of how he came into possession of $1,400. He recalls an apartment, a woman, an agreement to fix a portable radio, and a lot of drinking. He can't account for about an hour of the evening. His memory can't bring the hour back—but what should he do about the money?

If Sailor is Red Riding Hood, then Miss Goth (Susan Hayward) is the hunter skilled at dispatching wolves. New York is brand new to Sailor; to Miss Goth, the city is as drearily familiar as a bathtub ring. Nightly, she balances on aching feet as a taxi dancer, endlessly doing the fox-trot with lonely men who come at her clutching ribbons of dance tickets.

Sailor selects Miss Goth at the dance hall, and when he mentions that he's based in Norfolk, Virginia, Miss Goth perks up. *That's my home town*, she says. *If I give you my mother's address, will you look her up and tell her I'm doing great?*

That's okay with Sailor, who is mostly preoccupied with the apartment and the money. Miss Goth—who likes to say, "Call me June, rhymes with moon," as if June isn't really her name at all—urges Sailor to return the cash. She's suddenly in a happy and adventuresome mood, so she ignores her credo, "This is New York, where hello means goodbye," and offers to accompany Sailor on his journey, probably because Sailor is the first man in a long time who hasn't asked her for something.

The urban, picaresque adventure that follows is populated with unusual people, including a dead woman, Edna (Lola Lane), who is hazily recalled by Sailor; a sweating blind man (Marvin Miller) who had argued with the dead woman about $1,400; and a philosophical cab driver (Paul Lukas). All of these have had contact with the murdered Edna.

Various ancillary characters invoke war and war brides, bananas, a dead cat, baseball, a rubber check, and the good cop/bad cop routine. Then there is the late Edna's husband, a glaring mobster named Bartelli (Joseph Calleia), who can't pull his suspicious gaze from Sailor.

The New York that's traversed by Sailor and Miss Goth is curiously, almost magically deserted (and shot on atmospheric stages). The middle-aged cab driver, Mr. Hoffman, offers omniscient pronouncements on the unfolding situation, rather like the timeless Wise Old Man posited by Jung. Hoffman shares his maturity and insight by guiding the young couple; he particularly cautions them to be careful about their reactions to anything they may hear. After all, "speech was given to man to hide his thoughts."

The written word has its perils, too, as Edna kept a bundle of intimate letters that she may have used for blackmail. Who was she blackmailing? Does it matter?

As the unlikely allies piece together a rationale for the murder, the killer's identity grows more apparent. In the end, we learn that Edna was killed for that most precious of all things, love.

Deadline at Dawn is the only feature film directed by Harold Clurman, a progressive Broadway director and Group Theatre member who mentored the young Clifford Odets and later directed the New York premieres of *Awake and Sing!*, *The Iceman Cometh*, and *Long Day's Journey into Night*. Like Clifford Odets, he favored character over plot and was sympathetic to working-class concerns.

When Odets wrote *Deadline at Dawn* in 1945, he had been doing credited and uncredited script work on major Hollywood films for nearly ten years and had directed one of his own scripts, *None but the Lonely Heart* (1944). Clurman was new to cinema, but the form held no terror for Odets; or for Clurman's other key collaborator, cinematographer Nicholas Musuraca.

Deadline at Dawn is not the terror-noir of jagged shadows and unrelieved fear. Rather, this is noir of the unconscious, where the setting is real and yet unreal; where goals and priorities shift and change; where many characters have symbolic purpose; and where speech, although often elliptical and mannered, reveals the truth (or truths) rather than hides it. When Miss Goth is frightened by a door buzzer, she softly, rapidly intones, "Rain, rain, go away, come again some other day." She practices magical thinking. Sailor tells himself he doesn't think at all, as per his habit of tapping his head to ruefully explain, "*Non compos mentis.*"

And why do four of the principals and one minor character have European accents? Perhaps they are the Old World that will be swept aside by the New World hopefulness of Miss Goth and Sailor. *Deadline at Dawn* teases us with its peculiarities and invites us to think along unorthodox liners. The movie is unusually participatory.

By the time the adventure concludes, Sailor and Miss Goth have displayed their strengths and foibles. They know they complement each other. With dawn just minutes away, they are together.

Sweet Songs of Murder

Like so many of us on the cusp of critical moments, she was minding her own business. The train slowed for its approach into Grand Central, and when she put her mystery novel aside to glance from her window into a trackside building, she saw . . . murder. The police won't listen, so she decides to investigate on her own. Numerous people make no secret of their intense dislike of her, but she perseveres, with cleverness and courage that finally bring her close to the killer—so close, in fact, that she doesn't realize she's in dreadful danger.

That's one précis of *Lady on a Train* (1945), a frequently grim exercise in noir directed by Charles David, shot by Woody Bredell, and sharply plotted by mystery writer Leslie Charteris and scripters Edmund Beloin and Robert O'Brien.

Another, equally accurate, précis of the picture might go like this:

Universal Pictures proudly presents Deanna Durbin, who brings her beauty, charm, and exciting vocal ability to *Lady on a Train*, a tale of wealth and high-stakes homicide that combines comedy with thrills. Deanna is Nicki Collins, a headstrong girl who accidentally witnesses the murder of an industrialist and decides to uncover the killer's identity herself! Along the way, she impersonates a nightclub singer, takes a car ride that may be her last, and perplexes an already perplexed mystery novelist played by David Bruce—who struck sparks with Deanna in last year's *Can't Help Singing*. Deanna also explores the murdered man's creepy estate and runs into the squabbling heirs, including sinister Dan Duryea and charming Ralph Bellamy. You can bet that Deanna knows which one to avoid! Elizabeth Patterson is the family dowager who hasn't a nice word for anyone, least of all Deanna, and Edward Everett Horton is Deanna's stumble-footed attorney, who tries his best to keep her out of harm's way. And don't miss it when Deanna wraps her voice around "Gimme a Little Kiss, Will Ya, Huh?" "Night and Day," and the timeless holiday classic, "Silent Night." For music, laughs, danger, and Durbin, there's only one *Lady on a Train*!

Universal allowed its number-one star, singer Deanna Durbin, a change of pace with *Lady on a Train* (1945). Deanna is a chance witness to murder but can't prove the crime ever happened. Mystery writer David Bruce helps out.

My précis are very much at odds with each other, but *Lady on a Train* takes those disparate tones and blends them into an alternately delightful and disturbing whole. Besides the original story by Charteris (who wrote a paperback novelization of the film's screenplay for simultaneous release with the picture), key elements of *Lady on a Train* come from a 1940 British film called *Lady in Distress*, in which the person who witnesses murder from inside a train is male.

The mild spoofiness of the whole project is apparent right from the first scene, in which Nicki rides the train while reading aloud to herself from a gruesome mystery novel. To emphasize the assertion that mystery fiction is nothing like reality, the film brings in a famed author of whodunits (Bruce), who dictates prose so overheated that when he instructs his secretary (Jacqueline deWit) to "Type that up," she comes back with "Tear it up?" But no one is laughing later when the novelist and a nightclub manager (George Coulouris)—and well-utilized stuntmen—have a savage fistfight amidst the tottering shelves of a cobwebbed wine cellar. If the wrong man wins, Nicki may be done for.

Most of the supporting characters are stock types, and Durbin has no trouble establishing herself as the film's dominant presence (the whole point, since the singing star was Universal's number-one asset). The picture is driven by Durbin and by a briskly delivered plot that offers a cute climactic surprise that leads neatly into another, even better one. For a few crucial moments, amidst dark dialogue and waving of guns, innocent characters can't tell the murderer without a scorecard. We're especially impressed because during their careers, scripters Beloin and O'Brien wrote comedy almost exclusively.

Woody Bredell's crisp, high-contrast photography shimmers, and director Charles David kept the camera in graceful, often elegant motion. Key sequences, including Nicki's frantic scramble to hide in a car elevator and dodge a pursuer in the hills and valleys of a weirdly illuminated indoor mountain of grain, are gorgeous with menace.

Three years after *Lady on a Train*, Deanna Durbin walked away from her career. She craved more vehicles with an element of danger, but Universal returned her to sweetness 'n' light projects. Durbin knew better. She knew that some of the best popular art is informed by shadows.

What's Past Is Past—Sometimes

In the aforementioned *Deadline at Dawn*, a character loses a portion of his day. Well, it happens. *Total* amnesia is rare, but you wouldn't know it from movies and television, because the affliction (often called general amnesia) is a beautifully simple way to create conflict and drama. That's what writer-director Joseph L. Mankiewicz did with *Somewhere in the Night* (1946).

A GI (John Hodiak) has been severely injured in combat. When he awakes in an Army hospital, in pain from numerous surgeries, he has no idea who he is. Although angry and terrified, he keeps his affliction secret. People call him George Taylor and mention to him that he's from Los Angeles.

The only other clue to his past life is a Dear John letter he finds in his wallet. It's an angry, vituperative letter that casts Taylor as completely reprehensible. The woman wants no more to do with him and lets him know that she wishes him nothing but ill fortune.

Taylor is furious because his mind won't let him remember who he is—or was. How did he come to be such a terrible man? And who is the woman?

Physically recovered and now in LA, Taylor liberates a briefcase that he's had in storage for three years. Inside, he discovers a pistol and a note from an apparent friend, Larry Cravat, promising that George will find $5,000 deposited in his name at a particular bank. Taylor is unable to get at the money (he's spooked when the bank manager asks a lot of questions), so he's on his own with very little cash and no fresh clue to his past other than "Larry Cravat."

The remainder of the brisk, engaging narrative follows Taylor as he searches the city for Cravat, running afoul of various lowlifes who threaten, beat, and even try to kill him. "Larry Cravat" shapes up to be the password to personal disaster.

Taylor picks up a couple of allies: a self-possessed young singer named Chris Smith (Nancy Guild) and a prosperous and amiable club owner, Mel Phillips (Richard Conte). The search soon widens to encompass a phony clairvoyant (Fritz Kortner), his goon-like enforcer (Lou Nova), a high-tone insane asylum, and a subtly inquisitive police lieutenant named Kendall (Lloyd Nolan). Taylor hears tales of $2 million in hidden Nazi loot, a murdered bartender (Whit Bissell), an inaccessible and insensible witness (Houseley Stevenson) to a murder that Taylor may have committed, a waterfront mission, and the slimy underside of a San Pedro pier.

At 108 minutes, *Somewhere in the Night* is long for a film noir—and is almost completely satisfying. Mankiewicz, who cowrote the script with Howard Dimsdale, directs with smooth assurance that shows off the back lot and on-location capabilities of 20th Century-Fox. This is a slick and confident movie made by confident people.

Mankiewicz and his cinematographer, Norbert Brodine, used visual mood effects judiciously. This is not a noir that paints the entire city as a menacing place—just certain parts of it. Daytime footage at the pier is shot on location and in full light, like a documentary, but an important nighttime sequence there is shot on a carefully designed stage (art directed by James Basevi and Maurice Ransford) that is dank and claustrophobic, with the slapping water faintly illuminated to look like dirty milk.

A protracted nighttime sequence at the asylum is shadowed and pregnant with danger. Thrown out once, Taylor sneaks back inside, determined to find the witness. He negotiates blank hallways illuminated only by baseboard nightlights; has a quick, silent tussle with an attendant; and is shocked to see another man hurriedly exit the witness's room via a window. Is Taylor too late?

Other characters provide unsavory texture. Harry Morgan is amusingly unpleasant as a masseur who gives Taylor a hard time at a Turkish bath, and Margo Woode brings perverse sparkle to her role as Phyllis, a loud, flashily dressed dame who's in cahoots with the clairvoyant. Fritz Kortner is fine as the phony fortune teller, but there's something overdone, even precious, about not just his characterization but his very presence. With his heavy but unidentifiable European accent and dogged interest in the $2 million, he's unnecessarily exotic and seems to have slid in from another movie.

John Hodiak is in nearly every scene; the film is carried on his shoulders. Hodiak was up to the challenge, expressing Taylor's agitation and awful frustration. The character is tormented, angry, and confused. But he's gentle (as in a lovely, melancholy sequence with actress Josephine Hutchinson) and vulnerable, too, as in his scenes with his ally, smoky-voiced Chris. Actress Nancy Guild clearly

Trauma suffered during combat spurs the events of *Somewhere in the Night* (1946), in which an amnesiac GI (John Hodiak) wants to discover who he really is—and isn't. Here, the disoriented Hodiak asks Nancy Guild to tell him everything she knows.

functions as Fox's answer to Lauren Bacall, and she's good at the impersonation. Chris has intelligence and physical courage and expresses a sharply developed sense of loyalty. The film's trailer describes Chris/Guild as someone who "gives as good as she gets," and the trailer isn't lying. Richard Conte is smooth and ingratiating as the club owner—and if you make an early guess that he's not as he seems, you're right.

And Larry Cravat? Although his whereabouts are cleverly disclosed, the revelation is not a tremendous surprise, and it hardly matters. The point of *Somewhere in the Night* is that redemption and honest self-appraisal are possible and that the past can stay dead.

Forged Memories

As German forces rampaged across Europe during World War II, special units stole numberless paintings and other artworks from museums in conquered nations. Some pieces ended up in the private collections of Hermann Göring and other top Nazis, but most were simply stockpiled, often deep within salt mines. At war's end, an awful tangle of provenance delayed the return of many pieces to rightful owners. Meanwhile, art forgers of varying skill set about remedying shortfalls with their own versions of coveted works.

Art forgery grounds the plot of Irving Reis's *Crack-Up* (1946), but the real issues are criminal misdirection and misapprehension of reality. Adapted by John Paxton, Ben Bengal, and Ray Spencer from Fredric Brown's 1943 short story "Madman's Holiday," the picture was shot in deep, glorious darkness by Reis and cinematographer Robert de Grasse. We share the travails of museum executive George Steele (Pat O'Brien), who breaks into his museum very early in the film, tussles violently with a cop, and inadvertently destroys a sculpture—all of this after surviving a grinding train crash, which we experience with George, via flashback, after his arrest.

But there has been no crash.

Friends quietly speculate that Steele has battle fatigue from his time in the service—a judgment that won't help him convince anybody of anything. He catches a break when an associate, Traybin (Herbert Marshall), intercedes to keep him out of jail. Steele's girlfriend, Terry (Claire Trevor), and a sympathetic secretary, Mary (Mary Ware), subsequently help him determine whether the museum has unknowingly taken possession of forged paintings.

Not surprisingly, Steele is obsessed with the train crash. If he's to figure it out, he must work alone, retracing his steps, taking the same train, and hoping in vain that someone in the station or onboard will remember him. The investigation doesn't work out to Steele's satisfaction—can he be going crazy?

The murder at the museum of a curator who warned about forgeries leads to a peculiar interlude with Terry at a penny arcade, a dreadful fire that threatens paintings inside the hold of a ship at dock, and a terrible run-in with a supposed friend who wants to inject Steele with a narcosynthetic in order to learn the whereabouts of the genuine paintings. After a few additional twists to the narrative, Steele is vindicated.

Case File: Robert de Grasse (1900–71)

Because this busy cinematographer worked steadily from 1921 until 1968, he is among those Hollywood craftsmen who literally came of age along with the movies. During the 1930s and early '40s, de Grasse excelled with such "women's pictures" as *Alice Adams*, *Bachelor Mother*, and *Kitty Foyle*; did a quasi-noir, *The Leopard Man*, for producer Val Lewton; and jumped into the genre full on with a succession of strongly visualized RKO noir thrillers: *Crack-Up*, *Born to Kill*, *The Clay Pigeon*, *Follow Me Quietly*, and the brilliantly realized *The Window*.

De Grasse left features in 1953 for television, where he shot scores of episodes of *The Amos 'n Andy Show* and virtually the entire five-season run of *The Dick Van Dyke Show*. De Grasse retired in 1968.

Crack-Up is overplotted and too cute by half. And yet, because of the confident brazenness of the script and Irving Reis's direction, and a pleasingly underplayed central performance by Pat O'Brien, the film is good entertainment with a satisfying splash of danger.

The nighttime train-wreck sequence is outstanding, a cascade of light and noise that begins when Steele spots the other train and then stares in horrified disbelief as the heavy beam from the approaching headlight grows closer. The wheels turn loudly beneath Steele, and screams of whistles blast from both trains. In an overpowering close-up, Steele's features are splashed with intense, merciless light. He's frozen like a prey animal, seemingly hypnotized. The light grows brighter, closer, brighter. And then the collision, suggested via a cacophony of sound and a few quick cuts and disorienting camera angles.

Crack-Up is a B movie with a B-plus cast and a final surprise that will jolt you out of your seat. Although Claire Trevor is wasted, young Mary Ware has some engaging moments. The film really belongs to the men: O'Brien, Marshall, Ray Collins, Wallace Ford (playing an incisive, deceptively casual police detective), and young character player Robert Bray, as a silent, menacing presence who has the answers Steele is looking for.

But before Steele gets that satisfaction, there is the train—rushing, pumping, complicit.

Chasing Freedom

Crack-Up, Street of Chance, Somewhere in the Night, and other noir thrillers from the immediate postwar era reflect the public's hazy understanding of "battle fatigue," an affliction that often went untreated, partly because many GIs came of age during the Depression, when silent forbearance of suffering was a virtue. So it is that in Arthur Ripley's *The Chase* (1946), psychologically damaged ex-Navy man Chuck Scott (Robert Cummings) shuffles around Miami in a bad suit and a comically short tie, gazing hungrily into a restaurant window. When Scott discovers a wallet, he spends a dollar or two on breakfast and then returns the wallet to the owner, a violent but queerly refined thug named Eddie Roman (Steve Cochran). The sleek and handsome Roman is amused by Scott's rumpled honesty and gives him a job as a chauffeur. Soon, Scott meets the gangster's beautiful and desperately unhappy wife, Lorna (Michele Morgan). Because Scott's judgment became a little scrambled during the war, he's receptive when Lorna asks for his help in getting her to a fairy-tale destination, Havana, beyond the clutches of her husband. Scott is even more receptive when Lorna asks that he come to Havana with her, as her lover.

Is Eddie Roman going to sit still for this?

The Chase is based on Cornell Woolrich's 1944 novel, *The Black Path of Fear,* adapted to the screen by prolific writer (and later producer) Philip Yordan. In the novel (the fifth in Woolrich's "Black" series), Scott is annoyingly dim rather than psychologically compromised, and his misadventures in Cuba encompass run-ins with opium fiends and Chinese smugglers. The screenplay eliminates drug use, smuggling, and an unlikely ally Scott finds in Havana, but Woolrich's dramatic high point is retained, and it's a shocker.

Early in the film's Havana sequence, Scott and Lorna kiss passionately in the back of a hansom, their faces framed in tight close-up that suggests romanticism as well as romance. But when Scott is on the run, the presumed glamour of Havana shrivels and is shown to be mostly false. As lensed by Frank E. Planer, the city isn't the "Paradise Under the Stars" of tourist brochures but an old and dilapidated place full of unpleasant, sweating people, illness, and intimidating shadows.

Visual contrast is provided by Eddie Roman's spacious, ornate Miami mansion that has gorgeous statuary and a phonograph that plays only classical music. Steve Cochran brings a dangerous, self-educated charm to Roman, and Peter Lorre, as Gino, Roman's number one, is insouciantly, sleepily evil. It's an underwritten role that would be virtually nothing if not for the Lorre persona.

Roman has a dank wine cellar (where he bumps off a business competitor) and a back-seat gas pedal that allows him to take over the speed of his limousine. This is an unlikely but hugely amusing story gimmick that figures in the film's literally explosive climax, when Roman tries to coax a trick from Gino that Scott has already managed but that Gino can't. (Obvious miniature work compromises the sequence and is the clearest evidence of the film's modest budget.)

Michele Morgan, already one of the most famous film actresses in France, is radiant and startlingly intelligent as Lorna; you wonder how she got mixed up with a pretender like Roman and why she's attracted to Scott. The mild, Everyman persona that Robert Cummings brought to Hitchcock's *Saboteur* (1941; another innocent man wrongly accused story) is replicated here. The actor's diffidence and the character's frequent lack of urgency are peculiar but refreshing. Movies are larger than life, so it's novel to observe a protagonist who is merely life-sized.

A narrative twist about two-thirds of the way into the film replicates a device used by the novel, and it's to the credit of Arthur Ripley that he encourages us to swallow it and remain onboard for the climax. Ripley worked as an editor and director of photography before becoming a screenwriter, seeing particular success as a gag man at the close of the silent era. He wrote dramas, too, and finally got the nod to direct in 1938. But between 1938 and 1958, Ripley directed only five films, closing that phase of his career with the 1958 moonshine melodrama *Thunder Road*, an oddball Robert Mitchum vehicle that later achieved cult status.

The Chase was released by United Artists and eventually fell into public domain. Visual and sound quality of all but the 2004 VCI DVD release are awful, and even VCI struggled to patch together a watchable restoration. A truly peculiar noir, *The Chase* deserves full-blown restoration and more admirers, too.

Charlie Finds the Light

A loss of origins underscores *Somewhere in the Night*. Contrarily, in Abraham Polonsky and Robert Rossen's *Body and Soul* (1947), the Jewish origins of promising welterweight boxer Charlie Davis (John Garfield) are made explicitly apparent and help spur Charlie's ambition. His father (Art Davis) and mother (Anne Revere) run a narrow, dim candy store on New York City's East Side. The place was once a going concern, but the Davises hung on too long. Now the neighborhood has changed and the store and the streets outside crawl with thieving kids and violent gangsters. In the candy store, the dream shared by so many first- and second-generation Jews in America has gone sour. Hard work has brought daily aggravation, subsistence living, and, worse, a bitter, ungrateful son. The Davises have their pride, so when Charlie rails at his father for having amounted to nothing, you squirm with deep discomfort. Charlie angrily promises to become a success, which he measures by the bills he stuffs into his pockets. But in a commonplace, real-life irony, Charlie's Jewish roots and urban-American ambition collide with his urgent impatience and threaten to ruin him.

When Polonsky wrote *Body and Soul* in 1946–47, professional boxing was an enormously popular sport that united Americans at the neighborhood, regional, national, and ethnic levels. But boxing was a troubled sport, as well, that was in the thrall of dealmakers, fixers, gamblers, and gangsters—particularly when weight classes other than heavyweight came into their own and produced a colorful variety of fighters that excited the public, generating big gates and encouraging fervent gambling activity. In time, the money put down by bettors was considerably more substantial than the sport's legitimate income.

Then there was the issue of moral tone. Every professional sport is a business, of course, but boxing became a meat-processing plant that developed and chewed up young boxers. Purses were split into so many slices that fighters often ended up with next to nothing, and allegations of fixed fights designed to benefit bettors were common. Promoters, managers, trainers, syndicates—everybody took a big bite. By the time of *Body and Soul*, boxing's many improprieties were being investigated by the U.S. government.

Charlie Davis's ferocious skill protects him from obvious abuse until he becomes champ . . . and then comes the decree from Roberts (Lloyd Gough), the smooth, cynical promoter who has inveigled himself into a 50 percent share of the Charlie Davis money machine. Charlie is instructed to take a dive in his first title defense. During a grinding, eight-minute fight sequence that is the film's climax, Charlie appears to play along (he's been instructed to go the full fifteen rounds and lose on a decision), but when his opponent (played by former pro welterweight Artie Dorrell) tags him hard, Charlie summons his pride and his anger—and channels the frustrations of his parents, too—and punches his way to victory.

Polonsky and director Rossen were concerned with a subject greater than the boxing that is the ostensible subject of *Body and Soul*. Leftist activists who came out of New York's Group Theatre—as did cast members Garfield, Revere, Smith, Gough, Joseph Pevney, and Canada Lee—Polonsky and Rossen were preoccupied with predatory capitalism that rewarded the perfidious, and abused and exploited those who actually generated the income. As far as the writer and director were concerned, it wasn't sufficient that the fictional Roberts and the other moneymen be defied—they had to be defeated. With an almost guileless idealism, the film tells us that goodness can win. (For background about the picture's production entity, Enterprise Studios, see the discussion of *Force of Evil* in Chapter 5.)

Charlie has tenacity, bravery, and other positive qualities, including an ability to return the love of a gentle, good woman, Peg (Lilli Palmer), an unknown but talented painter (that is, a creature completely different from Charlie who nevertheless adores him). Peg encourages Charlie's better aspects and enfolds him—and the film—in common sense, warmth, and the firm morality of the unostentatiously saintly. In this, as Garfield biographer Larry Swindell has noted, Peg is the "Soul" of *Body and Soul*.

The "Body" is Alice (Hazel Brooks, an enticing, cat-eyed actress awarded an "And Introducing" title card). Alice is the carnal, uneducated mistress of a greasy minor fixer named Quinn (William Conrad, in a finely restrained performance), but as Charlie punches his way to the top, Alice gravitates to him. She's physical, greedy, and mostly id, designed by Polonsky and Rossen to function as the darkness that exists in counterpoint to Peg's beatific illumination.

John Garfield gives a typically forceful, fully invested performance that grows in intensity, but the real revelation of *Body and Soul* is Lilli Palmer, who (whether by her own decision or Rossen's) exhales her lines in fascinating rhythm: at first quickly, the words tumbling forth in a rush until an abrupt, brief halt, and then a resumption, with the words now slow and considered, as if Peg must force herself to marshal her enthusiasms. The character is remarkably *alive*.

Rossen and cinematographer James Wong Howe brought inventive camerawork to the eight-minute fight sequence mentioned earlier, combining handheld shots and setups that are intentionally out of focus, with poorly framed images (in the spontaneous manner of a newsreel cameraman), low angles bisected by ropes and turnbuckles, and setups in which the fighters' bodies stagger perilously close to the camera.

Body and Soul was well received by critics and the public, but many of its participants suffered later at the hands of baldly opportunistic, Red-baiting politicians involved in HUAC. Abraham Polonsky ran afoul of HUAC investigators in 1951, a year that also brought HUAC trouble to Robert Rossen, John Garfield, Art Smith, Lloyd Gough, and Anne Revere. Investigators had victimized Canada Lee in 1949. Each of these people suffered industry blacklisting of varying degrees and duration. The stress is widely thought to be a contributing factor to Garfield's 1952 death at age thirty-nine.

Significantly, perhaps, Garfield, Polonsky, Rossen, and Smith were Jewish. For them, the implications of the immigrant experience were mixed indeed.

Welcome Home, Soldier

Body and Soul is thematically complex and eager to be important. It succeeds admirably, but success comes at all levels of ambition. Take RKO's *Desperate* (1947), which is as direct and as bluntly effective as a good rabbit punch. It gave Anthony Mann the opportunity to direct his first film noir and brought character actor Steve Brodie (a young man with a lived-in face) a rare lead. *Desperate* is also an interestingly topical film that plays off of a number of immediate postwar concerns.

Truck driver Steve Randall (Brodie) is suckered by an acquaintance, Walt Radak (Raymond Burr), into hiring out his truck to transport stolen furs. Steve tries to signal a cop, and in the gun battle that follows, the cop is killed and Radak's guileless kid brother (Larry Nunn) is captured. *Desperate* runs just seventy-three minutes, and for most of that time, Steve and pregnant wife Anne (Audrey Long) are on the run from Radak. The kid brother, you see, has taken the fall and is scheduled to die in the electric chair. Radak, perhaps unreasonably, blames Steve for the whole mess. He's eager to kill Steve, and Anne, too.

Like *They Live by Night* (1948), *Gun Crazy* (1950), and other proto–Bonnie and Clyde fables, the young couple flees from the tumult and danger of the city to the succor of the country. The city may never let Steve and Anne become completely happy. In the country, on the farm belonging to Anne's aunt and uncle, life is (temporarily) peaceful, almost idyllic. A lengthy dance sequence, with bright lights, happy people, and exuberant movement, brings the harried couple some much-needed joy and recalls a similar sequence that served a similar dramatic purpose in John Ford's *The Grapes of Wrath* (1940).

Inevitably, of course, the single-minded Radak traces the young marrieds to the farm. After a minor ruckus that forces the principals back into an urban environment, Radak is dealt with and Steve is finally cleared.

Filming of *Desperate* wrapped in December 1946, just fifteen months after the end of World War II. Steve, like millions of his real-life counterparts, had been a GI, and like them he struggles with substandard housing, wages that can't keep up with inflation—even with a slimy used-car dealer (Cy Kendall) who tries to swindle Steve out of his purchase of a nearly junked '29 Ford.

Anthony Mann had directed ten films previously and was beginning to command his technique by 1946. Noir was apparently congenial for him right off the bat, for *Desperate* is directed with the élan and zest of a smart kid playing with a new toy. When Radak takes a poke at Steve's jaw, his follow-through sends his meaty fist arcing directly into the camera. A broken bottle carried to the lens is examined in minute, unnerving detail, and a fistfight in a room illuminated only by a swinging overhead light is a nightmare of flailing bodies, weirdly lurching shadows on walls and ceiling, and faces that go dark, then light, then dark again.

During the climactic gun battle, Mann and cinematographer George E. Diskant utilize a richly shadowed apartment-house staircase, with its carpeted steps, curved railings, and eerily quiet landings, as their focal point, creating a disorienting, Escheresque tangle of interior geometry.

Steve Brodie was one of those unflamboyant actors who never seems to be acting. Because he has no discernible technique, you never catch him at his craft, and *Desperate* shines because of that. Audrey Long, as the innocent wife, gives a credible and appropriately tentative performance, but Raymond Burr, just beginning to hit his stride as a screen villain, goes for the gusto as Radak. Jason Robards (the elder) is a small wonder as an insouciant police detective who plays poor Steve like a bass before finally exonerating him. Light-comedy actor Dick Elliot has surprising impact in a protracted cameo as a rural sheriff whose hayseed good humor turns to flat menace in a heartbeat.

Desperate is capable and entertaining, with one forgivable flaw that escapes many viewers. It certainly escaped Mann and scripter Harry Essex: Instead of going to the potentially risky bother of inveigling Steve to provide his truck, why don't Radak and his gang just steal one?

Because it's difficult to fashion a thriller from good common sense, that's why.

With Both Barrels

Less than a year after wrapping *Desperate*, Anthony Mann completed work on his first mature noir, *Railroaded!* (1947). Entertaining and (as we'll see) ambitious, it's a solid thriller and a milestone in the development of a great filmmaker.

Lies and double-cross define the scheming of beautician Clara Calhoun (Jane Randolph) and her gangster boyfriend, Duke Martin (John Ireland), who engineer a nighttime robbery of Clara's shop. Why a beauty shop? Because the back room conceals a cash-heavy betting parlor that's one of a string operated by Duke's boss, a gambling-club owner named Ainsworth (Roy Gordon). Duke manages that club for Ainsworth, but that's not enough—he wants to knock over his boss and take charge of the whole operation.

The robbery comes off, but a cop is killed, and Duke's accomplice, Kowalski (Keefe Brasselle), is mortally wounded. No physical evidence other than a bullet is found at the crime scene, but because Kowalski has a bad history with a local kid, a sailor named Steve Ryan (Ed Kelly), he fingers Steve as the shooter—on his deathbed, no less, a particularly ugly sort of revenge. It looks as if Steve is cooked.

A few things work in his favor: the loyalty of his sister, Rosie (the appealing Sheila Ryan); extra investigation by the detective, Mickey Ferguson (Hugh Beaumont); and the inevitable falling-out of Clara and Duke.

Not long after Clara inadvertently hands Ferguson proof of Steve's innocence, the detective and Duke have a brutal, final showdown in a shadowed nightclub.

A rare step up to a "class" production by poverty-row production and distribution house Producers Releasing Corporation (PRC), *Railroaded!* overcomes its origins. This was no *Swing Hostess, Machine Gun Mama,* or *The Devil Bat*—this was a concerted effort by PRC to match the quality of films from big studios' B units. John C. Higgins's screenplay, from a story by Gertrude Walker, has a familiar premise but crackles with terse, pointed dialogue and a simpatico collaboration of Mann and his director of photography, Guy Roe (*Try and Get Me!*, *Armored Car Robbery*).

The shooting is set off by the growing panic of Clara's helper, Marie (Peggy Converse), who becomes understandably frightened when Kowalski points a shotgun her way. Mann and editor Louis Sackin cut between increasingly close views of the woman's face and the double barrel of the moving gun, which practically touches our noses by the time Mann is done. When Marie screams, Kowalski whirls, sees the cop, and takes one in the lower jaw (an unusual and particularly excruciating wound). Duke comes back with a revolver shot that drops the cop and sends his body crashing through the glass door. The shock value is punched up with simple, declarative blocking that helps us keep all the participants straight as we're pulled into the action. Smart cutting helps, too, and there's an uncomfortably unique visual touch: twin tongues of flame that leap from the shotgun's barrels when the gun is fired.

In this sequence, and throughout *Railroaded!*, Mann exploits the frame from front to back, designing the action with objects prominent in the foreground (in one setup from the opening sequence, these are floor-model hair dryers), key action in the middle ground, and added information staged in the background—all of it in sharp focus. In other moments, our eyes are led from a slightly out-of-focus foreground element to sudden movement in the deep-focus background. *Railroaded!* hasn't the gloss of a B from MGM or Paramount, but it could easily pass for Universal or Columbia product. Score a big one for PRC.

John Ireland, on the verge of real (if relatively brief) stardom, brings a hard, quietly threatening edge to Duke. In a scene at the club, he leans in very close as he speaks with Rosie, crowding her to establish his dominance. He has a fetish, too, for carefully polishing his cigarette case and his gun with a perfumed handkerchief, as if engaging in foreplay or (more probably) masturbation. Although we want the wrongly accused kid to be exonerated, it is Duke, sleek and perverse, who engages our attention and holds it.

Hugh Beaumont is pleasingly understated as Ferguson, and Ed Kelly, a John Derek type only blond, is earnest as the wrongly accused Steve Ryan. Curvy Jane Randolph is terrific as Clara, a querulous, off-putting schemer who puts a lot of stock in her sex appeal (considerable) and her big brain (not as big as she thinks). *Railroaded!* is a nice showcase for an actress who was retired by 1948, a real apex for PRC, and one step closer to industry significance for Anthony Mann.

Those Tormenting Details of Murder

Vincent Grayson is tormented by a real-seeming nightmare of murder, in which
he imagines struggling with a man in a peculiarly octagonal, mirrored room
and stabbing him to death with an awl surrendered by a mysterious woman.
Upon awakening, Grayson discovers items on his person that relate directly
to the dream: a key, a button, a drop of blood on his wrist, and thumbprints
on his throat. Afraid, he confides in his brother-in-law, Cliff, a police detective
who initially dismisses Grayson's claim but gradually comes to believe that, yes,
Grayson *has* committed murder. The question is, was Grayson aware of the crime
as he was committing it?

This is the setup of Cornell Woolrich's 1941 short story, "Nightmare" (credited to a Woolrich pseudonym, "William Irish"). Writer-director Maxwell Shane's
movie adaptation, *Fear in the Night* (1947; an indie production picked up by
Paramount), follows the course of the short story almost precisely and emphasizes two key elements: Grayson's uncanny familiarity with a mansion where a
murder much like the one he described took place and a peculiar new neighbor,
Belnap (Robert Emmett Keane), a skilled hypnotist who mesmerized the sug-
gestible Grayson (DeForest Kelley) and sent him off to kill Mrs. Belnap and her
lover. Cliff (Paul Kelly) reasons that if he can encourage Belnap to hypnotize
Grayson again, the killer can be trapped and Grayson exonerated.

The love triangle that motivates the crime is familiar enough, and the mirror
motif—suggestive of bitter, unavoidable truths about oneself—is merely visually
clever. What is unusual, particularly for a film, is the essential, inherent weakness of the protagonist. Although young and unusually well toned in the arms
and torso (as we see during a protracted sequence in which the protagonist
pads around his small room in a sleeveless undershirt), Grayson is a reticent
man who labors mousily as a bank teller. He is diffident and passionless with
his girlfriend (Kay Scott), and his preferred mode of escape from stress is self-
induced unconsciousness—he faints with the regularity of a besieged heroine
in a Victorian novel. When he can't summon a faint, he tries to jump from a
window. (In Woolrich's story, Grayson slashes his wrists with a razor.)

So that Grayson doesn't hurt himself, Cliff spends the night in the adjoining double bed, a modest irregularity that, along with Grayson's nature, has
encouraged some film historians to cite *Fear in the Night* as a tale of repressed
homosexuality. That's a stretch, even though Woolrich's original magazine story
dances around the subject, most vividly when Grayson absently caresses the
mysterious key, which has peculiarities of shape and design that suggest a penis.
This subtext didn't interest Maxwell Shane because of Hollywood's Production
Code—and because he wasn't interested in it. Grayson is just weak, period.

He's also deeply frightened. Belnap functions not as a person but as an
instrument of fate, focused and unstoppable. In literal terms, the hypnotism
gimmick is frankly absurd, but Woolrich and Shane utilize it as a metaphor for
helplessness and complete lack of free will. That's malevolent determinism, and

that's enough to frighten anybody. (To emphasize this point of view, short story and film include a corker of a thunderstorm that, while a device that moves the story forward, is also a subliminal reminder that people are puny indeed.)

Maxwell Shane wasn't prolific, and he's little recalled today. He has no reputation as a visual stylist. Regardless, the dream sequence that is central to *Fear in the Night* is appropriately disorienting and claustrophobic, with the reflective, weirdly octagonal room (designed by F. Paul Sylos) captured by cinematographer Jack Greenhalgh with a subtle fish-eye lens. Another effect, the literal fragmentation of scenes into small, hurtling pieces is a striking (if obvious) representation of Grayson's stress. Noirish lighting effects are wisely reserved for the dream; the greater part of the movie is shot in a handsome but matter-of-fact manner that reinforces the dream's peculiar visual and emotional power.

Nine years later, writer-director Shane returned to the same source material for *Nightmare* (1956), a painfully inexpensive remake distributed by United Artists. Virtually a scene-for-scene redo of *Fear in the Night*, the modestly jiggered script transforms Grayson (Kevin McCarthy) into a New Orleans jazz clarinetist. Shane and cinematographer Joe Biroc shot cast and exteriors on location but on the cheap, without sound; traffic noise was laid in later. For exterior dialogue, the actors line up stiffly in front of process screens. There are no genuine New Orleans interiors, only small, pinched soundstages drably lit in flat grays. And in a fundamental mistake, the dream sequence is staged and photographed with considerably more clarity than in *Fear in the Night* and seems more literal than phantasmagorical.

Famed arranger Billy May, playing himself (woodenly), fronts an unadventurous jazz combo that undermines tension rather than excites it. Herschel Burke Gilbert's orchestral score, though strong, isn't at all suggestive of New Orleans. However, a recurring, five-note motif that Grayson knows he's heard somewhere before, and that is driving him crazy, is effectively utilized. (The resolution to this musical mystery, though awkwardly staged, is a clever stroke and one of the remake's few fresh ideas.)

Billed alone above the title, Edward G. Robinson is allowed to dominate every scene he's in. Kevin McCarthy, a fine, highly trained actor with stage experience, becomes invisible when he's on-screen with Robinson. The cop becomes the film's unavoidable focus, even though the script isn't written that way. (Promotional advertising favored Robinson, too. One poster says, "Edward G. Robinson shocks the screen awake in NIGHTMARE.")

Jowly character player Gage Clark is creepily devious as Belnap, and Marian Carr brings a seductive purr to her role as a good-looking barfly. Leading lady Connie Russell, a singer taking a stab at movies, is lost as an actress and as a character.

The film's most profound shortcoming is that McCarthy doesn't exude the mouse-like fright that's so well expressed by DeForest Kelley in the first film. Bigger and more traditionally handsome than Kelley, McCarthy may simply seem too "regular" to be in such a mess. Instead of a helpless creature terrified of being crushed by fate, he's just a man with an odd problem.

The Lawyer Needs a Lawyer

Lawyers aren't cut out to be bodyguards. That's the hard lesson learned by Bob Regan (Edmond O'Brien) in *The Web* (1947). His employer is a confident, wealthy man named Andrew Colby (Vincent Price), who is favorably impressed when Regan bursts into a board meeting to demand sixty-four dollars owed to a client. Regan's legal practice isn't exactly thriving, so he's open-minded when Colby explains that an angry former business partner who went to prison for selling counterfeit bonds has just been released. Colby worries that the ex-con may decide to bother or even harm him. He needs a bodyguard, and if his selection of Regan seems far-fetched, remember that in 1947 it was easy to assume that a young man had done time in the service during the war and was familiar with firearms. Regan, full of piss and vinegar, takes the job. Colby thoughtfully provides him with a gun, and Regan's misadventure begins. Before the young lawyer can say, "I'm in over my head," he's on the hook for murdering the former partner.

The Web is minor but entertaining, directed with smoothness but not a lot of style by Michael Gordon, a journeyman who became associated later with light romantic fluff the likes of *Pillow Talk*, *Boys' Night Out*, and *Move Over Darling*. The story, scripted by William Bower and Bertram Millhauser, sets up its premise on an unchallenging narrative grid that allows the viewer to stay a half-step ahead. Colby was complicit in the counterfeiting and set up his former partner so that Regan shoots him in self-defense. In the final moments, a clever cop (William Bendix) waits in the shadows as Colby makes a bad—and completely unnecessary—mistake. It's all satisfying enough (who doesn't like to see an arrogant rich guy take a fall?) but predictable.

The real pleasures of *The Web* are the performances. Edmond O'Brien, in one of the earliest tough-guy roles of the sort that sustained him into the 1950s, is brash and energetic. Regan knows he's not as clever as he'd like to be, but he's dogged in his effort to clear himself and finds a congenial ally in Colby's secretary, Noel Faraday (Ella Raines). Noel has worked for Colby for six years, and you get the idea that she'd like it if a real romance with her boss developed. It doesn't, but a subtle sexual tension informs the scenes shared by Raines and Price. Partly because of that and partly because of issues of loyalty, Noel needs a long time to warm up to Regan.

Raines made a remarkable impression a few years earlier in *Phantom Lady* (see Chapter 1). She's appealing in *The Web*, but the role has no snap, and in the hands of a lesser actress Noel would come off as little more than a plot device. Raines holds her own on-screen, of course, but the fact is that she's criminally wasted.

Vincent Price nearly walks off with the whole movie. Colby is skilled at hiding his criminality, and he's ruthless when he needs to be. Price had played a vaguely similar sophisticated fellow in *Laura* (1944; see Chapter 1) and by 1947 had a firm grasp of that sort of role. As Colby, he's at once archly amusing, contemptible, and deadly.

Money, a Priest, and Murder

In Fairfield, Connecticut, in 1924, Fairfield County State's Attorney Homer Cummings declined to prosecute an itinerant for the shocking Bridgeport murder of a beloved local priest. In fact, at the May 28 arraignment, Cummings picked apart, piece by piece, the foundation of what might have been his case. He demonstrated serious inconsistencies in an apparent ballistics match, the accounts of seven eyewitnesses, and the defendant's (coerced) confession. Cummings spoke for ninety minutes. When he finished, the gallery applauded. The accused, Harold Israel, was freed.

That story, a true-life "innocent man wrongly accused" tale, intrigued magazine writer Fulton Ourslur, who chronicled it in the *Reader's Digest*. The article was sold to 20th Century-Fox and adapted by screenwriter Richard Murphy, who called the tale *Boomerang!* (1947). The script adheres to the details of the murder and to virtually all of the evidential portions of the case against Israel. In the film, the accused is a bitter, unemployed World War II veteran named John Waldron (Arthur Kennedy). State's Attorney Henry Harvey (Dana Andrews) resists pressure from local politicos and follows his better instincts in order to get at the truth. Waldron is freed.

To enhance the drama, Murphy and director Elia Kazan developed the local-politics angle into a major plot point involving a reform government that's presently in power, ambitious machine politicians (and a sympathetic newspaper) that want to return to power, and a local Parks Commissioner, Paul Harris (Ed Begley), who secretly owns valuable real estate that will go unsold if the machine politicians make the reform government look foolish. In other words, Harris will be wiped out financially unless Waldron is convicted. At the film's climax, Harris shifts miserably in his gallery seat, reaches into his coat, and shoots himself.

Although a true noir, *Boomerang!* has virtually none of the visual stylistics that characterize the genre. Kazan shot in natural light on location in Connecticut (though the town is never identified by the stentorian voice-over narrator, Reed Hadley). The murder—quite shocking, as a hand that grips a pistol enters from frame right to point the barrel at the back of the priest's head—occurs at night, and there are one or two other nighttime sequences, but most of the story unfolds during working hours. We see real streets, real businesses, an actual courthouse, and people going about their everyday business. So un-noir is all this that, on one level, *Boomerang!* might be a documentary about small-town life in 1947 America.

Noir is served by virtue of the false accusation, the innocent man's growing panic and later resignation, and the powerful, pointedly self-interested forces arrayed against him. Things look bad, too, on the micro level, because one of the eyewitnesses, a hash house waitress (Cara Williams, in a tarted-up, attention-getting performance), is sore at Waldron because he dumped her. Now she wants to fix his wagon.

A small plot point, the inability of the state's attorney's wife (Jane Wyatt) to have children is invoked in just one brief scene but is important because it suggests that Harvey is likely to be sensitive to the unfair vagaries of fate and thus unwilling to ferociously go after a man who happened to wander into town one day.

Some sequences are almost revolting. The reform crowd dangles the prospect of the governorship before Harvey—if he plays along. In other scenes, local politicos and businessmen from both factions giddily drink and laugh, while a man who may be innocent stews in jail.

Besides Harvey, the film's conscience is provided by a machine reporter, played with subtle, jaundiced depth by Sam Levene.

Dana Andrews, a perennially underrated actor, is sterling, particularly in his handling of lengthy, difficult monologues. Good work is also done by Lee J. Cobb, as the chief of police; James Dobson, as a dim cub reporter; and Philip Coolidge, as a gangly, oddly bug-eyed local with some peculiar connections to the murdered priest.

A superficially similar movie, Alfred Hitchcock's bleak and measured *The Wrong Man* (1956), has a more consistent noir look but falls into the drama category because Hitch's fact-based story has no undercurrent of double-dealing cops or politicians, or collusion for personal aggrandizement. The title character's predicament is based entirely on innocent human error.

The Unfulfilled Male

Although some ten million American men were drafted for service during World War II, thousands of GIs spent the war stateside, in administrative, training, and other roles. They performed necessary duties, but for many of these men, their service was a personal disappointment. In Andre de Toth's *Pitfall* (1948), this is hinted at—barely—in a brief dialogue exchange between minor insurance executive Johnny Forbes (Dick Powell) and his young son, Tommy (Jimmy Hunt). The father of the kid next door, Tommy says, came home from the war with a Silver Star. Johnny's wife, Sue (Jane Wyatt), smilingly informs Tommy that *his* dad served in Colorado and was awarded the good conduct medal with oak leaf clusters. The moment is light and amusing, a throwaway that's never referred to again. But it's the cleverest and most subtle element of Karl Kamb's adaptation of *The Pitfall*, a 1947 novel by Jay Dratler. It explains why the happily married Johnny begins an affair with another woman, courts danger, and ultimately kills a man.

From the film's earliest scenes, we see that Johnny Forbes is bored, bored, bored. Although reasonably prosperous, Johnny feels his life is insignificant. His home and work routines never vary—they're so precise, in fact, that he can dryly tell Sue he'll be back from work to peck her on the cheek at precisely 5:50 pm. Sue is charming and patient, which makes Johnny all the more restless. He can't stand the secure predictability of his life. He wants to be a primal man.

While investigating the disbursement of articles purchased for the likable Mona Stevens (Lizabeth Scott) with money embezzled by her now-imprisoned boyfriend, Bill Smiley (Byron Barr), Johnny allows his professional mask to slip. In just a few days, he and Mona are on the road to becoming lovers.

But there's another man in Mona's life besides Smiley and Johnny: MacDonald (Raymond Burr), a burly private detective who has worked with Johnny on the Smiley case and develops a sexual obsession with Mona. Although roundly rejected by Mona, Mac can't take no for an answer. He begins to stalk Mona and visits the soon-to-be-released Smiley, "helpfully" informing him about Johnny. In a short time, Mac becomes Johnny's personal nightmare. In a pair of dramatic incidents, one at Johnny's house and the other at Mona's apartment, Mac and Smiley are shot. Smiley is dead; Mac has a slim chance to live.

Mona is a sympathetic figure (when she first kisses Johnny, she has no idea he's married and doesn't for some time). Smiley is an ill-tempered dope, and Mac will be pleased if Smiley or Johnny or both end up dead. These are flawed personalities, but the script never lets us forget that those flaws may never have been aggravated and magnified if not for Johnny's foolish restlessness. He's enjoyed Mona but also invited Mac's hatred and Smiley's jealous fury. None of the unpleasantness had to happen.

Case File: Jay Dratler (1911–68)

The career of this important noir screenwriter began in 1940 with trifles the likes of *Girls Under 21*, *Get Hep to Love*, and *Where Did You Get that Girl?* Dratler's adapted screenplay for *Laura* seems to have come out of nowhere, and he made the most of the opportunity with keen delineations of the Obsessive Male, a key element of film noir. *Laura* was followed by scripts for *The Dark Corner* and *Impact*. A Dratler novel, *The Pitfall*, was adapted for the screen by Karl Kamb and became director Andre de Toth's noir thriller *Pitfall*.

Dratler did tough, concise script work on conventional dramas: *Call Northside 777*, *The Las Vegas Story*, and *The Desperate Hours* (uncredited), and collaborated with Fred Allen and Alma Reville on the script of *It's in the Bag!*, one of the funniest comedies of the '40s.

Sue tells Johnny that although she considered divorce, she's willing to try to repair the marriage if Johnny will help her. He says he will.

Much of the picture's success comes from its air of plausibility. Nothing that happens is beyond the realm of everyday possibility. Women choose boyfriends who embezzle. Married men cheat. Other men get hung up on women and can't let go. Two men often pursue one woman. And in domestic squabbles, people sometimes get shot. *Pitfall* has no perpetually wisecracking hero, no mysterious black bird, no femme fatale whose home base is Macao. The people that populate *Pitfall* are homegrown.

Dick Powell brings a fine understatement to Johnny. The character is nothing like Powell's take on Philip Marlowe (*Murder My Sweet* [1944]; see Chapter 3). Johnny has a modest self-confidence, but there's nothing jaunty or purposely provocative about his personality. He speaks quietly and reflectively. At home, he's vaguely remote and disengaged. There's nothing of the grand gesture about him.

Mac is one of Raymond Burr's best inventions. Looking larger and bulkier than usual, his physicality alongside the petite Lizabeth Scott (a quietly melancholy presence) is automatically intimidating. Like Johnny, he never raises his voice. He wants things to fall his way and he's going to see that they do. The moment when Mac unexpectedly uncorks with a terrific punch to Johnny's middle, and then hits and kicks him after he falls, is a stunner that we don't see coming. The sequence is well directed by de Toth and sets up another sequence that we're delighted to have waited for: Johnny's revenge. Mac answers his doorbell one day, and Johnny's fists are in his face, in his gut, everywhere. (Throwaway dialogue has established that Johnny boxed in college.) Mac falls like a redwood.

Andre de Toth directed films with assurance and honesty, remaining mindful of story and character. Unlike many directors of mid-level Hollywood pictures, he developed effectively collaborative relationships with his actors. Their thoughts about character, and about how to play specific scenes, were important to him. He began his directorial career in Hungary in the late 1930s and was working in Hollywood by 1943. He directed many capable westerns (*Last of the Comanches* [1952] is particularly good); an aggressively effective, low-budget noir, *Crime Wave* (1954; discussed later in this chapter); and even the amusing, action-packed 1969 Michael Caine vehicle *Play Dirty*.

Typical of his output, de Toth doesn't strive for effect in *Pitfall*; the script is strong enough that it needs little in the way of visual amplification. Harry Wild's lighting is restrained throughout most of the film but has a splendid noir flourish at the climax, when a drunk, armed, and very angry Smiley besieges Johnny's shadowed house. Now Johnny will defend the home that he used to think was a prison. After Smiley momentarily vanishes, the camera executes an exceedingly slow, nearly 180-degree pan of the inside walls of the living room, as Johnny might see them. The camera stops at the French doors—and Smiley is there.

But not for long.

Even a Crook is Innocent of Something

Because insurance man Johnny Forbes is complicit in his own predicament, *Pitfall* invites an ambivalent viewer response. As we've seen throughout this book, ambivalence is a dominant dramatic and reactive force in noir, and few "victims of circumstance" make us more ambivalent than Joe Sullivan (Dennis O'Keefe), the escaped convict who is the unfairly abused protagonist of Anthony Mann's masterful and very important *Raw Deal* (1948). There's no doubt that Joe has been treated badly, but he set himself up for that mistreatment by making a living as a professional criminal. He's done time for a crime he didn't commit (he was framed by his cronies), but because he's a habitual lawbreaker, he's one of noir's least sympathetic victims. Still, nobody (including those of us in the audience) likes to be played for a chump and locked up. When that happens to you, you get angry. People are going to have to answer for the crap they put you through and for the lost time that you can never recover. *Raw Deal*, then, is predicated not on a momentary moral lapse of the protagonist but on the

Director Anthony Mann and cinematographer John Alton did superb work on *Raw Deal* (1948), a bitter account of a habitual criminal's desire for revenge against former cronies who framed him. The hood (Dennis O'Keefe) is foolishly focused on his goal. Only his fearless, loyal lover (Claire Trevor) possesses the insight needed to understand her man's obsession.

protagonist's poor character, his vexation, and a hot desire for revenge. Joe Sullivan is a crumb who is determined to settle the books.

Joe has two primary targets for his revenge: the lean, coolly trigger-happy Fantail (John Ireland) and Fantail's giant-sized boss, Rick Coyle (Raymond Burr), a midlevel crime lord who has a sadistic fascination with fire and an eagerness to wash Joe Sullivan out of his hair.

All of that is the strictly male portion of *Raw Deal*. The film's other conflicts, male-female ones, are embodied in the two women in Joe's orbit: Pat (Claire Trevor), Joe's pathetically loyal yet reflective blonde mistress, who provides the film's ghostly and knowing voice-over narration against composer Paul Sawtell's eerie theremin score; and brunette Ann (Marsha Hunt), who has had a peripherally sympathetic involvement with Rick during his trial and now is Joe's prisoner, forced to travel highways and back roads as a diversion (the cops are looking for an escaped con, not a man accompanied by two women).

This "female" element of *Raw Deal* slides into the psychosexual because of the particulars of the inevitable romantic triangle. Joe is grateful to the earthily sexual Pat (early in the film, she bravely holds her ground in an idling car as Joe scales the prison wall). But Joe is unable to return Pat's love, perhaps because, like him, she's part of "the life." Ann, on the other hand, is a "lady" with no links to criminality or the lifestyle. Because of that, and despite Joe's frequently expressed impatience with Ann, he's strongly attracted to her. And Ann—educated, articulate, thoughtful—wants Joe. She wants to be corrupted.

This marvelous stew of conflict and desire, scripted by John C. Higgins and Leopold Atlas, is impeccably visualized. *Raw Deal* is a particular thrill because of

Case File: Raymond Burr (1917–93)

One of the greatest and most enduring stars produced by television, Raymond Burr excelled as literal and figurative heavies in films noir and other thrillers made in the 1940s and '50s. As his weight fluctuated, Burr ranged from large to very large; his dark glower and sheer presence made him a fearsome adversary in many noir pictures: *Desperate, Ruthless, Raw Deal, Pitfall, Criss Cross, Red Light* (as a particularly nasty schemer who meets a spectacular end), *His Kind of Woman* (as a fiend who wants to literally steal Robert Mitchum's face), *The Blue Gardenia* (as a personable pinup artist who has rape on his mind), and *Crime of Passion*.

Among Burr's other career highlights are *Walk a Crooked Mile, Abandoned, M* (1951 version), *A Place in the Sun, The Whip Hand, Bride of the Gorilla, Meet Danny Wilson, Godzilla, King of the Monsters* (the cleverly Americanized 1956 version of *Gojira*), and *Rear Window* (as the oddly sympathetic murderer who resents James Stewart's snoopiness).

A 1957–66 run as TV's *Perry Mason* made Burr one of the most recognizable actors in the world. He reprised the role in twenty-six "event" TV movies made from 1985 to 1993. Another very successful show, *Ironside* (1967–75) further cemented Burr's enduring popularity.

the ways in which Anthony Mann and cinematographer John Alton present the nighttime urban environment via carefully composed frames dominated by clock faces, girders, walls, street signs, and rooftops. These things "are" the city, and they're unpleasant. The use of synecdoche carries on with repeated visualization of supposedly ambient light: automobile headlamps, flashlights, road flashers, the flare of a match, the trio of lights mounted on a policeman's motorcycle. And more: streetlamps, candles, a flambéed dessert that Rick abruptly tosses onto a chippie who has annoyed him (an act that presages the boiling coffee in *The Big Heat*; see Chapter 4).

Finally, uncontrolled fire threatens to consume a plush apartment and everybody inside.

Joe's failings are partially militated by references to his childhood act of heroism in which he saved other children from—inevitably—a fire. Young Joe was given an award for that, but the city's gratitude couldn't help him out of his daily circumstances. Exasperated, he tells Ann, "If you want to know what happened to that kid with the medal, he hocked it at sixteen. He got hungry."

Marvelous business onboard a dark ship allowed Mann and Alton to slip into the visually avant-garde, with dense diagonals of shadow, Pat's face (with veil) in striking close-up, and Joe and Pat's embrace in the light of an open bulkhead door, a moon-like porthole on the wall next to them, and the porthole's reflection in a mirror on the perpendicular wall. Joe has promised to marry Pat aboard the ship, and although she is thrilled, Joe's false enthusiasm is evident in Mann and Alton's claustrophobic, surreal compositions.

Ultimately, *Raw Deal* concerns itself with the city, the corruption of innocence, the loss of goodness, and the sacrifice of common sense. When a densely

Case File: John C. Higgins (1908–95)

Between 1935 and 1938, Winnipeg native John C. Higgins scripted six of MGM's laudably tough "Crime Does Not Pay" short subjects. The shorts—ostensibly public-service pieces but in reality entertainingly nasty mini-thrillers with tones purposely at odds with the typical MGM product—were used as training grounds for writers no less than for actors and directors. Higgins apparently found the genre compatible. In 1942, he wrote one of the first forensic thrillers, *Kid Glove Killer* (the American feature debut of director Fred Zinnemann), and scripted his first noir, *Railroaded!*, five years later. That was the beginning of a very important two-year collaborative relationship with director Anthony Mann, for whom Higgins wrote *T-Men, Raw Deal, He Walked by Night*, and a startling procedural, *Border Incident*. These screenplays are dominated by protagonists who, because of their work as cops or as excessively bold criminals, place themselves on the path to extinction.

Higgins also wrote *Shield for Murder*, a showy noir vehicle for director-star Edmond O'Brien; a shockingly tough prison melodrama, *Big House U.S.A.*; and one of the most amusing of all teenpics, *Untamed Youth*.

fogged-in city street is suddenly cut with a heavy shaft of illumination, you know that people are about to suffer for their foolishness and their foolish dreams.

An Efficient Way to Kill

The year 1948 brought the plain suburban reality of *Pitfall* and the grim hyper-reality of *Raw Deal*. In April, Paramount released John Farrow's *The Big Clock*, a glossy and remarkable exercise in violent murder laced with whimsy, a deep sense of menace, and satire. The last is seldom found in noir, and because the satire of *The Big Clock* is so pointed and so effectively presented, the film stands alone in the genre.

George Stroud (Ray Milland) is the highly paid editor of *Crimeways* magazine, which is part of a vast publishing empire ruled by Earl Janoth (Charles Laughton). Janoth is an arrogant and remote autocrat who intimidates his low-level employees and buys the loyalty of his top people.

When Janoth murders his willful mistress (Rita Johnson), he confides in his number one (George Macready) and turns the investigative resources of *Crimeways* into a spurious hunt for the killer. Stroud, who had been with the victim minutes before her death, realizes that the investigation will eventually point to him. Before that happens, he must uncover the true killer.

Nearly all of the action of *The Big Clock* is set at the Janoth Building, a modernist skyscraper where the palatial lobby is dominated by the enormous *moderne* clock that is Janoth's obsession. Efficiency, as measured in hours and minutes, absorbs him completely; early in the film, he tells his mistress that he'll see her later in the evening, "at 10:55."

The concept of time management was developed in the nineteenth century, concurrent with mass industrialization and new media that worked according to strict schedules. By 1948, "time management" was a relentless, much-hated buzz phrase of business. At Janoth Publications, it's carried to disquieting extremes. Every clock in the building is linked to the lobby clock. Deviation from schedule and routine is not allowed. Precision, efficiency. Do it now, do it smarter, see you at 10:55.

Art directors Roland Anderson, Hans Dreier, and Albert Nozaki, as well as set decorators Sam Comer and Ross Dowd, make vital contributions to the film's theme, creating grandly impressive but arid lobby and office sets that are built from what appear to be polished blocks of granite, dominated by Wrightish horizontals, and decorated with precisely placed modernist furniture. The whole place is simultaneously gorgeous and soul-killing. From these offices and an endless grid of corridors, Janoth employees labor on many magazines: *Crimeways*, *Airways*, *Sportsways*, *Styleways*, and *Newsways*. Janoth is the noir equivalent of Time-Life mogul and American tastemaker Henry Luce.

Jonathan Latimer's sparkling screenplay (from Kenneth Fearing's celebrated 1946 novel) suggests that Janoth, like Luce, specializes in breezy, predigested

Case File: Jonathan Latimer (1906–83)

Crime novelist Jonathan Latimer came to Hollywood in 1937 and scripted features and television until 1972. He wrote many crime and suspense thrillers, including some important noir pictures: *The Glass Key*, *Nocturne*, the fanciful *The Big Clock*, and the disturbingly deterministic *Night Has a Thousand Eyes*. These comprise Higgins's best work. Other notable scripts: *Alias Nick Beal*, *Submarine Command*, *Plunder of the Sun*, and *The Unholy Wife*, RKO's failed 1957 attempt to establish British blonde bombshell Diana Dors as a Stateside star.

---

news and information. Janoth Publications is prosperous because it plays to the limitations and lesser instincts of its readers.

The notion of a man profiting from pap fed to the masses brings one level of satire to *The Big Clock*. Another is the film's overt disapproval of work as salaried slavery. Much of the film's plot is driven by Stroud's not-unreasonable desire to take his wife (Maureen O'Sullivan) on a honeymoon—after nearly seven years of marriage. (In an amusing touch, George's wife is named Georgette, and their son is named George.) Stroud has worked for Janoth during those seven years, and every time he's broached the subject of time off, he's been shamed into forgetting the idea and doing his job. Now, working for $30,000 a year (in 1948 dollars, mind you), Stroud is more trapped than ever, and Janoth knows it. But given an ultimatum by his wife, Stroud insists on time off and is fired. When he describes his sacking to his wife, Milland and O'Sullivan play the moment as if it were news of a long-awaited promotion or a big win in the Irish Sweepstakes. Stroud will be blackballed throughout the industry and is destined to return to his beginnings as a reporter on a small newspaper in West Virginia.

The couple couldn't be happier.

The satire of *The Big Clock* becomes positively sinister near the climax, as Stroud dashes here and there throughout the building after being wrongly identified as the killer. He ends up in the elevated control room of the clock—or perhaps now we should say, the Clock. Director John Farrow and cinematographer John F. Seitz present the room as a small, weirdly shadowed turret, like the top of a lighthouse crammed with electronics. Stroud is bathed in the glow of lighted instruments and dials arrayed in neat rows from floor to ceiling. The place is silent, unearthly. This is atom-age science designed to destroy spirits and minds rather than bodies. Visually and thematically, the control room sequence recalls the mad machines of commerce in *Metropolis* (1926) and anticipates the intimidating hardware on view in some of the paranoid science-fiction thrillers of the 1950s.

Stroud appears overwhelmed by all this looming technology, but when he accidentally leans against a lever, the Clock is shut down and the whole building is thrown into disarray.

Many incidental characters, such as a dotty artist played by Elsa Lanchester (Charles Laughton's wife), are "characters" akin to the amiable oddballs indelibly captured at the time by writers Joseph Mitchell and A. J. Liebling: earthy cab drivers, an eccentric tavern owner, a timid art critic pressed into detective work, an undersized masseur, a lippy elevator operator, an out-of-work radio actor. There's real whimsy at work in the film, and the remarkable thing is that none of it detracts from the serious subtexts or from the grisly resolution of the plot.

The Stars Are Watching

The very title of *Night Has a Thousand Eyes* (1948) suggests the determinist bleakness that is the film's major preoccupation. Based on the 1945 George Hopley (Cornell Woolrich) novel, the film is remorselessly downbeat, yet not without moments of odd, literally awesome beauty. And it all has to do with the stars that fill the night sky.

In a desolate, deeply shadowed train yard, Elliott Carson (the uncharismatic John Lund) worriedly trails after Jean Courtland (Gail Russell), the woman he loves. Sure enough, he spies Jean far above him, on the edge of a railroad bridge, enveloped in steam and waiting to jump to her death as soon as an approaching train is beneath her. Carson vaults the steps to the bridge and pulls Jean to safety just as she relaxes her grip on the railing.

In a café immediately afterward, Jean and Carson are approached by a man they know, John Triton (Edward G. Robinson), a onetime professional clairvoyant, long out of the limelight, who brings the couple up to date on his activities. He abandoned show business twenty years ago when touched by visions that were disturbing—and accurate. A vision of his on-stage partner Jenny (Virginia Bruce) dying in childbirth was particularly unsettling, and true. After years of miserable, self-imposed exile, Triton returned to Los Angeles to keep an eye on Jenny's daughter, Jean, and the girl's father, Whitney Courtland (Jerome Cowan). Courtland had been Triton's loyal business manager, and when Triton had a vision of Courtland perishing in a plane crash, he felt obliged to contact the now-grown Jean.

Courtland died wealthy—in a plane crash. Devastated, Jean was pushed to the brink because Triton revealed yet another vision: one of Jean lying beneath a night sky sprinkled with stars.

Triton concludes his reminiscence. Carson is emotionally exhausted from his last-second rescue of Jean and resentful of Triton's unasked-for presence in Jean's life. And Carson is deeply suspicious of the circumstances surrounding Courtland's death. At his urging, an ambitious special prosecutor indicts Triton for murder. During a midnight gathering at the Courtland mansion, the true nature of the threat to Jean is revealed.

Written on a piece of paper found inside Triton's overcoat is his prediction of his own death.

Case File: Cornell Woolrich (1903–68)

The cleverness and bleak points of view put forth in the work of dominant noir novelist and short-story writer Cornell Woolrich are so popular that nearly thirty film and television adaptations of his work have appeared since his death in 1968. During his lifetime, Woolrich was unsurpassed as a source for noir and other suspense: Between 1929 and 1968, more than *eighty* adaptations of his work played on movie and television screens. During noir's golden age in the 1940s and '50s, no other source writer approached Woolrich's popularity with Hollywood screenwriters and story editors. Indeed, in all of Hollywood history, the only authors that are likely to have surpassed Woolrich's popularity as a source of story material are those who, like Edgar Allan Poe and Robert Louis Stevenson, long ago fell into the public domain. Cornell Woolrich is one of the best friends Hollywood ever had.

There's a cheap irony in that, because Woolrich was a reclusive man with few friends, unhealthily bound to his mother and deeply unhappy about his homosexuality. A 1928 Hollywood marriage to a producer's daughter was annulled, and Woolrich abandoned his brief career as a writer of titles and dialogue in silent and early sound cinema. He turned to novels and short stories, spending most of his life in emotional misery and physical disarray. He lived, with Mum, in a grungy Harlem apartment. Finally loath to leave his four walls, Woolrich allowed a leg injury to progress to gangrene—and lost the leg. He carried on, though he sank deeper into alcoholism and isolation following his mother's death in 1957. Because he had sold and continued to sell so many novels and stories to filmmakers, money never was a problem. The tragedy, as with many protagonists of his suspense tales, is that Woolrich was too tormented to enjoy life.

Woolrich's appeal as a writer lies not in his convoluted, often messy plotting, nor in his love of endless detail, but in his worldview: We exist, he insists, on the razor edge of disaster, victims of fate, circumstance, and the chance encounter, or of our foolish tendency to trust others. We will be visited by disaster and dissolution, and probably sooner rather than later. "First you dream," Woolrich wrote, "then you die."

Woolrich's work was adapted for key episodes of TV's *Alfred Hitchcock Presents*, *Thriller*, *Suspense*, *Playhouse 90*, and *Lux Video Theatre*. Big-screen adaptations of his stories and novels include *Street of Chance*, *Phantom Lady* (1944 film and 1950 TV adaptation for *Robert Montgomery Presents*, both starring Ella Raines), *Deadline at Dawn*, *Black Angel*, *The Chase*, *Fear in the Night*, *Night Has a Thousand Eyes*, *The Window*, *No Man of Her Own*, and *Nightmare*. Most famous among the non-noir adaptations is *Rear Window*. Other notable film credits are *Seven Footprints to Satan* (titles only, from the novel by Abraham Merritt), *The Leopard Man*, and *The Mark of the Whistler*.

The existential angst put forth by Woolrich translates well and has been adapted for features and television produced in France, Germany, Italy, Spain, the Soviet Union, Turkey, Brazil, and Argentina.

Director John Cromwell, working with cinematographer John F. Seitz, imbued the frankly fantastic story with a tone that moves between realism (Triton's ascent in the world of show business), atmospherics (the intimidating and foreboding train yard of the opening sequence), and the cornball dramatics of the final third, in which Triton and a gaggle of others inside the Courtland mansion become chess pieces in an old dark house mystery that might have been made in 1932. (There's even a mysterious *someone* who hides behind the drapes [nobody notices when the drapes visibly rustle!] and fingers that *move the hands of a clock forward*, so that midnight—the predicted time of Jean's demise—will seem to have come and gone, giving the killer fresh advantage. Amusingly, nobody checks a wristwatch during the run-up to twelve; all eyes are riveted on the compromised clock.)

The disparities of tone and visual approach are purposely peculiar and underscore the multiple meanings of "realities" that are alternately—and sometimes simultaneously—empirical and miserably existential.

Overarching over everything is a queasy determinism. When Triton wearily says, "I am what I am," he's not being glib or shallow; he's offering a profound explanation of his nature and his essential helplessness. His life is run by the stars. As Jean prepares for suicide, she gazes above at a starry blackness. The film's final shot, after Triton's death prediction has been fulfilled, is of another starry night sky, this one decorated with a few diagonal swatches of cloud.

This notion of unwholesome cosmic forces is right out of H. P. Lovecraft, of course, but neither Woolrich nor screenwriters Barré Lyndon and Jonathan Latimer allowed the story to become true horror. Instead, the narrative is a meditation on our inability to acknowledge and appreciate the nonempirical. Further, the story makes clear that not every aspect of our fates is necessarily written in stone. An empath like Triton can (despite, or because of, his determinedly Christian-symbolic name) alter the deterministic course of events. The power given to him may be latent in all of us.

Actress Gail Russell, a beguiling presence who died young, is ideally cast. Her enormous dark eyes, lit so that the expansive whites acquire a luminous glow, suggest Jean's deep melancholy as well as a reflective nature that opens her mind to the unknowable. Although suicidal as the story begins, Jean is not a hysteric. To the contrary, her thinking is very measured. A whole galaxy of intellect and emotion is visible in her gaze. She's positively otherworldly.

Collaboration and Other Crimes

Noir melodrama predicated on the topicality of returned war vets resurfaces in Richard Fleischer's *The Clay Pigeon* (1949), in which former sailor Jim Fletcher (Bill Williams) awakes in a Long Beach military hospital, recovering from a head injury. After a nurse insults him to his face, Fletcher discovers that, while a prisoner of the Japanese, he ratted out pals who were stealing food, causing their executions and ensuring his own survival. Now Fletcher is looking at a court-martial and a possible death sentence.

Like Sailor Williams in *Deadline at Dawn* (an earlier Bill Williams vehicle) and George Taylor in *Somewhere in the Night*, Fletcher is tormented because his sense of self is threatened by the judgments made against him by others. The final torment is that his injury has left him unable to recall important details of his military service. Fletcher is sure of one thing, though: He could never have sent his friends to their deaths. Following his escape from the hospital, and with Martha Gregory (Barbara Hale), the widow of one of the executed prisoners, in tow, Fletcher hurries to LA to clear his name.

American collusion with the enemy wasn't much discussed after World War II, so screenwriter Carl Foreman earns points for anticipating an unpleasantness that wouldn't become a hot topic for another four or five years, after the Korean War. (Personal responsibility was heavy on Foreman's mind at this time: While he fashioned *The Clay Pigeon* he also was developing his moralistic script for *High Noon*.) Bill Williams and Barbara Hale are capable and pleasant but strike no sparks. Third-billed Richard Quine, who later became an important director at Columbia, is merely adequate as Fletcher's old wartime buddy, Ted. Badly needed edge is provided by bit players Robert Bray and Ken Terrell, as goons intent on snuffing Fletcher; and by veteran character man Richard Loo, very well cast as a former camp guard named Tokiyama, a frequent tormentor of Fletcher during the war and now unaccountably in the United States.

Fleischer was only a couple of years into his feature-film career in 1949 but was already developing his penchant for swift movement and narrative urgency. A daytime foot chase though LA's Chinatown is well staged (most of the picture was shot on location), but the best moments are set at night, when the goons force Fletcher and Martha's car off the road; and onboard a train, when Tokiyama readies himself to shove Fletcher into the path of an oncoming locomotive (via process photography borrowed from *Crack-Up*). Although a counterfeiting angle is pretty cute, the identity of the fixer behind Fletcher's frame and persecution is embarrassingly obvious. (Hint: Early in the story, Fletcher says, "What a guy! I knew I could depend on Ted!")

Foreman's script is workmanlike and no more. A pointed but irrelevant mention of the U.S. Army's famed 442nd Regimental Command Team, composed mainly of Nisei (Japanese American) GIs, is an obvious sop intended to appease postwar viewers who might be offended because a key villain of the tale is Japanese (actor Richard Loo was of Chinese extraction).

The worst stumble is the speed with which Martha accepts Fletcher's story and forgives him for terrorizing her, tying and gagging her, and forcing her to travel with him. In the second act, when tension should be building, the two take a beachfront trailer and spend a week happily sunbathing and swimming! With this, the anguish caused by Fletcher's unfair harassment is fatally diminished. The picture's dramatic impact dissolves altogether at the fade-out, when Fletcher and Martha happily announce to the Navy that they've decided to get married.

RKO's B unit was famously competent and would build much of its reputation on two noir thrillers Richard Fleischer directed later, *Armored Car Robbery* and *The Narrow Margin*. The budget of *The Clay Pigeon* was tight even by the B unit's standards, and a sixty-three-minute running time marked the film as bottom-of-the-bill fare. Still, Fleischer delivered a good-looking thriller that's undone by things beyond his control.

Dark Poetry

During a recent screening of Nicholas Ray's *They Live by Night* (1949), a companion remarked to me that the young fugitive lovers, Bowie (Farley Granger) and Keechie (Cathy O'Donnell), "never look at each other." My companion was put off, she said, because the youngsters seemed not to make a believable emotional connection. Upon reflection, I decided that the remark was more or less correct. The young lovers spend a lot of time in embrace and looking over each other's shoulders, or observing each other, almost secretly, through windows. Direct, eye-to-eye communication is rare. In many scenes, their sight lines are oblique, as if each is embarrassed by even the modest intimacy of a shared gaze. Sometimes, one or the other youngster slips into dreamy monologue that doesn't require (or inspire) eye-to-eye contact. (Reveries are usually one's own, after all.) And yet for all this, the two are in love, and even marry.

Why are Bowie and Keechie hesitant to make eye contact? Why their avoidance of basic emotional connection? The answer is the fundamental theme, and heartrending tragedy, of *They Live by Night*: Bowie and Keechie, warily hopeful children of the poor South, have grown up in circumstances so mean and so impoverished that each is emotionally stunted. Abandoned by family and locked into rigid stratification of class, they cannot properly develop. Bowie's slide into criminality (he's just escaped from prison) is almost inevitable. The youngsters become lovers mainly because of propinquity and need.

They Live by Night was adapted by Nick Ray, and scripted by Charles Schnee, from Edward Anderson's 1937 Depression novel *Thieves Like Us*. Although the film is set in present-day 1947, numerous elements—the Southern setting, wardrobe suggestive of "Okies," dissolution of families, busted agriculture and manufacturing—deliberately harken back a full decade and more. (Former story man and first-time director Ray wrapped the shoot during the summer of '47, but turmoil at RKO, including the takeover of the studio by Howard Hughes, kept *They Live by Night* from general release until November 1949.) Partly because of the progressive, sympathetic sensibilities of executive producer Dore Schary, Bowie and Keechie yearn desperately to "live like other people" and "do things other people do"—and they may as well hope to emulate residents of another planet. The picture's interest in literal and figurative imprisonment inevitably recalls James Agee and Walker Evans's *Let Us Now Praise Famous Men*, a celebrated 1941 book about white sharecroppers.

Bowie's attempt to set up a sort of family with fellow escapees T-Dub (Jay C. Flippen) and one-eyed Chickamaw (Howard Da Silva), and with T-Dub's sister-in-law, Mattie (Helen Craig), is a pipe dream because T-Dub perpetually needs money, Chickamaw is a sociopathic drunk, and Mattie will do anything,

RKO's marketing department promoted Nicholas Ray's *They Live by Night* (1949) as a breathless teen melodrama. The film has a bit of that, but it's mostly a reflective, heartbreaking study of people doomed by their origins, and their tragic limitations of character and imagination.

including betray Bowie to the police, to earn her husband's release from prison. Bowie's dreams are illusions.

The film takes pains to suggest that the young lovers are innocents who face impossible odds in a corrupt and uncaring world. Police are professional, implacable, and everywhere. City crooks tell them to beat it back to the country. The sly, aged justice of the peace (Ian Wolfe) who perfunctorily performs a marriage ceremony for twenty dollars arranges for Bowie to buy a hot car and inaccurately boasts that if they can pay, he can get them safely into Mexico. (In the novel, this character is a judge, a gross corruption that the Production Code would not have allowed.) A plumber who has come to repair a leak in the couple's rental cabin (simply, heartbreakingly decorated by Keechie) identifies Bowie and hurries away to raise the alarm and claim a reward.

Rural exteriors were shot on the RKO ranch, and town scenes were filmed in Encino. Ray and special cameraman Paul Ivano devoted the first day of shooting

Case File: Nicholas Ray (1911–79)

With formal training in architecture, sculpture, and music, as well as experience as a stage actor and director, Nicholas Ray wasn't just one of the more broadly educated Hollywood film directors, but one who seemed destined to develop the humanism that informs so many of his projects. He was attracted to protagonists who mount ferocious struggles to overcome the bad hands dealt to them by circumstance and make their presence matter in an uncaring world.

Ray's directorial debut, *They Live by Night*, is noir that sees victory in struggle, if not in outcome. His other noir films are *In a Lonely Place*, *On Dangerous Ground*, and *Party Girl*.

Personally restless and either ill equipped or just disinclined to deal amicably with studio executives and other meddlers, Ray had some commercial success but felt trapped by projects that he felt had been imposed upon him. When he was invested in the material, as in *Rebel Without a Cause*, *In a Lonely Place*, *Bigger Than Life* (in which a gentle family man becomes a demon after taking the prescription drug cortisone), and *The Lusty Men* (a largely improvised modern-day western), characters and settings are evoked with grace and interludes of explosive confrontation. Ray was attracted to the drama of generational conflict and seems to have had a grand time exploring gender conflict in his wryly funny Freudian western *Johnny Guitar*.

Publicity surrounding Ray's marriage to noir queen Gloria Grahame—who divorced Ray in 1952 and married his son (her stepson) nine years later—raised eyebrows. During the shoot of 1963's *55 Days at Peking*, Ray openly battled alcoholism and then suffered a heart attack that caused him to be replaced by the uncredited Guy Green and Andrew Marton. Ray never directed another feature. He subsequently did some acting in Europe and capped his life and career with an unsettling (and posthumous) 1980 pseudo-documentary called *Lightning over Water*, in which he and director Wim Wenders chronicled the final stage of Ray's death by cancer.

to a striking series of helicopter shots of the small, moving figures of Bowie and the other men, and various automobiles that speed across roads and shorn fields. In one overhead tableau, Bowie collapses in front of a gaily illustrated billboard that invokes Depression-era billboards photographed, with all due irony, by Margaret Bourke-White. The sequences marked the first time a helicopter had been used to film action, and appear periodically throughout the film, making Bowie and the others seems like small things observed by an omniscient eye that never blinks.

In the boldly poetic pretitle sequence shot by cinematographer George E. Diskant, the young lovers are seen in close-up, faces bathed in comforting light and shadow. Words written in graceful script appear at the bottom of the screen: "This boy . . . and this girl. . . were never properly introduced to the world we live in." With that, the lighting becomes harsher. Granger and O'Donnell look up, startled, and the film's title erupts on the screen.

Little of this would have worked if not for the sincere, understated playing of Granger and O'Donnell. They make us care about the troubled lovers. At story's end, after Mattie has contacted the police, Bowie is cut down after going for his gun. Keechie, by now pregnant with Bowie's child, rushes from the cabin and retrieves a note he had written for her just minutes earlier. She whispers the words she sees on the paper: "I love you.—Bowie," and then she softly repeats them, with different emphasis: "I love you, Bowie." Keechie's face fills the screen in tender, intimate close-up. The girl's simple, unadorned beauty is breathtaking, her expression beatific. Gradually, gently, the light on her face dims until her features recede, as if behind a silken veil, forever. This may be the most moving final image of any film since Chaplin's *City Lights*. And like that masterpiece of a moment, it evokes the irrationality and fervor of an impossible love.

Case File: George E. Diskant (1907–65)

Perhaps better recalled as a TV cinematographer, Diskant, who didn't shoot a single feature for the last twenty-two years of his career, nevertheless devised fulsome, meaningful lighting for many stylish noir films: *Desperate*, *They Live by Night* (a remarkable aesthetic collaboration of Diskant and director Nicholas Ray), *Between Midnight and Dawn*, *The Racket*, *On Dangerous Ground*, *The Narrow Margin* (a textbook example of how to light and shoot in confined spaces), *Beware, My Lovely*, and *Kansas City Confidential*. Diskant was especially skilled at lighting close-ups, whether tenderly evocative (*They Live By Night*) or bluntly savage (*The Narrow Margin*).

Diskant shot some solid Tim Holt westerns and a variety of unsentimental dramas that include *Port of New York* and director Ida Lupino's *The Bigamist*. His television work is highlighted by a lengthy association with Dick Powell's Four Star Films and some of the better shows of the 1950s, including *Four Star Playhouse*, *The Rifleman*, *Dick Powell's Zane Grey Theater*, and *The Dick Powell Show*.

The Rat in the Mirror

Amnesia induced by brain trauma suffered during the war triggers the plot of *The Crooked Way* (1949), in which mild-mannered combat veteran Eddie Rice (John Payne) travels to Los Angeles, where he's rudely told by cops and thugs alike that he's really Eddie Riccardi, a hoodlum who, in years past, turned state's evidence on a local vice lord and former friend named Vince Alexander (Sonny Tufts). Understandably enough, Alexander is still sore about his brief stretch in the pen. As Eddie struggles to clarify his past, he has his hands full just staying alive and dodging a persistent police detective named Williams (Rhys Williams). When Eddie runs across angry Nina Martin (Ellen Drew), who pulls suckers to the gaming tables in Alexander's gambling club, he discovers that he and Nina had been married. Because of that, Alexander made life very tough for Nina, so—like everybody else in town—she's not pleased that Eddie has returned.

Richard H. Landau's script, based on a Robert Monroe radio play called "No Blade Too Sharp," is satisfyingly linear and direct. Eddie never does regain his memory, but through information provided by others, he's able to reconstruct his past—and know that he doesn't want to be that person again. The script is tight, has one moment that's a shocker, and chugs to the inevitable showdown between Alexander and Eddie.

French-born director Robert Florey worked in all Hollywood genres during a long career but displayed a special flair for horror with *Murders in the Rue Morgue* (1932), *The Face Behind the Mask* (1940), and *The Beast with Five Fingers* (1946). Florey was most at home with melodramatic material that encouraged him to become aggressive in his camera setups and narrative style.

Cinematographer John Alton was a perfect collaborator because nobody had a better understanding of the roles of light and shadow in the creation of mood and tension. Early scenes at the VA hospital, as Eddie is examined in darkened rooms, are unsettling and help us grasp the wounded soldier's confused unhappiness. Sequences inside Nina's house are similarly dark and claustrophobic. One setup, a close shot on Eddie's face, completely obscures his features with shadow, making him, at least for the moment, as unknowable to us as he is to himself.

A protracted nighttime sequence in which Eddie walks the crowded streets (Florey shot on location in LA), is an effective montage of flophouses, shooting galleries, headlights, and insistent neon. In this and other sequences, Florey and Alton made excellent use of deep focus that creates visual interest and advances the plot via people and objects in the extreme foreground, middle ground, and background. High and low camera angles emphasize the relative power of particular characters. One sequence, in which Eddie (who's been framed) wakes up in a dark car next to the slumped body of a murdered man, is frankly nightmarish.

The final set piece unfolds at night inside a warehouse that's a maze of shadows created by jumbles of crates, old furniture, and junk. The place is home to a tubercular little man called Petey (Percy Helton, in a performance that's at once repellent and sympathetic), and it's going to be where Eddie and Alexander have it out.

John Payne is typically stalwart and appealing, and Sonny Tufts, who made a nice impression as a corn-fed GI in his first picture, the World War II drama *So Proudly We Hail!* (1943), is a cauldron of venom as Alexander. The actor usually played amiable lugs, so this role allowed him to explore a character who is relentless and terrifying. Vince swings freely from whispered threats to out-and-out rages. He's very much a self-made man, so his fury at Eddie Riccardi is easy to understand.

God's Heavy Hand

Rage is the central emotion and motivator of *Red Light* (1949), a minor but provocative thriller that focuses on Johnny Torno (George Raft), a San Francisco trucking magnate crazily determined to find the killer of his brother Jess (Arthur Franz), a young priest. Central to the plot is that Jess, although mortally wounded in his hotel room, is able to tell his brother that he left a message for him inside a Gideon bible. But the bible has vanished, so Johnny rockets between San Francisco, Los Angeles, and Reno to locate the half-dozen hotel guests who had had access to the room.

As imagined by scripter George Callahan and directed by Roy Del Ruth, Jess is an ethereal, godly presence—closer to a symbol of beatitude than anything resembling a human being. He's false and annoying, and you want to give him a good, painful pinch.

So great is Johnny's fury over Jess's death that he allows his business go to hell, aggravates the woman (Virginia Mayo) whom he's hired to do legwork, and angrily renounces the Catholic faith that had once meant so much to him. As Johnny becomes more frustrated as his search for the bible drags on, he angrily tells a parish priest (Arthur Shields) that God had better give him "twenty-four-hour service," adding that mere faith is "bunk for your Sunday suckers!" With that, he hurls a candelabrum through a stained-glass window that he had donated to the church.

This was strong stuff in 1949, even for American audiences that were predominantly Protestant. Johnny's words and violent act suggest blasphemy and still have the power to knock you back in your seat.

The culprit behind all of this sadness and anger is Nick Cherney (Raymond Burr, at his most enormous), a Torno bookkeeper who had been sent to prison for embezzlement. Nearing the end of his sentence, he offers to pay Rocky (Henry Morgan), a reptilian inmate on the verge of release, to murder Johnny's brother. What better way to hurt his former employer than to take from him what he values most?

For pure, sickening astonishment, nothing in *Red Light* surpasses the fate of Johnny's faithful business manager, Warni (Gene Lockhart), who is killed in a dark staging yard when a jack holding a semi trailer is abruptly kicked free, bringing the whole thing down on him with a revolting, ground-shaking thud. Editor Richard Heermance held on the settled trailer for a beat and then cut to Nick, whose smiling face is starkly illuminated when he lights a cigarette.

When the bible is finally located, Johnny discovers that (despite three bullets in the belly) Jess had found the energy to write, "Thou shalt not kill," *and* circle *Romans* 12:19: "[A]venge not yourselves . . . for it is written, Vengeance is mine. . . ."

A lot of people aren't paying attention. In just one of the film's numerous and heavy-handed references to religion, Nick is surprised by Rocky, whom Nick has assumed to be dead after punching him right off the observation deck of a moving train. Now, like a battered, pissed-off Lazarus, Rocky is back, squinting up at Nick from the bottom of a dark stairway, with metaphoric blood in his eye.

Faith and God's love are still in play, though, as Johnny discovers when he finds a man (Philip Pine) who had had the hotel room before Jess. The man explains that just as he was about to leap from the window, he was saved by a window washer who seemed to have materialized from nowhere. Window washer. Sky. Angel. Get it?

In the very well-staged finale on the roof of Johnny's business, Nick carelessly fries himself as he clambers atop the neon sign that announces "TORNO FREIGHT LINES." Blinking underneath are the words, "24 Hour Service." The soundtrack swells with a heavenly chorus. Vengeance is mine, indeed!

George Raft is his usual on-screen self: one-dimensional but enormously charismatic. He pushes through the film like a bulldozer, in a constant state of irritable agitation. (Raft modeled parts of his characterization on a late friend, mobster Bugsy Siegel.) During one vulnerable moment, when Johnny cries over his slain brother, Raft is embarrassingly inadequate, but he was a movie star in the truest sense: You can't take your eyes off him.

The Kid Who Saw Too Much

Child actor Bobby Driscoll was the first human being put under contract by Walt Disney. Just nine years old when he made a strong impression in Disney's *Song of the South* (1946), he was loaned to RKO in the fall of 1947 to star in *The Window* (1949). The picture's release was delayed for about eighteen months, but its quality and box-office success made the wait worthwhile: *The Window*, based on Cornell Woolrich's 1947 novelette *The Boy Cried Murder*, was one of the year's top critical and commercial successes, and Bobby Driscoll was awarded a special Oscar for "best juvenile performance of 1949."

Because this noir protagonist is a small boy, he doesn't grapple with blackmail or infidelity. But he's forced by circumstance to think a lot about murder. *The Window* is a stinging examination of the helplessness of the small and marginalized.

Tommy Woodry (Driscoll) lives with his parents in a dingy walkup on New York's Lower East Side. Mr. Woodry (Arthur Kennedy) does unspecified night work; Mrs. Woodry (Barbara Hale) is a housewife. Tommy is a bright, imaginative kid with a penchant for tall tales of robbery, kidnappings, gun battles, and the like. His inveterate and enthusiastic storytelling puts him into a "boy who cried wolf" situation when he peeps beneath a window shade and mutely watches as the upstairs neighbors struggle with a man in their apartment and stab him to death.

Tommy's parents don't believe his story—in fact, they're more than a little fed up with him. The kid visits the local precinct house, where the cops don't believe him. His visit gets back to his folks, who become even more upset. When Tommy persists in his story, his mother unknowingly does the worst possible thing by marching him upstairs to apologize to Mrs. Kellerson (Ruth Roman). Although Tommy refuses to repeat what he's told his parents, young Mrs. Kellerson (although a cool customer in front of Mrs. Woodry) is sufficiently alarmed to mention the visit to her middle-aged husband (Paul Stewart). The pair finally abduct Tommy in the middle of the night, lose their grip on him, and finally chase him into a condemned, deserted apartment house. Inside, Tommy gets the fright of his life.

Director Ted Tetzlaff and cinematographer William Steiner created one of the most handsome and visually thoughtful of all noir thrillers, filming scenes in the Woodry apartment from a subtle, almost subliminally low vantage point, so that we view the place as Tommy does. Because of the low point of view, many scenes involving adults are shot subjectively, with impatient (or threatening) adults looking down at the camera and at Tommy. (Mrs. Kellerson's placid, fixed smile as she listens to Tommy's mother is a thing of horror.)

Tetzlaff filmed on gritty NYC locations, anticipating the thrilling immediacy of Morris Engel's 1953 "kid" docudrama, *Little Fugitive*. *The Window* presents the Lower East Side as a series of significant, potentially dangerous verticals: ascending and descending staircases and fire escapes; the steps that lead to an el platform; the tall, narrow spaces that separate adjoining buildings.

Windows are a persistent motif. Our first view of Tommy is a voyeuristic one from outside the Woodrys' window. When she wants to hang out her wash, Mrs. Woodry steps through a window onto the fire escape. Tommy witnesses the murder through the Kellersons' window (Tommy has crawled up to their fire escape in search of a cool place to sleep). Much later, his father locks Tommy in his room and nails the window shut. Mrs. Kellerson shows up outside and shines a flashlight through the same window. Abducted, Tommy sees a policeman through a car window and tries to call out. Later, in the condemned apartment, he looks through the empty window frame at the dark street below and sees his father and a policeman, who are too far away to hear him.

The climactic set piece inside the condemned apartment house is blocked, shot, and edited (by Frederic Knudtson) to brilliantly unnerving effect. Tommy knows the building—it's familiar to him and his playmates—but Kellerson is bigger, stronger, and motivated.

Case File: Comic Victims of Circumstance

A bellboy at a posh hotel is wrongly accused of murdering a guest, a pompous VIP named Strickland. Soon, the bodies of Strickland's male secretary and another man are discovered—in the bellboy's closet, in his bed, in the bathtub, in the elevator, everywhere. The corpses can't stay put, and the hapless bellboy, Freddie, must suffer the suspicious gaze of an aggressive police inspector. But there are other suspects, including a European femme fatale and a fake swami who might have stepped out of *Nightmare Alley*. With some help from the abrasive hotel detective, Casey, and after a harrowing misadventure with the killer inside a vast, eerie cavern, Freddie is cleared and the real murderer unmasked.

All of this is from Universal-International's inelegantly titled *Abbott and Costello Meet the Killer, Boris Karloff* (1949), a significant comic noir that arrived at about the midpoint of the noir cycle. Lou Costello is Freddie, of course, and Bud Abbott plays the impatient hotel dick. Director Charles T. Barton and writers Hugh Wedlock Jr., Howard Snyder, and peerless A&C gagman John Grant lift numerous noir tropes and turn them into jokes: Freddie is tricked by a flirtatious and dangerous beauty (Lenore Aubert) into writing and signing a confession; in order to survive a particularly hazardous interlude, Freddie must assume a disguise (as a maid) that's nearly blown when the aging, whiny-voiced night clerk (Percy Helton) puts the make on him; the swami forces his will on Freddie so that Freddie will leap to his death from a window (but instead of jumping *out* the window from the sill, the mesmerized Freddie jumps back *into* the room). On the deeply shadowed landing of a deserted utility staircase, Freddie struggles to transport two corpses in a laundry cart; Freddie throws back the covers of his bed and discovers the murder gun; in an effort to trap the killer, Freddie offers to sell an incriminating handkerchief; and Freddie is nearly boiled alive inside a steam cabinet (shades of *Raw Deal!*).

Charles Van Enger's cinematography is rich with diagonal slashes of shadow, figures and faces oddly illuminated by what seems to be a single source of light, and light-and-dark effects on the gorgeous and complex cavern set that incorporates matte paintings, split-screen, and deep focus, and that looks like a vast underground city. Labyrinthine and confusing, in moments it evokes some of the feel of the famed hall of mirrors of *Lady from Shanghai*.

In a sequence that's both absurd and genuinely horrifying, Freddie and Casey desperately play bridge with two of the corpses, which the boys have propped in chairs and given cards. Director Barton's visual setup is dominated at the left foreground by a lamp, which throws a sickly light that makes the dead men look *very* dead. Of course, others who enter the room don't notice that half the players are corpses—a cute gag in a sequence that expresses with unusual visual clarity the link between noir and the Hollywood horror genre. (In fact, Milton Schwarzwald's score picks up a lot of "spook" cues from Frank Skinner's score for the comics' 1948 triumph *Abbott and Costello Meet Frankenstein*.)

Noir's innocent man wrongly accused is usually an ordinary Joe, a patsy who is presumably powerless to expose his tormentors and clear his name. That's certainly

Femme fatale Jean Wallace coaxes ice cream peddler Jack Carson into some foolhardy behavior in *The Good Humor Man* (1950).

the case with Freddie the bellboy, as well as with Biff (Jack Carson), the ice-cream-bar salesman turned murder suspect in Lloyd Bacon's cheerfully schizophrenic *The Good Humor Man* (1950). Bacon had been an efficient director of melodramas at Warner Bros. before making this Columbia comedy that was written by former Warner cartoon director Frank Tashlin. As a live-action director, Tashlin had a career that engenders considerable cult interest today. Here, his themes and visual gags are so pushily vivid that Bacon hardly seems to have been present at all.

Biff is an amiable, childlike guy who hangs with local kids as a member of a Captain Marvel fan club. (The group's rallying cry, *Niatpac Levram!*, is "Captain Marvel!" backwards.) Most of this very funny picture is a framework for endless Tashlinesque gags, including Biff's inability to deliver a Good Humor to a coal stoker (in the superheated factory, only a forlorn stick remains by the time Biff reaches his customer); Biff's encasement in a mammoth block of ice and his subsequent ride along a watery curb and down a storm drain after thugs have stuffed him into the freezer compartment of his own truck; and a climactic nighttime chase through a dark high school where Biff and his girlfriend (Lola Albright) turn musical instruments and power tools into absurdly deadly weapons. (Visualize a thug with his neck caught by a trombone slide and an enormous circular saw that cuts its way through the shop room floor and drops itself and everybody into the swimming pool below. Once in the water, the saw pursues the hoodlums like a buzzing shark.)

Played straight, any of these bits would have been horrifying, and appropriate for what *The Good Humor Man* really is: a crime thriller. Noir elements come to the fore during a very effective sequence, beautifully lit by Lester White, in which Biff hides out in an empty suburban house with a gorgeous dead blonde (Jean Wallace) who isn't dead at all. Pale and sheathed in a black peignoir, her neck unappetizingly bruised by the fingerprints of somebody who tried to strangle her, the woman alternately seduces and threatens Biff (who wonders how he's going to explain all of this not just to the cops but to his girlfriend). The house has no power, so when night falls, the entire place is crisscrossed with disconcerting shadows that pull your eye back and forth across the frame and set you up for effective "scare" moments.

The knockabout comedy that characterizes *Abbott and Costello Meet the Killer, Boris Karloff* and *The Good Humor Man* is uniquely stylized, especially because so much of it is grounded in fear. When mated to the stylistics of noir, the results are unexpectedly congenial.

A violent, frightfully noisy collapse of a staircase (the pieces of which fall from a great height directly *on top of* the camera) is enormously startling, but Kellerson and Tommy haven't finished their business. A brilliant shock moment is followed by yet another dreadful collapse—but even after Kellerson is neutralized, Tommy remains in mortal physical danger. The film's climax, then, is a triple climax, and by the time it's all over, you feel like a dishrag.

Ted Tetzlaff was a high-profile cinematographer before becoming a director. In the former role, he did sterling work for major directors on pictures as varied as *The Criminal Code, My Man Godfrey, I Married a Witch,* and *Notorious.* His acute visual sense gives *The Window* particular power, but he was very good with his actors, too, coaxing natural, almost extemporaneous line readings, particularly from Barbara Hale and Ruth Roman. And Paul Stewart, with his dark eyes, trim physique, and deep voice, is a relentless and intimidating adversary. The horror of one moment, in which Kellerson waits patiently for the groggy Tommy to topple backwards to his death from a precarious perch atop a fire-escape railing, is almost too awful for the viewer to absorb.

Bobby Driscoll is enthusiastic, believable, and appealing. His career faded when he entered adolescence, and he soon fell into drug use. In a bizarre irony, he was found dead in an abandoned building in New York City in 1968. He was thirty-one.

Driscoll's fate is a cautionary tale from the adult world. *The Window* is very much about the "kid world" and its myriad unfair limitations and disadvantages. Like all youngsters, Tommy is more of a visitor than a fully empowered citizen. His predicament unfolds almost completely against his will, and he has virtually no power to defend himself. As far as he can tell, nobody cares.

On a hot night in New York, a little boy (Bobby Driscoll) peers through *The Window* (1949) and witnesses his neighbors commit murder. Trouble is, he can't get his parents or any other grown-up to believe him. Meanwhile, the killers (Paul Stewart and Ruth Roman) finally realize the kid has seen them. Well, what would *you* want to do about it?

Long Road to Justice

Gritty naturalism marks Jules Dassin's *Thieves' Highway* (1949), a melodrama with noir touches as well as clearly stated attitudes about honor, labor, and the immigrant experience in America. Scripter A. I. Bezzerides adapted his 1949 novel *Thieves' Market*, establishing a story structure modeled on classical quest adventures.

After returning home to Fresno after years in Asia, Nick Garcos (Richard Conte) is shocked to discover that his father (Morris Carnovsky) has lost his legs in a suspicious trucking accident. The truck was subsequently picked up on the cheap by another driver, Ed Kinney (Millard Mitchell), leaving the old man with almost nothing because he was cheated out of his final load by Mike Figlia (Lee J. Cobb), a produce wholesaler in San Francisco. Nick has come home with nearly $2,000, which he uses to buy back his father's truck, make an unwilling partner of Ed Kinney, and even buy a retired Army truck. Now with a fleet of two, the Garcos family is back in business.

Like his dad, the younger Garcos is a wildcatter—an independent trucker lacking the organizational and financial support of a large company. Like other wildcatters, he must anticipate the needs of the market, sniff out lucrative loads, and deliver them to wholesalers before he's beaten to the punch by other drivers. Nick and Ed's goal is San Francisco, and their mission is to deliver two loads of the season's first Golden Delicious apples to market before anybody else.

Nick is the first to arrive in San Francisco, where Figlia tries to help himself to the apples. He's thwarted, however, by Rica (Valentina Cortesa *née* Cortese), a sly Italian dame who warns Nick after having agreed to help Figlia pull the swindle. Although Nick insists upon, and gets, a fair price when he confronts Figlia, two of Figlia's goons beat Nick later and take back the money, despite Rica's best effort to stop the robbery.

WASP girlfriend Polly (Barbara Lawrence) shows up, intending to get married, shoots dark glances at rough-and-tumble Rica, and dumps Nick as soon as she learns his money is gone. The hero's golden girl is a fraud.

Nick is the real thing. His ex-Army truck still wears a white star on each door, like a *fleur-de-lis* or a talisman. He seems destined for greatness, but danger surrounds him. On the long drive to San Francisco, he and Ed battle the night, fatigue, and treacherous roads. When a jack slips as Nick tries to change a tire, the truck pins him in the dirt. Ed catches up and risks his life to save Nick's— redeeming himself for trying to cheat the apple grower.

Two other wildcatters, Slob (Jack Oakie) and Pete (Joseph Pevney), function as a Greek chorus, following Ed for hundreds of miles, good-naturedly dogging him about his failing truck, cracking jokes, and chronicling his journey. After Ed dies in a crash that scatters apples up and down a lonely hillside, Slob and Pete complete their function by relating the details to Nick. Because Figlia offers to pay anybody who retrieves the load, Nick breaks the schemer's hand and takes back the stolen money.

Dassin and cinematographer Norbert Brodine vividly delineated the San Francisco market and waterfront area. Nearly all of the key sequences are set at night, on the market's impossibly crowded and frantic main avenue, and on nearby cobbled, rain-slick streets that echo with the sounds of boat whistles and raucous music. Nick, who has seen great expanses of the world, is trapped and out of place in this proscribed environment. With Rica, he'll forge a new life elsewhere.

Thieves' Highway was the last film Jules Dassin made before director Edward Dmytryk named him during HUAC hearings as a Communist sympathizer. Dassin exiled himself to Europe, bowed but not broken.

"You've been murdered."

A man who has been fatally dosed with poison knows he has only a few hours to track and locate his killer. That's the nightmarish premise of *D.O.A.* (1950), a high-concept thriller before there was high concept. Although one might think the story originated on radio—the premise has that blunt, thirty-minute feel to it—*D.O.A.* was an original screenplay by Russell Rouse and Clarence Green.

Vital to the film's impact and point of view is the nature of the Everyman protagonist, Frank Bigelow (Edmond O'Brien, who is ideally cast), a CPA visiting San Francisco from his home in Banning, California. Like a lot of vets who put their asses on the line in Europe and Asia, he's come home and established a small business. Bigelow is a regular guy: nice-looking but not wildly handsome; reasonably prosperous but far from wealthy. He's single and has a sweet-natured secretary (Pamela Britton) who makes no secret of her desire to marry him. But Bigelow is still on the prowl, and the film's early San Francisco scenes put him in the middle of a hotel gathering of rowdy traveling salesmen and the good-looking women who buy from them. Bigelow doesn't know where to look first. He's entranced by the parade of dames. When he spies one, he leers, and the soundtrack lets loose with a goofy slide-whistle sound effect. The device is childish and obvious—and maybe that's the point: Bigelow's vacation has just started, and he's already enjoying life like a goofy kid.

Director Rudolph Maté shifted the tone when Frank accompanies some of his new friends to a smoky jive joint, where the jump jazz of the all-black combo transports white proto-beatniks to existential musical nirvana. In the middle of the din (which sounds fabulous to twenty-first-century ears), Bigelow cases the bar and puts the moves on an attractive blonde. He attempts a simple pickup, but the insistent music suggests that all is not right. *D.O.A.* was a United Artists release shot at the tail end of 1949, when the presence of black men on a theater screen was, frankly, a way to build tension and even a sense of incipient danger. Maté and his fine cinematographer, Ernest Laszlo, zeroed in hard on the gyrating (and thus sexualized) musicians, focusing closely on their perspiring faces and wild eyes. The players beat and blow their instruments with abandon, and you know that Bigelow is a long way from Banning.

Our attention is caught by another figure, a man seen only from the back, who wears a hat, a heavy topcoat, and a gaudily decorated scarf. He leans against the bar, near Bigelow's unattended drink, and then moves away. When Bigelow returns to his cocktail, he tells the bartender it doesn't taste right.

Bigelow feels a little unwell the next morning. He sees a doctor, who tells him he's fine. All that needs to be done is to quickly check the test results. And those results are devastating: Bigelow has been fatally dosed with a luminous poison that attacks the internal organs. There is no treatment. Bigelow may have a day, a week—two weeks at the outside.

Time for a second opinion. This doctor (Frank Gerstle) speaks even more bluntly than the first: "I don't think you fully understand, Bigelow. You've been murdered."

Very nearly all of the remainder of *D.O.A.* is shot on location, as Bigelow literally runs for his life in San Francisco and Los Angeles, trying to locate the salesmen, the blonde, anybody who might point him to his killer. By putting pieces together after increasingly frantic visits to surly people who are little inclined to help, Bigelow uncovers a complex scheme of murder and double-cross that caused deadly iridium to fall into the hands of criminals. He unknowingly became involved in Banning, when he notarized a spurious bill of sale.

The film develops a lot of colorful characters, including an erudite mobster (Luther Adler); a toothy, psychotic gunsel (Neville Brand, in his first film role);

Case File: Edmond O'Brien (1915–85)

Following stage experience that grew out of a boyhood interest in magic, Edmond O'Brien came to the movies in 1939, as the young male lead in the Charles Laughton version of *The Hunchback of Notre Dame*. He worked steadily in films and television until his retirement in 1974. Stocky but handsome, O'Brien flirted with leading man status during the first half of his career and moved easily into character parts—sometimes of the comic variety—when he put on pounds in the mid-1950s. A dominant presence with a big voice and plenty of bluster, O'Brien could steal scenes from the unwary and was at his best when challenged on-screen by equally forceful personalities (such as James Cagney in the noir gem *White Heat*). O'Brien appeared in a variety of films noir and had the leads in most, including what may be his single most famous picture, *D.O.A.* This is noir at its most bleak, with O'Brien perfectly cast as the amiable Everyman who discovers that, for reasons quite unknown to him, a stranger has murdered him with slow-acting, irreversible poison. O'Brien also shook up noir in *The Killers*, *The Web*, *Backfire*, *711 Ocean Drive*, *Between Midnight and Dawn*, *Two of a Kind*, *The Hitch-Hiker*, and *Shield for Murder* (and directed).

O'Brien's pugnacious masculinity made him well suited to westerns, where he excelled, notably in two of the very best, *The Man Who Shot Liberty Valance* and *The Wild Bunch*. He won the best supporting actor Oscar for his 1954 performance as a cowardly press agent in *The Barefoot Contessa*.

and the mobster's arrogant, raven-haired mistress (Laurette Luez). Effective set pieces include Bigelow's visit to a run-down photo studio (located, weirdly, in a sun-blasted industrial wasteland), a chase through the skeleton of an abandoned factory, and a nighttime pursuit along sidewalks and into a crowded drugstore. Many incidental moments, as when the exhausted Bigelow pauses at a newsstand that prominently displays copies of *LIFE*, are sardonically amusing.

The climactic sequence inside LA's fabulously baroque Bradbury Building brings Bigelow a measure of satisfaction—the last he'll ever have.

D.O.A. is mercilessly bleak. Bigelow knows how to handle a gun because, we surmise, he was in the service. What the hell was he fighting for? (Yes, it's a mantra of noir.) Business and crime seem to have coalesced into a single entity that strides invisibly through commerce and culture. Because of a few serendipitous moments during a typical day at work, Bigelow has been selected to die. His earlier confidence in the "rightness" of life, and his certitude that he has decades ahead of him, has discouraged him from telling his secretary that he loves her. When he does, it's by phone, with hoodlums on either side of him,

D.O.A. (1950): Insurance man Edmond O'Brien is stunned when a doctor (Frank Gerstle) informs him he's been fatally dosed with poison. How or why it happened is a mystery, but if the victim wants to find his killer, he'd better do it fast.

when he's dying. In the film noir canon, *D.O.A.* stands alone for its bitterness and its audacious suggestion that much of what we believe in is worse than an illusion: It's a hoax.

Because the film employs a framing device—the entire tale is related by Bigelow to police as a flashback—the inevitability of his doom is pounded home. The moment we meet Frank Bigelow, he's dead. Only details remain.

Murder and the Resurrection of Love

A failed San Francisco artist (Ross Elliott) who has witnessed a murder takes it on the lam, forcing his disaffected wife (Ann Sheridan) into uneasy, unasked-for alliances with the police and an aggressive reporter (Dennis O'Keefe)—all of whom want to locate the witness before the killer does. *Woman on the Run* (1950) is obscure and seldom discussed, and that's unfortunate because it's a noir sleeper that has unexpected thoughtfulness and moments of visceral power.

Director Norman Foster, who began as an actor and joined Orson Welles's Mercury Players before going behind the camera, learned his craft while directing Charlie Chan and Mr. Moto programmers in the 1930s and early '40s. He grasped the virtues of briskness and established the plot of *Woman on the Run* within seconds of the main title, as Frank Johnson pauses while on a late-night walk with his dog to look up at a coupe that has pulled to a stop at the crest of a hill. Inside the car, an amiable older gent (played with an avaricious twinkle by Thomas P. Dillon) lightly goads the unseen driver, mentioning that he'll take most of the $20,000 the driver had collected to cover up a bribe. With that, the passenger is shot. The driver's arm reaches across and opens the passenger door, and the victim falls halfway out of the car, now pleading for his life. There's an uncomfortable, sickly realism to this, and when the man is shot at point-blank range a second time, even the most experienced noir fancier will be horrified.

Johnson's dog barks from below, and the killer (still unseen to us) snaps off a couple of quick shots, missing his target. (Shadowplay during this sequence, lit by cinematographer Hal Mohr, is intimidating and startlingly dimensional.) Johnson stays around for the police but vanishes when the danger becomes apparent to him.

Foster (who cowrote the script with Alan Campbell) kept the remainder of the picture's seventy-seven minutes going in this vein of literal and figurative darkness. Attentive viewers will have noticed that, in the opening sequence, the unsuspecting victim calls the killer "Danny boy." With that, the film elects to pursue suspense instead of surprise, because when Eleanor Johnson (Sheridan) is approached by the hotshot reporter, he introduces himself as Danny Legget. Much later, when Legget holds his lighter out to police inspector Ferris (Robert Keith) in the same way the murderer held it to light his victim's cigarette, we know for certain that Eleanor and the cops are being played and that Frank Johnson may not live much longer.

The decision to abandon the notion of a surprise that wouldn't have been much of a surprise at all was a good one. The film distinguishes itself further by making clear that it's not really "about" crime but about the abeyance and resurrection of love. Johnson has left writings and other clues that gradually confirm for Eleanor his deep love for her. Eleanor is touched and surprised. The sharp quips that have characterized her conversations with the cops vanish because now she knows that she's valued and wanted. In other words, Frank Johnson isn't just a guy who might get himself killed but a man of depth and sensitivity. With that, Johnson ceases to be a plot device. Although Ross Elliott is on-screen only at the beginning of the film and at the climax, he becomes increasingly real to us. We "discover" and appreciate him in increments, just as Eleanor does.

Woman on the Run was produced inexpensively by Howard Welsch's Fidelity Pictures and picked up for release by Universal-International. Ann Sheridan had recently been dropped by her longtime employer, Warner Bros., and now, like many other established stars, worked freelance. She was a great beauty who gave many strong, tough-cookie performances during a very successful career, but she seldom had a role with as many layers as here. The complicated nature of marriage is suggested by the complex nature of Eleanor. Assumptions can be mistaken. Impatience has to be tempered with understanding. Love doesn't necessarily disappear; sometimes it just assumes a different shape or voice. Most unfortunate is that Eleanor's loneliness has been partly self-imposed—a tragedy when precious devoted companionship is still available to her.

Because of a verbal slip by Legget, Ferris realizes that the reporter is the killer. In a climax at a rowdy amusement park, lit mostly with available light, the four protagonists approach a shared destiny. Effective cross-cutting between Johnson, Ferris, the prowling Legget, and Eleanor (who is temporarily trapped on a hurtling roller coaster) bring the suspense to a boil.

Dennis O'Keefe lavishes his Irish charm on the colorful but underwritten role of Legget. Robert Keith, who has some subtly amusing dialogue, is excellent as the clever cop. During Chinatown sequences, Victor Sen Yung and Rako Sato are engaging and believable as a struggling dance team. But the picture belongs to Sheridan, who reminds us how and why she became a star.

Most of the movie was shot on location, without sound, in San Francisco. Street noise and dialogue (much of which is spoken when characters have their backs turned) were looped during postproduction. Nearly all of the close-up dialogue "exteriors" were shot in front of process screens. (In this cost-cutting, the picture is similar to *Nightmare.*) The final effect isn't awful, but it does mark this production as a second feature.

At this writing, *Woman on the Run* is commercially available, via a poor print, on budget DVD. A good print is hidden in a vault somewhere. Let's find it.

Fiendish and Funny

A man is shot in the forehead. Another is viciously beaten and nearly boiled alive by steam. A deported crime lord schemes to literally steal the face of a living man after destroying the donor's brain with deadly serum administered by a fugitive

Nazi. All of that and a great deal more happens in *His Kind of Woman* (1951), an RKO production that has a general quality of . . . delightfulness.

After some trouble with the LAPD, professional gambler Dan Milner (Robert Mitchum) is receptive to a mysterious offer of $50,000 if he leaves the country and travels to a plush resort in Mexico (gorgeous mid-century-modern design by art director Albert S. D'Agostino and set decorators Darrell Silvera and Ross Dowd). Once there, Milner meets a beautiful, amiable heiress named Lenore Brent (Jane Russell); an oversexed millionaire (Jim Backus); sadistic thugs (Charles McGraw and Anthony Caruso); a discredited plastic surgeon (John Mylong); a federal cop (Tim Holt); and a ham movie actor named Mark Cardigan (Vincent Price). And stewing aboard a yacht anchored in the bay is deported American criminal Nick Ferraro (Raymond Burr), who wants badly to come back to the USA.

Before things careen out of control, Milner pursues an easy, insouciant romance with Lenore (who turns out not to be an heiress); finds an enthusiastic new friend in Cardigan; and slowly realizes that there is no fifty grand. Ferraro wants Milner's identity—face and all, a plot point of 1947's *Dark Passage* taken to a murderous extreme.

While Milner struggles for his life aboard the yacht, Cardigan and a ragtag crew of sailors and Mexican police board the ship to aid our beleaguered hero.

His Kind of Woman is a delight for a lot of reasons. The easy byplay between Mitchum and Russell—RKO's two biggest assets and a perfectly matched pair—gives the film a sexy, relaxed charm. Tall and broad-shouldered, they seem at ease in their bodies, and with each other.

> LENORE
> I'm drinking champagne.

> MILNER
> I'm hip.

Much later, after Ferraro and the Nazi have been disposed of, Lenore makes an observation and asks a question:

> LENORE
> You turned out to be quite a hero. They tell me you killed
> Ferraro. How did it feel?

> MILNER
> He didn't say.

This kind of minimalist, wiseacre dialogue can easily fall flat. In order to work, it has to be driven as much by an actor's persona as by the actor's talent. Mitchum and Russell had persona, and screen presence, to spare. There's an unspoken connection between Milner and Lenore that you can see in their eyes and in the untroubled way they stand next to each other. They *fit*, like bookends. And because we like these two, the story's darkly menacing interludes carry added weight.

As Cardigan, the popular but hambone film star famed for swashbuckling roles, Vincent Price is splendid in one of his most endearing characterizations. In a film dominated by people who are not what they appear to be (phony heiress, undercover cop, affable but smarmy lech, the Nazi who masquerades

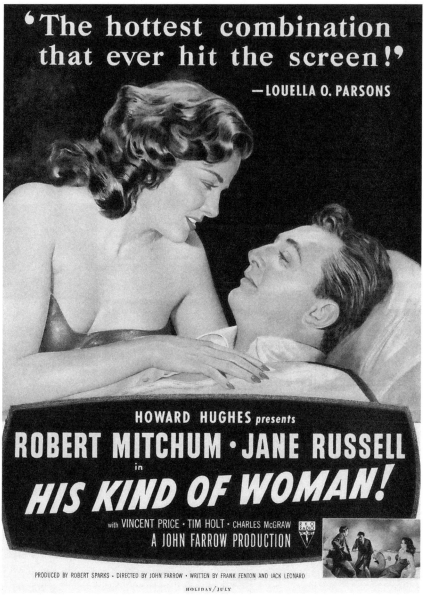

Handsome ad art for *His Kind of Woman* (1951), director John Farrow's combo platter of invented identities, violence, terror—and laughs. In the midst of escalating mayhem, Jane Russell and Robert Mitchum keep their cool.

as a writer, the criminal who wants to almost literally become another person), Cardigan is initially hard for us to figure out. He acts for a living. When he ingratiates himself with Milner, is he sincere or duplicitous?

He's sincere. The climactic rescue—which gets off to an aborted start when Cardigan's overloaded rowboat slowly, hilariously sinks beneath him and his party—allows the ham to assert himself as a man. Disaffected and a little ashamed of what he does for a living, he taps his inner resources, helps rid the world of tyrants, and humbly accepts the respect of his estranged wife (Marjorie Reynolds).

The complex, climactic set piece aboard the yacht was devised by three people who went without credit: RKO's micromanaging owner, Howard Hughes; writer Earl Felton; and contract director Richard Fleischer. Hughes wanted a longer, more exciting climax than the one devised by scripters Frank Fenton and Jack Leonard and credited director John Farrow. Fleischer agreed to do the reshoot only after Hughes promised to take Fleischer's long-completed *The Narrow Margin* (see Chapter 4) off the shelf and put it into release.

Case File: Robert Mitchum (1917–97)

The beauty of Robert Mitchum is that although he claimed not to be particularly invested as an actor (he once likened himself to "a Bulgarian wrestler"), he approached the craft with considerable seriousness. During a fifty-four-year screen career, he devised and frequently reinvented a larger-than-life persona, thrilling fans with his charisma and impressing critics with numerous performances that still have the capacity to startle.

Mitchum was the most important male star at RKO during the Howard Hughes years and dutifully did his job there, sometimes in films that weren't worthy of his talent. But even in the least of his pictures, this durable leading man commands the screen with a professionalism that appears deceptively easy.

Tall, broad-shouldered, and sleepy-eyed, with a deep, laconic voice to match, Mitchum is an indispensable figure in noir history. He won over men and women alike in *Crossfire* (just four years after his film debut, and where he matches up well, mano a mano, with the imposing Robert Ryan), *Out of the Past* (well loved and, in many ways, a textbook noir), *Where Danger Lives*, *His Kind of Woman*, *The Racket*, *Angel Face*, and *The Night of the Hunter* (his remarkable collaboration with another giant, director Charles Laughton).

Mitchum played in plenty of westerns and in a variety of dramas and melodramas. He's particularly effective in *Blood on the Moon*, *The Big Steal*, *The Lusty Men*, *Thunder Road* (a low-budget personal project), *Cape Fear*, *Ryan's Daughter*, *The Friends of Eddie Coyle* (giving one of his finest performances as an aging Boston hoodlum simultaneously squeezed by the mob and the cops), *The Yakuza*, and *The Last Tycoon*. Mitchum also played Philip Marlowe in a pair of intriguing neo-noirs of the '70s, *Farewell, My Lovely* and *The Big Sleep*.

Hughes loved what Fleischer put together (a hyperkinetic interlude of Milner being tortured below deck by belt, fists, and needle is pleasurably unpleasurable) but decided that he disliked the actor playing Ferarro—an actor who already had been put through his paces twice. After a complicated and time-consuming search, character man Robert J. Wilke (often seen as a western heavy) was hired to assume the role in redone Ferraro sequences. (This meant, of course, that Mitchum and many other players had to return, as well.) Fleischer had nearly finished with Wilke when Raymond Burr arrived on the set and announced to Fleischer that Mr. Hughes had hired *him* to play Ferarro. Wilke was paid off and everybody got together to do it all yet again. Mitchum, pushed to his limit, literally destroyed the set one day.

Harry J. Wild's cinematography, whether simulating sunlight (the entire picture was shot on stages) or oppressive night, is crisp and evocative. At 120 minutes, the film is long for a noir, but its energy never flags. An unfortunate misstep, though, is that Lenore isn't involved in the climax. In fact, Milner locks her in a closet before the action begins!

His Kind of Woman was well liked by the public, but the outrageous cost of reshoots meant a final loss of some $800,000. Hughes was undeterred and wisely stood by Mitchum and Russell for the remainder of their contracts. And they remained loyal to their eccentric employer.

Cutting Ties with the Syndicate

The real-life intersections of the movie business, organized crime, politics, and early television are vividly illuminated in *Hoodlum Empire* (1952), a Republic production that is part docudrama, part procedural, and, most intriguingly, part noir.

In 1950–51, U.S. Senator Estes Kefauver (D-TN) chaired the United States Senate Special Committee to Investigate Crime in Interstate Commerce—a mouthful that became popularly known as the Kefauver Committee. The hearings were televised live, and as Kefauver grilled such mobsters as Joe Adonis, Meyer Lansky, and, most famously, Frank Costello (whose compellingly writhing hands filled TV screens because he refused to allow his face to be shown), he uncovered a sophisticated, highly organized criminal syndicate that controlled vice from coast to coast.

To a naïve public, the many-tentacled organism revealed by Kefauver seemed like something out of a movie serial, driven by often-unseen forces to encourage and profit from our weaknesses. Not surprisingly, the committee's findings were hot topics around the nation's watercoolers. (All of this embarrassed the hell out of longtime FBI director J. Edgar Hoover, who had long maintained that organized crime was a myth.)

Republic was barely hanging on in 1952, slowing output of its serial and B-western units and struggling to survive in a changing Hollywood by offering fare that was timely and provocative. *Hoodlum Empire* is one of those, directed with flat competence by Joseph Kane, a longtime Republic contract director who helmed dozens of B westerns at the studio during a twenty-year span that began in the 1930s. By the late 1940s, Kane became producer or coproducer of the Republic pictures he directed.

Scripters Bruce Manning and popular feature journalist Bob Considine devised a key plot element that pushes *Hoodlum Empire* into noir territory: During a crusading U.S. senator's televised investigation of organized crime, mob chief Nick Mancani (Luther Adler) expects his nephew, Joe Gray (John Russell), to obfuscate if called to testify. Joe has no particular argument with his uncle, but he does want to get out of the life. Wartime experience with "regular guys" showed Joe that a decent existence removed from crime is possible. (Yes, this is another wartime-vet-in-conflict story.) Now Joe owns a modestly successful garage and diner, which marks him as a solid citizen in our eyes but to his uncle as a square and a fool.

Unlike *New York Confidential* (1955) and other superficially similar "exposé" pictures of the period, the central conflict of *Hoodlum Empire* isn't internal greed or Byzantine mob politics or even compromised investigators but a fundamental clash of moral philosophies arising from within the criminal organization. Joe had been raised by Nick and owes his uncle a certain debt of gratitude. Joe's ex-girlfriend, Connie (Claire Trevor, assuming a lively Southern accent and evoking real-life mob girl Virginia Hill), still revolves on the periphery of his life, and although Joe isn't tempted to resume the romance (he's happily married), he knows that he's out of the rackets, and he's going to stay out.

Tempers fray. In the film's most bluntly shocking sequence, Mancani's pissed-off number one, Charlie Pignatelli (Forrest Tucker), leads Joe's closest friend, the blind, reform-minded Reverend Simon (Grant Withers), through an office, out a side door, and into an open elevator shaft. In a disconcerting touch, the camera lingers on the clergyman's body as it tumbles and smashes to the bottom of the shaft.

Joe never does testify, so his final break from the mob must come in another way: secret tape recordings made by old flame Connie, which lead to her murder and the unexpected death of Mancani. Senator Stephens (Brian Donlevy, in "crusader" mode) gets hold of the tapes and sees that Joe is publicly exonerated.

The honest motivations of Joe Gray are reasonably fresh to the genre, but the film grammar of *Hoodlum Empire* is old school: Many sequences are bridged by vertical wipes, and the upward or downward travel of elevators is announced via trite horizontal wipes. Camera movement is modest and perfunctory, with most setups situated at eye level. To Kane's credit, frames are filled from front to back with visual information, encouraging our gaze to move freely. Attempts at symbolism suggest modest ambition; for example, the mobsters wear black suits while Joe often wears white coveralls. In the main, however, *Hoodlum Empire* seems a little dated. If Republic was intent on striding into the future, Joe Kane never got the memo.

He's Angry, and His Fists Are Deadly Weapons

As discussed earlier in this chapter, the character played by John Payne in *The Crooked Way* doesn't know who he is. Contrarily, in Phil Karlson's fiercely dynamic *99 River Street* (1953), ex-prizefighter Ernie Driscoll (Payne) knows very well who he is: He *isn't* the guy who killed his wife. Robert Smith's screenplay, based on a story by George Zuckerman, gets into rough action right away as we witness a flashback to what will be Driscoll's last fight. It's a heavyweight championship match, and Driscoll is beating on the champ like a tether ball. But late in the fight, the champion opens a cut over Driscoll's eye. His sight badly compromised, Driscoll is pummeled before the ref stops the bout. Banned, for his own good, from fighting again, Driscoll moves from celebrity and fortune to the anonymity and puny pay of driving a hack around Manhattan.

This displeases Driscoll's sexy but bad-tempered and selfishly disappointed wife, Pauline (Peggie Castle), and encourages Pauline's lover, a slick schemer named Vic Rawlins (Brad Dexter). Rawlins is a strong-arm jewel thief who blithely strangles Pauline with her own scarf because she's an unknowing impediment to his racket. Rawlins knows that Pauline and Driscoll's marital troubles are no secret—so he dumps Pauline's body in the back of Driscoll's cab.

With help from Linda (Evelyn Keyes), an actress who patronizes Driscoll's favorite diner, Driscoll makes plans to get his boxer's hands on Rawlins.

John Payne and director Phil Karlson had collaborated prior to *99 River Street*, on *Kansas City Confidential* (see Chapter 5), and would do a third picture together, *Hell's Island* (1955). As artists, they were well matched: Karlson, with his aggressive, keenly masculine style of visual storytelling; and Payne, with his boldly declarative line readings, the physique of a trained athlete, and the intimidating handsomeness of his face—which looked best when locked in a scowl.

Because Driscoll's cab and his dispatcher ally (Frank Faylen) are central to the plot, many sequences take place inside the car, which was utilized by Karlson as an unpleasant place of impatient confinement and tension. Indeed, the film's great shock sequence, the unexpected discovery of Pauline's body, is expressed via the reactions of Driscoll and Linda as they gaze down at something out of frame, followed by a shock cut to Pauline from Driscoll and Linda's point of view: sprawled across the cab's backseat, her eyes and mouth open. (We never see her killer, Rawlins, move the body, but the discovery scene is chillingly presaged much earlier, as the cab drives off with a triangle of decorative fabric peeping from the edge of the back door.)

With the excellent cinematographer Franz Planer, Karlson pushes and pulls us into the action, even when we think we might not enjoy going there. The opening fight sequence takes cues from the great battles in Robert Wise's 1949 boxing gem *The Set-Up* (see Chapter 5), with the camera alternately beneath the fighters' pumping arms, close on their faces as they absorb head shots, and even near the floor of the ring, wobbling like a handheld newsreel rig.

Case File: John Payne (1912–89)

A pleasing fixture of 20th Century-Fox musicals of the early 1940s and well-liked today as Maureen O'Hara's smart, sweet-natured suitor in *Miracle on 34th Street*, John Payne came to Hollywood in 1935 following dramatic training at Columbia, voice study at Juilliard, and brief vaudeville and stage experience. Audiences enjoyed him in musical fluff the likes of *The Dolly Sisters* and *Footlight Serenade*, but before the 1940s were out Payne had opportunities to experiment with heavier characterizations, notably in *To the Shores of Tripoli* and *The Razor's Edge*.

He began his reinvention as a movie tough guy in 1948, when he went to Universal to play a con man in *Larceny*. Payne's subsequent work in noir includes *The Crooked Way* and two for director Phil Karlson, *Kansas City Confidential* and the unremittingly ferocious *99 River Street*.

Besides musicals and melodramas, Payne was at home in westerns, and starred in a thoughtful TV oater, *The Restless Gun*, during 1957–59. Wealthy from investments, Payne worked only occasionally after 1960 and almost exclusively in episodic TV. (His 1955 option on Ian Fleming's James Bond thriller *Moonraker* is one investment that never panned out for the actor, because the rights to the other books were not then available.) Payne retired for good in 1975.

Characters repeatedly walk *to* the camera for close-up images, and when they continue to move laterally, the camera pulls back slightly and moves with them. Because this technique effectively locks us into the moment, much of *99 River Street* is told via subjective camerawork that's so subtle our perception of it is unconscious.

Driscoll's fistfight with a thug (Jack Lambert) is related via a pile-on of quick edits, shifting points of view, and sterling stunt work. (Payne, as in the boxing sequence, uses his hands and the rest of his body as a boxer would.) The battle, which leaves the thug liberally bloodied and insensible in a chair, isn't easy to absorb and presages the visceral brutality of Robert Aldrich's *Kiss Me Deadly* (1955; see Chapter 3).

In an astounding sequence that you may or may not buy, the film reflects on the nature of *performance* (boxing is just one sort) when Linda suckers Driscoll into believing she's killed a man and left his body on the stage of a darkened theater—all so that she can "act" the part of a panicked woman and impress the director and backers, who secretly watch from the shadows. (Keyes is impressive, pulling off the fevered, nearly three-minute monologue in a single take.) Driscoll is less than amused by the deception, not least because he's offered to help Linda by dumping the body in a remote quarry. He's further infuriated by the archly condescending attitude of a producer (Glenn Langan, taking a bit part far removed from his leading roles at Fox barely ten years earlier). In an instant, Driscoll lashes out, decking the producer and most of the other frightened "phonies" on the stage, forgetting in his anger that the police consider his boxer's hands deadly weapons. This fundamental mistake reinforces an assertion Driscoll made earlier: "The harder you're hit, the harder you *have* to hit."

Driscoll's climactic nighttime pursuit of Rawlins through a shipyard is big-scale action that swells with the sounds of distant tugs, foghorns, and lapping water. In a clever close-up touch, Driscoll's face falls against a taut chain after a punch from Rawlins, a clever redo of an image from the film's opening sequence, when Driscoll's face slams against one of the ring ropes as he's knocked to the canvas. In the ring and on the dark ship, Driscoll fights to preserve what he believes himself to be.

As the doomed Pauline, Peggie Castle is edgy and unwholesomely sexualized (Karlson takes an almost fetishistic interest in her fabulous legs and derriere). The role is an arresting showcase for this perceptive, generally unheralded actress. Husky, pale-eyed Brad Dexter has one of his best roles as the scheming, generally unflappable Rawlins.

United Artists' promotional material for *99 River Street* promised "battering-ram violence" and "sheer-negligee excitement"—low-level sell for a film that battles confidently to rise above it.

A vengeful, dispirited ex-pug (John Payne, right) who's been set up to take a murder rap momentarily forgets that Frank Faylen is his friend in Phil Karlson's knife-edged *99 River Street* (1953).

If You Like It, Swipe It

A cop who has lost his wife and young daughter to a car bomb intended for him exists only to take vengeance on the mobster who ordered the hit. That's a capsule summation of Fritz Lang's 1953 triumph, *The Big Heat* (see Chapter 4), and it also sums up a baldly imitative minor noir, *Cry Vengeance* (1954). One difference is that the cop no longer functions as a peace officer: He's been imprisoned in San Quentin on a phony bribery rap for three years. As the story opens, he's just been released.

After shaking down various punks across San Francisco, the improbably named Vic Barron (Mark Stevens) learns that his nemesis, Tino Morelli (Douglas Kennedy), has relocated to Ketchikan, Alaska. (A froze-ass wilderness town seems the last place an urban mobster would choose for retirement, but that's an issue for another day.) Vic emerges from a seaplane with blood in his eye—and awful scars up and down one side of his face, visible reminders of the botched bombing. He circulates around town, hoping for a lead on Morelli, who inadvertently comes to Vic at a local watering hole.

Vic is a little crazed, but he knows he can't ice Morelli in public. He'll wait. As the story continues to unreel, though, Vic rediscovers his humanity. He responds to the honest affection of a local woman, Peg (Martha Hyer), and is so taken with Morelli's little girl (Cheryl Callaway), and the bittersweet memories of his own daughter, that he can neither kidnap the child nor kill her father. Regardless, justice begins to be served when Roxey (Skip Homeier), a large, white-blond psychopath once associated with Morelli, pursues the hapless Morelli into a Ketchikan forest and shoots him dead. Roxey has happily reasoned that with Morelli out of the way, nobody can tell Vic the truth—that Morelli was innocent of the car bombing and that it was Roxey who executed and botched it.

A propitious phone call from Roxey's alcoholic girlfriend, Lily (Joan Vohs), tips Barron to the truth. Following a backwoods car chase, Barron and Roxey face off at a deserted paper mill.

Roxey is a brazen lift of the Lee Marvin character in *The Big Heat*, and Lily is a reinterpretation of the earlier film's Gloria Grahame character. Even Vic's touching moments with Morelli's little girl steal from *The Big Heat*'s family interludes.

Plagiarism is hardly unusual in Hollywood. *The Big Heat* obviously impressed scripters Warren Douglas and George Bricker (both veterans of the old Monogram factory), as well as producer Lindsley Parsons, another veteran of B and C movies. You can't really excuse their sticky fingers, but you can't be surprised, either.

Familiarity and clumsiness aside, what really hurts *Cry Vengeance* is Mark Stevens, who directed as well as starred. Small but fit, he was a tough undercover hero in a glossy 20th Century-Fox noir, *The Street with No Name* (1948; see Chapter 4). Although Stevens had promise, audiences never completely warmed to him, and he spent most of his long career in B and C pictures and on television. *Cry Vengeance* makes clear that Mark Stevens, director, had no gift at all with actors, including himself. Because dialogue (which is clumsily expository to begin with) is recited by nearly everybody at a snail's pace (Martha Hyer is a pleasing exception), scenes seem to be about a third longer than they need to be. When in character as Vic, Stevens holds his head in his hands and communicates in a gravelly, monotone whisper that's meant to be dramatic and intimidating but is mainly annoying and difficult to hear.

Outdoor scenes (shot on location in Ketchikan), particularly those with violent payoffs, are well staged, but too many interiors are blocked like stage plays with actors simply facing each other or striking poses.

Stevens's conflicted, vengeance-obsessed urban antihero is pure noir, of course, and so is an unintentionally amusing scene in which Vic poses in that most clichéd of noir tableaus, a shabby hotel room illuminated by a blinking neon sign. It's another of many chestnuts that *Cry Vengeance* roasts one more time.

Venus Goes the Distance

The adapted works of Mickey Spillane returned to film noir with *The Long Wait* (1954), producer-director Victor Saville's second treatment of Spillane (*I, the Jury* had been released the year before; see Chapter 3). *The Long Wait* was also the first adaptation not to feature the signature Spillane character, Mike Hammer. This time, the aggressive antihero (Anthony Quinn) is named Johnny McBride—or, at least he *thinks* that's his name, because a car crash has wiped his memory clean. Eventually, his travels take him to a small town called Lyncastle.

Spillane's 1951 novel focuses primarily on revenge, but as interpreted for the screen by writers Alan Green and Lesser Samuels, Johnny's main preoccupation is self-discovery, as in: *Who am I, and why does half the population of Lyncastle want to kill me?* Through dogged determination, and a willingness to take lumps from bad cops and a lot of other locals, Johnny learns that he's a onetime Lyncastle bank teller who apparently stole $250,000 and subsequently murdered the local district attorney. After that, Johnny and the dough did a fast fade and hadn't been seen since—until now.

The amnesia that torments Johnny intrigues the Lyncastle police. They don't buy it, but it does provide their investigation with a certain challenging novelty. What's more difficult for the cops to reckon with is the fact that Johnny has no fingerprints. You see, they were burned off in the car crash. Is he McBride or isn't he?

Pretty soon, an unseen shooter with a silenced handgun uses Johnny for target practice. Later, someone tries to knock him off at an isolated quarry, and there's a cute bit of business involving a small wooden box containing a handgun and a tripwire. But for real narrative complexity consider this: One of the four beautiful Lyncastle women who welcome Johnny into their orbits (and boudoirs) is Johnny's old flame, Vera. However, because she's had plastic surgery, *Johnny can't identify her.* Voice, physical attitude, scent—nothing gives Vera away to Johnny, or to local crime boss Servo (Brillo-haired Gene Evans), who wants to shake Vera down for information about the missing quarter million. Even assuming that plastic surgery was astonishingly advanced in 1954 (which it was not), to assert that a transformation could be thorough enough to fool a former lover is ridiculous. But it's a plot device, and we'll pretend to roll with it.

Here are the mystery women: Servo's secretary, Carol (Shawn Smith); a casino floorwalker named Wendy (Mary Ellen Kay); Servo's girlfriend, Troy (Dolores Donlon); and the local Venus, named Venus (Peggie Castle).

When Servo convinces himself that Venus is Vera, he and his goon (Bruno VeSota) spirit her to a dark, abandoned power station; tie her at her wrists and ankles; and toss her onto an empty floor that's illuminated by a large oval of light. Beyond that oval, all is blackness, and it's in the protracted sequence that begins here that *The Long Wait* becomes fully engaged with the visual stylistics and sick psychology of noir.

Franz Planer's camera eye is initially very high above the floor. Venus lies on her side far below, her wrists in front of her, her knees slightly bent. The angle is such that she looks as if she's going to do the impossible and slide off the floor (very much like Marilyn Monroe during the bell-tower sequence of the previous year's *Niagara*; see Chapter 2). Subsequent setups bring us closer to Venus's head, which dominates the frame in unusual tableaus that emphasize her hair or her jawline. These images are almost abstract.

During the most remarkable—and frankly unforgettable—portion of the power-station sequence, *The Long Wait* serves up pure sadomasochism. Servo steps from a far doorway and into the lighted oval. By this time, Johnny is in the lighted oval as well, tied to a chair. Death is coming, so Johnny says it would be nice if he could say goodbye to Venus. Servo gaily agrees, and so for the next *122 seconds* the bound Venus painfully drags herself across the hotly lighted floor toward Johnny, the camera preoccupied with the exertions evident on her face and the tortured exertions of her arms and upper body. Actress Peggie Castle was an extraordinarily beautiful woman, and the sequence slides deeper into the perverse because Saville and Planer contemplated Peggie like men who want to humiliate the woman they desire.

Venus locks her eyes on her goal and continues to inch across the floor, exhaling with the effort, biting her lip, grimacing, tossing her head to get her sweep of honey-blonde hair out of her face. The crawl goes on and on, with only one or two brief cutaways. In an especially nasty gesture, Servo uses his foot to shove a table into Venus's path. Even seasoned watchers of noir may begin to feel uncomfortable or somehow *used*. But is the sequence dramatically effective? Yes. (Keep in mind that "effective" isn't the same as "justifiable.")

Venus finally pulls herself onto Johnny's legs and finds his ankle gun, a little .25 that she uses to plug Servo, who fires back as he falls. Wounded, Venus has strength enough to shoot apart Johnny's bonds, so that he's free to turn the .25 on Servo's goon.

Case File: Peggie Castle (1927–73)

This tall, feline blonde from Appalachia, Virginia, one of the most poverty-stricken regions in America, settled in Los Angeles, where she modeled and got into movies in 1947 with unbilled bits. Although the roles soon became more prominent, the arc of Castle's career never was an arc at all but a continual series of peaks and valleys: leads and second leads in B-plus and A-minus pictures starring Randolph Scott, Van Johnson, and Mario Lanza, interspersed with protracted interludes of B westerns (Castle made more of these than any other kind of film) and cheapjack science fiction. The cycle repeated for ten years, until Castle left features in 1957 to concentrate on television. She retired in 1962, after a 105-episode run as saloonkeeper Lily Merrill on *Lawman*.

Peggie's charms enliven three noir thrillers: *I, the Jury*, Phil Karlson's blistering *99 River Street*, and *The Long Wait*. The actress is impressive in each, reveling in murderousness, adultery, and tortured masochism, respectively. In addition to extraordinary good looks, Castle had a distinctive voice and considerable on-screen intelligence. Unfortunately, alcoholism eventually got the better of her, and she died just a few months after the passing of her fourth husband.

With Servo and other murderous locals accounted for, *The Long Wait* finally deals with the who-is-Vera MacGuffin (for the record, Venus is not the woman) and makes everything right for Johnny. The municipal corruption that defines so many noir thrillers, and that has infected Lyncastle, presumably will be addressed. Toughness, courage, and debasement have won the day.

Extortion for Old Times' Sake

Andre de Toth's *Crime Wave* (1954) is driven by issues of character, specifically, whether a bad man is invariably bad, whether a mistake is grounds enough to be branded as bad in the first place, and how a good man can fall into bad behavior. Can people change and become better? As far as LAPD Det. Lt. Sims (Sterling Hayden) is concerned, criminal rehabilitation is a myth fashioned from pixie dust. Once a crook, always a crook—that's how Sims views his corner of the world, and that's why ex-con Steve Lacey (Gene Nelson) finds himself in a hard place.

Steve does good work as an airplane mechanic and dutifully reports to his sympathetic parole officer (James Bell). He shares an appealing apartment and a devoted relationship with his wife, Ellen (Phyllis Kirk), and just wants to forget a stretch he did at Q for his part in a robbery five years ago. When three of Steve's old playmates break out of the pen, Lt. Sims sees the possible connection and begins to harass Steve. Sure enough, the escapees make for LA and tap Steve for a place to hide after they've committed murder. Not long after, with Ellen held as insurance (and in the care of scene-stealing actor Timothy Carey), Steve is forced to participate in an ambitious bank robbery. Can the heist be stopped before anyone else is killed?

Andre de Toth (whose career is discussed earlier in this chapter vis-à-vis *Pitfall*) shot *Crime Wave* in thirteen or fourteen days (accounts vary) at the end of 1952. Former actor Crane Wilbur based his script on a *Saturday Evening Post* story by John and Ward Hawkins. When the project was in development at Warner Bros., Jack Warner wanted Humphrey Bogart to play Lt. Sims. De Toth preferred a quite different personality, Sterling Hayden. Warner agreed to Hayden but insisted that, because the picture would now be a B movie rather than an A, de Toth would have to work quickly on a reduced budget.

That was fine with de Toth, who avoided the expense and bother of sets by shooting on location in LA and suburban Glendale. The locations give *Crime Wave* a remarkable, visceral immediacy that's on view in the opening sequence, when the escapees pull a nighttime stickup of a gas station. The set piece is an assemblage of wonderful devices: a back-seat camera that puts us right in the car with the thieves as they pull into the station; the place's peculiarly overbright fluorescent lights, which turn people's faces into white masks; a mildly eccentric attendant (Dub Taylor, credited as "Dubb") who bobs in front of his radio to Doris Day's recording of "S'Marvelous"; the abrupt conking of the guy's skull by Morgan (Nedrick Taylor); and Morgan's half-assed impersonation of an attendant while Doc Penny (Ted de Corsia) and Hastings (Charles Buchinsky [Bronson]) rifle the till.

A coincidental pass-by of a motorcycle cop (Joe Bassett) causes the robbery to unravel disastrously. Not long after, Steve and the playmates are back together. Doc gets one look at Ellen and knows he has the leverage he'll need. If anything is more maddening to Steve than prison, it's this.

De Toth and longtime Warner staff cinematographer Bert Glennon made assured use of LA's Hall of Justice, a dimly lit apartment building, a spacious bank, scrubby alleys and side streets, and crowded city boulevards. Glennon's lighting is so unobtrusive, it's almost invisible. Interiors and nighttime exteriors have the immediacy given by available light. Daytime exteriors, under bright overcast, are similarly "real." Shadows are expressive without being contrived.

Yet stylization isn't avoided. When the door to Steve's apartment is abruptly kicked in by cops, the last detective through the doorway pauses there, an aggressively spraddle-legged silhouette framed against illumination from the hall outside. This is an ex-con's night fright personified.

In another, quite different moment, the camera holds close on a bedside phone as it begins to ring. A male hand enters from frame left and grips the receiver, but a woman's hand darts into frame almost simultaneously, gripping the underside of the male wrist. Ellen's voice comes from off-camera: "Don't answer it." This is urgent and imaginative, and pure cinema.

Gene Nelson, a stage and screen personality known before this as a dancer who acted a little, is the film's biggest surprise. His small, athlete's body is perpetually coiled, his face struck with resentment, his voice a low-register mutter.

Crime Wave (1954): Ex-con Steve Lacey (Gene Nelson) just wants to look after wife Ellen (Phyllis Kirk) and be left alone. But an unwanted visit from old prison playmates threatens everything Steve and Ellen have worked for.

His scenes with Phyllis Kirk, a Warner contract player who never again seemed as real or as earthily appealing, are revealing studies of easy, unforced intimacy. Ellen is a good woman who believes in her man, and we can see for ourselves that Lt. Sims's unreasonable attitude is going to be destructive.

Sims is among Sterling Hayden's most engrossing creations, a professional with restlessly roving eyes, a hard carapace of cynicism, and an encyclopedic grasp of the city's criminal activity. He enters the case as one sort of man and leaves it as quite another. Sims exists to show that even angry men can put aside their worst inclinations and maintain the pulse of their humanity. His evolution is pleasing and logical and has useful purpose: Steve Lacey isn't going to be victimized any more.

A Thousand Shades of Red

Chicago in the early 1930s. When principled club dancer Vicki Gaye (Cyd Charisse) falls for a brilliant mob attorney named Tom Farrell (Robert Taylor), she inspires him to think about setting up a legitimate practice. But Tom knows far too much about the organization and his boss, Rico Angelo (Lee J. Cobb), who makes clear that Tom's departure would be unhealthy for Tom—and for Vicki.

That's the boilerplate setup of an extravagant, romantic thriller, *Party Girl* (1958), directed by Nicholas Ray for MGM. Shot in CinemaScope and brilliant Metrocolor, *Party Girl* is one of the most handsome and eye-filling pictures of the '50s. A genre piece with unique aesthetics, it's a peculiar yet satisfying amalgam of noir themes and stylistics, with the visual splash of MGM musicals (particularly *Singin' in the Rain*) and the blunt, energetic moralism of *The Roaring Twenties* and other Warner Bros. gangster melodramas of the 1930s. *Party Girl* breaks no new ground except in its brazen combining of those disparate elements. In that, it's a significant achievement.

But *Party Girl* is a problematic film, too, particularly for auteur theorists who cannot reconcile Nick Ray's participation in what was a big-studio, work-for-hire assignment in which Ray's vision and personality were supposedly crushed beneath the weight of big-studio politics and decision making. In no sense was this movie a "personal" project. As if to leave no doubt about that, some fifteen years after *Party Girl*, Ray described the film as "shit."

That's not an accurate—or honest—qualitative judgment. Rather, it's an expression of the bitterness of a maverick filmmaker who accepted a fee to make a picture with a locked-down cast and script and no invitation to participate in the edit process. But great directors the likes of Michael Curtiz, Victor Fleming, Sam Wood, and Raoul Walsh worked that way for most of their careers and created a lot of brilliant pictures. Perhaps because *Party Girl* is neither as explosively timely as *Rebel Without a Cause*, nor as socially conscious as *They Live By Night*, nor as determinedly quirky and gender-bending as *Johnny Guitar*, nor as unexpectedly and uncomfortably shocking as *Bigger Than Life*—each an earlier Ray project—the director may have felt entitled to whine a little.

The *Party Girl* shooting script was written by George Wells, adapting the content of at least half a dozen earlier script drafts by others that grappled with an unpublished, 270-page story by Leo Katcher. The final draft rests on two compatible, and familiar, tropes: the tribulations of an outsider who is victimized by events as she struggles to reshape her man, and the corrupted authority figure who is redeemed by the woman's love. MGM and other studios were filming stories like this one since the early sound era. Although a gangster-film revival began a couple of years after *Party Girl* (*The Rise and Fall of Legs Diamond, The George Raft Story, Portrait of a Mobster, Mad Dog Coll*, many others), the Ray film isn't predictive of that coming new wave. To the contrary, it resolutely looks backward—except, as suggested, in its unique mixing of ingredients.

Ray had made effective, often symbolic use of color in *Rebel, Johnny Guitar*, and other projects but never with the uninhibited boldness he uncorked for *Party Girl*. "Gangster thriller" sums up the film's plot, but its tone and attitude

In *Party Girl* (1958), Nicholas Ray's splashy and pictorially inventive epic of the Roaring Twenties, dancer Vicki Gaye (Cyd Charisse) wants to choose her own friends, but a mob triggerman (John Ireland, center) and his boss nevertheless insert themselves into Vicki's life.

are best described with "red." Working with cinematographer Robert Bronner and "Color Consultant" Charles K. Hagedan, Ray utilized red hues to suggest the urgency of love and sexual passion, the flame of violence, the primal allure of a big city, resoluteness of character, and utter despair.

Cyd Charisse, a gorgeous woman and a brilliant dancer, was a rather inexpressive actress. But when we gaze on Vicki Gaye in an unending succession of scarlet dresses, hats, and dance costumes, we can see that Ray was helping Charisse express emotions that existed beyond her range. In an especially vivid moment, Vicki lifts a bouquet of red roses and fans them across her lower face, closing her eyes and surrendering to the love she has for Tom. The imagery has the sleek elegance of a *Vogue* shoot and expresses as much about romance and longing as five pages of dialogue. Throughout *Party Girl*, image is indispensable content.

Existing in sharp contrast to Vicki is the attorney, who lives in a big-money world colored by leather and mahogany. When his relationship with Vicki is still developing, Tom's clothing and surroundings are in browns and cool blues. Vicki, of course, is all about red, and we can guess that Tom's world isn't going to be cool blue for much longer. Robert Taylor was a much better actor than he ever is given credit for, and he's intriguing here in throaty-voiced middle age. Taylor didn't need Ray's help, but the color schemes undeniably give the troubled attorney added dimension.

During a perfunctory montage that suggests Vicki and Tom's whirlwind tour of Europe, Tom wears red for the first time. Rico (played by Cobb with unabashed enthusiasm) doesn't wear red, but he holds court in an enormous chair that looks like a scarlet throne. In his club, the faces of revelers are bathed in a perpetual red glow.

When Vicki's roommate, Joy (Myrna Hansen)—unmarried and three months pregnant—commits suicide, the camera lingers on the red bathwater that covers the girl's body. (Another 1958 release, William Castle's absurd and wonderful *The Tingler*, revels in the shock of a bathtub filled to the brim with blood, but that full-color moment in an otherwise black-and-white movie is a goof, a gimmick. In *Party Girl*, the red water is uncomfortably real and is nearly unprecedented in respectable pictures of the day.)

Rico decides to scar Vicki's face with acid as payback for what he considers Tom's perfidy. To demonstrate the stuff's potency, he sadistically dribbles some onto a decorative red crepe bell, which melts and turns black. The deserted nightclub set where this takes place is a sickly combination of red and a color we haven't seen to this point, green. Green, of course, is the literal opposite of red, so the visual and psychological impacts are jarring. And although very little is shown when Rico accidentally splashes his own face with the acid, we can guess what color his flesh will be.

Dance and backstage sequences show off a succession of lovely costumes that include Vicki's provocative, slit-leg leopard-skin outfit and a pink gown with a blood-red train (which for a moment flutters, as if caught by a magical wind, to completely fill the screen). Costume designer Helen Rose's antic side is apparent when we meet a downstate mob of thugs led by Cookie LaMott (Corey Allen, who had worked with Ray in *Rebel*). LaMott and his boys dress with such flashy cheapness that they look like something out of Damon Runyon or a Harlem musical revue. They're really quite delightful.

On the other hand, because Rico's schemes hang over the narrative like a poisonous cloud, *Party Girl* is pregnant with violence. A cathartic montage of mob killings is beautifully staged by Ray and sharply edited by John McSweeney Jr. The sequence unreels—bam bam bam—and hits us right in the gut. Victims are caught in hallways and on stairs. Tommy gun bullets that catch a mobster inside a phone booth tear into him with such force that his body is blown right through the glass. In the montage's final tableau, two thugs who run to catch a train are beckoned forward and then ripped apart by a machine gunner who abruptly leans into frame from the extreme right foreground. *Party Girl* may be a rehash of a lot of familiar carryings-on, but it's a slick and effective one.

Although more than one historian has determined that *Party Girl* is self-indulgent, the film has no more of that quality than Ray's overstated (and over-rated) *Rebel Without a Cause* or the sublimely mannered *Johnny Guitar*, which are widely accepted as masterpieces. Ray was keenly aware of his *Party Girl* stylistics and his rationales for them. Very much a personal project because it makes something wonderful from very little, *Party Girl* unites victims and victimizers beneath a scrim of unearthly beauty.

7

The Unsprung Mind

"Go on, sit on any chair you wanna sit in. . . . I want you to consider yourself my guest. We'll have a couple of drinks. And then I'm gonna knock your teeth out."

—William Bendix to Alan Ladd, *The Glass Key* (1942)

T he temporary insanity that torments the young protagonist of Boris Ingster's *Stranger on the Third Floor* (1940) is not innate or deep-seated but is thrust upon him by racking guilt. Testimony by reporter Michael Ward (John McGuire) has helped to convict a cabbie named Briggs (Elisha Cook Jr.) of the violent murder of a cafe owner. Ward did not witness the slaying but encountered Briggs at the scene, with a knife and the body. The case is circumstantial but strong. However, things are amiss: The judge pays almost no attention to the proceedings, and one of the jurors falls asleep. Briggs's attorney is plainly inept.

As Briggs is led from the courtroom after the guilty verdict is read, he shrieks like a frightened animal: "I didn't kill him! I didn't kill him! I didn't! I didn't!"

Those cries haunt Ward, who frets and suffers in his furnished room and alarms his girlfriend, Jane (Margaret Tallichet), with stories of a mysterious, bulgy-eyed stranger (Peter Lorre) he's seen prowling the stairs in his building, and on the stoop outside. But the man, whoever he is, is damnably elusive and thus one more thing to prey on Ward's mind.

Ward begins to unravel. Even everyday encounters with stairs, closed doors, shadowed walls, empty streets, and rain disturb him profoundly. And then there's the guy next door, Meng (Charles Halton), a pinch-faced busybody who long ago decided to dislike Ward. The long-simmering tension explodes when Meng and the landlady stalk into Ward's room just as Ward is drying Jane's bare, rain-soaked feet and legs. (As the girl peels off her stockings and allows Ward to take the towel to her bare flesh, the screen quivers with an electric charge of eroticism.) In essence, Ward and Jane have been interrupted in the middle of sex. Ward is understandably furious.

Late that night, Ward grows paranoid because he can't hear Meng snore. Meng *always* snores. Is something wrong? Ward discovers Meng's body, and is arrested for murder.

And the stranger? Ward knows the stranger is out there somewhere.

Ingeniously, the script by Frank Partos (with an uncredited polish by novelist and RKO staff writer Nathanael West) doesn't allow the celebrated, eight-minute dream sequence of this sixty-four-minute thriller to be inserted into the film capriciously. We've been shown the portents.

Stranger on the Third Floor (1940): A reporter (John McGuire) who had been a witness in a capital murder case is tormented by visions of a peculiar upstairs neighbor (Peter Lorre) and then suffers excruciating, paranoid nightmares. This early noir has roots equally dug in German Expressionism and the American crime thriller.

Ward dreams. His body is crisscrossed and squeezed by narrow, closely spaced stripes of shadow that evoke prison bars. He often appears small and isolated at the back of the frame, overwhelmed by odd rectangles of light that dominate the foreground. He dreams that Jane is desperately upset, her slender body a fragile thing beneath menacing skyscrapers that tower behind her in outrageous forced perspective.

Ward dreams of his upcoming trial, where the jurors sit unmoving, heads deeply bowed. The gallery, a vast expanse of peculiarly white seats, is empty except for the pop-eyed stranger, who climbs over seatbacks to get a better view of Ward's misery.

When the dreaming Ward is found guilty, newspapers proclaim MURDER! in absurd 100-point type. At the death house, Ward is mocked by Meng, whose presence startles Ward into hysteria. The murdered man is alive!

In the death chamber, the dreaming Ward withers beneath the enormous shadow of the electric chair. Implacable forces much larger than he are about to destroy him. He's going to die. But he's innocent! Innocent! The stranger did it! Find the stranger!

The efforts of Boris Ingster, who directed only two other small films, mustn't be minimized. Ingster's friend Nathanael West credited him with a superb story sense and a sharp grasp of character. Still, it's plain to see that Ingster's chief collaborators on *Stranger*, cinematographer Nicholas Musuraca (who shot numerous noir thrillers and other intriguing films) and longtime RKO art director Van Nest Polglase, made essential contributions. The stark sets, shadowplay, semiabstract expressionism, and off-kilter camera angles are at once beautiful and upsetting. Camera movement is supple, and frames burst with visual information: foreground, middle ground, and background.

Peter Lorre, who worked on *Stranger* for just a few days, is an effectively furtive presence in a characterization that has echoes of the child murderer the actor played in Fritz Lang's *M* (1931). Although much of *Stranger on the Third Floor* explores Ward's unwholesome imagination, the stranger turns out to be very real. The denouement, in which the dying stranger exonerates Ward, isn't much of a surprise and wasn't intended to be. Mostly, it's a relief.

The leading man of *Stranger*, perennial bit player John McGuire, is more than competent, and doe-eyed Margaret Tallichet brings a tenderness that softens this artful curiosity of a movie and keeps it grounded. *Stranger on the Third Floor* is just real enough to be psychologically valid, and unforgettable.

The Perverse Urge to Hurt

The Glass Key (1942), adapted from the 1931 Dashiell Hammett novel by writer Jonathan Latimer and director Stuart Heisler, is a story of statewide political corruption and the things that accompany it: racketeering, marriage trouble, murder, nonlethal violence, cover-up, and suicide. The story is convoluted, and not nearly as intriguing as it first seems, but that was hardly the point. Paramount

Ah, a nibble of steak for demented, egg-sucking Jeff (William Bendix, right), who will shortly go back to beating the hell out of captive Alan Ladd in *The Glass Key* (1942). The *rotisseur* next to Bendix is Eddie Marr.

put the picture together to capitalize on the sudden popularity of the studio's two most beautiful contract players, Veronica Lake and Alan Ladd. The pair made a fabulous impression in *This Gun for Hire* (1942), which had been released just five months before *The Glass Key*, and Paramount wanted to recreate the magic. Thus, Lake and Ladd in *The Glass Key*. And, yes, the magic is recreated, but that's not why we're discussing the film in this chapter.

Political boss Paul Madvig (Brian Donlevy) relies on his unflappable number-one boy, Ed Beaumont (Ladd), to keep tabs on enemies and allies. Ed knows his job but has a tricky time negotiating the minefield laid down by gambling boss Nick Varna (Joseph Calleia) and practically everybody in the powerful Henry family: Senator Henry (Moroni Olsen), a finagling politician; Taylor Henry (Richard Denning), a whiny spendthrift; and Janet Henry (Lake), a cool, level-headed beauty who is Madvig's fiancée. Ed's worry is that Janet is engaged to Madvig only for his political gain.

When Taylor Henry is murdered, suspicion falls on Madvig. The whispers of accusation grow louder, and Ed realizes that his friend is being set up for the murder by Varna. Reason: Madvig supports a spurious reform ticket that will crack down on gambling and cripple Varna. Ed forces a split from Madvig and pretends to go to work for Varna, so that he can undercut the frame.

Varna finally discovers what Ed is up to and hands him over to Jeff (William Bendix) for punishment.

"Jeff" is such a friendly, accessible name, isn't it? Jeff. But this Jeff is wildly malevolent, and over the course of days, in a small room atop a grimy warehouse (menacingly lit by Theodor Sparkuhl), he batters Ed like a tetherball. You get the impression, though, that what Jeff—who is plainly psychotic—is up to isn't strictly business but his way of working out his ambivalent feelings for Ed. Plainly put, Jeff can't keep his hands off the guy. He paws Ed's shoulders and he hugs him. He calls him "Sweetheart," and then beats his face for a while. He runs his hands over Ed's chest, calls him "Baby," and then pounds on his abdomen. One day shades into the next, and Ed's face looks like an eggplant.

Clearly, Jeff is a sadist. Director Heisler and makeup man Wally Westmore took great pains to display what Jeff has done to Ed's beauty. Why does Jeff hit with such glee, and why does Ed take it?

Just as we're meant to admire Ed's good looks, we're invited to loathe Jeff's physical grossness. He's a squat, fleshy guy who looks like a stevedore. His curled hair is an unruly marvel, like a Brillo pad with a cowlick. Clothes don't hang on him well, and his appearance doesn't improve when he gets to the warehouse and strips down to his undershirt. Physically, he's the antithesis of Ed.

Jeff hammers Ed because he hates him—and because he loves him. It's a deranged, crazy love, with sexual longing sublimated into violence and Jeff's keen jealousy masked with bitterly humorous quips and small talk. Jeff wants to *be* Ed. He can't, so he hits him. Jeff loves Ed, but because this is 1942 and inclinations of that sort just aren't indulged publicly, Jeff's dilemma won't be solved until Ed is no longer desirable. For that to happen, Jeff has to destroy Ed's good looks.

The film doesn't hint as to why Ed takes all this abuse. The script establishes that he's brave, clever, loyal, and vaguely amoral (he seems unbothered by the fact that he has a passive hand in a man's suicide). Beyond that, he's a bit of a blank. In the Hammett source novel, Ed is considerably more complicated, carrying the baggage of alcoholism and even a suicide attempt. From that, we can infer that the Ed of Hammett's imagination submits to Jeff's abuse because he wants to be punished.

Well, Paramount wasn't likely to allow Alan Ladd to be seen in that light, so the reasons for the passivity of movie-Ed must remain mysteries.

Ed eventually escapes the warehouse (in a literal crashout involving a great, glassy fall, sterling stunt work, and sharp photography and editing). The killer of Taylor Henry comes forward; Madvig is off the hook and is agreeable when Janet and Ed become a couple.

Jeff is going to go to prison but not before he fondles Ed one more time and calls him "Cuddles." What a romantic.

A Monster in the Family

Alfred Hitchcock had a deep interest in deviant personality, specifically, as exhibited by characters that took what they wanted because of psychosis, usually without fear, and often with preening self-righteousness. Those qualities define many noir protagonists, yet Hitchcock isn't primarily regarded as a noir director, at least not in the sense of Anthony Mann or Fritz Lang. Hitchcock's body of work has caused him to be placed in his own critical and historical category: Hitchcock.

Hitchcock was British, of course, but because *Shadow of a Doubt* (1943) is set in sunny, gracious Santa Rosa, California, and populated by Americans with all-region accents, the film is one of the director's most pointedly "American." (Coscripter Thornton Wilder created the film's uniquely small-town feel. Others who contributed to the script were playwright Sally Benson; Hitchcock's wife and frequent collaborator, Alma Reville; and Hitch himself.) At the time of the shoot, Santa Rosa was a sleepy town with a charming central square and tree-lined residential streets. On-screen, it suggests nothing specifically Californian. To the contrary, it's very much like the archetypal Midwestern American town and thus as American as American can be.

Into this sleepy place comes Uncle Charlie (Joseph Cotten), a murderer of wealthy widows who has returned to family in Santa Rosa because he's on the run from police. Fashionable, genial, and generous, he immediately captures the heart of his teenage niece and namesake, Charlie (Teresa Wright). The girl is thrilled. At last, something exciting has happened to Santa Rosa!

Charlie imagines that she and Uncle Charlie are twins, not simply in the sameness of their names but psychically. In Charlie's globe-trotting adventurism, worldliness, and social grace, Charlie sees herself as she'd like to be.

Not surprisingly, the gloss wears off the relationship as Uncle Charlie makes little slips: he gives Charlie an emerald ring with a inscription he hadn't noticed; he shows queer interest in a particular newspaper story; he lets loose with a startling, barking response to Charlie when he feels she's intruded on his space; and he indulges himself in a calm but horrible diatribe at the family dinner table against wealthy widows ("faded, fat, greedy women"). After a close call with a broken stair step, and with a running automobile in a locked garage, Charlie *knows*.

Uncle Charlie's fiendish sociopathic nature is more than just frightening. It's a sad thing, too, because it destroys so many of Charlie's assumptions, and her innocence. Because Charlie's mother (warmly played by sweet-smiling Patricia Collinge) adores her baby brother, Charlie's dilemma isn't just a matter of self-protection but her responsibility to protect her mother, who would be irrevocably devastated by the truth.

Two police detectives (Macdonald Carey and Wallace Ford) are snooping around under a clumsy pretext, and Charlie has become chummy with the younger of them. Uncle Charlie knows it's time to make a concerted effort to

Case File: Alfred Hitchcock (1899–1980)

Hitchcock looms so large on the cinema landscape that any attempt to deal with his legacy is fated to be inadequate. Hitch himself made evaluation difficult because of his flair for self-promotion and concomitant public face, which was that of an amiably ghoulish uncle. He was fun, he was accessible. His plummy British voice and rotund figure further cemented this aspect of his uniqueness and disguised the fact that he was not simply a sexually repressed, extraordinarily private man but a shrewd, hardnosed businessman whose profit participation eventually included considerably more than his director's fee.

As a filmmaker, he was deeply involved in every aspect of his films' preproduction, taking active roles in budgeting, acquisition, concept, script, location scouting, storyboarding, and casting. When the films were ready for release, Hitchcock hurled himself into promotion and exploitation, making personal appearances, granting interviews, and sometimes appearing in his pictures' trailers. (The trailer for *Psycho*, in which Hitch conducts a protracted, tongue-in-cheek "tour" of the Bates Motel, is fiendishly funny.)

Much critical attention (and dime-store psychoanalysis) has been paid to Hitch's recurring motifs, particularly paranoia, voyeurism, horror that hides in plain sight, and the innocent man wrongly accused. All of that, as well as his preoccupation with coolly sophisticated female characters who are sexual tigresses beneath the mink, inform, to varying degrees, many of his movies and completely dominate some of them.

It can be convincingly argued that Hitchcock invented the suspense/thriller genre as we experience it today and was the first filmmaker to aggressively challenge, even "stalk," his audiences.

Although not generally known as a noir director, Hitchcock made vivid contributions to the genre: *Shadow of a Doubt*, *Notorious*, *Strangers on a Train*, and *Vertigo*, as well as *Psycho*, the brazen, deceptively thoughtful entertainment that simultaneously capped noir's golden age and brought it to an end.

---

kill his niece—the daughter of the sister who adores him. This time, he's going to shove Charlie to her death from a train as he leaves town.

The film's recurring motifs, such as an image of whirling, nineteenth-century dancers and variations of the "Merry Widow" waltz theme, are splendid. Little has been written, however, about a sequence in which Uncle Charlie imposes himself on a local bank (that employs Charlie's father [Henry Travers]) and blithely deposits $40,000. Uncle Charlie has murdered for that money, but he passes it off as spare cash that he just wants out of his hair. His performance for the bank manager is a marvel of cheek and arrogance.

Hitchcock's most pointed, and repeated, use of symbolism is his linking of Uncle Charlie to blackness, specifically, the ebony locomotive that delivers the killer to Santa Rosa, the inky smoke that belches from its stack, and the heavy shadow cast over the station (and, metaphorically, on the family and all of Santa

Evil comes to a small town dressed in an amiable package called Uncle Charlie (Joseph Cotten) in Alfred Hitchcock's *Shadow of a Doubt* (1943). Only one person figures out that Uncle Charlie is a murderous fiend—his perilously vulnerable namesake niece, Charlie (Teresa Wright).

Rosa) as the engine slows and stops. Wherever Uncle Charlie goes, he brings with him the bottomless, dark void of eternity.

Hitchcock often cited *Shadow of a Doubt* as his favorite of the films he made. His daughter, Pat, has said that Hitch was attracted to the notion of evil living amidst the innocents of a small town. That's perfectly reasonable, but a guess is that her father held the film in high regard for another reason, too: because it confronted his own anxieties and desires. After Uncle Charlie's death (and an adoring, first-class sendoff by Santa Rosa), the detective says to Charlie, "[The world] seems to go a little crazy now and then. Like your Uncle Charlie." That's a clear reference to World War II, which was still unfolding in Germany's favor when *Shadow of a Doubt* was filmed during the summer and early fall of 1942. Although the Soviets offered stiff resistance, the outcome of the war was very much up in the air. Hitchcock's ailing mother lived in England, and Hitch was unable to travel home to be with her. All of that was scarifying and discombobulating. War is focused but, ultimately, irrational. Like Uncle Charlie.

Hitchcock's real-life treatment of women has been much discussed. His ongoing casting of "cool blondes" was no accident, and at least one of those actresses, Tippi Hedren, suffered beneath Hitchcock's clumsy attempts at seduction. Hitchcock may not have been a misogynist, but attractive women troubled and perplexed him. In Uncle Charlie, he found a vehicle with which to express and work out some of those troubles.

When Uncle Charlie loses his grip on his niece and falls from the moving train into the path of an oncoming one, Hitchcock wasn't just sparing young Charlie and giving us a measure of relief. He was rescuing himself.

He Likes to Look—and Kill

And now that film-school favorite, "the male gaze," and its expression in John Brahm's splendid period noir thriller, *The Lodger* (1944). This is the best of numberless film speculations about the legendary Jack the Ripper, who murdered women with knife or scalpel in East London in the 1880s. As played here by the physically imposing Laird Cregar, the title character is an emotionally isolated research pathologist who continually gazes at faces, as if in them are the answers to whatever it is that troubles him. After engaging rooms with the Bontings (Cedric Hardwicke and Sara Allgood), he stares at his own face in water, frequently examines a miniature self-portrait done by his late brother (a young man of feminine beauty), and compulsively observes women from windows, through doorways, from a theater audience, and even in mirrors. He is especially interested in a friend of the Bontings, a music-hall star named Kitty Langley (Merle Oberon).

Barré Lyndon's script (from the 1913 novel by Marie Belloc Lowndes) leaves no doubt that the lodger sexualizes the objects of his gaze, his late brother included, which suggests a propensity to morbidly unwholesome attachments. By pinning people with a look, the lodger hopes to dominate and keep them.

A particularly amusing aspect of *The Lodger* is that the film coyly refuses to commit to whether the lodger is the Ripper. In some moments (as when he complains about the insidious nature of female beauty), we're convinced of his guilt. At other interludes, characters ascribe logic to the lodger's actions, and we're tempted to believe that the lodger is innocent after all and a mere red herring.

Existing in neat counterpoint to the lodger's dreamy turn of mind and Kitty's artistic temperament is the cool logic of Scotland Yard's Inspector Warwick (George Sanders, at his most urbane and appealing). By the time the inspector puts his clues together, the film has revealed its point of view, and its villain.

We've had the surprise; now comes suspense, as Kitty is unaware that she's in deadly danger.

Some sources note that *The Lodger* is a remake of the 1927 Alfred Hitchcock silent of the same name, but there really is no relation between the two other than that the Ripper murders are employed to motivate the plot of each. In Hitchcock's paranoiac film, the title character is innocent and wrongly accused; in Brahm's, the lodger most certainly could be the killer (though no one has accused him of anything).

In the latter-day *The Lodger*, the man who might be the Ripper is the dominant figure. All other characters are his satellites, even the one played by the confident and very beautiful Merle Oberon, who was seldom a satellite to anybody during her prime. But then, she'd never worked before with Laird Cregar, a tall, heavyset young character player who got into movies in 1940, at age twenty-seven. Before *The Lodger* he'd gained attention in *I Wake Up Screaming* (see Chapter 6), *This Gun for Hire* (Chapter 5), *Heaven Can Wait*, and others. His physical heft was an on-screen asset, and he also possessed a remarkably acute psychological presence.

Cregar seems to have been born to be an actor in movies, where directors could come in close on his fevered eyes, place him in menacing shadow, and shoot him from below to emphasize his potential for menace—all of which Brahm and cinematographer Lucien Ballard (who was Merle Oberon's husband from 1945 to early 1949) did during the shoot of *The Lodger*. Shot entirely on the Fox back lot, the film is lusciously dank and menacing in its many nighttime sequences, with black doorways, rain-slick cobbles, curling mist, and female figures traipsing to their doom. The most violent murder sequence, set inside a victim's flat instead of on the street, simulates a handheld camera for a subjective view as the fiend (and we) moves closer to his victim (played with uncomfortably real terror by Helena Pickard).

The film's climax is set amidst the maze of catwalks in a theater, and is a rouser. Terror, fury, animal defiance—all of those and more are on display. In the final moments, the setting is tight and constricting, like the ceaseless, malevolent thoughts that crowd the killer's brain.

Composition for Piano and Death

Laird Cregar returned to Victorian London in *Hangover Square* (1945), another teaming with director John Brahm and the first time Cregar enjoyed top billing (above fellow Fox players Linda Darnell and George Sanders). In matters of visual stylization, the film is a reiteration of what *The Lodger* had established the previous year, with atmospheric use of nighttime sequences, rainy streets, and high-contrast cinematography (this time by Joseph LaShelle) that makes particularly effective use of faces in close-up. Additionally, Brahm and returning screenwriter Barré Lyndon added some fresh elements: the inevitably unhappy collision of art and commercialism, and psychopathic dementia with a physical cause. It's a provocative stew that is further highlighted by a splendid score—that includes a sweeping piano concerto—composed by Bernard Herrmann.

Well-regarded, soft-spoken composer George Harvey Bone (Cregar) struggles to complete his long-anticipated piano concerto. His serious work is derailed, however, by the insincere attentions of a selfish music-hall entertainer, Netta Longdon (Linda Darnell), who beguiles George into wasting his time and talent on trifling new songs for her vulgar act. Unaware that he's being manipulated, George falls in love and then goes a little crazy after discovering that he's been had. The consequences are particularly bad because, in addition to romantic obsession, George has a problem with impulse murder (as we witness in the film's startling opening sequence). A hypersensitivity to sharp noises literally blurs his vision, turns the world a little tipsy, and sends him into murderous blackouts—all of which we experience via subjective camera, making us complicit as well as righteously shocked. George is a split personality, a condition neatly suggested by an early, low-angle camera setup in which the killer's gaze is fixed on a knife he holds, his features vertically bisected by the blade.

Hangover Square is satisfying for many reasons, not least because it explores the fragility of the creative process and the various pressures an artist must overcome in order to produce quality work. Offhand dialogue establishes that

In John Brahm's atmospheric *Hangover Square* (1945), neighborhood night watchman Clifford Brooke (left) suspects something unwholesome is afoot. He's right about that, because composer George Harvey Bone (Laird Cregar) has surrendered his musical gifts to madness—and murder—after being betrayed in love.

George isn't yet in serious music's top rank. He's close, however, and if the completed concerto is as good as available fragments suggest, George will be regarded as a genius. Friends innocently remind him that what he produces may make his career. George tries to concentrate, but Netta inevitably shows up to tempt and distract him.

Tick tock, time to complete the concerto is running out, so when George discovers that Netta is engaged, he garrotes her—and then, in one of the greatest and most awful interludes in all of Hollywood melodrama, he brazenly carries her shrouded corpse through crowded, festive streets to a towering wood pyre that's been prepared for Guy Fawkes Day. As George struggles up a ladder with his burden, a gaudy mask he has placed over Netta's face begins to slip, exposing her mouth and jaw. The moment has a dread suspense, but no one notices that George carries a human body. He finishes the climb, deposits the corpse at the very top of the pyre, and then watches, almost hypnotized, as the fire is lit, consigning what remains of the beautiful temptress to ash.

The film's other great set piece, when George goes fully, irrevocably mad in the concert hall, also invokes metaphoric cleansing by flame, as the place becomes an inferno while George is at the piano. More and more flames surround George as the camera executes a majestic, overhead pullback. After a few moments, smoke obscures our view and George is gone.

Cregar dominates the screen with barely suppressed agitation, which is expressed in his eyes and in body language that alternately suggests a haughty artistic temperament or clumsy sexual desire. Linda Darnell, almost always a much better actress than she was ever credited for being, is lubricious and vile as the scheming entertainer. Like Cregar, Darnell used her eyes with sharp effectiveness, suggesting false seduction and dismissive boredom. (Still, *Time* magazine wasn't off the mark when it described Darnell in its review of *Hangover Square* as "Hollywood's most rousing portrayer of unhousebroken sex.")

Fresh-faced Faye Marlowe is appealing as a young woman with honest feelings for George, and Glenn Langan has a good bit as a supercilious fop. George Sanders, playing a physician who becomes curious about George's state of mind, is suitably bright-eyed and engaged.

Laird Cregar never lived to see the release of *Hangover Square*. Despite Fox's interest in him as a character actor, Cregar had dreams of becoming a romantic leading man. He put himself on a harsh diet and lost eighty pounds between the shoots of *The Lodger* and *Hangover Square*. Subsequent dieting took off another twenty pounds, but the strain was too much for his heart. Cregar died in December 1944, just thirty-one years old.

Fashionably Murderous

Four elements mesh very satisfactorily in *Leave Her to Heaven* (1945): Technicolor and Gene Tierney (this was the actress's first color film); and romantic melodrama and director John Stahl. Stahl became a 20th Century-Fox contract

324 Film Noir FAQ

director in 1943, after establishing himself at Universal in the 1930s, where he did *Back Street, Only Yesterday, Imitation of Life,* and *Magnificent Obsession*—each an important "women's picture" that focused keenly on uniquely female concerns and predicaments. Because Stahl had experience as a producer-director dating from 1914, he possessed a thorough understanding of his craft. He wasn't overwhelmed by over-the-top emotion; to the contrary, he possessed a lucid, unshowy visual sense and brought to even the most fevered material intelligence and relative restraint. *Leave Her to Heaven,* though far from a traditional women's picture, is nevertheless well suited to Stahl's talents, mainly because it has a female lead so potent, and so relentlessly focused on by script and Technicolor camera, that she reduces her male costar to a plot device.

Successful novelist Richard Harland (Cornel Wilde) marries Ellen Berent (Tierney), a wealthy beauty who adores him. She adores him so much, in fact, that she resents the presence of others in his life and even comes to resent his work. If Harland isn't giving her 100 percent of his attention, Ellen feels cheated, and becomes petulant . . . and murderous. Ellen, you see, is quite insane.

Because female sexuality is a potent force that is feared nearly as strongly as it is desired, we're quick to accept a beautiful woman as a killer. Somehow, in our shared cultural consciousness, it makes sense. Generations of fictions, and the occasional true-life story, have convinced us that beauty and perfidy go together, like sugar and arsenic (more about that later).

Case File: Gene Tierney (1920–91)

The beautiful, intriguingly remote actress who played *Laura* began her film career at 20th Century-Fox in 1940, after two years of Broadway experience. Her feline eyes and striking facial structure encouraged the studio to cast her early on as exotics, such as a South Seas islander in *Son of Fury,* and an Arab beauty in *Sundown.* Tierney caused a stir (and is very good) as the unashamedly coarse Ellie Mae in *Tobacco Road* and then settled into a succession of prestige pictures the likes of *Heaven Can Wait, Dragonwyck, The Razor's Edge,* and *The Ghost and Mrs. Muir.*

Tierney's box-office punch waned after 1950 (in 1954's *Black Widow,* she's wasted in a "wife" role and is upstaged by, of all people, Peggy Ann Garner). Tierney's bankability evaporated altogether during 1955–60, when the actress's struggle with deep depression prevented her from working.

On-screen, there's something elusive about Tierney, as if she's unwilling to fully reveal herself—a quality that was perfect for *Laura* and for Tierney's second noir, *Leave Her to Heaven,* in which she plays a charming woman whose secret is that she's a serial murderer. Tierney hasn't a lot to do in *Where the Sidewalk Ends* but is incisive and intelligent in *Night and the City,* in a small but well-drawn role as a woman who can't completely untie herself emotionally from a conniving hustler. But *Laura* will be Tierney's enduring achievement.

Leave Her to Heaven (1945): Mad love prompts wealthy Ellen Berent (Gene Tierney) to marry novelist Richard Harland (Cornel Wilde)—and woe unto anyone who takes an iota of her husband's time. You see, Ellen murders innocent interlopers, including Harland's disabled younger brother.

A cute trick of Jo Swerling's script (from the 1944 novel by Ben Ames Williams) is that not even the barest confirmation of Ellen's disturbed state appears until well past the 30-minute mark of this 110-minute thriller. Until then, the story unfolds in a very traditional Hollywood manner, complete with a "meet cute" aboard a sunny train, obliquely romantic chitchat, and eye-filling locations in Northern and Southern California, as well as Flagstaff and Prescott, Arizona (variously filling in for Maine, New Mexico, and Georgia).

As in so many big-budget romances, *Leave Her to Heaven* establishes a rarefied world of wealth and privilege; everyone seems to own a ranch or a lakefront lodge or a cut-stone mansion in the desert, and when they relax after dark, the men dress as though they're at a board meeting and the women look like debutantes. Harland even smokes a pipe. It's all rather giddy in its sophisticated opulence.

Ellen adores her late father, and you soon suspect that there are unresolved "daddy issues" here, but the real trouble begins when Ellen meets her husband's disabled younger brother, a teenager named Danny (Darryl Hickman, in an ingratiating performance). Ellen appears to take a shine to him but can barely conceal her regret when Harland invites Danny to stay with Ellen and him at the lodge in Maine. In a peculiarly effective sequence, Ellen chats with Danny's physician (Reed Hadley) about the boy's treatment—and then impatiently lets out with, "But after all, he's a cripple!" Dead silence from the doctor as Ellen nervously tries to backpedal.

Later, Danny swims in the glorious piney lake as Ellen rows alongside. She encourages him to attempt a long swim (Danny has been planning to surprise Harland with the feat), but when the kid cramps up and begins to struggle, Ellen—having slipped on ominous-seeming sunglasses—impassively watches from the canoe as Danny cries for help, goes under once, twice, and then vanishes for good.

The murder is particularly potent because Danny is a sweet kid who's very fond of Ellen, and because the sylvan setting (gorgeously shot by Leon Shamroy) seems about the last place you'd expect to witness such heartlessness. The drowning is unforgettably upsetting (the boy's fright is palpable) and, frankly, a risk for Gene Tierney, who was willing to challenge her image so that she could play a fiend.

Harland silently blames Ellen for the "accident," and as he grows increasingly remote, Ellen contrives to get pregnant. Yes, a baby will bring her husband back to her! But Ellen dislikes being pregnant and fakes a fall down a staircase *so that she'll miscarry.* If this isn't as punishing on the audience as the drowning, it's only because a fetus can't holler for help.

With the baby out of the picture, Ellen has achieved her short-term goals, but because her psychosis is now out of control, she admits to Harland that she let Danny drown and that she killed the baby. (By this time, you notice that most of Ellen's beautiful clothes are boldly monogrammed. In Ellen's world, almost nothing matters but Ellen.) Despite a benumbed response from Harland that makes it clear the marriage is over, Ellen turns her spider gaze on her adopted sister, Ruth (Jeanne Crain). Ruth and Harland enjoy each other's company too much to suit Ellen, who prepares a mix of sugar and arsenic and takes everybody on a picnic.

During a high-pitched murder trial that consumes the picture's final fifteen minutes, the narrative's momentum unravels. The trial is predicated on a startling plot twist, but we're shoved, nevertheless, into completely fresh dramatic territory that's restricted to a (handsome) soundstage.

Further, it's absurd to believe that the district attorney (a florid and righteously upset Vincent Price) would be allowed to try the case—he was engaged to Ellen before she threw him over for Harland!—and his browbeating of witnesses is comically unrealistic.

Cornel Wilde is stolid and capable as the male lead, but he's no match for Price's theatrics or for Tierney's piercing blue eyes and lush mouth. Wilde seems more "visible" in scenes opposite red-haired Jeanne Crain, a wholesomely beautiful woman who, like Tierney, is smashing in Technicolor.

When you step back a bit, you realize that *Leave Her to Heaven* is as preoccupied with gloss and surfaces as with the story it tells. Resplendent in color so luscious you want to bite it, the picture is equal parts travelogue, thriller, and marital horror story. If *Holiday* magazine had done a special issue in partnership with *Master Detective*, it would look and feel like *Leave Her to Heaven*: chic, cold, and murderous.

A Child's Garden of Insanity

At the beginning of *The Locket* (1946), just minutes before his marriage, a pleasant young man named Don (Gene Raymond) is visited by Dr. Blair (Brian Aherne), a psychiatrist who explains that Don's fiancée, Nancy (Laraine Day), has destroyed the lives of various men and had in fact been *his* wife for five years.

Blair relates his tale via flashback. In it, Blair describes his professional relationship with a promising young artist named Norman Clyde (Robert Mitchum, at ease in an atypical role). During one session, Clyde tells Blair that Nancy is a murderer.

The Clyde-Nancy relationship is related by Clyde as a flashback-within-a-flashback, thus establishing *The Locket*'s narrative structure, which recalls the dependent pieces of a Russian nesting doll, each piece building on the one immediately before.

Nancy had become Clyde's muse and inspired him to create paintings that attracted the attention, and money, of New York's art *cognoscenti*. When Clyde discovers that Nancy has stolen a valuable necklace while at a society party, Nancy tries to explain why, going all the way back to her childhood in a flashback that exists within Clyde's flashback within Blair's flashback.

How did Blair meet Nancy? Through Clyde.

As more plot points are elucidated, the course of the flashbacks is finally reversed (the doll is put back together again) and returns us from Nancy's story to Clyde's, and then to Blair's. Finally, we are back in the present, as Don tries to absorb everything Blair has told him. In a few minutes Don and Nancy will be married. How much—if any—of Blair's tale should Don believe?

Because of Blair's personal involvement with Nancy, and his knowledge of her childhood and later relationship with Clyde, Blair becomes nearly as important to the narrative as Nancy. The fact that he's a highly competent psychiatrist—objective and capable of detached assessment—brings clarity and establishes a reliable narrative voice.

All credit goes to writer Sheridan Gibney (a 1936 Oscar winner for *The Story of Louis Pasteur*), whose script keeps the discrete sections of narrative not only clear and distinct but vivid, as well. Director John Brahm, famed for *The Lodger* and *Hangover Square*, successfully chases after characterization rather than startling visual effects. By the time all the flashbacks are over, we've learned that the perpetually cheerful Nancy, though a habitual liar with a capacity to kill, has no real malice in her. (Yes, the character is fascinatingly contradictory.)

Her mother's heartless return of a much-loved locket given to Nancy by a wealthy playmate has warped Nancy's mind, turning her into a habitual thief and murderer whose machinations cause, among other things, an innocent man to be sentenced to the electric chair.

Clyde has been involved in that last calamity. Stricken with love for Nancy and tormented by his conscience, Clyde gives Dr. Blair his earliest portrait of Nancy—a gorgeous and frightening blank-eyed Cassandra—and then finds emotional rest in one of noir's great shock moments. (A figure of Greek myth, the beautiful Cassandra has the gift of doom-laden prophecy, and eventually descends into schizoid madness.)

Bridegroom Don is not fully persuaded by Blair, but during final preparation for the ceremony, Nancy is visited by visual and aural ghosts of her past, some of which hinge on savage ironies that will not be revealed here. As she descends the staircase, Brahm and cinematographer Nicholas Musuraca focused with uncomfortable closeness on the terrified face beneath the veil, and then, with marvelous subjective camerawork, on the walls and ceilings as Nancy sees them, and on the ornately patterned rug that unreels beneath her feet as she walks.

When she shrieks and collapses, Blair stands ready to return her to a sanitarium.

Unlike the Jean Simmons character in the later *Angel Face* (see discussion in this chapter), Nancy isn't flamboyantly cuckoo. Generally, she's disinterested in big, bold action. Because of Laraine Day's ability to carry a film and Brahm's smartly tempered direction, Nancy is perpetually the emotionally stricken little girl denied a prized possession because of social class. With her sunny, unostentatious beauty, ingratiating charm, and generally well-hidden motivations, Nancy is very nearly an innocent, a striver who wishes to do no harm but sometimes does because, after all, she's psychotic.

Let Steve Do It

"Pick-Up Girls on a Ride to Love with Satan Behind the Wheel!" That's the shy sell line on the front cover of Avon's 1949 paperback edition of Robert DuSoe's *The Devil Thumbs a Ride*, a novel that first appeared, as a paperback original, in Britain in 1941. The editors at Avon even floated the crimson head of Satan himself above the tableau of a crazed driver and frenzied passengers, just to reinforce the unpredictable nature of hitchhikers.

The Devil Thumbs a Ride (1947): Wherever glib hitchhiker Steve Morgan (Lawrence Tierney) travels, he leaves a wake of confusion, mayhem, and murder. His luck has held for quite a while, but for how much longer?

Case File: Lawrence Tierney (1919–2002)

In all of noir, perhaps no one has been as consistently scary as Lawrence Tierney, a tall, rugged college athlete who began his acting career on the stage. His earliest movie roles were unbilled bits, but just two years after his debut he took the title role in *Dillinger* (1945). The picture established Tierney as RKO's go-to guy for violent, intimidating toughs. The peculiar "genuineness" of Tierney is that he lived a lot of that life offscreen, famously getting into public brawls and playing the angry drunk. The only Hollywood figure who ever got Tierney to shut up and behave himself was the diminutive actor—and real-life war hero—Audie Murphy.

Dillinger was followed by a war film and a western, and then noir beckoned in 1947, when Tierney took the starring roles in *The Devil Thumbs a Ride* and *Born to Kill*—two studies of antisocial misfits who bully, scheme, and murder. Another, later noir, 1955's *Female Jungle*, is disjointed and minor. Tierney also starred and costarred in standard crime melodramas, including *San Quentin*, *Bodyguard*, *Shakedown*, *The Hoodlum*, and *Kill or Be Killed*.

Tierney was increasingly active in episodic television after 1956 and enjoyed a latter-day renaissance, returning to features as a bald, bear-like growler who looked nothing like his earlier self. But he still bristled with the familiar toughness. See him in *Prizzi's Honor*, *Tough Guys Don't Dance*, and (most memorably) in Quentin Tarantino's *Reservoir Dogs*. Tierney remained active until 2000.

In the opening scene of RKO's 1947 adaptation, San Diego forger and stickup artist Steve Morgan (Lawrence Tierney) callously drills an elderly bank messenger in the back. That's devilish, but Steve has amusingly annoying, "everyday" qualities, too. He doesn't have a job, likes to have things done for him, and thinks he's God's gift to women. He has an insult for everybody and takes charge of every situation with such bossy decisiveness that the timid souls in his orbit mumble, "Gee, Steve, I guess you're right" and "Yeah, I guess that's the best thing to do."

Traveling brassiere salesman Jimmy "Fergie" Ferguson (Ted North) innocently gives Steve a ride when the shot-up bank messenger is still warm. Things are all right for a while (Fergie is quite a chatterbox and enjoys having company), but Fergie should give Steve the boot the moment he discovers that two dames hitchhiking at a gas station have been invited into the car. It's been established that Fergie is crazy about his wife. Why should he want this kind of trouble?

Okay, Fergie lets Steve's bit of presumption slide, but maybe he should tell Steve to get lost when Steve speeds like a maniac (yes, Steve has maneuvered himself into the driver's seat in more ways than one). How about when Steve backs up over a motorcycle cop who wants to write them a ticket? No, not then, either.

Steve speeds off. Fergie, and even the girls, are alarmed but Steve says the cop isn't hurt (how does *he* know?), and anyway, other cops will be there pretty soon to help the guy.

Well, that makes sense to Fergie, who shows mounting evidence of being developmentally disabled.

Steve wants to lay low and talks Fergie into making a midnight stop at a beach house owned by Fergie's boss. Inside, the booze starts to flow. Steve dismisses high-mileage "bad girl" Agnes (Betty Lawford) by calling her "Grandma" and tries to put the squeeze on "good girl" Carol (Nan Leslie). Not long after Fergie calls his wife to give her some bunk about a bum carburetor—and never mind the swing music and female braying you hear in the background, honey—Carol turns up dead in shallow waters of the lagoon outside. The death tableau is very well shot night-for-night by cinematographer J. Roy Hunt and is one of the great movie shock moments of the 1940s. It's especially effective because we do not see the murder take place and because writer-director Felix Feist resisted the urge to turn it into something visually extravagant. The scene is covered in a medium shot that simply records Fergie's attempt to pull the body onto shore. No close-ups, no bizarre angles—just a sour dose of reality.

While Steve and the others are having their misadventure, frequent and lively crosscutting to a hardnosed old cop (Harry Shannon) keeps us current with the authorities' northerly pursuit along the California coast. The cop has a young gas station attendant (Glen Vernon) in tow, a very bright, quietly funny kid who can ID the killer. This parallel story underscores Steve's devious energy and keeps the narrative cooking.

Lawrence Tierney is familiarly big, cold-eyed, and predatory. The gruff Tierney delivery is fun, if your idea of fun is to be intimidated. He's really an actor you don't want to warm up to, but he's ferociously good here, throwing sidelong glances to keep tabs on Fergie and positioning himself within arm's reach of a hidden gun.

Longtime character player Andrew Tombes gets laughs as a gullible night watchman who drops by the beach house to see what all the ruckus is about.

Tidy at a mere sixty-two minutes, *The Devil Thumbs a Ride* purrs along pretty nicely until the car-crash climax, which is bungled because RKO had no money, no time, or no stock footage to do it properly. Instead, the camera holds on a police car while the one that's being pursued crashes *offscreen*, with an over-dubbed sound effect of squealing tires and smashing glass. What just happened? Whatever it was, maybe it was Steve's idea.

Well, gee, Steve, I guess that's an okay way to handle it, sure.

Made for Each Other

Barely nine weeks after the February 20, 1947, release of *The Devil Thumbs a Ride*, Lawrence Tierney was back for more bad mischief, in Robert Wise's *Born to Kill* (1947). This is probably RKO's most unrelentingly grim noir thriller, with a dark plot motivated by the greed, deceit, and violence of its two protagonists.

But if your disposition is steely, *Born to Kill* is also a perverse pleasure.

While in Reno to fulfill residency requirements for a divorce, Helen Brent (Claire Trevor) catches the eye of handsome, broad-shouldered Sam Wild (Tierney). Although Helen is intrigued by this preternaturally self-confident fellow, she keeps her distance because she's engaged to a wealthy San Franciscan (Phillip Terry) who will give her all the material things she longs for. When Sam cleverly courts and marries Helen's wealthy foster sister, Georgia (Audrey Long), he guarantees his proximity to Helen. The two begin a secret romance, but the whole deal explodes, messily, because of Sam's insane jealousy. And we mean *insane*.

Early in the story, Helen discovers the bodies of a man and woman. She doesn't know Sam is the culprit, but she doesn't flinch at the sight of death, either—even though the young female victim was an acquaintance. Helen just wants to get back to San Francisco without any fuss. This peculiar, self-serving reaction is our first clue that Helen isn't quite right in the head, either.

Why did Sam commit double murder? Because the young woman, Laury (vivacious Isabel Jewell), dated another guy after she'd dated Sam. That's all.

Back at home, Sam's friend, Mart (Elisha Cook Jr., in one of his best-ever roles), is exasperated because this sort of thing has apparently happened before.

MART
You just can't go around *killin'* people! It just ain't feasible!

SAM (angrily)
Why isn't it?

Case File: Claire Trevor (1910–2000)

The sly intelligence in Claire Trevor's eyes and the firm set to her mouth suggest that she's to be taken seriously in the world of noir. Although for much of her career a B-picture actress and never a major star, Trevor nevertheless became popular and respected. She even won the best supporting actress Oscar, for *Stagecoach* in 1939; worked continually through 1967; and then returned for another burst of film and TV activity during 1982–87.

Claire Trevor had some Broadway experience before getting into the movies in 1931. She made an unforgettable impression as Humphrey Bogart's pathetically dissolute, tubercular ex-girlfriend in 1937's *Dead End*, a superb social-problem melodrama. By the 1940s, Trevor was a busy leading lady with the chops of an accomplished character actress. She appeared in a variety of films, including a lot of noir treasures: *Street of Chance*; *Murder, My Sweet*; *Johnny Angel*; *Crack-Up*; *Born to Kill* (in which she doesn't take any guff from Lawrence Tierney); *Raw Deal*; and *Hoodlum Empire*.

Trevor is also fondly remembered for her work in the fine quasi-noir *Key Largo* (in which she's at odds with Edward G. Robinson), *The High and the Mighty*, and a late King Vidor project, *Man Without a Star*. In 1959 Trevor was a lively Ma Barker in the "Ma Barker and Her Boys" episode of *The Untouchables*.

Mart has established himself as Sam's protector, which puts him at odds with a bleary Reno landlady named Mrs. Kraft (Esther Howard), who has hired a two-bit private detective (Walter Slezak) to look into the death of her friend Laury. In a spooky sequence that's strikingly well staged by Wise and cinematographer Robert de Grasse, Mart takes Mrs. Kraft on a late-night drive to examine some nonexistent evidence. At a dark, windswept crossroads surrounded by dunes, Mart tries to knife the old lady but is knocked on his ass when she head-butts his stomach and sticks his leg with a hat pin. Just as Mart recovers from these indignities, Sam shows up and kills his pal because he's wrongly assumed that Mart is chasing after Helen.

The terror in Mrs. Kraft's face and eyes as all of this is going on captures our fright of physical harm and death with the sort of brute power that B films often summon with considerably more effectiveness than A pictures. Liberated from the need to be circumspect or "respectable," Wise and scripters Eve Greene and Richard Macaulay (adapting James Gunn's 1942 novel *Deadlier than the Male*) were free to go for the jugular.

There's more visceral horror later, when Helen pays the old lady a visit to chat about the wisdom of engaging a private detective.

MRS. KRAFT
Are you trying to scare me?

HELEN (coolly)
I'm just trying to warn you. Perhaps you don't realize—it's painful being killed. A piece of metal sliding its way into your heart or a bullet tearing through your skin, crashing into a bone. It takes a while to die, too. Sometimes a very *long* while.

MRS. KRAFT
But I don't want to die!

HELEN
I tell you, you will!

MRS. KRAFT (with loathing)
...I wouldn't trade places with you if they sliced me into little pieces!

HELEN (glaring)
Do you want to live or die?

MRS. KRAFT (rising from her chair and then falling back, weeping)
Laury! Laury, I've failed you!

Robert Wise came to *Born to Kill* just a handful of years after fruitful associations with Orson Welles (as an editor) and producer Val Lewton (as a director). He already had a sure command of the medium and an awareness of how to sting an audience. Heavy use of medium and close-up two-shots subliminally suggests the intimate nature of Sam's brand of mayhem: strangulation, beating, stabbing, bludgeoning. As *Born to Kill* plays out, you feel increasingly threatened.

Lawrence Tierney, a real-life Hollywood brawler, is a hearty presence as Sam, skating on the edge of parody but capturing the creepiness of a completely uninhibited psychopath. Claire Trevor, her hair a bit darker than usual, seems to have had fun playing Helen, a practiced, fiendish manipulator. She and Sam were made for each other.

May they cohabit happily in hell.

Squealers and Squirts

Sam of *Born to Kill* enjoys murder, but he really isn't very disciplined about it. His violence serves no larger purpose than to satisfy the impulse of angry self-gratification. Paradoxically, the mad killer of Henry Hathaway's *Kiss of Death* (1947), although more cartoonish than Sam, is considerably more "real." Tommy Udo, one of noir's greatest inventions, kills because he sees the big picture.

Although not the central figure of *Kiss of Death*, the giggling and sadistic Udo (Richard Widmark) gives the film its poisoned center and exemplifies the twisted morality that sometimes motivates professional criminals. Udo is upset because a longtime heist man named Nick Bianco (Victor Mature) has turned state's evidence in order not to spend years in prison, separated from his second wife, Nettie (Coleen Gray), and two young daughters. Udo hates "squealers" even more than he loathes "squirts," and he's particularly upset because he had imagined that he and Nick were "pals." Perpetually agitated and hyperactive, and marked by sunken eyes, death's-head features, and an indignant, piping voice, Udo fancies himself an exemplar of the criminal code that says *You never rat out a pal.* Udo feels obligated to exact revenge. Police records will say that Nick is no less a professional criminal than Udo, but the difference between them is soul. Udo doesn't have one.

A pragmatic, fair-minded assistant DA named D'Angelo (Brian Donlevy) is keen to put the screws to Udo, a three-time loser who is a known killer. If Udo is busted for any felony at all—such as simply *carrying* a gun—he goes away for life. Nick's mandate is to report infractions to D'Angelo, but when Udo explicitly threatens Nick's family, Nick feels forced to risk his life in order to literally put a gun in Udo's hand. He phones D'Angelo and tells him he'd better show up with the cops in exactly two minutes. If Nick plays it right, Udo will make the biggest mistake of his life.

Shot on location in Queens and elsewhere in New York by director Henry Hathaway and cinematographer Norbert Brodine, *Kiss of Death* has an air of documentary authority. Office buildings, restaurants, walk-up apartments, the train station, a boxing arena, traffic-choked streets, even Sing Sing—they're all real. The light-and-dark patterns of nighttime sequences are skillfully lit by Brodine to suggest a natural light that's more piquant than the real thing but no less real (we imagine) than what we would see for ourselves on those same

An uncharacteristically quiet interlude in *Kiss of Death* (1947), as psychotic hood Tommy Udo (Richard Widmark, left) treats new pal Nick Bianco (Victor Mature) to a night of revelry at a high-class bordello. Soon, though, Nick will give evidence against Udo, arousing a frothing murderousness that might consume Nick's whole world.

locations. The sound quality during some interior sequences is agreeably hollow and lets us imagine that we're listening in on things we're not really supposed to hear. Because the crackling script by Ben Hecht and Charles Lederer immerses us in the criminal milieu and mind, blending docudrama with crime a full seven months before *The Naked City*. *Kiss of Death* (and 20th Century-Fox) took noir in a new direction.

Widmark, fresh from Broadway and radio experience, is electric and queerly intimidating. A lover of black shirts, white ties, and enormous, padded overcoats, Udo makes a banty-rooster kind of first impression, but when he shoves a help-less middle-aged woman—wheelchair and all—down a steep flight of stairs, we're prepared not to underestimate him. His gleeful verbal and physical abuse of others and the mad glitter in his eyes suggest that he's not simply a dangerous adversary but a potentially unbeatable one.

Part of the shock of all this is that Udo looks like he can't weigh more than 145 pounds soaking wet; Nick, by way of contrast, is burly and muscular, seem-ing to have been chiseled from Renaissance stone. And yet the two seem evenly matched. Victor Mature, an indelible screen presence and a far more nuanced actor than people realize, embodies the humanity that the film must have if Nick's past is going to be satisfyingly accounted for, and if Udo is to be more than a grotesque.

The wheelchair sequence has justifiably become movie folklore. Other par-ticularly effective set pieces include Nick's silent anguish in an impossibly slow elevator after he's pulled a heist; a spontaneous display of joyful ardor between Nick and Nettie in their kitchen; and a circumspect but nevertheless very bold scene in which Udo happily treats Nick to a first-class whorehouse.

Coleen Gray, as Nettie, the guileless, intensely loving young woman who has adored Nick since childhood, is a revelation in her first notable role (two of her previous parts were uncredited bits, and a third ended up on the cutting-room

Case File: Ben Hecht (1894–1964)

A great newspaper reporter and columnist, Ben Hecht wowed Broadway with *The Front Page*, the 1928 seriocomedy he cowrote with Charles MacArthur. Hecht's heroic alter ego, reporter Hildy Johnson, has the story of the year stumble into his lap, and then must figure out how to keep an innocent man from the gallows and shield him from corrupt lawmen, politicians, and publishers.

The play's jaded, cynical tone and wisecracking dialogue helped define popular writ-ing of the 1930s and gave Hecht and MacArthur the juice needed to go to Hollywood, where they wrote original scripts and worked, without credit, as script doctors on many major pictures.

Hecht claimed to have no respect at all for Hollywood, but he was happy to accept the industry's money—and the fact is that he did a lot of very good work in the movies. His noir scripts include *Gilda* (uncredited), *Notorious*, *Kiss of Death*, *Ride the Pink Horse*, *Where the Sidewalk Ends*, *Strangers on a Train* (uncredited), and *Angel Face*.

floor). In too many genre films, the "wife" role is a throwaway, but Nettie is formed with pathos and insight and played by Gray with such quiet fervor that you can't imagine the film without her.

The final moments of *Kiss of Death* were later appropriated by writer Steve Fisher and producer-director John H. Auer for use in an occasionally atmospheric but generally inept Republic noir called *Hell's Half Acre* (1954). In it, a former Honolulu gang boss (Wendell Corey) goads a murderous associate (Philip Ahn) into shooting him, so that waiting cops can make the collar.

The Boiling Point

A key preoccupation of Richard Brooks's 1945 novel *The Brick Foxhole* is that when men are engaged in military duty, trained to fight, and then have no opportunity to do so, their latent aggressiveness might be inappropriately expressed in places other than the battlefield. The novel creates a vivid portrait of Jeff Mitchell, a Marine in a stateside propaganda unit who becomes furious after coming to believe (on poor evidence) that his wife has cheated in him. So virulent is his rage that others in his unit are "infected." When a homosexual civilian is murdered, the unhappy husband, now vanished, becomes the chief suspect. But Mitchell has killed no one. His best friend tries to get to him before the police.

RKO producer Adrian Scott purchased *The Brick Foxhole* and gave it to director Edward Dmytryk, who filmed it as *Crossfire* (1947), a "message" noir of intelligent, unpleasant power. Mindful of moviegoers' tolerances, and eager to avoid time-wasting conflict with the Breen Office, Scott and screenwriter John Paxton scuttled the adultery angle and focused on a Jewish, rather than homosexual, victim. In the film, Mitchell (George Cooper) is a mild man with no hate—only an incomplete, boozy memory of what happened after he accompanied two GI pals, Floyd (Steve Brodie) and Montgomery (Robert Ryan), to the apartment of a civilian named Samuels (Sam Levene). Samuels happens to be Jewish, and during a flashback just thirty minutes into the film, he's being roughed up by Montgomery and Floyd as Mitch wobbles from the apartment. The dramatic tension of *Crossfire* doesn't relate to the identity of the killer—we know that Montgomery is the culprit—but to how long the police will buy Montgomery's "cooperative" act as they search for Mitch.

Police captain Finlay (Robert Young) has no real reason to believe Mitch is the killer. However, Finlay becomes very interested in Montgomery, who periodically spices his helpfulness with non-sequitur invocations of "Jewboy." Although not explicitly stated, it's probable that Montgomery, like Mitchell and the others in his unit, never saw combat. In the lingo of Psych 101, Montgomery is overcompensating. (Robert Ryan never saw action, either. The Marines recognized his stateside value and shaped him into a drill instructor. The actor hated war but apparently had no difficulty understanding Montgomery's demented frustration.)

The narrative eventually splits into four branches: Finlay's investigation of the murder; Montgomery's evolving scheme to cover himself (which includes his murder of his pal Floyd); Mitch's aimless, late-night wanderings through the city; and the search for Mitch undertaken by his even-tempered friend Keeley (Robert Mitchum). As these characters interact, and offer and interpret their own versions of the truth, we become increasingly absorbed in Montgomery and the sorry consequences of hate.

Edward Dmytryk grasped the "danger" of Ryan's presence as well as anybody. When Montgomery faces a guileless GI (William Phipps) who has pissed him off, and waits while the kid stoops to retrieve something he's dropped, J. Roy Hunt's camera is positioned somewhere near Ryan's knees, shooting up on his face at an angle so unflattering and extreme that Montgomery looks like a glowering cannibal god. We expect his knee to come up, or his fist to come down, or both. Neither of those things happens, but the point of the sequence is that they could have.

Robert Ryan read *The Brick Foxhole* and later met Richard Brooks at Camp Pendleton (near San Clemente, California) while waiting to be mustered out of the Marines. Ryan told Brooks he wanted to play the killer if the book were ever sold to the movies. When the role came Ryan's way, he handled it superbly. Montgomery is smooth with the authorities, quick-thinking, and skillful at hiding in plain sight. But when he feels no need to put up a façade, Montgomery is inevitably on edge, like an angry man doing a fast dance on a razor. So convincing is the performance that the course of Ryan's career was altered: His interpretation of Montgomery propelled him to lifelong stardom but proscribed the breadth of his career. Ryan would remain a top-billed personality but an intimidating one, and frequently a heavy. Costars Robert Young and Robert Mitchum moved easily between light and serious roles, but Ryan was locked into a dark persona early on.

Every performance in *Crossfire* is insightful and shrewdly underplayed, though some roles, like Robert Mitchum's Keeley and Sam Levene's Samuels, are underwritten. In the key role of Captain Finlay, Robert Young displays the intelligence and relaxed charisma that characterize his best work. Gloria Grahame and Paul Kelly express weary dignity as an unhappily married couple living on life's margins, and small-part actor George Cooper, in an important opportunity as Mitchell, is earnest and appealing. Jacqueline White, who later costarred in *The Narrow Margin* (1952; see Chapter 4), is a warm presence as Mitchell's concerned wife.

Hunt's cinematography is moody in the RKO house style (he did exemplary work on Val Lewton's 1943 thriller *I Walked with a Zombie*), with effective use of shadow and some clever, knife-edged double exposure suggesting the drunkenness that prevents Mitchell from being a reliable witness. The film's opening sequence, the murder of Samuels, is a harshly lit agitation of moving legs, kicked-over lamps, and boiling shadows.

If there's a problem with *Crossfire*, it's that Captain Finlay "explains" bigotry to assorted GIs in a didactic and overlong monologue predicated on the indignities suffered by Finlay's Irish ancestors. The sequence doesn't play well today, though it may have been necessary in 1947, when the USA was only just coming out of its provincialism. A side trip into social studies couldn't have hurt.

Three's a Crowd

In Jean Negulesco's *Road House* (1948), a long-established marriage is threatened by the spouses' reactions to a seductive stranger. Passions build until revenge and finally madness control events. This psycho-emotional terrain is eminently familiar to devotees of noir. The fascinating aspect of *Road House* is that, although the longtime marriage is very real, it is noted in no book nor consecrated by any church. The partners are men, and they're not even consciously aware of being married. And neither, obviously, was Hollywood's regulatory Breen Office, which would never have allowed the sexual dynamics of *Road House*—that is, if the office had been sharp enough to perceive them.

The volatile but loving couple is comprised of Paul (Cornel Wilde) and Jefty (Richard Widmark). The two have been together since boyhood, and now, in their early thirties, Jefty owns and operates Jefty's Road House, a stunningly good-looking mid-century-modern nightclub/restaurant/bowling center located on the woodsy outskirts of a small town just fifteen miles from the Canadian border. Paul is the place's very competent live-in manager, whose work ethic and precision are major reasons why the place prospers.

Jefty is the "husband." He's handsome in an intense, unorthodox way—a sharp dresser with a taste for good times and dalliances with the succession of dames he brings into the club as singers, to Paul's continual disapproval. Jefty likes to shoot, hunt, and carouse with his pals and leaves the roadhouse for long periods. He's successful but not very responsible. (Consider the little-boy quality of his name.) Fortunately, Jefty has Pete to keep the house in order.

Pete regards the roadhouse with great seriousness. After all, the place is his home. With the help of a trusted cashier, Susie (Celeste Holm), Pete maintains precise, accurate books. He knows how much money comes into the place and how it goes out. Whenever Jefty expresses a desire to "spruce the place up a little" with fresh paint or an expanded bowling area, it's up to Pete to figure out how to pay for it.

Like many wives who function mainly as homemakers, Pete is a fastidious, frequently fussy housekeeper. His upstairs office/apartment is spotless and very well organized, and he imposes similar order on the place's public areas. Pete's furious battle with an abusive, giant-size drunk (Louis Bacigalupi) has the psychological resonance of an indignant housewife chasing a pack of screaming kids from her living room. And not long after Jefty's latest songbird shows up, Pete is dismayed to see that she's in the habit of resting her cigarettes on the top edge of the piano, where they burn grooves into the wood.

Pete is mortified.

The singer is Lil (Ida Lupino, in her first freelance work after a seven-year association with Warner Bros.), a self-possessed dame with a sexy shape, a husky way with a song, and a lifetime of experience in her eyes. (In this, Lupino essentially plays the rootless, dangerous male figure typical of many melodramas.) Although Lupino was younger than Widmark and Wilde, Negulesco and cinematographer Joseph LaShelle took some care to subtly suggest that Lil is older than Jefty and Pete, emphasizing the hoarseness of her voice and a mask-like set to her features.

Because the marriage of Jefty and Pete is strictly subtext, both men are susceptible to Lil's considerable charms. In a bit of a genre turnabout, Lil doesn't actively pursue either man. In more traditional terms, she's not out to break up a marriage. She's taught herself to be independent and self-sufficient, qualities that allow her to quietly resist Jefty's cheerful but ceaseless courting. She just isn't interested. But as sometimes happens in life, and more frequently in movies, she's drawn to Pete, the man who initially mistrusts and rejects her. While Jefty is away on a hunting trip with the boys, Lil and Pete fall in love. There is no perfidy; it just happens.

As the third act approaches, the central questions of Edward Chodorov's crackling script are these: How will Lil and Pete tell Jefty about their romance, and how will Jefty react?

When *Road House* was released in September 1948, audiences had already seen Richard Widmark in his film debut, *Kiss of Death* (August 1947), and *The Street with No Name* (June 1948; see Chapter 4). *Road House* was the actor's third film (and third for 20th Century-Fox). He remained typed as a volatile psychopath. Part of the genius of *Road House* is that for two-thirds of the running time Jefty is an appealing fellow: upbeat, generous, amused and amusing. But when he decides to punish Pete and Lil, he lets the mask drop by framing Pete for robbing the club and then appealing to the judge to give Pete probation and assign him to Jefty's custody. The judge finds Jefty's offer commendably generous but warns Pete that if he makes a single slip, he'll be off to state prison for ten years.

Now Jefty has a puppeteer's complete control. He demands that Pete and Lil (and sometimes even Susie) go where he goes so that he can torment and belittle them, and restore his sense of self. He flashes the smile of a man who revels in causing the misery of his betrayers. He's the *ne plus ultra* of the archetypal betrayed husband.

At Jefty's well-appointed cabin deep in the woods (fulsomely shot on a gorgeous and ornate soundstage, complete with mist, water, towering trees, and the postproduction cries and thrips of night birds and insects), the court-ordered structure of the relationship collapses into a wild melee of fists, bullets, and pursuit. Drunk, giggling, and dangerously confident, Jefty's violent pathology bursts forth, and we're rewarded with the madness we've been waiting for.

When Pete momentarily gets the upper hand and batters Jefty's face, Jefty appears to crave the pain. His sobbing hint of a smile looks like gratitude. Despite his angry insanity, he still loves Pete and wants to be punished.

Via a good trick pulled off by Pete and clever, blood-freezing twists involving Lil and Susie, Jefty's impromptu reenactment of "The Most Dangerous Game" ends disastrously for him.

Pete's marriage is over. Maybe he'll enjoy better luck the second time around.

The Misery of Guilt, the Madness of Retribution

Even before the progressive Dore Schary was appointed production chief of MGM in 1949, the studio took steps to reverse the financial decline that had become critical by 1947. MGM's boss of bosses, New York–based Nicholas Schenck, retained studio head Louis B. Mayer—for the time being—but approved a shift into dramas that were grittier and more economically budgeted than had traditionally been encouraged by the studio. One of those pictures was Fred Zinnemann's Act of Violence (1948), a potent think piece that combines noir existentialism and visual cues with a subject that was anathema to the flag-waving Mayer: American soldiers' collusion with the enemy during World War II.

One of the leading citizens of a small California town somewhere outside Los Angeles is Frank Enley (Van Heflin), a handsome, affable builder who has been instrumental in pushing through a much-needed development of affordable new homes. The community respects him, and his wife, Edith (Janet Leigh), adores him.

One man has a different opinion. This is Joe Parkson (Robert Ryan), a lean, limping war vet who served as Enley's bombardier during Air Corps missions over Europe. Silent and spookily focused, Parkson arrives from out of town to stalk Frank. His presence makes Enley unreasonably paranoid (he won't call the police), frightens the hell out of Edith, and eventually forces a terrible truth into the open.

Before his final confrontation with Parkson, Enley feels he must unburden himself. He explains to Edith that he and Parkson were held in the same German POW camp. When rations were cut to almost nothing, Enley and the others began to starve. A desperate group that included Parkson dug an escape tunnel that Enley urged them to abandon because a similar attempt in the camp's British section ended with the deaths of all who participated. Undeterred, Parkson and the others continued with their plan. Desperate to save his buddies, Enley approached the camp's commandant, an SS colonel, and revealed the tunnel's existence after getting an assurance that the would-be escapees would not be harmed.

When Parkson and his companions emerged from the tunnel days later, the Germans didn't fire a shot. Instead, they set upon the Americans with bayonets and dogs. Parkson escaped with his life, but ten others were killed in the slaughter.

Visibly agitated on the back stairs of a Los Angeles hotel where Edith has found him, Enley finally drops his carefully cultivated pretense:

> ENLEY *(miserably)*
> I hadn't done it just to save their lives. I talked myself into
> believing it, that he'd keep his word. But in my guts from the
> start I think I knew he wouldn't. Maybe I didn't even care.
> They were dead and I was eating, and maybe that's all I did it
> for, to save *one* man, me.
> [pause] There were six widows, ten men dead, and I couldn't
> even stop eating.
>
> EDITH [sobs]
>
> ENLEY
> Go on. Go on home. You don't have to say anything.

Robert L. Richards wrote the screenplay, adapting a story by Collier Young. Four moral issues drive events: the wrongness of self-interest when others are harmed; the trap of dishonest rationalization; the justification and efficacy of revenge; and the limits of self-forgiveness and the forgiveness of others. Frank's transgression has driven him into a permanent state of denial, and Parkson exists somewhere very near madness. The film's pretitle sequence, in which Parkson hefts a government-issue .45, slams the clip home, and methodically inspects the breech, suggests that he's hardly a man at all but a killing machine. He's propelled by the certitude that only Enley's death will restore some sense of justice to the world.

Edith, a very young woman apparently full of illusions, struggles to understand what her husband has done, and what her reaction should be. And Parkson, at a critical moment, must decide whether he'll dispense vengeance or mercy.

A narrative detour to LA's Skid Row, where Enley meets a variety of highly symbolic characters, doesn't ring true but does set up a notion that helps shape the climax: For $10,000, a shifty thug (Berry Kroeger) will assassinate Parkson. When the two antagonists and the inept hired killer come together at a train station (where journeys begin and end), somebody shouts a warning, guns go off, and a careening car crashes and bursts into flames. Some sort of justice has been served, but the survivors don't seem very happy about it.

Fred Zinnemann suggests the characters' inner agitation with thoughtful blocking that encouraged the actors to move restlessly in small spaces and to frequently address each other obliquely rather than face to face. Much of the narrative is about illusions that will be shattered if characters peer too directly at one another, so the sense of physical avoidance is very strong. (A similarly handled marriage of theme and bodily movement is apparent in a later Zinnemann picture, *High Noon* [1951].)

In the early stages of *Act of Violence,* when the narrative focus is on Enley's tidy, leafy community, Robert Surtees's photography shimmers with sunlight and literal and figurative warmth. (The philosophical brightness is cleverly violated when Parkson delivers himself to Edith's door one sunny afternoon.) Later sequences unfold at night inside shadowed rooms with single sources of light and on deserted, rain-slick streets. One set piece, Enley's shrieking dash through an empty, oddly lighted highway tunnel, is straight out of Freudian nightmare. Other key sequences have sharp, high-contrast lighting that gives brilliant whites, deep blacks, and a full range of grays.

So strong are the film's successful elements that Bronislau Kaper's thoughtful score is used sparingly, and for great stretches is not heard at all. We don't need musical cues to tell us how to feel because the boundaries of the human heart and mind—all the certitude and ambiguity—are there in front of us, plain to see and consider.

"What do you do when you get excited?"

Follow Me Quietly (1949), an early RKO credit for director Richard Fleischer, has no pretensions. It runs a mere fifty-nine minutes and is headlined by William Lundigan and Dorothy Patrick, appealing but minor actors who seldom enjoyed leading roles. Sets, though handsomely finished, are small; the picture doesn't open up visually until the "chase" climax. The movie was intended as bottom-of-the-bill product, tossed off quickly to fill time in theaters owned by the studio. And yet *Follow Me Quietly* is a crowd-pleaser that rises to a special weirdness.

The city is terrorized by a strangulation murderer who kills only when it rains. The murderer sends taunting notes to the police and signs them "The Judge." Detective Lt. Harry Grant (Lundigan) leads the investigation and picks up an unwanted partner, a smart and perky true-crime writer named Ann Gorman (Patrick). The Judge is an arrogantly confident killer who has left shoe prints, hair, fibers, a hat, cigarette butts, and other physical evidence at the scenes of his crimes. Working with this material, his imagination in high gear, Grant creates a full-sized dummy that accurately recreates The Judge in all aspects save the most important: the face. The dummy is reproduced on countless photographs handed out to cops, and the manhunt begins in earnest.

Grant goes about his job as efficiently as he knows how. He's frustrated by The Judge's elusiveness but suffers none of the torment or obsession that dog many noir heroes. His brainstorm about creating a dummy is plainly ridiculous, but we swallow it precisely *because* Grant has no neuroses. The dummy isn't a symptom of mental imbalance—it's just the best idea Grant can come up with. (As his boss says, "Oh, well, wouldn't hurt to try.")

The Ann Gorman character is an evolution of the brassy "news hen" career girl played many times by Glenda Farrell at Warner Bros. during the 1930s. In a nod to more modern sensibilities, though, Ann doesn't work for a newspaper but for a lurid magazine called *Four Star Crime.* Such magazines were coming into their own in 1949, to satisfy the jaded tastes of young veterans of World War II. (Just a year after the release of *Follow Me Quietly,* American periodical publishing exploded with horror comics, another medium favored by young men and one in which The Judge would have been right at home.)

Although referenced with just a few lines of tossed-off dialogue, the relationship of crime coverage to the commission of crime is a subtext. Significantly, The Judge buys used copies of *Four Star Crime* at a neighborhood bookstore, and keeps a shelf in his simple room filled with books about crime and criminal psychosis. According to the simplistic shorthand of facile cause-and-effect, The Judge has been corrupted by what he reads.

But what about the killer's affinity for rain? The quirk is never explained.

Follow Me Quietly came early in Richard Fleischer's career and is obviously the work of a young director in love with visual storytelling. When Grant exclaims that he'd give anything to see The Judge's face, Lundigan aggressively strides to the camera until *his* face fills the screen. A bit later, when the dummy Judge is on display (with its back turned) for the entire detective squad, Grant asks, "What do you do when you get excited?" The PA system reverberates with a hollow voice that answers, "I *kill!*" At that, the camera rapidly dollies in as the dummy (somehow) wheels around to confront the lens, its horrid blank face caught at enormous size in a startling freeze frame.

The climactic sequence, in which Grant chases The Judge (played by mournful-looking character actor Edwin Max) along the ladders, pipes, and catwalks of a refinery, is exciting, with dramatic, varied coverage by Fleischer and sharply timed cuts by editor Elmo Williams. The sequence is emotionally liberating—at last, the fiend has been flushed out! The fact that the killer is a mousy little guy disappoints some viewers but is in line with a recurring tenet of noir: The killer might be beside you, quiet and unassuming but deadly beyond your imagination.

A Gangster for the Atomic Age

More than a dozen people meet violent deaths in Raoul Walsh's *White Heat* (1949), a clever and pugnacious combination of police procedural and noir that gives a great star, James Cagney, one of his signature roles. Warner Bros. had abandoned the gangster genre about ten years before, but postwar, with increased artistic freedom and deeper characterizations possible because of the public's newly sophisticated mindset, Warner was willing to revive the genre, with a twist. This time, the outlaw protagonist wouldn't simply be amoral; he'd be insane.

Heavier in the face and thicker in the body than in 1939, the fiftyish Cagney brought literal weight to the role of the highly skilled heist man Cody Jarrett, whose father died in an insane asylum. The film opens with a brazen daylight robbery of a payroll train and then develops into a cat-and-mouse thriller, as

Cody outthinks the feds, violently puts down dissension in his own ranks, and accepts Vic Pardo (Edmond O'Brien), a new member of the group, as if Pardo were a little brother, or a son. (Family is very important to Cody.) But Cody's hold on reality is tenuous. He has a psychopathic attachment to his bloodless mother (Margaret Wycherly), who lives only for her son. When Ma is killed, Cody begins to slide over the edge, and he snaps completely when he discovers that his wife, Verna (Virginia Mayo), has cheated on him *and* that Pardo is a federal agent. Cody's simulacrum of family has fallen to pieces, and now he's alone and unloved. In a final spasm of violence at a gas refinery that was to be the gang's greatest heist, Cody wildly sprays bullets, igniting enormous tanks beneath him. In what has become movie folklore, Jarret echoes his mother by shouting, "Made it, Ma! Top of the world!" An instant later, the tanks explode, blowing Jarret to bits.

White Heat can be discussed from two perspectives: as exemplary film craft and as a study of perverse psychosis. On both counts, the picture is matchless. It was directed by Raoul Walsh, a longtime mainstay of the Warner Bros. lot who was responsible for numerous triumphs of the 1930s and '40s: *The Roaring Twenties, They Drive by Night, High Sierra, They Died with Their Boots On, Strawberry Blonde, Desperate Journey, Gentleman Jim,* and *Objective Burma.* A rough-and-tumble, larger-than-life figure of huge talent, Walsh had few real peers. He was an auteur in the physical rather than philosophical sense. He was compelled to make actors and events *move,* as if he were crouched behind his cast, his crew, and the audience, irresistibly pushing forward. You don't simply watch a Walsh picture, you surrender and let it carry you along.

Ivan Goff and Ben Roberts's screenplay (from a story by Virginia Kellogg) gave Walsh and cast ample opportunity for lively set pieces: the carefully executed train robbery that's marred by a couple of impromptu murders and an unexpected blast of steam that scalds the face of one of the gang; the great comfort Cody finds when he sits on Ma's lap; a documentary-like study of a police tail on Ma Jarrett's car; Cody's brazen escape from the penitentiary; and his reckoning with the sluttish Verna and the gang's scheming number two, Big Ed (Steve Cochran).

The complex preparation and execution of the gas-refinery holdup, which places the gang inside an empty tanker truck à la the Trojan horse, is detailed and fascinating. Police-procedural elements come to the fore, because the truck carries a radio transmitter that allows the feds to track the truck to its final destination.

Cody's offhanded ventilation of a car trunk (via .45 automatic) that holds a punk who'd given him a hard time in prison is fondly recalled, but few sequences in film history have the eye-opening impact of Cody's violently psychotic reaction during prison mess when relayed whispers inform him that Ma is dead. Cagney uses his dancer's body brilliantly here, as Walsh wisely avoids bravura camerawork that might distract from his star. Even before Cody is finally restrained and snugged into a strait-jacket, we know that he's hopelessly, dangerously mad.

Whether or not *White Heat* is among the greatest films ever made is debatable (this writer votes in the affirmative). What is indisputable is that Cagney, one of the screen's imperishable personalities, summoned a performance that may be unrivaled for conviction, frightfulness, and sheer manic energy.

A Furious Race to the Grave

White Heat was a considerable box-office hit that excited audiences. Although Cagney had returned to the gangster genre reluctantly, he appreciated the picture's commercial success, particularly because the independent film company he owned with his brother, William Cagney Productions, was struggling to recover from losses incurred by a 1948 flop called *The Time of Your Life*. Because of the popularity of *White Heat*, Warner Bros. was prepared to work with Cagney Productions on any project that had the feel of the earlier film. That willingness was the genesis of *Kiss Tomorrow Goodbye* (1950), in which Cagney is Ralph Cotter, an articulate, small-time heist man with an inflated sense of his own cleverness. Whether interacting with members of his gang or abusing the public, Cotter displays unquenchable recklessness and frightening sadism. He isn't as nuts as Cody Jarrett, but he's definitely unbalanced, and audiences anticipate his inevitable comeuppance.

Although Cotter gives the story its motive power, the moral focus is Holiday (Barbara Payton), who lost her brother in a jailbreak that freed Cotter. She has no real interest in Cotter except as somebody who was present when guards shot the kid dead in a muddy potato field. Holiday has no criminal record—yet. But she was present at the periphery of the break, firing a revolver and taking out a guard. Now she's a murderer.

She's also blonde and very good looking, which encourages Cotter to want her as his girl. She resists but finally gives in, not because she has warm feelings for Cotter (who's about twice her age) but because she's frightened. "I'm so alone!" she wails in Cotter's arms. "I'm so alone!"

The fact that Cotter exploits the kid's grief to shack up with her marks him as the worst sort of opportunist. Naturally, we assume that the two are having sex, and we see for ourselves that Holiday keeps house for him and makes his sandwiches. Soon, she thinks she loves him.

Cotter knocks over a supermarket payroll with help from a local joker called Jinx (Steve Brodie), only to be shaken down by a crooked police inspector named Webber (Ward Bond). Cotter consults an unsavory attorney called Cherokee Mandon (slyly played by Luther Adler) and blackmails Webber with a secret recording made during their second meeting. While all of this is going on, Cotter romances and marries Margaret Dobson (Helena Carter), the daughter of the wealthiest and most powerful man in the state—so that he can meekly agree to her father's demand for an annulment, win the old guy over, and profitably remain in Margaret's life.

Cotter murders three runners who work for a local crime boss, and although Webber is handed twenty large when the job is over, he's furious because the victim is supposed to be protected against things like this. But with the incriminating recording in hand, Cotter and Webber are partners, and they're going to stay partners.

Cotter is clever, but Holiday eventually discovers his relationship with Margaret. Worse, she learns what we see for ourselves early in the film: Cotter executed the hapless brother (Neville Brand) during the break, after the kid was wounded. During a climax that Cagney plays with maniacal energy, Holiday manufactures her own brand of justice.

The Ralph Cotter of Horace McCoy's first-person novel is a Phi Beta Kappa with a high-flown vocabulary and a fondness for classical allusion. Director Gordon Douglas and scripter Harry Brown toned that down and added a clever framing device in which Holiday and six more defendants are on trial simultaneously for murder and other crimes committed during their association with Cotter. Most of the story unfolds in flashback.

Except for a bravura, dolly-in close-up of Webber's shadowed face as Cotter plays the incriminating recording, *Kiss Tomorrow Goodbye* (which was shot by

Sociopathic heist man Ralph Cotter (James Cagney) handles lonely, unfulfilled Holiday (Barbara Payton) with cynical confidence in *Kiss Tomorrow Goodbye* (1950). But Cotter makes a misstep when his ambition overrules caution and he takes up with another woman.

J. Peverell Marley) has few of the visual stylistics of noir. The film's power comes from Douglas's confident, straightforward direction and Cagney's interpretation of incipient, reckless madness. In the book, Cotter is scared to death when the thrill-seeking Margaret Dobson takes him for a midnight drive at one hundred miles per hour. In the film, Margaret is no less wild, but as she accelerates the convertible to nearly a hundred, Cotter grins weirdly and mashes his foot atop hers, making the car go even faster.

Early in the story, Cotter beats the hell out of Mason (Rhys Williams), a cynical, club-footed garage owner who has bankrolled Cotter's escape and makes the mistake of telling Cotter, "You're stark, staring nuts!" During the supermarket job, Cotter pistol-whips the place's owner so ferociously that the man later dies; and at home, just to establish the chain of command, he brutally whips Holiday with a wet, rolled-up towel.

Former model Barbara Payton was a new Warner Bros./William Cagney Productions contract player who had just a year's experience and a few small film roles to her credit when she was tapped to play Holiday. Payton's performance as a woman who accepts brutality in order to be loved is vulnerable and heartrending. At the film's climax, when Holiday faces Cotter and her revolver clicks on an empty chamber, the profound, frightened surprise that transforms her face seems completely genuine. She's been unhappily surprised by life since she was born, and here's another surprise that might be fatal.

Barbara Payton had the looks and talent needed for stardom, but bad behavior quickly made her a darling of scandal magazines and a pariah in the picture business. Her film career ended in 1955. Just a dozen years later, beset by alcoholism, poverty, and a history of prostitution, Payton died. She was thirty-nine. Holiday's climactic monologue, delivered to Cotter, is eerily predictive of Payton's own fate:

HOLIDAY
You only said one true thing in your life. And that was when you said you were going away tonight. And you are. Three miles out of town and six feet down. All alone. With nobody to lie to. And you can kiss tomorrow goodbye.

Smother Love

Nicholas Ray's *In a Lonely Place* (1950) is a grim portrait of Dixon Steele (Humphrey Bogart), a longtime Hollywood screenwriter whose unpleasant irascibility and propensity to hit people—women included—have exiled his career to the Phantom Zone. Thanks to some industrious groveling by his agent, Mel (Art Smith), Dix has been awarded the assignment to adapt a crummy best seller for the screen. It's clear that this plum job may be his last chance to jump back into the big time.

He's inspired in this new assignment because of his feelings for his new lover, Laurel Gray (Gloria Grahame), a self-possessed blonde who lives in the apartment across the garden courtyard. On very short acquaintance, because she "likes his face," Laurel provides Dix with an alibi for murder. The victim is a hat-check girl named Mildred Atkinson (Martha Stewart), a brainless sweetheart whom Dix takes home with him one night because she's offered to "tell him" the novel he's so loath to read. Because Mildred dies later that night (we do not see the crime), Dix is a natural suspect. He is closely questioned and then released. As the police investigation continues, Dix exhibits his violent dark side, beating a motorist and nearly killing him with a rock as Laurel looks on; driving like a maniac; knocking Mel's glasses from his face with a cruel backhand swipe in a crowded restaurant; and encouraging married friends to physically reenact Mildred's strangulation. (The down-to-earth husband [Frank Lovejoy] is an old Army buddy *and* one of the detectives assigned to the Atkinson case.) Through all of this, neither Dix's gaze nor his hands ever waver or shake. He's preternaturally calm.

After awhile, Dix's paranoiac gaze fixes on his muse, Laurel. He smothers her with an engagement ring and talk of a new house. He's in a rush to be loved, but Laurel doesn't want to move so fast. Later, Dix bursts into her apartment, repeatedly answers her phone, and puts his hands around her throat. Finally put off because she's afraid, and because she realizes she doesn't know Dix at all, Laurel ends the relationship. For the first time, Dix's hands tremble with fear.

In a Lonely Place was produced for Columbia by Bogart's own company, Santana. The fifty-year-old actor was at the top of his game and eager to take professional (and box-office) risks to explore characters that would allow him to expand on his "principled loner" persona. Dix Steele is indeed an elaboration of the "loner" component of the Bogart myth but has nothing in the way of principles to recommend him other than a self-centered desire to do work of substance. In every other aspect, Dix is dangerously unbalanced. If not a murderer, he has the inclination to be one. He may have come close to killing people in the past; we can't be sure. Dix is a vivid and reasonably complex figure but an enormously unsympathetic one, too.

For Gloria Grahame—at this time Mrs. Nicholas Ray but separated from her husband—the film was an important step up and an acknowledgment that Grahame had qualities special enough to do a picture with Bogart and match him, moment for moment. As scripted (and frequently revised) by Andrew Solt, Laurel is bright and pleasant, but the fact that she lives well in Beverly Hills, with nothing more on her résumé than some bits in B pictures, seems not to arouse Dix's curiosity. During a peculiar sequence that puts Laurel naked on her stomach beneath a thin sheet, her muscled, frankly butch masseuse, Martha (Gloria Mitchell), warns that Dix has a bad history. The relationship with him isn't going to be "as easy to get out of as it was with Mr. Baker"—the last man to have kept her. By shooting up on Laurel's face so that Martha looms very tall behind her, Ray encourages us to wonder about the limits of Laurel's submissiveness and her definition of love.

Although very modern in its examination of a psychotic protagonist and a sexually ambiguous (or just adventurous) female lead, *In a Lonely Place* does display the relative inexperience of Nicholas Ray. Group Theatre alumnus (and later blacklist victim) Art Smith was encouraged, or allowed, to overplay as Mel, and a washed-up, proto-Barrymore drunk (Robert Warwick), who enunciates faux Shakespearean dialogue instead of real words, turns up much too frequently and becomes incredibly tiresome and ham-handed. Why is he part of the story? To show us the deleterious effects of Hollywood? Of booze? That nobody stays on top forever? We already know all that.

The Mildred Atkinson character, played with idiot charm by Martha Stewart, is a far more successful device. She exists not simply as somebody who will be murdered to propel the plot but as the embodiment of everything that Dix hates: ignorance, cheap sentimentality, inarticulateness, a brainless yearning for sophistication, subservience, and a general love of the tired and hackneyed. As such, Mildred is a hugely condescending creation—and it's up to individual viewers to determine whether the film condemns that sort of Hollywood arrogance, or whether Ray and Solt felt like congratulating themselves for their sophistication and were convinced that *In a Lonely Place* was high art.

The final shot of Dix, as he follows the course of a garden walkway made of geometrically laid stone squares, suggests a diagram and the predetermined course of events that Dix himself has set in motion. *In a Lonely Place* is a very good film with some brilliant elements. It's also precisely the sort of diagrammatically ironic melodrama that Mildred would have loved.

The Wrath of a Maniac

White Heat, Kiss Tomorrow Goodbye, and *In a Lonely Place* showcase veteran stars in successful career reinventions. Conversely, producer Hal Wallis designed *Dark City* (1950) as a presentation piece showcasing a charismatic, twenty-seven-year-old Broadway and TV actor named Charlton Heston. Although seldom discussed today, *Dark City* is justifiably notable as Heston's big-screen debut (he'd earlier appeared in a pair of ambitious amateur movies shot in 16 millimeter). *Dark City* also is mildly intriguing because it draws from *And Then There Were None* and other artificial who-will-die-next thrillers of the 1930s and early '40s, *and* offers a violent sort of plot twist that would become hugely popular in the 1980s and defines a great proportion of Hollywood melodrama to the present day.

In a smoky, harshly lit room in New York City, professional gambler Danny Haley (Heston) and his two-bit pals sucker out-of-towner Arthur Winant (Don DeFore) into an evening of rigged poker and relieve the poor schlub of a $5,000 cashier's check that belongs to his employer. For Danny and the others, it's a small, low-down victory with huge consequences. As they learn a day or two later, Winant returned to his hotel room, scribbled a note, and hanged himself.

Worse, the victim has a protective older brother who got to the body and the note before the cops. Now he's likely to want revenge.

The setup already has the ingredients for an engaging thriller, but scripters John Meredyth Lucas and Larry Marcus upped the ante with a couple more pieces of sobering news: The big brother (delicately named Sidney) is a psychopathic killer.

And nobody, apparently, knows what he looks like.

Let the retribution murders begin.

Today, you can't go to the movies without tripping over the psycho killers, but the notion was fairly novel in 1950—and no less contrived. In one set piece after another, Danny's pals are strangled and *then* hanged. In order that we're kept on the edge of our seats, we hardly have a clearer visualization of the brother than Danny does; all we see is a very large hand adorned with an onyx ring. Danny's best hope is to try to find Sidney before Sidney finds *him*.

Director William Dieterle made his name with prestige Warner Bros. projects of the 1930s, including *A Midsummer Night's Dream* and *Juarez,* as well as a whole slate of sober biopics: *The Story of Louis Pasteur, The Life of Emile Zola,* and *Dr. Ehrlich's Magic Bullet.* Postwar, Dieterle made *Portrait of Jennie* (1948) and the self-spoofing *Rope of Sand* (1949). He had some trouble with Hollywood Red-baiters but continued to work, displaying his outstanding technical competence on projects of gradually diminishing importance.

Dark City is as well crafted as its modest budget allowed (a lot of stage and process work hampers the illusion of reality) but is truly successful only in moments: the angry dismay of gambler Barney (Ed Begley) when wiseass Augie (Jack Webb) serves him milk in a dribble glass (a particularly eccentric and satisfying sequence); Augie's contemptuous treatment of the slow-witted gofer named Soldier (Harry Morgan); an explosively staged police raid on the gamblers' betting parlor; and the heartbreaking naïveté of Winant as his stack of chips dwindles to nothing. For the last, Dieterle and cinematographer Victor Milner shot very close on the actors' faces and hands, emphasizing the smallness of the card table and trapping us with them in the tightness of the room.

One character's nighttime investigation of strange noises has a jolting payoff; likewise Danny's visit to an apparently deserted motel room and his struggles during the film's climax.

Numerous insert shots of the onyx ring tell us that Sidney follows Danny all over the place and often positions himself mere feet away, without Danny ever noticing. That's a stretch because Sidney (as we see very late in the story) is played by 6'5" Mike Mazurki, who has "homicidal maniac" written all over him. (Mazurki is well recalled as the demented bruiser in *Murder, My Sweet*; see Chapter 3.) How much better it would have been if Sidney turned out to be an ordinary-looking guy, or even a shrimp! (Director James Whale made this kind of reversal work in *The Old Dark House* [1932], in which the violent maniac who escapes from a locked room is revealed to be a tiny, timid-seeming fellow.)

Danny's relationship with a nightclub singer (Lizabeth Scott) is intrusive (too many songs) and perfunctory, even though Scott is appealing and at her least mannered. Winant's widow (Viveca Lindfors), whom Danny contacts under false pretenses in hopes of getting a photograph of Sidney, has considerably more dramatic significance. Lindfors works with sincerity and quiet dignity, embodying the emptiness left after the premature death of a mate and providing a nice offset to young Heston's already-stolid screen persona. (Lindfors, in innocent collusion with the film's male cast members other than Heston, takes our young star to acting school and is at the center of the picture's most honest moments.) The widow's relationship with Danny builds nicely but then is allowed to peter out, which is disappointing.

The worst sin of *Dark City* is that Danny is let off the hook because he had no idea the poker game was rigged. This cynical guy who carries a gun, hangs out with a professional crew in an illegal enterprise, and says things like, "What's going on in the world stinks!" has no clue that his pals are taking unfair advantage of the mark that Danny delivered to them in the first place!

Danny's ignorance is a whopper, and so is the late-revealed fact that he's a graduate of Cornell. That explains his non-sequitur allusion to the River Styx but doesn't make him any more appealing. Regardless, Danny gets the girl, has his cake, eats it, and is one of those unaccountably lucky movie characters who meets a psycho and lives to tell the tale.

Like Two Animals in Heat

Gun Crazy (1950) is a triumph partly because its brilliant leading lady, Peggy Cummins, failed in Hollywood. A teenage film star in England, the Irish Cummins struck the fancy of 20th Century-Fox executive Darryl F. Zanuck, who cast her in the highly coveted title role in *Forever Amber*, Fox's "event" production for 1947. But after thirty-nine days of shooting, Zanuck was unhappy with the rushes. He halted production and Cummins was replaced by Linda Darnell. Cummins remained under contract to Fox and had the female leads in a pair of quality productions, *Escape* and *Green Grass of Wyoming* (both 1948), but her dismissal from *Amber* was a death blow to her Hollywood ambitions. *Gun Crazy*, which was independently produced by vending-machine magnates the King Brothers (Maurice, Frank, and Herman), was Peggy's final American picture.

Greeted as a retelling of the Bonnie and Clyde story, *Gun Crazy* differs in that its small-time criminal protagonists, Bart Tare (John Dall) and Annie Laurie Starr (Cummins), are doomed not by the poverty and ignorance that helped kill Bonnie and Clyde but by severe psychological failings. Both are articulate and bright; Bart, in particular, has not-unreasonable aspirations to middle-class American life. He also has a fetishistic attachment to guns that goes back—as we see in well-wrought flashbacks—to adolescence. He shoots purely for the love of it and because his incredible prowess makes him feel "like somebody." He kills only once—the victim is a baby chick shot by the young Bart—and he can't bring himself to kill again.

A whirlwind of sex, violence, and fetishism is central to Joseph H. Lewis's *Gun Crazy* (1950), a high point of American cinema. Bart and Laurie (John Dall and Peggy Cummins) have guns and the moxie needed to steal. Worst of all, though, is that they have each other.

We know less about Laurie's background, except that she's nearly as skilled with guns as Bart and that she once killed a man in St. Louis. A star attraction with a traveling carnival, Laurie (the "Annie" part of her name is apparently for the show only) performs her trick shots with swaggering arrogance. She loves guns, too, but as tools to get what she wants, rather than as objects of desire. Like Bart, she craves a normal existence, but her capacity for it is stuffed deep into the dark sack of her mind. As is made clear in pointed, well-played scenes involving Bart's married sister (Anabel Shaw), Laurie is ill at ease in domestic situations and regards small children with confusion and distaste. In keeping with the nature of sexual roles of 1950, *Gun Crazy* suggests that Laurie isn't completely female. Although intensely sexual (and sexy), her primary virtues are masculine ones. Bart, conversely, is feminized. He's the one who cannot kill; he's the one who hesitates before firing on a pursuing police car. If Laurie is the pair's id, Bart is its (tortured) soul.

The pair's drift into armed robbery, and finally into murder, seems inevitable. At the climax, Bart and Laurie are out of options, trapped in a foggy mountain swamp surrounded by police.

Forever Amber makes a pretense of being sexy but is just a guttering flame when regarded alongside the scorchingly sexual conflagration that is *Gun Crazy*.

In one of the film's most celebrated sequences, Bart gets his first look at Laurie at her workplace, a carnival. Director Joseph H. Lewis set up the sequence cleverly, keeping Laurie off the makeshift stage until she can be properly introduced by the carnival owner (Berry Kroeger): "So appealing! So dangerous! So lovely to look at! Miss! Annie! Laurie! Starr!" With the camera shooting up at the stage from Bart's point of view, Laurie strides into the frame from the bottom, the six-guns that she fires above her head visible first and then her face and body. She's immediately enticing and challenging.

Onstage with Laurie a few minutes later, Bart challenges her in a shooting contest, speculatively eyeing Laurie with blatant sexual interest (he literally walks all the way around her)—while Laurie looks at him in just the same way. Bart joins the show that day.

During a celebrated three-minute, twenty-seven-second uninterrupted take, as Laurie looks for a place to park so that Bart can rob a bank, the lovers are

Case File: Joseph H. Lewis (1907–2000)

The superb B-film director Joseph H. Lewis never got very famous outside of Hollywood, and he never directed a "big" movie, but he forged a good, steady career; died as the owner of a yacht; and is revered by generations of filmmakers, historians, and buffs. His 1950 thriller *Gun Crazy*—a stylish and delirious mash-up of violence, fevered love, compulsion, and obsession—exists at the summit of film noir.

Lewis had a lot going for him, including a flair for striking, often ingenious visual storytelling and a gift for making his points and achieving his dramatic effects while mindful of his budgets, which were never generous. If he came in very close on the faces of two people, part of the reason might have been that there was virtually no set around them!

Lewis started as an editor in 1935 at Mascot, a Poverty Row outfit that limped along on Rin Tin Tin movies starring Rinty's son. Lewis got his first directorial assignment in 1937, at Universal, and subsequently worked for Columbia (directing many superior B westerns featuring Charles Starrett), Warner Bros., MGM, Monogram, PRC, and RKO, as well as for numerous indie production companies, such as King Brothers, Security Pictures, Darmour, Seltzer Films, and others that released through United Artists and Allied Artists.

For twenty-two years, Lewis made adventures, war films, crime thrillers, westerns, horror films, and oddities the likes of *Secrets of a Co-ed* (1942). *Gun Crazy* appeared in the latter portion of Lewis's big-screen career, but before he left features for television in 1959, he directed another great noir, *The Big Combo*—still working with élan and ingenuity, disguising budget shortfalls, and getting strong, nervy performances from his cast.

Lewis's fans also revere his great 1949 police procedural *The Undercover Man*; a novel western, *Terror in a Texas Town* (in which a Swedish whaler uses a harpoon to deal with land-grabbers); and *The Halliday Brand* (father-son western conflict). During 1958–63, Lewis directed more than fifty episodes of the superior western series *The Rifleman*.

attired as cowboys. (The town is having a western-style celebration.) The western garb suggests the unpredictable danger of the Old West, as well as Bart and Laurie's own instability. Similarly, the pair's intermittent periods of privation suggest the urgency of a Great Depression story, but that, too, is past. This is 1950 (*Gun Crazy* was shot the previous year), when the American economy was on a postwar rebound (inflation notwithstanding) and jobs were becoming plentiful. It's not just that Bart and Laurie are anachronisms reminiscent of the Old West and the Depression—the truth is that they're lazy. In a telling moment, Bart himself sums it up when he remarks to Laurie, with a mixture of disgust and disbelief, "Two people dead. Just so we can live without working."

Russell Harlan's cinematography is breathtaking and varied: documentary-like during the robberies and deeply expressionistic when the lovers suffer and love together. Bodies are bisected or swallowed by shadows, and many close-ups are startling in their emotional immediacy. Lewis was enamored of the faces of both of his stars and pulled us unusually close to them, so that we want them to succeed, to get away clean.

Gun Crazy was written by MacKinlay Kantor (adapting his *Saturday Evening Post* short story) in collaboration with blacklisted writer Dalton Trumbo. (Original-release prints credited Kantor and Trumbo's "beard," Millard Kaufman.)

John Dall was a stage actor who was hired by Alfred Hitchcock to costar in *Rope* (1949) because of what Hitchcock claimed was an inherently weak quality. Hitch was on to something because the weakness of Bart Tare is palpable. Dall was a handsome actor who easily suggested diffident indecision. Whatever "Bart Tare" is, very little of him exists beyond his passions for guns and Laurie.

Laurie adores Bart, but she has his number, too. Lewis helped Peggy Cummins use her small, curvy body, pouty face, and penetrating eyes to exquisitely chilling effect—little wonder that some prints of *Gun Crazy* are titled *Deadly Is the Female*.

Love Him to Death

RKO produced a greater number of fine noir films than any other studio. In an odd turn, one of the best, John Farrow's *Where Danger Lives* (1950), is seldom discussed today. This critical inattention may partly be due to persistent bad mojo associated with the picture's leading lady, Faith Domergue, a dark-eyed protégé of Howard Hughes. Through no fault of Domergue's, what was to have been her star-making RKO "debut" (she'd done a couple of bits previously), a nineteenth-century Corsican melodrama called *Columba*, needed *four years* to grind its way through production. Along the way, the project encouraged Hughes to end his business partnership with a key *Columba* player, Preston Sturges, and dictate his wishes to three directors, only one of whom, Mel Ferrer, was credited. (The others, both dismissed by Hughes, were Max Ophuls and Stuart Heisler. Sturges's script was dismissed, too, after a great deal of it had been shot.) When *Columba* was finally released during the last week of 1950, it was called *Vendetta*—and the public didn't care. Four years of ceaseless publicity about Faith Domergue had worn everybody out. (On top of that was confusion about the proper pronunciation of Domergue's name, which was variously given as doo-MERG, DOE-merg, doe-MAIRG, doe-MERG, and doe-MYURE.)

This nationwide epidemic of Domergue-overload didn't help the prospects of *Where Danger Lives*, which came to theaters four months before *Vendetta*. The irony, as you may already have guessed, is that the sultry actress is terrific, interpreting Charles Bennett's script with fevered conviction and holding her own with Robert Mitchum and Claude Rains.

A young intern, Dr. Jeff Cameron (Mitchum), falls for a beautiful patient who has attempted suicide. The woman is Margo Lannington (Domergue), who tells Jeff that she wants to be with him but can't because she's a virtual prisoner of her wealthy father. In a meeting that quickly goes sour, Jeff is informed by Lannington (Claude Rains) that Margo isn't his daughter but his wife.

Oh cripes.

Jeff grasps that Margo is a little bit mental, and he starts to leave, intending to chalk the whole thing up to horny enthusiasm. But he returns to the drawing room when Margo screams. She claims that Lannington has physically hurt her, and in the escalation that follows, Margo becomes hysterical and Lannington beats Jeff about the back and head with a poker, until he's shoved to the floor by Jeff and knocked cold. Jeff steps out to examine his damaged noggin, and when he returns to check Lannington, the older man is dead. Now Jeff is really on the hook.

A dexterous fillip by Bennett is that the blows to the skull have left Jeff seriously concussed, and for the rest of the story, he deteriorates physically and mentally. By the time events come to a head in Nogales, Arizona, where Margo is determined to get across the border alone, Jeff's judgment is shot and his whole left side is paralyzed (a disturbing invocation of an early scene in which Jeff examines a paralyzed little girl [Sherry Jackson] who is confined to an iron lung). Barely mobile, Jeff stumbles into the street to follow Margo, unaware that police are closing in or that his erstwhile sweetheart has a sweet little gun.

To the credit of director John Farrow (whose wife, Maureen O'Sullivan, appears in an unrewarding cameo), Jeff's failing health is *not* suggested via ever-worsening subjective shots of the world as Jeff groggily sees it. Instead, Mitchum delivers a carefully considered performance that not only keeps the narrative engine going but subtly chronicles the alarming decline of Jeff's faculties. On the run with Margo because he believes the cops have already found Lannington's body, Jeff is easily taken advantage of by a trio of unprincipled capitalists: a braying used-car dealer (Tol Avery), a scheming pawnbroker (Ralph Dumke), and a white-collar border mule (Philip Van Zandt). Jeff is too dulled to realize that Margo is monopolizing the radio (she doesn't want him to hear updates about her husband), and he can't discern that a desert roadblock is just a plant-quarantine checkpoint. He's also very slow to come around to what we've suspected and what Margo finally cops to: When Jeff left the drawing room on the night of the argument, Margo polished off her husband by holding a pillow over his face.

This gruesome revelation comes full circle, after Jeff's body has broken down and Margo holds a pillow over *his* face. (Fortunately, she doesn't hold it for too long.)

We explicate Jeff's difficulties here because a great deal of critical comment about *Where Danger Lives* charges that Mitchum is miscast because Jeff is an

Where Danger Lives (1950) was one part of a scheme by RKO owner Howard Hughes to make a star of newcomer Faith Domergue. The campaign failed, but Domergue is creepily good as a wealthy psychotic who goes on the run with Robert Mitchum and nearly kills him.

indecisive weakling. That's precisely the wrong reading, and misses the vital reversal: Here is a strong man who *is made weak* when he's physically battered into insensibility. That's uncomfortable and frightening; it also gives Mitchum one of his best and most involving early roles.

John Farrow had a reputation as a driven, often unpleasant directorial presence. Some actors feared him; others just wanted to punch him in the nose. But Farrow was kind to Domergue and worked with her on the nuances of her performance, well aware that the character she played is the story's emotional and narrative center. Domergue and Mitchum are on-screen almost continually, and because Farrow favored long takes to delineate key sequences, the acting challenges were considerable. (A two-minute, twenty-five-second take at about the hour mark that places Margo and Jeff in a dumpy motel room involves precise blocking that brings the pair in and out of shadow and key lights, plus pans and dolly shots, and elegant moves from two-shots to close-ups and back again. Margo's restless checking and rechecking of the radio news when Jeff has gone into the bathroom is particularly well executed.)

Cinematographer Nicholas Musuraca brought immense artistry to *Where Danger Lives*, shooting in brilliant, high-contrast black and white with a fulsome range of grays. The film stock shimmers, bringing hard emotional weight to carefully lit interiors and withering desert exteriors. A recurring mirror motif is nicely handled—and begins, cheekily enough, with views of the face of the child confined to the iron lung. Much later, a re-creation of the dusty, neon-lit main drag of Nogales, Arizona, shot night-for-night on a carefully dressed street set, is seedy and gorgeous.

Case File: Nicholas Musuraca (1892–1975)

This highly respected cinematographer shot his first picture in 1923 and remained busy for forty years. Like other shooters with careers spanning many eras, Musuraca was fearlessly versatile, taking assignments as they came and handling them with great skill. Dramas, westerns, comedies (including many short subjects), mysteries, and crime thrillers occupied him for twenty years, before a 1943 association with RKO producer Val Lewton. He shot five important Lewton pictures, including two that are particularly beautiful to look at, *Cat People* and *The Seventh Victim*. Musuraca got into noir with an early example, the boldly visual *Stranger on the Third Floor*, and later shot many important pictures in the genre: *Deadline at Dawn*, *The Locket*, *Out of the Past*, *Where Danger Lives*, *Roadblock*, and *The Hitch-Hiker*. As confident with outdoor shooting as with soundstages, Musuraca was an indefatigable talent. Unfortunately, the collapse of the studio system helped prompt Musuraca's move into episodic television, where he worked almost exclusively from 1954 until his retirement in 1966.

Among non-noirs shot by Musuraca are *The Tuttles of Tahiti*, *Back to Bataan*, *The Spiral Staircase*, *Bedlam*, *Blood on the Moon*, *The Whip Hand*, *Clash by Night*, and Dick Powell's crazy-entertaining A-bomb thriller, *Split Second*.

One result of Farrow's attention to Domergue is that Margo Lannington isn't just smashingly beautiful but manipulative and cunning, a creature completely dedicated to her own interests. Even better, Bennett's script is sufficiently layered so that Margo is more than just a caricature. The real sadness of the tale is that Margo loves Jeff, powerfully and deeply. If she were normal, she might not love him as fiercely, but she'd love him better.

The Unreadable Face

MGM production chief Dore Schary stuck it to Louis B. Mayer yet again with *Dial 1119* (1950), an unnerving, low-budget hostage thriller, with significant noir overtones, that is not at all in the previous MGM mode. As in numerous other films noir, the protagonist is a young war vet who has been psychologically damaged by his experiences.

Dial 1119 establishes a simple premise that is developed concisely, without pretension or irrelevant side issues. A handsome escaped mental patient named Gunther Wyckoff (Marshall Thompson) shoots and kills a bus driver one night and takes refuge inside a neighborhood tavern in an unidentified city (probably New York). He holds the bartenders and patrons hostage and informs the police outside that he'll kill his prisoners unless he can speak with Dr. John Faron (Sam Levene). Faron has had past dealings with Wyckoff, arguing with such persuasion about Wyckoff's crippled mental state that the young man was spared execution for the crime of murder. Now, Faron may hold the fate of his patient's hostages, too.

A number of things distinguish *Dial 1119*. First is the lovely economy with which the picture was made. All exteriors were shot on the MGM lot, where sound and (especially) nighttime-lighting effects could be strictly controlled. The effect is vaguely artificial—and that's good because the whole setup is like a stage play, with modest physical movement and unusually intense emotional investment in the central situation and in the unique motivations and reactions of each character.

Second, director Gerald Mayer worked effectively with what is essentially a two-set picture—the bar and the street outside—mixing shots, moving the camera with effective subtlety, and allowing visuals to tell large portions of the story. Mayer made only a handful of features (the Dorothy Dandridge-Harry Belafonte drama *Bright Road* is one) before embarking on a thirty-year career in television.

Third, screenwriter John Monks Jr., adapting a story by Hugh King and Don McGuire, created characters that are sufficiently "stock" to be quickly understood, yet not without their surprises. For example, a middle-aged, blowhard businessman (Leon Ames) spends the early part of the story transparently romancing his much younger secretary (Andrea King), with whom he's connived an illicit weekend getaway. The old roué sells himself to the girl as a man of the world, a take-charge kind of fellow who laughs at obstacles. Your expectation is

Dial 1119 (1950) follows the loosely wrapped Gunther Wycoff (Marshall Thompson), who has been released from the veterans' hospital too soon. Now he's in New York, killing people, holding hostages, and demanding to see the psychiatrist who treated him. The unlucky bus driver is John Damler.

that this man will melt into jelly—or worse—when confronted by Wyckoff, but he remains calm, if a little nervous. Part of the point is that the character is neither good, bad, nor hopeless—he's just a cipher whose intense self-involvement apparently precludes, in his mind, the possibility that he may not get out of the evening alive.

A female barfly (Virginia Field) also goes against type. Rather than the worn and dissolute female drinker we've seen many other times, she's beautiful, defiantly glamorous, and very funny—self-amused as well as profoundly amused by others. The gunman scares the hell out of her, but there's nothing to suggest that she's a tragic figure or has regrets in her moment of danger. She just likes to drink a lot.

Richard Rober (a rugged, very promising leading man before his death in 1952 at age forty-two) is the police detective in charge of the detail that surrounds the bar. As a character, he's pleasing because he's a flexible improviser. If one tack doesn't work, he tries another. As circumstances change inside the tavern, his mode of thought changes, too.

Last, there is the central performance of MGM contract player Marshall Thompson, as Wyckoff. Playing without affect, in a kind of benumbed stasis, he's more like a force of nature than a person. He can't be reasoned with, he can't be cajoled, and he can't be threatened. Wyckoff stares flatly at the world and kills without compunction (the murders of the bus driver [John Damler] and one of the bartenders [William Conrad] are deeply shocking). Yet he has moments of weird, uncanny patience. For Thompson, who came up in the mid-1940s, usually filling agreeable "juvenile" roles, Wyckoff was a startling, and artistically successful, turnabout.

Although never dealt with in explicit terms, the subtext of *Dial 1119* (the number rings the police emergency line, by the way) concerns the human wreckage left behind by the unrealistic, often romanticized notions encouraged by governments during war. A climactic revelation about Wyckoff's service drives that idea home with pitiless force.

People who are tricked and betrayed often fall into a dark place that encourages them to make their unhappiness known. Somebody has to answer for the illusive lies about happiness and glory. Accounts have to be settled.

Cuddly Crazy

In Alfred Hitchcock's *Strangers on a Train* (1951), noir is plumbed for a generous helping of deception, miscommunication, murder, guilty feelings of the (partially) innocent, and smugly innocent feelings of the (totally) guilty. Because of splendid source material (Patricia Highsmith's 1950 novel, her first), Hitchcock's thorough command of the material, and a peerless central performance, *Strangers* is one of noir's most ringing entertainments.

Two young men who meet on a train pass the time with idle, silly talk about "exchanging murders"—each doing away with a bothersome person in the other's life and getting away with it because of lack of motive. To tennis player Guy Haines (Farley Granger), it's all nonsense that he thoughtlessly agrees to, but wealthy dilettante Bruno Anthony (Robert Walker) is dead serious. Sure enough, Bruno murders Guy's estranged wife and then demands that Guy keep his part of the presumed bargain by knocking off Bruno's father. If Guy refuses, Bruno will set him up to take the fall for his wife's death.

Central to Guy's dilemma is that, although he never commits murder, he's hardly innocent. First, he's romantically involved with the daughter of a U.S. senator. This being 1951, nothing in the film explicitly suggests that the two are having sex—but of course they are, and that's adultery. Second, Guy finds the idea of getting rid of his wife, Miriam (Laura Elliott), appealing. He hasn't the constitution for murder, yet the thought of Miriam being no longer on the planet, and no longer able to hang onto him out of spite, doesn't horrify him. With her absence, he could marry Anne Morton (Ruth Roman), be mentored by Senator Morton (Leo G. Carroll), and one day abandon his tennis career with nary a care. Third, Guy unconsciously grasps that he and Bruno are like Janus: different but the same. Their desires and aspirations are unnervingly similar. Each wants the prestige of wealth, its material accoutrements, and the delicious, unfettered freedom that comes with it.

Robert Walker's Bruno is handsome in a broad-forehead, too-intense-a-gaze kind of way, and he brims with brio and self-confidence. Irrepressibly sunny and eager to please, he also has the determination of a bulldozer. He dogs Guy mercilessly (and always with a smile) when it appears that Guy won't hold up his part of the "bargain." Guy peers from a window at Anne's Washington flat and spies Bruno waiting in the shadows across the street. Guy works himself into an overheated lather at a tennis match (he has to finish quickly, before Bruno has the opportunity to commit specific mischief); when Guy glances at the crowd, there's Bruno, staring dead-straight at him while every other head turns this way and that to follow the course of the ball. (This is a marvelous visual joke.)

Hitchcock designed things so that Guy remains a sort of neuter—neither here nor there as a male presence, and as dull and earnest as an underwriter. Bruno, on the other hand, is sexually ambiguous rather than a blank. He's lively, provocative, and funny. We're willing to forgive his craziness because he inherited it from his mother (Marion Lorne), and because Mum has failed to help Bruno wriggle from beneath the thumb of his father.

Hitchcock never intended for us to like Bruno. He intended for us to love him—and we do. Bruno is that archetype: the grinning Bad Little Boy, all grown up. We're hard-wired to be attracted to him. He has such twinkle, such élan, that we'd be pleased if, as he's threatened to do, he manages to plant Guy's lighter at the scene of Miriam's murder. We'd be pleased because we admire Bruno's resourcefulness and envy his brazen courage. (He even maneuvers himself spookily close to Anne and her father.)

Hitchcock and his screenwriters—Raymond Chandler, Ben Hecht (uncredited), and Czenzi Ormonde (a Hecht associate who came bundled with Hecht)—arranged Strangers on a Train so that it's dominated by sterling set pieces. Guy and Bruno's initial meeting on the train is one of these; another is the tennis match, and yet another is Bruno's agonized attempt to get his fingers on the all-important lighter after it's fallen through a storm grate. Bruno and Guy's climactic battle aboard a madly spinning, out-of-control merry-go-round is memorably suspenseful and strange. (If the craziness of a merry-go-round climax seems to you suggestive of Bruno's whirligig of a brain, you're on the right track.)

The picture's greatest set piece, Bruno's murder of Miriam, is propelled equally by Hitchcock, Walker, and Laura Elliott (known throughout much of her career as Kasey Rogers). An earlier scene with Miriam and Guy establishes that the brunette Miriam, oddly pretty with her thick, cat's-eye glasses and defiant tilt of her head, radiates sex like a hot radiator in a small room. It's easy enough to grasp why Guy got mixed up with her. She barters, cajoles, and punishes with one thing, and a long time ago she snared her tennis player. Miriam's damp eroticism is the closest Hitchcock had yet come to acknowledging his interest in "dirty" sex without covering it in blonde sophistication. (He would do it again later in the decade, with the redheaded "Judy" character in Vertigo.)

Satisfied that we have a basic understanding of Miriam's inclinations, Hitchcock builds to her murder with what is essentially foreplay, teasing us with a mildly unsavory nighttime carnival setting that allows Bruno and Miriam to exchange flirty glances near a bus, in a Tunnel of Love, and on the shore of a lake. (Never mind that Miriam is being squired around by not one but two young swains.) The consummation comes on a dark, isolated island (lit with crawling menace by Robert Burks), where Bruno finds Miriam alone, as if waiting for him. Held by the camera's tight, uncomfortably close-up gaze, he illuminates the lenses of her glasses with Guy's lighter, flirtatiously confirms Miriam's name, and then strangles her, using his square body to slowly force her to the ground. Her fallen spectacles reflect and distort this act, this intimate union of two people.

Bruno has a scare after the murder, when he meets Anne Morton's bespectacled sister (Patricia Hitchcock, in a quirkily wrought small role). He imagines the dance of the lighter's flame in the sister's glasses, and for a moment he's startled and overcome. He recovers quickly and soon gets back to planning his own life and arranging Guy's. He's busy and enterprising, and you just want to hug him.

Bullied, Alone, and Hopeless

The Wyckoff character of *Dial 1119* invokes mental illness, wartime service, and the disturbed protagonist's desire to be cured. The same elements come together, with dramatically different emphasis, in *The Sniper* (1952), directed by Edward Dmytryk for Columbia release.

Every weekday morning Eddie Miller (Arthur Franz) gets into his truck and delivers clean laundry across San Francisco. He's soft-spoken and deferential. But Eddie has a secret: Locked in the top drawer of his bureau is an M1 rifle with a scope and a folding stock. For some time now, Eddie has been using it across the city to ambush and kill women.

Eddie isn't happy about what he's been doing. He wants help from the psychiatrist that treated him in prison, but on the day Eddie calls, the doctor can't be reached. Eddie needs help *now*. He can't wait. So he continues to kill women until two detectives (Adolphe Menjou and Gerald Mohr) put a few clues together and corner him in his small flat. (À la real-life killer William Heirens, Eddie sends the police a note: STOP ME—FIND ME AND STOP ME I'M GOING TO DO IT AGAIN. For more on the Heirens case, see this chapter's discussion of *While the City Sleeps*.)

Like many other noir protagonists we've met in this book, Eddie returned home from war well practiced in firearms and killing. As police discover, he's served time for nonlethal assaults against women. He was treated during his most recent incarceration, but when his sentence was up, he was turned loose. Eddie has had no further course of treatment, but he has a lot of unfinished business. A police psychiatrist (Richard Kiley) comes to that conclusion because, since all of the sniper's victims have been brunette women in their late twenties,

Mild, introverted Eddie Miller (Arthur Franz) is *The Sniper* (1952), whose loneliness and psychosis drive him to serial rifle murders of innocent women. Singer Jean Darr (Marie Windsor) knows Eddie only as the shy guy who delivers her dry cleaning. Eddie decides to deliver a lot more.

the shooter is "killing the same woman, over and over again, and he'll keep on killing her." (A remark tossed off by Eddie—"My mother never gave me anything!"—confirms rather too glibly the source of his angst.)

The psychiatrist demands early intervention with men who assault women. He's a liberal crusader, created by screenwriter Harry Brown (from an Oscar-nominated story by Edna and Edward Anhalt), and very much in keeping with the inclinations of producer Stanley Kramer, one of Hollywood's more politically progressive producer-directors. Just prior to *The Sniper*, Kramer had explored institutionalized racism (*Home of the Brave*), the challenges faced by disabled veterans (*The Men*), and the tragedy of working-class illusions (*Death of a Salesman*). Kramer continued in this vein for the rest of his long career, and if his projects eventually grew bloated and self-important (*On the Beach, Inherit the Wind*), and even embarrassingly false and contrived (*Pressure Point, Guess Who's Coming to Dinner?*), his social and political instincts never wavered.

The Sniper is a brilliant thriller directed by Dmytryk with craft. Although most successful as a genre piece, the picture also succeeds as a study of bottled-up anger and self-imposed loneliness. In this, the picture is squarely within the thematic boundaries of noir, even though cinematographer Burnett Guffey shot the greater part of it outdoors, in the natural light of bright overcast.

At its conclusion, *The Sniper* elevates itself above genre. As the police burst through a door, the killer sits passively on his bed, his gun harmless in his lap, his eyes filled with tears, a mournful gaze locked on the cops, and on us. Audiences who expected a climactic shoot-out went home disappointed, but the final, intimately close image of Eddie's face, while admittedly theatrical and manipulative, puts an appropriate cap on the story. Eddie is guilty as hell, and he's going to pay, one way or another, but he's a victim, too.

Dmytryk was very conscious of Eddie's physical environment as a reflection of character and of his mental dilemma. The narrative repeatedly places him in narrow hallways, inside confining rooms, in the low-ceilinged rear of his claustrophobic truck, behind windows, and bracketed by fencing. San Francisco itself, densely packed and crisscrossed with vertiginous streets, is another kind of prison.

Not everything in *The Sniper* is symbolic. The image of a woman's head, bisected by the crosshairs of Eddie's scope, is pure (and purposely revolting) exposition. Eddie's later assassinations of a club singer (Marie Windsor) and a steeplejack affixed to the side of a faraway smokestack are among the most upsetting and powerfully staged set pieces in all of noir.

The film's cleverest stroke is that it turns us into Eddie's accomplices, and not simply via subjective use of the rifle's scope. Eddie's supervisor at the laundry is a well-dressed, disagreeable woman (Geraldine Carr) who continually demeans and bullies him. She's remorselessly cruel, and we begin to think, *Eddie should kill her. Why doesn't Eddie wait for her and kill her?*

We've been encouraged to cross a moral frontier and become the sniper's little helpers, like the miniature devils that pop up on the shoulders of cartoon characters to goad them into bad behavior. Trouble is, in the world created for and by the sniper, there are no counterbalancing angels.

The Agonizing Struggle to Cope

This is the tricky balancing act pulled off by Harry Horner's *Beware, My Lovely* (1952): A homicidally violent central character earns our sympathy without contrivance or undue theatrics. We don't root for the dangerous man on the screen, but we don't hate him, either. In his yearnings, he strikes a chord that touches us. Unusually honest in many of its facets, this modestly produced thriller is like a fine painting done in miniature.

In a prosperous small town shortly after World War I, schoolteacher and war widow Helen Gordon (Ida Lupino) hires itinerant handyman Howard Wilton (Robert Ryan) to do routine chores around her house. Helen is unusually patient with Howard's quirks of personality (he slips into fugue states without warning) but becomes frightened and finally terrorized when Howard succumbs to his paranoia and locks both of them inside the house. The film has opened with a chilling vignette at another house, in another town, in which Howard opens a closet door and is shocked to find the staring, twisted corpse of a woman—but he shouldn't be surprised at all, because he killed her.

Howard has a very interesting problem with recollection. Because his short-term memory is deeply damaged, he has no awareness of what he may have said or done just minutes earlier. The aberration leads to see-saw behavior that alternates between homicidal fury and bemused, soft-spoken confusion. If Helen is going to leave her home alive, she'll have to craft and modulate her own behavior and appeal to Howard during one of his interludes of calm.

Central to the film's themes of loneliness and alienation are Helen's widowhood and Howard's rejection by the military for wartime service. Inevitably, a widow, no matter how well liked, becomes alienated in her community. Helen

The moods of a mentally scarred handyman (Robert Ryan) swing wildly, from mute blankness to aggressive fury. A widowed homeowner (Ida Lupino) never knows which persona will confront her next. All she knows for sure is that the handyman has locked the two of them in the house in *Beware, My Lovely* (1952).

is different from what she was before, and social opportunities that once were open to her are now closed. She is "the widow Morgan."

Although Howard isn't stupid, he is crippled by a pathetic literalness and the determined but myopic focus of a child. Denied the opportunity to join society by performing what was trumpeted as noble duty, his self-regard shriveled and he came to doubt himself as a man. (In a scene played with spiteful glee by young actress Barbara Whiting, Howard is taunted by a local teenage girl for scrubbing floors—"woman's work!") Howard's struggle to redeem and define himself is heartbreaking. Ryan's interpretation of the character isn't just frightening but oddly sweet. Howard is an innocent in a world that has no inclination to understand him.

Beware, My Lovely was scripted by Mel Dinelli, adapting his own Broadway play, *The Man*, which had had a respectable run of ninety-two performances during the winter and early spring of 1950. Dorothy Gish and Richard Boone starred. In the play, the widow is finally murdered. That wouldn't do in a movie, of course, but Ida Lupino, always on the lookout for provocative ideas she could purchase and bring to the screen under her Filmmakers banner, liked the play's intensity and (if handled properly) commercial possibilities. As an actress, she was ready to express the wide swing of emotions displayed by the widow. Robert Ryan, inevitably eager to subvert his leading-man status for art, was attracted to the handyman's unpredictable, essentially tragic nature.

Although Lupino had already directed four features by 1951, she offered the director's chair to Harry Horner, an Oscar-winning production designer (*The Heiress*; 1949) who had worked on The Filmmakers' *Outrage* (1950). So that the play would work as a movie, Horner had to open it up visually. A few well-utilized outdoor sequences are one obvious solution; the other is that Horner varied his setups and lighting and allowed George Diskant's camera to move freely about Helen's house. The fact that *Beware, My Lovely* is essentially a two-person story suggests its stage origins, but nothing about the visual treatment shouts "theater."

Horner had a very keen eye (and in fact created the *Beware, My Lovely* production design, without screen credit). Howard is often viewed from floor level, which underscores the character's innate menace as well as Helen's vulnerability. Also, as in *The Lodger*, we have a male protagonist with a propensity to gaze. Howard stares at Helen, at her departing boarder (Taylor Holmes), and at neighborhood children. He frequently peers through windows and from behind drapes and solemnly regards himself in a mirror and even in a bucket of water. In a striking variation near the film's climax, Howard's distorted figure is reflected in Christmas tree ornaments that dominate the right side of the frame as Howard creeps in to ambush Helen from behind.

When Horner had to temporarily leave *Beware, My Lovely* because of family illness, Lupino directed several sequences. The shoot wrapped in August 1951, but because RKO owner Howard Hughes was—as usual—preoccupied with myriad things other than the studio (including business deals, various lawsuits, and Hollywood's Red Scare), the picture sat on the shelf for a year. When it finally was released in August 1952, it was consigned to the lower half of double bills because of RKO's disinterest, its modest seventy-seven-minute running time, and Hughes's new antipathy for left-leaning Robert Ryan, who was released from his contract in 1952.

What foolishness.

Not every Hollywood leading lady could stand tall against Ryan's brand of talent, of course, but Ida Lupino could. She saved money by casting herself (she probably deferred or took a diminished salary), but she also knew she could express Helen's bittersweet melding of the tragic and the hopeful, the gentle and the tough. Helen is determined to survive, and if she can do it without harming her captor, all the better.

Savage Beneath the Beauty

Otto Preminger's *Angel Face* (1952) is among the strangest and most puzzling of all films noir. It's a thriller with no suspense, a murder whodunit with no mystery, and a romantic triangle that plays out in a peculiarly low-key fashion. And yet more may be going on than is apparent on the narrative's surface.

Angel Face is also scary as hell, because of Jean Simmons's central performance and because the Robert Mitchum character never seems to grasp the sort of awful danger he's in.

People in the orbit of heiress Diane Tremayne (Simmons) die in a freak accident, and although Diane and reluctant lover Frank Jessup (Mitchum) are brought to trial for double homicide, they freely walk from the courthouse, pronounced not guilty. After the verdict, Diane confesses the crime to her defense attorney but is informed about double jeopardy and sent on her way.

Frank begins to mend his relationship with his former flame Mary (Mona Freeman). Trouble is, he can't stay completely away from Diane.

Frank Nugent and Oscar Millard's script is more successful as a dispassionate examination of insanity than as a completely engaging melodrama. Diane—dark and with a lush, provocatively asymmetrical beauty—initially seems merely reserved, but after director Otto Preminger (who also produced) gives us numerous shots of her tinkling at the piano, her unfocused eyes staring ahead at nothing, we get the idea that she's not quite right. And we're correct about that because the secret Diana seethes like a volcano. Although she adores her penniless father (Herbert Marshall), she abhors her wealthy stepmother, Catherine (Barbara O'Neil).

Diane becomes acquainted with Frank when he shows up at the estate on an ambulance call. A loose gas jet in the bedroom of the stepmother has nearly shuttled the matriarch into oblivion. By the time Frank runs into Diane in town a few days later, he's thinking of quitting the ambulance business and setting up a garage for exotic cars. He's intrigued by Diane's low-slung Jaguar XK Le Mans and boasts that he can turn it into a real screamer.

One day, Diane takes a good, long look into the sunlit abyss that leads down from a sheer precipice at the back of the estate's driveway. When Diane's father and stepmother get into the family sedan later, Catherine puts the car in drive and promptly accelerates *backwards* over the precipice and into a grinding, fatal crash. It's a great shock moment.

A technical expert at Frank and Diane's trial explains that just a cotter pin prevents an automatic transmission from being in the gear shown on the cockpit indicator. With a minute of instruction, even Diane could have fiddled with the works and sent her parents to their deaths. (The courtroom sequence is nearly as off-kilter as Diane; the sedan's steering column and transmission box makes for a very declarative Exhibit A, attorneys on both sides seem ignorant of the rules of courtroom decorum, and a juror is allowed to stand up and question a prosecution witness.)

Acquitted, Frank wants to end the quickie marriage that was arranged by the defense attorney so that he and Diane would appear more sympathetic to the jury. He wants to disappear into Mexico, alone, which kills any idea we may have had that Frank, and not Diane, is the murderer. With divorce or annulment, he'll have access to none of the family fortune; if he killed, he surely wouldn't have done it for nothing.

Diane pulls up in the Jag and offers to drive Frank to the bus station. In one of the dumbest decisions a guy has ever made, Frank gets in. Then, in one of the most blatantly telegraphed "surprises" in film history, Diane sends the Jag, herself, and Frank backwards over the precipice, and to gory deaths. (Shots of the tumbling, smashing car are horrifying.)

Diane is a perplexing character, a violently insane person who has mastered the art of hiding her madness and moving through society with seeming normalcy. Costume designer Michael Woulfe repeatedly puts Diane in chic outfits that are black, or white, or both, all to suggest the sharp dichotomy and layers of the character's personality.

Frank plays it cool throughout, laconic in the famed Mitchum matter. You get the impression that he doesn't care if he ever sees Diane again and that he's just as happy eating hash as he is sharing sumptuous dinners at the big house. He's essentially disconnected from life, which probably explains his thoughtless willingness to get into the Jaguar with Diane.

Except for pinpoints of light in Diane's eyes when she goes into her fugue states, cinematographer Harry Stradling shot in a straightforward manner that isn't at all atmospheric. The general visual tone is sunny, almost cheerful, and paradoxically heightens the dark emotions roiling within the house. Set design is handsome but unremarkable.

The real drama of *Angel Face* takes place between Diane's ears, but we're not privy to enough of that to get the full story.

The Eye That Never Closes

Two pals on vacation near Mexicali pick up a hitchhiker who terrorizes them during a forced drive across the desert to the Gulf coast. That single sentence sums up the narrative, and the narrative implications, of Ida Lupino's frighteningly grim *The Hitch-Hiker* (1953), the first noir directed by a woman and that rarity of the genre: a noir picture without subtext or overt morality. It simply unreels, expertly, like a documentary treatment of a particular crime.

The only moral note is mild and is mainly a reproach of Roy (Edmond O'Brien) and Gil (Frank Lovejoy): *If you'd gone to where you told your wives you were going instead of detouring to carouse in Mexico, none of this would have happened to you.* That's the small extent of the victims' moral trespass, which is greeted with an outsize punishment—a near-death experience with an armed madman (William Talman).

Lupino wasn't just a brilliant film actress but one of the more captivating American writer-directors of the 1950s. In partnership with her husband, writer-producer Collier Young, Lupino's company, The Filmmakers, made incisive, low-budget films revolving around such subjects as unmarried pregnancy, police corruption, the life-altering nature of polio, destructive mother love, and bigamy. Lupino was drawn to strong, engaging stories in which characters had to

The narrative of Ida Lupino's merciless *The Hitch-Hiker* (1953) unreels with the linear clarity of a piece of rope pulled taut and tied to a stick of dynamite. Two pals (Frank Lovejoy and Edmond O'Brien, right) offer a stranger (William Talman) a ride—and hope they'll live to regret it.

manage unusual pressures that they often created themselves. She was intrigued by the notion of culpability, but the heavy hand of moralizing seems not to have interested her; indeed, the pregnant girl of *Not Wanted* and the title character of *The Bigamist* are treated with nonjudgmental sympathy.

Lupino naturally disapproved of bad cops, and of kidnap killers, too, but there was no arguing against the dramatic possibilities in the true-life story of heavy-lidded Oklahoman Billy Cook, a sharecropper's son who murdered seven people, including a family of five *and* the family dog, during a hitchhike-and-abduction winging across the American west and southwest during 1950–51. Impulsive and heartless, he developed an inflated notion of himself and life on the run. "I'm gonna live by the gun and roam," he said.

Like Cook, roving killer Emmett Myers (Talman) has inexplicable feelings of self-importance. A small-time guy to his core, he nevertheless congratulates himself for his presumed cleverness and calls his latest hostages "suckers" because they're tied to families, jobs, and mortgages.

As written by Young and Lupino, Myers is a localized force of nature, whose damaged right eye never closes, even when he's asleep. Or is he asleep at all? Roy and Gil never know for sure because the eye keeps staring, which inhibits most thoughts of escape. Only one thing seems sure: The friends are going to die, as soon as they get Myers to where he wants to go or as soon as the fiend hears a radio report that ties him to his hostages. And Myers insists that the radio be on almost all the time.

The central visual trope of *The Hitch-Hiker* is Roy and Gil's car, a bulbous 1950 Plymouth, a workingman's car, that makes its way through tortuous desert country on roads, quasi-roads, and no roads at all, leaving rooster tails of dust and looking inadequate and very, very hot. Because "the American road" and "the American West" are shorthand for masculine freedom and independence of thought and movement, Roy and Gil's predicament is a contravention not just of specific laws but of the very *idea* of America.

Lupino and cinematographer Nicholas Musuraca shot on location at California's Alabama Hills, in the Sierra Nevada range west of Lone Pine. This is rough, toweringly rocky country interrupted with great swaths of scrubby flatland. Life here is harsh, and only hardy organisms are going to survive. In the film's early going, before Myers, the camera eye takes medium views of the car's body and close views of the two pals inside (most of the latter are process work, but a few are accomplished with very effective in-car cameras, with natural light). After Myers enters the story and asserts himself, some setups are shot on the road from a camera car positioned ahead of the laboring Plymouth, but many more are coolly omnipotent, regarding the car from high above and far away. In such moments—and *The Hitch-Hiker* has many of them—the automobile is small and lost, and what does that say about the innocent men trapped inside?

Of course, the corollary is that Myers is small and lost, too. He pumps himself up with the gun and with the effect his rough features and staring eye have on his victims, but the moment he loses control of the gun, he looks like a rabbit.

Case File: Ida Lupino (1918–95)

To reflect that somebody was so gifted they "had it all" is trite, but that's undeniably true of Ida Lupino. She was favored with a family acting pedigree going back two hundred years, as well as bold, unusual beauty and a quick mind. She excelled as a performer, filmmaker, writer, and business executive. In the early and middle 1950s, when no other women were directing Hollywood feature films, Lupino—a co-owner of her own production company, The Filmmakers—financed, directed, and occasionally appeared in movies that made waves because of their boldness and lack of sentimentality. She tackled some heavy topics, including polio, careerism, rape, unwed motherhood, bigamy, and corrupt police.

Lupino was born in London and was already active as an actress in British cinema at fifteen. She came to America at the invitation of Paramount in 1934 and was a popular Warner Bros. contract star throughout the 1940s. Intellectually and artistically restless by 1949, she partnered with husband Collier Young to make films that mattered to her.

The Hitch-Hiker is Lupino's preeminent contribution to noir. It's a nerve-jangling thriller (loosely based on truth) that Lupino directed with a merciless sort of competence, creating a powerful sense of place while she examined not just criminality but the visceral terror of helpless victims. Lupino's other noir credits are *Road House* (acted only), *On Dangerous Ground* (acted only), *Beware, My Lovely* (acted and produced), *Private Hell 36* (acted, cowrote, produced), and *While the City Sleeps* (acted only).

Ida moved aggressively into TV, directing dozens of episodes for a great variety of series. In 1962 she directed Lee Marvin and James Caan in "A Fist of Five," an especially potent episode of TV's roughest and toughest show, *The Untouchables*.

In a mild turnabout, nobody perishes during the picture's nighttime climax. Roy and Gil are in one piece (though Edmond O'Brien's Roy is particularly wrung out), and Myers reacts with silent horror when a Mexican cop snaps cuffs on him. Aghast and unbelieving, the killer yanks his locked wrists to his chin, his eyes darting as he struggles to process the concept of "capture."

Ida Lupino heard the complimentary "You direct like a man!" often enough to want to rap people on the head. Inevitably, the subject matter and sensibility on view in *The Hitch-Hiker* are more apt to engage men than women. That doesn't mean that Lupino directed like a man. It means that she understood the crimes and terrors of people.

Dante Knew This Place

In writer-director John J. Parker's *Dementia* (1955), there is no tomorrow, only yesterday and the very unpleasant *right now*. Dismissed by many, lauded by some, this fifty-seven-minute cheapie cranks up the intensity of familiar film noir tropes until we stare hard at the squirming, unsavory relationship of noir to horror.

A plain, hard-faced young woman described in the credits only as "The Gamin" (Adrienne Barrett) has been psychologically crippled by the childhood abuse levied against her by her father. When she ventures forth into the night-time city from her furnished room, she passively allows herself to be picked up by a depraved rich man (Bruno VeSota), only to stab him to death and shove his body from a window of his flat. Pursued by police, she's momentarily rescued when a weasel-like man pulls her into an after-hours jazz joint. (Without evidence, some sources credit VeSota as the writer-director of *Dementia*.)

Inside the club, the girl acquires an evening gown and gives herself over to the music. Just when she seems on the verge of emotional release, the man she killed appears at a window to taunt her. The club crowd laughs and surrounds the girl, hands groping for her with such fervor that there's no hope of escape.

Dementia (which was rereleased to no good purpose, with voice-over narration and some cuts, as *Daughter of Horror*) was shot silent, with mild sound effects and some murmured dialogue added in postproduction. The film has a dream-like quality that might easily encourage viewer confusion or even distaste. Action is evenly split between small but nicely dressed stages, and location shooting in Los Angeles. The skillful night-for-night cinematography is by the prolific and quite unheralded William C. Thompson, who brought photographic sophistication to many B and Z movies, including *Glen or Glenda?* and six others directed by the remarkable Edward D. Wood Jr.

Dementia, which was shot in 1953 and distributed to theaters by Exploitation Pictures two years later, abounds in noir touches: a crummy furnished room with a HOTEL sign that continually blinks outside the window, dark alleys, faceless warehouses, a dwarf newsboy (Angelo Rossitto), winos, and a dissolute flower girl. Other iconographic images include a switchblade knife, a .38 revolver, a chauffeured Cadillac, endless cigarettes, a falling body, a prowl car with a spotlight that mercilessly pins a fleeing figure against the sides of buildings, a bankroll that is flashed with the unspoken suggestion that it might buy sex, and a hot jazz combo (Shorty Rogers and His Giants) that sends onlookers into an uninhibited, sexualized frenzy (as in *Phantom Lady*; see Chapter 6).

And finally, there is loneliness: brutal and (literally) maddening. One flabbergasting sequence, in which the girl busily saws at a dead man's wrist in order to get at something gripped in his hand (she'll just take the whole appendage, thank you), combines the roughest face of noir with the surrealism of Dali and Bunuel. The tableau is, almost literally, insane.

Dementia takes a sharp left turn into psychosexual horror when the girl observes her resurrected parents (one a drunk, the other a doxy) amidst overstuffed furniture arrayed in a misty graveyard. When the father's sexual advances are rebuffed by the mother, he shoots her. The girl, now dressed like a child, steps behind her father and stabs him in the back.

Because *Dementia* opens and closes with an image of a starry night sky, the unspoken insistence is that our fates are preordained and inescapable. Insistence? Yes, because when the girl suddenly awakens from the dream that has provided the narrative to that point, she opens her dresser drawer and discovers a severed, writhing hand.

All the Contradictions of Madness

James Agee and Charles Laughton's screenplay for *The Night of the Hunter* (1955) is based on Davis Grubb's best-selling 1953 novel about a spurious "preacher" who roams America's rural South during the Depression. Because Agee and Laughton both were deeply preoccupied with storytelling—Agee as an essayist, critic, and screenwriter (*The African Queen*); Laughton as an actor, monologist, and Broadway director—their script is every bit as much about storytelling as it is about the story it tells.

Preacher (Robert Mitchum, giving a rich, frequently funny, and completely unexpected performance) arrives in a small town with LOVE tattooed across one set of knuckles and HATE tattooed across the other. In a general store, he delivers a simplistic but mesmerizing account of love's duel with hate, using his own massive hands as props, clasping the fingers tightly, working the hands this way and that, allowing hate momentary advantage before giving the gathered listeners what they want, a turnabout, as love levers hate to the tabletop. "Hot dog, Love's a-winnin'! Yes sirree, it's Love that won."

Preacher is the Devil's own hypocrite.

Outside of town, in a house on the river, Rachel Cooper (Lillian Gish) takes in children who have been dispossessed by hard times. Rachel is a storyteller, too. She regales her charges with the stories of Moses and Jesus, and King Solomon and the dangers of false prophets. Without conceit or ulterior motive, she tells stories of love and wisdom and honest justice.

Preacher knows that a local man named Ben Harper has been hanged for murder, but not before Harper hid $10,000 in stolen money. Preacher also knows that the money should be his, because it will be the climax of his personal narrative.

Here are the nasty secrets of Preacher's story: Preacher is insane. He has married and then killed numerous widows for their money. To each, he has told the tale of his righteousness, and then he has taken their lives and their few dollars and moved on. But $10,000! Preacher can scarcely contain his joy.

He courts and marries Willa Harper (Shelley Winters), who has been made mournful and lonely by her husband's execution, and left with two young children, John (the immensely talented Billy Chapin) and Pearl (Sally Jane Bruce). With marriage, perhaps Willa's neighbors will stop creating and repeating their own version of her story, and perhaps the local children will stop their sing-song narrative about Ben, the one that goes *Hing hang hung/See what the hangman done/Hung hang hing/See the robber swing.*

Perhaps with marriage to Preacher, Willa can begin to tell her own story again, and in her own way.

But she's doomed, and the boy, John, senses it.

Willa's body isn't immediately found, and Preacher is left in sole charge of the children. But John has promised his father that he'll never reveal the money's hiding place. Preacher perseveres, growing angrier and more comically frustrated, and only managing to encourage John and Pearl to set off on the river. Preacher eventually locates them, but it seems apparent that he's never run up against the likes of Rachel Cooper before. His attempt to lay siege to her house fails, and when he's captured and exposed, the townsfolk's easy piety metastasizes into the unreasoning rage of a lynch mob. Preacher is saved from this violent hypocrisy only because deputies hustle him out the jail's back door.

The Night of the Hunter (1955) is the great lyric poem of film noir. Because it concerns itself with philosophies, specifically, divergent ways of looking at life, it subtly mimics the meter of lyric verse by offering a continual counterbalance, and choice, of one philosophy against another, the life of the dark and the life of spiritual illumination: Preacher's way and Rachel Cooper's way, deceitful stories and honest ones. The film arcs between these with ease and immense grace, lighting the ebony places of our souls *and* bringing forth the brilliance of our capacity for goodness.

Charles Laughton had never directed a film before. During preproduction, he surprised his brilliant cinematographer, Stanley Cortez, with quick assimilation of technical information; together, they established the film's bold, high-contrast monochrome visual style. Classic noir devices—heavily shadowed rooms, silhouetted figures, the visual unease of the night—are employed and always in service to the familiar, yet wholly unorthodox, story.

Many images are symbolic and magical: Rachel's face afloat in a starry night sky; the innocent animals that observe from the bank (in the extreme foreground of frames) as the children drift downriver in a simple skiff; and the nave-like walls and ceiling of Willa and Preacher's unhappy bedroom (Preacher has made Willa ashamed of her sexuality). When Willa is calmly recumbent on her bed, she's illuminated within a pointed arch of light that mimics a Gothic church window. A snake is killed with a blow from a shovel, and (offering a quite different tone) the sparkling, luminous river that flows past Rachel's house seems like the River of Life.

And the money is hidden inside a plain, sweet thing: Pearl's doll.

In this film of strikingly realized moments, two justly famed sequences stand out: Preacher's escalating, siren-like scream of rage when the children evade his grasp by inches as they push off in the skiff; and the elegiac vision of the murdered Willa's body, tied in a white sheet and submerged in a lake behind the wheel of her flivver, sunlight slanting through the water, Willa's long hair gently waving in the current, like sea grass.

Walter Schumann's brilliant score is built on an ominous, four-note theme that announces Preacher and segues into full-bodied melodies that are alternately charming and ominous. Hymns are used, to ironic effect. (Much of Schumann's score is on a 1955 RCA Victor LP with ardent spoken-word narration by Laughton. The album was reissued on CD by Germany's Bear Family label in 1999.)

Mixed critical reaction to *The Night of the Hunter*, and indifferent public response, conspired to kill Laughton's directorial career before it could properly begin. When the miserable box-office results came in, he was at work on an adaptation of Norman Mailer's epic novel of World War II, *The Naked and the Dead.* The project was taken from Laughton, who never directed another film.

Leave a Beautiful Corpse

The mental illness festering at the core *The Hitch-Hiker, Dementia,* and *The Night of the Hunter* is concertedly coarse and ugly. Contrarily, in Gerd Oswald's *A Kiss Before Dying* (1956), the illness is sleek and prettified. This glossy thriller was shot in DeLuxe color and CinemaScope and features a quartet of male and female ingénues on loan from Fox to indie producer Robert L. Jacks, for United Artists release.

Oswald insisted that we become thoroughly preoccupied with the well-scrubbed appeal of his beautiful, impeccably well-dressed young stars. Shot mostly in full sunlight in and around Tucson during the early summer of 1955, the film radiates a perverse glow of radiant physical health. In today's argot, *A Kiss Before Dying* is all about crazy, sexy murder.

When Dorie, the (beautiful) wealthy girlfriend of penniless (and pretty) college undergrad Bud Corliss, becomes pregnant, she tells Bud that she'll be disinherited the moment her hard-case father finds out. Still, Bud promises to marry her right away. Early in what will be their secret wedding day, Bud (Robert Wagner) and Dorie (Joanne Woodward) enjoy the sun atop the roof of an office building. They squeeze each other and pledge their love.

And then Bud shoves Dorie into eternity.

Because Bud has tricked up a "suicide" note, the death goes on the books that way. That, plus the fact that Dorie never told her family a word about him, leaves Bud free to seek out and romance Dorie's (beautiful) older sister, Ellen (Virginia Leith). After beguiling Ellen and charming her normally cynical father (George Macready), Bud is on the verge of joining the family. And then Ellen begins to piece together stray bits of information uncovered by a skeptical, young (and pretty) police detective (Jeffrey Hunter). When Ellen uses idle conversation to trick Bud into making a telling verbal gaffe, she sets herself up to be the next unlucky number on Bud's hit parade. How handy that the two of them have driven out to see the family smelting works and parked near the edge of a bottomless gravel pit . . .

Although Lawrence Roman's slick adaptation of Ira Levin's 1953 novel reduces the number of sisters from three to two, clever use is made of many elements from the book, notably that Bud is never mentioned by name in the story's first half, not even by Dorie or his mother (Mary Astor). The trick allows for a creepy moment of surprise much later, when Ellen's fiancé is introduced

And his hair was perfect: Icy charmer Bud (Robert Wagner) assures pregnant girlfriend Dorie (Joanne Woodward) that he'll marry her right away. Dorie is happy—for the last time in her life in *A Kiss Before Dying* (1956).

as "Bud" and turns to greet a visitor. We see that the fiancé is our pathologically murderous protagonist.

There are bumps. When Bud asks hapless, pregnant Dorie to translate a Spanish assignment for him, she hands it back to him in her own handwriting—never mind that the words comprise a suicide note. And she never wonders why Bud is suddenly foisting mysterious pills on her. Well, we didn't say that she was brilliant, just rich.

Gerd Oswald, directing his first feature after a nearly twenty-year career as a B-picture assistant director and associate producer, made good use of the CinemaScope frame, placing his cast amidst, variously, athletic bleachers, library shelves, colorful rows of chemical bottles, gardens at an expansive country estate, and, near the climax, the rocky landscape and distant peaks near Inspiration, Arizona. Cinematographer Lucien Ballard softened and tamed natural sunlight so that exterior colors fade to delicate pastels. Interiors have the fulsome hues of a Sirk film, and the young cast never looks anything less than gorgeous.

Because Oswald's coverage during a final stunt is inadequate, action involving a massive truck and that cliff edge we mentioned is spatially confusing and difficult to follow, despite the best efforts of editor George Gittens to cut it together. (In Levin's novel, the denouement involves a vat of molten metal!)

Neither Wagner nor Hunter can command the screen, and veteran character player George Macready is uncharacteristically remote. The young women fare best: Woodward, who captures Dorie's pathetic hopefulness; and Leith, because of her ability to display some edge and insist on our attention.

Finally, a gold star to hairdresser Kay Shea, who gave Robert Wagner a towering pompadour with the curvature and stiff swirls of a conch shell.

A Kiss Before Dying is glam-noir.

Media and Murder

RKO launched its own take on glamour in 1956, when it promoted Fritz Lang's *While the City Sleeps* with lively announcements of the picture's "10 Top Stars!" The cast is headlined by Dana Andrews, Rhonda Fleming, and George Sanders, and while neither they nor any of the other seven were exactly "top" in 1956, they had marquee value and give this underbudgeted thriller most of the small energy it possesses.

The film is based on the true-life crimes of William Heirens, a handsome Chicago teenager who murdered women and a little girl in the late 1940s and famously used a lipstick to scrawl at a crime scene, "For heavens [sic] sake catch me before I kill more I cannot control myself." The case was made for the movies.

Media mogul Amos Kyne has died, leaving his empire, including the *New York Sentinel,* to his dilettante son, Walter (Vincent Price). Walter knows nothing about the newspaper business, but he does come up with an exploitable idea calculated to humiliate top Kyne executives who have made a habit of condescending to him. The *Sentinel's* next executive editor will be chosen following an in-house competition among three top men: managing editor Jon Day Griffith (Thomas Mitchell); Kyne wire service chief Mark Loving (Sanders); and photo director Harry Kritzer (James Craig). (The top woman employed by Kyne, Mildred Donner [Ida Lupino], is a mere gossip columnist, and has been slotted to remain one.)

Another likely candidate, *Sentinel* columnist and Kyne Broadcasting star Edward Mobley (Andrews) doesn't wish to compete because he likes his lucrative, relatively undemanding routine. But when the focus of the competition, New York's fiendish "Lipstick Killer" (a twitchy John Barrymore Jr.), selects Mobley as his conduit to the police and public, what had been three competitors becomes four.

Fritz Lang was a lifelong admirer of gaudy pulp magazines. The rude, the excessively colorful, the outré—all of this fascinated him. Sex was another of the director's lifelong preoccupations. By 1955, when *While the City Sleeps* was shot, Lang wasn't turning down many projects; he took what was offered. Still, the William Heirens link in the Casey Robinson script (based on Charles Einstein's 1953 paperback original, *The Bloody Spur*) piqued his interest.

Lang explored compulsive criminality in many of his films, most enduringly in *M* (1931), in which a killer of little girls is endlessly tortured by voices in his head. (And doesn't the gigantic, illuminated "K" at the summit of the Kyne Building recall the "M" iconography of the earlier film?) Lang deftly made the "M" killer pitiable, but the Lipstick Killer of *While the City Sleeps* is a slouchy postadolescent dressed in black leather and unwholesomely absorbed in crime comic books. By the mid-1950s, educators, mental health professionals, and opportunistic politicians frequently noted that crime comics were virtual step-by-step templates for mayhem. Lang's film considers this supposed link between criminal behavior and comic books and makes it explicit.

The amusing, calculated irony of *While the City Sleeps* is that the Killer doesn't become really absorbed in his work until goaded by the Kyne media machine. When Mobley goes on TV and calls the Killer "a mama's boy" (right on the mark, by the way), and the *Sentinel* publishes a drawing of the Killer with a provocatively featureless face, the kid cooks up a plot to murder Walter Kyne's wife (Rhonda Fleming) and Mobley's fiancée, Nancy (Sally Forrest).

In a startling and thoroughly disagreeable twist, Mobley schemes to use Nancy as bait to lure the Killer. Mobley can't have sex with her (she refuses him), so she might as well do *something* for him. With Mobley's blessing, a front-page *Sentinel* account of the investigation is accompanied by a boxed announcement of Mobley's engagement! (If Mobley was really on the ball, he'd have mailed the Killer the keys to Nancy's apartment, wrapped in a map.)

The world of *While the City Sleeps* is thoroughly corrupt. No sympathy at all is whipped up for the Killer, and there's nothing to like about the Kyne people who are hunting him. When they're not double-crossing each other, they're cheating on their partners and trading sex among themselves for some temporary advantage. Only Walter Kyne, the dilettante, looks better as the narrative goes on, but that's mostly by comparison only. He's still subverting his newspaper's public duty.

The picture has a well-designed shocker of an opening, an aggressively staged car crash later, and a climactic chase through a dark subway tunnel. Otherwise, the ninety-nine-minute film is static and burdened with talk. Ernest Laszlo's lighting is mostly flat and perfunctory, and the Killer—the linchpin of the story, after all—sleepwalks through the proceedings, which is Lang's fault, not Barrymore's.

The "bloody spur" of the source novel is the bloody spur of ambition. Lang captured that well enough but forgot that his beloved pulps attracted him because of their pugnacious energy and outsized flair. Lacking those qualities, *While the City Sleeps* seems only half-finished.

Fast, Tough, and Ruthless

Four years after directing the 1954 pilot for a CBS TV series called *The Lineup*, Don Siegel was contracted by Columbia to direct an original, film-length spin-off for theatrical release. Predictably enough, the picture is called *The Lineup*

(1958) and features the star of the series, Warner Anderson, as San Francisco Detective Lt. Ben Guthrie. Young character lead Eli Wallach is Dancer, a professional killer; Robert Keith is Julian, Dancer's older mentor; and Richard Jaeckel is Sandy, a professional getaway driver. The plot is propelled by simultaneous police and criminal searches for statuettes and other items filled with heroin, which have been unknowingly brought into the country by returning tourists.

Although some attention is paid to lab work and other police procedure, the greater part of *The Lineup* is concerned with the activities of the criminals, in particular, the peculiar relationship between the arch, pretentious Julian and his frankly psychotic partner, Dancer. *The Lineup* is a noir thriller that utilizes a procedural element for irony.

As a team, Julian and Dancer have a history of great competence, with strict adherence—very much like the police—to discipline, rules, procedure, and protocol. One novel aspect of the pair's professionalism is that while Julian is thoroughly schooled in the proper ways to fulfill a contract, Dancer is still learning. Julian wants the younger man to have an effective grasp of grammar and syntax, and to know how and when to use force. Implicit in Julian's mentoring is that violence is best reserved for the final moment—that is, for the act that fulfills a murder contract. And no one is as interested in the final moment as Julian, who keeps a macabre written record of victims' last words. ("Oh, I *like* that," he says after one killing.)

In a bit of a hitch, Dancer is childishly impulsive. He rather unnecessarily plugs a stupid sailor in a steam room and shoots a houseboy dead when the polite approach fails. Similarly, a suave, lightly amusing approach that allows Dancer to get close to a young mother (Mary La Roche) and her little girl (Cheryl Callaway) goes for naught when Dancer loses his cool after learning that the child had found the "powder" inside her Japanese doll and used it to powder the dolly's face.

Mother and daughter are bundled into the killers' car and taken to San Francisco's Sutro's Museum and ice rink. There, Dancer intends to explain to "the Man" (Vaughn Taylor, oddly imposing in a wheelchair) why the shipment of H is short.

But the Man, a weasel-eyed, high-level mob functionary, doesn't buy Dancer's explanation about the "face powder." He especially doesn't like it that Dancer has seen him. "*Nobody* sees me," the Man warns. "You're dead. Dead! Now get out!" He slaps Dancer across the face, and when Siegel and editor Al Clark cut suddenly to a tight close-up of Dancer's infuriated expression, the back of his hand bent like a claw against his injured cheek, you know that something bad is going to happen.

Indeed.

In one of the great shock moments of latter-day noir, Dancer levers his leg against the wheelchair and shoves the Man backwards through a railing and into an upside-down plummet that ends with a sickening crunch on the ice far below. (For extra shock value, Siegel's camera follows Man and chair all the way down to the ice, with no cutaway until after the impact, when we see the sprawled body from Dancer's overhead POV.) Unlike the famed, vaguely similar moment with Richard Widmark in *Kiss of Death*, the victim here isn't an innocent but an important part of the killer's carefully structured professional world.

Now things fall apart.

A car chase from the north end of San Francisco all the way west to the Golden Gate Bridge is paused when the crooks' big Plymouth roars up a freeway bridge that's still under construction. The bridge curves and then just *ends*, hanging in space, and only Sandy's considerable skill brings the car to a skidding stop and prevents it from plunging hundreds of feet. (This was a real-time stunt, with no matte work or other trickery. Siegel and director of photography Hal Mohr nervously shot it from the fifth floor of an adjacent YMCA.)

Finally trapped a few minutes later on an on-ramp that narrows to nothing, Dancer takes a hostage and guns Julian. Then the real fun begins.

Dancer's last stand was shot, like all of *The Lineup*, on location and in natural sunlight. The final spasms of action are viewed from above, from below, and from eye level; in close-up and at considerable distances. Aggressive tracking shots mix well with stationary setups in which people and objects travel so that the borders of the frame are violated. Without being unnecessarily showy, the sequence *moves*. Don Siegel was an unpretentious storyteller with instincts that made him one of Hollywood's greatest thriller directors. He would return to San Francisco again, thirteen years later, for his much-celebrated *Dirty Harry*.

Consorting with the Dead

Vertigo (1958) is about obsession. This is how the obsession unfolds:

Retired San Francisco police detective Scottie Ferguson (James Stewart) is haunted by the rooftop death of a uniformed officer—a death that Scottie may have been able to prevent if not for his debilitating acrophobia. Restless and emotionally isolated, he accepts a job from an old friend, Gavin Elster (Tom Helmore), who worries that his chic wife, Madeleine (Kim Novak), is so unwholesomely absorbed with a female ancestor that she may commit suicide. Scottie shadows Madeleine and saves her when she leaps into San Francisco Bay. The two fall deeply in love, but Madeleine's obsession with her ancestor grows worse. Finally, because Scottie's crippling fear of heights prevents him from ascending a bell tower, Madeleine leaps to her death. Scottie is devastated—in a way, he's killed the woman he loved. But the male mind is endlessly adaptable in matters of sex, and Scottie begins to recover when he approaches a stranger, a red-haired shopgirl named Judy (Novak), who bears a remarkable resemblance to Madeleine. Judy is pathetically starved for love and reluctantly allows Scottie to remake her in Madeleine's image: wardrobe, makeup, hair color, hair style,

Psychological necrophilia with A-picture gloss—that's one way to describe Alfred Hitchcock's *Vertigo* (1958), a disturbing and challenging psychodrama about a police detective (James Stewart) whose shaky mental state grows even more tenuous when he becomes obsessed with a dead lover (Kim Novak). He wants to remake another woman (also Novak) so that his lover can come back to him, but will the other woman allow such sick impertinence?

everything. Scottie is in love with a dead woman, and now he's readying himself to resume sex with her—a remarkable notion by any standard and one of indescribable boldness in 1958.

Scottie's only oversight is that the dead nearly always stay dead.

Vertigo was directed by Alfred Hitchcock, and scripted by Alec Coppel and Samuel Taylor, who adapted *D'entre les Morts* aka *The Living and the Dead*, a 1954 novel by Pierre Boileau and Thomas Narcejac. (In 1952, the pair collaborated on *Celle qui n'etait plus* aka *The Woman Who Was No More*, which was filmed in 1955 by Henri-Georges Clouzot as *Les Diaboliques*. That brilliant, low-budget shocker encouraged Hitchcock to make *Psycho*.) The central twist of *Vertigo* is that Madeleine and Judy are the same woman, and that neither is the real Mrs. Elster. Scottie has been duped into a murder plot. He's never seen the real Madeleine, but it was she who took the fatal tumble from the bell tower, as Elster and Judy waited at the top, hidden, confident that Scottie's acrophobia would prevent him from climbing close enough to see them.

Of course, *Vertigo* isn't really about Gavin Elster's frankly fantastic murder scheme, the likes of which we encounter only in movies and pop novels. The film's real subject is the all-consuming passion of a damaged man and his outrageous, pitiable attempt to fashion his lover anew, so that both of them can cheat death.

Bernard Herrmann's score veers from soaring melody to agitated chops of sound and suggests the wild swings of Scottie's mind and emotions. Cinematographer Robert Burks, who shot eleven other Hitchcock pictures between 1951 and 1964, created a sickly color palette dominated by greens and reds—violent opposites—to express Scottie's disconnectedness. Costumes, hair styling, and makeup contribute to the film's visualization of two archetypes, one cool and the other carnal. Can a lovestruck man accept that both are the same woman? Would he care?

When the transformed Judy steps into Scottie's line of sight, attired like Madeleine and bathed in those reds and greens, Scottie's face is a remarkable meld of awe and worship, the indescribable pleasure felt by a child, and the naked lust of a man who has had numerous women but has wanted to fully possess and resurrect only one.

Vertigo's sick little jokes, other than that the acrophobic protagonist lives in the up-and-down terraform of San Francisco, are Elster's casting of the faux Madeleine as an obsessive, as if in anticipation of Scottie's obsessive nature; and the subtle pursuit of Scottie undertaken by Midge (Barbara Bel Geddes), a direct, enormously appealing woman who hasn't the decadent, sickly mystery of Madeleine/Judy, and thus cannot excite Scottie's interest. Scottie's problem, then, isn't just that he's not normal but that he can no longer respond to normalcy.

As noted in this chapter's discussion of *Strangers on a Train*, Hitchcock was fascinated—preoccupied, even—with visual and emotional cues that, to him, signaled the impropriety of sex. Like many men, he was drawn to the "whore in the bedroom" notion. The mindset is tiresome and embarrassingly adolescent, but who ever said male sexual obsession is an indicator of maturity? Scottie Ferguson, for all of his intelligence and sophistication, is a little boy. Hitchcock knew that little boy well because he lived and agonized with him every day.

James Stewart's "neurotic" antihero roles in Anthony Mann's westerns from earlier in the 1950s helped prepare audiences for Scottie's mental illness. The actor may never have been better or more vulnerable. Whatever Stewart's own feelings about the material and the character, Scottie is devastatingly real. And Kim Novak, a potent screen presence and star who has yet to receive her due as an actress, captures to stunning effect the emotional consequences suffered by women who are the objects (and I use the word advisedly) of obsessive male desire, whether or not those women are complicit in the obsession. "Couldn't you like me—just me—the way I am?" Judy plaintively asks. "If I let you change me, if I do what you tell me, will you love me?"

All of that is very difficult for Judy. The capper is that she's being asked by a sick man to become a woman who 1) never existed in the first place and 2) was Judy all along. This is identity crisis cut into small pieces and thrown into a revolving drum. Although both of these people are victims—Scottie because of his insistence on transformation and false identity, and Judy because of her deception and acquiescence—the more profoundly damaged one is Judy. Because of that, it is she, and not Scottie, who is the central, essential figure of *Vertigo*.

The situation also makes the film as much Kim Novak's as Hitchcock's. James Stewart, for all of his excellence here, is a secondary figure.

After being held in trust by Hitchcock and his family, *Vertigo* was finally rereleased to theaters at the end of 1983 (three years after Hitchcock's death). Rave reviews acknowledged the picture as one of the director's masterpieces (initial critical reaction had been mixed), and a key film in the history of world cinema. The reputation of *Vertigo* grew further following a fabulous, frame-by-frame restoration that was seen in 1996.

Numberless words have been devoted to this audacious and challenging work, and we really needn't belabor the movie here. It's sufficient to say simply that the unrestrained human heart, a driving force of noir, has seldom been revealed in the starkly honest and disquieting terms that frame *Vertigo*.

There's Always Mom

The classic era of film noir ends with *Psycho* (1960). Alfred Hitchcock's most celebrated achievement utilized numerous noir conventions—doomed romance, the self-isolated male, the woman with a guilty secret, the atavistic terrors of night, the deceptive freedom of the American highway, emotional turnabout, violence. But instead of using these tropes merely to elaborate on the genre, *Psycho* utilized them to simultaneously heighten noir and annihilate it. Neo-noir thrived after 1960, but because of *Psycho*, all of those films that came later are inevitably self-referential. Unlike the noir films of the 1940s and '50s, the neo-noir pictures didn't follow industry trends. Instead, they *resisted* business as usual by looking backward for inspiration. By definition, neo-noir is artificial, and *Psycho* is the reason why. After *Psycho*, traditional noir had nowhere left to go. The genre had been exploded. After 1960, filmmakers who wanted to recreate noir looked to pictures made before *Psycho*, because that was where noir tradition lay.

A disaffected Phoenix office worker named Marion Crane (Janet Leigh) steals $40,000 from her employer because she wants to marry her broke boyfriend. Exhausted after driving hundreds of miles into northern California, she stops at an isolated motel and shares a meal and conversation with the young owner, Norman Bates (Anthony Perkins). Without being aware of it, Norman convinces Marion to return to Phoenix with the money. But in the motel shower minutes later, Marion is stabbed and hacked to death by Norman's insane mother, who lives in a Gothic house that overlooks the motel. Shocked, Norman disposes of Marion's car and body, and then must suffer visits from an aggressive private detective, Arbogast (Martin Balsam); Marion's lover, Sam Loomis (John Gavin); and Marion's fearless sister, Lila (Vera Miles).

With *Psycho* (1960), Alfred Hitchcock brazenly redefined the relationship of film-makers to audiences, exploded the noir genre, and terrified two generations of moviegoers. Joining Hitch on this ad mat are Anthony Perkins (lower left), Janet Leigh (upper right), Vera Miles (upper left), and John Gavin (lower right). And, of course, there's always Mother, ensconced in the gloomy house on the hill.

Worried for Mother after she ambushes and kills Arbogast, and compelled to protect her, Norman hurries to the house moments after Lila has entered. In a dank root cellar, Mother makes her stand.

The goofy, wonderfully peculiar, cross-dressing revelation of *Psycho* is folklore, but when the picture was released in the summer of 1960, Hitchcock insisted that no one be admitted after the film began. Audiences of the day were accustomed to coming into movies well after the beginning, watching through the end, waiting for the next showing, and leaving at the point at which they came in. That sort of viewing would, of course, have spoiled *Psycho*'s great surprise and would also encourage latecomers to blab the ending to people on their way in. Hitchcock's wasn't having any—and besides, his dictum was a terrific gimmick calculated to get people talking.

Psycho has hardly been discussed to death (it's so *alive* that that is an impossibility), but it certainly has been exhaustively probed, dissected, turned this way and that, shaken, and observed with a lot of grave interest. It has been made into a metaphor for heterosexual frustration, warped family dynamics, and the latent assaultive potential of cinema itself. (Pauline Kael famously remarked that *Psycho* was the film that turned audiences into prey.)

In industry terms, the picture has been rightly praised for its effective use of a modest budget, a no-star cast, and the craft of Hitchcock's fast-working television crew (including a great cinematographer, John L. Russell). Joseph Stefano's script, which brings vast improvements to the 1959 Robert Bloch source novel, is a model of intelligent construction. The cast, particularly Perkins and Leigh, has been applauded, and Bernard Herrmann's strings-only score has been acknowledged for its perfect, shattering brilliance (sonic and otherwise).

And, of course, there is Hitch's contribution: his misdirection and manipulation of our expectations and allegiances, the masterful construction and cutting (editor: George Tomasini) of the shower sequence, and deft use in it of Leigh and her body double, Marli Renfrow. Hitchcock's display of cheeky black humor is well loved; likewise, his adroit exploitation of Marion's paranoia and our own (the impassive face of the highway patrolman [Mort Mills] framed in Marion's car window pricks every viewer).

Most impressive of all is Hitchcock's uncanny ability to negotiate the thin thread separating the credible from the absurd. The too-glib explanation of the psychiatrist (Simon Oakland) is intended to help us make sense of everything we've experienced, and if you don't know too much about psychiatry, I suppose it does. What might have been risible becomes, with this coda, well, *possible*. (Producer-director William Castle, who quickly threw together a *Psycho* imitation called *Homicidal* [1961], was unable to manage that tightrope. Although *Homicidal* is lively and a lot of fun, it's also silly in the extreme.)

Finally, there is Hitchcock's defiance of convention. What kind of filmmaker kills off the leading lady less than halfway through the picture—in a brightly lit shower, no less—and leaves the audience emotionally and intellectually adrift? (Well, American director John Moxey, with British writer George Baxt, did just that, coincidentally, in *City of the Dead*, an atmospheric Brit thriller set in present-day New England and released just weeks after *Psycho*. And the murder of Moira Shearer in Michael Powell's fine and highly upsetting *Peeping Tom* [also 1960] has a similar, but not identical, effect on audiences.)

Film scholars and fans marvel at *Psycho*'s cheek and its simultaneous pall of dread. The film really is a remarkable exercise, and it all boils down to this familiar noir dilemma: A young man and a young woman who love each other haven't the financial wherewithal to marry. On impulse, the woman decides that theft and flight are good ideas.

Even if her scheme fails, how bad could the punishment be?

Afterword
New-Generation Noir

Even before film noir was pushed in a new direction by *Psycho* in 1960, the genre underwent an important evolution. The term *film noir* had been coined in France in the mid-1940s. By the early '50s, as the "classic noir" era began to wind down in America, a coterie of young European filmmakers that had been greatly influenced by the auteur theory and American B movies consciously borrowed noir stylistics and (especially) themes and attitudes, and grafted them onto local sensibilities. These are the first true neo-noirs. The three most notable, arguably, are Henri-Georges Clouzot's *The Wages of Fear* (1952) and two that came later, Jean-Luc Godard's *Breathless* (1959), which Godard dedicated to Monogram Pictures; and Francois Truffaut's *Shoot the Piano Player* (1961), which adapted *Down There*, a 1956 novel by David Goodis.

After neo-noir took hold in Hollywood around 1964, American filmmakers undertook noir assignments not as simple genre projects but as conscious evocations of an earlier time and sensibility. This means that Hollywood neo-noir is inevitably self-conscious and referential (not necessarily bad qualities at all). Don Siegel remade Robert Siodmak's *The Killers* as a TV-movie in 1964, but the picture was so lively in its antisocial tendencies that the remake was sent to theaters rather than to the small screen. The picture gave Ronald Reagan (in his final screen role) a startling opportunity to shoot Angie Dickinson; more importantly, *The Killers* became a marker on Lee Marvin's road to stardom. He had played the thug Vince Stone a decade earlier in Fritz Lang's *The Big Heat*, and now he was *The Killers'* hyperaggressive leading man. Marvin would solidify his big-screen stardom a few years later with an electrifying performance in John Boorman's *Point Blank* (1967), a super-stylish, existential neo-noir about a professional criminal who has been selected for elimination by the elusive criminal cabal that employs him. And after that, in Michael Ritchie's very violent and deliriously loopy *Prime Cut* (1972), city gangster Marvin battles country kingpin Gene Hackman in a parodist tale of adultery, revenge, and double-cross.

In Paul Bogart's *Marlowe* (1969), Raymond Chandler's famed PI is played with self-deprecating wryness by James Garner. And in Peter Yates's *Bullitt* (1968), cop Steve McQueen, the biggest male star of the day, runs up against corrupt politics while trying to shield a witness. The famed car chase across San Francisco signaled the arrival in neo-noir of the automobile, which joined the gun as a fetish object. George Peppard, making his own bid for important stardom, played a PI in John Guillermin's brutal *P.J.* (1968), with support from noir stalwarts Raymond Burr and Coleen Gray.

A few other figures from classic noir became involved in new interpretations from the '60s: Edmond O'Brien directed *Man-Trap* (1961), a perfectly mad robbery-gone-wrong thriller with David Janssen and the estimable Stella Stevens. Mickey Spillane played his own creation, Mike Hammer, in a U.S.-British coproduction, *The Girl Hunters* (1963). Glenn Ford teamed once again with Rita Hayworth in a satisfyingly glum neo-noir cop thriller called *The Money Trap* (1966); and Craig Stevens, a supporting player in *Where the Sidewalk Ends*, reprised the TV role that made him famous, in *Gunn* (1967).

Writer-director Sam Fuller, cut loose by major studios in the early 1960s, made ferocious thrillers as an independent, most famously the revenge noir *Underworld U.S.A.* (1961) and the hyperemotional *The Naked Kiss* (1964), in which neither the sweet-natured heroine nor the postcard-pretty town she adopts as her home are what they appear to be.

Jack Smight's tough and wryly amusing *Harper* (1966) features Paul Newman as Ross Macdonald's popular private eye. (A 1975 follow-up starring Newman, Stuart Rosenberg's *The Drowning Pool*, is considerably less satisfying.) Conspiracy, double-cross, and amiable killers that hide in plain sight propel Buzz Kulik's *Warning Shot* (1967), in which cop David Janssen struggles to clear himself of a fatal shooting he knows he couldn't have done.

Police detective David Janssen runs into unexpected obstacles—and the helpful Stefanie Powers—as he scrambles to clear himself of murder in *Warning Shot* (1967).

Rogue cops (not always easy to sneak past the Code in the old days) have their moment in Don Siegel's *Dirty Harry* (1971) and its not-bad follow-up, Ted Post's *Magnum Force* (1973), both with Clint Eastwood and his brazenly sexualized .44 Magnum.

As the 1970s progressed, neo-noir continued, usually in straight-up variations of classic noir, as in Robert Culp's effectively bleak PI thriller *Hickey & Boggs* (1972), James Goldstone's decidedly postmodern *They Only Kill Their Masters* (1972; with James Garner as a smart but perpetually off-balance small-town sheriff), and Don Siegel's *Charley Varrick* (1973; with Walter Matthau as a mob-baiting bank robber whose hangdog demeanor conceals a razor-sharp mind).

For *The Outfit* (1973), director John Flynn worked with top-billed Robert Duvall (playing a double-crossed professional criminal obsessed with revenge) and a whole clutch of personalities from noir's golden age: Robert Ryan, Jane Greer, Timothy Carey, Marie Windsor, Elisha Cook Jr., Roy Roberts, and Emile Meyer.

Some other films of the period were startlingly revisionist in tone (Robert Altman's *The Long Goodbye*, 1973; with Elliott Gould as a now-generation Marlowe, fencing with noir icon Sterling Hayden) and a pair of Chandler adaptations starring a furrowed Robert Mitchum, *Farewell My Lovely* and *The Big Sleep*; the latter transposes the action not just to the present day but to London.

Two of the most important films of the '70s are neo-noir. Roman Polanski's *Chinatown* (1974) evokes late-'30s LA and the city's real-life land-grab and water scheme, topping off the tale with a highly disturbing revelation of incest. The picture established Robert Towne as a preeminent screenwriter and Jack Nicholson as the most charismatic star of the day.

The other landmark movie of this period is Martin Scorsese's blistering *Taxi Driver* (1976), in which the psychotic title character (Robert De Niro) fixates on a twelve-year-old prostitute and commits mass murder in order to save her. The public and the cops, not grasping the truth of the situation, hail the demented cabbie as a hero.

Chinatown and *Taxi Driver* bookended another great (and underrated) neo-noir, Arthur Penn's *Night Moves* (1975), in which even a deeply jaded PI (Gene Hackman) is shocked by human ugliness while attempting to retrieve a runaway nymphet from the Florida Keys. The movie is satisfying as a thriller, as an assemblage of character studies, and as an existential think piece. It's among the finest of all neo-noirs, and the one that remains most faithful to tenets set down by the genre in the old days.

During the 1980s and beyond, neo-noir grew increasingly self-conscious and evocative of the past. Chandler, Goodis, Cornell Woolrich, Jim Thompson, and other hard-boiled novelists were enjoying a renaissance (which still shows no sign of abating), and films that emphatically set their tales in period (such as Bob Rafelson's overlong and unnecessary 1981 remake of *The Postman Always Rings Twice*) were joined by others that co-opted and caricatured such noir conventions as eerily shadowed rooms (Alan Parker's exhaustingly stylish *Angel Heart*, 1987);

An LA private detective (Gene Hackman) locates a missing girl in Florida, only to become tangled in a complex scheme of murder, smuggling, and conspiracy, in Arthur Penn's elegant and important *Night Moves* (1975). Here, Hackman tries to wring the truth from James Woods.

the voice-over narrator adrift in a soulless city (Ridley Scott's magnificently visual *Blade Runner,* 1982); and the dumb guy who's eaten alive by a brazenly wicked femme fatale (Lawrence Kasdan's *Body Heat,* 1981 and Paul Verhoeven's quite awful *Basic Instinct,* 1992).

Against All Odds (Taylor Hackford; 1984) is an effective redo of *Out of the Past,* with costarring roles filled by Jane Greer (star of the earlier picture) and Richard Widmark. And Jim McBride's deceptively laconic *The Big Easy* (1987) successfully evokes the slippery morality of modern-day New Orleans.

Michael Mann directed *Thief* (1981; ace safecracker dreams of a normal life) and the majestic neo-noir thriller, *Heat* (1995; big-score heist man is compelled to tie up one last loose end). Both films deal with different sorts of compulsion and how one's better judgment can be overruled. In their examinations of illegal vocations and character flaw, then, the Mann pictures are clear extrapolations of classic noir.

The Coen Brothers (Joel and Ethan) took neo-noir in fresh directions with some eccentric, absorbing gems: *Blood Simple* (1984; Texas double-cross to the *n*th degree); *Fargo* (1996; a blackly funny catalog of incredibly dumb decisions that precede and follow a Minnesota murder); *The Man Who Wasn't There* (2001; in the 1950s, a small-town barber becomes mixed up in mayhem); and the disturbing and perversely funny *No Country for Old Men* (2007; evil embodied as a man). Similarly, David Lynch brought his nightmarish, obsessive sensibilities and marvelously overbearing style to a pair of neo-noir masterpieces, *Blue Velvet* (1986; callow youth falls in with a hilariously appalling "bad crowd") and *Mulholland Drive* (2001; innocent girl newly arrived in LA has dire, dreamlike misadventures). Lynch's densely plotted *Lost Highway* (1997) is less successful. And then there is the director's first feature, *Eraserhead* (1977), a frankly experimental exercise that is undeniably noirish in its pitiless depiction of disaffection, loneliness, the vagaries of fate, and suffocating disappointment.

Onetime video-store clerk Quentin Tarantino invigorated neo-noir with *Reservoir Dogs* (1992), a darkly funny thriller (with onetime RKO noir star Lawrence Tierney in an important supporting role) about the aftershocks of a bloody heist and the tension that bubbles up between the gathered members of the gang. Not only are they hotter than hell, there's a special problem, too: One of the group is a policeman. But who? Two years later, with the violent, profane, and very amusing *Pulp Fiction* (1994), Tarantino paid homage to noir via criminal protagonists who have to keep dancing in order to stay a step ahead of powerful forces that want to eliminate them. With elements of *The Killers*, *Kiss Me Deadly*, and other classic noir thrillers, *Pulp Fiction* is a unique mash-up of traditionalism and post-modernism.

John Dahl's *Red Rock West* (1993) is a very pure descendant of classic noir, in which an ordinary guy hits a small Texas town and is mistaken for a hit man. A year later, Dahl's *The Last Seduction* (1994) cast Linda Fiorentino (a riveting actress who never achieved the importance she deserved) in a plum role as a sociopathic, astonishingly clever con artist who uses her brain and her considerable sexual wiles to dupe or destroy men who imagine that *they're* in charge.

Stephen Frears's *The Grifters* (1990, from the 1963 novel by Jim Thompson, with screenplay by crime novelist Donald E. Westlake) is similarly pure and remorseless, with smart performances by John Cusack, Anjelica Huston, and Annette Bening as an unwholesome family of con artists who decide that to con each other would be a good idea.

Novelist James Ellroy became a lively and popular literary force in the 1980s and helped to encourage a fresh round of "period" neo-noir. The most important film adapted from an Ellroy work, Curtis Hanson's *L.A. Confidential* (1997), is an assured and brilliant re-creation of early 1950s Los Angeles, with a plot drawn from the LA police scandals of those days. With its collision of corrupt and straight-arrow cops, high-end pimps and call girls, and a morally fuzzy central romance, *L.A. Confidential* is big in all ways: aesthetically, emotively, and thematically. The movie also signaled that neo-noir wasn't necessarily simple genre product but big-time mainstream moviemaking; *L.A. Confidential* elevated Russell Crowe to major stardom, made a (lesser) star of Guy Pearce, and propelled Kim Basinger to a best supporting actress Academy Award.

Neo-noir's preoccupation with period is evident in Carl Franklin's *Devil in a Blue Dress* (1995), which features Denzel Washington as novelist Carl Mosley's hardscrabble PI, Easy Rawlins. Rawlins was the first black protagonist in the genre since Harry Belafonte's Johnny Ingram, who figures in one of the last of the classic-era noir thrillers, *Odds Against Tomorrow.*

Linda Fiorentino is an oversexed thief who plays men like mandolins, while variously flummoxing, eluding, and killing her numerous pursuers, in John Dahl's *The Last Seduction* (1994).

Bryan Singer's pleasingly convoluted *The Usual Suspects* (1995) returned neo-noir to the present day, with a study of a group of habitual criminals picked up and grilled for a crime they apparently didn't commit. One trouble: Astute viewers will pick up on the climactic revelation after about thirty minutes!

Since the mid-'90s, neo-noir has freely moved between contemporary treatments and period stories, achieving generally good results with both tacks. On the contemporary side, Robert Benton's *Twilight* (1998) is dominated by a late starring role for Paul Newman, as an aging, down-on-his luck investigator who takes up residence in the Hollywood home of wealthy friends Gene Hackman and Susan Sarandon, only to fall into nasty intrigue as well as fallout generated by the rekindling of an old romance. With *Memento* (2001), director Christopher Nolan explicates a murder mystery through the distorted lens of a man who has lost his short-term memory and becomes hopelessly lost in what for most of us are everyday negotiations through time and simple recollection. It's all frankly improbable and yet classically noirish in its treatment of the mental confusion and torment of a sympathetic protagonist.

Training Day (Antoine Fuqua; 2001) and *Narc* (Joe Carnahan; 2002) assault us with corrupt veteran cops who masquerade as compelling antiheroes (Denzel Washington and Ray Liotta, respectively) and are deleterious influences on younger partners. In that, the pictures are direct descendants of Edmond O'Brien's *Shield for Murder* and other classic noirs about lawless police.

Wayne Kramer's *The Cooler* (2003) is a quirky, subtly comic neo-noir set in the world of high-stakes casino gambling, where schlub William Macy—the Vegas equivalent of *Li'l Abner*'s congenital jinx Joe Btfsplk—is regularly sent onto the floor by his boss to derail the runs of big winners simply by standing near them. But when the cooler falls in love, he loses his magic powers and his usefulness, becoming that familiar noir figure, the man who's flailing because he's in over his head.

Obsessive attention to period detail gives a splendid, nostalgic sheen to *Mulholland Falls* (Lee Tamahori; 1996), but the film is overplotted and only fitfully successful as a riff on the LAPD's real-life "Hat Squad" of the 1950s: four nattily dressed detectives who had jurisdiction across the city and won the grudging respect of many of the professional criminals they ran out of town.

Another period piece, Bob Rafelson's *Poodle Springs* (1998), was based on a fragment of a novel left by Raymond Chandler at his death in 1959 and completed forty years later by latter-day PI novelist Robert B. Parker. James Caan is the aging Philip Marlowe, who's about to get married in 1963 Los Angeles, only to become sidetracked by murder, blackmail, and a future father-in-law who is probably going to be trouble.

Brian De Palma's *The Black Dahlia* (2006; from James Ellroy's 1987 novel) is a textured but mannered and overly complex reimagining of the infamous 1947 murder-mutilation of LA party girl Elizabeth Short. Like many of De Palma's pictures (including 1976's *Obsession*, a stylish variation on Hitchcock's *Vertigo*), *The Black Dahlia* works best during some bravura set pieces. It's undone by weak central performances and a script that withers into tortured improbability. (*True Confessions* [Ulu Grosbard; 1981] utilized the Short case, with somewhat better results, as a springboard for a noirish exploration of the inevitable conflict between two brothers, one a police detective, the other a Catholic monsignor.)

One of the best American films of 2006, Allen Coulter's fact-based *Hollywoodland*, considers—but does not attempt to conclusively explain—the 1959 shooting death of actor George Reeves (played with a weary, bruised dignity by Ben Affleck). Set in the days and weeks after the actor's death, increasingly complicated and opaque developments are viewed through the eyes of a small-time, opportunistic private detective (Adrien Brody) who inserts himself into the investigation and later becomes heavily invested in it. Did TV's Superman commit suicide (the official ruling), or was he murdered because of his longtime romantic relationship with Toni Mannix (Diane Lane), the wife of a powerful MGM executive and a woman so in love with Reeves that she turned him into her kept man?

Martin Scorsese played with memory and the nature of reality to bring a nightmarish spin to *Shutter Island* (2010), set almost completely at the title location—what we used to call an "insane asylum." It's 1954, and cop Leonardo DiCaprio travels to the island with a partner to unravel the seemingly impossible disappearance of a patient. As reality twists and bends, the increasingly frustrated cop begins to believe that he's been told only a small part of the story.

Shutter Island is flamboyantly disturbing. It cleverly undermines reality, but its hyperaggressive stylishness divorces it from the relatively restrained (and "realistic") tone of classic noir films. (Clearly, that was Scorsese's intention.) That outcome was avoided by director Michael Winterbottom's 2010 adaptation of Jim Thompson's 1952 paperback original *The Killer Inside Me*. This very well-crafted film set in small-town Texas during the early 1950s marks the high point of neo-noir. The story has a has a grim kicker: The boyish, soft-spoken deputy sheriff played by Casey Affleck is a psychotic killer. Like some of his breed, he's become very good at hiding that fact from his friends and neighbors. He's deferential and quietly focused on his work. He gets on well enough with the local power bosses and is liked and respected by the citizenry. He has two women in his life, and he loves both of them deeply. So deeply, in fact, that he's genuinely regretful when circumstances, as he perceives them, force him to kill his lovers with his fists. Because the first victim is a known prostitute, the deputy is able to see that another man is blamed. The murder of the second, a prototypical noir "good girl," is going to be more problematic for the deputy. It's certainly problematic for the viewer—not just because of the act's cruelty but for its remorseless, insane "logic."

These female characters are fully humanized in the script and are well shaded by a pair of appealing actresses, Kate Hudson and Jessica Alba. The women exist in separate compartments of the deputy's life, and each trusts her lover completely. The murders are agonizingly protracted, as well as brutal, brutalizing, and chillingly low-key. The deputy never raises his voice and uses

Japanese trade ad for Michael Winterbottom's *The Killer Inside Me* (2010), with Kate Hudson, Casey Affleck, and Jessica Alba. Dark in intention and remorseless in execution, this highly disturbing exercise may be the ultimate expression of the noir mindset.

his fists in an oddly dispassionate way, like a machine. The murders bring three ingredients of classic noir—a compromised lawman, insanity, and the destruction of innocents—to an end point that's logical only to the killer but may have been inevitable in the artistic progression of neo-noir.

Among other plot elements are an extortion scheme and townies who have secrets, but the story's malevolent center is the deputy's psychosis. After *The Killer Inside Me*, nothing may remain to be explored by neo-noir. Whatever follows, no matter how excellent, may be superfluous.

Selected Bibliography

Books (nonfiction)

Adamson, Joe, ed. *Byron Haskin*. Scarecrow Press. Metuchen, NJ: 1984.

Alton, John. *Painting with Light*. University of California Press. Berkeley: 1995.

Auiler, Dan. *Vertigo: The Making of a Hitchcock Classic*. St. Martin's Press. New York: 1993.

Barlett, Donald and James B. Steele. *Empire: The Life, Legend, and Madness of Howard Hughes*. W. W. Norton. New York: 1979.

Behlmer, Rudy. *Memo from Darryl F. Zanuck*. Grove Press. New York: 1993.

Borde, Raymond and Etienne Chaumeton. *A Panorama of American Film Noir, 1941–1953*. City Lights Books. San Francisco: 2002.

Buntin, John. *L.A. Noir*. Harmony Books. New York: 2009.

Callahan, Dan. *Barbara Stanwyck: The Miracle Woman*. University Press of Mississippi. Jackson: 2012.

Curcio, Vincent. *Suicide Blonde: The Life of Gloria Grahame*. Morrow. New York: 1989.

Davis, Ronald L. *Hollywood Beauty: Linda Darnell and the American Dream*. University of Oklahoma Press. Norman, OK: 1991.

Donati, William. *Ida Lupino: A Biography*. University Press of Kentucky. Lexington: 1996.

Dowdy, Andrew. *"Movies Are Better than Ever": Wide-Screen Memories of the Fifties*. Morrow. New York: 1973.

Eisenschitz, Bernard. *Nicholas Ray*. Faber and Faber. London: 1993.

Fishgall, Gary. *Against Type: The Biography of Burt Lancaster*. Scribner. New York: 1995.

Fleischer, Richard. *Just Tell Me When to Cry*. Carroll & Graf. New York: 1993.

Ford, Peter. *Glenn Ford*. University of Wisconsin Press. Madison, WI: 2011.

Freeman, Lucy. *"Before I Kill More . . ."* Crown. New York: 1955.

Fuller, Samuel. *A Third Face: My Tale of Writing, Fighting, and Filmmaking*. Knopf. New York: 2002.

Hagen, Ray and Laura Wagner. *Killer Tomatoes*. McFarland. Jefferson, NC: 2004.

Halliday, Jon, ed. *Sirk on Sirk*. Viking. New York: 1972.

Halliwell, Leslie. *Halliwell's Filmgoers and Video Viewers Companion*, 9th ed. Scribner's. New York: 1988.

Higham, Charles. *Charles Laughton: An Intimate Biography*. Doubleday. New York: 1976.

Hirsch, Foster. *Otto Preminger*. Knopf. New York: 2007.

Jarlett, Franklin. *Robert Ryan*. McFarland. Jefferson, NC: 1990.

Jones, Preston Neal. *Heaven & Hell to Play With: The Filming of The Night of the Hunter*. Limelight Editions. New York: 2002.

Katz, Ephraim. *The Film Encyclopedia*, 2nd ed. Harper Perennial. New York: 1994.

Kobal, John. *Rita Hayworth*. W. W. Norton. New York: 1978.

Lanchester, Elsa. *Elsa Lanchester Herself*. St. Martin's Press. New York: 1983.

Linet, Beverly. *Ladd*. Arbor House. New York: 1979.

Maltin, Leonard, ed. *Movie Guide 2012*. Plume. New York: 2011.

McGilligan, Patrick. *Fritz Lang: The Nature of the Beast*. St. Martin's Press. New York: 1997.

Muller, Eddie. *Dark City Dames*. Regan Books. New York: 2001.

Nevins, Francis. *Cornell Woolrich: First You Dream, Then You Die*. Mysterious Press. New York: 1988.

O'Dowd, John. *Kiss Tomorrow Goodbye: The Barbara Payton Story*. Bear Manor Media. Albany, GA: 2006.

Price, Victoria. *Vincent Price*. St. Martin's Press. New York: 1999.

Rode, Alan K. *Charles McGraw: Biography of a Film Noir Tough Guy*. McFarland. Jefferson, NC: 2008.

Siegel, Don. *A Siegel Film*. Faber and Faber. London: 1993.

Silver, Alain and Elizabeth Ward, eds. *Film Noir*. Overlook. Woodstock, NY: 1979.

Silver, Alain and James Ursini. *What Ever Happened to Robert Aldrich?* Limelight Editions. New York: 1995.

Sperber, A. M. and Eric Lax. *Bogart*. Morrow. New York: 1997.

Spoto, Donald. *The Dark Side of Genius: The Life of Alfred Hitchcock*. Little, Brown. Boston: 1983.

Stephens, Michael L. *Film Noir*. McFarland. Jefferson, NC: 1995.

Sterritt, David and John Anderson, eds. *The B List*. Da Capo Press. Cambridge, MA: 2008.

Swindell, Larry. *Body and Soul: The Story of John Garfield*. Morrow. New York: 1975.

Welles, Orson and Peter Bogdanovich. *This is Orson Welles*. HarperCollins. New York: 1992.

Wolfe, Donald H. *The Black Dahlia Files*. Regan Books. New York: 1999.

Youngkin, Stephen D. *The Lost One: A Life of Peter Lorre.* University Press of Kentucky. Lexington: 2005.

Books (fiction)

Cain, James M. *Mildred Pierce.* Vintage. New York: 1978.
————. *Three of a Kind* [*Career in C Major, The Embezzler, Double Indemnity*]. Knopf. New York: 1943.
Chandler, Raymond. *The Big Sleep and Farewell, My Lovely.* Modern Library. New York: 1995.
Gresham, William Lindsay. *Nightmare Alley.* Rinehart. New York: 1946.
Hammett, Dashiell. *Dashiell Hammett, Complete Novels* [*Red Harvest, The Dain Curse, The Maltese Falcon, The Glass Key, The Thin Man*]. Library of America. New York: 1999.
Hughes, Dorothy B. *In a Lonely Place.* Bantam. New York: 1979.
————. *Ride the Pink Horse.* Bantam. New York: 1979.
Kersh, Gerald. *Night and the City.* Simon and Schuster. New York: 1946.
McCoy, Horace. *Kiss Tomorrow Goodbye.* Midnight Classics. London: 1996.
Polito, Robert, ed. *Crime Novels: American Noir of the 1930s and 40s* [Cain: *The Postman Always Rings Twice*; Anderson: *Thieves Like Us*; Fearing: *The Big Clock*; Gresham: *Nightmare Alley*]. Library of America. New York: 1997.
Spillane, Mickey. *Kiss Me, Deadly.* E.P. Dutton. New York: 1952.
————. *The Mike Hammer Collection, Volume 1* [*I, the Jury, My Gun is Quick, Vengeance Is Mine!*]. New American Library. New York: 2001.
Wallis, J. H. *Once Off Guard.* E. P. Dutton. New York: 1942.
Wolfert, Ira. *Tucker's People.* L. B. Fischer. New York: 1943.
Woolrich, Cornell. *The Black Path of Fear.* Doubleday, Doran and Co. Garden City, NY: 1944.

Essays

Clark, Mark. "Stranger on the Third Floor." *Actors Series: Peter Lorre.* Gary Svehla and Susan Svehla, eds. Midnight Marquee Press. Baltimore: 1999.
Hogan, David J. "Detour." *Magill's Cinema Annual 1986.* Frank N. Magill, ed. Salem Press. Pasadena: 1986.
————. "Quicksand." *Actors Series: Peter Lorre.* Gary Svehla and Sue Svehla, eds. Midnight Marquee Press. Baltimore: 1999.
————. "While the City Sleeps." *Actors Series: Vincent Price.* Gary Svehla and Susan Svehla, eds. Midnight Marquee Press. Baltimore: 1998.

Loren, Scott. "Dead Fathers and Other Detours: Ulmer's Noir." *Edgar G. Ulmer.* Gary D. Rhodes, ed. Lexington Books. Lanham, MD: 2008.

Savage, Guy. "Striking Back: The Have-Nots in the Sordid Underbelly of British B Noir." *Noir City Sentinel Annual #3.* Donald Malcolm, ed. Film Noir Foundation. San Francisco: 2010.

Silver, Alain. "Kiss Me Deadly: Evidence of a Style." *Film Noir Reader.* Silver & James Ursini, eds. Limelight Editions. New York: 1996.

Silver, Alain and James Ursini. "John Farrow: Anonymous Noir." Ibid.

Smith, Imogen Sara. "British Noir: A Climate of Fatalism." *Noir City Sentinel Annual #3.* Donald Malcolm, ed. Film Noir Foundation. San Francisco: 2010.

———. "A Common Language: American Expatriate Directors in British Noir." Ibid.

Wood, Robin. "Creativity and Evaluation: Two Film Noirs of the Fifties." *Film Noir Reader 2.* Alain Silver and James Ursini, eds. Limelight Editions. New York: 1999.

Magazine article

Hogan, David J. and Ted Okuda. "Peggie Castle: Green Eyes Crying." *Filmfax.* October-November, 1994.

Websites

www.archive.org
www.filmnoir.com
www.filmnoirblonde.com
www.filmnoirfoundation.org
www.filmsnoir.net
www.glamourgirlsofthesilverscreen.com
www.imdb.com
www.youtube.com

Index

Page numbers in **boldface** refer to photographs or other images.

THE FAQ SERIES

Lucille Ball FAQ
*by James Sheridan
and Barry Monush*
Applause Books
978-1-61774-082-4
$19.99

The Beach Boys FAQ
by Jon Stebbins
Backbeat Books
978-0-87930-987-9
$19.99

Black Sabbath FAQ
by Martin Popoff
Backbeat Books
978-0-87930-957-2
$19.99

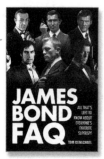

James Bond FAQ
by Tom DeMichael
Applause Books
978-1-55783-856-8
$22.99

Doctor Who FAQ
by Dave Thompson
Applause Books
978-1-55783-854-4
$22.99

The Doors FAQ
by Rich Weidman
Backbeat Books
978-1-61713-017-5
$19.99

Fab Four FAQ
*by Stuart Shea and
Robert Rodriguez*
Hal Leonard Books
978-1-4234-2138-2
$19.99

Fab Four FAQ 2.0
by Robert Rodriguez
Hal Leonard Books
978-0-87930-968-8
$19.99

Jimi Hendrix FAQ
by Gary J. Jucha
Backbeat Books
978-1-61713-095-3
$22.99

KISS FAQ
by Dale Sherman
Backbeat Books
978-1-61713-091-5
$22.99

Led Zeppelin FAQ
by George Case
Backbeat Books
978-1-61713-025-0
$19.99

Pink Floyd FAQ
by Stuart Shea
Backbeat Books
978-0-87930-950-3
$19.99

Bruce Springsteen FAQ
by John D. Luerssen
Backbeat Books
978-1-61713-093-9
$22.99

Star Trek FAQ
by Mark Clark
Applause Books
978-1-55783-792-9
$19.99

Three Stooges FAQ
by David J. Hogan
Applause Books
978-1-55783-788-2
$19.99

U2 FAQ
by John D. Luerssen
Backbeat Books
978-0-87930-997-8
$19.99

Neil Young FAQ
by Glen Boyd
Backbeat Books
978-1-61713-037-3
$19.99